PRICE GUIDE TO

Flea Market Treasures

FOURTH EDITION

HARRY L. RINKER

Published by

**krause
publications**

700 E. State Street • Iola, WI 54990-0001
Telephone: 715/445-2214

Please call or write for our free catalog.
Our toll-free number to place an order or obtain a free catalog is 800-258-0929
or please use our regular business telephone 715-445-2214
for editorial comment and further information.

ISBN: 0-87069-748-X

Printed in the United States of America

Contents

PART ONE: A Flea Market Education

Chapter 1: What is a Flea Market?

Chapter 2: Finding and Evaluating Flea Markets

Chapter 3: Top 25 U.S. Flea Markets

Chapter 4: Flea Market Survival Guide

Part Two: Flea Market Treasures

Part Three: Flea Marketer's Annotated Reference Library

CATEGORIES

PREFACE

Welcome to a somewhat unconventional price guide. It is designed to serve the non-traditionalist independent buyer and collector, as well as the person collecting in "established" categories. The approach is informal. When you read the category introductions and carefully scan the listings, you will find a fair amount of humor. Do not be afraid to laugh. This book is about the pure fun and joy of collecting.

The third edition of *Price Guide to Flea Market Treasures* was the first edition to be published in this large format. The results surprised and pleased everyone. Sales the first six months surpassed the total, two-year sales of the second edition. Thanks for this tremendous vote of confidence.

The flea market and garage sale markets are huge, far larger than the collector, dealer and decorator markets to which more than 90% of the books about antiques and collectibles cater. The more flea markets and garage sales I visit, the more I realize that 70% top 80% of the material I find cannot be researched in a general antiques and collectibles price guide. This title seeks to correct that problem.

Price Guide to Flea Market Treasures contains dozens of unconventional categories. It offers the opportunity to test the waters with a new collecting category and have a little fun at the same time. Some categories eventually will work their way into my *The Official Harry L. Rinker Collectibles Price Guide*, while others will fall by the wayside. Alas, some collecting categories only enjoy a brief moment in the sun. This is why there are dozens of new categories included in this book for the first time and why some categories from previous editions are missing.

Criteria

Availability and affordability are the primary factors determining what collecting categories do and do not appear in this book. Objects do not have to be 25, 50 or 100 years old to be included. If it is collected and offered for sale in quantity at a number of flea markets, I have tried to cover it. Because many objects appeal to multiple buyers, I urge you to become familiar with the index. The object about which your are seeking information may be in this book. You may not be looking in the right collecting category.

Discounted contemporary merchandise, manufacturer and store overstock and holiday remnants are not included. Tube socks, cheap Japanese knockoffs, clothing odds and ends, cassette tapes and CDs and handcrafted products, all too common at some flea markets, are not collectible. This book is not a price guide to junk.

In between the third and fourth edition of this title, Dana Morykan and I authored *Garage Sale Manual and Price Guide*, published by Antique Trader Books. It is designed to be a companion volume to this title. It covers recycled or reusable goods. A sampling of these items are found in this book's "Secondhand Rose" category.

Goodbye, Harry Jr.

In the Foreword to the third edition of *Price Guide to Flea Market Treasures*, I wrote: "This is the last Foreword that I plan to write for Harry Jr.'s *Price Guide To Flea Market Treasures*. Time to cut Harry Jr. loose and let him fend for himself." These words proved far more prophetic than I imagined.

This time, I am writing the Preface and my name appears as author. There have been a number of significant changes during the past two years at Rinker Enterprises. The same holds true for those responsible for publishing of this book. The changes are positive ones. All have resulted in making this fourth edition of *Price Guide to Flea Market Treasures* a very much improved new model.

As this book goes to press, Harry Jr., is in Hungary. He has been a member of the Army Reserves for almost a decade. Duty called, and he answered. His transportation unit is helping to supply the United Nations troops in Bosnia. While it would be nice to suggest that this is why Harry Jr., no longer authors this title, such an impression would be false. Harry Jr., simply was unable to love it all, something that is necessary when you author or edit a general price guide. He preferred only working on projects that interested him—militaria, firearms, Star Wars, photography and computer graphics and design. Harry Jr., asked to be relieved as author more than a year ago, and I agreed.

Team Effort

As noted in previous editions, *Price Guide to Flea Market Treasures* is a team effort. Dana Morykan—my co-author for *Warman's Country* and *Garage Sale Manual and Price Guide* and my No. 1 (to borrow a Star Trek term) and I made the final selection of categories. I made the decision to add category advisors and revised and rewrote the front matter and back matter.

Kathy Williamson prepared the category listings. Dana reviewed and revised the heads and supervised the selection and captioning of photographs. Nancy Butt, our staff librarian, is responsible for the accuracy of reference and collectors' club listings. Debra Tutka, an intern from Kutztown University, did the preliminary research for the revision of the trade paper list. Harry Jr., took the vast majority of the photographs. Virginia Reinbold acted as guardian of the accounts.

The initial editing and production of this book occurred at Chilton Books in Radnor, Pa. Troy Vozzella began the editing of the manuscript, and Edna Jones supervised production. Both had worked on previous editions. When Krause Publications acquired Chilton Books and its Warman and Wallace-Homestead imprints, the remaining editing and production was moved to Iola, WI. Deborah Faupel, Acquisition Editor, served as project liaison. Jon Brecka completed the editing, and Don Gulbrandsen supervised production. The Rinker Enterprises, Inc., staff looks forward to working with these and other Krause employees on many future projects.

As much as I would like this book to be perfect, it is not. We all make mistakes. If you spot information that you believe is incorrect or have a suggestion to make that you think will improve the next edition, I encourage you to send your comments and/or criticisms to: Harry L. Rinker, Rinker Enterprises, Inc., 5093 Vera Cruz Rd., Emmaus, PA 18049.

Harry L. Rinker
Vera Cruz, PA
March 1997

INTRODUCTION

GOOOOD MORNNNNINGGGG, Flea Marketeers! Welcome to *Price Guide to Flea Market Treasures*. Today's specials are the very best goodies, tidbits and knickknacks found in every flea market throughout the good old U.S. of A. It's all here—neatly printed and organized for your use and reading pleasure.

Sound a bit like a carnival barker? It should. Going to a good flea market will produce as much fun, enjoyment, treasures and memories as a visit to any carnival. Flea marketing is a grand adventure. You have an idea of what to expect, but you know there will be a number of surprises. If you are lucky, you will grab a brass ring.

This fourth edition of *Price Guide to Flea Market Treasures* is the second edition of this book to appear in its larger format. I was concerned prior to the publication of the third edition that readers who were familiar and comfortable with the smaller 6" by 9", two-column format of the first two editions would not accept this larger, three-column format. Was I wrong. Within six months of publication, sales of the third edition exceeded the total two-year sales of the second edition.

There is no sense arguing with success. This fourth edition continues the fine-tuning process found in the third edition. A major effort was made to change the majority of objects listed in each collecting category. Why duplicate some object listings from edition to edition? There are two principal reasons. First, some objects are so common that anyone using this book as a reference expects to find them in it, and they should. Second, some categories have a limited number of listings. If they are not repeated, the category needs to be dropped. Finally, prices can stagnate. This is information worth knowing.

First Look

Like its predecessors, *Price Guide to Flea Market Treasures, Fourth Edition,* also provides a first look at many potential collecting categories. Collectibility is tested at the flea market level. Dealers are continually offering material not seen previously. The successful sale of new groups of items immediately attracts the attention of other dealers. Their enthusiasm spreads. Before long, a new collecting category enters the established market. Many collecting categories first presented in this book are now regular entries in general antiques and collectibles price guides.

Not all efforts to establish a new collecting category succeed. This is why some categories that appeared in previous editions of *Price Guide to Flea Market Treasures* have been dropped from this edition. A few others have become so pricey that they have been moved up into *The Official Harry L. Rinker Price Guide to Collectibles* rather than retained in this book.

Category advisors were used sparingly in the first three editions of this work. This edition marks a significant change in approach. In an effort to add breadth and diversity to the categories appearing in this book, more than 75 specialized collectors were approached and asked to contribute information about their collecting specialty. More than 40 responded positively. When an advisor is responsible for the information in a category, his full name and address is listed at the end of the category introduction.

This book follows the same approach as previous editions, which is to combine basic information about flea marketing with price listings by category. Those familiar with previous editions will renew their acquaintance with an old friend. Those discovering this book for the first time have an opportunity to make a friend for life.

Three Parts

Price Guide to Flea Market Treasures is divided into three principal parts.

1. The first part is a guide for flea marketers. It helps you identify a "true" flea market, tells you how to find and

evaluate flea markets, provides a list of the top 25 flea markets nationwide, gives tips for surviving the flea market experience and honing your shopping skills and provides in-depth analysis of the current flea market scene. Much of the information is duplicated from previous editions. You will find minor changes in the sections dealing with general guides to flea market locations, trade papers and top 25 flea markets. Chapter 6, "The Flea Market Scene Today," has been totally rewritten to reflect changes within the flea market scene over the past two years.

In talking with individuals who purchased earlier editions of this book, I was surprised to learn how many "experienced" flea marketers had skipped this first part. They made a mistake. Even the most experienced flea marketer will find something of value. One of the worst mistakes you can make in the antiques and collectibles field is to assume that you know all you need to know.

2. The second part of the book is devoted to price listings by category. Previous users are advised to thumb through the categories and not rely on the assumption that they know what the book contains. This fourth edition of *Price Guide to Flea Market Treasures* contains more than 50 new categories.

You deceive yourself if you assume this book is just another antiques and collectibles price guide. Not true. This book was prepared using the premise that everything imaginable turns up at a flea market—from the finest antiques to good reusable second-hand items. *Price Guide to Flea Market Treasures* contains several dozen categories that are not found in any other antiques or collectibles price guide.

In a few categories, you will not find specific priced items. Instead you are provided with general information that allows a broad understanding of the category. Occasionally, you are referred to specialized books on the subject. One of the great joys about working on the categories in this book is that so many are supported with collectors' clubs, newsletters and periodicals. You will find full addresses for these listed in the appropriate category before the price listing.

Price Guide to Flea Market Treasures provides the Rinker Enterprises, Inc., staff and me an opportunity to let our hair down. If you are comfortable with a formal traditionalist price guide approach this price guide is not for you. Category introductions range from serious to humorous to sublime. If the key to a great flea market is that it evokes these emotions and more within you, why should this book do any less?

3. Although I am not certain why, the third part of this book, which contains reference material for flea marketers, including the "Flea Marketer's Annotated Reference Library" and a list of "Antiques and Collectibles Trade Papers," is often overlooked by purchasers of this book. I strongly recommend that you become familiar with this section. The information not only helps you become highly proficient as a flea marketer but also serves as your introduction to many other wonderful areas within the antiques and collectibles field.

Let's Go!

It is time to honor the cry of the circus ringmaster: "On with the show." Take a moment and read the program (the first section) before you watch the acts in the center ring (the second section) and then relive the memories (the third section). Most of all, don't forget—the entire purpose of the performance is for you to have fun.

PART ONE

A
Flea Market
Education

CHAPTER ONE

What Is a Flea Market?

It is difficult to explain the sense of excitement and anticipation felt by collectors and dealers as they get ready to shop a flea market. They are about to undertake a grand adventure, a journey into the unknown. Flea markets turn the average individual into an explorer in search of buried treasure. The search is not without adversity—conditions ranging from a hostile climate to intense competition as one waits with other collectors and dealers for the gates to open may be encountered. Victory is measured in "steals" and bargains and in stories that can be shared at the end of the day over dinner with friendly rivals.

Flea markets provide the opportunity for prospective collectors to get their feet wet in the exciting world of antiques and collectibles and for novice dealers to test their merchandise and selling skills at minimal expense. Many first contacts, some of which last a lifetime, are made between and among collectors and dealers there. More than any other aspect of the antiques and collectibles trade, the flea market is the one forum in which everyone is on equal footing.

Before you learn how to find, evaluate and survive flea markets, it is important that you understand exactly what a flea market is, how it fits into the antiques and collectibles market and the many variations of it that exist. This is the first step to identify the flea markets that are most likely to provide the greatest opportunities for you.

Defining a Flea Market

Few terms in the antiques and collectibles field are as difficult to define as "flea market." If you visit the Rose Bowl Flea Market in Pasadena, Calif., you will find discontinued and knock-off merchandise, handmade crafts, clothing (from tube socks to dresses), home-care items, plants of all types and specialty foods more in evidence than antiques and collectibles. On the other hand, if you visit the Ann Arbor Antiques Market in Michigan, you will find primarily middle- and upper-level antiques and collectibles. Both are flea markets, but they are light-years apart.

The flea market concept is generations' old. As it spread throughout the world, each country changed and adapted the form to meet its own particular needs. Regional differences developed. In New England, the Mid-Atlantic States and throughout the Midwest, the term generally is used to describe a place where antiques and collectibles are sold. In the South and Southwest, the term is more loosely interpreted, with the emphasis on secondhand and discounted goods.

It is not hard to see where the confusion originates. Check the dictionary definition for "flea market." *Webster's Ninth New Collegiate Dictionary* (Springfield, MA: Merriam-Webster, Inc., 1984) defines a flea market as "a usually open-air market for secondhand articles and antiques." Individuals involved with antiques and collectibles make a big distinction between secondhand (recycled or reusable) goods and antiques and collectibles. Although the dictionary may lump them together, collectors and dealers clearly differentiate one from the other.

The flea markets described in this book fit a much more narrow definition than the dictionary definition. When collectors use the term "flea market," they mean a regularly scheduled market, held either indoors or outdoors, in which the primary goods offered for sale are those defined by the trade as antiques or collectibles. Occasionally, you will find some handcrafted products and secondhand goods among the offerings, especially in the seasonal and roadside flea markets, where professional flea market dealers mix with individuals selling on a one-shot basis.

The problem with trying to define "flea market," even when limited to the antiques and collectibles perspective, is that a multiplicity of flea market types exist. There are the great seasonal flea markets, such as Renninger's Extravaganza (Kutztown, Pa.) and Brimfield's (Brimfield, Mass.), the monthlies, such as the Metrolina Expo (Charlotte, N.C.), and numerous weeklies scattered across the country.

One of the best ways to understand what an antiques and collectibles flea market encompasses is to discuss how it differs from three other closely related institutions in the antiques and collectibles trade: the mall, the garage sale and the show. While the differences may appear subtle, they are significant to collectors and dealers.

Prior to the arrival of the mall, there was a clearly defined ladder of quality within the antiques and collectibles community, which progressed from garage sale or country auction to flea market to small show to major show or shop. This is how most goods moved through the market. This is the route many dealers used to establish themselves in the trade. Two things changed the equation: collectors recognized the role flea markets played as the initial source of goods and actively participated in flea markets to eliminate the "middleman," and the antiques and collectibles mall came into existence.

Antiques and collectibles malls arrived on the scene in the early 1980s. As the decade of the 1990s ends, the trend is toward the Super Mall, a mall with more than 200 dealers that offers a full range of services, from direct sales to auctions. Malls resulted because many flea market and weekend dealers wanted a means of doing business on a daily basis, without the overhead of their own shops. They also needed an indoor environment, free from the vagaries of weather. Additionally, the buying public wanted to find as many sellers as possible in one location when shopping for antiques and collectibles. Antiques and collectibles malls bring together a number of dealers—from 10 to hundreds—in one location.

Malls differ from flea markets in that they are open daily for business (a minimum of five and often seven days a week), the display and sales process is often handled by a manager or other representative of the owner of the items, a more formal business procedure is used, and the quality of material is somewhat higher than that found at flea markets. The main drawbacks are that the buyer generally has no contact with the owner of the merchandise, and price negotiation is difficult.

Garage sales are usually one-time events, often conducted by people with no pretensions of being antiques or collectibles dealers—they are merely attempting to get rid of used or damaged goods that they no longer find useful. While it is true that some antiques and collectibles enter the market through this source, most individuals conducting garage sales have enough good sense to realize that this is the worst way to sell these items.

A recent development in the garage sale area is the annual or semi-annual community garage sale. A promoter rents a large hall or auditorium and sells space to any individual wishing to set up. Usually, there is a rule that no established antiques and collectibles dealers are allowed to take part. However, many dealers sneak in with friends or simply use a different name to rent a space in order to "pick" the merchandise during the set-up period. Although community garage sales fit the dictionary definition of a flea market, the large volume of secondhand merchandise distinguishes them from the flea markets discussed in this book.

An antiques or collectibles show consists of a number of professional dealers (weekend, full-time or a combination of both) who meet in a fixed location on a regular basis, usually two to three times each year, to offer quality antiques and collectibles primarily to collectors, interior decorators and others. Once an antique or collectible reaches the show circuit, the general assumption is that it is priced close to book value. Flea markets thrive on the concept that merchandise priced for sale is significantly below book value. While this concept is more myth than reality in the 1990s, it still prevails.

Confusion arises because a number of monthly flea markets have dropped the term "flea market" from their titles. They call themselves "shows" or "markets. They do not use "flea," because of a growing list of problems, ranging from unscrupulous dealers to an abundance of unmarked reproductions, that plague flea markets in the 1990s. Calling yourself something else does not change what you really are. Most monthly markets and shows are nothing more than flea markets in disguise.

Seasonal Flea Markets

Seasonal flea markets are those held a maximum of three times a year. Theoretically, they are held outdoors. However, many sites now provide either indoor or pavilion shelters for participants, especially those whose merchandise is expensive or susceptible to damage by weather. Most have clearly established dates. For example, Renninger's Extravaganza is held the last weekend in April, June and September.

If there is a Mecca in the flea market world, it is Brimfield. The name is magic. You are not an accomplished flea marketeer until you have been there. Actually, Brimfield is not a flea market, it is an event. For the second full week in May, July and September, more than 15 separate flea markets open and close. On Fridays, the dealer count exceeds 1,500. Area motel rooms are booked more than a year in advance. Traffic jams last hours.

For the past several years Renninger's has been promoting seasonal markets during the winter months at its Mount Dora, Fla., location. They are an important stop on the Southern winter circuit. Although there are a few seasonal markets in the Midwest, none are on a par with the Renninger's Extravaganzas and the Brimfield weeks.

Monthly Flea Markets

The strength of monthly flea markets rests on a steady dealer clientele, supplemented by other dealers passing through the area, a frequency that allows dealers enough time to find new merchandise and a setting that is usually superior to the seasonal and weekly flea markets. The monthlies range from the upscale Ann Arbor Antiques Market to the mid-range antiques and collectibles show (the Fairgrounds Antiques Market in Phoenix) to the something-for-everybody flea market (Kane County Flea Market in St. Charles, Ill.).

Most monthly flea markets have outdoor spaces. The Kentucky Flea Market in Louisville and the Fairgrounds Antiques Market in Phoenix are two exceptions. Flea markets with outdoor space operate only during warm weather months, generally April through November. A few of the larger operations (e.g., the Springfield Antiques Show & Flea Market in Springfield, Ohio) operate year-round. Double-check the schedule of any flea market you plan to visit between November and April, with the possible exception of those located in the Deep South or the Southwest.

Monthly flea markets attract a large number of dealers who appear on a regular basis; hence, collectors and dealers have time to cultivate good working relationships. A level of buying trust is created because the collector knows that he or she will be able to find the seller again, if questions develop.

Weekly Flea Markets

The weekly flea markets break down into two types: those held on a weekday and those held on a weekend. The weekday markets are primarily for dealers. Monday flea markets at Perkiomenville, PA, and Wednesday

flea markets at Shipshewana, IN, are legends. These markets begin in the pre-dawn hours. The best buys are found by flashlight, as participants check merchandise when it is still being unpacked. Most selling ends by 9 a.m. These markets are designed primarily for individuals actively involved in the resale of antiques and collectibles. Most collectors prefer something a bit more civilized.

Renninger's in Adamstown, PA, shows the staying power of the weekend flea market. Within driving distance of several major population centers, yet far enough in the country to make the day an outing, Renninger's combines an ever-changing outdoor section with an indoor facility with primarily permanent dealers. Renninger's has survived for years by opening only on Sundays, except for Extravaganza weekends. However, because buyers like to shop for antiques and collectibles on Saturdays as well, Renninger's Promotions created Renninger's in Kutztown, Pa.

Weekend flea markets are now a fixture across the country and constitute the largest segment of the flea market community. It is not unusual to find several in one location, as each tries to capitalize on the success of the other. However, their quality varies tremendously.

The biggest problem with weekend flea markets is merchandise staleness. Many dealers add only a few new items each week. Most collectors shop them on a four- to eight-week cycle. The way to avoid missing a shot at a major new piece is to maintain a close working relationship with the dealers at the flea markets who specialize in the category of items you collect. Most weekend flea market dealers do get to shop the market. They can be your eyes when you are not there.

As with the monthly flea markets, you can buy from indoor dealers knowing that you are likely to find them if a problem develops later. You must be much more careful when purchasing from the transient outside dealers. Get a valid name, address and phone number from anyone from whom you make a purchase at a flea market.

One of the things I like best about large weekend flea markets is that they feature one or more book dealers who specialize in antiques and collectibles books. I always stop at these booths to check on the latest titles, including the large stock of privately published titles. In some cases, I find a book I never saw advertised in the trade papers. Some of the dealers offer search services for out-of-print titles. Spending time getting to know these book dealers is something I never regret.

Roadside Flea Markets

I ignored roadside flea markets until this point because the merchandise they offer is usually secondhand and of garage-sale quality. This is not to say that I have not experienced some great finds at roadside markets. However, when I consider the amount of time that I spend finding these few precious jewels, I quickly realize I can do much better at one of the more traditional flea markets.

Chances are that you collect one or two specific categories. If so, not every type of flea market is right for you. How do you find the best markets? What type of evaluation can you do in advance to avoid the frustration of coming home empty-handed? These questions and more are answered in the next chapter.

CHAPTER TWO

Finding and Evaluating Flea Markets

To attend a flea market, you have to locate one. It is not as easy as it sounds. To thoroughly research the available markets in any given area, you will have to consult a variety of sources. Even when you have finished, you are still likely to spot a flea market that you missed in your research. I told you there was a strong sense of adventure in flea marketing.

Flea Market Guides

There are three national guides to U.S. flea markets: *The Original Clark's Flea Market U.S.A.: A National Directory of Flea Markets and Swap Meets* (Clark Publications, 419 Garcon Point Rd., Milton, FL 32583); *The Official Directory to U.S. Flea Markets, Fifth Edition,* edited by Kitty Werner (House of Collectibles, Division of Random House, 201 E. 50th St., New York, NY 10022); and *U.S. Flea Market Directory, Second Edition,* edited by Albert LaFarge (Avon Books, Confident Collector Series, 1350 Avenue of the Americas, New York, NY 10019). Buy them all.

Newly published since the last edition of this book is the four-edition set entitled *Goodridge's Guide to Flea Markets,* edited by Jim Goodridge (Adams Publishing, 260 Center St., Holbrook, MA 02343). The four editions are: Northeast/Mid-Atlantic, Southeast, Midwest, and West/Southwest. Buy the one that covers your local area and make certain to acquire those editions that correspond to your favorite vacation spots.

Clark's, issued quarterly, lists more than 2,000 flea markets and swap meets. The guide is organized alphabetically by state. The secondary organization is city or town closest to the flea market within the state. You will find information on name, address, days and (occasionally) hours of operation and telephone number. Information provided about each market varies greatly. Completely missing are directions for hard-to-find markets. I buy an issue every year or two as a safety check against my regular sources. A one-year subscription is $30. Single copies are available from the publisher at $8 (includes postage and handling).

The Official Directory, under Kitty Werner's direction, gets better with each edition. The book covers more than 850 flea markets in the United States and Canada. Yes, Canada—it's time someone paid attention to our northern neighbor. Each listing contains information about a flea market's dates, hours, admission, location, a very detailed description of the type of merchandise found, dealer rates and a telephone number and full address for the chief contact person. I especially like the list of "Other Flea Markets" found at the end of most state listings. These are markets that did not respond to the questionnaire. Werner advises users to call to make certain they are open. You can purchase a copy of this guide in most larger bookstores. It is a bargain at $6.99.

The second edition of *U.S. Flea Market* is welcome. Designed to compete with *The Official Directory,* it provides detailed information that includes maps and travel directions, days and times, number of dealers, description of goods sold, dealer information and other useful tidbits for about 1,000 flea markets nationwide. As one might expect, LaFarge covers many of the same flea markets that are found in *The Official Directory*. However, there are enough differences to make both books a must-buy. *U.S. Flea Market* retails for $6.99 and is available at most bookstores.

The *Goodridge* guides obviously offer broader coverage than *The Official Directory*. However, information listings contain much less detail. Actually, the *Goodridge* guides contain sections on three distinct business communities: flea markets (includes Swap Meets, Trade Days, and Farmer's Markets), antiques and craft malls, and auctions. Since flea market shoppers welcome diversity, the ability to check out the auction scene with a phone call or two is a valued plus. Each edition is sprinkled with collecting tips and other helpful advice. Each is priced at $9.95.

In the late 1990s, a day "antiquing" means visiting a variety of different selling markets. A flea market stop is combined with a visit to two or three nearby antiques and collectibles malls. For this reason, I recommend acquiring a copy of Judy Lloyd's *No-Nonsense Antique Mall Directory*. It covers 5,200 malls throughout the United States. It is available only by mail order. Send a check for $20.50, the price includes fourth class postage, to FDS Antiques, P.O. Box 188, Higginsport, OH 45138.

Antiques and collectibles flea markets are not unique to the United States. In fact, the modern antiques and collectibles flea market originated in Paris. Flea markets play a vital role throughout Europe, especially in France, Great Britain, and Germany.

Travel Keys (P.O. Box 16091, Sacramento, CA 95816) has published separate flea market price guides for France, Great Britain and Germany, each edited by Peter B. Manston. Although badly in need of revision, the books still have value if you are traveling abroad. First, many of the flea markets are decades old—same time, same place. Double-check before setting out, if possible. Once at a market, ask dealers to recommend other flea market venues. Second, the introductory material is a must read, especially the section on export laws and regulations. This is information you will not find anywhere else.

Regional Shop Guides

A number of specialized regional guides for locating antiques and collectibles flea markets, malls and shops exist. Most are published by trade papers. A few are done privately. None focus solely on the flea market scene.

The *AntiqueWeek Central Antique Shop Guide* and *AntiqueWeek Eastern Antique Shop Guide* (Antique Week, P.O. Box 90, Knightstown, IN 46148) are typical.

Organization is by state, region and alphabetically by city and town within a region. Brief listings for each business are supplemented by display advertising. Each edition covers flea markets, malls, shops, shows and more. Each year, the coverage gets better. The principal problem with these guides is that you have to pay a fee to be listed. As a result, coverage is limited to those willing to pay. However, they are a great starting point and a bargain at $3.50 each.

David Maloney Jr.'s *Maloney's Antiques and Collectibles Resource Directory* (4th edition due out in 1997, Antique Trader Books, P.O. Box 1050, Dubuque, IA 52004) contains category listings for antique shops and flea markets. The listings include address and telephone number. Hopefully, you own a copy of Maloney's book. If you do not, you should. Make a resolution—right now—to buy a copy the next time you visit a bookstore or the stand of an antiques and collectibles bookseller at a flea market. It is the best investment anyone in the trade can make. If you do not think so, I will give you your money back.

When planning to visit a new area, contact some of the trade papers that serve the region and ask if they publish a regional guide or know of such a guide. Regional guides are inexpensive, ranging from $5 to $15. Many of the businesses listed in the guide sell it across the counter. I always pick up a copy. The floor behind the front seat of my car is littered with road maps and regional guides, most of which show signs of heavy use.

Trade Newspapers

The best source of flea market information is advertisements in trade newspapers. Some papers put all the flea market advertisements in one location, while others place them in their appropriate regional section. Most trade papers' events calendars include flea markets with the show listings. Once again, the problem rests with the fact that all advertising is paid advertising. Not all flea markets advertise in every issue of a trade paper. Some advertise in papers outside their home area because the locals know where and when to find them. Flea markets that operate between April and September usually do not advertise in December and January. The only way to conduct a complete search is to obtain a four- to six-month run of a regional paper and carefully scan each issue. When doing this, keep your eyes open for reports and features about flea markets. As advertisers, flea markets expect to get written up at least once a year.

The following is a list of national and regional trade papers that I recommend you consult for flea market information. You will find their full addresses and phone

Here is an example of a national trade paper.

numbers (when known) in the listing of trade newspapers at the back of this book.

National Trade Papers

Antique Trader Weekly, Dubuque, IA
AntiqueWeek, Knightstown, IN
Antiques & the Arts Weekly, Newtown, CT
Collector News, Grundy Center, IA
Maine Antique Digest, Waldoboro, ME
Warman's Today's Collector, Iola, WI

Regional Trade Papers

New England
Antiques & Collectibles and the Long Island Arts Review Magazine, Westbury, NY
Cape Cod Antiques & Arts, (Register Newspaper) Orleans, MA
The Hudson Valley Antiquer, Rhinebeck, NY
MassBay Antiques/North Shore Weekly, Ipswich, MA
New England Antiques Journal, Ware, MA
New Hampshire Antiques Monthly, Farmington, NH
The Western CT/MA Antiquer, Rhinebeck, NY

Unravel The Gavel, Ctr. Barnstead, NH

Mid-Atlantic States
American Antique Collector, Murrysville, PA
Antique Country, Berryville, VA
Antiquer's Guide to the Susquehanna Region, Sidney, NY
Antiques & Auction News, Mount Joy, PA
Eastern Seaboard Antique Monthly, Burtonsville, MD
The New York Antique Almanac of Art, Antiques, Investments & Yesteryear, Lawrence, NY
New York—Pennsylvania Collector, Fishers, NY
Northeastern Antique Buyer's Guide, Rochester, NY
Renninger's Antique Guide, Lafayette Hill, PA
Treasure Chest, New York, NY

South
Antique Gazette, Nashville, TN
The Antique Press, Tampa, FL
The Antique Shoppe, Belleview, FL
Carolina Antique News, Charlotte, NC
Cotton & Quail Antique Trail, Monticello, FL
MidAtlantic Antiques Magazine, Henderson, NC
The Old News Is Good News Antiques Gazette, Hammond, LA

Southern Antiques, Decatur, GA
20th Century Folk Art News, Buford, GA

Midwest
The American Antiquities Journal, Springfield, OH
Antique & Collectible News, Anna, IL
The Antique Collector and Auction Guide, Salem, OH
Antique Review, Worthington, OH
The Collector, Heyworth, IL
Collectors Journal, Vinton, IA
Discover Mid-America, Kansas City, MO
Great Lakes Trader, Williamstown, MI
Indiana Antique Buyers News, Silver Lake, IN
Midwest Illinois Antiques Gazette, Winchester, IL
Old Times, Minneapolis, MN
Yesteryear, Princeton, WI

Southwest
The Antique Traveler, Mineola, TX
Antiquing Texas, The Woodlands, TX
Arizona Antique News, Phoenix, AZ

Rocky Mountain States
Mountain States Collector, Evergreen, CO

West Coast
Antique & Collectables, El Cajon, CA
Antique Journal, Union City, CA
Antiques Today, Carson City, NV
Antiques West, San Francisco, CA
Cochran's Art, Antiques & Collectibles, Petaluma, CA
Country Pleasures Magazine, Centralia, WA
The Flea Market Shoppers Guide, Maywood, CA
Old Stuff, McMinnville, OR
West Coast Peddler, Whittier, CA

This list is by no means complete. I am certain that I have missed a few regional papers. However, these papers provide a starting point. Do not be foolish and go flea marketing without consulting them.

Which Flea Market is Right for You?

The best flea market is the one at which you find plenty to buy at good to great prices. This means that most flea markets are not right for you. Is it necessary to attend each one to make your determination? I do not think so.

I am a great believer in using the telephone. If long-distance rates jump dramatically as a result of the publication of this book, I plan to approach AT&T and ask for a piece of the action. It is a lot cheaper to call than to pay for transportation, lodging and meals—not to mention the value of your time. Do not hesitate to call promoters and ask them about their flea markets.

What type of information should you request? First, check the number of dealers. If the number falls below 100, think twice. Ask for a ratio of local dealers to transient dealers. A good mix is 75% local and 25% transient for monthly and weekly markets. Second, inquire about the type of merchandise being offered for sale. Make a point not to tell the promoter what you collect. If you do, you can be certain that the flea market has a number of dealers who offer the material (when, in fact, it might not be true). Do not forget to ask about the quality of the merchandise. Third, ask about the facilities. The more indoor space available, the higher the level of merchandise is likely to be. What happens if it rains? Finally, ask yourself this question: Do you trust what the promoter has told you?

When you are done talking to the promoter, call the editor of one of the regional trade papers and ask his or her opinion about the market. If they have published an article or review of the market recently, request that a copy be sent to you. If you know someone who has attended, talk to that person. If you still have not made up your mind, try the local daily newspaper or chamber of commerce.

Do not be swayed by the size of a flea market's advertisement in a trade paper. The Kane County advertisement is often less than a sixteenth of a page. A recent full-page advertisement for Brimfield flea markets failed to include J&J Promotions or May's Antique Market, two of the major players on the scene. This points out the strong regional competition between flea markets. Be suspicious of what one promoter tells you about another promoter's market.

Evaluating a Flea Market

After you have attended a flea market, it is time to decide if you will attend it again and how frequently. Answer the following 19 questions "yes" or "no." In this test, "no" is the right answer. If more than half the questions are "yes," forget about going back. There are plenty of flea markets from which to choose. If 12 or more are answered "no," give it another chance in a few months. If 17 or more answers are "no," plan another visit soon.

Flea Market Quick Quiz

1. Was the flea market hard to find? ___ Yes ___ No

2. Did you have a difficult time moving between the flea market and your car in the parking area? ___ Yes ___ No

3. Did you have to pay a parking fee in addition to an admission fee? ___ Yes ___ No

4. Did the manager fail to provide a map of the market? ___ Yes ___ No

5. Was a majority of the market in an open, outdoor environment? ___ Yes ___ No

6. Were indoor facilities poorly lighted and ventilated? ___ Yes ___ No

7. Was there a problem with the number of toilet facilities or with the facilities' cleanliness? ___ Yes ___ No

8. Was your overall impression of the market one of chaos? ___ Yes ___ No

9. Did collectibles outnumber antiques? ___ Yes ___ No

10. Did secondhand goods and new merchandise outnumber collectibles? ___ Yes ___ No

11. Were reproductions, copycats, fantasy items and fakes in abundance? (See Chapter 5.) ___ Yes ___ No

12. Was there a large representation of home crafts and/or discontinued merchandise? ___ Yes ___ No

13. Were the vast majority of antiques and collectibles that you saw in fair condition or worse? ___ Yes ___ No

14. Were individuals that you expected to encounter at the market absent? ___ Yes ___ No

15. Did you pass out fewer than five lists of your wants? ___ Yes ___ No

16. Did you buy fewer than five new items for your collection? ___ Yes ___ No

17. Were more than half the items that you bought priced near or at book value? ___ Yes ___ No

18. Was there a lack of good restaurants and/or lodging within easy access of the flea market? ___ Yes ___ No

19. Would you tell a friend never to attend the market? ___ Yes ___ No

There are some flea markets that scored well for me, and I would like to share them with you. They are listed in the next chapter.

CHAPTER THREE

Top 25
U.S. Flea Markets

The first two editions of *Price Guide to Flea Market Treasures* contained a list of the "Top 20 U.S. Flea Markets." Deciding which markets would and would not be on the list was not easy. There are thousands of flea markets throughout the United States. In each edition there were four to six markets that I excluded simply because of the arbitrary number that I selected. Subsequent travels have provided me with the opportunity to visit many flea markets that I knew previously only by reputation. When making the final selection for the third edition, I could not narrow the list to 20, hence the "Top 25 U.S. Flea Markets."

Adding five more flea markets to the list did not silence all my critics. Everyone has regional favorites that failed to make the cut. I wish I could list them all, but that is not the purpose of this price guide. In making my choices, I used the following criteria. First, I wanted to provide a representative sample from the major flea market groups—seasonal, monthly and weekly. Since this price guide is designed for the national market, I made certain that the selections covered the entire United States. Finally, I selected flea markets that I feel will inspire a prospective or novice collector. Nothing is more fun than getting off to a great start.

This list is only a starting point. Almost every flea market has a table containing promotional literature for other flea markets in the area. Follow up on the ones of interest. Continue to check trade paper listings. There are always new flea markets being started.

Finally, not every flea market is able to maintain its past glories. Are there flea markets that you think should be on this list? Have you visited some of the listed flea markets and found them to be unsatisfactory? As each edition of this guide is prepared, this list will be evaluated. Send any thoughts and comments that you may have to: Harry L. Rinker, Rinker Enterprises, Inc., 5093 Vera Cruz Rd., Emmaus, PA 18049.

The "Top 25" list contains the following information: name of flea market, location, frequency and general admission times, type of goods sold and general comments, number of dealers, indoor and/or outdoor, special features, 1997 admission fee, and address and phone number (if known) of manager or promoter.

Seasonal Flea Markets

1. **America's Largest Antique and Collectible Sale**

   Portland Expo Center, Portland, OR; exit 306B off I-5; Saturday and Sunday, early March, mid July and late October; antiques and collectibles; 1,250+ dealers in March and October, indoors; 1,500+ dealers in July, indoor/outdoor; admission—$5 per person; parking—$4; Palmer/Wirfs & Associates, 4001 N.E. Halsey, Portland, OR 97232, (503) 282-0877.

2. **America's Largest Antique and Collectible Sale**

   Cow Palace, San Francisco, CA; exit off Highway 101; Saturday and Sunday, February, May, August and November, usually mid-month, Saturday 8 a.m. to 7 p.m., Sunday 9 a.m. to 5 p.m.; antiques and collectibles; 400+ dealers, indoors; admission—$5 per person; parking—$3; Palmer/Wirfs & Associates, 4001 N.E. Halsey, Portland, OR 97232, (503) 282-0877.

3. Brimfield

Route 20, Brimfield, MA 01010; six consecutive days in May, July and September; antiques, collectibles and secondhand goods; 3,000+ dealers; indoor/outdoor; includes more than 20 individual antiques shows with staggered opening and closing dates, most shows with different promoters; admission—varies, according to field, ranging from free admission to $3; average parking fee—$3

Brimfield Acres North, P.O. Box 397, Holden, MA 01520, (508) 754-4185 or (413) 245-9471.

Central Park Antiques Shows, P.O. Box 224, Brimfield, MA 01010, (413) 596-9257.

The Dealers' Choice and Faxon's Treasure Chest-Midway Shows, P.O. Box 28, Fiskdale, MA 01518, (508) 347-3929.

Heart-O-The-Mart, P.O. Box 26, Brimfield, MA 01010, (413) 245-9556.

J&J Promotions, P.O. Box 385, Brimfield, MA 01010, (413) 245-3436 or (508) 597-8155.

Jeanne Hertan Antiques Shows, P.O. Box 628, Somers, CT 06071, (203) 763-3760 or (413) 245-9872.

Mahogany Ridge, P.O. Box 129, Brimfield, MA 01010, (413) 245-9615.

May's Antique Show, P.O. Box 416, Brimfield, MA 01010, (413) 245-9271.

New England Motel Antiques Market, Inc., P.O. Box 186, Sturbridge, MA 01566, (508) 347-2179.

Quaker Acres, 62 W. Main St., Norwich, NY 13815, (607) 336-7355 or (413) 245-9549.

Shelton Antiques Shows, P.O. Box 124, Brimfield, MA 01010, (413) 245-3591.

Sturtevant, P.O. Box 468, Brimfield, MA 01010, (413) 245-7458.

You can subscribe to the *Brimfield Antique Guide* from Brimfield Publications, P.O. Box 442, Brimfield, MA 01010, (413) 245-9329. Three issues are $9.95.

4. Renninger's Extravaganza

Noble Street, Kutztown, PA 19530; Thursday, Friday and Saturday of last full weekend of April, June and September, Thursday opens at 10 a.m. for pre-admission only ($40 per car carrying one to four people), Friday and Saturday, 7 a.m. to 5 p.m.; antiques and collectibles; 1,200+ dealers; indoor/outdoor; admission—$5 on Friday, $3 on Saturday; Renninger's Promotions, 27 Bensinger Dr., Schuylkill Haven, PA 17972; call Monday through Friday at (717) 385-0104, Saturday at (610) 683-6848, and Sunday at (717) 336-2177.

Monthly Flea Markets

5. Allegan Antiques Market

Allegan Fairgrounds, Allegan, MI 49010; last Sunday of the month, April through September, 7:30 a.m. to 4:30 p.m.; antiques and collectibles; 170+ dealers indoors/200 dealers outdoors; admission—$3; Larry L. Wood and Morrie Fulkerson, 2030 Blueberry Dr., N.W., Grand Rapids, MI 49504, (616) 453-8780 for show information or (616) 887-7677.

6. Ann Arbor Antiques Market

5055 Ann Arbor-Saline Rd., Ann Arbor, MI 48103; May through August and October (third Sunday of the month), April and September (Saturday and Sunday, weekend of third Sunday of month); November market usually occurs second Sunday of month, 7 a.m. to 5 p.m.; antiques and select collectibles; 350+ dealers; all under cover; locator service for specialties and dealers; admission—$5; M. Brusher, Manager, P.O. Box 1512, Ann Arbor, MI 48106, (313) 662-9453.

7. Birmingham Fairgrounds Flea Market

Birmingham Fairgrounds, Birmingham, AL 35208; Exit 120 off I-20/59, follow signs for Alabama State Fair Complex; first weekend of every month, year-round, plus second and third weekends in December, Friday, 3 p.m. to 9 p.m. and Saturday and Sunday, 9 a.m. to 6 p.m.; antiques, collectibles and new merchandise (somewhat swapmeet-like); 600+ antique market dealer spaces; mostly indoors; admission and parking—free; Birmingham Flea Market, 621 Lorna Sq., Hoover, AL 35216, 800-362-7538.

8. Burlington Antiques Show

Boone County Fairgrounds, Burlington, KY 41005; third Sunday of the month, April through October, 8 a.m. to 3 p.m.; antiques and collectibles; outdoor; admission—$2, early buyers 5 to 8 a.m.—$5; Paul Kohls, P.O. Box 58367, Cincinnati, OH 45258, (513) 922-5265.

9. Centreville Antiques Market

The St. Joseph County Grange Fairgrounds, State Route 86, Centreville, MI 49032; one Sunday per month, May through October, excluding September, 7 a.m. to 4 p.m.; antiques and collectibles (all merchandise guaranteed); 500+ dealers; admission—$4; Robert C. Lawler Management, 1510 N. Hoyne, Chicago, IL 60622, (773) 227-4464.

10. Fairgrounds Antiques Market

Arizona State Fairgrounds, 19th Avenue & McDowell, Phoenix, AZ 85009; third weekend of the month, year-round, except December (second weekend), no show in October, Saturday 9 a.m. to 5 p.m. and Sunday 10 a.m. to 4 p.m.; antiques, collectibles and crafts; antique glass and clock repairs; about 200 dealers; indoor; admission—$1; parking—$4; Jack Black Shows, P.O. Box 61172, Phoenix, AZ 85082-1172, (800) 678-9987 or (602) 943-1766.

11. Gordyville USA Flea Market & Auction

Rantoul, IL 61866; Route 136, 7.5 miles east of I-57; second weekend (Friday, Saturday, Sunday) of each month, first weekend in December, Friday 4 p.m. to 9 p.m., Saturday 9 a.m. to 6 p.m., and Sunday 9 a.m. to 4 p.m.; antiques, collectibles, vintage items, arts, crafts; indoor/outdoor; Saturday and Sunday auctions start at 11 a.m.; admission—free; Gordon Hannagan Auction Company, P.O. Box 490, Gifford, IL 61847, (217) 568-7117.

12. Kane County Antiques Flea Markets

Kane County Fairgrounds, Randall Road, St. Charles, IL 60175; first Sunday of every month and preceding Saturday, except New Year's and Easter, year-round, Saturday 1 to 5 p.m. and Sunday 7 a.m. to 4 p.m.; antiques, collectibles and some crafts (a favorite in the Midwest, especially with the Chicago crowd); indoor/outdoor; country breakfast served; admission—$4 (children under 12 free); Helen Robinson, Manager, P.O. Box 549, St. Charles, IL 60174, (708) 377-2252; Internet address: http://www2.pair.com/kaneflea/

13. Kentucky Flea Market

Kentucky Fair and Exposition Center at junction of I-264 and I-65, Louisville, KY; three- or four-day show, dates vary, check trade papers; Friday noon to 8 p.m., Saturday 10 a.m. to 8 p.m. and Sunday 11 a.m. to 5 p.m.; antiques, collectibles, arts and crafts and new merchandise; about 1,000 booths; indoor (climate-controlled); admission—free; parking—$2 at facility; Stewart Promotions, 2950 Breckinridge Lane, Ste. 4A, Louisville, KY 40220, (502) 456-2244.

14. Long Beach Outdoor Antiques & Collectible Market

Veterans Stadium, Lakewood Boulevard and Conant Street, Long Beach, CA; third Sunday of each month, 8 a.m. to 3 p.m., first Sunday in November, last Sunday in June; antiques and collectibles (including vintage clothing, pottery, quilts, primitives, advertising); 800+ dealers; admission—early admission (5:30 to 6:30 a.m.) $10, general admission $4.50; Americana Enterprises, Inc., P.O. Box 69219, Los Angeles, CA 90069, (213) 655-5703.

15. Metrolina Expo

7100 N. Statesville Rd., Charlotte, NC; first and third Friday, Saturday and Sunday of every month, year-round, 8 a.m. to 5 p.m. Friday and Saturday, 9 a.m. to 5 p.m. Sunday; antiques and collectibles; indoor/outdoor; first weekend about 1,500 dealers; third weekend between 800 and 1,000 dealers; Metrolina hosts three Spectaculars yearly—April, June and November—which feature more than 5,000 dealers; admission—first weekend $3 per day, third weekend $2 per day and spectaculars $5 per day; early buyer's fee and sneak preview fee are available; Metrolina EXPO Center, P.O. Box 26652, Charlotte, NC 28221, (704) 596-4643 or 800-824-3770.

16. Sandwich Antiques Market

The Fairgrounds, State Route 34, Sandwich, IL 60548; one Sunday per month, May through October, 8 a.m. to 4 p.m.; antiques and collectibles; 600+ dealers; admission—$4; Sandwich Antiques Market, 1510 N. Hoyne, Chicago, IL 60622, (773) 227-4464.

17. Scott Antiques Market

Ohio Expo Center, Columbus, OH; Saturday 9 a.m. to 6 p.m. and Sunday 10 a.m. to 5 p.m., November through June (weekend dates vary, check Scott advertisements in the trade papers); antiques and collectibles; 1,200 booths; indoor; admission—free; parking—$3; Scott Antiques Market, P.O. Box 60, Bremen, OH 43107, (614) 569-4112. [Scott also conducts a second monthly flea market—The Scott Antique Market, Atlanta Exposition Centers, adjacent north and south facilities, I-285 to Exit 40 at Jonesboro Road, two miles east of Atlanta airport—second weekend of every month.]

18. Springfield Antiques Show & Flea Market

Clark County Fairgrounds, Springfield, OH; third weekend of the month, year-round, excluding July (December market is held the second weekend of the month), Saturday 8 a.m. to 5 p.m. and Sunday 9 a.m. to 4 p.m.; Extravaganzas are held in May and September; more than half the market is antiques and collectibles; 400 dealers indoors/900 dealers outdoors for monthly market in warm weather; admission—$2 (children 12 and under free); Extravaganza admission—$3; early admission for Extravaganza (Friday morning)—$5; Bruce Knight, P.O. Box 2429, Springfield, OH 45501, (513) 325-0053.

Weekly Flea Markets

19. Adamstown

Route 272, Adamstown, PA 17517; Sundays; antiques, collectibles and secondhand material; admission—free; three major markets (information and dealer reservations, 717-484-4115):

Black Angus; year-round, 8 a.m. to 5 p.m.; indoor/outdoor; Carl Barto, 2717 Long Farm Ln., Lancaster, PA 17601, (717) 569-3536 or (717) 484-4385.

Renninger's; year-round, 7:30 a.m. to 5 p.m.; indoor/outdoor; Renninger's Promotions, 27 Bensinger Dr., Schuylkill Haven, PA 17972; phone on Sunday, (717) 336-2177.

Shupp's Grove; April through October, 7 a.m. to 5 p.m.; outdoor; Shupp's Grove, 1686 Dry Tavern Rd., Denver, PA 17517.

20. Antique World and Marketplace

10995 Main St., Clarence, NY 14031 (Main Street is Route 5); Sunday 8 a.m. to 4 p.m.; three buildings (one devoted to antiques and collectibles, one to flea market material and one as exhibition building); 350 dealers in winter/650 dealers in summer; indoor/outdoor; admission—free; Antique World, 10995 Main St., Clarence, NY 14031, (716) 759-8483.

21. Atlanta Antiques Center and Flea Market

5360 Peachtree Industrial Blvd., Chamblee, GA 30341; Friday and Saturday, 11 a.m. to 7 p.m. and Sunday noon to 7 p.m.; antiques, collectibles, reproductions, oriental rugs and gift items; 165 booths. indoor; admission—free; Atlanta Antiques Center and Flea Market, 5360 Peachtree Industrial Blvd., Chamblee, GA 30341, (770) 458-0456.

22. First Monday Trade Days

Canton, TX 75103 (two blocks from downtown square); Friday through Sunday (Friday before the first Monday of each month) 7 a.m. to dusk; antiques, collectibles, new merchandise, crafts (Note: This belongs in the book—not because it is a great source for antiques and collectibles, but because it is the best known swap meet-flea market in the world); 4,000+ booths; antiques and collectibles located on three-acre plot north of Courthouse; admission—free; parking—$3; City of Canton, P.O. Box 245, Canton, TX 75103. (903) 567-6556.

23. Lambertville Antiques Flea Market

Route 29, 1.5 miles south of Lambertville, NJ 08530; Wednesday, Saturday and Sunday, 6 a.m. to 4 p.m.; antiques and collectibles; 150 dealers; indoor/outdoor; admission—free; Robert Errhalt, 1864 River Road, Lambertville, NJ 08530, (609) 397-0456.

24. Renninger's Antiques Center

Highway 441, Mount Dora, FL 32757; Saturdays and Sundays, 9 a.m. to 5 p.m. (indoor opens at 9 a.m.); Extravaganzas on third weekend of November, January and February, Friday 10 a.m. to 5 p.m., Saturday 8 a.m. to 5:30 p.m. and Sunday 8 a.m. to 5 p.m.; antiques and collectibles; 500+ dealers; indoor/outdoor; admission—free; Extravaganza admission—three-day pass $15, Friday $10, Saturday $5 and Sunday $3; Florida Twin Markets, P.O. Box 1699, Mount Dora, FL 32757, (352) 383-8393.

25. Shipshewana Auction and Flea Market

On State Route 5 near the southern edge of Shipshewana, IN 46565; Wednesdays, 6 a.m. to dusk from May through October, 7:30 a.m. to dusk from November through April; antiques, collectibles, new merchandise and produce (you name it, they sell it); can accommodate up to 800 dealers; indoor/outdoor; admission—free; Shipshewana Auction, Inc., P.O. Box 185, Shipshewana, IN 46565, (219) 768-4129.

Thus far, you have learned to identify the various types of flea markets, how to locate them, the keys to evaluating whether or not they are right for you and my recommendations for getting started. Next you need to develop the skills necessary for flea market survival.

CHAPTER FOUR

Flea Market Survival Guide

Your state of exhaustion at the end of the day is the best gauge that I know to judge the value of a flea market—the greater your exhaustion, the better the flea market. A great flea market keeps you on the go from early morning, in some cases 5 a.m., to early evening, often 6 p.m. The key to survival is to do advance homework, have proper equipment, develop and follow a carefully thought-out shopping strategy and do your follow-up chores as soon as you return home.

If you are a Type-A personality, your survival plan is essentially a battle plan. Your goal is to cover the flea market as thoroughly as possible and secure the objectives (bargains and hard-to-find objects) ahead of your rivals. You do not stop until total victory is achieved. Does not sound like you? No matter. You also need a survival plan if you want to maximize fun and enjoyment.

Advance Homework

Consult the flea market's advertisement or brochure. Make certain that you understand the dates and time. You never know when special circumstances may cause a change in dates and even location. Check the admission policy. It may be possible to buy a ticket in advance to avoid the wait in line at the ticket booth.

Determine if there is an early admission fee and what times are involved. It is a growing practice at flea markets to admit collectors and others to the flea market through the use of an early admission fee. In most cases, the fee is the cost of renting a space. The management simply does not insist that you set up. Actually, this practice had been going on for some time before management formalized it. Friends of individuals renting space often tagged along as helpers or assistants. Once inside, the urge to shop superseded their desire to help their friend.

Review the directions. Are they detailed enough to allow you to find the flea market easily? Remember, it still may be dark when you arrive. If you are not certain, call the manager and ask for specific directions. Make certain of parking provisions, especially when a flea market takes place within a city or town. Local residents who are not enamored with a flea market in their neighborhood take great pleasure in informing police of illegally parked cars and watching the cars get towed away. In some cases, I have found locating parking to be more of a problem than locating the flea market. Avoid frustration and plan ahead.

Decide if you are going to stay overnight, either the evening before the flea market opens or during the days of operation. In many cases, local motel accommodations are minimal. It is common for dealers, as well as collectors, to commute 50 miles each way to attend Brimfield. The general attitude of most flea market managers is that accommodations are your problem, not theirs. If you are lucky, you can get a list of accommodations from a local chamber of commerce. The American Automobile Association regional guidebooks provide some help. However, if you attend a flea market expecting to find nearby overnight accommodations without a reservation, you are the world's biggest optimist.

If possible, obtain a map of the flea market grounds. Become familiar with the layout of the spaces. If you know some of your favorite dealers are going to set up, call and ask them for their space numbers. Mark the location of all toilet facilities and refreshment stands. You may not have time for the latter, but sooner or later you are going to need the former.

Finally, try to convince one or more friends, ideally someone whose area of collecting is totally different from yours, to attend the flea market with you. Each becomes a second set of eyes for the other. Meeting at predesignated spots makes exchanging information easy. It never hurts to share the driving and expenses. Best of all, war stories can be told and savored immediately.

Flea Market Checklist

To have an enjoyable and productive day at the flea market, you need the right equipment, ranging from clothing to packing material for your purchases. What you do not wear can be stored in your car trunk. Make certain that everything is in order the day before your flea market adventure.

Clothing Checklist

___Hat

___Sunglasses

___Light jacket or sweatshirt

___Poncho or raincoat

___Waterproof work boots or galoshes

Field Gear Checklist

___Canvas bag(s)

___Cash, checkbook and credit cards

___Wants lists

___Business (collector) cards

___Magnifying glass

___Swiss Army pocket knife

___Toilet paper

___Sales receipts

___Mechanical pencil or ball-point pen

___This price guide

Car Trunk Checklist

___Three to six cardboard boxes

___Newspaper, bubble-wrap, diapers and other appropriate packing material

___Sun-block

___First-aid kit

___Cooler with cold beverages

Clothing

Most flea markets you attend will either be outdoors or have an outdoor section. If you are lucky, the sun will be shining. Beware of sunburn. Select a hat with a wide brim. I prefer a hat with an outside hat band as well. First, it provides a place to stick notes, business cards and other small pieces of paper that I might otherwise lose. Second, it provides a place to stick a feather or some other distinguishing item that allows my friends to spot me in the crowd. Some flea marketers use the band as a holder for a card expounding their collecting wants. Make certain that your hat fits snugly. Some flea market sites are quite windy. An experienced flea market attendee's hat will look as though it has been through the wars. It has.

I carry sunglasses, but I confess that I rarely use them. I find that taking them on and off is more trouble than they are worth. Further, they distort colors. However, I have found them valuable at windswept and outdoor markets located in large fields. Since I usually misplace a pair a year, I generally buy inexpensive glasses.

The key to dressing for flea markets is a layered, comfortable approach. The early morning and late evening hours are often cool. A light jacket or sweatshirt is suggested. I found a great light jacket that is loaded with pockets. Properly outfitted, it holds all the material I would normally put in my carrying bag.

You must assume that it is going to rain. I have never been to Brimfield when it was not raining. Rain, especially at an outdoor flea market, is a disaster. What is astonishing is how much activity continues in spite of the rain. I prefer a poncho over a raincoat because it covers my purchases as well as my clothing. Most flea markets offer ponchos for sale when rain starts. They are lightweight and come with a storage bag. Of course, you have to be a genius to fold them small enough to get them back into their original storage bag. One I purchased at Kane County lasted years. Mrs. Robinson, being a shrewd promoter, just happened to have them imprinted with information about her flea market. I had a great time there, so I have never objected to being a walking bulletin board on her behalf.

The ideal footwear for a flea market is a well-broken-in pair of running or walking shoes. However, in the early morning, when the ground is wet with dew, a pair of waterproof work boots is a much better choice. I keep my running shoes in the car trunk and usually change into them by 9 a.m., at most flea markets.

Rain at outdoor flea markets equals mud. The only defense is a good pair of galoshes. I have been at Brimfield when the rain was coming down so fiercely that dealers set up in tents were using tools to dig water diversion ditches. Cars, which were packed in the nearby fields, sank into the ground. In several cases, local farmers with tractors handsomely supplemented their income by pulling out the stuck autos.

I always go to a flea market planning to buy something. Since most flea market sellers provide the minimum packaging possible, I carry my own. My preference is a double-handled canvas bag with a flat bottom. It is not as easy an item to find as it sounds. I use one to carry my field gear along with two extra bags that start out folded. I find that I can carry three filled bags comfortably. This avoids the necessity of running back to the car each time a bag is filled.

If you are going to buy something, you have to pay for it. Cash is always preferred by the sellers. I carry my cash in a small white envelope with the amount with which I started marked at the top. I note and deduct each purchase as I go along. If you carry cash, be careful how you display it. Pickpockets and sticky-fingered individuals do attend flea markets.

Since I want a record of my purchases, I pay by check whenever I can. I have tried to control my spending by only taking a few checks. Forget it. I can always borrow money on Monday to cover my weekend purchases. I make certain that I have a minimum of 10 checks.

Most flea market sellers will accept checks with proper identification. For this reason, I put my driver's license and a major credit card in the front of my checkbook before entering the flea market. This saves me the trouble of taking out my wallet each time I make a purchase.

A surprising number of flea market sellers are willing to take credit cards. I am amazed at this practice, since the only means they have of checking a card's validity is the canceled card booklet they receive each week. They wait until later to get telephone authorization, a potentially dangerous practice.

I buy as much material through the mail as I do at flea markets. One of the principal reasons I attend flea markets is to make contact with dealers. Since flea markets attract many dealers from other parts of the country, I expand my supplier sources at each flea market I attend.

The key is to have a wants-list ready to give to any flea market seller that admits to doing business by mail. My wants-list fills an 8-1/2 inch by 11 inch sheet of writing paper. In addition to my wants, it includes my name, post office box address, UPS (i.e., street) address and office and home telephone numbers. I also make it a point to get the full name and address of any dealer to whom I give my list. I believe in follow-up.

Not every dealer is willing to take a full-page wants-list. For this reason, I hand out my business card. The back of my business card contains an abbreviated list of my wants and a blank line for me to add additional information. Do not waste this valuable space by leaving it blank. Most take it as a courtesy. However, I have received quotes on a few great items as a result of my efforts.

I carry a simple variety-store 10-power magnifying glass. It is helpful to see marks clearly and to spot cracks in china and glass. Ninety-nine percent of the time, I use it merely to confirm something that I saw with the naked eye. Jewelers' loupes are overkill, unless you are buying jewelry.

Years ago, I purchased a good Swiss Army pocket knife, one that contains scissors as part of the blade package. It was one of the smartest investments that I made. No flea market goes by that I do not use the knife for one reason or another. If you do not want to carry a pocket knife, invest in a pair of operating-room surgical scissors. They will cut through almost anything.

I am a buyer. Why do I carry a book of sales receipts? Alas, many flea market sellers operate in a nontraditional business manner. They are not interested in paper trails, especially when you pay cash. You need a receipt to protect yourself. More on this subject later.

I keep a roll of toilet paper in the car and some in my carrying bag. Do not laugh. I am serious. Most outdoor flea markets have portable toilets. After a few days, the toilet paper supply is exhausted. Even some indoor facilities give out. If I had $5 from all the people to whom I supplied toilet paper at flea markets, I would be writing this book in Hawaii instead of Pennsylvania.

I carry a mechanical pencil (a ball-point pen works just as well). When I pick up someone's business card, I note why on the back of the card. Use the pencil to mark dealer locations on the flea market map. I do not always buy something when I first spot it. The map helps me relocate items when I wish to go back for a second look. I have wasted hours at flea markets backtracking to find an item that was not located where I thought it was.

Anyone who tells you they know everything about antiques and collectibles and their prices is a liar. I know the areas in which I collect quite well. But there are many categories where a quick source-check never hurts. Every general price guide is different. Find the one that best serves your needs and use it consistently. You know you have a good command of your price guide when you do not have to use the index to locate the value for the item you are seeking. I scored some major points with dealers and others when I offered to share information with them.

From the Car Trunk

My car trunk contains a number of cardboard boxes, several of which are archival file boxes with hand inserts on the side. I have them because I want to see that my purchases make it home safe and sound. One of the boxes is filled with newspaper, diapers and some bubble-wrap. It supplements the field wrapping, so that I can stack objects on top of one another. I check the trunk seals on a regular basis. A leaking car trunk once ruined several key purchases I made on an antiquing adventure.

A wide-brim hat may protect the face and neck from the sun, but it leaves the arms exposed. I admire those individuals who can wear a long-sleeved shirt year-round. I am not one of them. In the summer, I wear short-sleeved shirts. For this reason, I keep a bottle of sun-block in the trunk.

I also have a first-aid kit that includes aspirin. The most used object is a Band-Aid for unexpected cuts and scratches. The aspirin comes in handy when I have spent eight or more hours in the sun. My first-aid kit also contains packaged cleaning towelettes. I always use one before heading home.

It does not take much for me to get a flea market high. When I do, I can go the entire day without eating. The same does not hold true for liquid intake. Just as toilet paper is a precious commodity at flea markets, so is ice. I carry a small cooler in my trunk with six to a dozen cans of my favorite beverage. The fastest way to seal a friendship with a flea market dealer is to offer him or her a cold drink at the end of a hot day.

How to Shop a Flea Market

After attending flea markets for a number of years, I would like to share some of the things that I do to bag the treasures found in the flea market jungle. Much of what I am about to tell you is no more than common sense, but we all know that this is probably one of the most ignored of all the senses.

Most likely, you will drive to the flea market. Parking is often a problem. It does not have to be. The general rule is to park as close to the main gate as possible. However, since most flea markets have a number of gates, I usually try to park near a secondary gate. First, this allows me to get closer than I could by trying for the main gate. Second, I have long recognized whatever gate I use is "my" main gate and it serves well as home base for my buying operations.

As soon as I arrive at the flea market, I check three things before allowing my buying adrenaline to kick into high gear—the location of the toilets and refreshment stands and the relationship between outdoor and indoor facilities. The latter is very important. Dealers who regularly do the flea market are most likely to be indoors. If I miss them this time around, I can catch them the next. Dealers who are just passing through are most likely set-up outdoors. If I miss them, I may never see them again.

I spend the first half hour at any flea market doing a quick tour to understand how the flea market is organized, spot those dealers that I would like to visit later and develop a general sense of what is happening. I prefer to start at the point farthest from my car and work my way to the front, just the opposite of most flea market shoppers. It makes trips back to the car shorter each time and reduces the amount of purchases that I am carrying over an extended period of time.

Whenever I go to a flea market to buy, I try to have one to four specific categories in mind. If one tries to look at everything, one develops "antiques and collectibles" shock. Collectors' minds short-circuit if they try to absorb too much. They never get past the first aisle. With specific goals, a quick look at a booth will tell me whether or not it is likely to feature merchandise of interest. If not, I pass it by.

Since time is always at a premium, I make it a practice to ask every dealer, "Do you have any...?" If they say "no," I usually go to the next booth. However, I have learned that dealers do not always remember what they have. When I am in a booth that should have the type of merchandise that I am seeking, I take a minute or two to do a quick scan to see if the dealer is right. In about 25% of the cases, I have found at least one example of the type of material for which I am looking.

I eat on the run, if I eat at all. A good breakfast before the market opens carries me until the evening hours, when dusk shuts down the market. I am at the flea market to stuff my bag and car trunk, not my face.

When I find a flea market that I like, I try to visit it at least once in the spring and once in the late summer or early fall. In many flea markets, the same dealers are located in the same spot each time. This is extremely helpful to a buyer. I note their location on my map of the market. When I return the next time, I ask these dealers if they have brought anything that fills my needs. If they say "yes," I ask them to hold it for an hour or two. Some will, some won't. Those who have done business with me previously and know my buying pattern are more willing to accede to my wishes than those who do not. I do not abuse the privilege, but I do not hesitate to take advantage of it, either.

Guarantees

There is an adage among collectors that "if you bought something at a flea market, you own it." I do not support this approach. I believe that every seller should unconditionally guarantee his or her merchandise. If I find a piece is misrepresented, I take it back.

I try to get a receipt for every purchase I make. Since many individuals who sell at outdoor flea markets are part-time dealers, they often are unprepared to give a receipt. No problem. I carry a pad of blank receipts and ask them to fill one out.

In every case, I ask the dealers to include their name, shop name (if any), mailing address and phone number on the receipt. If I do not think a dealer is telling me the truth, I ask for identification. If they give me any flack, I go to their vehicle (usually located in their booth) or just outside their indoor stand and make note of the license-plate number. Flea market dealers, especially the outdoor group, are highly mobile. If a problem develops with the merchandise I bought, I want to reach the dealer to solve the problem.

Whenever possible, the receipt should contain a full description of the merchandise, along with a completeness and condition statement. I also ask the dealer to write "money back guaranteed, no questions asked" on the receipt. This is the only valid guarantee that I know. Phrases such as "guaranteed as represented" and "money back" are open to interpretation and become relatively meaningless if a dispute develops. Many dealers are reluctant to provide this guarantee, afraid that the buyer will switch a damaged item for a good one or swipe a part and return the item as incomplete. Any selling situation has to involve trust by both parties.

Shopping Around

I always shop around. At a good flea market, I expect to see the same merchandise in several booths. Prices will vary, often by several hundred, if not several thousand, percent. I make a purchase immediately only when a piece is a "real" bargain, priced way below current market value. If a piece is near current market value, I often inspect it, note its location on my map and walk away. If I do not find another in as good condition, at a cheaper price, or both, I go back and negotiate with the dealer.

I take the time to inspect carefully, in natural sunlight, any piece I buy. First, I check for defects, such as cracks, nicks, scratches and signs of normal wear. Second, if the object involves parts, I make certain that it is complete. I have been known to take the time to carefully count parts. The last two times that I did not do this, the objects that I bought turned out to be incomplete.

I frequently find myself asking a dealer to clean an object for my inspection. Outdoor flea markets are often quite dusty, especially in July and August. The insides of most indoor markets are generally not much better. Dirt can easily hide flaws. It also can discolor objects. Make certain you know exactly what you are buying.

I force myself to slow down and get to know those dealers from whom I hope to make future purchases. Even though it may mean that I do not visit the entire flea market, I have found that the long-term benefits from this type of contact far outweigh the short-term gain of seeing every booth.

Flea Market Food

Flea market food is best described as overcooked, greasy and heartburn-inducing. I think I forgot to mention that my first-aid kit contains a roll of antacid pills. Gourmet eating facilities are usually nonexistent. Is it any wonder that I often go without eating?

Several flea markets take place on sites that also house a farmer's market. When this is the case, I take time to shop the market and eat at one of its food counters or buy something that I can eat while sitting in my car. I make a point to spot any fast-food restaurants in the vicinity of the flea market. If I get desperate, I get in the car and drive to one of them.

I do make it a point to inquire among the dealers where they go to have their evening meals. They generally opt for good food, plenty of it, at inexpensive prices. At the end of the day, I am hungry. I do not feel like driving home, cleaning up and then eating. I want to eat where the clientele can stand the appearance and smell of a flea marketer. I have rarely been disappointed when I followed a flea market dealer's recommendation.

The best survival tactic is probably to bring your own food. I simply find this too much trouble. I get heartburn just thinking about a lunch sitting for several hours inside a car on a hot summer day. No thanks; I will buy what I need.

Follow Up

Immediately upon returning home, or the next day, unpack and record all your purchases. If you wait, you are going to forget important details. This is not the fun part of collecting. It is easy to ignore. Discipline yourself to do it. Get in the habit. You know it is the right thing to do, so do it.

Review the business cards that you picked up and notes that you made. If letters are required, write them. If telephone calls are necessary, make them. Never lose sight of the fact that one of your principal reasons for going to the flea market is to establish long-term dealer contacts.

Finally, if your experiences at the flea market were positive or if you saw ways to improve the market, write a letter to the manager. He or she will be delighted in both instances. Competition among flea markets for dealers and customers is increasing. Good managers want to make their markets better than their competitors'. Your comments and suggestions will be welcomed.

CHAPTER FIVE

Honing Your Shopping Skills

Earlier, I mentioned that most buyers view flea markets as places where bargains and "steals" can be found. I have found plenty. However, the truth is that you have to hunt long and hard to find them; in some cases, they evolve only after intense bargaining. Shopping a flea market properly requires skills. This chapter will help shape and hone your shopping skills and alert you to some of the pitfalls involved in buying at a flea market.

What Type of Dealer Are You Dealing With?

There are essentially three types of dealers found at flea markets: the professional dealer, the weekend dealer and the once-and-done dealer. Each brings a different level of expertise and merchandise to the flea market. Each offers pluses and minuses. Knowing which you are dealing with is advantageous.

So many flea markets developed in the 1980s and 1990s that there are now professional flea market dealers who practice their craft on a full-time basis. Within any given week, you may find them at three or four different flea markets. They are the modern American gypsies; their living accommodations and merchandise are usually found within the truck, van or station wagon in which they are traveling. These individuals survive on shrewdness and hustle. They want

to turn over their merchandise as quickly as possible for the best gain possible and are willing to do whatever is necessary to achieve this end.

Deal with professional flea market dealers with a questioning mind; i.e., question everything they tell you about an object, from what it is to what they want for it. Their knowledge of the market comes from hands-on experience. It is not as great as they think, in most cases. They are so busy setting up, buying, selling and breaking down, that they have little time to do research or follow trade literature. More than any other group of dealers in the trade, they are weavers of tales and sellers of dreams.

The professional flea market dealer's circuit can stretch from New England to California, from Michigan to Florida. These "professionals" are constantly on the move. If you have a problem with something one of these dealers sold you, finding him or her can prove difficult. Do not buy anything from a professional dealer, unless you are absolutely certain about it.

Judge the credibility and integrity of the professional flea market dealer by the quality of the merchandise he or she displays. You should see middle- and high-quality material in better condition than you normally expect to find. If the offerings are heavily damaged and appear poorly maintained, walk away.

Do not interpret what I have said to imply that all professional flea market dealers are dishonest. The vast majority are fine individuals. However, as a whole, this group has the largest share of rotten apples in its barrel—more than any other group of dealers in the flea market field. Since there is no professional organization to police the trade, and promoters do not care as long as their space rent is paid, it is up to you to protect yourself.

The antiques and collectibles field works on the principle of *caveat emptor,* "let the buyer beware." Just remember that the key is to beware of the seller as well as the merchandise. It pays to know with whom you are doing business.

Weekend flea market dealers are individuals who have a full-time job elsewhere and are dealing on the weekends to supplement their incomes. In most cases, their weekday job is outside the antiques and collectibles field. However, with the growth of the antiques mall, some of these weekend dealers are really full-time antiques and collectibles dealers. They spend their weekdays shopping and maintaining their mall locations, while selling on the weekend at their traditional flea market location.

In many cases, these dealers specialize, especially if they are in a large flea market environment. As a result, they are usually familiar with the literature relating to their areas of expertise. They also tend to live within a few hours' drive of the flea market in which they set up. This means that they can be found if the need arises.

Once-and-done dealers range from an individual who is using the flea market to dispose of some inherited family heirlooms or portions of an estate to collectors who have culled their collection and are offering their duplicates and discards for sale. Bargains can often be found in both cases. In the first instance, bargains result from lack of pricing knowledge. However, unless you are an early arrival, chances are that the table will be picked clean by the regular dealers and pickers long before you show up. Bargains originate from the collectors, because they know the price levels in their field. They realize that to sell their discards and duplicates, they will have to create prices that are tempting to dealer and collector alike.

The once-and-done dealers are the least prepared to conduct sales on a business basis. Most likely, they will not have a receipt book or a business card. They almost never attempt to collect applicable sales tax. There is little long-term gain in spending time getting to know the individual who is selling off a few family treasures. However, do not leave without asking, "Is there anything else you have at home that you are planning to sell?"

Spend time talking with the collector. If you have mutual collecting interests, invite him or her to visit and view your collection. What you are really fishing for is an invitation to view his or her holdings. You will be surprised how often you will receive one when you show genuine interest.

What Is It?

You need to be concerned with two questions when looking at an object: What is it? and How much is it worth? To answer the second question, you need a correct answer to the first. Information provided about objects for sale at flea markets is minimal and often nonexistent. In many cases, it is false. The only state of mind that protects you is a defensive one.

There are several reasons for the amount of misidentification of objects at flea markets. The foremost is dealer ignorance. Many dealers simply do not take the time to do proper research. I also suspect that they are quite comfortable with the adage that "ignorance is bliss." As long as an object bears a resemblance to something authentic, it will be touted with the most prestigious label available.

When questioning dealers about an object, beware of phrases such as "I think it is an...," "As best as I can tell...," "It looks exactly like...," and "I trust your judgment." Push the dealers until you pin them down. The more they vacillate, the more suspicious you should become. Insist that the sales receipt carry a full claim about the object.

In many cases, misidentification is passed from person to person, because the dealer who bought the object trusted what was said by the dealer who sold the object. I am always amazed how convinced dealers are that they are right. I have found there is little point in arguing with them. The only way to preserve both individuals' sanity is to walk away.

If you do not know what something is, do not buy it. The general price guide and any specific price guides that you have in your carrying bag can point you in the right direction, but they are not the final word. If you simply must find out right that minute and do not have the reference book you need, check with the antiques and collectibles book dealer at the market to see if he has the title you need.

Stories, Stories and More Stories

A flea market is a place where one's creative imagination and ability to believe what is heard are constantly tested. The number of cleverly crafted stories to explain the origin of pieces and why the condition is not exactly what one expects is endless. The problem is that they all sound plausible. Once again, I come back to the concept upon which flea market survival is founded: a questioning mind.

I often ask dealers to explain the circumstances through which they acquired a piece and what they know about the piece. Note what I said, I am not asking the seller to reveal his or her source. No one should be expected to do that. I am testing the openness and believability of the dealer. If the dealer claims there is something special about an object (e.g., it belonged to a famous person or was illustrated in a book), I ask to see proof. Word-of-mouth stories have no validity in the long run.

Again, there are certain phrases that serve as tip-offs that something may be amiss. "It is the first one I have ever seen," "You will never find another one like it," "I saw one a few aisles over for more money," "One sold at auction a few weeks ago for double what I am asking," and "I am selling it to you for exactly what I paid for it" are just a few examples. If what you are hearing sounds too good to be true, it probably is.

Your best defense is to spend time studying and researching the area in which you want to collect before going to flea markets. Emphasis should be placed equally on object identification and an understanding of the pricing structure within that collecting category. You will not be a happy person if you find that, although an object you bought is what the seller claimed it was, you paid far more for it than it is worth.

Period, Reproduction, Copycat, Fantasy or Fake

The number of reproductions, copycats and fantasy and fake items at flea markets is larger than in any other segment of the field. Antiques and collectibles malls run a close second. In fact, it is common to find several dealers at a flea market selling reproductions, copycats and fantasy items openly. When you recognize them, take time to study their merchandise. Commit the material to memory. In 10 years, when the material has begun to age, you will be glad that you did.

Although the above terms are familiar to those who are active in the antiques and collectibles field, they may not be understood by some. A period piece is an example made during the initial period of production. The commonly used term is "real." However, if you think about it, all objects are real, whether period or not. "Real" is one of those terms that should set your mind to questioning.

A reproduction is an exact copy of a period piece. There may be subtle changes in areas not visible to the naked eye, but it is essentially identical to its period counterpart. A copycat is an object that is similar, but not exactly like the period piece it is emulating. It may vary in size, form or design elements. In some cases, it is very close to the original. In auction terms, copycats are known as "in the style of." A fantasy item is a form that was not issued during the initial period of production. An object licensed after Elvis's death would be an Elvis fantasy item. A Chippendale-style coffee table, a form which did not exist during the first Chippendale period, is another example.

The thing to remember is that reproductions, copycats and fantasy items are generally mass-produced and begin life honestly. The wholesalers who sell them to dealers in the trade make it clear exactly what they are. Alas, some of the dealers do not do so when they resell them.

Because reproductions, copycats and fantasy items are mass-produced, they appear in the market in quantity. When you spot a piece in your collecting area that you have never seen before, quickly check through the rest of the market. If the piece is mint, double-check. Handle the piece. Is it the right weight? Does it have the right color? Is it the quality that you expect? If you answer "no" to any of these questions, put it back.

The vast majority of items sold at any flea market are mass-produced, 20th century items. Encountering a new influx of never-seen-before items does not necessarily mean they are reproductions, copycats or fantasy items. Someone may have uncovered a hoard. The trade term is "warehouse find." A hoard can seriously affect the value of any antique or collectible. Suddenly, the number of available examples rises dramatically. So usually does the condition level. Unless the owner of a hoard is careful, this sudden release of material can drive prices downward.

A fake is an item deliberately meant to deceive. They are usually one-of-a-kind items, with many of them originating in shops of revivalist craftspersons. The folk-art and furniture market is flooded with them. It is a common assumption that reproductions, copycats, fantasy items and fakes are of poor quality and can be easily spotted. If you subscribe to this theory, you are a fool. There are some excellent examples out there. You probably have read on more than one occasion how a museum was fooled by an object in its collection. If museum curators can be fooled, so can you.

This is not the place for a lengthy dissertation on how to identify and differentiate period objects, reproductions, copycats, fantasies or fakes. There are books on the subject. Get them and read them. What follows are a few quick tips to put you on the alert:

1. If it looks new, assume it is new.

2. Examine each object carefully, looking for signs of age and repair that should be there.

3. Use all appropriate senses—sight, touch, smell and hearing—to check an object.

4. Be doubly alert when something appears to be a "steal."

5. Make copies of articles from trade papers or other sources that you find about period, reproduction, copycat, fantasy and fake items and keep them on file.

6. Finally, handle as many authentic objects as possible. The more genuine items you handle, the easier it will be to identify impostors.

What's a Fair Price?

The best selling scenario at a flea market is a buyer and seller who are both happy with the price paid, and a seller who has made sufficient profit to allow him or her to stay in business and return to sell another day. Reality is not quite like this. Abundance of merchandise, competition among dealers and negotiated prices often result in the seller being less than happy with the final price received. Yet, the dealers sell because some money is better than no money.

Price haggling is part of the flea market game. In fact, the next section discusses this very subject in detail. The only real value an object has is what someone is willing to pay for it, not what someone asks for it. There is no fixed price for any antique, collectible or second-hand object. All value is relative.

These considerations aside, there are a few points relating to price and value that the flea marketeer should be aware of. Try to understand these points. Remember, in the antiques and collectibles field, there are frequently two or more sides to every issue and rarely any clear-cut right or wrong answer.

First, dealers have a right to an honest profit. If dealers are attempting to make a full-time living in the trade, they must triple their money to cover their inventory costs, pay their overhead expenses (which are not inconsequential) and pay themselves. Buy at 30 cents and sell at $1. The key problem is that many flea market dealers set up at flea markets not to make money, but simply to have a good time. As a result, they willingly sell at much lower profit margins than those who are trying to make a living. It is not really that hard to tell which group is which. Keep the seller's circumstances in mind when haggling.

Second, selling is labor- and capital-intensive. Check a dealer's booth when a flea market opens and again when it closes. Can you spot the missing objects? When a dealer has a "good" flea market, he or she usually sells between 15 and 50 items. In most cases, the inventory from which these objects sold consists of hundreds of pieces. Do not think about what the dealer sold, think about what was not sold. What did it cost? How much work is involved in packing, hauling, setting up and re-packing these items until the objects finally sell?

Flea market sellers need a high profit margin to stay in business.

Third, learn to use price-guide information correctly. Remember that the prices are guides, not price absolutes. For their part, sellers must resist the temptation to become greedy and trap themselves in the assumption that they deserve book-price or better for every item they sell. Sellers would do better to focus on what they paid for an object (which, in effect, does determine the final price) rather than on what they think they can get for it. They will make more on volume sales than they will trying to get top dollar for all of their items.

Price guide prices represent what a "serious" collector in that category will pay, provided he or she does not already own the object. An Elvis Presley guitar in its original box may book for more than $500, but it has that value only to an Elvis Presley collector who does not already own one. What this means is that price guide prices tend to be on the high side.

Fourth, the IRS defines fair-market value as a situation that includes a willing buyer and seller, both of whom are equally knowledgeable. While the first part of this equation usually applies, the second usually does not. There is no question that knowledge is power in the flea market game, and sharing it can cost money. If money were the only issue, I could accept the idea of keeping your mouth shut. However, I like to think that any sale involves transfer of information about the object, as well as the object itself. If there was a fuller understanding of the selling situation by both sides, there would be a lot less grousing about prices after the deal is done.

Finally, forget about book value and seller's value. The only value an object has is what it is worth to you. This is the price that you should pay. The only person that can make this judgment is you. It is a decision of the moment. Never forget that. Do not buy if you do not think the price is fair. Do not look back if you find later that you overpaid. At the moment of purchase, you thought the price was fair. In buying at a flea market, the buck stops in your heart and wallet.

Flea Market Haggling

Few prices at a flea market are firm prices. No matter what anyone tells you, it is standard practice to haggle. You may not be comfortable doing it, but you might as well learn how. The money you save will be your own.

In my mind there are only three prices: a bargain price, a negotiable price and a ridiculous price. If the price on an object is already a bargain, I pay it. I do this because I like to see the shocked look on a seller's face when I do not haggle. I also do it because I want that dealer to find similar material for me. Nothing encourages this more than paying the price asked.

If the price is ridiculous, marked several times above what it is worth, I simply walk away. No amount of haggling will ever get the price to where I think it belongs. All that will happen is that the dealer and I will become frustrated. Who needs it? Let the dealers sit with their pieces. Sooner or later, the message will become clear.

I firmly believe it is the responsibility of the seller to set the asking price. When an object is not marked with a price, I become suspicious that the dealer is going to set the asking price based on what he or she thinks I can pay. I have tested this theory on more than one occasion by sending several individuals to inquire about the value of an unmarked item. In every case, a variety of prices were reported back to me. Since most of the material that I collect is mass-produced, I walk away from all unpriced merchandise. I will find another example somewhere else. This type of dealer does not deserve my business.

I have too much to do at a flea market to waste time haggling. If I find a piece that is close to what I am willing to pay, I make a counter-offer. I am very clear in what I tell the seller. "I am willing to pay 'x' amount. This is my best offer. Will you take it?" Most dealers are accustomed to responding with "Let's halve the difference." Hard though it is at times, I never agree. I tell the dealer that I made my best offer to save time haggling, and I intend to stick by it.

If the flea market that I am attending is a monthly or weekly, I may follow the object for several months. If the object has gone unsold at the end of four to five months, I speak with the dealer and call attention to the fact that he has been unsuccessful in selling the object for the amount asked. I make my counter-offer, which sometimes can be as low as half the value marked on the piece. While the dealer may not be totally happy selling the object at that price, the prospect of any sale is often far better than keeping the object in inventory for several more months. If the object has been sold before I return, I do not get upset. In fact, I am glad the dealer received his price. He just did not get it from me.

In Summary

If you are gullible, flea markets may not be for you. While not a Darwinian jungle, the flea market has pitfalls and traps that must be avoided for you to be successful. The key is to know that these pitfalls and traps exist.

Successful flea marketing comes from practice. There is no school or seminar in which you can learn the skills you need. You fly by the seat of your pants, learn as you go, wing it. The tuition that you pay will be the mistakes that you make along the way.

You can lessen your mistakes by doing homework. Research and study what you want to collect before you start buying. Even the most experienced buyers get careless or are fooled. Buying from the heart is much easier than buying from the head.

Never get discouraged. Everyone else you see at the flea market has experienced or is experiencing exactly what is happening to you. When you become a seasoned veteran, you will look back upon the learning period and laugh. In the interim, at least try to smile.

CHAPTER SIX

The Flea Market Scene Today

While the flea market scene continually evolves, changes occur so gradually that they almost escape notice. My report of the flea market scene in the third edition of *Price Guide to Flea Market Treasures* began: "The current status of today's flea markets can be summarized in one sentence: Little has changed in the past two years." After rereading the full reports I wrote for the second and third edition, I was tempted to begin the same way again. On the surface, little appears to have changed. Beneath the surface—well, that is an entirely different matter.

There have been a number of significant changes over the past four years in the flea market scene, almost all of them positive. Flea markets are experiencing a renewed vitality. Optimism abounds. The mood is definitely upbeat.

Young Buyers

Two new buying groups are partially responsible for this resurgence. The first is a group of younger buyers who are shopping flea markets for objects they can use on a daily basis. Many are in the process of furnishing their apartments or homes. They are not collectors. They have no intention of putting pieces on a shelf or in a cabinet beside similar objects. They are buying secondhand, reusable goods. Once again, it is cheaper to buy at a flea market than to buy new. This accounts for the growing demand at flea markets for items ranging from dinnerware and pots and pans to furniture and decorative wall accessories.

There seems to be less junk for sale at flea markets in the late 1990s than there was in the early 1990s These younger buyers are the reason. They have little or no interest in objects that need repair or restoration. "Like new" is their buying creed. They want objects that are ready to use or display. The burden of putting an object in this condition now rests squarely on the shoulders of the seller.

Collectors also have become highly condition conscious. Many older collectors feel the pendulum has swung too far to the right. It is not reasonable to expect an object that is 25 or more years old to look as though it just came off the assembly line. Emphasis on period packaging further complicates the issue. The key date is 1980. Objects made after that date are considered incomplete if their period packaging is missing.

Decorators

Professional decorators have returned to the flea market scene. This second group is providing a major cash infusion. Many remember the boom times of the early 1980s when decorator money fueled an inflationary spiral. Things are under control at the moment. The spending free-for-all of the early 1980s remains a distant memory.

The do-it-yourself decorator also is having an impact on the flea market scene. Everyone is looking for decorative accent pieces. While the primary emphasis is on big, showy, pizzazz-oriented pieces, these amateur decorators are showing an increasing interest in tabletop smalls, especially when the object speaks to a specific time period, e.g., an early 1960s Venetian abstract glass ashtray or a plaster figural string holder.

Individuals buying primarily for decorating purposes act as a counter to the condition demands of young buyers and collectors. Decorators are after a look, an ambiance. It does not have to be pristine. They are willing to buy items that appear nice, but are in less than fine condition.

Flea Market Operations

Flea market expansion has slowed significantly, so also has flea market failures. The mid-1990s flea market owners, managers and dealers placed an emphasis on operating in a more business-like manner. Everyone benefited. Owners are investing in new facilities and other amenities designed to make the flea market experience more pleasant for everyone.

There has been a major increase in the number of antiques malls that are establishing their business on the coattails of well-established regional flea markets, especially those held weekly. The antiquing town is giving way to the antiquing strip. Adamstown, Pa., is an excellent example. In the space of a few miles on Route 272, there are now more than a dozen large antiques malls and more than six flea markets. The trade has discovered that the way to draw the largest crowd of buyers is to provide more shopping opportunities than can be covered in a day's time.

Everyone is getting into the "extravaganza" act. Most major flea markets now hold three or more each year. The end result is that the uniqueness of these massive dealer assemblages has been diluted. There is at least one extravaganza somewhere every weekend. Their current role may have more to do with providing a vehicle for social interaction for dealers working the flea market circuit on a regular basis, rather than serving customers.

Flea market dealers do not seem as greedy as they did in the early 1990s. Most have accepted the fact that the flea market environment is not a top-dollar environment. It is often the first or second step up the price ladder. Further, today's flea market customers are comparison shoppers and bargain hunters. If they do not find an object in the condition they want at a price they are willing to pay, they pass on it. Buyers are far quicker to say no in the late 1990s than they were in the late 1980s.

Hot Stuff

Are the 1950s passé in the flea market scene? You bet they are. In 1997, David Letterman, Farah Fawcett and Kareem Abdul-Jabbar all turned 50. Does this make you feel old? It does me. Most flea market shoppers view the 1950s as ancient history.

The "hot" period is the mid-1960s through the late 1980s. The Age of Aquarius has struck the flea market. A request for television memorabilia from "Charlie's Angels," "The Brady Bunch" or "Hogan's Heroes" is far more common than a request for material from "Leave It to Beaver" or "Dr. Kildare." Sheet music featuring Perry Como or Eddie Fisher goes begging, while Elvis and Beatles sheets sell briskly.

When an era achieves a stable secondary collectibles market for its objects, toys and television-related memorabilia lead the way. Records, paper, dinnerware and kitchenware follow. Record album covers with strong psychedelic art, magazines covers featuring 1960s and 70s sports heroes and television/movie stars, Melmac and melamine dinnerware and Pyrex are current "hot" collecting topics.

Surprisingly, living- and dining room accessories lag behind. While the market for 1950s toys, television and personality memorabilia and dinnerware is flat, the market for 1950s living- and dining room accessories is hot. 1950s textiles, wall hangings, end table lamps, smoking paraphernalia and maple, Scandinavian and sectional furniture are experiencing strong sales. Formica kitchenette sets continue to sell well. Heaven help us all when the era of K-Mart and Walmart collectibles arrives.

Earlier, I mentioned the growing interest in tabletop knickknacks. No where is this more evident than the increasing number of figurine collectors, especially on the West Coast. Five years ago you could not give away a piece of Kay Finch or a Josef figurine. Today, some sell in the hundreds of dollars. While the figurine collecting craze even has caused a renewed interest in Made in Occupied Japan, Japanese and other cheap imported figurines, it has had no stimulating effect on the Hummel market, which is still very much in the doldrums.

Some Negatives

Having talked about the positives, it only fair to talk about some of the negatives. A major parasite, the toy scalper, has become an integral part of the flea market scene. These greedy individuals capitalize on artificial toy shortages, especially around the holiday season, and sell contemporary toys at four to five times their initial retail cost. In almost every instance, the bubble eventually bursts. The scalpers win, the buyers lose. Refuse to buy from them. Encourage the management to throw them out.

Reproductions (exact copies), copycats (stylistic copies), fantasy items and fakes continue to be a major problem. While obvious to the experienced buyer, they continue to fool novice collectors and the casual buyer. Alas, most flea market owners and managers are more concerned about renting space than they are vetting the merchandise being sold. Once again, refuse to buy from these individuals and complain to the management about their presence.

The tax man is coming. Several states have begun an active crackdown on flea market sellers, especially out-of-state vendors, who do not collect and file the proper state sales taxes. Look for this trend to continue as states seek new ways to replace the reduction in Federal revenues to the states. Buyers, when asked to pay sales tax, do it willingly.

A Final Note

In previous editions, Harry Junior closed his current market report with the final paragraphs from the market report in the first edition. I intend to continue that tradition.

"Permit me one final thought. The key to having an enjoyable experience at a flea market does not rest with the manager, the dealers, the physical setting or the merchandise. The key is you. Attend with reasonable expectations in mind. Go to have fun, to make a pleasant day of it. Even if you come home with nothing, savor the contacts that you made and the fact that you spent a few hours or longer among the goodies.

"As a smart flea marketeer, you know the value of customers to keep flea markets alive and functioning. When you find a good flea market, do not keep the information to yourself. Write or call the regional trade papers and ask them to do more stories about the market. Share your news with friends and others. Encourage them to attend. There is plenty for everyone."

Happy Hunting from all of us at Rinker Enterprises, Inc.

PART TWO:

Flea Market Treasures

Price Notes

Flea market prices for antiques and collectibles are not as firmly established as those at malls, shops and shows. As a result, it is imperative that you treat the prices found in this book as "guides," not "absolutes."

Prices given are based on the national retail price for an object that is complete and in "fine condition." These are "retail prices." They are what you would expect to pay to purchase the objects. They do not reflect what you might realize if you were selling objects. A "fair" selling price to a dealer or private collector ranges from 20% to 40% of the book price, depending on how common the object is.

Prices quoted are for objects that show a minimum of wear and no major blemishes to the display surface. The vast majority of flea market objects are mass-produced. As such, they survive in quantity. Do not buy damaged or incomplete objects. It also pays to avoid objects that show signs of heavy use.

Regional pricing is a factor within the flea market area, especially when objects are being sold close to their place of manufacture. When faced with higher prices due to strong regional pricing, I offer the price an object would bring in a neighboring state or geographic area. In truth, regional pricing has all but disappeared, due to the large number of nationally oriented antiques and collectibles price guides, magazines, newspapers and collectors' clubs.

Finally, "you" determine price; it is what "you" are willing to pay. Flea market treasures have no fixed prices. What has value to one person may be totally worthless to another. Is it possible to make sense out of this chaos? Yes, but to do so, you have to jump in feet first: attend flea markets and buy.

Happy Hunting! May all your purchases turn out to be treasures.

Abbreviations

These are standard abbreviations used in the listings in *Price Guide to Flea Market Treasures.*

3D	three-dimensional	mfg	manufactured
adv	advertising	MIB	mint in box
C	century	MIP	mint in package
c	circa	MISB	mint in sealed box
circ	circular	mkd	marked
cov	cover or covered	MOC	mint on card
d	diameter or depth	MOP	mother of pearl
dec	decorated or decoration	No	number
dj	dust jacket	orig	original
ed	edition	oz	ounce or ounces
emb	embossed	pc	piece
expo	exposition	pcs	pieces
ext	exterior	pgs	pages
ftd	footed	pkg	package
gal	gallon	pr	pair
h	height, high	pt	pint
hp	hand painted	qt	quart
illus	illustrated, illustration or illustrations	rect	rectangular
imp	impressed	sgd	signed
int.	interior	SP	silver plated
j	jewels	SS	sterling silver
k	karat	sq	square
l	length, long	vol	volume
lb	pound	w	width, wide
litho	lithograph or lithographed	yg	yellow gold
MBP	mint in bubble pack	yr	year

Abingdon Pottery

Over the years, Roseville and Weller pottery—favorites of old-time traditionalist collectors of mass-produced pottery wares—have become more and more expensive. In the 1970s and 1980s, collectors with limited budgets began concentrating on firms such as Gonder, Hall, Hull, McCoy, Stangl and Vernon Kilns. Now this material is going up in value. Stretch your dollar by concentrating on some of the firms that still have limited collector appeal. Abingdon Potteries, Inc., Haeger Potteries and Pfaltzgraff Pottery Co., are a few suggestions. I'll bet you can think of many more.

The Abingdon Sanitary Manufacturing Co., began manufacturing bathroom fixtures in 1908 in Abingdon, Ill. In 1938, they began production of art pottery made with a vitreous body. This line continued until 1970 and included more than 1,000 shapes and pieces. Almost 150 colors were used to decorate these wares. Given these numbers, forget about collecting an example of every form in every color ever made. Find a few forms that you like and concentrate on them. There are some great ones.

Club: Abingdon Pottery Club, 210 Knox Hwy. 5, Abingdon, IL 61410.

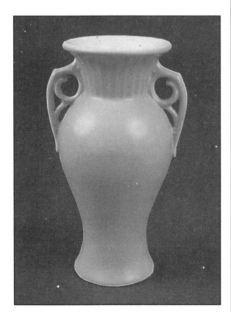

Vase, urn shape, matte pink glaze ext., white int., $15.

Vase, nautical motif, green, 10" h, $10.

Bookends, pr
Cactus, 6" h 60.00
Dolphin, planter, 5-1/2", decorated . 30.00
Dolphin, planter, 5-1/2", solid colors 20.00
Horse Head, figural, 6-3/4" h, black,
    #441 . . . . 45.00
Scottie, 7-1/2", black 115.00
Scottie, 7-1/2", Other colors 70.00
Sea Gull, solid colors, 6" 65.00

Cookie Jars
Cookie Time Clock, 9" h, #653 . . . . 75.00
Daisy Jar, "COOKIES" with daisies as O's,
    8" h, #677 . . . . 30.00
Little Girl, 9-1/2" h, #693 . . . . 40.00
Money Bag, "$Cookies" 7-3/4" h,
    #588 . . . . 60.00
Mother Goose, 12-1/4" h 300.00
Pineapple, 10-1/2" h, #664 . . . . 70.00
Sunflower 15.00

Planters
Fan-shape, raised bow at base, 4-3/4" h, 9"
    l, rect, dark green glaze, #4844 . 10.00
Mexican and Cactus, hand decorated,
    6-1/2" h, #616D 50.00
Sailing Ship, raised design, 7-1/2" h, imp
    rope handles, sea green glaze . . 18.00

Vases
Art Deco-style, 10" h, dusty rose,
    #114 . . . . 25.00
Beta, maroon, #102 . . . . 58.00
Flattened oval-shape, 7" h, emb sailing
    ship on sides, ball column handles, blue
    glaze, #494 . . . . 20.00
Hour Glass, 9" h 15.00
Scroll, 9" h, soft green, flared 5.00
Wreath, 8" h 30.00

Wall Pockets
Dutch Boy, 10" h 90.00
Dutch Girl, 10" h 90.00
Ivy Hanging Basket, 7" h 60.00
Morning Glory, double, 7-3/4" h . . . 20.00

Action Figures

Action, action, action! Action is the key to action figures. Action figures show action. You can recognize them because they can be manipulated into an action pose or are modeled into an action pose. There is a wealth of supporting accessories for most action figures, ranging from clothing to vehicles, that is as collectible as the figures themselves. A good rule is the more pizzazz, the better the piece.

This is a relatively new collecting field. Emphasis is placed on pieces in mint or near-mint condition. The best way to find them is with their original packaging. Better yet, buy some new and stick them away. Unless noted, prices quoted are for action figures out of their packaging.

Club: The Classic Action Figure Collector's Club, P.O. Box 2095, Halesite, NY 11743.

Periodicals: *Action Figure News & Toy Review*, 556 Monroe Turnpike,

The Tramp, Dick Tracy Coppers and Gangsters, Playmates, The Walt Disney Company, $5.

Monroe, CT 06468; *Tomart's Action Figure Digest*, Tomart Publications, 3300 Encrete Ln., Dayton, OH 45439; *Toy Shop*, Krause Publications, 700 E. State St., Iola, WI 54990.

Batman Dark Knight, Kenner, 1990
Batcopter........................6.00
Batmobile 20.00
Batwing 15.00
JokerCycle 6.00

Beetlejuice, Kenner, 1989, Series 1
Beetlejuice figure, 5" h, spinhead 3.00
Beetlejuice figure, 12" h 15.00

Captain Action, Ideal, 12" h figures
Action Boy, First Issue, #3420,
    1967 ....600.00
Action Boy, Second Issue.......475.00
Captain Action, Second Issue, #3400,
    1967.....................500.00
Captain Action, Third Issue......650.00
Dr. Evil, second issue, deluxe
    lab set 1,000.00

Captain America, figures
Lakeside, bendie..............120.00
Marx, 6" h, plastic, 1966 ....15.00
Mego, 8" h, orig box, 1974 ......175.00
Mego, 12-1/2" h, fly away action...125.00
Remco, 9" h, energized..........60.00
Transogram, flying figure 70.00

Ghostbusters, Kenner, 1988, Series 1
Accessory, ECTO 1..............30.00
Figure, Slimer, with three pieces
    food 14.00
Figure, StayPuft, 6" h, carded.....15.00

He-Man Masters of the Universe, Mattel, 1982
Accessory, Castle Grayskull 35.00
Figure, Series 1, 5" h, Beastman ...10.00
Figure, Series 1, 5" h, He-Man 10.00

Mighty Morphin Power Rangers, Bandai, 1993, figures
Pink Ranger 10.00
Red Ranger....................7.00

Rambo, Coleco, 1985, 5" figures
Chief 10.00
Rambo.........................5.00
Sgt. Havoc....................5.00

Roger Rabbit, LJN, 1988, 6" bendies"
Jessica 15.00
Roger Rabbit...................3.00
Talking Roger Rabbit 8.00

Simpsons, Mattel, 1990, 5" figures
Bart 5.00
Lisa 8.00

Star Trek III, ERTL, 1984, 3-3/4" figures
Kirk..........................12.00
Klingon.......................15.00
Scotty........................15.00
Spock........................10.00

WWF, Hasbro Toys, 1990, Series 1, 5" h figures
Andre The Giant "Giant Jolt" 55.00
Hulk Hogan "Gorilla Press" 8.00
Jake the Snake "Python Punch" 5.00

X-Men, Toy Biz, 1991, 2" h figures
Apocalypse 2.00
Colossus 2.00
Storm.........................10.00
Wolverine......................2.00

Adventure Games

Adventure games have been played for hundreds of years. In an adventure game, each player is asked to assume the role of a character. The character's fate is determined by choices that he and other players make. The rules are often very complex; games can last for days, even months.

There are many different game scenarios ranging from sports and entertainment or war and conflict, to finance and fortune. The principal marketing source for current games is the comic book shop. Some comic book shops also handle discontinued games.

Collectors fall into two groups—those who buy discontinued games to play them and those who buy them solely for the purpose of collecting them. Both groups place strong emphasis on completeness. Many of the games contain more than 100 different playing pieces. Few take the time to count all the parts. This is why adventure games tend to be relatively inexpensive when found at garage sales and flea markets.

A small group of individuals have begun to collect playing pieces, many of which are hand painted. However, rarely does the price paid exceed the initial cost.

Club: American Game Collectors Association, 49 Brooks Ave., Lewiston, ME 04240.
Acquire, Avalon Hill, 1976 ....10.00
Business Strategy, Avalon Hill 20.00
Confrontation, Gamescience Corp. .20.00
Dark Tower, Milton Bradley, 1981 ..30.00
Diplomacy, Games Research Inc.,
    1971 ....20.00
Divine Right, TSR, 1979..........30.00
Dragonhunt, Avalon Hill, 1982 .....12.00
Executive Decision, Avalon Hill,
    1981.....................10.00
Fantasy Forest, TSR, 1980 ....10.00
Feudal, 3M, 1969 ....15.00
Sorcerer, Simulations Publications Inc.,
    1975 ....10.00
Venture, Avalon Hill, 1983 ....12.00

Advertising Items

Divide advertising items into two groups: items used to merchandise a product and items used to promote a product. Merchandising advertising is a favorite with interior decorators and others who want it for its mood-setting ability. It is often big, splashy and

Double Game Board Lincoln Highway and Checkers, Parker Bros., $75.

showy. Promotional advertising (give-aways) are primarily collector-driven.

Almost every piece of advertising appeals to more than one collector. As a result, prices for the same piece will often differ significantly, depending on who the seller views as the final purchaser. Most advertising is bought for the purpose of display. As a result, emphasize theme and condition. The vast majority of advertising collectibles are two-dimensional. Place a premium on large three-dimensional objects.

Clubs: Antique Advertising Association of America, P.O. Box 1121, Morton Grove, IL 60053; National Association of Paper and Advertising Collectors, P.O. Box 500, Mount Joy, PA 17552; The Ephemera Society of America, P.O. Box 95, Cazenovia, NY 13035; The Trade Card Collector's Association, P.O. Box 284, Marlton, NJ 08053; Tin Container Collectors Association, P.O. Box 440101, Aurora, CO 80044.

Periodicals: *Paper Collectors' Marketplace*, P.O. Box 128, Scandinavia, WI 54977; *The Advertising Collectors Express*, P.O. Box 221, Mayview, MO 64071.

Banks
Del Monte, clown, figural 28.00
Pepsi Cola, cooler-shape, "Pepsi Cola Ice Cold Sold Here," 3-3/4" by 3" 55.00
Pepto-Bismol, 24 Hour Bug, 1970s, molded vinyl, 7" 35.00

Blotters
Chase & Sanborn Coffee & Tea, multicolored, woman sipping from mug, 6" by 3-1/2" 6.00
Joel H. Woodman Seating Co., Hoboken, NJ, 6-3/4" by 3-1/4" 45.00
Kellogg's Co., box next to bowl of flakes with sliced banana 18.00
Morton's Iodized Salt, 1930s, ice skating scene, "Children Are Becoming More Healthy" 21.00
Mould's Women's Wear, Reading, PA, 3" by 6" 30.00
Nehi, "Drink Nehi, Bottled Energy!" . .11.00

Box labels, inner lid
Little Lord Cigars, young boy holding whip, 1895, 6" by 9" 25.00
Lord Delaware Cigars, Lord Delaware flanked by Harbor & Shoreline, 6" by 9" .40.00
Madie Cigars, peasant girl, 6" by 9" .12.00

Mark Twain Cigars, portrait of Mark Twain superimposed over fishing scene, 6" by 9" 5.00

Calendars
Collins Baking Co., Celebrated Bread, 1909, 8" by 8" 25.00
Dr Pepper, The Friendly Pepper Upper, girl at bowling alley 25.00
Dr Pepper, 75th Anniversary, 1960 . 35.00

Clocks
Charlie the Tuna, 1969 . . . . 125.00
Coca-Cola, "Drink Coca Cola In Bottles," 1939-40, wood frame 160.00
Pepsi-Cola, bottle cap, molded plastic 325.00
Westinghouse Television, round, name in center 55.00

Cookbooks
Alaga Syrup, 15 pages, 1920s 5.00
Heinz, *Heinz Book of Meat Cookery*, 1930, paperback, 54 pages 8.00
Maxwell House Coffee, 1927, 22 pages 7.00
Sleepy Eye Bread Loaf 250.00

Cookie Jars
Blue Bonnet Sue 50.00
Keebler Elf, sitting 75.00
Mr. Peanut 40.00
Pepperidge Farm 60.00

Dolls
Chiquita Banana 20.00
Del Monte, Shoo Shoo Trudy 15.00
Del Monte, Sweet Pea, 12" h 10.00
Del Monte, Jack Frost, 19" h 12.00
Del Monte, Wurlitzer Fun Maker . . . 12.00

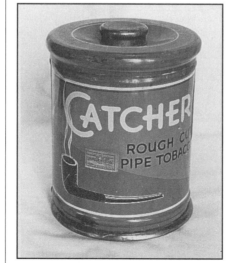

Tin, Catcher Pipe Tobacco, Brown & Williamson Tobacco Corp., Louisville, humidifier-style can, 6" h, 5" d, $40.

Fan, Haines, The Shoe Wizard, cardboard, wood handle, $10.

General Mills, Count Chocula, 1975. 20.00
General Mills, Slippin' Sam 15.00
Life Savers, Mike-E-Mint, with comb, scented, 1981 . . . . 15.00
Nabisco, Mr. Salty, cloth, 11" h 10.00
Nestle, Little Hans the Chocolate Maker, cloth, Chase Bag Co., 13" h 58.00
Nestle Quik, bunny, 1985 . . . . 15.00

Matchsafes
Banquet Hall and Bouquet Cigars, brass, 2-1/2" by 1-1/2" 65.00
John Hohenadel Brewery, Philadelphia, metal and celluloid, 3" by 1-1/2" . 85.00
M. Stachelberg & Co., Havana Cigar Makers, brass and paper, 1-1/2" by 1-3/4" 65.00

Mirrors
Friedand Reineman Packing Co., 1-3/4" by 2-3/4" 60.00
Mascot Crushed Cut TobacCo., Whitehead and Hoag, 2-1/4" 40.00
Seely's Celeste, The New Perfume, 1-3/4" 65.00

Oat Boxes
Aunt Sally Quick Cooking Oats, 1940s 55.00
Fairway Rolled Oats, 1930s 70.00
Red Owl Quick Cooking Oats 35.00

Playing Cards
Dolly Madison Selected Ice Cream, blue, red, and white graphics, yellow ground 5.00
Knox Gelatin, "Get to Know Knox, The Real Gelatin," white ground, gold and blue border 5.00
Kool Milds 8.00

Maull's Barbeque Sauce, red on white with red and gold decorative border . . .8.00

Pocket Mirrors
Franklin Glass and Mirror Manufacturing, 3-3/8" 10.00
Mascot Crushed Cut TobacCo., celluloid .30.00
Ted's Root Beer, pictures baseball player and labeled bottle 15.00

Radios
Dr Pepper, figural can 40.00
Hamburger Helper, Helping Hand. . .30.00
Miracle Whip Salad Dressing, figural jar 40.00

Signs
Dutch Boy Paints, die-cut cardboard.60.00
Greyhound, porcelain, red border, white top, blue bottom, 1940-50, 24" by 40" 100.00
Holoway's London Dry Gin, tin, 1920s, 14" by 11-1/2" 65.00
Hood's Penuchi Ice Cream, paper . .45.00
John Deere, emb metal, green and yellow, 11" by 15" 10.00
Royal Crown Cola, tin, 1930s, 12" by 29-3/4" 40.00
Silver Spring Ale, tin, 9" by 19-1/2" . .30.00
Stroh's, plastic on tin, late 1940s, 15" by 6" 150.00
Tower Root Beer, tin, 13" by 19" 95.00

Thermometers
Coca-Cola, 100th Anniversary, metal 25.00
Frostie Drink, painted metal 25.00
Pfaff's Lager, wood, 21" by 5" 25.00
Royal Crown RC, metal. 50.00
Winston, "Tastes Good...Like A Cigarette Should," 6" by 13-1/2", emb metal 28.00

Thimbles
Hershey's Chocolate, porcelain, gold logo, Franklin USA 15.00
Iten's Biscuit Co., aluminum, black band. 4.00
John Deere, plastic 3.00

Tins
Johnson's Baby Powder, sq, 3" by 11" 20.00
Scarless Gall Remedy, team of horses pulling plow 10.00
St. Joseph's Aspirin, counter top display. .75.00
WH Baker Best Cocoa, 3-3/4" h 2.00

Trays
7-Up, The Uncola, metal, 12" d 7.00
Miller High Life, The Champagne of Bottled Beer, metal, 12" d 48.00

Old Reading Brewery, Inc., Reading, PA, metal, 12" d 30.00

Other
Ashtray, Barbasol, clear glass jar on metal tray, 3-1/2" d, 3" h 15.00
Ashtray, General Electric, heavy, white ceramic, embossed, figural fluorescent bulb, platinum ends. 50.00
Broom Holder, Gold Medal Flour, wood, tin front insert, "Use Cigarette Lighter, Hi-C Fruit Drinks," Zippo, table top, Hi-C logo, blue and red, 4" 55.00
Display Box, Alka Seltzer, paper lined, 25-1/4" by 6-1/2" 5.00
Frisbee, Kodak Film, "For The Time of Your Life". 10.00
Glass, Pepsi Cola, 1973 Collectors Series, Tweety Bird. 10.00
Knife, Goodwill Shoes, Hollistion, Mass., Germany, 3" 75.00
Pail, Light House Peanut Butter, logo of boat and lighthouse, slip lid, bail handle, 4" by 4" 150.00
Gold Medal Flour, Washburn-Crosby Co., 41". 150.00
Pencil, Coca-Cola, 1950s, 7-1/2". . . . 2.50
Pin, Heinz, figural pickle, green plastic, 1" l 20.00
Pocket Knife, Home Insurance Co., New York, 2-1/4" l 85.00
Pocket Knife, Traveler Insurance Co., Hartford, CT, 3-1/4" l 85.00
Puzzle, Baby Ruth Candy Bars, 45 pieces, die-cut cardboard, double-sided, 1930s, 6" by 8" 12.00
Ruler, Coca-Cola, 1930s, wood. 3.00
Sharpening Stone, Bull Brand's Feeds, litho cow 16.00
Shoe Buttonhook, The Savings Store, Kalamazoo, MI 12.50
Shot Glass, Montreal Malt Rye 17.00
Sleeve Patch, Citgo, cloth, 2-3/8" sq . 5.00
Tape Measure, Frigidaire, celluloid, retractable, 1" d 30.00
Tape Measure, Merchant's Savings Bank, Holyoke, MA 15.00
Tea Bin, A&P, wood, 30" h 210.00
Toy Truck, Hershey's, Winross, metal, rubber wheels, orig box 25.00
Tumbler, Miller High Life, glass, 6" h 16.00

Airline Pilot and Crew Collectibles

The flight crew members of the world's airlines have left behind a wide range of collectibles for the airline enthusiast. It is strongly recommended that the collector focus his or her efforts on a particular category, as the range of collectibles in this area is daunting. Some examples are: a particular airline company, regional-commuter carriers, airlines of a particular geographic region or start-up airlines that are now out of business.

The serious collector will study the wealth of material available to familiarize him- or herself with the history of a particular airline or group of airlines. Knowing the logo history of an airline can greatly aid in dating an item. Airlines have very distinct logos that generally span a 10- to 20-year period. Studying pictures of crew members in uniforms from different eras is invaluable in period dating. Attending airline memorabilia shows will greatly assist the novice collector in seeing the wide range of items available and market prices.

Airline crew collectibles can be broken down into five eras, depending on the age of an item: 1920-30, Pioneer Era; 1930-45, Growth and War Era; 1945-60, Post-War Era; 1960-78, The Jet Age; and 1978-present, Deregulation Era. Generally, the older the item, the more valuable it is. However, an item from a recent, but well-known smaller airline that has gone out of business, may command a higher price. The Trump Shuttle is such an example. Items from a heavily collected airline such as Pan American will also be higher. So enjoy finds from the romantic "when flying was really something special" eras to the current fast-paced jet era.

Advisor: Dr. Charles C. Quarles, 204 Reservation Dr., Spindale, NC 28160, (704) 286-3224.

Jacket Wings, Stewardess, gold single wing, "PAA Stewardess," 1945, $85.

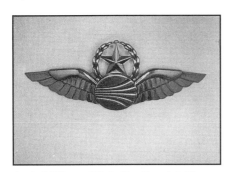

Jacket Wings, Pilot, Continental Airlines, gold, 1990, $20.

Club: World Airline Historical Society, 13739 Picarsa Dr., Jacksonville, FL 32225.

Periodical: *Airliners*, P.O. Box 521238, Miami, FL 33152.

Crew Bag Tags
Eastern Airlines, plastic, c1970 . . . . . .7.00
Mid-Continent Airlines, metal, c1950 10.00
U.S. Air, paper, 1995 . . . . .7.00

Hat Badges
Pilot, American Airlines, sterling "AA" with eagle, 1960 . . . . .50.00
Pilot, Delta-C&S, gold metal with red enamel, 1954 . . . . .95.00
Pilot, Eastern Air Transport, metal with enamel, 1930 . . . . .250.00
Pilot, U.S. Air, silver with red, 1994. .12.00
Stewardess, United Air Lines, 1-3/4" sterling single wing with red and blue enamel logo, pinback, 1938 . . . . .85.00

Jacket Wings
Flight Attendant, Trump, gold wings, "T" with name bar 35.00
Flight Attendant, Western Airlines, gold wings, "W," 1980 . . . . .15.00
Pilot, Braniff International, silver with white enamel "BI," 1970 . . . . .45.00
Pilot, Continental Airlines, gold, 1990 . . . . .20.00
Pilot, Eastern Airlines, black felt with metal enamel center disc, 1955 . . . . . . .95.00
Pilot, Lake Central Airlines, sterling with red and black lettering, 1960 . . . .95.00
Pilot, PAA, silver with blue "PAA," 1928 . . . . .350.00
Pilot, Transcontinental and Western Air, gold, 1940 . . . . .95.00
Stewardess, National Airlines, gold single wing, red and white enamel "NAL Stewardess" 75.00
Stewardess, PAA, gold single wing, "PAA Stewardess," 1945 . . . . . . .85.00

Uniforms
Flight Attendant, complete with jacket, hat, skirt/pants, blouse/shirt, wings, and hat emblem, male or female, Northwest Airlines, 1988 . . . . 50.00
Pilot, complete with jacket, hat, pants, tie, wings and hat emblem, Delta Airlines, 1990 . . . . 45.00
Pilot, Trans World Airlines, 1955 . . 150.00
Stewardess, complete with jacket, hat, skirt/pants, blouse/shirt, wings, and hat emblem, Northeast Airlines, 1958 . . . . 150.00
Stewardess, PSA, hot pants uniform, 1972 . . . . 75.00

Other
Ashtray, commemorative, ceramic, United Airlines Caravelle jet design in center, pilot's name on rim, c1962, 7" by 7" 20.00
Certificate, commemorative, "Braniff Airways Junior Hostess," 1949 . . 15.00
Cigarette Lighter, commemorative, "Piedmont Airlines F-27 Propjet," 1959 . . . . 20.00
Hat, pilot, no insignia 5.00
Jacket, pilot, no insignia 5.00
Log Book, pilot, Piedmont Airlines, 1948-65 . . . . 20.00
Model Airplane, commemorative, Capital Airlines Constellation, metal display model, 24" l, complete with propellers and stand 500.00

Akro Agate Glass

When the Akro Agate Co., was founded in 1911, its principal product was marbles. The company was forced to diversify during the 1930s, developing floral-ware lines and children's dishes. Some collectors specialize in containers made by Akro Agate for the cosmetic industry.

Akro Agate merchandised many of its products as sets. Full sets that retain their original packaging command a premium price. Learn what pieces and colors constitute a set. Some dealers will mix and match pieces into a false set, hoping to get a better price.

Most Akro Agate pieces are marked "Made in USA" and have a mold number. Some, but not all, have a small crow flying through an "A" as a mark.

Club: Akro Agate Art Association, P.O. Box 758, Salem, NH 03079.

Ashtrays
Car, suction cups, 2-1/2" 45.00
Ellipsoid, dark jade 5.00
Hexagonal, 4-1/2" 30.00
Leaf, 4-1/8" 8.00
Shell 8.00

Children's Dishes
Cereal Bowl, marbleized blue and white 32.50
Cup, Concentric Ring, green & white . 4.00
Cup, Houzex Opaque, blue 45.00
Interior Panel, Cobalt and pumpkin . 20.00
Interior Panel, Lemonade and oxblood 35.00
Interior Panel, Raised Daisy, opaque 20.00
Plate, Concentric Rib, green 3.00
Saucer, Concentric Rib, white 3.00
Sugar, cov, Houzex Opaque, blue . . 55.00
Teapot, cov, Interior Panel, lemonade and oxblood 85.00

Cold Cream/Cigarette Jars
Marbleized 40.00
Solid color .35.00

Cornucopias, 3-1/4", turned-up foot
Black 35.00
Common colors 6.00
Crystal 35.00
Niagara colors 20.00

Flower Pots
Ribbed, 2-1/4", all colors 6.00
Type 1, 3", smooth top, sgd on bottom "The Akro Agate Company, Clarksburg, W. Va.," marbleized colors 25.00
Type 1, Solid colors 25.00

Other
Cigarette Holder, all colors 8.00

Powder jar, Mexicali with hat, marbleized, $35.

Curtain Tie Back 18.00
Demitasse Cup and Saucer,
    orange and white 12.50
Dresser Set, handles, with mirror . . .35.00
Dresser Set, without mirror 20.00
Jardiniere, narrow ledge vase, 4-1/2",
    marbleized. 30.00
Lamp, ivory, without shade 30.00
Lamp, wall lamp, all colors 35.00
Mexicali Jar, hat lid, marbleized orange
    and brown 25.00
Nasturtium Bowl, 6" d, Graduated Darts,
    pumpkin, ftd 15.00
Powder Box, Colonial Lady, blue . . .55.00
Powder Box, Treasure Trunk, crystal,
    5-1/2". 40.00
Sugar Bowl, crystal 30.00
Urn, 3-1/4" h, orange and white, ftd . .6.50
Vase, graduated Dart, 6-1/4", Type II,
    scalloped. 50.00
Vase, tab-handled, 6-1/4",
    solid colors 30.00

Aladdin

The Mantle Lamp Co., of America, founded in 1908 in Chicago, is best known for its lamps. However, in the late 1950s through the 1970s, it also was one of the leading producers of character lunch boxes.

Aladdin deserves a separate category because of the large number of lamp collectors who concentrate almost exclusively on this one company. There is almost as big a market for parts and accessories as for the lamps themselves. Collectors are constantly looking for parts to restore lamps in their possession.

Club: The Mystic Light of the Aladdin Knights, 3935 Kelley Rd, Kevil, KY 420532.

LAMPS

Floor
Model B, 270, green and silver,
    1936 .200.00
Model B, 293, antique ivory lacquer,
    1939-42. . . . . .225.00
Model B, 1254. . . . . .175.00
Model B, 1258, bronze, 1945 . . . . .175.00

Hanging
Model 2, 203 shade. 375.00
Model 6, 215 shade, harp with chimney
    tube 250.00
Model 12, four post, parchment
    shade .250.00

Model 21C, aluminum hanger and font,
    white paper shade 50.00
Model B, Flat steel frame, parchment
    shade 300.00
Model B, Tilt frame, 716 glass
    shade. 275.00

Table
Model A, 102, Venetian, peach,
    1932 . . . . 75.00
Model B, 106, Colonial, amber crystal,
    1933 . . . . 200.00
Model B, 107, Cathedral, clear crystal,
    1934 . . . . 125.00
Model B, 108, Cathedral, green crystal,
    1934-35. . . . . 150.00
Model B, B-25, Victoria, decorated china,
    oil fill, 1947 . . . . 500.00
Model B, B-29, Simplicity, green font,
    1948-53. . . . . 75.00
Model B, B-39, Washington Drape, round
    base, clear crystal, 1939. . . . . . . 55.00
Model B, B-134, Orientale, bronze,
    1935-36 . . . . 110.00
Model B, B-138, Treasure, nickel,
    1937-53 . . . . 90.00
Model C, Brazil, quilted font,
    steel foot 85.00

Other
Bracket, Model 12 . . . . 80.00
Bracket, Model B, Alacite font,
    ring foot 150.00
Caboose, Model 21C, shade 55.00
Caboose, Model B, shade 90.00
Candle, Aladinette, Glass chimney, two
    shapes 150.00
Candle, Aladinette, Revolving shade
    holder, paper shade. 175.00
Parlor, Model 3 . . . . 750.00
Parlor, Model 4 . . . . 450.00
Practicus 185.00
Vase, Model 12, crystal, 1930-35,
    variegated verde, 12". 175.00
Wall Pocket 125.00

PARTS AND ACCESSORIES

Shades
Glass, 201, Opal white, Bullseye . . 150.00
Glass, 203, Opal, plain,
    hanging lamp 70.00
Glass, 301, Satin white or enamel,
    Chippendale. 125.00
Glass, 401, Satin white, fancy,
    table lamp 110.00
Glass, 681, Satin white, Dogwood,
    decorated. 45.00
Glass, 682, Satin white, Violet,
    decorated. 60.00
Glass, 716, Opal, hanging 175.00
Paper, Aladdinite Parchment, 15" d, table
    or hanging lamp, 1929-33. . . . . 175.00

Paper, Alpha, plain, 14" d, table lamp,
    1960s. 4.00
Paper, Whip-O-Lite Parchment, 14" d,
    table lamp, plain, 1933-56 . . . . . 75.00

Other
Burner, Model 5, old-style. 125.00
Burner, Model 21C 30.00
Ceiling Extension Hanger No. 3,
    nickel 90.00
Ceiling Extension Hanger No. 3,
    rose gold. 150.00
Chimney, ball-style, logo 85.00
Chimney, extension tube 25.00
Electronic Converter, N 185,
    new-style 20.00
Flame Spreader, Model 4A. 150.00
Flame Spreader, Model 11 . . . . 15.00
Gallery, Model 4 . . . . 70.00
Gallery, Model 23 . . . . 10.00
Mantle, Welsbach. 15.00
Wall Bracket 40.00
Wick, Model 6, orig box 12.00
Wick Raiser, Model B. 5.00

Albums

The Victorian craze has drawn attention to the Victorian photograph album that enjoyed an honored place in the parlor. The more common examples had velvet or leather covers. However, the ones most eagerly sought by collectors are those featuring a celluloid cover with motifs ranging from floral to Spanish American War battleships.

Photo Album, magnetic pages, $15

Photo Album, music box inside, celluloid cov, $125.

Most albums housed "family" photographs, the vast majority of which are unidentified. If the photographs are head and shoulders or baby shots, chances are they have little value, unless the individuals are famous. Photographs of military figures, actors and actresses and other oddities are worth checking out further.

Cardboard albums still have not found favor with collectors. However, check the interior contents. In many cases, they contain post cards, clippings, match covers or photographs that are worth far more than the album.

8-1/2" by 10-1/2", plain red velvet
  covers 30.00
8-1/2" by 10-3/4", crushed velvet covers, orange and red floral dec on front, plain green back, brass closure 65.00
8-1/2" by 10-3/4", raised floral design on cream-colored celluloid front cover, red velvet back cov..............85.00
10" w, 14" h, emb gold "Album" and floral design on cream-colored celluloid front cov, orange and dark green floral pattern on crushed velvet back cov, emb brass clasp, gold-edged heavy cardboard pages.................65.00
10-1/2" w, 14-1/2" h, red velvet covers, emb scroll design trim on front cov, emb brass clasp, gold-edged heavy cardboard pages.................55.00
Cartes de Visite, 8" by 10", 41 cartes de visite, leather, gilt border, one clasp missing, 1860s.............625.00

Aliens, Space-Related

IEEEEKK!! As the scream goes up for extra terrestrials, so does their collectibility. From "War of the Worlds" to "My Favorite Martian," aliens have been landing in our collections. Aliens have gained in popularity with the influence of television and advances made in movie special effects. The "Mork and Mindy" show, starring comedian Robin Williams as a fun-loving extra terrestrial, and the "Star Wars" trilogy, with its strange alien creatures, are just two prime examples of alien familiarity.

So what is an alien? The alien is any creature, character, or being that is not of this planet. Aliens appear in many shapes and sizes so be careful, you never know where an alien will turn up.

Alien
Glow Putty 10.00
Halloween Costume, Alien, Ben Cooper, 1979 ....60.00
Jigsaw Puzzle, Alien, illus, HG Toys, 1979 ....20.00
Movie Viewer, Kenner, 1979 ......90.00
Puzzle, egg 15.00
Trading Cards, Topps, 1979,
  set of 84..................30.00

Puzzle, jigsaw, "Close Encounters of the Third Kind," Milton Bradley, $10.

Battle Star Galactica
Action Figure, "Imperious Leader," Mattel, 1978 ....5.00
Lunch Box, steel, Aladdin, 1978....20.00
Photo Necklace, orig display box, Mattel, 1978 ....10.00
Space Station Kit, General Mills, 1978 ....50.00

Close Encounters of the Third Kind
Button, "I've Seen One" 1.00
Record 8.00
Sheet Music 4.00
Thermos, King Seeley, 1978 ....8.00
Trading Cards, Wonder Bread, 1977, set of 24 ....8.00

Dune
Calendar, 1985..................7.00
Coloring and Activity Book, Grosset & Dunlap, 1984 ....3.00
Newsletter, fan club 3.00
Poster, "A World Beyond Your Dreams".................3.00
Vehicle, Sand Roller, battery operated 10.00

E.T.
Figure, reading book, 2" h 3.00
Fun Art, coloring set 6.00
Jewelry, pin and necklace 2.00
Pinback Button, photo 3.00
Shrinky Dinks 6.00
Tee Shirt, Hershey's.............12.00
Trading Cards, Topps, set of 88.....7.00

Lost In Space
Game, Milton Bradley, 1965.......40.00
Puzzle, Milton Bradley, 1966 ......33.00

Outer Limits
Comic book, Dell 7.00
Costume, Collegeville, 1964......140.00
Model Kit, Golden Era Models, Inc. .50.00

Planet of the Apes
Lunch box, Aladdin, emb steel 40.00
Mini Playset, Multiple Toymakers, 1967 ....35.00
Model Kit, Dr. Zaius, plastic, snap together, Addar, 1973.................20.00

Aluminum Cookware

Hand-wrought aluminum has been a popular collectible for several years, with prices rising steadily. It only stands to reason that aluminum cookware, hand-wrought aluminum's poorer relation, should spark collector interest, as well.

Wok, turned wood handles, three pcs, $5.

Prices are currently very reasonable and examples are plentiful. Look for pieces with unusual decorative elements, preferably made by the same companies which produced the giftware items found in the next section.

Butter Warmer, 6 oz, wood handle . . .2.00
Cake Pan, 8" d 1.00
Casserole, cov, turned wood finial,
    1-1/2 or 2 qt. 5.00
Coffeepot, percolator, five pcs 5.00
Double Boiler, cov, three pcs 10.00
Dutch Oven, cov, 5 qt, three wood
    handles 10.00
Egg Poacher, cov, single-egg size . . .1.00
Fondue, 1-1/2 quart, wood handles .10.00
Pie Plate, 9" d 1.00
Pressure Cooker, cov, 6 qt 12.00
Skillet, 10" d 5.00
Stock Pot, cov, 8 qt 10.00
Tea Kettle, whistling, Bakelite handle .7.50
Wok, wood finial and handles 5.00

Aluminum, Hand-Wrought

With increasing emphasis on post-World War II collectibles, especially those from the 1950s, hand-wrought aluminum is enjoying a collecting revival. The bulk of the pieces were sold on the giftware market as decorative accessories.

Do not be confused by the term "hand-wrought." The vast majority of the pieces were mass-produced. The two collecting keys appear to be manufacturer and unusualness of form.

There is an enormous difference between flea market prices and prices at a major show within driving distance of New York City. Hand-wrought aluminum is quite trendy at the moment.

Club: Hammered Aluminum Collectors Association, P.O. Box 1346, Weatherford, TX 76086.

Periodical: *The Continental Report*, 5128 Schultz Bridge Rd., Zionsville, PA 18092.

Basket, Canterbury Art, Sutherland Collection, square-knot handle, fern . . . 16.00
Belt, H. Ponerantz Inc., NY, Planetelle,
    flower pattern 60.00
Bookends, De Ponceau, 6" by 5-1/2", pine
    pattern. 100.00
Bowl, De Ponceau, petaled design forming
    points around edge, center water lilies
    pattern. 35.00
Brooch, unmarked 30.00
Butter Dish, Rodney Kent 15.00
Candelabra, unmarked, half circle
    sections 60.00
Candle Holders, pr, Kensington, aluminum
    with crystal ball 35.00
Candy Jar, unmarked, aluminum holder,
    berry pattern 35.00
Chafing Dish, Everlast 45.00
Coaster, Clayton Sheasley, daffodil
    design 4.00
Creamer & Sugar, Shup Laird, stylized leaf
    handle. 30.00
Crumber Set, brush and tray, grape cluster
    design. 20.00
Ice Bucket, Buenilum, double wall, beaded
    edge around lid 30.00
Napkin Holder, World Hand Forged,
    intaglio rose pattern 18.00
Pencil Holder, Wendell August Forge,
    pheasants in flight over grain field,
    3" d, 4" h 30.00
Pie Plate and Server, Edem Craft, tiny
    stylized flowers and leaves 45.00
Plate, Buenilum, 9" d, 6" blue and white tile,
    satin smooth finish 22.00
Punch Ladle, unmarked. 25.00
Relish Tray, Everlast, 11-1/2", grape
    pattern in each corner, double-bail
    handle with square knot. 20.00
Silent Butler, Everlast, 5", hammered edge
    and horse heads on lid,
    wooden handle 20.00
Trivet, Clayton Sheasley, coach and four
    design. 30.00

Amusement Parks

From the park at the end of the trolley line to today's gigantic theme parks such as Six Flags Great Adventure, amusement parks have served many generations. No trip to an amusement park was complete without a souvenir, many of which are now collectible.

Prices are still modest in this new collecting field. When an item is returned to the area where the park was located, it often brings a 20-percent to 50-percent premium.

Club: National Amusement Park Historical Association, P.O. Box 83, Mount Prospect, IL 60056.

Ashtrays
7-1/2" d, Disneyland, ceramic, brown,
    green marbleized recessed center section, raised images of Haunted Mansion, Monorail, Sleeping Beauty Castle, Jungle Cruise, and Mark Twain,
    c1960 . . . . 25.00

Lunch Boxes
Disneyland Monorail, Aladdin,
    1960 . . . . 275.00
Ludwig Von Drake in Disneyland, emb
    steel, orig thermos, Aladdin, 1961
    copyright, slight use wear 100.00

Pinback Buttons
Atlantic City, 1911-20, multicolored . 12.00
Disneyland 30th year, 1970s,
    multicolored 10.00
Long Beach Park, 1901-10, blue and
    white 15.00
Ontario Beach Park, 1901-10,
    multicolored 15.00

View-Master Reels
Disneyland/Fantasyland, 4-1/2" sq color
    envelope, three reels, sealed package,
    Sawyer, c1960. . . . . 30.00

Ticket, Palisades Amusement Park, admission and five rides, double-folded, orange and blue, expires June 1, 1951, 4" by 9", $7.50.

Mickey Mouse Club Circus Visits
Disneyland, color envelope,
three reels #856-A-B-C, 1956 Disney
copyright 35.00

Other
Game, Disneyland, It's A Small World,
Parker Brothers, 1965 . . . . .18.00
Game, Kooky Carnival Game, Milton
Bradley, 1969 . . . . .15.00
Medal, Coney Island, steeplechase race,
orig ribbon, 1924 . . . . .90.00
Map, Giveaway Map/Guide Folders,
Disneyland, 1955 . . . . .35.00
Photograph, Coney Island, 1941,
set of six 17.00
Playing Cards, Disneyland castle
photo 5.00
Postcard, Shooting the Chutes, Sylvan
Beach, NY, 1928 . . . . .5.00
Poster, Coney Island, 1911
Mardi Gras 450.00
Salt and Pepper Shakers, pr, Disneyland,
orig 2" by 4" tray with raised name,
white metal, silver and gold metallic
finish, fit together to form castle, orig
cork and "Japan" sticker, c1950. .35.00
Sheet Music, "If I Loved You," from
"Carousel", Rogers & Hammerstein,
carousel illus, 1945 . . . . .10.00
Trade Card, Atlantic City, multicolored,
boardwalk scene, Maizena National
Starch Co. adv, printed in
Germany 75.00

Animal Dishes, Covered

Covered animal dishes were a favorite of housewives during the first half of the 20th century. Grandmother Rinker and her sisters had numerous hens on nests scattered throughout their homes. They liked the form. It did not make any difference how old or new they were. Reproductions and copycats abound. You have to be alert for these late examples.

Look for unusual animals and forms. Many early examples were enhanced through hand-painted decorations. Pieces with painting in excellent condition command a premium.

Cat, hamper base, chocolate, chip on
base, Greentown Glass 200.00
Clamshell, colorless, three clamshell feet
on base 35.00
Collie, floral base, old gold paint, sgd
"Vallerystahl" on base 265.00
Deer, fallen tree base, sgd "E.C. Flaccus
Co., Wheeling, WV" 175.00
Dog, detailed leaves and tassel pressed on
cover, reclining dog finial,
George Duncan & Sons. 75.00
Dolphin, chocolate, beaded rim,
fish finial. 315.00
Duck, pressed details, nonlead glass,
Challinor, Taylor & Co., Ltd. 75.00
Fish, 6-1/2" h, 7-1/2" d rim, opaque,
Atterbury 150.00
Hen, 3", introduced 1967, marked 1973,
mint green, Degenhart 25.00
Rooster, opaque white, Challinor,
Taylor & Co. 50.00
Turkey, introduced 1971, marked 1972,
amber, Degenhart. 35.00

Animal Figures

Animal collectors are a breed apart. Collecting is a love affair. As long as their favorite animal is pictured or modeled, they willingly buy the item. In many cases, they own real life counterparts to go with their objects. My son's menagerie includes a cat, dog, tarantula, lovebird, two rabbits, a Golden Ball python, and three tanks of tropical fish.

Boar, hp porcelain, $18.

Clubs: Cat Collectors, 31311 Blair Drive, Warren, MI 48092; The Frog Pond, P.O. Box 193, Beech Grove, IN 46107; The National Elephant Collectors Society, 380 Medford St., Somerville, MA 02145.

Newsletters: *Canine Collectibles Newsletter*, 736 N. Western Ave., Ste. 314, Lake Forest, IL 60045; *Jumbo Jargon*, 1002 W. 25th St., Erie, PA 16502.

Periodical: *Hobby Horse News*, 5492 Tallapoosa Rd., Tallahassee, FL 32303.

Angel Fish, bookend, crystal,
8-1/4" h 70.00
Bear Cub, head turned, crystal, 3" h
, New Martinsville 50.00
Bird, frosted glass, Westmoreland,
2" by 3-1/2" 12.50
Bulldog, doorstop, solid glass, green mist,
Tiffin Glass 425.00
Bunny, "Cottontail," ears down, 5" h . 95.00
Butterfly, 2-1/2" h, mkd "Maruri
Masterpiece, Bone China" 9.00
Cat, green, 8" h, Viking Glass 45.00
Pelican, commemorative, opal iridescent,
1988, Fostoria 40.00
Donkey with cart, crystal, Haley, large,
4-1/2" h 20.00
Donkey with cart, crystal, Haley,
small 15.00

Hen, basketweave base, clear, red comb and wattle, 4-1/4" l, $35.

Cat, white milk glass, $25.

Wood Duck, Heisey, $550.

Duck, head up, orange, 13-1/2" h, Viking
    Glass 35.00
Ducks, three, swimming, crystal, 9-1/2" l,
    Haley 40.00
Eagle, bookend, crystal, 7-1/2" h,
    Fostoria. 90.00
Elephant, bookend, crystal, 5-1/2" h,
    New Martinsville 75.00
Epic Rooster, 9-1/2" h, Viking Glass .45.00
Fish, medium blue, 10" h,
    Viking Glass 45.00
Horse & Rider, bookend, crystal, 6" h,
    Haley. 40.00
Leopard, porcelain, 4-3/4" by 6-1/2",
    Germany 100.00
Mallard, wings half, caramel slag, 5" h,
    Imperial 30.00
Owl, jar, two-piece, horizon blue carnival
    with glass eyes, Imperial 40.00
Penguin, topaz, 4-5/8" h, Fostoria. .115.00
Pouter Pigeon, 2-1/2" h, crystal,
    Westmoreland. 20.00
Rabbit, amber, 6-1/2" h, Viking
    Glass. 30.00
Ringneck Pheasant, crystal, 11-1/2" h,
    Haley. 25.00
Scottie, bookend, 6-1/2" h,
    Cambridge 90.00
Seal, topaz, 3-7/8" h, Fostoria. 125.00
Seal Cub with ball, ruby glass, 4-1/2" h,
    New Martinsville. 50.00
Squirrel, two-piece set, amber,
    Fostoria. 35.00
Swan, bowl, crystal, 6-1/2" l, New
    Martinsville 20.00

Anti-Axis Collectibles

    The Golden Rule may tell us to turn
the other cheek, but during World War
II we learned to hate our enemies.
Anti-Axis material, items which were
derogatory of the leaders of Germany,
Japan, and Italy, was plentiful and
many American families showed their
patriotism through the display of these
humorous novelties.

Advisor: Ken Fleck, 496 Second St.,
Highspire, PA 17034, (717) 939-8441.

Ashtrays
"Burn The Axis," glass, set of three.250.00
Hitler Face, flat, redware, Art
    Deco-style 175.00
Hitler Face, flat, redware,
    Open Mouth 150.00
Mussolini Head, standup, painted flesh
    tones, open mouth, 4-3/4" 100.00

**Figure, Hitler skunk, chalkware, swasti-
ka on tail, 3-1/2" h, 4-3/4" w, $125.**

Pinback Buttons
1-1/4", celluloid, "Kick 'Em In The Axis,"
    Uncle Sam kicking the word "Axis," red,
    white and blue. 35.00
1-1/4", celluloid, "To Hell With Hitler" 25.00
1-5/8", Uncle Sam hanging Hitler, "Let's
    Pull Together," multicolored litho tin,
    mechanical 75.00
2-1/2", celluloid, "Jap Hunting License,"
    red, white and blue 35.00

Sheet Music
Der Fuehrer's Face, Walt Disney. . . 50.00
We've Got To Stick Together. 35.00
You're A Sap Mr. Jap. 35.00

Other
Advertising, Interwoven Sock Box, GI
    chasing Japanese soldier with
    bayonet 95.00

**Sheet Music, "We've Got To Stick To-
gether," $35.**

Bank, figural, Bomb, various slogans and
    names, chalk 125.00
Bank, figural, Pig with Hitler's Face, "Save
    For Defense-Make Him Squeal," yellow
    composition 250.00
Chamber Pot, miniature, Hitler's face
    inside, ceramic, 2" d 35.00
Cigar Box, "MacArthur Cigar-Every Puff A
    Jap Rebuff" 175.00
Figure, skunk, Hitler's head, chalk, black
    and white 175.00
Game, Victory Rummy, cards depict three
    Axis leaders. 50.00
Nail Apron, "One Down-Two To Go,"
    pictures three Axis leaders in sinking
    boat 175.00
Panties, miniature, "Shoot The Pants Off
    The Japanazi" 35.00
Pencil, bullet-style, Uncle Sam punching
    Hitler and Tojo, "Now-You'll Remember
    Pearl Harbor," red, white
    and blue 45.00
Pennant, "Pack Up Japan, The Yanks Are
    Coming," felt, 24" l. 75.00
Pincushion, Adolph Hitler, 4-5/8" h, chalk,
    "Hotzi-Notzi" 125.00
Pincushion, Two-Faced Rat, Hitler and
    Tojo, 5-1/4" h, chalk. 175.00
Punch Board, anti-Hitler, "Take A Punch,"
    cardboard, 1-cent 15.00
Push Toy, Canadian, GI fist punching Hitler
    in eye, wood and paper litho . . .375.00
Toothpick Holder, figural, Hitler bending
    over, toothpick stick in backside,
    4-1/4" h, chalk. 175.00
Toy, Krak-A-Jap, machine gun, wood and
    cardboard 175.00

Appliances, Electrical

    Nothing illustrates our ability to take
a relatively simple task—e.g., toast a
piece of bread—and create a wealth of
different methods for achieving it quite
like a toaster. Electrical appliances are
viewed as one of the best documents
of stylistic design in utilitarian form.

    Collectors tend to concentrate on
one form. Toasters are the most commonly collected, largely because several books have been written about
them. Electric fans have a strong following. Waffle irons are pressing
toasters for popularity. Modernistic
collectors seek bar drink blenders from
the 1930s through the 1950s.

Clubs: Porcelier Collectors Club, 21
Tamarac Swamp Rd., Wallingford, CT

06492; The Electrical Breakfast Club,
P.O. Box 306, White Mills, PA 18473.

Mixers

Hamilton Beach, 1930s, Model G, cream-
colored metal, black Bakelite handle,
"mix guide" in window below handle, removable portable mixer head, two white
glass bowls 35.00
KitchenAid, Hobart Corp., cream-colored
body, aluminum trim and handle, meat
grinder, dough hook, wire whisk,
1939 .50.00
Sears Kenmore, Model 322-8220, portable
hand mixer, cream-colored plastic
body, original box and booklet,
1940 .25.00

Toasters

Knapp-Monarch, rounded chrome body,
bakelite handles, 1930s 20.00
Montgomery Ward & Co., square body,
rounded corners, chrome, bakelite
handles, 1930s 18.00
Perc-O-Toaster, Armstrong Mfg., model
PT, nickel, two plug, cabriole legs,
slip-out toast rack in sq base,
1918 .60.00
Proctor, two-slice, Color Guard, Model
1468C. 45.00
Westinghouse, style #231570, nickel body,
wire doors, pierced warmer top, cord
with china plug, 1910s 35.00

Waffle Irons

Coleman Lamp & Stove Co., Model 17,
round chrome body, 14" oval base,
black bakelite handles,
7-1/2" d plates 30.00
Empress, Fitzgerald Mfg. Co., 1928 .20.00
Knapp-Monarch, dessert size, black
wooden knobs, 1930s,
6" d plates 15.00

Whippers

Dorby, Model E, chrome motor housing,
black bakelite handle, clear glass,
1940s .25.00
Knapp-Monarch, Moderne, high-speed
whipper, 1930s, 3-cup clear glass
bottom, cream-colored top, green open
handle, 8" h 20.00

Other

Baby Bottle Warmer, Universal, Landers,
Frary & Clark, 1912 . . . . .8.00
Blender, Silex, Philadelphia, PA #D2606,
cream-colored sq metal base,
one- speed, push-button switch, 4-cup
sq tapered glass top, vertical Art Deco
center design and measuring
increments, soft black plastic lid,
early 1940s 12.00

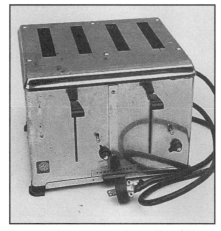
Toaster, Toastmaster, four slice, $25.

Broiler, Farberware, chrome, black
wooden handle, 1920s 20.00
Chafing Dish, #K-601, high-style Art Deco
design, chrome, round tray/hot plate,
hot water dish, bowl and lid, black
bakelite handles, three prong hi/lo plug,
1925 . . . . 45.00
Clock Timer, Montgomery Ward & Co.,
cream body, flat swivel base, silver and
red, 1940s. 15.00
Coffee Maker, Farberware, Model #208,
chrome with garland drape, black wood-
en handles, late 1930s, 12-1/2" h 15.00
Coffee Service, four pcs, E-9119, nickel
chrome, classical urn on flared base,
creamer, cov sugar and tray, open
handles with flat tops, large glass insert,
black wooden handle spigot . . . 125.00
Coffee Urn, classical design, nickel,
cabriole legs, tall curved handles, flat
top, lid with large swirled glass insert,
15-1/2" h 35.00
Curling Iron, General Electric Hotpoint,
chrome-plated, 1935-36 . . . . 12.00
Egg Cooker, The Rochester, egg-shaped
nickel body, four pcs 35.00
Frying Pan, steel, cord in wooden handle,
inverts to hot plate, 6" d, 1911 . 150.00
Hot Plate, Westinghouse, round plate,
round green porcelainized metal top,
1920s 20.00
Iron, Edison Iron, nickel body, wooden
handle, detachable cord, 1906 . . 5.00
Iron, Steam-O-Matic, Waverly Products,
hammered aluminum body, black
bakelite handle, 1931-44 . . . . . . 20.00
Juicer, Vita-Juicer, Kold King Dist.,
Los Angeles, Hoek Rotor Mfg.,
Reseda, CA, cream-painted cast metal,
fitted lid, nickel handle, 10" h . . . 35.00
Knife Sharpener, Handy Hannah, red and
cream body, 1930s, 4-1/2" d. . . . 10.00

Marshmallow Toaster, Campfire Bar-b-Q,
two pc metal body, pierced flattened
pyramid top, loop-wire legs with rubber
encased cushion feet, three small metal
two-prong forks, 3" sq 55.00
Popcorn Popper, U.S. Manu. Co., one pc,
red and silver, 1930 . . . . 20.00
Sandwich Grill, unmarked, triple, nickel
body, black wooden handles,
1920s. 25.00
Tea Kettle, Mirro, flared base, squatty,
black wooden holder, 1910 . . . . . 45.00
Washing Machine, portable, aluminum
body, iron handles, clip-on wringer,
tub 75.00

Ashtrays

Most price guides include ashtrays
under advertising. The problem is that
there are a number of terrific ashtrays
in shapes that have absolutely nothing
to do with advertising. Ashtrays get a
separate category from me.

With the nonsmoking movement
gaining strength, the ashtray is an endangered species. The time to collect
them is now.

Club: Ashtray Collectors Club, P.O.
Box 11652, Houston, TX 77293.

**Floor Model, Duralod, chrome stand, 10-
7/8" d, brown glass insert, $35.**

Advertising

Chesterfield Cigarettes, tin, 1930-50,
6" l 20.00
Coca-Cola, bakelite 30.00
Coors, white porcelain 4.00
Fatima Turkish Cigarettes, ceramic,
3-1/4" 100.00
Frisch's Big Boy, glass, orange graphics,
3" d 30.00
General Streamline Jumbo, tire-shape,
emb glass insert 25.00
Good Year, tire-shape, 7" d 20.00
Greyhound, glass 7.00
Michelin, 1970s, 5" 95.00
Miller Tires, emb rubber tire-shape, glass
insert, 7" d 42.00
Moxie, ceramic, white edge,
multicolored 100.00
Mr. Peanut, ceramic 60.00
Smirnoff Vodka, clear glass, red and black
lettering on white bottom 3.00
Playboy Club, glass, orange, black
lettering and key, 4-1/4" 32.00
Union Pacific, sq, glass 12.00
Ushers Ale, glass diamond logo, sq .15.00
Victor, RCA, porcelain, set of four . . .15.00

Other

Alligator, art deco, 4-3/8" by 1-3/4" . .20.00
Apple, metal, 3" by 4-1/4" by 4-1/4" .10.00
Baggage Cart, lighter, ashtray and
cigarette holder set, enameled,
rubber wheels 125.00
Banjo, silver-plated, gold lined 15.00
Book, red and black enameling,
glass lined 20.00
Cat, green onyx tray, bronze figural cat,
silver finish 35.00
Cigarette Box/Ashtray Combination, black
and silver enameled covered box,
cedar lined 30.00
Cowboy Hat, copper 10.00
Dog, figural, Akro Agate 25.00
Goose, metal, 6" h 35.00

Art Deco, Puss 'n Boots, Vienna bronze, alabaster base, mkd "Austria," 5-3/4" by 4" by 5-7/8", $375.

Golfer, metal, 10-1/4" by 7-1/4" 40.00
Horse, metal 40.00
Mouth-shaped, white 20.00
Naughty, oval, copper, emb man patting
nude woman on behind 12.00
Owl, alabaster, multicolored, stylized owl in
center, 6" d 18.00
Playing cards, porcelain, 5-1/2" by
6-3/4" 15.00
Scottie Dog, aluminum, hand-forged 10.00
Shoes, made in India 10.00
Television, lighter set 20.00
Tray and Lighter, green onyx 60.00

Autographs

Collecting autographs is a centuries' old hobby. A good rule to follow is the more recognizable the person, the more likely the autograph is to have value. Content is a big factor in valuing autograph material. A clipped signature is worth far less than a lengthy handwritten document by the same person.

Before spending big money for an autograph, have it authenticated. Many movie and sports stars have secretaries and other individuals sign their material, especially photographs. An "autopen" is a machine that can sign up to a dozen documents at one time. The best proof that a signature is authentic is to get it from the person who stood there and watched the celebrity sign it.

Clubs: Manuscript Society, 350 Niagara St., Burbank, CA 95105; Autograph Collectors Club, P.O. Box 6181, Washington, DC, 20044.

Periodicals: *Autograph Collector*, 510-A S. Corona Mall, Corona, CA 91720; *Autographs & Memorabilia*, P.O. Box 224, Coffeyville, KS 67337; *Autograph Times*, 2303 N. 44th St., #255, Phoenix, AZ 85008; *The Autograph Review*, 305 Carlton Rd., Syracuse, NY 13207; *The Collector*, P.O. Box 255, Hunter, NY 12442.

Aikman, Troy, Lil Riddell Mini
Helmet 95.00
Aldrin, Buzz, 24" by 36" color
limited-edition poster 80.00
Ali, Muhammad, signed sketch 50.00
Alomar, Roberto, baseball 30.00
Anderson, Loni, 8" by 10" color
photo 25.00

Burt Reynolds, black-and-white photo, $20.

Barkley, Charles, basketball 145.00
Barrymore, Lionel, sgd letter 120.00
Berra, Yogi, book, *It Ain't Over* 35.00
Bowie, David, sgd card 35.00
Capote, Truman, document, boldly signed,
dated 1980 . . . . 150.00
Carter, Jimmy, Book,
Always a Reckoning 42.00
Carter, Jimmy, Photo 75.00
Cosby, Bill, sgd *TV Guide* cover 15.00
Crawford, Cindy, 11" by 14"
black-and-white nude photo . . . 250.00
Cunningham, Randall, football 65.00
Cunningham, Walt, 8" by 10" color NASA
photo 24.00
Davis, Jim, boldly sgd letter 50.00
Derek, Bo, 8" by 10" black-and-white
photo 32.00
Diamond, Neil, sgd record album . . . 40.00
Dole, Bob, *Spirit of '76* first day cover,
boldly sgd 30.00
Eastwood, Clint, 4" by 6" photo 10.00
Eisenhower, David and Julie, 8" by 10"
black-and-white photo 25.00
Ford, Whitey, sgd sketch 60.00
Gaye, Marvin, sgd contract dated
Sept 1977 . . . . 200.00
Gershwin, George, musical
quotation 500.00
Gifford, Frank, 3" by 5" card 20.00
Ginsburg, Allen, self portrait 15.00
Hamill, Dorothy, sgd photo 25.00
Hanks, Tom, 8" by 10" color glossy photo,
Forest Gump sitting on
park bench 39.00

Jackson, LaToya, 5" by 9" color Playboy
    photo 19.00
Jong, Erica, photo 15.00
Kelly, Gene, 8" by 10" black-and-white
    photo 150.00
Kennedy, Ted, sgd sketch. 50.00
LaFontaine, Pat, puck 27.00
Leonard, Sugar Ray, sgd sketch. . . .50.00
Lewis, Jerry, comic book 20.00
Maddux, Greg, batting helmet. 150.00
Mantle, Mickey, sgd sketch 200.00
Martin & Lewis, 8" by 10" color photo,
    red pen signature 70.00
Mills, Donna, sgd magazine cover . .10.00
Norris, Chuck, sgd black-and-white
    photo 25.00
Rockerfeller, Nelson, sgd document .44.00
Savalas, Telly, sgd document 7.00
Schmidt, Mike, bat. 150.00
Schwarzenegger, Arnold, sgd letter .25.00
Winfrey, Oprah, sgd sketch. 50.00

Automobile Collectibles

An automobile swap meet is 25-percent cars and 75-percent car parts. Restoration and rebuilding of virtually all car models is never-ending. The key is to find the exact part needed. Too often, auto parts at flea markets are not priced. The seller is going to judge how badly he thinks you want the part before setting the price. You have to keep your cool.

Two areas that are attracting outside collector interest are promotional toy models and hood ornaments. The former have been caught up in the craze for 1950s and 1960s Japanese tin. The latter have been discovered by the art community, who view them as wonderful examples of modern streamlined design.

Clubs: Hubcap Collectors Club, P.O. Box 54, Buckley, MI 49620; Spark Plug Collectors of America, 2115-51st St. Apt. D, Lubbock, TX 79412

Periodicals: *Automobilia News*, P.O. Box 3528, Glendale, AZ 85311; *Hemmings Motor News*, P.O. Box 256, Bennington, VT 05201; *Mobilia*, P.O. Box 575, Middlebury, VT 05753.

Auto Parts and Accessories
Ashtray, metal, Snap-On Tools,
    5" by 7". .10.00
Catalog, JC Whitney, 1959 . . . . . . .20.00
Cigarette Lighter, Casco, knob glows when
    lighter is hot 25.00

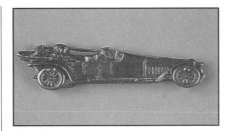

**Pocket Knife, German silver, two
blades, $65.**

Clock, neon, "NAPA Auto Parts," blue and
    yellow logo 45.00
Drive-In Speakers, good condition with
    wiring 30.00
First-Aid Kit, Johnson & Johnson, tin, orig
    contents, 5" by 7" box 25.00
Flag Holder, gold colored, red and blue
    enamel, 1927 . . . . 75.00
Fuzzy Dice, 4" w, white with black
    dots 5.00
Gasoline Gauge, Atwater Kent,
    1909 . . . . 30.00
Gearshift Knob, simulated onyx, brass
    Saint Christopher medal center . 25.00
Gloves, pr, long gauntlet-style, black
    leather. 35.00
Hood Ornament, Liberty Bell, 1926 . 16.00
Hood Ornament, Moon, crescent-shape,
    1912-28. 65.00
Hubcaps, set of four, Flipper,
    chrome 90.00
Hubcaps, set of four, Pasco, screw-on,
    nickel-plated brass 50.00
License Plate, District of Columbia, 50th
    President Inaugural. 20.00
License Plate, Pennsylvania, school bus,
    1969 . . . . 10.00
License Plate Tag Topper, American
    Automobile Association 10.00
License Plate Tag Topper, Cat 26.00
License Plate Tag Topper, State Farm
    Insurance 13.00
Mirror, Argus, rearview 45.00
Mirror, Vanity visor, bakelite frame, birds
    and flowers 20.00
Owner's Manual, Buick Electra, Le Sabre
    and Wildcat, 1972. . . . . 7.00
Owner's Manual, Ford Thunderbird,
    1961 . . . . 15.00
Owner's Manual, Plymouth, 1931 . . 15.00
Radiator Ornament, Ford, 1936,
    greyhound. 200.00
Reflector, red plastic, litho tin, 1950s 15.00
Sign, tin, Champion Spark Plugs . . . 55.00
Spark Plug, Blue-topped porcelain . 15.00
Spark Plug, Motormaster Blue Crown 5.00
Steering Wheel Knob, ivory colored glass,
    blue and yellow swirls, "Rotary
    International" center 45.00

**Magazine Tear Sheet, Fisk Cord Tires,
The Liberty Digest, April 24, 1920, $5.**

Sunshade, cobalt blue, 1930s,
    heavy. 50.00
Tissue Dispenser, swing-out model,
    Hollywood brand 50.00
Tray, carhop, 1950s 25.00
Sales and Promotional Items
Ashtray, Chrysler Corporation, copper,
    1933 World's Fair 40.00
Badge, AAA Membership, white
    porcelain 30.00
Badge, Humble Oil, plastic, red and
    silver 15.00
Bell, Pontiac, hand held 30.00
Bird, Ford Falcon, plastic, 1960 . . . .75.00
Blotters, Dodge/Plymouth, 1947. . . .10.00
Blotters, Firestone Tires, 1920s roadster,
    unused. 8.00
Blotters, GMC Heavy Duty Trucks, 1951,
    unused. 5.00
Calendar, Chevrolet, hanging,
    1920 . . . . .145.00
Calendar, Pennsylvania Ford, pocket,
    1939 . . . . .10.00
Candy Container, 1930s sedan-shape,
    glass 15.00
Coffee Mug, Chevrolet, white ceramic, red
    and blue lettering. 10.00
Coin, commemorative, 1954 Corvette, gold
    colored. .15.00
Coloring Book, Buick, 1958 . . . . . . .10.00
Cookie Cutter, metal, Chevrolet bowtie
    trademark 5.00
Fan, Ford, cardboard with wooden
    handle 10.00

Flashlight, Mopar Parts, red plastic,
pocket size 10.00
Fork, Cadillac crest, silver-plated . . .35.00
Ice Scraper, Pontiac, red plastic 5.00
Key Ring, Chevrolet, 1962 . . . . .15.00
Magazine, Buick, May 1951 . . . . .5.00
Magnet, Mustang horse, vinyl 5.00
Matchbook, Plymouth, 1956 . . . . .4.00
Medallion, Chrysler, brass, 1939 . . . .20.00
Pencil, mechanical, Pontiac, 1930s .35.00
Pinback Button, Chrysler Motors. . . .26.00
Playing Cards, Jeep Golden Eagle . .15.00
Pot Holder, Dodge, apple-shaped. . .10.00
Puzzle, Chevrolet, die-cut, 35 pcs,
8" by 14", 1932 . . . . .60.00
Ruler, Pontiac, wood, 1938 . . . . .30.00
Service Mats, Chevrolet, paper,
1964 . . . . .10.00
Screwdriver, Chevrolet, metal handle,
bowtie logo 25.00
Sign, Chrysler Motors/Mopar Parts, metal,
flange 185.00
Sign, ESSO/Put A Tiger In Your
Tank 110.00
Sign, Good Year Tires, emb painted
metal 55.00
Sunglasses, Chevrolet, 1962 . . . . . .10.00
Thimble, Indiana Chevrolet, plastic,
1960s 5.00
Tray, Pontiac, tin, 1957 . . . . .50.00
Thermometer, Buick, porcelain,
1915 . . . . .275.00
Visor, Chevrolet, blue and white 5.00
Windshield Scraper, Pontiac, 1957 . . .5.00

Auto Racing

Man's quest for speed is as old as time. Automobile racing dates to before the turn of the century. Many of the earliest races took place in Europe. By the first decade of the 20th century, automobile racing was part of the American scene.

The Indianapolis 500 began in 1911 and was interrupted only by World War II. In addition to Formula 1 racing, the NASCAR circuit has achieved tremendous popularity with American racing fans. Cult heroes such as Richard Petty have become household names. This is a field of heroes and also-rans. Collectors love the winners. A household name counts. Losers are important only when major races are involved. Pre-1945 material is especially desirable since few individuals were collecting these items prior to that time.

The field has problems with reproductions and copycats. Check every item carefully. Beware of paying premium prices for items made within the last 20 years. Although interest in Indy 500 collectibles remains strong, the current market is dominated by NASCAR collectibles. In fact, the market is so strong that racing collectibles have their own separate show circuit and supporting literature. Because racing collecting is in its infancy, price speculation is rampant. Market manipulators abound. In addition, copycat, fantasy and contemporary limited edition items are being introduced into the market as quickly as they can be absorbed. A shake-out appears to be years in the future. In the interim, check your engine and gear up for fast action.

Clubs: Auto Racing Memories, P.O. Box 12226, Saint Petersburg, FL 33733; National Indy 500 Collectors Club, 10505 N. Delaware St., Indianapolis, IN 46280.

Periodicals: *Collector's World*, P.O. Box 562029, Charlotte, NC 28256; *Quarter Milestones*, Oxhaven Apartments, Apt. C-38, Oxford, PA 19363;

Coca-Cola Can, Mario Andretti, 1994, $7.

Racing Collectibles Price Guide, P.O. Box 608114, Orlando, FL 32860.

Games
Cannonball Run, 1981 . . . . .17.00
Circle Racer, 1988 . . . . .12.00
Hot Wheels Wipe-Out, Mattel, 1968. 30.00
Thunder Road, Milton Bradley, 1986 25.00

Other
Autograph, Mario Andretti, photo . . . 20.00
Bottle, Fan Fuelers sports drink, 32 oz,
Kyle Petty 6.00
Bumper Sticker, Thunderbird, NASCAR
Birds of Prey 5.00
Clipboard, black plastic, Chevy Racing, red
bowtie 10.00
Decal, STP, checkered flag, Novi Indy race
car, 1950s 25.00
Glass, Indianapolis 500, 1951 . . . . .20.00
Hat pin, Jimmy Bryan, 200, 1986 . . .10.00
Helmet, brown leather, some aging . 75.00
Key Fob, Indianapolis car, brass,
1950s 35.00
Mug, Indianapolis 500, frosted glass,
Roger Ward, metal race car replica on
handle, 1950s 35.00
Order Form, flyer, Daytona 500 tickets,
1965 . . . . .5.00
Patch, jacket, Demolition Derby 2.00
Plate, ceramic, Dale Earnhardt, 23k gold
border, 6-1/2" d 30.00
Playing Cards, Hallmark, The Great
Race 10.00
Newspaper, National Dragster,
1964 issue 2.00
Program, Late Model Championship Stock
Car Race, 1958 . . . . .20.00
Rule Book, American Hot Rod Association,
1970 . . . . .15.00

Autumn Leaf

The Hall China Co., developed Autumn Leaf china as a dinnerware premium for the Jewel Tea Co., in 1933. The giveaway was extremely successful. The "Autumn Leaf" name did not originate until 1960. Previously, the pattern was simply known as "Jewel" or "Autumn." Autumn Leaf remained in production until 1978.

Pieces were added and dropped from the line over the years. Limited production pieces are most desirable. Look for matching accessories in glass, metal and plastic made by other companies. Jewel Tea toy trucks were also made.

Gravy Boat, $25.

Club: National Autumn Leaf Collector's Club, 7346 Shamrock Dr., Indianapolis, IN 46217.

Baker, French, 3 quart 10.00
Bean Pot, New England,
    two handles 150.00
Bowl, Oval, cov 30.00
Bowl, Round, 9" d 38.00
Butter, cov, 1/4 lb 65.00
Cake stand, metal base 100.00
Candy, metal base 225.00
Canister, 8-1/4" h 25.00
Clock, battery 250.00
Coffeepot, Rayed, 8-cup 35.00
Cookie Jar, Ziesel 55.00
Creamer and Sugar. 50.00
Fruit Dish. 5.00
Marmalade, three pcs 70.00
Mixing Bowl, #5, Radiance 13.00
Mug, Conic 20.00
Mug, Irish Coffee. 42.00
Mustard, three pcs 70.00
Percolator, electric 170.00
Pie Baker. .22.00
Pie Lifter 45.00
Sugar, J-Sunshine. 40.00
Tidbit, three-tier. 38.00
Warmer, round 80.00
Vase 100.00

Aviation Collectibles

Now is the time to get into aviation collectibles. The airline mergers and bankruptcies have produced a wealth of obsolete material. There were enormous crowds at Eastern's liquidation sale in spring 1991. I have a bunch of stuff from Piedmont and Peoples, two airlines that flew off into the sunset in the 1980s.

The wonderful thing about airline collectibles is that most of them initially were free. I try to make it a point to pick up several items, from bathroom soap to playing cards, each time I fly. Save the things most likely to be thrown out.

Pamphlet, Lindbergh's Flight No. 2-1-4, Nila B. Smith and Rhoda C. Schwieg, illus by Barry Bart, Silver Burdett Co., softcover, 1938, 18 pgs, 5-1/4" by 7-1/4", $18.

Clubs: Aeronautica & Air Label Collectors Club, P.O. Box 1239, Elgin, IL, 60121; World Airline Historical Society, 13739 Picarsa Dr., Jacksonville, FL 32225.

Periodical: *Airliners*, P.O. Box 521238, Miami, FL 33152.

Ashtray, TWA, china, Rosenthal . . . 20.00
Blanket, North Central Airlines. 25.00
Book, *The Airline Handbook*, Paul K
    Martin, 600 pgs. 18.00
Calendar, Lufthansa, 1956, color,
    Constellation aircraft in
    upper right. 35.00
Cap Badge, TWA, lightweight metal 35.00
Coaster, Delta Airlines, metal 1.00
Flatware, Pacific Northern, spoon,
    silver-plated, 1950s. 10.00
Flight Bag, Ozark, 7" by 4" h 5.00
Glass, Eastern Airlines, brandy, crystal,
    made by Schott Zweisel,
    Germany. 16.00
Glass, Regent Air, heavy leaded crystal,
    Atlantis 35.00
Lithograph, Aeromexico, color,
    8" by 10" 5.00
Manual, Ozark Air Lines, DC-10 . . . . 3.00
Menu, TWA, 1960s 4.00
Pin, Britt Airways, stewardess 35.00
Pin, Frontier, wings, red,
    porcelain ground. 50.00
Pin, Northeast Airlines, Pilgrim logo 150.00
Pitchers, coffee and cream, silver-plated,
    Oneida, price each 18.00

Program, Reading Municipal Airport Air Show, 23 pgs, 8-1/2" by 11", $3.

Plate, china, blue and yellow, seahorse
    dec, Limoges. 25.00
Playing Cards, Air Atlanta, yellow name
    and logo, red ground 5.00
Poster, Colonial Airlines, 1950s,
    27" by 41" 350.00
Poster, Pan Am, Honolulu clipper, 1930s,
    27" by 41" 950.00
Poster, Western Airlines, 11" by 16". 35.00
Ring, American Airlines, child's 10.00
Safety Cards, U.S. Air, 1970s. 2.00
Serving Tray, United, International Silver
    Co., 1960s. 75.00
Sign, Delta-C&S, metal. 100.00
Storybook Cards, Pan Am 3.00
Teapot, American Airlines, glass,
    3-1/2" h 50.00
Tray, TWA, bakelite, 1940s 20.00

Avon Collectibles

Avon products, with the exception of California Perfume Co., material, are not found often at flea markets any longer. The 1970s were the golden age of Avon collectibles. There are still a large number of dedicated collectors, but the legion that fueled the pricing fires of the 1970s has been hard hit by desertions. Avon material today is more likely to be found at garage sales than at flea markets.

Club: National Association of Avon Collectors, Inc., P.O. Box 7006, Kansas City, MO 64113.

Periodical: *Avon Times*, P.O. Box 9868, Kansas City, MO 64134.

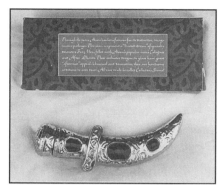

Dagger, Windjammer After Shave Lotion, $15.

Aladdin's Lamp, glass, green, bath oil,
7-1/2" l, 1971-73. . . . . .7.00
Alligator, plastic, green, 1978-79. . . . .3.50
Autumn's Color Porcelain Egg, 3" h,
wood base 15.00
Baby Bassett, glass, amber, 1978-79 .3.00
Big Mack, Windjammer After Shave,
1973-75 .8.00
Bunny Fluff Puff, plastic, children's talc,
1979-80 .3.50
Christmas Bells, red glass, 1979-80 . .3.00
Country Jug, gray paint over clear,
1976-78 .5.00
Cupid Candle Holder, 3-1/4" h, white
glazed porcelain, 1995. . . . . .5.00
Dachshund, frosted glass, 1973-74 . .5.00
Dolphin, frosted glass, 1968-69 . . . . .5.00
Duck, aftershave, glass, painted ducks,
1971. . . . . .4.00
Dueling Pistol 1760, glass, brown,
1973-74 .8.00
Hammer, glass, amber, Wild Country After
Shave, 1978. . . . . .5.00
Eagle, Pride of America, porcelain, figural,
7-3/4" h, 1982-83 . . . . .30.00
Electric Charger, black glass, after shave,
1970-72 .8.00
Flamingo, clear, gold cap, 10" h,
1971-72 .7.00
Fluffy Chick, glass, yellow flocking, Hello
Sunshine cologne, 1980. . . . . .4.00
Four Seasons, calendar plate, porcelain,
9" d, 1987. . . . . .15.00
Gingerbread, candle, brown and white,
frankincense and myrrh fragrance,
1977-79 .5.00
Giving Thanks, bell, porcelain, pumpkin,
4-1/2" h, 1990. . . . . .15.00
Graceful Giraffe, clear glass, plastic top,
1976. . . . . .6.00
Grapefruit, candle, 1974-76 . . . . .5.00
Ice Cream, lip pomade, flavored, fruitti,
1974-76 .3.00
Jeep Renegade, black glass, decals, tan
plastic top, 1981-82 . . . . .7.00

King Pin, set, red and green, two 4-oz
aftershave bottles, 1953 . . . . 45.00
Liberty Bell, glass, amber, brown cap,
1971-72. 7.00
Little Lamb, baby lotion, plastic, white,
blue cap, 1968-69 . . . . 5.00
Snoopy, soap dish, plastic, 1968-76 . 4.00
Toofie Train, red plastic train, yellow plastic
cup, red and blue toothbrushes, Toofie
toothpaste, 1974-75 . . . . 5.00
Turn A Word, plastic, pink, white cap,
green letters, bubble bath,
1972-74. 3.00
Unicorn, glass, clear, gold cap,
1974-75. 5.00
Weather Vane, clear glass painted red,
black horse top, Wild Country,
1977-78. 7.00
Year To Year Birthday Candle, ceramic,
clown, 4-1/2" h, 1983-84 . . . . 10.00

Badges

Have you ever tried to save a name tag or badge that attaches directly to your clothing or fits into a plastic holder? We are victims of a throwaway society. This is one case in which progress has not been a boon for collectors.

Commemorative, Member, Dewey Fire Co. No. 1, Hellertown, PA, $25.

Fortunately, our grandparents and great-grandparents loved to save the membership, convention, parade and other badges that they acquired. The badges' colorful silk and cotton fabric often contained elaborate calligraphic lettering and lithographed scenes in combination with celluloid and/or metal pinbacks and pins. They were badges of honor, often having an almost military quality about them.

Look for badges with attached three-dimensional miniatures. Regional value is a factor. I found a great Emmaus, Pa., badge priced at $2 at a flea market in Florida; back home, its value is more than $20.

Advertising
Dean and Barry Liquid Paint, 1920,
multicolored. 12.00
Old Kentucky Whiskey, 1901-10,
multicolored. 20.00
Sears, Roebuck & Co., 1920, tan. . .20.00

Civil War
Lincoln Thank Offering-Freedmans Aid
Society, 1" d, black and white,
1880 .100.00
Maryland Sixth Corps, silver,
cross-shaped, T-bar 140.00
Merrimac First Ironclad, iron,
heart-shaped, 1862. . . . . .40.00

Military
Canadian, submarine, cloth, two dolphins,
maple leaf, red wreath,
multicolored. 25.00
German, Naval U-boat, gold and gray,
solid swastika 84.00
Russian, campaign, 1853-56, 28mm d,
bronze, orange ribbon, three black
stripes .45.00
U.S., Naval Shore Patrol, 43mm by 61mm,
nickel. 95.00
WWI, Royal Flying Corps, hat, brass 29.00
WWII, French Bomber Pilot, multi-piece,
lug-back. 20.00
WWII, French Cross of Valor, bronze,
striped ribbon, back reads "Croix de la
Valeur Militaire" 20.00

Political
Eisenhower, 4", red, white and blue, white
ribbon, 1953 . . . . .50.00
Nixon, 2", red, white and blue, gold ribbon,
1969 . . . . .20.00
Reagan, 2-1/2", multicolored, 1981 . .5.00
Roosevelt, 3-1/2", sepia, ribbon,
1905 . . . . .150.00
Truman, brass, pink ribbon, 1949. . .50.00

Bakelite

This is a great example of a collecting category gone price-mad. Bakelite is a trademark used for a variety of synthetic resins and plastics used to manufacture colorful, inexpensive, utilitarian objects. The key word is inexpensive, which can also be interpreted as cheap. There is nothing cheap about Bakelite collectibles in today's market. Collectors, especially those from large metropolitan areas who consider themselves design-conscious, want Bakelite in whatever form they can find it.

Buy a Bakelite piece because you love it. The market has already started to collapse for commonly found material. Can the high-end pieces be far behind?

Jewelry
Brooch, 1-3/4" d, carved black ship's
    wheel, 1935 . . . . .45.00
Buckle, 4-3/8" w by 2-1/8", brass, two-pc,
    red 95.00
Pin, white, Scottie dog. 12.00
Ring, blue-green, marbleized, black-dot
    center, 1940 . . . . .55.00
Jewelry Box, aqua. 25.00

Radio
Burgundy Spartan, 1946 . . . . .85.00
Tom Thumb, brown, 1948 . . . . . . .100.00
Silvertone, Sears, transistor, black, leather
    case, 1959 . . . . .30.00
Zenith, brown 75.00

Other
Adding machine, 7" h, 12-1/2" d,
    1920 . . . . .150.00
Ashtray, brown, mkd "USA" 35.00
Baby Dish, yellow handles 20.00
Bar Utensil Set, five-pc set, green
    handles. 40.00
Cigarette Dispenser, musical, white .50.00
Coffee Warmer, Vaculator Hill Shaw Co.,
    black handle and base 30.00
Corn Cob Holders, "Kob Knobs,"
    green 17.00

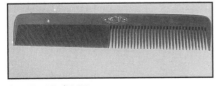

Comb, 9", $7.50.

Door Knocker, Amsonfurtsch Corp. . 20.00
Dresser Set, 10-pc, velour box 40.00
Flatware, six-pc, green handles. . . . 50.00
Hair Dryer, Oyster Air Jet,
    black stand 30.00
Pie Server, yellow and green handle . 6.00
Poker Chip Caddy, round, brown. . . 15.00
Server, hot and cold, brown handles
    and knob. 20.00
Shaving Brush, Klenzo, two-part
    handle 8.50
Salt and Pepper Shakers, pr, yellow and
    aqua 13.00
Teapot, stainless steel, electric, black
    handles and knob 55.00
Telephone, brass base, mkd "Strongberg
    Carlson" 200.00

Bandannas

Women associate bandannas with keeping their hair in place. Men visualize stage coach holdups or rags used to wipe the sweat from their brows. Neither approach recognizes the colorful and decorative role played by the bandanna.

Some of the earliest bandannas are political. By the turn of the century, bandannas joined pillow cases as the leading souvenir textile found at sites, ranging from beaches to museums. Hillary Weiss's *The American Bandanna: Culture on Cloth from George Washington to Elvis* (Chronicle Books, 1990), provides a visual feast for this highly neglected collecting area.

The bandanna played an important role in the Scouting movement, serving as a neckerchief for both Boy Scouts and Girl Scouts. Many special neckerchiefs were issued. There is also a close correlation between scarves and bandannas. Bandanna collectors tend to collect both.

Benjamin Harrison/Levi Morton, 19" by 20",
    silk, flag, bright colors, 1888 . . . 100.00
Buck Jones, 4-3/4" by 5-1/4", 1934 . 35.00
Cleveland/Thurman, 21" by 24", black and
    white, red backing. 90.00
Garfield/Arthur, 1880 . . . . 100.00
George McGovern for President, beige,
    red and black 120.00
Hancock/English, 1880 . . . . 100.00
Herbert Hoover, silk 110.00
Hopalong Cassidy, rayon, white, black
    and red 100.00

McGovern for President, beige design,
    blue map outline of United States,
    "Come Home America
    Come Home" 120.00
Roy Rogers and Trigger, 17" by 7", red
    and white, 1950s 75.00
Stevenson, "All the Way With Adlai,"
    1952 . . . . 120.00
Taft/Sherman, 16" by 17", red, white, blue
    and sepia, 1908 . . . . 180.00
Teddy Roosevelt, 19-3/4" by 18", red and
    white, initials "TR," center hat . . . 50.00

Banks, Still

Banks are classified into two types—mechanical (action) and still (non-action). Chances are that any mechanical bank you find at a flea market today is a reproduction. If you find one that you think is real, check it out in one of the mechanical bank books before buying it.

The still or non-action bank dominates the flea market scene. There is no limit to the methods for collecting still banks. Some favor type (advertising), others composition (cast iron, tin, plastic, etc.), figural (shaped like something) or theme (Western).

Beware of still-bank reproductions, just as you are with mechanical banks, especially in the cast-iron sector. Most banks were used, so look for wear in places you would expect to find it. Save your money and do not buy if you are uncertain of a bank's authenticity.

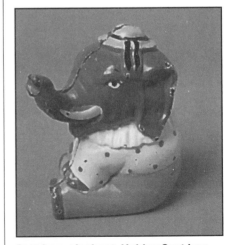

Cast Iron, elephant, Hubley Cast Iron Toys, 1940s, $175.

Club: Still Bank Collectors Club of America, 4175 Millersville Rd., Indianapolis, IN 46205.

Advertising

AC Spark Plugs, cast metal, wheels 120.00
Bokar Coffee, tin 12.00
Cincy Stoves, 4", cast iron, blue, porcelain enamel 40.00
Cinnamon Toast Crunch, General Mills, 6", plastic, musical, 1988. . . . . .10.00
Donald Duck Orange Juice, 4", cardboard, metal ends 5.00
Frigidaire, 4" by 2", pot metal 30.00
Frisch's Big Boy, 9", soft vinyl, 1973 .25.00
Hamm's Beer, 11", ceramic, 1980s. .25.00
Heinz 57, Ertl, metal, Model T Van, 1970s 70.00
Hershey's Syrup, pottery, can-shape, silver and brown 30.00
Kellogg's Pop-Tarts, 5", plastic, 1980 . . . . .50.00
Kentucky Fried Chicken, 13" 12.00
Land O' Lakes Butter, wood 25.00
Metz Beer, ceramic, barrel-shape . . .20.00
Mobiloil, glass, Pegasus emblem . . .25.00
Nestle Quik, Bunny Money 12.00
Orkin Exterminating Co., 8", papier-mâché, 1960s 350.00
Pillsbury, Poppin' Fresh, 7-1/2", ceramic, 1987 . . . . .25.00
Red Goose Shoes, tin, green, paper label 110.00
Royal Gelatin, 10", molded vinyl, 1970s 50.00

Metal, Northern Life Tower Bank, Seattle, silver-colored, #439, 3" by 2-7/8" by 5-1/4" h, $65.

Sinclair Gasoline, 4", figural gasoline pump, tin 30.00
Star-Kist Tuna, 9-1/2", ceramic, 1988 . . . . 20.00
Wolf's Head Motor Oil, 4" by 2", cardboard cylinder, metal ends, wolf head logo 12.00

Cast Iron

Apple 25.00
Automobile, miniature, Banthrico, 1910 Stanley 22.00
Bird House, 7" 55.00
Bust, Benjamin Franklin, bank advertising 12.50
Car, Montgomery Ward, 1905 . . . . . 15.00
Frog, 4-1/8" l, 1973 . . . . 55.00
Spitz, 4-1/4" by 4-1/2" 225.00

Character

Charlie Brown, 8-1/2" h, ceramic, 1969 . . . . 40.00
Donald Duck, plastic, 1979 . . . . 15.00
Howdy Doody, 9" h, plastic 40.00
Huckleberry Hound, 10" h, vinyl, 1960 . . . . 15.00
Popeye, plastic, 1972 . . . . 6.00

Glass

Bear, Snow Crest. 10.00
Kewpie, barrel, 3". 40.00
WWI Globe 50.00

Pottery

Acorn, 3" h, stoneware, 1910-20 . . . 80.00
Apple, 4" d, redware, 1879-81 . . . . . 70.00
Barrel, 4" h, yellow ware, 1860-90 . 160.00
Jug, 3" h, center spout, wire bail handles, spongeware, 1885-1905 . . . . . . 250.00

Tin

Andy Gump 15.00
Cash Box, Chein 7.50
Safe, The Empire Strikes Back, West Germany, 1980 . . . . 7.00

Other

Ceramic, mammy, 6-1/2" h 25.00
Chalkware, Santa in chimney, 11" h, 1950s 25.00
China, cat, 4" h, sitting with ball, wrapped tail 35.00
Metal, 2" by 2" by 8", rocket, "Mercury" on side, "Metropolitan Federal Savings, Los Angeles" decal 45.00
Papier-mâché, Snoopy, Joe Cool, Ideal, 1977 . . . . 20.00

Barbed Wire

Barbed wire is a farm, Western or military collectible. It is usually collect-

ed in 18-inch lengths and mounted on boards for display. While there are a few rare examples that sell in the hundreds of dollars for a piece, the majority of strands are common types that sell between $2 and $5 per sample.

Club: American Barbed Wire Collectors Society, 1023 Baldwin Rd., Bakersfield, CA 93304.

Periodical: *Barbed Wire Collector*, 1322 Lark, Lewisville, TX 75067.

Barbershop and Beauty Parlor Collectibles

Let's not discriminate. This is the age of the unisex hair salon. This category has been male-oriented for far too long. Haven't you wondered where a woman had her hair done in the 19th century? Don't forget drug store products. Not everyone had the funds or luxury to spend time each day at the barbershop or beauty salon.

Club: National Shaving Mug Collectors Association, 320 S. Glenwood St., Allentown, PA 18104.

After Shave Talc, Palmolive 7.50
Antiseptic Container, 8" h, plated brass 40.00
Ashtray, 5" d, William Marvy barber supplies giveaway 10.00
Atomizer, Tetlow's, pistol-shape . . . 150.00

Bottles, LeVarn's Shampoo and Hair Tonic, label under glass, German silver spouts, 8-1/2" h, price for pair, $125.

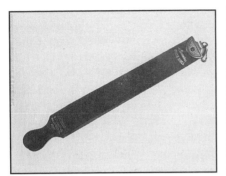

Strop, gold stamped "Genuine Horse Shell, M.S. Young & Co., Allentown, PA, ZS632," 22-3/4" l, $18.

Barber Bottle, Milk Glass, 7-1/2", hexagonal base, "W.H." on front 65.00
Barber Bottle, Opaline, 6-3/4" h, squatty base, fluted panels, stenciled lettering 30.00
Chair, oak, metal rim, Congress Pedestal Hydraulic Chair. 500.00
Clipper, Eureka, 1903 . . . . .25.00
Display Case, 4" h, wood and glass, Gillette, 1940s 30.00
Hair Tonic, Rexall 30.00
Hair Tonic, Watkins Dandruff Remover. 25.00
Jacket, black and white striped, three pockets. .80.00
Lather Brush, Genuine Badger, bone handle 15.00
Mug Rack, 36" h, oak 200.00
Mug Rack, 38" h, pine. 140.00
Mug Rack, 41" h, wood, revolving. .125.00
Neck Brush, satinwood handle, bleached bristles 25.00
Postcard, shop exterior, color, 1900 .18.00

Seat, child's, wood, imitation leather. 125.00
Shaving Cream, Burma Shave, unused, orig box 3.00
Shaving Cream, Williams, unused, 1930s 2.00
Shaving Mirror, 10" h, celluloid, silver-plated trim, beveled glass. 60.00
Shaving Mug, Fraternal, Masonic, DC Reynolds, gold letters, mkd "Limoges," yellow and gold tools 75.00
Shaving Mug, Occupational, blacksmith, John D. Singer, horseshoe with protruding black nails, horse head in center 45.00
Shaving Stand, 14" h, silverplated, beveled mirror, 1920 . . . . 25.00
Shears, French Black Beauty 10.00
Sign, Beauty Shop, globe, 16", illuminated 100.00
Sign, Ladies and Childrens Hair Bobbing Our Specialty, 12" by 24", red, white and blue 175.00
Sign, Shampoo DeLux, cast aluminum, 12" l, 1930s 40.00
Sign, Shaving, pole, 21" by 10", wood, white and blue. 100.00
Spittoon, 10" d, brass, two pc 30.00
Sterilizer Cabinet, oak frame, glass panels 60.00
Strop Container, silverplated, Art Nouveau-style 12.00
Thermometer, Tru-Value adv, 1940. 90.00
Token, Gillette, King Gillette, slogan on front, razor and slogan on back . 28.00
Travel Set, six-pc, aluminum, wood box 20.00
Travel Set, 18-pc, ivory brush and comb, silver-trimmed accessories and mirror, wood case, 1840. . . . . 700.00

Barbie Doll Collectibles

As a doll, Barbie is unique. She burst upon the scene in the late 1950s

Ponytail Barbie, #850, wearing #971 Easter Parade Coat, 1961, price for doll, $300.

and has remained a major factor in the doll market for more than 40 years. No other doll has enjoyed this longevity. Every aspect of Barbie is collectible, from the doll to her clothing to her play accessories. Although collectors place the greatest emphasis on Barbie material from the 1950s and 1960s, there is some great stuff from the 1970s and 1980s that should not be overlooked. Whenever possible, try to get original packaging. This is especially important for Barbie material from the 1980s forward.

Club: Barbie Doll Collectors Club International, P.O. Box 586, North White Plains, NY 10603.

Newsletters: *Barbie Fashions*, 387 Park Avenue South, New York, NY

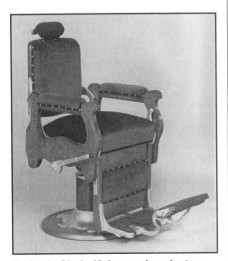

Barber's Chair, Koken, oak, velvet upholstery, c1900, $450.

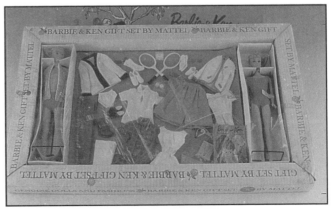

Barbie and Ken Gift Set, c1962, $1,000.

Greek Barbie, International, 1986, $125.

10016; *Collector's Corner*, 519 Fitzooth Dr., Miamisburg, OH 45342.

Periodicals: *Barbie Bazaar*, 5617 6th Ave., Kenosha, WI 53140; *Miller's Barbie Collector*, P.O. Box 8722, Spokane, WA 99203.

Clothing Accessories, MIB

Barbie, Ballerina, #989, 1961 . . . . . .30.00
Barbie, Beau Time, #1651, 1965 . . .40.00
Barbie, Dancing Doll, #1626, 1964 . .55.00
Barbie, Drum Majorette, #0875,
    1963 . . . . .50.00
Barbie, London Tour, #1661, 1965 . .80.00
Barbie, New Disco-Dater, #1807,
    1966 . . . . .75.00
Barbie, Miss Astronaut, #1641,
    1964 . . . . .200.00
Barbie, Sleeping Pretty, #1636,
    1964 . . . . .50.00
Ken, Army and Air Force, #0797,
    1963 . . . . .100.00
Ken, Campus Hero, #0770, 1963 . . .50.00
Ken, Cheerful Chef 35.00
Ken, Ken in Mexico, #0823, 1963 . . .75.00
Ken, Masquerade, #0794, 1963 . . . .40.00
Ken, Mr. Astronaut, #1415, 1964 . .200.00
Ken, Sleeper Set, #0781, 1962 . . . . .20.00
Ken, Roller Skate Date, #1405,
    1963 . . . . .35.00
Beach Bus, 1974 . . . . .30.00
Book, *The Island Resort Adventure*,
    electronic storybook, Golden Sound
    Story, 1992 . . . . .10.00
Cake Pan, Wilton, 1992 . . . . .12.00
Camera, 35mm, Kalimar, 1994 . . . . .15.00

Car, Classy Corvette, 1976 . . . . . . 125.00
Charm Bracelet, 18k gold-plated, Peter
    Brams Designs 100.00
ColorForms, Barbie Dress Up Kit,
    1970 . . . . 40.00
Coloring Book, 15-1/2" by 20", Merrigold
    Press, 1984 . . . . 12.00

Dolls

Barbie, 1967, Standard 175.00
Barbie, 1971, Talking 125.00
Barbie, 1976, Ballerina Barbie
    on Tour 60.00
Ken, 1964, bendable legs 250.00
Ken, 1969, Talking 75.00
Ken, 1973, Mod Hair Ken 45.00

Other

Case, Mountain Ski Cabin, Mattel,
    1972 and 1974 . . . . 40.00
Case, Skipper, 1964 . . . . 25.00
Game, Dream Date, Golden-Western
    Publishing, 1992 . . . . 10.00
Game, Keys to Fame, Mattel, 1963 . 35.00
Game, Miss Lively Livin', Mattel,
    1970 . . . . 30.00
Game, We Girls Can Do Anything, Western
    Publishing, 1986 . . . . 15.00
Hanger, MIB 12.00
Jewelry Box 20.00
Nurse Kit, Pressman 75.00
Olympic Gymnast Set, Barbie and PJ,
    MIB 25.00
Paper Dolls, Barbie and Ken, all sports
    tournament, Whitman, unused,
    1976 . . . . 25.00
Pencil Case, ADI, 1983 . . . . 5.00
Piano, electronic, Mattel, 1982 . . . . 90.00
PJ, New N' Groovy, talking, 1969,
    MIB 90.00
Record, *Barbie Sings*, six songs, three
    records, 1961 . . . . 30.00
Salt and Pepper Shakers, pr, Barbie and
    Ken, bisque, Enesco Corp.,
    1995 . . . . 40.00
Suitcase, Hollywood, Ero Industries, Inc.,
    1993 . . . . 12.00
Tea Set, miniature, porcelain, set of four,
    gray suede box, pink lined
    interior 40.00
Trading Cards, jumbo, 1962 . . . . . . 45.00
View-Master, Barbie and The Rockers,
    1986 . . . . 15.00
View-Master, Barbie: Featuring Superstar
    Barbie, 1989 . . . . 10.00
Watch, Barbie For Girls, 1990 . . . . . 15.00

Baseball Cards

Collecting baseball cards is no longer just for kids. It is an adult game.

Recent trends include buying and stashing away complete boxed sets of cards, placing special emphasis on rookie and other types of cards, and speculation on a few "rare" cards that have a funny habit of turning up on the market far more frequently than one would expect from such rarities.

Baseball cards date from the late 19th century. The earliest series are tobacco company issues dating between 1909 and 1915. During the 1920s American Caramel, National Caramel, and York Caramel issued cards.

Goudey Gum Co. (1933 to 1941) and Gum, Inc.(1939), carried on the tradition in the 1930s. When World War II ended, Bowman Gum of Philadelphia, the successor to Gum, Inc., became the baseball giant. Topps, Inc., of Brooklyn, N.Y., followed. Topps purchased Bowman in 1956 and enjoyed almost a monopoly in card production until 1981 when Fleer of Philadelphia and Donruss of Memphis challenged its leadership.

In addition to sets produced by these major companies, there are hundreds of other sets issued by a variety of sources, ranging from product manufacturers, such as Sunbeam Bread, to Minor League teams. There are so many secondary sets now issued an-

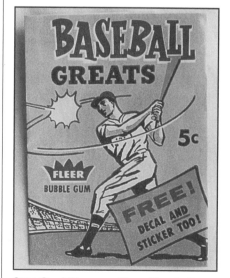

Gum Card Wrapper, Fleer, Baseball Greats, 1961, $25.

nually that it is virtually impossible for a collector to keep up with them all. The field is plagued with reissued sets and cards, as well as outright forgeries. The color photocopier has been used to great advantage by unscrupulous dealers. Never buy cards from someone that you can't find six months later.

The listing below is simply designed to give you an idea of baseball card prices in good to very good condition and to show you how they change, depending on the age of the cards that you wish to collect. For detailed information about card prices, consult the following price guides: James Beckett, *Beckett Baseball Price Guide No. 18*, Beckett Publications, 1996; Bob Lemke, ed., *Standard Catalog of Baseball Cards*, Fifth Edition, Krause Publications, 1995; and *Sports Collectors Digest Baseball Card Price Guide*, 10th Edition, Krause Publications, 1996. Although Beckett is the name most often mentioned in connection with price guides, I have found the Krause guides to be more helpful.

Periodicals: *Beckett Baseball Card Monthly*, 15850 Dallas Parkway, Dallas, TX 75248; *Sports Cards* and *Sports Collectors Digest*, 700 E. State St., Iola, WI 54990.

Bowman
1950, Complete Set 2,500.00
1950, 11 Phil Rizzuto 46.00
1950, 58 Carl Furillo 20.00
1950, 67 Willie Jones 12.00
1951, Complete Set 6,000.00
1951, 1 Whitey Ford 240.00
1951, 80 Pee Wee Reese 42.50
1951, 186 Richie Ashburn 16.50
1989, Complete Set 4.75
1989, 6 Gregg Olson 08
1989, 26 Roger Clemens 14
1989, 126 Bo Jackson 10

Donruss
1984, Complete Set 130.00
1984, Common Player 05

Fleer
1981, Complete Set 60.00
1981, Common Player 90
1983, Complete Set 40.00
1983, Common Player 02

Leaf
1948, Complete Set 9,000.00

1948, 127 Enos Slaughter 217.00
1948, 168 Phil Cavaretta 105.00
1991, Complete Set 12.00
1991, 8 Dave Martinez 03
1991, 44 Lee Smith 04

Score
1989, Complete Set 6.00
1989, Common Player 01

Topps
1955, Complete Set 2,000.00
1955, 47 Hank Aaron 90.00
1955, 166 Hank Bauer 10.00
1955, 194 Willie Mays 120.00
1955, 202 Jim Owens 9.00
1959, Complete Set 1,500.00
1959, 1 Ford Frick 12.00
1959, 10 Mickey Mantle 120.00
1959, 35 Ted Kluszewski 3.00
1959, 207 George Strickland 1.25
1962, Complete Set 1,300.00
1962, 5 Sandy Koufax 45.00
1962, 29 Casey Stengel 6.00
1962, 49 Hal Jones 1.00
1962, 85 Gil Hodges 5.25
1964, Complete Set 750.00
1964, 97 Jim Fregosi 1.00
1964, 120 Don Drysdale 6.00
1964, 125 Pete Rose 43.00
1964, 293 Phillies Team 1.75
1989, Complete Set 6.00
1989, 2 Wade Boggs 05
1989, 200 George Brett 12
1989, 240 Greg Maddux 14
1989, 300 Darryl Strawberry 06
1991, Complete Set 6.00
1991, 1 Nolan Ryan 15
1991, 100a Don Mattingly 25
1991, 170 Carlton Fisk 04

Upper Deck
1990, Complete Set 12.00
1990, Common Player 03
1990, 20 Mike Schmidt 20
1990, 119 Brett Butler 04
1990, 256 Orel Hershiser 04
1992, Complete Set 12.00
1992, 102 Hector Villanueva 02
1992, 112 Dave Magadan 03
1992, 650 Ken Griffey Jr 20

Baseball Memorabilia

What a feast for the collector! Flea markets often contain caps, bats, gloves, autographed balls and photos of your favorite all-stars, baseball statues, regular and world series game programs and team manuals or rosters. Do not overlook secondary mate-

Book, *Frank Merriwell's New Boy*, Merriwell Series #134, Burt Standish, paper cov, $12.

rial such as magazine covers with a baseball theme. Condition and personal preference should always guide the eye.

Be careful of autograph forgeries. The general feeling among collectors is that more than 50 percent of the autographed baseballs being offered for sale have faked signatures. But do not let this spoil your fun. There is plenty of good stuff out there.

Periodical: *Sports Collectors Digest*, 700 E. State St., Iola, WI 54990.

Autographed Baseball
Carlton Fisk 25.00
Casey Stengel 480.00
Goose Goslin 800.00
Joe Jackson 13,000.00
Mickey Lolich 20.00

Matchbook Cover, Washington American League Baseball Club, home game schedule, $15.

Press Badge, 1914 World Series, Philadelphia Athletics, 5" l, $650.

Reggie Jackson. 32.00
Richie Ashburn 30.00
Rod Carew .29.00
Steve Garvey 22.00

Book

Baseball's Most Valuable Players, George
    Vecsey, Random House, 1960s. .10.00
Connie Mack, *My 66 Years in the Big
    Leagues*, Universal House, first edition,
    1950s 50.00
Joe DiMaggio, *Lucky to Be a Yankee*,
    Bantam, 1940s. 20.00
1964 Official Baseball Almanac,
    paperback, Gold Medal Books. . .15.00

**Starting Lineup Figures, Kenner,
1988, MIB**

Darryl Strawberry 13.00
Don Mattingly 20.00
Dwight Gooden 15.00
Nolan Ryan 120.00
Pete Rose .30.00

Other

Annual, *Who's Who In Baseball*, 36th Edi-
    tion, 1951 . . . . .20.00
Ashtray, metal, Detroit Tigers,
    1930s 100.00
Bank, Cincinnati Reds, glass, 1950s.25.00
Bank, Philadelphia Phillies, 5", ceramic,
    1960s 25.00
Bat, Mike Schmidt, autographed. . .100.00
Bobbin' Head Doll, Los Angeles Dodgers,
    boy's head, square blue base,
    1962 . . . . .90.00

Bobbin' Head Doll, Pittsburgh Pirates,
    mascot, round gold base,
    1967-72 . . . . 80.00
Cap, Cal Ripken. 75.00
Clock, Philadelphia Phillies, Medford
    Meats, 16" by 16", 1970s 30.00
Cup, Yankees, Icee, plastic, 3-1/2" by 7",
    1984 . . . . 6.00
Drinking Glass, Philadelphia Phillies,
    Connie Mack Stadium, 1960s. . . 10.00
Glove, Reggie Jackson 350.00
Key Tag, John Mize, 1-1/2", leather,
    1950s 15.00
Magazine, *Life*, Joe DiMaggio cover, Time,
    Inc., May, 1939 . . . . 15.00
Magazine, *Sports Stars*, Phil Rizzuto
    cover, August 1951. . . . . 10.00
Matchbook Cover, Don Drysdale, Diamond
    Match Co. 10.00
Package, Bat Chewing Tobacco,
    1920 . . . . 50.00
Record, Richie Ashburn, 7" by 7-1/2",
    1952 . . . . 20.00
Schedule, Yankees, 2-1/2" by 4", red, white
    and blue, 1987 . . . . 1.00
Shoes, spikes, Mike Schmidt, worn in
    game, autographed. 300.00
Soda Can, Philadelphia Phillies, Canada
    Dry Ginger Ale, 1976 . . . . 1.00
Uniform, Yankees, flannel, Tommy Hen-
    rich, 1951 . . . . 650.00
Watch, Jose Torres, 1970 . . . . 50.00
Yearbook, Kansas City A's, 8-1/2" by 11",
    52 pgs, 1955. . . . . 200.00

Basketball

As the prices of baseball cards and
baseball memorabilia continue to rise,
collectors are turning to other sports
categories based on the affordability of
their material. Basketball and football
are "hot" sport collecting fields.

**Puzzle, jigsaw, 1992 USA Olympic Bas-
ketball "Dream Team," Golden, #5159,
$10.**

Gum Card Wrapper, Topps, 1975, $10.

Collecting generally centers around
one team, as it does in most other
sport collecting categories. Items have
greater value in their "hometown" than
they do "on the road." You know a category is gaining strength when its secondary material starts to bring
consistently strong prices.

Periodicals: *Beckett Basketball Card
Magazine,* 15850 Dallas Parkway,
Dallas, TX 75248; *Sports Cards* and
Sports Collectors Digest, 700 E. State
St., Iola, WI 54990.

Autographs

Billy Cunningham, sgd basketball. . .30.00
Bob Cousy, 8" by 10" photo 55.00
Earl Monroe, 3" by 5" card 12.00
Wilt Chamberlain, 8" by 10" photo . .75.00

Games

Harlem Globetrotters, Milton Bradley,
    1971 . . . . .35.00
Real-Life Basketball, Gamecraft,
    1974 . . . . .10.00
Sports Illustrated Pro Basketball, Avalon
    Hill, 1981 . . . . .15.00

Pennants

Charles Barkley 5.00
Larry Bird 8.00
Michael Jordan. 10.00
Shaquille O'Neal. 6.00

Posters

Elvin Hayes, 1970. . . . . .35.00

Reed, Willis, 1968-71 . . . . .20.00

Shoes
Charles Barkley 400.00
Dennis Rodman 150.00
Moses Malone 175.00

Starting Lineup Figures, Kenner, 1988, MIB
Charles Barkley 20.00
Kareem Abdul-Jabbar 24.00
Larry Bird .24.00
Moses Malone 45.00
Patrick Ewing 15.00

Ticket Stub, NBA All-Star Game
1960, Philadelphia 25.00
1972, Los Angeles 8.00
1982, New Jersey 8.00

Baskets

A tisket, a tasket, who's got the basket? Baskets, ranging from old timers to contemporary craft types, are readily found at flea markets.

Easter, braided rim and handle, 10-1/2" w, 9" h, $25.

Backpacking, 9" by 18", ash splint, heavy straps 65.00
Beehive, 16" by 16", rye 16.00
Bell, 6" by 6", rattan 8.00
Berry, 4-1/2" by 7", white oak splint 125.00
Bread, 6" by 12", willow, oblong 9.00
Cake, 10" by 9", rattan 30.00
Clothes Pin, 9-1/2" by 13", oak splint, low handle .140.00
Compote, 12" by 6-1/2", ash splint, wrapped handles, reinforced base 60.00
Feather, 13-1/2" by 12", ash splint .150.00
Half, oak splint, painted white 40.00

Picnic Basket, oak splint, swivel handles, hinged lid, $20.

Jigger, 2" by 2-1/2", ash splint, sweet grass 25.00
Melon, 7" by 12" by 11", oak splint, white 250.00
Strawberry, 5" by 3-1/2", ash splint and sweet grass, red and green 30.00
Turtle, 2-3/4" by 4-1/2" by 2", pine needle, raffia 20.00
Yarn, 7" by 11", grass, ash, covered 45.00

Batman

"Galloping globs of bat guano, Caped Crusader!" and similar cries may be heard as the Dark Knight and his sidekick are summoned to restore peace to Gotham City.

The saga of the search for Batman and Robin-related items began with Batman's appearance in 1939 in issue #27 of Detective Comics. Today, Boy Wonder and Caped Crusader collectibles are found in almost every medium imaginable. Local flea markets offer a large variety of batgoodies capable of making any batcollector go batty!

Club: Batman TV Series Fan Club, P.O. Box 107, Venice, CA 90294.

Action Figures
Batgirl, 5" h, bendable, 1972, Mego. 65.00
Batman, 7" h, bendie, 1989, Bully . . 20.00
Batman, 15" h, with stand, Applause 25.00
Bruce Wayne, Batman Returns, 1992-93, Kenner 15.00
Catwoman, 5" h, bendable, 1972, Mego 90.00
Joker, 3" h, plastic, blue, 1966, Ideal 15.00
Robin, 5" h, rubber, bendable, 1973, Mego 7.00

Other
Activity Book, 8" by 11", 20 pgs, dot-to-dot, 1967 . . . . 25.00

Ashtray, 5" d, ceramic, white, Batman and Robin center, 1966, Salex 50.00
Batcopter, Dark Knight, 1989, Kenner 50.00
Batmobile, Bandai, 1980s 60.00
Batmobile, Toy Biz, remote control, 1989 . . . . .45.00
Batscope Dart Launcher, 1966, Tarco 55.00
Beach Towel, 34" by 58", white, color illus, Batman hitting crook 25.00
Belt, child's, elastic, bronze logo buckle, 1960s 45.00
Brochure, Please Touch Museum, four pgs, yellow and black, 1989 . . . . .7.00
Cereal Bowl, Joker, 5" d, plastic 15.00
Chair, inflatable, 1982, MIB 25.00
Chewing Gum, 25-pack box, 1989, Lott 70.00
Costume Pattern, paper envelope, 1960s, *McCall's* .20.00
Fork and Spoon Set, stainless steel, emb 1-1/2" figure on handle, 10" by 4" display card, 1966 . . . . .25.00
Game, Capture The Joker, 9" by 18", board game, 1965, Hasbro 50.00
Game, Target Game, 9" by 12", litho tin, plastic revolver, rubber-tipped darts, 1966, Hasbro 100.00
Gotham City Stunt Set, 1989, Tonka 55.00
License Plate, 4" by 7-1/4", emb metal 30.00
Marionette, 1977, Madison 50.00
Mask, 6" by 8-1/2", paper, 1943 . . .175.00

Colorforms, 1966, $45.

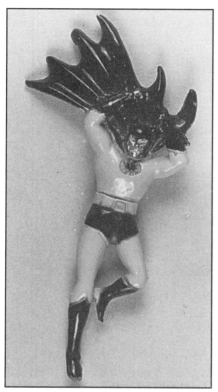

Pin, enameled, black cape, trunks and boots, gray suit, 3" l, $25.

Mittens, child's, blue, plastic vinyl, logo, 1973 . . . . .20.00

Music Box, Riddler, ceramic, figural, 1978 . . . . .50.00

Nite-Lite, 2" by 3", hard plastic, logo, electric, 1966, Snap-It 20.00

Notebook Binder, three-ring, vinyl, yellow, logo, 1966 . . . . .25.00

Pajamas, blue, two-pc set, logo on chest, 1966, Wormser 700.00

Party Hat, 7" h, cardboard, 1972 . . . . .8.00

Pencil Box, gun-shaped box, 1966, Empire Pencil 40.00

Pennant, 11" by 29", felt, color illus, 1966 . . . . .25.00

Pin, 3" l, metal, Batman leaping, display card 25.00

Pinback Button, metal, color litho, Charter Member-Batman and Robin Society, 1966, Buttton World 35.00

Placemat, 13" by 18", Robin, vinyl, multi-color, 1966 . . . . .50.00

Puzzle, frame tray, 11" by 14", Batman, Robin and Joker, 1966, Whitman 200.00

Radio, AM, Batmobile, 1970s, Bandai 80.00

Ray Gun, 7" l, blue and black, 1960s 140.00

Sheet Music, 9" by 12", six pages, 1966, Miller Music 15.00

Stickers, Official Bat Signals, 8" by 5" poly-bag, eight stickers, 1966, Alan-Whitney 20.00

T-shirt, white, cotton, red, white-and-black logo 50.00

Wallet, yellow vinyl, 1966, Standard Plastics 25.00

Watch, Catwoman, digital, 1991 . . . 12.00

Bauer Pottery

J.A. Bauer established the Bauer Pottery in Los Angeles in 1909. Flowerpots were among the first items manufactured, followed by utilitarian items. Dinnerware was introduced in 1930. Artware came a decade later. The firm closed in 1962.

Newsletters: *Bauer News*, P.O. Box 91279, Pasadena, CA 91109; *Bauer Quarterly*, P.O. Box 2524, Berkeley, CA 94702.

La Linda, 1939-59
Cookie Jar 65.00
Creamer 7.00
Gravy 15.00
Jug 40.00
Saucer 3.00
Tumbler, 8 oz 13.00
Vegetable Bowl, 8", oval 20.00

Monterey, 1936-45
Bowl, 8", fruit, footed 25.00
Cake Plate, pedestal 100.00
Candlestick 40.00
Coffee Server, 8-cup, wood handle . 35.00
Creamer 10.00
Jug, 2 qt 65.00
Relish, 10-1/2" 40.00
Saucer 7.00

Ring, c1931
Ashtray, 2" 35.00

Creamer, La Linda, medium green, imp "Bauer USA" on bottom, 4-3/4" w, 3" h, $7.

Canister, 4-1/2" 60.00
Casserole, 9-1/2", metal holder 75.00
Chop Plate, 12" 40.00
Cigarette Jar 150.00
Coffeepot, 8-cup 150.00
Cookie Jar 200.00
Creamer 15.00
Eggcup 70.00
Goblet 65.00
Jug, 2 qt, metal handle 75.00
Mixing Bowl, 1 gal 55.00
Mixing Bowl, 1 pint 25.00
Mixing Bowl, 1-1/2 qt 30.00
Pickle Dish 20.00
Refrigerator Jar, open 20.00
Salt and Pepper Shakers, pr, barrel-shape 50.00
Teapot, 6-cup, wood handle 75.00
Vase, 10", cylindrical 75.00
Water Bottle 75.00

Beatles

Ahhh! Look, it's the Fab Four! The collector will never need Help to find Beatle memorabilia at a flea market—place mats, dishes, records, posters and much more. The list is a Magical Mystery Tour. John, Paul, George and Ringo can be found in a multitude of shapes and sizes. Examine them carefully. They are likely to be heavily played with, so conditions will vary from poor to good.

Clubs: Beatle Fan Club, 397 Edgewood Ave., New Haven, CT 06511; Beatles Connection, P.O. Box 1066, Pinellas Park, FL 34665; Beatles Fan Club of Great Britain, Superstore Publications, 123 Marina, St. Leonards on Sea, East Sussex, England TN38 OBN; Working Class Hero Beatles

Trading Card, Topps, black-and-white photo, printed signature, 1964, Series 2, $2.

Club, 3311 Niagara St., Pittsburgh, PA 15213.

Periodicals: *Beatlefan*, P.O. Box 33515, Decatur, GA 30033; *Instant Karma*, P.O. Box 256, Sault Ste. Marie, MI 49783; *Strawberry Fields Forever*, P.O. Box 880981, San Diego, CA 92168.

Bank, ceramic, 1968 . . . . .115.00
Blanket, 54" by 72", cotton,
   silk-screen 250.00
Brooch, 2", metal. 60.00
Calendar, pocket size 20.00
Charm Bracelet, group photo 65.00
Christmas Seals, 4" by 7", 100 seals 40.00
Coin, commemorative, 1964 tour . . .15.00
Cufflinks, pr, orig card 125.00
Doll, Ringo Starr, 5" h, rooted hair, black
   suit, without instrument, 1964,
   Remco .40.00
Drinking Glass, 6" h. 90.00
Game, Flip Your Wig, 1964, Milton
   Bradley. 140.00
Hair Brush, plastic, red, white and blue,
   1964. . . . . .20.00
Harmonica, 4" by 1-1/4", orig box, 1964,
   Hohner 90.00
Hummer, plastic, blue 70.00
Key Chain, 2-1/2" by 6", plastic, 1968, King
   Features. .15.00
Lunch Box, vinyl, oval, top zipper, no
   thermos 250.00
Mug, 4" h, plastic. 80.00
Necklace, 1-3/4", ceramic-like pendant,
   photo on front. 90.00
Nodder, Paul McCartney, 8" h, ceramic,
   1964, Carmascot 90.00
Pin, brass, 1-1/2", four heads around body
   of guitar, 1964 . . . . .35.00
Pinback Button, 2-1/2" d, 3-D flasher 10.00
Pinback Button, 3-1/2" d, inscribed "I'm 4
   Beatles" .8.00
Pennant, "I Love The Beatles" 40.00

Record Player, four-speed, blue case, 17-1/2" by 10" by 6", $560.

Postcard, 10" by 14", 1968, King Features,
   set of six 7.00
Soaky, 12" h, plastic, Paul 45.00
Stickers, color, 100 per pkg, 1964,
   Hallmark 30.00
Switchplate Cover, 6" by 10-1/2", Meanie,
   1968, Dal, King Features 25.00
Three-Ring Binder, 10" by 12", 1964,
   Loose-leaf. 100.00
Tumbler, plastic, paper insert, kissing lips
   on top 70.00
Underwear, Made in UK 80.00
Watercolor Set, 6" by 8" pictures, 1968,
   Craft Master, MIB, set of four . . . 60.00
Wig, 1964, MIB 60.00

Beatnik and Hippie Memorabilia

The "Beatniks," or "Beats" arose from the post-World War II disillusionment with conventional society. Bohemian nonconformity in thinking and appearance produced new poetry, literature, music and art. Books, records, posters, pamphlets, leaflets and other items made during this period (1948-1962) are highly collectible. The most prominent Beat authors are Jack Kerouac, Allen Ginsberg and William Burroughs, and items by or about them are especially prized.

In the early 1960s, folk musicians such as Bob Dylan continued this alternative culture. The Free Speech Movement in Berkeley (Calif.) was the beginning of student involvement in politics. Political groups such as the Yippies, Students for a Democratic Society, Black Panthers and Weathermen demonstrated against the Vietnam War. Author Ken Kesey and his Merry Pranksters on the West Coast and Harvard professor Timothy Leary on the East Coast began experimenting with hallucinogenic drugs (legal at the time).

The youth culture culminated in the "Summer of Love" in 1967 in San Francisco's Haight-Ashbury district. Items produced during this time that are sought are: underground newspapers and comics, posters for political or musical events, such as concerts at the Fillmore or Avalon Ballroom; and magazines, books, bumper stickers,

pinback buttons, records (both musical and spoken word), handbills and leaflets. Some collectors concentrate on items related to a specific musical group such as the Grateful Dead, Jefferson Airplane or Quicksilver Messenger Service.

Advisor: Richard M. Synchef, 16 Midway Ave., Moll Valley, CA 94941 (415) 381-4448.

Books

Brown, William, *Beat, Beat, Beat,* Signet,
   NY, 1959, paperback with cartoons of
   Beatnik life. 25.00
Cohen, John (ed.), *The Essential Lenny
   Bruce*, Douglas, NY, 1970, hardbound,
   dust jacket, 1st edition. 50.00
Feldman, Gene and Max Gartenberg
   (eds.), *The Beat Generation and the
   Angry Young Men*, Dell, NY, 1959,
   comprehensive anthology with
   Kerouac, Burroughs and Ginsberg,
   paperback, 1st edition 35.00
Kerouac, Jack, *Tristessa*, Avon, NY, 1960,
   paperback original 60.00
Krim, Seymour (ed.), *The Beats*, Fawcett,
   Greenwich, Conn., 1960, important
   early Beat anthology, paperback, 1st
   edition 40.00
Max, Peter, *Paper Airplane Book*, Pyramid
   Books, 1971 . . . . 50.00

Magazines

Evergreen Review, Issue #2, "The San
   Francisco Scene," Grove Press, NY,
   1959, exposed Beat Generation writers
   to nation. 40.00
Man From Utopia, San Francisco Book
   Co., San Francisco, 1972, highlights
   famous '60s artist
   Rick Griffin's work 35.00
Ramparts, "The Social History of the
   Hippie," March 1967, comprehensive
   photo-filled account of growing hippie
   movement in San Francisco 40.00
The Realist, Paul Krassner (ed.), Issue
   #90, May-June 1971, "An Impolite
   Interview with Ken Kesey". 40.00
Life, March 25, 1966, LSD cover story with
   photos, published when LSD
   was still legal 35.00
Life, Oct. 21, 1969, marijuana cover story
   with photos 20.00

Records

Dick Gregory at Kent State, two LP album,
   Poppy, 1970, describes May 4, 1970,
   Kent State shooting 50.00
Is Freedom Academic?, LP recording,
   KPFA Radio, Berkley, CA, 1964 . 50.00

L.S.D., Timothy Leary, LP recording, Pixie
Records, NY 1966 . . . . .120.00
San Francisco Poets, LP recording,
Hanover, NY 1959, readings by
Ginsberg, Ferlinghetti, McClure,
etc. 65.00

Other

Bumper Sticker, Lyndon's Bridge Is Falling
Down, blue lettering, orange ground,
early 1968, 15" by 3" 35.00
Bumper Sticker, McCarthy for President,
1968 . . . . .25.00
Cigarette Holder, Beatnik, plastic, black,
c1950s, 12" l, cardboard display
backing. 20.00
Comics, underground, Robert Crumb,
Homegrown Funnies, Kitchen Sink
Press, 1971 . . . . .45.00
Comics, underground, Robert Crumb, *Your
Hytone Comix*, apex Novelties,
1971 . . . . .35.00
Flyer, "Dick Gregory for President," 1968,
size and format similar to U.S.
$1 bill 20.00
Jigsaw Puzzle, Nixon/Agnew, two-sided,
The Puzzle Factory, NY, c1970,
22" by 15". 30.00
Map, Hippieville, street map of
Haight-Ashbury area, San Francisco,
W,T. Samhill, Sausilito, CA, 1967,
folding, 17" by 22" 35.00
Pinback Button, "Free Speech" and
"F.S.M.," Berkeley, CA, 1964, blue
ground, white letters. 35.00
Pinback Button, "March on Washington-
San Francisco April 24-Out
Now-NPAC," 1971, yellow, blue and
red, 1-5/8" d 20.00
Playbill, Hair, first run at Biltmore Theatre,
NY, 72 pgs 50.00
Poster, Antiwar, "Out Now. Stop the
Bombing. March Against the War,"
issued by Student Mobilization
Committee, Berkeley, CA, 1970,
22" by 14". 50.00
Poster, Human Be-In, The Bindweed
Press, San Francisco, Jan. 10, 1967,
artists Kelly and Mouse, possibly the
classic poster of '60s announces first
counterculture "be-in". 450.00
Program, movie Woodstock, Warner
Brothers, 1970, 48 pgs. 50.00
Sheet Music, "San Francisco (Be Sure to
Wear Flowers in Your Hair)," Scott
McKenzie, Trousdale Music Publishers,
Inc., 1967 . . . . .35.00
Ticket, Woodstock, 1969,
one- or three-day admission,
Globe Ticket Co. 100.00
Tour Book, Jefferson Airplane, 1967, 32
pgs, full-color photos 50.00

Beer Cans

Beer can collecting was very popular in the 1970s. Times have changed. The field is now dominated by the serious collector and most trading and selling goes on at specialized beer can-ventions.

The list below contains a number of highly sought-after cans. Do not assume these prices are typical. Most cans fall in the 25-cent to 50-cent range. Do not pay more unless you are certain of the resale market.

There is no extra value to be gained by having a full beer can. In fact, selling a full can of beer without a license, even if only to a collector, violates the liquor laws in a large number of states. Most collectors punch a hole in the bottom of the can and drain out the beer.

Finally, before you ask, Billy Beer, either in individual cans, six packs or cases, is not worth hundreds or thousands of dollars. The going price for a can among collectors is between 50 cents and $1. Billy Beer has lost its fizz.

Club: Beer Can Collectors of America, 747 Merus Ct., Fenton, MO 63026.

Alpine, 12 oz, flat-top 60.00
American Beer, Pittsburgh Brewing Co., 12
oz, tab-top, white can, metallic red
diamond-shaped label 2.00
Bavarian Flavor Pilsner, 12 oz, flat-top,
mountain scene, red circle 30.00
Ballantine, Newark, NJ, 16 oz,
flat-top. 10.00

Mulheim draft beer, 12 oz, $10.

**Lowenbrau, German distribution, 11 oz,
$2.**

Black Label, 14 oz, tab-top, red can, black
label, white outline 10.00
Brown Derby Lager, San Antonio, 12 oz,
white can, red label, brown outline 2.00
Carling Black Label, Fort Worth, TX, 12 oz,
red can, black label 15.00
Dart Premium Light, Eastern Brewing Co.,
12 oz, tab-top 10.00
Dixie Beer, Mountain Brewing Co., 12 oz,
flat-top, metallic gold can,
white label 150.00
Fisher, three cities, 16 oz, pull-top . . . 4.00
Fox Deluxe, G. Heilman Brewing Co., 12
oz, tab-top, white can, metallic-gold
band 3.00
Genesee Cream Ale, 12 oz, tab-top, green
can, white label 3.00
Gibbons Ale, Wilkes Barre, PA, 12 oz,
cone top. 150.00
Goebel, 12 oz, gold can, blue-and-white
label. 3.00
Heidelberg, 12 oz, tab-top, gold and red
can. 3.00
Holland Brand Ale, Eastern Brewing Co.,
12 oz, flat-top, woodgrain can,
white label 65.00
Lone Star Draft, two cities, 12 oz,
pull-top. 5.00
Manheim Premium, Reading, PA, 12 oz,
tab-top, white can, gold and
red label. 8.00
Meister Brau Premium, Miller Brewing Co.,
16 oz, tab-top, gold can,
white label 3.00
Miller High Life, 10 oz, tab-top, gold can,
white label outlined in green 10.00
National Bohemian, Baltimore, 12 oz,
pull-top. 2.00

Old Dutch Brand, The Good Beer, 12 oz,
    tab-top, white can, multicolored
    label 3.00
Olde Virginia, Roanoke, VA, 12 oz, cone
    top, blue can, white label 100.00
Pabst Blue Ribbon, 12 oz, flat-top, white
    can, red ribbon 5.00
Piels Draft Ale, 12 oz, tab-top, green can,
    red and white 25.00
Pikes Peak Ale, Pueblo, CO, 12 oz,
    pull-top .35.00
Robin Hood Cream Ale, Pittsburgh,
    12 oz 50
Tuborg Brewed Light, 12 oz, tab-top, gold
    can, red label, blue outline 5.00

Bells

Bell collectors are fanatics. They tend to want every bell they can find. Admittedly, most confine themselves to bells that will fit on a shelf, but there are those who derive great pleasure from an old school bell sitting on their front lawn.

Be alert for wine glasses that have been converted into bells. They are worth much less than bells that began life as bells. Also, collect limited-edition bells because you like them, rather than with the hope they will rise in value. Many limited edition bells do not ring true on the resale market.

Clubs: American Bell Association, Alter Rd., P.O. Box 386, Natrona Heights, PA 15065; American Bell Association International, Inc., P.O. Box 19443, Indianapolis, IN 46219.

Brass
Desk, 3-1/2" d, 1856 . . . . .20.00
Door, 7" d, cast iron back 135.00
Hand, wood handle 90.00
Servant's, 13" h, mid 1800s 145.00
Ship, 9" h. .850.00
Turkey, 1-1/4" d. 15.00

Other
Advertising, Sterling Beer, 4-3/4" by
    14-3/4", metal. 60.00
Animal, cast iron, 3" d 15.00
Boxing, 10" d, trip hammer 75.00
Cow, hardwood, wood clapper, 7" h .40.00
Farm, cast iron 75.00
Japanese, foil-covered cardboard, mid
    20th century 10.00
Lady, china, 4-1/2" h, pink, yellow and
    white dress, holding
    floral bouquet 65.00

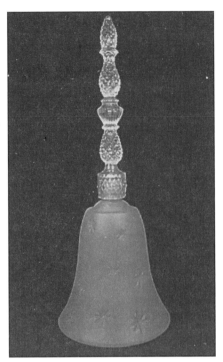

Heavenly Cherub Hostess Bell, Avon, 1979-80, $7.

Liberty Bell, glass, candy container . 85.00
WWII, 6" h, metal, emb Roosevelt,
    Churchill and Stalin heads 60.00
Yacht, 5-1/4" h, brass 40.00

Belt Buckles

This is a category loaded with reproductions and fakes. Beware of any cast buckle signed Tiffany. Surprisingly, many collectors do not mind the fakes. They like the designs and collect them for what they are.

A great specialized collection can be built around military buckles. These can be quite expensive. Once again, beware of recasts and fakes, especially Nazi buckles.

Club: Buckle Buddies International, 501 Dauphin St., Riverside, NJ 08075.

Military
Austrian, steel, gray painted finish. . 55.00
Bavarian, steel, gray paint, black leather
    belt, steel nook 115.00
French Infantry, 2-1/2" by 2-1/4", rect,
    brass plate 65.00
Prussian, 50mm, brass, nickel roundel,
    DRGM stamped on prong bar. . . 35.00

Other
Bee Gees, brass, logo 15.00
Bull's Head, lady's size. 35.00
KISS, brass, logo, 1976 . . . . 25.00
Panama Red. 25.00
Wells Butterfield 65.00

Bibles

The general rule to follow is that any Bible less than 200 years old has little or no value in the collectibles market. For a number of reasons, individuals are reluctant to buy religious items. Bibles are proof positive that nothing is worth anything without a buyer.

Many have trouble accepting this argument. They see a large late 19th century family Bible filled with engravings of religious scenes and several pages containing information about the family. It is old and impressive. It has to be worth money. Alas, it was mass-produced and survived in large quantities. The most valuable thing about it is the family data and this can be saved simply by copying the few pages involved on a photocopier.

An average price for a large family Bible from the turn of the century is between $25 and $50. Of course, there are Bibles that sell for a lot more than this. Never speculate when buying a Bible, God would not like it.

1850, Philadelphia, Bible, woodcut illus,
    English medical recipe (Pow-Wow)
    broadside on rear paste down, Petre
    family record 35.00
1854, Philadelphia, Holy Bible: Comprehensive Bible, gilt leather cov . . .35.00
1866, 23rd Psalm, Hurd Houghton, NY,
    seven chromolithographs,
    gilt binding 45.00

Bicentennial

America's 200th birthday in 1976 was PARTY TIME for the nation. Everyone and everything in the country had something stamped, painted, printed, molded, cast and pressed with the commemorative dates 1776-1976. The American spirit of "overdo" and "outdo" always puts our nation in a great mood. We certainly overdid it during the Bicentennial.

The average flea market will have a wide variety of Bicentennial goodies. Prices have come down in recent years as the patriotic spirit waned and the only buyers left in the market were the collectors. Remember the Bicentennial was only 20 years ago. This is one category where you only want to buy in fine or better condition.

Bank, 2" by 3" h, American Can Co.,
   Signers of Declaration of
   Independence 14.50
Coin, Half Dollar, 1976S, silver clad . .4.00
Coin, $1 Coin, 1976D, copper-nickel clad
   variety I, representation of Liberty Bell
   superimposed against moon 14.00
Coin, Proof Set, 1976, silver clad,
   three pcs 20.00
Pinback Button, Maryland Spirit, red,
   white and blue 3.00
Pinback Button, Philadelphia Bicentennial,
   10,000 trees, green and white 3.00
Plate, Battle of Concord 55.00
Plate, Paul Revere's Ride 115.00
Plate, Victory at Yorktown 55.00

Bicycles

Bicycles are divided into two groups—antique and classic. Chances of finding an antique bicycle, such as a high wheeler, at a flea market are slim. Chances of spotting a great balloon tire classic are much greater.

Do not pay much for a bicycle that is incomplete, rusted, or repaired with non-original parts. Replacement of parts that deteriorate, e.g., leather seats, is acceptable. It is not uncommon to heavily restore a bicycle, i.e., to make it look like new. If the amount of original parts is less than half, question an extremely high price.

There is a great market in secondary material from accessories to paper ephemera in bicycle collectibles. Since most bicycle fanatics haunt the automobile flea markets, you might just get lucky and find a great bicycle item at a low cost at an antiques and collectibles flea market.

Clubs: Classic Bicycle & Whizzer Club of America, 35769 Simon Dr., Clinton Township, MI 48035; International

Veteran Cycle Association, 248 Highland Dr., Findlay, OH 45840; National Pedal Vehicle Association, 1720 Rupert, NE, Grand Rapids, MI, 49505; The Wheelmen, 55 Bucknell Ave., Trenton, NJ 08619.

Newsletter: *Classic Bike*, 5046 E Wilson Rd., Clio, MI 48420.

Periodicals: *Antique/Classic Bicycle News*, P.O. Box 1049, Ann Arbor, MI 48106; *Classic Bicycle & Whizzer News*, P.O. Box 765, Huntington Beach, CA 92648; *National Antique & Classic Bicycle*, P.O. Box 5600, Pittsburgh, PA 15207.

Bicycles

Columbia
Cheeto's Easy Rider, 24", prize giveaway,
   1980s 400.00
Mad Mach, 1969 . . . . 300.00
SS Five, 1969 . . . . 450.00

Elgin
Custom Boardwalk Cruiser, 1937 . 750.00
Girl's Sport Model, 4 star, 1040 . . . 650.00
Motorbike, 28", 1920s 300.00

J.C. Higgins
1948 . . . . 300.00
Jet Flow, 1956 . . . . 900.00
Regal Deluxe, 1951 . . . . 350.00

Monark
Lady's Deluxe, 26", 1948 . . . . 400.00
Rocket, 1946 . . . . 600.00
Super Deluxe, 1953 . . . . 750.00
Zephyr, 1958 . . . . 300.00

Murray
Aero-Line, 1953-55 . . . . 300.00
AMC VIII, 26" 300.00
Chopper, 20", 1970s 250.00

Roadmaster
1930s, 26" 350.00

Silver King, 1936, $1,700.

1948-50, 26" 250.00
1950 . . . . .500.00
Jet Pilot, 1965. . . . . .300.00
Luxury Liner, 1952 . . . . .700.00
Roadmaster Jr., 1955. . . . . .300.00
Sky Rider, 26". 150.00

Schwinn
Bantam, 1970s 100.00
Continental, 10-speed, 1973 . . . . .300.00
Fastback, 1969 . . . . .200.00
Hornet, 1950. . . . . .225.00
Lil Chik 20", 1976 . . . . .200.00
Little Tiger, 12", 1970s 25.00
Pixie Stingray, 1973 . . . . .250.00
Run-A-Bout, 20" 400.00
Spartan, lady's, 26" 150.00
Starlet, 1958 . . . . .200.00
Toronado, 1949 . . . . .250.00

Shelby
Flying Cloud, 1947 . . . . .650.00
Pre-War, 26". 400.00
Western Flyer Hi-Lo, 16" 350.00

Other Bicycles
Colson, Tandem, 1930s 400.00
Colson, Tricycle, 1920s 200.00
Dayton, 1930s 800.00
Firestone, 500, 1950s. 300.00
Firestone, Speed Cruiser Deluxe . .600.00
Hawthorne, 26", 1941. . . . . .650.00
Huffy, 20", 1940s 50.00
Huffy, Custom Liner, 1955 . . . . . . .200.00
Iver Johnson, 1937. . . . . .500.00
Manton & Smith, 26", 1936. . . . . . .600.00
Mattel, Vrroom, 20", 1961. . . . . . . .300.00
Mead, Pathfinder, 28", wood rims,
   1922 .200.00
Raleigh, Chopper, 1969 . . . . .350.00
Rollfast, 1956 . . . . .350.00
Rollfast, 1958 . . . . .300.00
Sears, 1965, 29". 350.00
Sears, Spaceliner, 1960s 400.00
Yamaha, BMX Bike Suspension,
   1970s. 500.00

Bicycle-Related
Advertising Trade Card, Clark Bicycle Co.,
   Christmas, Santa on high wheeler,
   1880 . . . . .20.00
Brochure, Crescent Bicycles, 1899 . 20.00
Bubblegum Cards, BMX Bikes,
   59 cards. 3.00
Catalog, Indian Motorycles and Bicycles,
   1915 . . . . .50.00
Catalog, Iver Johnson Bicycle &
   Motorcycle Supplies, 1909 . . . . .35.00
Chain, Diamond 10.00
Child Carrier, wicker, 1920s 120.00
Horn, Yoder, 1950s 7.00
Lapel Stud, Superb Bicycles, purple,
   white inscription and illus, profile of
   cyclist on bike 30.00

Lapel Stud, Wolff American High Art Cycle, pale pink, inscription, illus of running wolf 15.00

Lapel Stud, Zimmy, black and yellow symbol, inscription "Ask To See A Zimmy" 20.00

Light, Schwinn Phantom, chrome, battery operated. 60.00

Pedals, Schwinn, girl's, glass reflectors 50.00

Pinback Button, American Traveler, 1898-1900, red, white and blue . .20.00

Pinback Button, Champion of the Wheel, DF Green, 1896-1900, sepia 20.00

Pinback Button, Franklin's Bicycle Polish, 1896-1900, black and white 10.00

Pinback Button, Indian Bicycle, 1901-1910, red, white and blue. 20.00

Poster, Ce Michelin Est Indechirable, 31" by 40", lithograph, linen, Indian biting tire 350.00

Poster, Cycles Favor, 62" by 46-1/2", male figure holding up bicycle and motorcycle, 1957 . . . . .750.00

Poster, Triumph Cycles-Coventry, 30" by 46", lithograph, woman in large hat standing beside bicycle, 1907 . .750.00

Saddle Pin, replica of bicycle seat, short stickpin soldered on back, late 1890s Mesinger, 3/4" by 7/8", die-cut tin 30.00

Sign, Iver Johnson Cycles, 10" by 20-1/2", tin 2,000.00

Sign, The Cyclists' Touring Club, 16" by 16", porcelain 50.00

Stickpin, Olympic Bike, 3/4", celluloid and metal, green victory wreath border around small red slogan "Good As Gold," black title bar "Olympic Cycle Mfg's Co. NY". 35.00

Stickpin, The Hoffman Bike, die-cut brass, emblem title plate featuring letter "H" at center over "Cleveland Ohio" 25.00

Big Little Books

The first Big Little Book was published by Whitman Publishing Co., in 1933. As with any successful endeavor, copycats soon appeared. Saalfield Publishing Co., was first with the introduction of its line of Little Big Books. Lesser known and less successful, imitators include Engel-Van Wiseman, Lynn Publishing Co., Goldsmith Publishing Co., and Dell Publishing Co.

Condition and story content are the keys to determining value. Prices listed are for books in fine condition.

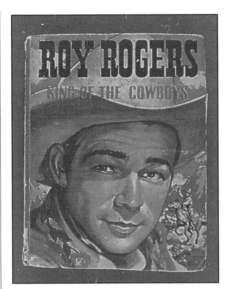

Roy Rogers, King of the Cowboys, #1476, $20.

Club: Big Little Book Collectors Club of America, P.O. Box 1242, Danville, CA 94526.

Alice in Wonderland, #759. . . . . 30.00
Arizona Kid, The, #1192 . . . . 10.00
Betty Boop in Miss Gulliver's Travels, #1158 . . . . 65.00
Blondie, Count Cookie in Too, #1430 . . . . 20.00
Buck Jones in Ride 'Em Cowboy, #1116 . . . . 20.00
Buck Rogers on the Moons of Saturn, #1143 . . . . 65.00
Charlie Chan: Villainy on the High Seas, #1424 . . . . 35.00
Clyde Beatty Daredevil Lion and Tiger Tamer, #1410 . . . . 20.00
Dick Tracy and the Bicycle Gang, #1445 . . . . 30.00
Donald Duck and Ghost Morgan's Treasure, #1411 . . . . 40.00
Don Winslow of the Navy vs. the Scorpion Gang, #1419 . . . . 20.00
Ellery Queen, The Adventure of the Last Man Club, #1406 . . . . 30.00
Flying the Sky Clipper with Winsie Atkins, #1108 . . . . 20.00
G-Man and the Radio Bank Robberies, #1434 . . . . 15.00
Houdini's Magic, #715 . . . . 40.00
Jackie Cooper in "Gangster's Boy," #1402 . . . . 25.00
Kazan in Revenge of the North, #1105 . . . . 15.00
Li'l Abner Among the Millionaires, #1401 . . . . 35.00
Little Orphan Annie in the Movies, #1416 . . . . 45.00

Lone Ranger and the Menace of Murder Valley, #1465. . . . . .25.00
Men of the Mounted, Adventures of the Canadian Royal Mounted, #755 . 25.00
Mickey Mouse and the Lazy Daisy Mystery, #1433 . . . . .45.00
Nancy and Sluggo, #1400 . . . . 45.00
Popeye and Caster Oyl the Detective, #1497 .35.00
Shadow and the Ghost Makers, #1495 .80.00
Tarzan Lord of the Jungle, #1407. . .30.00
Texas Kid, The, #1429 . . . . .15.00
Tillie the Toiler and the Wild Man of Desert Island, #1442. . . . . .45.00
Uncle Wiggily's Adventures, #1405 . 20.00
Zane Grey's Tex Thorne Comes Out of the West, #1440 . . . . .20.00

Bisque

Every time I look at a bisque figure, I think of grandmothers. I keep wondering why I never see a flea market table labeled "Only things a grandmother would love."

Bisque is pottery ware that has only been fired once and not glazed. It is a technique that is centuries' old and is still being practiced today. Unfortunately, some of today's figures are exact copies of those made hundreds of years ago. Be especially aware of bisque piano babies.

Collectors differentiate between Continental (mostly German) and Japanese bisque with premiums generally paid for Continental pieces. However, the Japanese made some great bisque. Do not confuse the cheap five-and-dime "Occupied Japan" bisque with the better pieces.

Figures
Baby and Egg, 5" h, artist sgd, Heubach. 250.00
Baby in Barrel, blue eyes, blonde hair, closed mouth, white barrel 55.00
Bathing Beauty, 3-1/2" l, Germany . 120.00
Boy, wearing sailor suit, 3-1/2" h, with toy boat 45.00
Girl with bow, pleated baskets on side. 75.00
Kewpie Groom, 4-1/2" h, wearing tuxedo 200.00
Lady and Man, 5" h, dressed as rooster and hen, embracing pose, Germany 240.00

Figure, angel, green highlights, 12-1/2" h, $50.

Mickey Mouse riding Pluto, 2-1/8" h,
    repainted, c1930 . . . . .75.00

Other
Animal Covered Dish, brown chick with
    broken shell, domed green glass cover,
    white basketweave base 500.00
Bank, Elmer The Elephant, movable trunk,
    gray, yellow and red 275.00
Cigar Holder, 4-1/4" h, tree stump, bird
    chasing insect, natural colors,
    Germany, 19th C 35.00
Game Dish, cov, two birds, basketweave
    base 100.00
Match Holder, Frowning Old Man,
    #5691 incised on back 55.00
Match Holder, Ugly Old Woman, 3-1/8" h,
    strikers on sides and rear. 65.00
Nodder, 4-1/2" h, seated lady, white and
    turquoise Oriental-style robe, gold trim,
    holding fan 150.00

Nodder, 4-3/4" h, poodle and bulldog, oval
    base 145.00
Pitcher, Jug type, Pink Rose
    pattern. 95.00
Pitcher, Milk, 6" h, chrysanthemum
    dec 90.00
Vase, 7-1/2" h, 5" w, woman in purple
    dress standing by tree 50.00
Whimsy, 2-3/4" by 3-1/4", two frogs sitting
    in front of two eggs 75.00

Bizarre Art

There is some really great stuff made by senior citizen groups and community organizations that can be found at local bazaars, church rummage sales and so on. Of course, after a few years, these items often turn up at flea markets.

Some bazaar craftspeople also create unique decorative accessories that may hold some resale value. Other stuff is just "stuff" and can be had for pennies on the dollar. Perhaps some day this tacky stuff will catch a decorator's eye and skyrocket in value!

Artificial Rose, painted seashell on plastic
    stem, price per dozen 5.00
Bread Basket, swan, made from plastic
    milk jug 50
Christmas Tree Ornament, Rudolph Head,
    brass bell, pipe cleaner antlers, glue
    facial features 50

Centerpiece, egg-carton flowers, beaded centers on long corsage pins which attach flower to Styrofoam ball center, gold painted metal base, 7" h, 25 cents.

Vase, bead, brass and safety pin, with plastic flowers, $5.

Christmas Tree Ornament, Santa and Mrs.
    Claus, painted cinnamon sticks, price
    for pair 2.00
Christmas Tree Ornament, Sled, painted
    popsicle sticks 1.00
Dish Towel, crocheted hanger, button
    attached. 2.00
Door Knob Hanger, needlepoint on plastic
    mesh, Christmas greetings 2.00
Footstool, fabric cov over large
    juice cans 2.00
Honey Do List Holder, wood, figural
    hammer, hand-painted, clip to hold list
    of things to do 3.00
Lamp Shade, plastic bottle with colorful
    beads and cutout work 2.00
Picture Frame, needlepoint on plastic
    mesh, colorful border. 1.00
Pinecone Wreath, large, well-made and
    decorated 5.00
Plant Hanger, macramé 50
Pot Holder, crocheted. 1.00
Rag Doll, Boo Boo Bear, made from
    washcloth 50
Tissue Box Holder, needlepoint on plastic
    mesh, colorful design 3.00
Toilet Paper Cover, crocheted,
    hat-style. 2.00

Black Memorabilia

Black memorabilia is enjoying its second renaissance. It is one of the

Magazine Tear Sheet, Aunt Jemima Pancake Flour, *Saturday Evening Post*, **1920s, 10" by 13", $15.**

"hot" areas in the present market. The category is viewed quite broadly, ranging from slavery-era items to objects showing ethnic stereotypes. Prices range all over the place. It pays to shop around.

Because Black memorabilia embodies a wide variety of forms, the Black memorabilia collector is constantly competing with collectors from other areas, e.g., cookie jar, kitchen and salt and pepper shaker collectors. Surprisingly enough, it is the collectors of Black memorabilia who realize the extent of the material available and tend to resist high prices.

Reproductions, from advertising signs (Bull Durham Tobacco) to mechanical banks (Jolly Nigger), are an

increasing problem. Remember—if it looks new, chances are that it is new.

Club: Black Memorabilia Collector's Association, 2482 Devoe Ter., Bronx, NY 10468.

Periodical: *Blackin'*, 559 22nd Ave., Rock Island, IL 61201.

Banks
Boy and House, 3-1/2" h, cast iron, mechanical, push-broom on side of house, boy flips upside down . . 200.00
Lucky Joe, 4-1/4" h, glass 30.00
Mammy, 5-1/4" h, cast iron, 1930s 125.00
Minstrel, 7" h, wall bank, terra cotta. 85.00

Books
Black Sampson, 1909 . . . . 30.00
Bulls-Eye Bill, 1921 . . . . 50.00
Ezekiel Travels, 1938 . . . . 100.00
Frawg, 1930. . . . . 100.00
Little Black Sambo, cloth, 1942 . . . . 25.00
Little Brown Koko Has Fun, 1945 . . 70.00
Little Pickaninnies, 1929 . . . . 45.00
Minstrel Jokes, 1916 . . . . 25.00
Mo and Koko in the Jungle, pop-up storybook, 1961 . . . . 25.00
Nicodemus Helps Uncle Sam, 1943 75.00
Pinky Marie, 1938 . . . . 25.00
Topsy Turvy's Pigtails, 1930 . . . . . . 25.00
Turkey Trott, 1942 . . . . 75.00
Uncle Remus Stories, 1934 . . . . 20.00
Uncle Tom's Cabin, German version, 1897 . . . . 80.00
Watermelon Pete, 1927 . . . . 40.00

Cookie Jars
Aunt Jemima, plastic, 1950 . . . . . . 275.00
Chef, ceramic, Japan, 1980 . . . . . . 50.00
Mammy, White Dove Pottery, 1980 . 75.00
Mandy, ceramic, copyright Omnibus Japan, 1980 . . . . 175.00

Salt and Pepper Shakers, pr
Boy and girl on drums, wood 45.00
Boy's head and melon, ceramic. . . . 55.00
Calypso figures, plaster 35.00

Chef and mammy, ceramic, 1990. . . 30.00
Chef holding two coffeepots, ceramic, Japan. 40.00
Kissing natives 35.00
Native on corn, ceramic 55.00

Other
Ashtray, Boy with donkey 10.00
Ashtray, Outhouse, "You Are Next," Japan. 18.00
Apron, cotton, mammy face appliqué on pocket 40.00
Box, Fun To Wash Soap Powder . . . 35.00
Box, Licorice Babies, candy, 1940-50 . . . . 35.00
Broom Cover, mammy, cotton dress, 1980 . . . . 40.00
Cup and Saucer, man playing banjo on cup, lady dancing on saucer, China 50.00
Decanter Set, ceramic, alligator, cork-lined boy's head in its mouth, emb alligators on shot glasses 100.00
Doll, 10" h, cloth, flowered red turban, yellow blouse, red lace sleeves, green shawl, blue flowered skirt, black and orange flowers, white pearls 35.00
Doll, 14" h, Topsy Turvy, black girl and white girl, lamb's wool hair, red and blue striped dresses, rickrack trim. . . . 40.00
Doorstop, Mammy, Cast Iron 90.00
Doorstop, Glass, bottle type 65.00
Egg Timer, chef, ceramic 60.00
Figure, Boy in clown outfit holding accordion, bisque, Germany, 1900-20 . . . . 120.00
Figure, Maid holding scrubber and brush, 6" h, wood 20.00
Jar, Old Black Joe, Hancock Axle grease, with lid 85.00
Laundry Bag, Mammy washing clothes 38.00
Magazine, *Life*, Jackie Robinson cover, May 8, 1950. . . . . 30.00
Magazine, *Time*, Martin Luther King Jr. cover story, Jan. 3, 1964 . . . . 40.00
Matches, 1-1/2" by 2", Coon Chicken Inn, showing face 30.00
Match Holder, man with watermelon, chalk 25.00
Note Pad Holder, Aunt Jemima, red and yellow plastic 70.00
Note Pad Holder, Mammy, 8" h, wood 40.00
Note Pad Holder, Mammy, 11" by 14", copper, magnetic. 70.00
Pillow, silk, girl's head, yarn hair with bows 75.00
Postcard, Coon Chicken Inn, linen, 1930-40 . . . . 25.00
Postcard, "I'm Afraid Of The Dark," 1914 . . . . 30.00

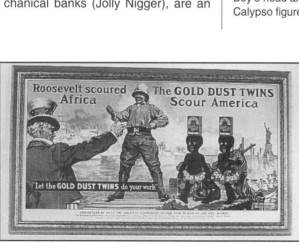

Poster, Gold Dust Washing Powder, paper, Uncle Sam and Teddy Roosevelt welcoming Gold Dust Twins, framed, 20" w, 10-1/2" h, $1,375.

Pot Holder Plaque, boy and girl eating watermelon, plaster, painted, metal hooks 30.00
Puzzle, Little Black Sambo 10.00
Salad Set, Calypso figures 35.00
Spoon Rest, chef, ceramic 65.00
Stamp, George Washington Carver, 3 cents, four-block, 1948. . . . . . . .10.00
Stamp, Martin Luther King Jr., 15 cents, four-block, Jan 1979. . . . . .40.00
Teapot, elephant with native, 7-1/2" by 8", china. 100.00
Tea Towel, Butler and Mammy, cotton .40.00
Tea Towel, Boy eating watermelon, linen 45.00
Thermometer, native boy and girl, china, Japan, 1940-50 . . . . .50.00
Toaster Cover, 12", cardboard mammy holding stack of pancakes, wearing cotton dress 40.00
Wall Pocket, chef with cooking utensils, ceramic. 130.00
Whisk Broom, Mammy 40.00

Blue Ridge

Southern Potteries of Erwin, Tenn., produced Blue Ridge dinnerware from the late 1930s until 1956. Four hundred patterns graced eight basic shapes.

Club: Blue Ridge Collectors Club, Rt. 3, P.O. Box 161, Erwin, TN 37650.

Newsletter: *National Blue Ridge Newsletter*, 144 Highland Dr., Blountville, IN 37617.

Periodical: *The Daze*, P.O. Box 57, Otisville, MI 48463.

Soup, blue and yellow flowers, 8" d, $17.50.

Platter, $18.

Bowls
Corsage, soup 17.50
Mardi Gras, Fruit 5.00
Mardi Gras, Vegetable. 8.00
Skyline-shape, children's ware 55.00

Pitchers
Abby, earthenware. 70.00
Grace, pale yellow 55.00
Helen, china. 90.00
Sculptured Fruit, china. 75.00
Virginia, 6-1/2", china. 80.00
Watauga 160.00

Plates
Cherry Cobbler, 9" 11.00
Cherry Tree Glen, 6" d 5.00
Children's Ware 85.00
Christmas Tree, 10" d 60.00
Mardi Gras, 7" d 9.00
Rustic Plaid, 9" d 11.00

Platters
Crab Apple, oval, 13" 14.00
Nocturne 20.00
Rooster 95.00

Other
Candy Box, Calico 175.00
Creamer, Mardi Gras. 6.00
Cup and Saucer, Christmas Tree . . 55.00
Cup and Saucer, Mardi Gras. 10.00
Egg Cup, double, Valley Violet 30.00
Jug, Chick 95.00
Mug, children's ware, 2-3/4" 50.00
Pie Baker, Julie 25.00
Relish, Palisades 40.00
Salt and Pepper Shakers, pr, Apple 15.00
Salt and Pepper Shakers, pr, Chicken, 2-1/4" 90.00
Snack Set, Petunia, plate and cup. . 20.00
Sugar, Rustic Plaid 12.00
Teapot, Fantasia, Skyline-shape . . . 65.00
Teapot, Good Housekeeping, ceramic. 95.00
Vase, Gladys, boot-shape, 8" h 80.00
Vase, Mood Indigo 80.00

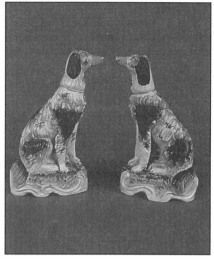

English Setters, pottery, painted, $250.

Bookends

Prices listed below are for pairs. Woe to the dealer who splits pairs apart!

Anchor, bronze 35.00
Bull Dog, Bradley & Hubbard, cast iron. 400.00
Dancing Girl, Art Nouveau, white metal 90.00
Dutch Girl, pails 55.00
Eagle, shield, cast iron 75.00
Girl's head, Art Deco, wood, 1930s .60.00
Jungle Scene, silvered background, bronze border, Heintz 135.00
Knight on Horse, cast iron 40.00
Nude Lady, on sea shell, chalkware. 48.00
Owl, 5-1/4" by 3-1/2", cast iron 65.00
Pagoda, brass, 6-1/2" h, 4" w, brass 95.00
Parrot, 5" h, cast iron 70.00
Parrot, Pentagonal-form, Heintz . . .120.00
Peacock, 5-1/2" by 5-1/4", cast iron 150.00
Pierrot and Lady with fan, cast iron .80.00
Pointer, 4-1/2" by 5-1/4" 400.00
Rooster, 6" by 5", cast iron 140.00
Russian Wolfhound, bronze, 1929 . .80.00
Scotties, Hubley #S217, cast iron. .130.00
Spirit of Freedom, 6" by 6", cast iron 75.00
Unicorn and Lion, 6" h, 5-1/2" l, brass 40.00

Bookmarks

Don't you just hate it when you lose your place in that book you've been reading? Bookmarks can help keep your sanity and they're easy to find, easy to display and fun to own.

Bookmark collecting dates back to the early 19th century. A bookmark is any object used to mark a reader's place in a book. Bookmarks have been made from a wide variety of materials, including celluloid, cloth, cross-stitched needlepoint in punched paper, paper, sterling silver, wood and woven silk. Heavily embossed leather markers were popular between 1800 and 1860. Advertising markers appeared after 1860.

Woven silk markers are a favorite among collectors. T. Stevens of Coventry, England, manufacturer of Stevensgraphs, is among the most famous makers. Paterson, N.J., was the silk weaving center in the United States. John Best & Co., Phoenix Silk Manufacturing Co., and Warner Manufacturing Co., produced bookmarks. Other important U.S. companies that made woven silk bookmarks were J.J. Mannion of Chicago and Tilt & Son of Providence, R.I.

The best place to search for bookmarks is specialized paper shows. Be sure to check all related categories. Most dealers file them under subject headings, e.g., Insurance, Ocean Liners, World's Fairs and so on.

Club: Antique Bookmark Collector's Association, 2224 Cherokee, St. Louis, MO 63118.

Newsletter: *Bookmark Collector*, 1002 W. 25th St., Erie, PA 16502.

Silk

Administration Building, Chicago, 1893 . . . . .65.00
For A Good Boy, I had a little doggy, Stevens .60.00
George Washington, Phoenix Silk, World Columbian Exhibition, 1893 . . . .100.00

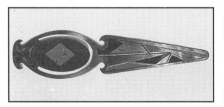
Art Deco-style, enameled brass, 4-1/2" h, $4.50.

Little Bo Peep, Stevens 50.00
John Best & Co. Manufacturer, Paterson, NJ 40.00
Landing of Columbus, commemorative, Phoenix. 50.00
The Late Earl of Beaconsfield, Peace with Honour, Stevens 25.00

Other

Cardboard, Yellow Kid, 2-1/2" by 6-1/4", die-cut, issued by "A No. 1 Candy Company," full color, late 1890s . 60.00
Celluloid, Bell Piano adv, die-cut, owl-shape, upright piano. 90.00
Celluloid, Royal Insurance Co., adv, 1905 . . . . 15.00
Celluloid, Tappen Shoe Mfg. adv, die-cut, White & Hoag Litho. 48.00
Felt, embroidered "Merry Christmas", 19th C 35.00
Leather, "Season's Greetings," 1900 . . . . 10.00
Metal, Cracker Jack, litho tin, 2-1/4" h, brown terrier 18.00
Metal, Taft-Sherman, die-cut aluminum, Teddy Bear-shape, cutout heart with Taft portrait, Sherman portrait on reverse 75.00
Valentine Heart, sterling silver, Tiffany, 1930 . . . . 75.00

Books

There are millions of books out there. Some are worth a fortune. Most are hardly worth the paper they were printed on. Listing specific titles serves little purpose in a price guide such as this. By following the 10 guidelines below, you can quickly determine if the books that you have uncovered have value potential.

1. Check your book titles in *American Book Prices Current*, which is published annually by Bancroft-Parkman, Inc., and is available at most libraries, as well as Huxford's *Old Book Value Guide*, Eighth Edition (Collector Books, 1996). When listing your books in preparation for doing research, include the full name of the author, expanded title, name of publisher, copyright date and edition and/or printing number.

2. Examine the bindings. Decorators buy handsomely bound books by the foot at prices ranging from $40 to $75 per foot.

3. Carefully research any children's book. Illustration quality is an important value key. Little Golden Books are one of the hottest book areas in the market today. In the late 1970s and early 1980s, Big Little Books were hot.

4. Buy all hardcover books about antiques and collectibles that you find that are less than $5. There is a growing demand for out-of-print antiques and collectibles books.

5. Check the edition number. Value, in most cases, rests with the first edition. However, not every first edition is valuable. Consult *Blank's Bibliography of American First Editions* or Tannen's *How to Identify and Collect American First Editions*.

6. Look at the multi-faceted aspects of the book and the subject that it covers. Books tend to be collected by type, e.g., mysteries, westerns, etc. Many collectors buy books as supplements to their main collection. A Hopalong Cassidy collector, although focusing primarily on the objects licensed by Bill Boyd, will want to own the Mulford novels in which Hopalong Cassidy originated.

7. Local histories and atlases always have a good market, particularly those printed between 1880 and 1930. Add to this centennial and other celebration volumes.

8. Check to see if the book was signed by the author. Generally an author's signature increases the value of the book. However, it was a common practice to put engraved signatures of authors in front of books during the last part of the 19th century. The Grant signature in the first volume of his two-volume memoir set is not original, but printed.

9. Book-club editions have little or no value with the exception of books done by George and Helen Macy's Limited Editions Club.

10. Accept the fact that the value of most books falls in the 50-cent to $2 range and, that after all your research is done, this is probably what you'll get.

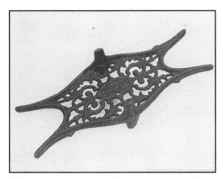

Filigree center, cast iron, double-ended, Pat. May 18, 1869, 12", $40.

Bootjacks

Unless you are into horseback riding, a bootjack is one of the most useless devices that you can have around the house. Why do so many individuals own one? The answer in our area is "just for nice." Actually, they are seen as a major accessory in trying to capture the country look. Cast iron reproductions are a major problem, especially for "Naughty Nellie" and "Beetle" designs.

Cast Iron

Advertising, Musselman's Plug Tobacco,
    ornate .150.00
Beetle, painted 30.00
Bug, projecting feelers 60.00
Intertwined scrolls form letter M,
    11-1/2" l .25.00
Naughty Nellie, 9-3/4" l, old worn
    polychrome repaint. 45.00
Tree center, 12" l, ftd. 30.00
Vine design, 12" l 35.00

Wood

Board with V-shaped cutout,
    raised end 15.00
Forked Stick, primitive. 8.00
Maple, 13" l, hand hewn 15.00
Pine, 24" l, rose head nails, pierced for
    hanging 40.00
Pine, 25" l, oval ends, sq nail
    construction 30.00
Walnut, 22" l, heart and diamond
    openwork 40.00

Bottle Openers, Figural

Although this listing focuses on cast iron figural bottle openers, the most sought-after type of bottle openers, do not forget the tin advertising openers. Also known to some as church keys, the bulk still sell between $2 and $10, a very affordable price range.

Clubs: Figural Bottle Opener Collectors Club, 117 Basin Hill Rd., Duncannon, PA 17020; Just For Openers, 3712 Sunningdale Way, Durham, NC 27707.

Advertising

Burgermeister Beer 10.00
Coca-Cola, metal catch, original box 70.00
Duff Norton Jacks, Pittsburgh USA,
    cast iron 60.00
Holland Brand Beer, wood,
    figural bottle 10.00
Orange Crush 25.00
Pabst Blue Ribbon, die-cut steel,
    color bottle, 1930s 20.00
Pepsi-Cola, figural bottle, litho tin . . 35.00
7-Up, cast iron 15.00

Cast Iron, Figural

Canadian Goose 75.00
Canvasback Duck 70.00
Clown, 4-1/2" by 4" 75.00
Cocker Spaniel, black 65.00
Dilly Dentures 150.00
Elephant, 2-1/2" by 3-1/2" 75.00
Gamecock 70.00
Sailor 65.00
Seahorse 80.00
Springer Spaniel 70.00
Toucan 350.00
Trout 75.00

Other

Ceramic, boxing glove, dark purple, white
    decal, silvered metal opener,
    4-1/2" l 15.00
Wood, Scottie dog, moveable
    mouth 15.00

Bottles

Bottle collecting is such a broad topic that the only way one can hope to survive is by specialization. It is for this reason that several bottle topics are found elsewhere in this book. Bottles have a bad habit of multiplying. Do not start collecting them until you have plenty of room. I know one person whose entire basement is filled with Coca-Cola bottles bearing the imprint of different cities.

There are many bottle categories that are still relatively inexpensive to collect. In many cases, you can find a free source of supply in old dumps. Before getting too deeply involved, it pays to talk with other bottle collectors and to visit one or more specialized bottle collector shows.

Beverages

Hillside Dairy Milkpt 13.00
Hires Improved Root Beer, 10" h . . .35.00
Jim Beam, Blue Goose, 1979. . . . . .12.00
Lieberman's, Allentown, PA, clear, blob
    top, 8" h 22.50
Miller 1000 Beer, 12 oz. 2.00
Quaker Maid Whiskey, clear, pt 9.00
Red Top, emb top, qt 10.00
White Nun, miniature 20.00
Witter Springs, amber, paper label. .18.00
Yoo Hoo Chocolate Drink, clear,
    yellow label, 3" h 5.00

Food

Acker Merrall & Condit Cafe De Luxe,
    amber, screw cap 45.00
Chas Gulden, mustard 1.50
Corbin, Sons & Co., cinnamon extract,
    color lithograph label 15.00
Crisco, 1/2 gal, screw cap 3.00
Dr. Price's Flavoring Extract, three bottles,
    1/2 oz. 5.00
Eiffel Tower Fruit Juices, aqua, 4" h . .2.00
Forbes Delicious Flavoring Extract. . .4.00
Grand Union Tea Co., 5" h, clear 2.00
Hallocks Pure Extract, 6" h 1.50
Lake Horseradish 10.00
Mrs. Chapin's Mayonnaise, clear, pt .3.00
Old Style Mustard, clear, pt 5.00

Household, gold dec, ground stopper, late 18th/19th C, $75.

Medicine, clear glass with cork stopper, 80cc, 5-1/4" by 2" by 1-1/4", $7.

Smucker's Jelly, round, clear, 1-3/4" h 5.00
Wine Cured Pickles, Manhattan
 Pickle Co. 4.00

Health and Beauty
Bromo Seltzer, cobalt blue, 6" 5.00
Caldwells Syrup Pepsin, 3" h 4.00
Cauvins Syrup for Babies 22.00
Citrate of Magnesia, blob top,
 8-1/4" h. .9.00
Colts Foot Expectorant, 6" h 3.00
Craigs Kidney & Liver Cure,
 9-1/2" h. 100.00
Cushing Medical Supply Co., alcohol,
 paper label, qt 25.00
Dr. Thatchers Worm Syrup 7.00
Elys Cream Balm, hay fever
 catarrah .14.00
Halls Balsam for the Lungs, aqua 5.00
Iodine, amber, 2-1/4". 2.00
Johnson & Johnson Oil, aqua, 5" h . . .4.00
Kemps Balsam for Throat & Lungs,
 aqua, 5-1/4" h. 4.00
Listerine, varying sizes, clear 2.00
Mitchells Eye Salve, blue 60.00
Races Indian Blood Renovator 30.00
Scotts Emulsion Cod Liver Oil, with lime
 soda, aqua 6.00
Smiths Green Mountain Renovator, oval,
 aqua, 7-3/4" h. 70.00

Spohns Distemper Cure, 5" h 8.00
Turkish Liniment 5.00

Household
Ammonia, SF Gaslight Co., yellow amber,
 9-1/8" h 50.00
Bullard's Soap 10.00
Carbona, aqua, 5" h. 2.00
Eastman Kodak Chemicals, amber,
 5-1/4" h 6.00
E-Z Stove Polish, clear 4.00
French Gloss 1.00
Holy Water, Behold The Heart That Love
 Men, 6" h. 45.00
Lake Shore Seed Co., 5-1/2" h 1.00
Lazell's Sachet Powder 20.00
National Casket Co., clear, emb eagle and
 Capitol. 20.00
Prof. Callans World Renowned, aqua,
 4" h 2.00
Saratoga Dressing, figural shoe, aqua,
 4-1/2" h 30.00
Special Battery Oil, Thomas Edison,
 4-1/2" h 3.50
Sperm Sewing Machine Oil, clear,
 4-3/4" h 2.00

Boxes

We have reached the point with some 20th century collectibles where the original box may be more valuable than the object that came in it. If the box is colorful and contains a picture of the product, it has value.

Boxes have always been a favorite among advertising collectors. They are three-dimensional and often fairly large in size. The artwork reflects changing period tastes. Decorators like the pizzazz that boxes offer. The wood box with a lithographed label is a fixture in the country household.

Advertising, Minneopa Tooth Picks, cardboard, $20.

Advertising
Borax, wood .5.00
Bromo-Seltzer, 8-1/2" by 10-3/4" by
 9-1/4" 10.00
Butterkist, popcorn, blue and white . . 3.00
Cheerios, single portion, 1940s 14.00
Chesterfield, carton, 1940s. 35.00
Churn Baking Soda, unused, 1920s. 10.00
Dr. Blumer's Toothpaste,
 blue and green 2.00
Detmer Woolen, 29" by 21" 50.00
Franco-American Purgative Tablets,
 wood 5.00
Hi-Hat Jockey Club Face Powder,
 contents intact 8.00
Honor Bright Soap, cardboard 5.00
La Reclama Habana Cigars, wood. . 20.00
Ladies Crimped Collar & Cuffs, round 6.00
Moo Girl, butter, 1925. . . . . .5.00
Log Cabin Brownies, figural cabin,
 cardboard 50.00
Montgomery Ward Tea, cardboard,
 tin lid, 1913 . . . . 40.00
Peachey Tobacco, yellow. 4.50
Popeye Bubble 'N Clean 15.00
Reynold's Rat Driver, cardboard,
 c1900. . . . . 4.50
Rocky Mountain Tea, 3" by 5", paper . 3.00
Sweet Caporal Candy Cigarettes,
 cardboard 5.00
Van Houten's Cocoa, wood, paper label,
 stamped lettering on sides 75.00
Walko Tablets, c1930. . . . . 6.00

Other
Bible, 17-1/4" l, pine, chip carved design on
 facade, old dark patina, rose head
 wrought iron nail construction,
 replaced hinges 120.00

Advertising, Federal Cartridge Corp., box of 25, 12-gauge Hi-Power Shot Shells, $15.

Jewelry, 8" l, two drawers, gold-painted cutout design with red cloth backing, white porcelain pulls, cigar-box backboard 35.00

Pencil, Dondi, cardboard, red, Hasbro, 1961 . . . . .20.00

Pencil, Felix the Cat, cardboard, color litho paper design on lid, Hasbro, 1950s 35.00

Huckleberry Hound, cardboard, red, snap-open lid, Hasbro, 1960 . . . .20.00

Spice, 9" l, cherry, dovetailed, four compartment int., sliding lid, refinished 110.00

Boyd Crystal Art Glass

The Boyds, Bernard and his son, purchased the Degenhart Glass Factory in 1978. Since that time, they have reissued a number of the Degenhart forms. Their productions can be distinguished by the color of the glass and the "D" in a diamond mark. The Boyd family continues to make contemporary collectible glass at its factory in Cambridge, Ohio.

Club: Boyd Art Glass Collectors Guild, P.O. Box 52, Hatboro, PA 19040.

Newsletters: *Boyd's Crystal Art Glass*, P.O. Box 127, 1203 Morton Ave., Cambridge, OH 43725; *Jody & Darrell's Glass Collectibles*, P.O. Box 180833, Arlington, TX 76094.

Animal

Balloon Bear, 2" h, Patrick, Alexandrite 6.00

Balloon Bear, 2" h, Patrick, Country Red 6.50

Bernie The Eagle, 2-1/2" h, limited to 30 colors, Cardinal Red Carnival 9.00

Bull Dog Head, Ice Green 10.00

Butterfly, ruby, originally Cambridge mold. 30.00

Ducklings, Crown Tuscan 2.75

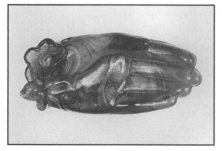

Hand, brown-and-white slag, 5" l, $12.

Ducklings, Light Rose 2.50
Kitten on Pillow 15.00
Lucky Unicorn 12.00
Sammy the Squirrel, Autumn Beige. . 5.00
Sammy the Squirrel, Mulberry Carnival 6.00
Sammy the Squirrel, Shasta White . . 5.00
Scottie Dog, mold retired in 1988, marked with "R," Vaseline carnival 10.00
Woodchuck, Bermuda Slag 10.00
Zack Elephant, Crystal. 12.00
Zack Elephant, Lilac 14.00

Other

Boyd Airplane, 4" l, 3-1/4" w, 2" h, introduced November 1991, first color, classic black 15.00
Candy Dish, Dawn 12.00
Chuckles The Clown, Baby Blue 7.00
Chuckles The Clown, Pistachio 7.50
Chuckles The Clown, White Opal . . . 8.00
Jeremy, 2-1/4" h, 1-1/4" l, Vaseline . . 6.00
Joey, leaping pony, "B" in diamond trademark, Lavender. 12.00
Joey, Ruby. 25.00
Joey, Zack Boyd Slag 12.00
Santa, bell, Cardinal Red Carnival. . 17.00
Santa, bell, Olde Lyme 15.00
Santa, bell, Rubina 16.00

Boy Scouts

This is another collecting area in which adults dominate where you would normally expect to find kids. When I was a Boy Scout, emphasis was on swapping material with little concern for value. One-for-one trading was the common rule.

Today, old Scouting material is viewed in monetary terms. Eagle badge books go for $75 or more. The key is to find material that was officially licensed. Unlicensed material is generally snubbed by collectors. Boy Scout collecting is so sophisticated that it has its own shows or swap meets. Strong retail value for Boy Scout material occurs at these shows. Flea market prices tend to be much lower.

Clubs: American Scouting Traders Association, Inc., 2300 Fairview Rd., #G202, Costa Mesa, CA 92626; International Badgers Club, 2903 W Woodbine Dr., Maryville, TN 37801; National Scouting Collectors Society, 806 E. Scott St., Tuscola, IL 61953.

Patches, 1960s, price each, $10-25.

Periodicals: *Fleur-de-Lis*, 5 Dawes Ct., Novato, CA 94947; *Scout Memorabilia*, P.O. Box 1121, Manchester, NH 03105.

Book, *Scouting For Boys*, 1935 . . . . 17.50
First Aid Kit, Johnson and Johnson, green cov, New York City, orig contents 15.00
Game, Boy Scout Progress Game, Parker Brothers, 1924. . . . . 45.00
Handbook, *Boy Scout Handbook*, 6th edition, 1st printing 5.00
Hat, 1993 National Jamboree. 3.00
Insignia, Life, heart-shaped 12.00
Insignia, Scoutmaster, round, green background 3.00
Insignia, Tenderfoot, tan background, folded under 20.00
Medal, God and Country, blue ribbon. 20.00
Medal, Pinewood Derby, car on medallion 1.00
Medal, Presidents Trail, Washington DC 6.00
Mug, 1981 National Jamboree 5.00
Neckerchief, 1953 National Jamboree 30.00
Official BSA Firebuilding Kit 50.00

Book, *The Boy Scouts First Camp Fire*, Herbert Carter, hard cover, $25.

Patch, 50th Anniversary Achievement
   Strip 5.00
Patch, 1960 National Jamboree,
   pocket. 20.00
Patch, 1973 National Jamboree,
   pocket. 3.00
Patch, Northeast Region, rect 4.00
Patch, State Stripe, red and white, any of
   50 U.S. States 1.00
Pocket Knife, Imperial, four blades, raised
   1st class shield, metal emblem . .13.00
Pocket Knife, Remington, four blades,
   brown bone handle. 25.00
Sewing Kit, plastic cov, orig contents .4.00
Silva Compass, clear plastic base . .10.00
Toilet Kit, canvas cov, orig contents .15.00
Yucca Backpack, canvas 20.00

Brass

Brass is a durable, malleable and ductile metal alloy, consisting mainly of copper and zinc. It appears in this guide because of the wide variety of objects made from it.

Bookends, pr, 6" h, 5-1/2" l, unicorn and
   lion design 40.00
Box, 6-3/4" l, hanging, emb
   floral dec. 25.00

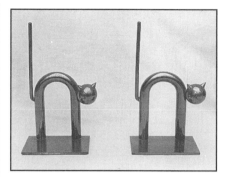

Bookends, pr, Art Deco cats, mkd "Chase," 7-1/2" h, $350.

Candelabrum, 16" h, five light, emb floral
   design base, Art Deco-style,
   c1930 . . . . 55.00
Candleholder, 9-1/2" h, 4" d base, English,
   c1800 . . . . 110.00
Coal Bucket, 13" h 85.00
Dipper, 13" l, 4-1/2" d bowl 75.00
Door Handles, pr, 16" l, sq elongated form,
   cast floral dec 10.00
Fire Screen, masted ship in relief . . 55.00
Hatpin, four kittens, 9" l 85.00
Inkwell, with tray 40.00
Jardiniere, 6" h, globular form, incised
   geometric and floral motif,
   19th C 20.00
Kerosene Lamp, 10" h, satin glass
   shade 75.00
Key, Door, 5" l, standard bow and bit 8.00
Key, Watch, 1" l, plain, swivel 2.00
Plant Stand, gilded, white onyx shelf
   and top 50.00
Slipper Box, 14" h, 16-1/2" l, 11" d,
   mounted on casters, emb tavern
   scene 70.00
Suppository Mold 80.00
Toasting Fork, pierced design, figural cat
   handle 25.00

Bread Boxes

Bread boxes are too much fun to be hidden in a Kitchen Collectibles category. There are plenty of great examples, both in form and decoration. They have disappeared from the modern kitchen. I miss them.

Graniteware, Green and White, 19" l,
   1920s 95.00
Graniteware, White, stenciled 30.00
Metal, White, red rose pattern 18.00
Metal, Yellow, flower decal 15.00
Tin, stenciled, "BREAD," imitation graining,
   wire handles 30.00

Tin, stenciled, Leaf design, 12" w, hinged
   lid. 30.00
Wood, 12-1/2" h, carved "Give Us This
   Day". 80.00

Breweriana

Beer is liquid bread, or so I was told growing up in Pennsylvania German country. It is hard to deny German linkage with the brewing industry when your home community contained the Horlacher, Neuweiler and Uhl breweries.

Brewery signs and trays, especially from the late 19th and early 20th century, contain some of the finest advertising lithography of the period. The three-dimensional advertising figures from the 1930s through the 1970s are no slouches either. Brewery advertising has become expensive. Never fear. You can build a great breweriana collection concentrating on barroom accessories such as foam scrappers, coasters and tap knobs.

Clubs: American Breweriana Association, Inc., P.O. Box 11157, Pueblo, CO 81001; National Association of Breweriana Advertising, 2343 Met-Tu-Wee Ln., Wauwatosa, WI 53226.

Sign
Budweiser, 20" by 17",
   red and white. 90.00
Coors, 22" by 23", red, white and
   gold 90.00
Old Topper Ale, 12" h, 12" w, glass,
   illuminated 44.00
Schlitz, 10-1/2" by 33-1/2", white . . . 60.00

Serving Tray, Schaefer Beer, $5.

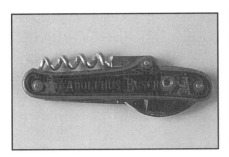

Pocket Knife, Busch Beer Co., adv, $150.

Statue

Ballantine, wood, white, red and
gold 18.00
Budweiser, wood, black, white and
red 20.00
Hamm's, ceramic, black, white and
red 18.00
Pabst, ceramic, white, black, red . . .18.00
Piels, plastic, brown, gold, white and
red 7.00

Steins

Budweiser, emb, red letters, brown banner,
1980 . . . . .100.00
Coors, brewery illus, holiday, 1988 . .18.00
Tap Handle, Schmidt City Club Beer,
multicolored enamel design 85.00

Trays

Ballantine's Ale, 12" d, 1940s 40.00
Bartels, 12" d, bakelite 50.00
Chester Pilsner, Ale and Porter, 12" d, blue
and gold .75.00
Columbia, Preferred Beer, 12" d, red, white
and gold .60.00
Eagle Brewery, Catasauqua Beer, 12" d,
eagle illus 150.00
Genesee Cream Ale, 12" d, black, green
and white .5.00
Hohenadel Beer-Ale, 13" d 45.00
Kaier's Beer, 12" d, green and white.20.00
Old Reading Beer, Reading, PA,
12" d. 40.00
Neuweiler's Ale, Allentown, PA, 13" d,
1940s 35.00
Pabst Blue Ribbon, emb plastic, blue .8.00
Stegmaier's Beer, 13-1/4" d, red, black and
gold 12.00
Tru-Blu Beer, Northampton Brewing Co.,
12" d, horse and dog llus 50.00

Other

Ashtray, O'Keefe's Old Vienna Beer,
6" d. 5.00
Ashtray, Tuborg Beer, white milk
glass. 15.00
Bank, Coors, aluminum, figural can . .5.00
Beer Can, Pabst, miniature, full 6.00
Belt Buckle, Stroh's 5.00

Blotter, Schlitz 4.00
Charm, Budweiser, commemorative,
wood 12.00
Cigarette Lighter Sleeve, Budweiser, 3" h,
metal, can replica, holds
disposable lighter 3.00
Clock, Piels 90.00
Drinking Glass, Pabst Blue Ribbon,
8 oz 4.00
Employee Badge, silvered brass 8.00
Foam Scraper, Stegmaier's Beer,
celluloid 16.00
Magazine Ad, Hamm's Beer 4.00
Matchbook Cover, Bubb's Beer, red and
white, 20 strike 5.00
Matchbook Cover, Miller High Life, 20
strike, front strike 5.00
Mug, Budweiser, ceramic, eagle logo
center, gold rim 25.00
Mug, Coors, pottery, logo 15.00
Pinback Button, American Beverage Co.,
"Hop Ale", red, white and blue . . 20.00
Pinback Button, Bohemian Export,
multicolored 12.00
Pinback Button, Gluek's Beer, blue and
white, 1911-20 . . . . 7.00
Playing Cards, Schlitz 1.50
Postcard, Genesee Brewing Co.,
Rochester, NY, linen. 5.00
Postcard, Pabst, aerial factory view,
1935 . . . . 2.50
Puzzle, Pabst Brewing Co., two-sided,
beer cans on geometric background
illus, nine pcs 30.00
Recipe Book, C Schmidt & Sons Brewing
Co., woman in hat holding glass of beer
cov illus, eight pgs 7.00
Salt and Pepper Shakers, pr, glass, Fort
Pitt Beer, miniature figural bottle. 12.00
Thermometer, Tannhauser Beer, brass
case, paper dial, eagle logo,
1896 . . . . 95.00

Breyer Horses

The Breyer line of model plastic horses has been on the market since the 1950s. During that time, Breyer also produced several wild animals, farm animals, cats and dogs. In 1984, the company was sold to Reeves International. The company moved from its old plant in Chicago to New Jersey. The company still produces a line of horses and animals.

The line consists of four different sizes of horses. The largest, (Traditional) stand about 9 inches tall. The next size (Classic) are about 6 inches tall. The third size (Little Bits) are

Texas Longhorn Bull, #75, $35.

about 5 inches tall. The final size (Stablemates) range from 1/2-inch to 3-inches tall.

There are two keys to collecting model horses. The first is the mold. A majority of the molds first tooled in the 1950s and 1960s are still being used today. Therefore, the rarity of the color, as well as condition, play the most important role in pricing Breyers.

Advisor: Antina Richards, 5838 Darlene Dr., Rockford, Il 61109.

Club: Breyer Collectors Club, P.O. Box 189, Pequannock, NJ 07440

Newsletter: *The Model Horse Trader*, 143 Mercer Way, Upland, CA 91786.

Periodicals: *Hobby Horse News*, 5492 Tallapoosa Rd., Tallahassee, FL 32303; *Just About Horses*, Reeves International, 14 Industrial Rd., Pequannock, NJ 07440.

Traditional Series
Arabian in Costume, porcelain 200.00
Clydesdale Stallion, #80, bay 30.00

Family Arabian Stallion, #907, woodgrain, $55.

Family Arabian Foal, #909,
woodgrain. 40.00
Family Arabian Stallion, #907,
woodgrain. 55.00
Fighting Stallion, #30, alabaster 31.00
Grazing Mare and Foal, #141 and #143,
bay, price for set. 55.00
Jasper the Market Hog, #355, gray and
white, NIB. 16.00
Jumping Horse with Stone Wall,
#300, bay 36.00
Lying Foal #165, black Appaloosa . .24.00
Lying Foal #166, buckskin. 35.00
Misty, #20, palomino pinto, NIB 18.00
Moose, #79, brown 28.00
Mustang, semi-rearing, #87,
buckskin. 28.00
Pacer, #46, dark bay 32.00
Poodle, #68, white. 46.00
Rearing Stallion, #183, palomino,
NIB 21.00
Running Mare, #848, brown pinto,
NIB. 40.00
SILVER, *70097, commemorative for 1989
edition of 5,000, NIB. 80.00
Scratching Foal, #168, black
appaloosa. 30.00
Shetland Pony, #21, black and white
pinto 21.00
Texas Longhorn Bull, #75, brown . . .35.00

Other

Classic Series, U.S. Equestrian Team,
#3055, set of three, MIB. 45.00
Little Bit Series, Little Bit Unicorn,
#9020, white. 12.00
Stablemate Series, Arabian Stallion,
#5016, alabaster 8.00
Stablemate Series, Thoroughbred Mare,
#5030, bay 8.00

British Royalty Collectibles

This is one of those categories where you can get in on the ground floor. Every king and queen, potential king and queen and their spouses is collectible. Buy commemorative items when they are new. I have a few Prince Harry items. We may not have royal blood in common, but...

Most individuals collect by monarch, prince or princess. Take a different approach—collect by form, e.g., mugs, playing cards, etc. British royalty commemoratives were made at all quality levels. Stick to high-quality examples.

It is fun to find recent issues at flea markets for much less than their original selling price. Picking is competitive. There are a lot of British Royalty commemorative collectors.

Album, Queen Elizabeth II and Prince Philip, 6-1/2" by 5", spiral bound, color portraits 15.00
Ashtray, King Edward VII and Queen Alexandra, multicolor, gold rim,
Wedgwood 45.00
Bank, Gregory and Elizabeth, oval,
tin 25.00
Beaker, Queen Elizabeth 60th birthday,
color portrait, gold handles 50.00
Bell, Andrew and Fergie, 5-1/2" h, 3" d,
Herbert Pottery 25.00
Bell, Silver Jubilee, brown, beige,
pottery. 30.00
Bowl, King Edward VII and Queen
Alexandra, 2-1/2" h, 4-1/2" d, multicolor,
gold rim. 60.00
Bowl, Silver Jubilee, 5-1/2" d, ftd, bone
china. 35.00
Brooch, King Edward VIII, ribbon, red,
white and blue. 30.00
Brooch, Queen Elizabeth, black-and-white
portrait, multicolor decoration,
silver tone 28.00
Bucket, King George coronation, raised
silhouette, miniature, brass. 35.00
Coaster, Charles and Diana,
black-and-white portrait, multicolor
dec, cork back. 7.00

Coin, Charles and Diana obverse,
Queen Elizabeth II reverse,
silver-tone metal 3.00
Compact, Queen Elizabeth II, color
portrait 42.00
Creamer and Sugar, playset, Princesses
Elizabeth and Margaret, color portrait,
orange trim 50.00
Cup and Saucer, milk glass, color dec,
Prince Charles wedding to
Lady Diana 27.00
Dish, Princess Anne wedding to Mark
Phillips, crystal, 6-1/4" d 50.00
Dish, Prince Charles 1969 Investiture as
Prince of Wales, gold-and-black,
4-1/2" d 18.00
Dish, St. Lawrence Seaway Opening 1959,
4-1/2" d 31.00
Egg Cup, Prince Henry birth, 2-1/4" h,
color, gold trim. 15.00
Figurine, Queen Elizabeth and Duke of
Edinburgh, 4" h, white-and-black,
plastic 35.00
Handkerchief, King Edward VIII, profile,
red or blue 25.00
Handkerchief, Princesses Elizabeth and
Margaret, black-and-white, color
flowers. 50.00
Jigsaw Puzzle, cardboard, multicolor,
Princess Anne, 400 pcs. 60.00
Jigsaw Puzzle, Queen Elizabeth,
500 pcs 32.00
Jug, King Edward VIII Coronation, sepia,
square 50.00
Jug, King George V, color portrait, 3-1/2" h,
bone china. 45.00

TV Guide, July 25-31, "The Royal Wedding: What It Means to Us," multicolor, black-and-white and color photos, $15.

Lighter, Queen Elizabeth, 3-1/4" h,
white-and-blue jasperware,
Wedgwood 65.00
Matchbook Cover, Queen Elizabeth, 2-1/4"
by 1-1/2", red-and-blue enamel, white
metal, chrome 20.00
Matchsafe, King Edward, "Long Live the
King" on reverse, silver plate 56.00
Model, Queen Elizabeth, 90th birthday,
1-1/2" h, Rolls Royce, die-cast metal,
purple with lavender top 30.00
Pocket Knife, King George V and Queen
Mary, raised design, silver tone . .60.00
Plate, Queen Elizabeth, 80th birthday,
black-and-white portrait, color
decoration 37.00
Mug, Prince Charles 1969 Investure as
Prince of Wales, red and green, Welsh
dragon illus, int. commemorative
design, gold lettering 30.00
Mug, Prince William Birth, gold dec, bone
china. 37.00
Playing Cards, Silver Jubilee, color, double
deck 60.00
Postcard, King Edward VII and Queen
Alexandra, color portraits 10.00
Postcard, King George V and Queen Mary,
black-and-white portraits 9.00
Silent Butler, Silver Jubilee, 11-1/2" l, 3" w,
brass 50.00
Tea Towel, Silver Jubilee, 30" by 18", color,
cotton 17.00
Thimble, Charles and Diana,
blue-and-white jasperware,
Wedgwood, boxed 20.00
Thimble, Prince William birth, gold profile,
Caverswall, bone china 23.00
Thimble, Royal family, set of eight, color
portrait, gold trim 40.00
Tin, King George VI and Queen Elizabeth,
color portrait, gold-and-blue dec .35.00
Tin, Prince Charles, color, gold
tone base 22.00
Tin, Prince Charles Wedding to Lady
Diana, color 20.00

Bubblegum Trading Cards

Based on the publicity received by baseball cards, you would think that they were the only bubble-gum cards sold. Wrong, wrong, wrong! There is a wealth of nonsport bubblegum cards. Prices for many of these card sets are rather modest. Individual cards often sell for less than $1. Classic cards were issued in the 1950s, but many more recently released sets are sure to become collectible.

Gum Card Wrapper, Donruss, The Flying Nun, 1968, $15.

Club: United States Cartophilic Society, P.O. Box 4020, St. Augustine, FL 32085.

Periodicals: *Non-Sport Update*, 4019 Green St., P.O. Box 5858, Harrisburg, PA 17110; *Non Sports Illustrated*, P.O. Box 126, Lincoln, MA 01773; *The Wrapper*, P.O. Box 227, Geneva, IL 60134.

Adventures in 'Toon World, 100 cards,
Upper Deck, 1993 . . . . 10.00
Aladdin, 90 cards, SkyBox, 1993 . . . 16.00
An American Tail: Feivel Goes West, 150
cards, Impel, 1991 . . . . 15.00
Animaniacs, 72 cards, 12 foil stickers,
Topps, 1995 . . . . 10.00
Beauty and The Beast, 95 cards, Pro Set,
1992 . . . . 14.00
Beavis and Butt-head, 150 cards, Fleer,
1994 . . . . 20.00
Berenstein Bears Story Cards, 72 cards,
Ken-Wis, 1992 . . . . 8.00
Casper Ultra, 119 cards, Fleer, 1995 16.00
Cinderella, 90 cards, SkyBox, 1995. 12.00
Cyndi Lauper, 33 cards, 33 stickers,
Topps, 1985 . . . . 10.00
Desert Storm, series 1, 60 cards, Spectra
Star, 1991 . . . . 8.00
Dinosaurs, 24 cards, First Glance
Productions, 1993 . . . . 8.00
Dr. Who, series 1, 110 cards, Cornerstone,
1994 . . . . 15.00
Fern Gully, 100 cards, Dart Flipcards,
1992 . . . . 12.00
Flintstones, 110 cards, Cardz, 1993 16.00

Garfield, 100 cards, 9 tattoos, SkyBox,
1992 . . . . 15.00
Ghostbusters II, 88 cards, 11 stickers,
Topps, 1989 . . . . 12.00
Goonies, 88 cards, Topps, 1985 . . . 12.00
Gremlins, 82 cards, 11 stickers, Topps,
1984 . . . . 15.00
Home Alone 2, 66 cards, 11 stickers,
Topps, 1992 . . . . 12.00
Howard The Duck, 77 cards, 22 stickers,
Topps, 1988 . . . . 15.00
Indian Motorcycles, series 2, 25 cards,
hologram, bandanna, 1993 . . . . . 12.00
Jurassic Park, 88 cards, 11 stickers,
Topps, 1993 . . . . 13.00
Kiss, 66 cards, Donruss, 1978 . . . . . 45.00
Lion King, 90 cards, SkyBox, 1994. . 11.00
Mad Magazine, 55 cards, Lime Rock,
1992 . . . . 7.00
Monty Python's Flying Circus, 108 cards,
Cornerstone Comm., 1995 . . . . . 18.00
Muppets, 60 cards, Cardz, 1994 . . . 10.00
National Lampoon, 100 cards. 15.00
Night Of The Living Dead, 60 cards,
Imagine, 1987 . . . . 25.00
Nightmare Before Christmas, 90 cards,
SkyBox, 1993 . . . . 12.00
Pagemaster, 90 cards, SkyBox,
1994 . . . . 12.00
Pin-Up Girls, 50 cards, 21st Century
Archives, 1992. . . . . 12.00
Pocahontas, 90 cards, 12 pop-ups,
SkyBox, 1995 . . . . 12.00
Power Rangers, 72 cards, 10 caps,
Collect-A-Card, 1994. . . . . 13.00
Ren and Stimpy, 110 cards, Dynamic
Marketing, Australia, 1995. . . . . . 20.00
The Simpsons, 88 cards, 22 stickers,
Topps, 1990 . . . . 15.00

Burma Shave

The famous Burma Shave jingle ad campaign was the brainstorm of Allan Odell, son of Burma-Vita's founder, Clinton M. Odell. The first sets, six signs placed 100 feet apart, appeared in 1926 on a stretch of road from Minneapolis to Albert Lea. Success was instantaneous and the Burma Shave name was fixed in the minds of drivers across the country. If You...Don't Know...Whose Signs These Are...You Haven't Driven...Very Far...Burma Shave.

Advisor: Steve Soelberg, 29126 Laro Dr., Agoura Hills, CA 91301, (818) 889-9909.

Aerosol Can 65.00

Shaving Foam, $50.

After Shave 30.00
Blades 5.00
Gift Set 40.00
Jar, empty, with lid 10.00
Jar, empty, without lid 5.00
Letterhead .25.00
Lotion Bottle, empty 15.00
Lotion Bottle, full 40.00
Printer's Blocks 50.00
Shaving Cream Tube 15.00
Sign, roadside, individual 100.00

Blockade Deodorant for Men, $65.

Sign, roadside, set of six 500.00
Talc 30.00
Toy Truck, metal 50.00
Trolley Ad 100.00

Buster Brown

R.F. Outcault could have rested on his Yellow Kid laurels. Fortunately, he did not and created a second great cartoon character—Buster Brown. The strip first appeared in the Sunday, May 4, 1902, *New York Herald.* Buster's fame was closely linked to Tige, his toothily grinning evil-looking bulldog.

Most of us remember Buster Brown and Tige because of Buster Brown Shoes. The shoe advertisements were popular on radio and television shows of the 1950s. "Look for me in there, too."

Club: R.F. Outcault Society, 103 Doubloon Dr., Slidell, LA 70461.

Banner, Buster Brown Children's Clothes, 35" by 58", cloth, red, black and yellow, white ground, red border 30.00
Bank, cast iron, Buster Brown and Tige, 5-1/4" h, dull gold repaint 77.00
Bank, Plaster, Buster and Tige 15.00
Birthday Card, Buster Brown Shoes, 1960s 15.00
Booklet, Buster Brown Cameras-How to Make Photographs, Ansco Co., 12 pgs. 7.50
Calendar Plate, 7" d, 1909 . . . . 48.00
Coat Hook 28.00
Coloring Book 34.00
Comic Strip, 10 segment, 1909 . . . . 12.00
Decal, 5" by 7", 1960s, framed 32.00

Camera, Anthony & Scoville Co., c1905, 4" by 4" by 6", $50.

Dish, 5-1/2" d, china, full color illus, German, c1905 . . . . .75.00
Drawing Book, 3-1/2" by 4-7/8", color cov, int. cov art signed by RF Outcault, copyright 1906 Kaufmann & Strauss Co. 50.00
Fork, dog on handle 8.00
Game, Ring Toss, cardboard, 7" . . .40.00
Gyroscope, Buster Brown Shoes, MIB 25.00
Hatchet, 13-1/4" l, Buster and Tige image, emb metal head, wood handle . .35.00
Ink Blotter, "Buster Brown Shoes, For Boys, For Girls," 3-1/2" by 6-1/4", 1930s. .12.00
Jacks, orig ball, c1920 . . . . .10.00
Key Chain, 2" sq, brown, plastic, emb image of Buster and Tige 40.00
Mask, half, die-cut paper, "Buster Brown Shoes" on hat, c1905 . . . . .75.00
Pinback Button, Buster Brown Bread, 1-1/4" d 38.00
Pinback Button, Buster Brown Hose Supporter, multicolored, c1900 . .15.00
Pitcher, 3-1/4" h 30.00
Plate, Buster Brown and Tige, china 55.00
Playing Cards, USPC, miniature, 52 cards, 1908. . . . . .35.00
Shoe Tree, plastic, 4-1/2" l 35.00
Tin, Buster Brown All Spice, paper label, round 25.00
Tote Bag, Buster Brown Shoes, 1960 . . . . .40.00
Wallet, 1946 . . . . .22.00
Whistle, 1-1/2" l 35.00
Yo-Yo, litho tin 24.00

Calculators

The Texas Instruments TI-2500 Datamath entered the market in the early 1970s. This electronic calculator, the marvel of its era, performed four functions—addition, subtraction, multiplication and division. This is all it did. It retailed for over $100. Within less than a decade, calculators selling for less than $20 were capable of doing five times as many functions.

Early electronic calculators are dinosaurs. They deserve to be preserved. When collecting them, make certain to buy examples that retain their power transformer, instruction booklet and original box. Make certain any calculator that you buy works. There are few around who know how to repair one.

Royal LD 40, eight-digit, solar and battery powered, EZ Vue tilting lens, sliding cover, c1994, $2.

It is a little too early for a category on home computers. But a few smart collectors are starting to stash away the early Texas Instrument and Commodore models.

Club: International Association of Calculator Collectors, 14561 Livingston St., Tustin, CA 92680.

Calculators

Four Functions	10.00
Five or More Functions	5.00
30 or More Functions	20.00
Solar-powered	3.00
Not Working	0.00

Calendar Plates

Calendar plates are one of the traditional, affordable collecting categories. A few years ago, they sold in the $10 to $20 range; now that figure has jumped to $35 to $50.

Value rests with the decorative motif and the place for which it was issued. A fun collection would be to collect the same plate and see how many different merchants and other advertisers utilized it.

Newsletter: *The Calendar*, 710 N. Lake Shore Dr., Barrington, IL 60010.

Bi-plane, adv, 1900s, $40.

1908, Cat Faces, Merry Christmas, 9-1/4" d, BL Schermerhorn, Lowville, NY	39.00
1908, Lady Portrait center, Detroit, Michigan, adv	50.00
1909, Gibson Girl	40.00
1910, Girl and Horse Heads center	25.00
1910, Scenic	35.00
1911, scene of hunter, dog and quail center	39.00
1912, Airplane, glider	25.00
1912, Flowers and Cherubs center, 8-1/2" d	25.00
1912, Indian Maiden, sitting by fire husking corn, Home Bank, De Witt, Arkansas, adv	85.00
1912, Owl on open book, calendar on pgs, 7-1/2" d	35.00
1913, rose garland and holly border, calendar months center	20.00
1914, Sandpiper center, 9-1/2" d, sgd RK Beck	45.00
1914, Washington's Tomb	35.00
1916, man in canoe center	35.00
1919, flag center, Lubbers Co., East Saugatuck, Michigan adv	35.00
1922, game birds and hunting dog center	45.00
1932, fish in center	45.00

Hot air balloon, adv, 1912, $50.

Calendars

The primary reason calendars are collected is for the calendar art. Prices hinge on quality of printing and the pizzazz of the subject. A strong advertising aspect adds to the value. A highly overlooked calendar collecting area is the modern art and photographic calendar. For whatever reason, there is little interest in calendars dating after 1940. Collectors are making a major mistake. There are some great calendars from this later time period selling for less than $2.

"Gentlemen's" calendars did not grace the kitchen wall, but they are very collectible. Illustrations range from the pinup beauties of Elvgren and Moran and the Esquire Vargas ladies in the 1930s to the Playboy Playmates of the 1960s. Early Playboy calendars sell for $50-plus.

But what's the fun of having something you cannot display openly? The following list will clear corporate censors with no problems.

1890, Aetna Insurance Co., framed	290.00
1890, Ivory Soap	65.00
1898, Betsy Ross sewing American flag, colorful	25.00
1898, John Hancock Insurance	25.00
1900, Springfield Breweries Co., center oval with girl surrounded by calendar months	225.00
1902, patriotic theme, General Stark at Battle of Bennington, VT	25.00
1903, Grand Union, young girl and roses	150.00

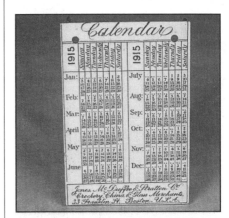

1915, Jones McDioffee & Stratton Co., Crockery, China, & Glass Merchants, 33 Franklin St., Boston USA, ceramic tile, 4-1/2" by 3-1/4", $85.

1957, Chessie, Chesapeake & Ohio Railway, $60.

1903, Melotte Cream Separators,
  framed 65.00
1904, Equitable Life Insurance 25.00
1905, Grand Union Tea Co., die-cut,
  lithograph 90.00
1906, Rice Seed Co., girl, orchid border,
  December pad, framed 40.00
1906, The John Beth & Sons Co., Choice
  Groceries & Provisions,
  Green Bay, WI 55.00
1908, De Laval Cream Separators, girl
  hugging cow, framed 350.00
1911, Pratts Veterinary Remedies, woman
  feeding horse, full pad 225.00
1915, Magic Yeast, boy carrying yeast and
  stick 225.00
1919, American Red Cross, 28" by
  10-1/4" .35.00
1919, United States Cartridge Co.,
  hunter .150.00
1919, Woodrow Wilson 10.00
1924, Pompeian Co., beautiful lady and
  man 16.00
1928, Harrisburg Pilot, gypsy girl . . .90.00
1929, Star Brand Shoes, woman by
  stained glass window, framed . .140.00
1930, Winchester Arms Co., hunter
  holding pages of calendar 300.00
1935, Lone Ranger and Silver 75.00
1939, Dionne Quintuplets, Five Little
  Sweethearts, full pad 28.00
1941, Earl Moran illus, "Out In Front," 11"
  by 23" 80.00
1944, Farmers Oil Co., full pad 7.00
1944, Sinclair Gasoline, 12 wildlife
  photos .20.00

1946, Washington's Prayer,
  historical art 25.00
1947, Rolf Armstrong illus, "See You
  Soon," September pad, salesman's
  sample 45.00
1949, Princess Elizabeth, 8-1/2" by
  4-3/4" 40.00
1950, Movie Star Calendar For 1950 22.00
1952, Mobil Oil, red Pegasus logo . . . 8.00
1955, Marilyn Monroe, full pad 25.00
1961, TWA, six sheets 15.00

California Raisins

California Raisins are those adorable claymation raisins seen on television commercials sponsored by the California Raisin Advisory Board. The American viewing public fell in love with the Raisins' conga-line performance of Marvin Gaye's hit single "I Heard It Through The Grapevine." The exploitation of these wrinkled raisins soon followed, much to the delight of the Advisory Board. California Raisins were soon found dancing their way across a myriad of merchandise from address books to welcome mats.

Advisor: John D. Weatherhead, 5224 S. Guerin Pass, New Berlin, WI 53151, (414) 425-4481.

Activity Book, by Helene Hovanec,
  1988 . . . . 6.00
Address Book, yellow, conga line,
  1988 . . . . 10.00
Air Freshener, orange sunglasses, Medco,
  1988, in seal 5.00
Auto Sunshield, Michael Jackson raisin,
  1988 . . . . 15.00
Back Pack, three raisin figures, maroon
  and yellow, 1987 . . . . 55.00
Badge, plastic, "Grapevine Tour 88" 14.00
Balloon, conga-line, multicolor, 1987 . 7.00
Bandanna, raisin characters, blue border,
  grape outline, 1988 . . . . 20.00
Bank, plastic, Sunkist and raisin base,
  1987, MIP 75.00
Baseball Cap, 1988 . . . . 10.00
Belt, lead singer with microphone on
  buckle, 1987 . . . . 15.00
Billfold, yellow plastic, 1988 . . . . 20.00
Board Game, 1987 . . . . 25.00
Book, Raisins in Motion, illus by Pat Paris
  Productions, 1988 . . . . 20.00
Bookmark, California Raisin Reading Club,
  1989 . . . . 10.00
Bubble Bath, Rockin Raisin, purple,
  24 oz 10.00

Cake Decoration, prepackaged kit with
  Michael Jackson raisin, 1988 . . . 30.00
Candy Dish, seven raisin figures, blue
  letters, 1989 . . . . 50.00
Cereal Box, Post Raisin Bran, cassette
  offer, 1988 . . . . 20.00
Chalkboard, singer and conga-line, Rose
  Art, 1988, MIP 35.00
Clay Factory, Rose Brand, 1988 . . . 40.00
Coffee Mug, 4-3/4" h, plastic, blue lid, no
  spill type, 1987 . . . . 9.00
Doll, 6" h, with microphone, 1988 . . . . 4.00
Doll, 7" h, orange glasses, 1987 . . . . 10.00
Halloween Costume, Collegeville Flag &
  Mfg. Co., child size, 1988, MIB . . 20.00
Keychain, graduate, both hands up,
  thumbs touch head, 1988 . . . . . . 40.00
Pillow Sham, Sears, 1987, MIP 20.00
Puzzle, American Publishing, 75 pcs,
  7" by 9", 1988 . . . . 15.00
Radio, AM, posable arms and legs, orig
  box, 1988 . . . . 150.00
Rain Coat, purple, three raisin ladies in
  Rolls Royce, 1988 . . . . 40.00
Refrigerator Magnets, three baby raisins,
  made in China, 1988 . . . . 60.00
Sunglasses, Imperial Toy Co., green,
  1987, MIB 15.00
Umbrella, 1988 . . . . 50.00
Watch, official fan club watch, three
  different bands, Nelsonic, 1987,
  MIB 150.00
Welcome Mat, 1988 . . . . 115.00

Camark Pottery

Camark Pottery derives its name from its location in Camden, Ark. The company was organized in 1926 and produced decorative and utilitarian items in hundreds of shapes, colors and forms. The pottery closed in 1986.

Figures
Bulldog, USA N91, 12" by 10-1/2" . 125.00
Bunny, 9" h 50.00
Cat, USA N62, 10" h 60.00
Elephant, USA 784, miniature, 3" w . 22.00
Hen on Basket, USA R55, two-pc . . 50.00
Horse, USA 567, 9" by 8" 50.00
Praying Woman, kneeling, 6" h 35.00

Planters
USA 140A, 4" w 15.00
USA 166, 14" w 22.00
USA 378, diaper, figural 30.00
USA 620, 6" by 3" 20.00

Vases
Boot, figural, USA 565 . . . . 20.00
Miniature, USA 674, gold trim, hp,
  3" h 25.00

Morning Glory, USA 801M, 8" by 11" 85.00
Morning Glory, USA 810K, two handles,
   10-1/2" w 100.00
Rose, USA 545D, 7" by 8" 65.00
Swan, figural, USA 115, gold trim,
   9-1/2" h. 75.00

Wall Pockets
Cup and Saucer, gold trim, hp 30.00
Flour Scoop, figural, USA Camark N-45,
   10" h. 40.00
Torch, figural, USA N22, 6" h 20.00

Other
Basket, USA 028, 4-1/2" h 24.00
Bowl, Morning Glory, USA 804M, 14" by
   7-1/2" .125.00
Bowl, Rose, USA 553D, 11" by 5",
   hp 75.00
Candlesticks, pr, Double Swirl, Rose, USA
   269, 5" h. 35.00
Cigarette Holder, USA R61, 4" h. . . .35.00
Console Bowl, double swan, USA 116, 14"
   by 6-1/2". 100.00
Creamer, round, USA 898, 2" h 18.00
Cup, tree trunk design, USA 255 . . .23.00
Deviled Egg Plate, USA 015. . . . . .24.00
Jewelry Box, USA 211, two-pc,
   8" by 3". 40.00
Mug, hillbilly picture center, 5-1/2" h .30.00
Oaken Bucket, USA R39, sticker . . .38.00
Pitcher, USA 088, cat handle, 7" by
   7-1/2" 75.00
Saucer, petal design, 4-1/2" d. 8.00
Soap Dish, bathtub, figural, USA 232,
   4" by 2". 16.00
Teapot, USA 265, swirl design,
   two-pc. .35.00
Wall Plaque, Bowl and Pitcher, figural,
   USA 157, two-pc, 12" w 50.00

Cambridge Glass

The Cambridge Glass Co., of Cambridge, Ohio, began operation in 1901. Its first products were clear table-

Rose Point, bowl, handled, 5-1/2" w, $45.

Ice Bucket, clear, hammered-aluminum handle and orig tongs, $25.

wares. Later, color, etched and engraved pieces were added to the line. Production continued until 1954. The Imperial Glass Co., of Bellaire, Ohio, bought some of the Cambridge molds and continued production of these pieces.

Club: National Cambridge Collectors, Inc.,
   P.O. Box 416, Cambridge, OH 43725.

Apple Blossom
Basket, pink 18.00
Console Bowl. 19.00
Salt and Pepper Shakers, pr 30.00

Caprice
Ashtray, blue, with place card 14.00
Bonbon, blue, low, ftd, 6" sq 50.00
Bowl, 11" l, oval, handle, alpine blue 95.00
Bowl, 11" l, oval, handle, blue 110.00
Bowl, 11" l, oval, handle, crystal . . . 45.00
Cabaret Plate, blue, 11" d,
   three-toed 70.00
Candlesticks, pr, crystal, three-light. 60.00
Candy Dish, cov, crystal, three-toed 45.00
Cigarette Box, cov, crystal, 3-1/2" by
   2-1/2" 20.00
Compote, 7" d, low, ftd, alpine blue . 50.00
Compote, 7" d, low, ftd, blue 50.00
Console Set, pink, 13" d ftd bowl, pr
   candlesticks with prisms 250.00
Creamer and Sugar, individual, blue 50.00
Creamer and Sugar, individual,
   crystal 25.00
Cruet, stopper, crystal, 3 oz. 30.00
Cup and Saucer, blue 40.00
Cup and Saucer, crystal 15.00
Plate, 8-1/2" d, blue 35.00

Plate, 8-1/2" d, crystal 15.00
Plate, 11" d, ftd, blue 75.00
Plate, 11" d, ftd, crystal. 50.00

Chantilly
Bonbon. 17.50
Cocktail Shaker, metal top 95.00
Water Goblet 20.00

Diane
Bowl, 11" d 35.00
Salt and Pepper Shakers, pr 42.50
Sherbet, amber, tall 20.00

Rose Point
Basket, 6" sq 65.00
Bowl, 12" d, four-toed. 125.00
Bud Vase, 10-1/2" h, ftd 165.00
Butter, cov, 5-1/2". 275.00
Candlesticks, pr, 5" h 115.00
Candy Dish, cov, 6" h, blown . . . 275.00
Celery, 12" d. 175.00
Champagne 25.00
Cheese and Cracker Set 115.00
Cocktail Icer 70.00
Compote, 6" d. 55.00
Corn Dish 60.00
Creamer and Sugar, individual size . 95.00
Cup and Saucer 35.00
Plate, 6-1/2" 55.00
Plate, 9-1/2" d, dinner. 150.00
Marmalade, cov 195.00
Salt and Pepper Shakers, pr 65.00
Sherbet, 6 oz 30.00
Tumbler, 5 oz, ftd 50.00

Wild Flower
Champagne 30.00
Cup and Saucer 20.00
Pitcher 95.00
Plate, 10-1/2" d. 40.00
Sugar 14.00

Cameos

Cameos are a form of jewelry that has never lost its popularity. Cameos have been made basically the same way for centuries. Most are dated by their settings, although this is risky, since historic settings can be duplicated very easily.

Normally, one thinks of a cameo as carved from a piece of conch shell. However, the term cameo means a gem that is carved in relief. You can find cameos carved from gemstones and lava. Lava cameos are especially desirable.

Ring, Atlas, silver mounting, Wedgwood, $250.

Beware of plastic and other forms of copycat and fake cameos. Look carefully at the side. If you spot layers, shy away. A real cameo is carved from a single piece. Your best defense when buying a cameo is to buy from a dealer that you can find later and then have the authenticity of the cameo checked by a local retail jeweler.

Agate, brooch, bust of woman with flowers in hair, Victorian, gold-knife edge and beadwork frame, 18k yg setting .800.00
Hobe Shell, earrings, rhinestones and smoked crystals 45.00
Lava, bracelet, various color panels, Victorian 14k yg mounting . . . 1,300.00
Opal, carved, stickpin, gold frame, ruby and diamond highlights, 14k yg setting, marked "Tiffany & Co.". 650.00
Onyx, compact, marcasite ring, yellow guilloche enamel 400.00
Pearl, button, bust and Lily of the Valley dec 10.00
Stone, necklace, silver filigree chain with jet beads, marked "Czech". 65.00

Cameras

Just because a camera is old does not mean that it is valuable. Rather, assume that the more examples of a camera that were made the less likely it is to be valuable. Collectors are after unusual cameras or examples from companies that failed quickly.

A portion of a camera's value rests on how it works. Check all bellows cameras by shining a strong light over the outside surface while looking at the inside. Check the seating on removable lenses. It is only recently that collectors have begun to focus in on the 35mm camera. You can still build a collection of early models at a modest cost per camera.

There is a growing market in camera accessories and ephemera. A camera has minimum value if you do not know how it works. Whenever possible, insist on the original instruction booklet as part of the purchase.

Clubs: National Stereoscopic Association, P.O. Box 14801, Columbus, OH 43214; Photographic Historical Society, P.O. Box 9563, Rochester, NY 14606.

Eastman Kodak Camera
Automatic Kodak Junior, No. 2C, 1916-27 . . . . 15.00
Boy Scout Camera, 127 roll film, green vest pocket, emb on bed, 1930-34 . . . 40.00
Bullet, 127 roll film, c 1935 . . . . 15.00
Instamatic, 314, lever wind, light meter, flash cubes, 1968-71 . . . . 12.00
Monitor Six-16, anastigmat special f4.5 lens, 2-1/2" by 4-1/4" exp, 616 roll film, c1939-46 . . . . 15.00
Pony, 135, Kodak Anaston f4.5 lens, 1950-54 . . . . 10.00
Weno Hawk-Eye Box, #7 . . . . 25.00

Other Cameras
Advertising, Parliament 12.00
Ansco, Rediflex 10.00

Photavit-Werk, 33mm, Germany, box winder, c1938, $85.

Bell & Howell, Autoset Movie Camera, 8mm, interchangeable lenses, c1957 . . . . 15.00
Bell & Howell, Filmo Turret Movie Camera, 8mm, triple lens holder, variable speeds, c1938 . . . . 15.00
Character, Donald Duck, Herbert George Co. 50.00
Candid Camera Corp. of America, Perfex 44, 35mm, c 1939-40 . . . . 80.00
Canon, Canonflex RP, fixed finder, canomatic lenses, 1960-62 . . . . 150.00
Ciro Cameras Inc., Delaware, OH, 35 rangefinder for 35mm film, 1949 . 15.00
Nikon, Nikkorex Zoom-8, 8mm movie camera, f1.8 lens 25.00
Revere, Ranger Model 81, 8mm movie camera, c1947 . . . . 10.00
Samei Sangyo, Japan, Samoca, 35mm, c1958 . . . . 35.00
Schneider Xenar, 70mm, f4.5 lens, c1934 . . . . 45.00
Scovill Mfg. Co., Klondike, c1898 . . . 50.00
Spartus 35, 35mm, bakelite viewfinder, c1950 . . . . 10.00
Universal Camera Corp., Univex AF, compact, collapsing for Number 00 roll film, cast metal body 15.00
Vitar, 35mm, Flash Chronomatic shutter 15.00
Zeiss, Ikon, Tenax I, East Germany, 1948-53 . . . . 60.00

Camera-Related
Book, *Guide to Kodak Retina, Retina Reflex, Signet and Pony*, Kenneth S. Tydings, 128 pgs, soft cov, 1952. . . . 8.50
Box, Eastman Kodak Developing Powders, "For Use in Brownie Tank Developer," c1900. . . . . 8.50
Catalog, Korona, 52 pgs, 1926. . . . . 25.00
Manual, Leica Reflex Housing, nine pgs, 1956 . . . . 5.00

Cameras, Novelty

Over the years, collectors of cameras have been a serious bunch, with a hierarchy interested in sophisticated, top-end equipment or beautiful antique pieces. Recently, more interest has been drawn to cameras exhibiting vibrant multicolor designs with a flair for grabbing one's attention.

Plastic cameras that depict cartoon characters are a fun collecting area that can really brighten up a shelf. The most striking are the "face" cameras resembling some of these characters,

Can Camera, Budweiser, Eiko, $35.

clowns, bears or Santa Claus and even a full figure Charlie Tuna.

Early 1930s Kodak box and folding cameras can be found in red, blue, brown, green, pink and some even more exotic colors. The challenge exists in finding an example of each model in each color. What an admirable display! The Art Deco crowd will want both sizes of the Beau Brownies and the diamond, lightning bolt and step patterns of the folding Petites.

Collecting the cardboard-covered disposable cameras is the new craze that is just beginning to catch on. Here, the re-wrapped and reloaded models advertising products such as Winchester bullets, Playboy, Budweiser, college sports teams, cereals, etc., are the most desirable. Their graphic art designs are colorful, making them stand out in any collection.

Prices listed are for cameras in excellent condition.

Advisor: Richard Ogden, P.O. Box 210, Chapman, NE 68827, (308) 986-2247.

Box

AGFA-Ansco, various colors, sizes
   2 and 2A .30.00
Kodak, Beau Brownie, Art Deco front, sizes
   2 and 2A, pink 175.00
Kodak, Beau Brownie, Art Deco front, sizes
   2 and 2A, other colors 75.00
Kodak, Brownie, various colors, sizes 2
   and 2A .40.00

Kodak, Rainbow Hawkeye, various colors,
   sizes 2 and 2A 30.00
Kodak, Target Hawk-Eye, various models
   and colors 30.00

Can, figural

Budweiser, EIKO 35.00
Coca-Cola, Tizer 75.00
Gent Coffee, EIKO 35.00
Pepsi, EIKO 35.00

Character

Barbie Cameramatic, 126 film 30.00
Brenda Starr Cub Reporter, black Bakelite,
   127 film 100.00
Bugs Bunny, plastic, "Eh-Doc Smile,"
   126 film 50.00
Charlie Tuna, figural, plastic,
   126 film 60.00
Davy Crockett, black box, face plate with
   Davy and rifles 50.00
Dick Tracy, black Bakelite, 127 film . 50.00
Donald Duck, Donald, Huey, Dewey and
   Louie on back, 127 film, black . . 35.00
Donald Duck, same as previous, but olive
   drab. 45.00
Fred Flintstone, Fred's face on front, lens in
   his mouth 30.00
Holly Hobbie, white plastic, decals, 126
   film 30.00
Hopalong Cassidy, black plastic box with
   Hoppy and Topper, camera and
   flash 150.00
Incredible Hulk, 126 film 30.00
Mick-A-Matic, plastic, Mickey's head with
   camera behind and lens in nose. 50.00
Mickey Mouse, riding toy train 40.00
Mickey Mouse, head and bowtie,
   110 film 35.00
Punky Brewster, red plastic,
   110 film 15.00
Roy Rogers, black plastic box, Roy riding
   Trigger on face plate, 120 film . . 50.00
Roy Rogers Jr., black plastic,
   127 film 40.00
Snoopymatic, dog house-shape, Snoopy
   on top 50.00
Spider Man, plastic, 126 film 30.00
Yogi Bear, Yogi's head, lens in
   mouth 30.00

Disposable

Budweiser 15.00
Cinnamon Toast Crunch 8.00
Harley Davidson, "Let The Good
   Times Roll" 20.00
J.C. Whitney, "Everything
   Automotive". 12.00
Party Cam, red, yellow and blue
   balloons 10.00
Playboy Playmate, 40th anniversary, used
   for "Photograph your own Playmate"
   contest 30.00

Mighty Morphin Power Rangers 15.00
Sonic & Knuckles 15.00
Time Magazine 10.00
University of Nebraska, Herbie Husker,
   "Huskers" on front 12.00
Winchester, "Because Every Shot Counts,"
   camouflage cov 30.00

Folder, Kodak

Folding Cartridge Hawk-Eye,
   No. 2 . . . . 40.00
Folding Rainbow Hawk-Eye, sizes
   2 and 2A 80.00
Petite, with Art Deco door plate and orig
   colored bellows 450.00
Petite, With orig colored bellows . . 150.00
Petite, With replacement black
   bellows 75.00
Pocket Jr., No. 1 and 1A. 50.00
Pocket Kodak, No. 1 and 1A, blue, brown,
   green and gray 40.00
Pocket Kodak, Series II, No. 1A, beige,
   blue, brown, green and gray 40.00
Vest Pocket Rainbow Hawk-Eye . . 125.00
F4c18F.doc

Campbell's Soup

Mmm, mmm good. That's what Campbell's Soup collectibles are.

Club: Soup Collectors Club, 414 Country Lane Ct., Wauconda, IL 60084.

Newsletter: *Campbell's Soup Link*, 311 Cambridge Dr., Dimondale, MI 48821.

Dolls

Campbell Kid, 5" h, bisque, jointed
   shoulders, molded and painted hair,
   painted side-glancing eyes, molded
   clothing, marked "Made in Germany"
   on back 300.00
Campbell Kid, 10" h, vinyl head, one pc
   Magic Skin body, molded and painted
   hair, painted side-glancing eyes,

Puzzle, frame tray, cardboard, $17.

Magazine Tear Sheet, *Woman's Home Companion*, **November 1923, 10-3/4" by 13-3/4", $9.**

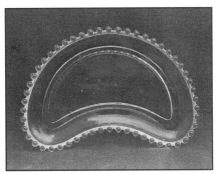

Salad, crescent, 400/120, $45.

Photograph, black and white, Tootsie Roll Industries delivery truck, 1916, $50.

smiling watermelon type mouth, orig red and white cotton dress, apron, chef's hat, nylon socks and plastic shoes, marked "Campbell Kid, Made by Ideal Toy Corp." 50.00

Campbell Kid, 12-1/2" h, composition, socket head, jointed shoulders and hips, molded and painted hair, painted side-glancing eyes, closed smiling watermelon mouth, orig white dress with diamond design around bottom and matching bonnet, marked "A Petite Doll," American Character Doll dress label reads "Campbell Kid". 400.00

Other

Cookbook, Campbell Soup Kids, 64 pgs 30.00

Display, Campbell Kid figure, die-cut cardboard standup. 15.00

Doorstop, 8-1/2" h, cast iron, Campbell Kids with dog, worn polychrome paint 160.00

Jigsaw Puzzle, The Campbell Kids Schooltime, Jaymar Kiddie Puzzle, #319, 28 pcs. 28.00

Salt and Pepper Shakers, pr, 4-1/2" h, plastic, girl and boy Campbell Kids, 1950s 35.00

Candlewick

Imperial Glass Corp. issued its No. 400 pattern, Candlewick, in 1936 and continued to produce it until 1982. In 1985 the Candlewick molds were dis-

persed to a number of sources, e.g., Boyd Crystal Art. More than 650 items and sets are known. Shapes include round, oval, oblong, heart and square. The largest assortment of pieces and sets were made during the late 1940s and early 1950s. For a list of reproduction Candlewick pieces, check the Candlewick category in *Warman's Americana & Collectibles*.

Club: The National Candlewick Collector's Club, 275 Milledge Ter., Athens, GA 30606.

Bowl, 400/63B, 10-1/2" d, bellied. . . 50.00
Bud Vase, 400/25 . . . . 40.00
Bud Vase, 400/107 . . . . 65.00
Cake Stand, 400/103D, 11" d 35.00
Candleholders, pr, 400/80, 3-1/2" h. 25.00
Candy, cov, 400/260, three-part . . 150.00
Celery Tray, 400/105, 13-1/2" l 30.00
Deviled Egg Tray, 400/154 . . . . . . 100.00
Goblet, 3400, 9 oz 15.00
Ice Tub, 400/63 . . . . 95.00
Mayonnaise Set, 400/49, three pcs . 45.00
Pitcher, 400/19, 40 oz, juice 250.00
Pitcher, 400/24, 80 oz 175.00
Plate, 400/5D, 8" d, salad 10.00
Plate, 400/10D, 10-1/2" d, dinner. . . 35.00
Punch Set, 400/20 bowl, 12 400/37 cups, 400/128B base and 400/91 ladle 250.00
Relish Dish, 400/268, 8" l, oval, two-part. 20.00
Salt and Pepper Shakers, pr, 400/96, beaded ft. 35.00
Tumbler, 400/19, 5 oz, juice 25.00

Candy Collectibles

Who doesn't love some form of candy? Forget the chocoholics. I'm a Juicy Fruit man. Once you start looking for candy-related material, you are

quickly overwhelmed by how much is available. Do not forget the boxes. They are usually discarded. Ask your local drugstore or candy shop to save the more decorative ones for you. What is free today may be worth money tomorrow.

Bank, Hershey's, 6-1/2" h, ceramic, 1983 . . . . .70.00
Box, Fanny Farmer Easter Candies, 4 oz, cardboard, bunny and chick design. 25.00
Box, Hershey Nougat-Almond 10.00
Box, Kate Litters Candy Shop, pralines, mammy illus 50.00
Candy Container, Clock, missing paper face dial. 300.00
Candy Container, Egg, tin, Dutch girl illus on front 15.00
Candy Dish, Schrafft's Chocolate, 4" by 7" d, name etched in base 60.00

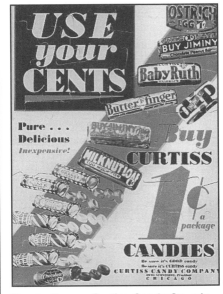

Puzzle, jigsaw, Curtiss Candy Co. adv, cardboard, $38.

Candy Dispenser, Little Imps, devilish
face illus .50.00

Display, Baby Ruth, candy bar illus
front 25.00

Display, Life Savers, metal, five slanted
shelves 25.00

Doll, Hershey's Kisses, 8" h, stuffed, plush,
candy figural, embroidered face . . .8.00

Folder, Whitman's Chocolates, color,
c1920 . . . . .18.00

Game, Tootsie Roll Rocket Game, 17" by
20", 1962 . . . . .25.00

Jar, Baby Ruth, glass, barrel-shape, red
and white, tin lid 15.00

Magazine Tear Sheet, Baby Ruth, *Boys'
Life*, sailor on phone illus 6.00

Ornament, M&M's, plastic, M&M wearing
Santa hat .2.50

Playing Cards, Life Savers, illus rows of different flavors 5.00

Sign, Samoset Chocolates, litho tin, gold,
blue, red and black 50.00

Sign, Wrigley's Double Mint Gum,
cardboard, standup, girl holding
cigarette behind pack of
gum illus .40.00

Sign, Yoo-Hoo Chocolate, Yogi Berra and
rock band cartoon illus, 1970s . . .35.00

Puzzle, Baby Ruth, 45 pcs, die-cut cardboard, two children under umbrella
eating candy with dog watching,
1930s 12.00

Tin, Bunte Candy, gold, 5 lb 25.00

Tin, Hershey's, Hershey's Hometown
Series, #4, 1990 . . . . .5.00

Tin, Sunny South Chocolate Peanut, black
face illus 175.00

Tin, Whitman White Cap Mints, round,
8 oz 10.00

Wrapper, Home Run Candy, baseball
game illus, 1936 . . . . .45.00

Wrapper, Wrigley's Licorice Gum . . .12.00

Cap Pistols

Classic collectors collect the one-shot, cast-iron pistols manufactured during the first third of the 20th century. Kids of the 1950s collect roll-cap pistols. Children of the 1990s do not know what they are missing. Prices for roll-cap pistols are skyrocketing. Buy them only if they are in working order. Ideally, acquire them with their appropriate accessories, e.g., holsters, fake bullets, etc.

Club: Toy Gun Collectors of America, 175 Cornell St., Windsor, CA 95492.

Edison

Matic 45, 24", plastic, 1980s 10.00

Sharkmatic, 6", automatic, 1980s . . 15.00

Susanna 90, 12 shot, 9", ring caps, black,
plastic wood grips, 1980s 15.00

Harvel-Kilgore

Flintlock Jr., 7-1/2", plastic, brown,
1955 . . . . 15.00

Harvel-Kilgore, Marshal, 9-3/4", die-cast,
nickel finish, scrollwork, brown and
white plastic grips 35.00

Rodeo, 7-1/2", white plastic grips,
1950s 35.00

Hubley

Midget, 5-1/2" l, die-cast, metal flintlock,
silver finish, 1950s 20.00

Tiger, 6-7/8" l, mammoth caps, metal,
1935 . . . . 35.00

Winner, 4-3/8" l, pop-up magazine release,
nickel finish, 1940 . . . . 80.00

Kilgore

Big Horn, 7", metal, disc caps, silver finish,
1950s 100.00

Cheyenne, side-loading, Sure-K plastic
grips, silver finish, 1974 . . . . . . 10.00

Clip 50, 4-1/4" l, black bakelite 75.00

Hawkeye, metal, side-loading, silver finish,
1950s 20.00

Mountie Automatic, 6" l, pop-up magazine,
nickel finish, black plastic grips . . 20.00

Mustang, chrome finish, plastic grips 30.00

Leslie-Henry

Marshal Cap Pistol, revolving cylinder
chambers, Nichols-style bullets,
1950s 35.00

Marshal Matt Dillon, "Gunsmoke" Cap
Pistol, 10" pop-up cap magazine,
scrollwork, bronze steer-head grips,
1950s 50.00

Nichols

Stallion .22 cap pistol, 7", revolving cylinder
chambers, five two-pc cartridges, black
plastic stag grips, 1950s 30.00

Tophand 250 cap pistol, 9-1/2", black
finish, brown plastic grips, 1960 . 10.00

Pecos Kid cap pistol, 9", silver-chrome
finish, brown plastic grips, 1970s Lone
Star 10.00

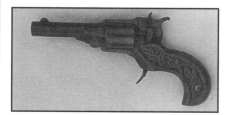

Stevens, Comet, 1885, $100.

Pony, metal, nickel finish, eagle illus on
grip, Actoy, 1950s 25.00

Stevens

49er cap pistol, 9", cast iron, nickel finish,
white plastic figural grips, 1940 . 100.00

Billy The Kid, 8" 55.00

Cowboy cap pistol, 3-1/2", cast iron,
1935 . . . . 20.00

Other

Automatic Cap Pistol, 6-1/2", silver,
simulated walnut grip, 1950s,
National 60.00

Derringer, die-cast, copper finish, twin
swivel barrel, Esquire Novelty,
1960 . . . . 20.00

Dick Cap Pistol, 4-3/4", automatic,
side-loading, black finish, Benton
Harbor Novelty, 1950s 20.00

Dragnet, plastic, die-cast, black, gold,
6-3/4", Knickerbocker 50.00

Gene Autry Dummy Cap Pistol, cast iron,
gray gunmetal finish, white plastic grips,
Kenton, 1939 . . . . 90.00

Lone Rider, 8" die-cast, white plastic inset,
1950s 35.00

Carnival Chalkware

Carnival chalkware is my candidate for the kitsch collectible of the 1990s. No one uses quality to describe these inexpensive prizes given out by games of chance at carnivals, amusement parks and ocean boardwalks.

The best pieces are those depicting a specific individual or character. Since most were bootlegged (made

Eagle, mkd "God Bless America," $25.

Siamese Cat, glitter collar, $20.

without permission), they often appear with a fictitious name, e.g., "Smile Doll" is really supposed to be Shirley Temple. The other strong collecting sub-category is the animal figure. As long as the object comes close to capturing the appearance of a pet, animal collectors will buy it.

Bag Pipe Girls, 6" by 15" 25.00
Betty Boop, 4" by 13" 45.00
Blue Birds, 8" by 8", red and blue . . .15.00
Cat, 6" by 17", yellow, black hat 10.00
Charlie McCarthy, 3" by 7" 30.00
Clown, 6" by 12-1/2" 15.00
Cowboy on Horse, 9" by 10" 30.00
Elephant, 9" by 10-1/2" 15.00
Ferdinand the Bull, 5" by 9" 15.00
George Washington, 6" by 7-1/2" . . .15.00
Gnome, 13-1/2" 40.00
Huey Duck, 4" by 7" 10.00
Hula Girl, cloth skirt, 4" by 15" 35.00
Indian, 3" by 8" 10.00
Lion, 10" by 12" 25.00
Lone Ranger, 6" by 15" 50.00
Mary Had A Little Lamb, 7" by 16",
    blue and yellow 35.00

Sailor, 3" by 8" 10.00
Tiger, 10" by 12", mouth open 35.00
WWII Dog, 4" by 5" 15.00
WWII Civil Defense Man, 5" by 14" . 50.00

Cartoon Collectibles

This is a category with something for each generation. The characters represented here enjoyed a life in comic books and newspaper pages or had a career on movie screens and television. Every collector has a favorite. Buy examples that bring back pleasant memories. "That's All Folks."

Banana Splits, 45 rpm record, 7" by 8" illus
    sleeve, Kellogg's cereal premium,
    1969 . . . . 30.00
Barney Google, hand puppet 50.00
Blondie, coloring book, 8-1/2" by 11",
    1954, Dell Publishing, unused . . 20.00
Bugs Bunny, Bank, hard plastic, emb full
    color Bugs and Elmer Fudd, talking
    mechanism, Janex, 1977 . . . . . . 55.00
Bugs Bunny, Necktie, 10-1/2" l, clip-on,
    c1940 . . . . 50.00
Casper and Friends, Cereal Bowl, 5" d,
    Westfield, early 1960s 25.00
Casper and Friends, Game, Casper The
    Ghost Electronic Adventure Game,
    built-in game board, four plastic
    mountain tunnels and pot of gold, orig
    box, Tarco, 1962 . . . . 225.00

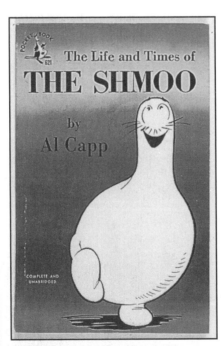

Li'l Abner, book, *The Life and Times of The Shmoo*, Al Capp, Pocketbook Co., $16.

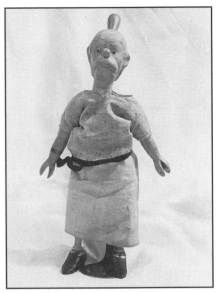

Maggie and Jiggs, Maggie figure, composition face, wood hands and feet, orig costume, Schoenhut, 9" h, $250.

Casper and Friends, Mug, cream-colored
    glass, orange, white and black illus,
    Westfield, early 1960s 25.00
Dick Tracy, Candy Bar Wrapper, color
    picture, premium offer, 1950s . . . 10.00
Dick Tracy, Hand puppet, 1961 . . . . 75.00
Elmer Fudd, figure, 7" h, hard plastic,
    moveable head, full color, Dakin,
    1968 . . . . 50.00
Felix the Cat, Game, playing pcs, spinner
    and picture cards, Milton Bradley,
    1968 . . . . 35.00
Felix the Cat, Clicker, litho tin, Germany,
    1929 . . . . 25.00
Foxy Grandpa, handkerchief, 1920 . 40.00
Fred Flintstone, bubblegum machine,
    figural head 40.00
Garfield, Christmas ornament, round,
    1981, orig box 9.00
Herman and Katnip, two-sided game
    board, cardboard playing pcs and
    cheese, mousetraps and elevator,
    unused, Saalfield, 1960 . . . . 35.00
Jetsons, activity book, 11" by 13", The
    Jetsons Color-By-Number, perforated
    pgs, Whitman, 1963 . . . . 45.00
Joe Palooka, lunch box, litho tin,
    1948 . . . . 45.00
King Leonardo and His Short Subjects,
    jigsaw puzzle, Jaymar, 1962 . . . . 25.00
Krazy Kat, bank, wearing graduation
    outfit 55.00
Little Audrey, doll, 15" h, plastic, soft-vinyl
    painted head, red western dress, brown
    suede cowboy boots, gun and holster,
    Fillmore, 1950s 120.00

Maggie and Jiggs, salt and pepper shakers, pr, 2-1/2" h, figural, marked "Made In Japan," 1930s 65.00

Moon Mullins, nodder, 3-7/8" h, bisque, Germany 60.00

Pebbles Flintstone, bubble bath, 24 powdered soap packets, orig box with pop-up display lid, Popeye, Charm, 1-1/4" w, celluloid, brass loop, orange, pink, black and green, Japan, 1930s 20.00

Popeye, Colorforms, Popeye The Weatherman, vinyl die-cut pcs, instruction booklet, orig box, 1959 . . . . .40.00

Popeye, Pencil Sharpener, tin, dated 1929 . . . . .95.00

Roclar, 1963 . . . . .85.00

Quick Draw McGraw and Friends, lamp shade, 9" d, full color stiff paper, Western desert scene, 1960 . . . .40.00

Ricochet Rabbit and Droop Along Coyote, board game, playing pcs, 12 cards, orig box, Ideal, 1964 . . . . .295.00

Scooby Doo, Soap, figural, orig box, un-used, Hewitt, 1977 . . . . .20.00

Smitty, nodder, bisque 85.00

Snoopy, pen holder. 65.00

Tom & Jerry, radio, hard plastic, figural, die-cut Tom's head, carrying strap and earphone, orig box, Marx, 1972 . .70.00

Uncle Walt, Gasoline Alley, pinback button, 13/16" d, litho 12.00

Underdog, lunch box 300.00

Yellow Kid, ice cream mold, 4-3/4" h, full figure, hinged 185.00

Yosemite Sam, hand puppet, 1960s 25.00

Cash Registers

If you want to buy a cash register, you better be prepared to put plenty of money in the till. Most are bought for decorative purposes. Serious collectors would go broke in a big hurry if they had to pay the prices listed below for every machine they bought.

Beware of modern reproductions. Cash registers were meant to be used. Signs of use should be present. There is also a tendency to restore a machine to its original appearance through replating and rebuilding. Well and good. But when all is said and done, how do you tell the refurbished machine from a modern reproduction? When you cannot, it is hard to sustain long-term value.

National

#4, nickel-plated brass, tape dispenser, extended oak base, 20" w, 20-1/2" h, 16-1/2" d 150.00

#7, detail adder, candy store model 325.00

#312, candy store model 475.00

#317, candy store model, extended base, tape dispenser, ornately emb, orig marquee, 17-1/4" w, 21" h, 15-1/2" d 550.00

#321, brass, 17-1/4" by 17" by 16", extended base, 1916 . . . . 650.00

#452-2, oak, two drawer, crank . . . 850.00

#1040, patent date, 8-30-1913 . . . 300.00

Other

Western, Verdic-Corbin Co., Detroit, barbershop, plated cast iron, heavily emb, 5 cents to $1, restored, castings replated, marquee and number tabs replaced, 9" w, 21" h, 15" d . . . 750.00

Cassette Tapes

Flea markets thrive on two types of goods—those that are collectible and those that serve a second-hand function. Cassette tapes fall into the latter group. Buy them for the purpose of playing them. The one exception is when the promotional pamphlet covering the tape shows a famous singer or group. In this case, you may be paying for the piece of paper ephemera rather than the tape, but you might as well have the whole shooting match.

Several times within recent years there have been a number of articles in the trade papers about collecting eight-tracks. When was the last time you saw an eight-track machine? They are going to be as popular in 30 years as the wire tape recorder is today. Interesting idea—too bad it bombed.

Average price. . . . . 50 cents to $2

Cast Iron

This is a category in which you should be suspicious that virtually everything you see is a reproduction or copycat. More often than not, the object will not be original. Even cast iron frying pans are being reproduced.

One of the keys to spotting the newer material is the rust. If it is orange in color and consists of small pinpoint flakes, forget it. Also, check paint patina. It should have a mellow tone from years of exposure to air. Bright paint should be suspect.

Cast iron is a favorite of the country collector. It evokes memories of the great open kitchen fireplaces and wood/coal burning stoves of our ancestors. Unfortunately, few discover what a great cooking utensil cast iron can really be.

Club: Griswold & Cast Iron Cookware Association, 54 Macon Ave., Asheville, NC 28801.

Newsletters: *Cast Iron Cookware News*, 28 Angela Ave., San Anselmo, CA 94960; *Kettles 'n Cookware,* Drawer B, Perrysburg, NY 14129.

Basin, 11-1/4" d, pitted, pinhole 40.00

Bottle Opener, Duff Norton Jacks, Pittsburgh, USA adv, 4-1/2" by 1-1/4" 70.00

Bottle Opener, Goose, 1-3/4" by 3-3/4" 75.00

Cardholder, elephant 65.00

Cuspidor, 13-1/2" l, turle, painted black, missing int. pan 95.00

Door Knocker, Basket of flowers, 4" by 3", oval 70.00

Door Knocker, Woodpecker, 3-3/4" by 2-1/2" 70.00

Door Stop, Boxer Dog, D.J. Murray Manufacturing Co., Wausau, WI, adv. 50.00

Door Stop, Roosting Hen 45.00

Ink Well, 5-1/2" h, stag's head, clear glass well 135.00

Mortar and Pestle, 6-3/4" h, flared foot 55.00

Lawn Sprinkler, frog, 4" by 4-1/2" . . . 75.00

Paperweight, Amish Couple, 4" by 1-1/2", red and black 70.00

Paperweight, Kansas Jayhawk, 3-3/4" by 2-1/2", marked Kansas on one side, Jayhawk on other 75.00

Pencil Holder, Penguin. 70.00

Pencil Holder, Three Bears 70.00

Plate, 2-7/8" d, two children with hoops, alphabet edge. 150.00

Scale, oval brass pan marked "Fairbanks" 145.00

Soap Dish, turtle. 70.00

Tobacco Cutter, emb John Finzer & Brothers, Louisville, KY 125.00

Trivet, 7-1/2" l 90.00

Trivet, 9" l, floral, star handle 75.00

Trivet, 9-1/2" l, George Washington . 75.00

Windmill Weight, rooster. 70.00

Cat Collectibles

It is hard to think of a collecting category that does not have one or more cat-related items in it. Chessie the Cat is railroad oriented; Felix is a cartoon, comic and toy collectible. There rests the problem. The poor cat collector is always competing with an outside collector for a favorite cat item.

Cat collectors are apparently as stubborn as their pets, because I have never seen a small cat collectibles collection. Also, unlike most dog collectibles collectors, cat collectors are more willing to collect objects portraying other breeds of cats than the one that they own.

Club: Cat Collectors, 33161 Wendy Dr., Sterling Heights, MI 48310.

Card Game, The Black Cat Fortune Telling Game, Parker Brothers, 1897, 24 playing cards and instruction sheet, orig box 100.00
Comic Book, Pat Sullivan's Felix the Cat, Toby Press, #36, 1953, 7" by 10-3/8" .8.00
Egg Cup, 3" h, black cat, Japan paper label 20.00
Kite, paper, Morris the Cat, Hi-Flier, 9-Lives Cat Food premium, "I Always Fly First Class," 29" w, 35-1/2" h 20.00
Little Golden Book, *Ruff and Reddy*, Harvey Eisenburg and Al White illus, written by Ann McGovern, first printed in 1959, 24 pgs 10.00
Match Holder, cat scene, ftd, marked "Wavecrest" 225.00
Mirror, pocket, White Cat Union Suits adv, 2-3/4" l, black and white, celluloid, cartoon illus, early 1900s 65.00
Pez, Tom & Jerry, marked "Made in Hong Kong," 1980s, 4-1/4" h Tom, 4-1/8" h Jerry, price each 10.00

Towel Holder, silk-screened print on aluminum, wire hangers, $45.

Pinback Button, Morris For President, multicolored photo portrait, bright red, white and blue border, 9-Lives Cat Food, 1988, 2-1/4" d 10.00
Planter, 6-3/4" h, kitten with basket, Hull 15.00
Print, 14" by 11", two cats in hat, titled "A Love Song," J. Ottmann Litho, 1894 . . . . 25.00
Puzzle, Little Roquefort and Percy Puss, frame tray format, die-cut cardboard, Terrytoons, Inc., E.E. Fairchild Corp., Rochester, NY #1600-s, late 1950s, 11" by 8-1/2" 20.00
Puzzle, Tom and Jerry, die-cut cardboard, copyright 1971 by Metro-Goldwyn-Mayer, Inc., 12" by 15-1/2" 12.00
Puzzle, Top Cat, frame-tray format, die-cut cardboard, #4457, Whitman Publishing Co., Hanna-Barbera Pictures, 1961, 10-3/8" by 14-1/2" 25.00
Salt and Pepper Shakers, pr, comical Siamese, paper label marked "Norcrest Japan," 4" h 10.00
Soakie, Felix the Cat, black, red and blue, 1980s, 10-1/4" h 12.00
Stuffed Toy, Kitten, Steiff, 1970s-80s, 12" l 15.00
Toothpick Holder, kitten and boot . . 10.00
Toy, Tailspin Tabby, Pop-Up Kritter, Fisher Price, No. 455, wood, c1940, 10-3/4" l 75.00

Tapestry, velour, rayon, waste cotton and cotton, made in Lebanon, 20" by 40", $10.

Celluloid

Celluloid is the trade name for a thin, tough, flammable material made of cellulose nitrate and camphor. Originally used for toilet articles, it quickly found a use as inexpensive jewelry, figurines, vases and other household items. In the 1920s and 1930s, it was used heavily by the toy industry.

Be on the look-out for dealers who break apart dresser sets and sell the pieces individually as a way of getting more money. Also, check any ivory or tortoise shell piece that is offered to you. Both were well-imitated by quality celluloid.

Animal Figures
Bulldog, 3-5/8" l 20.00
Elephant, 4" l 25.00
Fish, 1-1/2" l 12.00
Hippo, 4" l .20.00
Horse, 4-1/2" l 22.00
Rabbit, 3" h, floppy ears, sitting, radish in mouth, Japan 30.00

Jewelry
Pin, Fox 40.00
Pin, Girl, painted dec 68.00
Stickpin, pearlized pink 30.00

Other
Autograph Album, emb cov, dark turquoise, velvet binder, 19th C. . .25.00
Badge, Gene Autry, 1-1/4" d, Official Gene Autry Club, center portrait, black, white and orange, c1940 . . . . .65.00
Bookmark, Calendar, fabric insert, flower design, hand painted 20.00

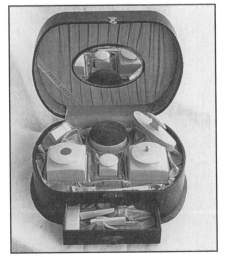

Dresser Set, French Ivory, $30.

**Jewelry Box, 2-1/2" by 4-1/2" by 5",
$125.**

Bookmark, University of Marurg in
    Germany, painted logo, 19th C . .25.00
Card, George Washington, ribbon tied,
    engraved portrait 30.00
Charm, Betty Boop, 1", tinted colors, brass
    loop at top, 1930s. 30.00
Clicker, Hasting's Bread adv 8.00
Clock, Cream colored, Art Deco,
    Telealarm Jr. 28.00
Clock, Green, speckled, 8" h, molded
    columns, cream trim, 1920. . . . . .30.00
Comb, tortoiseshell, blue
    rhinestones. 80.00
Crochet Hook 4.00
Crochet Hook Set, cream handle, blue,
    gold-lined case. 40.00
Desk Set, green, cream trim 85.00
Fan 30.00
Letter Opener, Black man's head, adv on
    blade 25.00
Letter Opener, Lion-shaped top, painted
    details. .67.00
Magnet, Scottie dog, 3/4", pr. 20.00
Manicure Set, travel, pink and white,
    six pcs .20.00
Man's Travel Set, wood grain accessories,
    mirror, burgundy soap dish 40.00
Mirror, blue 22.00
Napkin Ring, Scottie dog. 15.00
Nodder, donkey, 3" h. 30.00
Notepad, cream. 20.00
Photo Album, emb birds on cover,
    1895. . . . . .60.00
Razor, straight, black, marked "Torrey
    Razor Co., Worchester MA". 30.00
Recipe Butler, Art Deco, red and
    black. 60.00
Religious Statue, pink, Art Deco-style,
    metal medallion center, Milano,
    1930s 25.00
Ruler, Folding, marked "The Golden
    Rule". 15.00
Shaving Mirror, folding, brown and black,
    striped, milk glass insert, with real
    bristle shaving brush 65.00
Tape Measure, Cass Dairy Farm, Inc.,
    Jersey & Ayshire Milk. 28.00

Tape Measure, Sears Roebuck Plows,
    multicolored, David Bradley Plow
    illus. 75.00
Toy, Rattle, clown, 1900s 48.00
Toy, Roly-Poly 68.00

Cereal Boxes

There is no better example of a collectible category gone mad than cereal
boxes. Cereal boxes from the first half
of the 20th century sell from $15 to $50
range. Cereal boxes from the 1950s
through the 1970s can sell for $50 and
up. Where's the sense?

Club: Sugar-Charged Cereal Collectors, 92B N. Bedford St., Arlington, VA
22201.

Periodical: *Flake*, P.O. Box 481,
Cambridge, MA 02140.

Cheerios, Hall of Fun Jack Oakie,
    1949 . . . . 65.00
Cocoa Puffs, General Mills, front with
    aircraft carrier and jet launcher toy,
    cutout on back, 1950s. 65.00
40% Bran Flakes, Post, Li'l Abner Name
    Honest Abe's Sweetheart contest,
    1950s 65.00
Kellogg's Corn Flakes, sample size,
    c1920 . . . . 15.00
OK's, Kellogg's, Snack Pack, Brawny
    character on front, OK info on back,
    1960s 25.00
Quaker Muffets Shredded Wheat, 3" by 6"
    by 7", side panel adv "Authentic Model
    Civil War Cannon," 1960s. 40.00

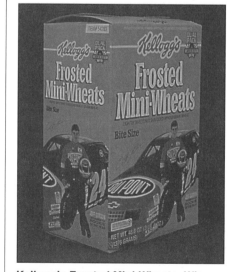

**Kellogg's Frosted Mini-Wheats, Win-
ston Cup Rookie of the Year Jeff Gordon, $15.**

Quaker Puffed Rice, 5 oz, 1919 . . . . 20.00
Rice Krispies, Kellogg's, Snack Pack,
    repeated red-lettered Kellogg's design,
    Snap, Crackle and Pop on front and
    back, 1960s. 25.00
Sugar Pops, Andy Devine and Guy
    Madison 85.00

Cereal Premiums

Forget cereal boxes. The fun rests
with the goodies inside the box that
you got for buying the cereal in the first
place. Cereal premiums have changed
a great deal over the past decade. No
self-respecting manufacturer in the
1950s would have included as their
premium a tube of toothpaste. Yuck!

Collectors make a distinction between premiums that came with the
box and those for which you had to
send away. The latter group is valued
more highly because the items are often more elaborate and better-made.

Club: Sugar-Charged Cereal Collectors, 92B N. Bedford St., Arlington, VA
22201.

Periodical: *Flake*, P.O. Box 481,
Cambridge, MA 02140.

Figures
Cap'n Crunch, 8" h, vinyl, 1971 . . . . 35.00
Crackle, Rice Krispies, jointed 15.00
Huckleberry Hound, plastic, removable
    head with secret storage space,
    1960s. 30.00

**Puzzle, die-cut cardboard, Quisp Cere-
al, $35.**

Wiggle Pictures, Walt Disney's Hippy the Hippo and Dumbo, Cheerios, price each, $4.

Puppets
Banana Splits, Bingo, plastic, 1969. .10.00
Snap, Crackle, Pop, Kellogg's Rice
    Krispies 25.00
Trix Rabbit, 12" h, cloth and vinyl,
    1960s .30.00

Rings
Captain Crunch, whistle, 1970s 45.00
Frankenberry, flicker, 1980s 75.00
Tom Mix Magnet Ring, Ralston, metal,
    1940s .100.00
Wheat Chex, decoder, paper,
    1940s .45.00
Wheaties, compass, 1940s 30.00

Other
Bowl, Tony The Tiger, Kellogg's Frosted
    Flakes, 5" d, figural, hard plastic, white,
    orange plastic feet-shape base,
    Kellogg's, 1981. . . . . .15.00
Car, Post Cereal, Chitty Chitty Bang Bang,
    plastic, two-tone, cardboard wings,
    1968 . . . . .30.00
Comic Book, Sugar Crisp, Baseball Facts
    & Fun, 52 pgs. 30.00
Cookie Cutter, Quaker Oats, standing
    bear, flatback, handle,
    yellow plastic 3.00
Decoder, Fruit Loops, 3" l, cutout, Toucan
    Sam, figural, plastic, 1970s 10.00
Decoder Card, Post, red and green .15.00
Doll, Crackle, Kellogg's Rice Krispies,
    15" h, cloth, 1930s 78.00
Doll, Mama Bear, Kellogg's. 75.00
Game, Quisp, Space Match Card Game,
    color illus box, 1968 . . . . .25.00
Glass, Frosted Flakes, Tony The
    Tiger. 12.00
Handbook, Quaker Puffed Wheat Sparkies
    and Rice Sparkies, Little Orphan Annie,
    Secret Guard, paper sheet, decoder,
    clicker, orig mailing envelope 90.00
Mug, Cheerios, plastic, three different
    black and white illus, 1950s 30.00
Postcard, Cheerios, Lone Ranger, 3" by 6",
    photo with signature, 1956. . . . . .10.00

Radio, Kellogg's Frosted Flakes, Tony the
    Tiger, 8" h, figural, plastic, 1970s 20.00
Record, Archies, 33-1/3 rpm, Jingle-
    Jangle, 1968-70 . . . . 5.00
Rocket Firing Star Fighter Jet and
    Exploding Light Tank, Cheerios,
    1950s 12.00
Sea Cycle, Cap'n Crunch, plastic, Cap'n
    Crunch and Seadog figure, rubber band
    powered, orig mailing box, unused,
    1960s 60.00
Songbook, Kellogg's Rice Krispies, Snap,
    Crackle and Pop, 1937 . . . . 5.00
Spoon, Kellogg's, Dennis the Menace,
    silver plate. 20.00
Wall Plaque, Cap'n Crunch, Oath of
    Allegiance, 8" by 10", color illus, paper,
    unused, 1960s 24.00
Wristwatch, chrome luster case, black
    leather straps, Sugar Bear image on
    dial, 1970s 75.00

Chase Chrome and Brass Company

The Chase Chrome and Brass Co., was founded in the late 1870s by Augustus S. Chase. Through numerous mergers and acquisitions, the company grew and helped it to expand its product line to chrome, copper, brass and other metals. Several name changes occurred until the company was sold as a subsidiary of Kennecott Corp., in its merger with Standard Oil in 1981. One of the most popular products this company made was the chrome Art Deco line which really appealed to housewives in the 1930-1942 period.

Chase items can be found with some really neat styling and are usual-

ly marked. Just like the aluminum wares, it does not need polishing and is becoming just as hot with today's collectors.

Club: Chase Collectors Society, 2149 W. Jibsail Loop, Mesa, AZ 85202.

Ashtray, Humpty Dump 125.00
Ashtray, Smokeless 75.00
Bank, plastic barrel, transparent, key-open
    lock 45.00
Bridge Scorer, 8" by 3-1/2" l, spring clip,
    brass 125.00
Candle Holders, pr, 1-3/4" by 3-3/8". 55.00
Cigar Humidor, holds 25 cigars . . .125.00
Cigarette Box, satin nickel finish, mounted
    on four ball bearings, wood veneer
    lining, top etched concentric
    circles .150.00
Cigarette Server and Ash Tray, black
    glass, 8" l, 4" w, three rests 110.00
Flower Pot Holder, saucer, 5-3/4" by
    4-1/2" 50.00
Skewers, 9-3/16" l, set of four 28.00
Table Bell, Brittany 80.00
Tray, Meridian, 7-7/8" d, 3/8v h 65.00
Vanity Mirror, 2-3/8", colored enameled
    back. 95.00
Vase, flared top, 3" by 9" 75.00
Zodiac Lamp, 12 signs of Zodiac displayed
    on center ring, blue center, brass stars,
    17" h 195.00

Children's Book Series

Most of these children's book series, often referred to as young adult books, are collected by series. Not surprisingly, books whose main character is male are generally collected by men—those with a heroine are collected by women. Obtaining a complete run of a particular series is possible and would make for an interesting collection. Happy hunting!

Cherry Ames, Helen Wells, author
At Hilton Hospital, #20, 1959 . . . . . . .7.50
Chief Nurse. 6.00
Department Store Nurse, 1956. . . . .16.00
Flight Nurse 7.00
Senior Nurse. 6.00

Dana Girl, Carolyn Keene, author
1957, *Winking Ruby Mystery*, #19 . .18.00
1959, *Haunted Lagoon*, #21 . . . . . . .18.00

Hardy Boys Series, Franklin Dixon, author
1928, *Shore Road Mystery*. 10.00

Merriwell Series, Burt L. Standish, author, Dick Meriwell's Test, No. 104, $15.

1929, *Secret of the Caves*. 10.00
1934, *Mark on the Door* 15.00
1939, *Twisted Claw*. 10.00
1953, *Crisscross Shadow* 15.00
1953, *Yellow Feather Mystery*. 10.00
1959, *Flickering Torch Mystery*, #22 .25.00
1959, *Hardy Boys' Detective
    Handbook*. 30.00

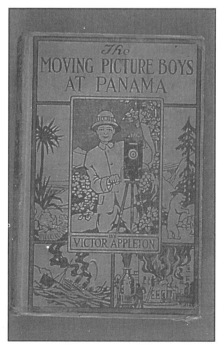

Moving Picture Boys Series, Victor Appleton, author, The Moving Picture Boys At Panama, $8.

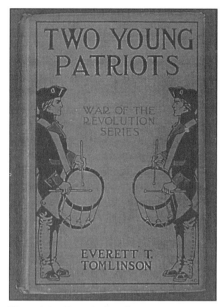

War of the Revolution Series, Everett T. Tomlinson, author, Two Young Patriots, $11.

Jerry Todd, Leo Edwards, author
1925, *Jerry Todd & the
    Talking Frog* 10.00
1925, *Jerry Todd & the Waltzing
    Hen*. 12.00
1964, *Riddle of the Frozen Fountain*,
    #26 . . . . 30.00

Nancy Drew, Carolyn Keene, author
1934, *Clue of the Broken Locket*,
    #11 . . . . 35.00
1936, *Mystery of the Ivory Charm*,
    #13 . . . . 20.00
1937, *Haunted Bridge*, #15 . . . . 75.00
1941, *Hidden Staircase*, #2 . . . . 45.00
1943, *Clue in the Jewel Box*, #20 . . 50.00
1944, *Secret of the Old Attic*, #21 . . 30.00
1949, *Clue of the Leaning Chimney*,
    #26 . . . . 40.00
1959, *Secret of the Golden Pavilion*,
    #36 . . . . 50.00

Tom Swift, Victor Appleton, author
1910, *Tom Swift & His Motorcycle*. . 15.00
1928, *Tom Swift & His Talking
    Pictures*. 50.00
1934, *Tom Swift & His Ocean Airport* 5.00
1941, *Tom Swift & His Magnetic
    Silencer*. 55.00
1954, *Tom Swift & His Atomic Earth
    Blaster*, #5. . . . . 10.00
1958, *Tom Swift Jr. & the Race for the
    Moon*. 15.00
1961, *Tom Swift & Electric
    Hydrolung* 12.00

Children's Collectibles

Mothers of the world unite. This category is for you. The children who used it hardly remember it. It's the kind of stuff that keeps your children forever young in your mind.

There is virtually nothing written about this collecting category, so what to collect is wide open. One collector I know has hundreds of baby planters.

Books
All About Cinderella, Gruelle/Johnny,
    1916 . . . . .90.00
Adventures of Humpty Dumpty, 1877,
    baking soda giveaway 28.00
Child's Garden Of Verses, Robert Louis
    Stevenson, 1908 . . . . .85.00
Little Red Riding Hood, litho, Star Soap
    giveaway 28.00
Rhymes For Kindly Children,
    Fairmont/Ethel, 1928 . . . . .85.00
The Three Bears, Platt & Munk 15.00

Cookbooks
General Foods: The New Jell-O-Book of
    Surprises, 1930 . . . . .7.00
Kenner's Easy Bake Cook Book,
    1964 . . . . .7.00
Kitchen Fun: A Cook Book For
    Children .7.00
Knox Gelatin: Dainty Desserts for Dainty
    People, 1924 . . . . .6.00
Pillsbury's Cook Book, 1920. . . . . . . .6.00

Tea Set
Britannia, emb design, flowers and
    butterfly emb saucer 150.00
Children's Tea Set, Dutch girl and boy
    skating deco, Ohio Art Co.,
    1939 .125.00
Royal Dresden Rose Tea Set, metal, white,
    green, gold trim, roses, Wolverine
    Supply and Manu. Co. 85.00

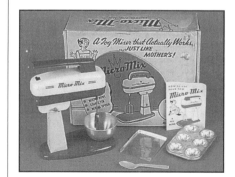

Toy, Micro Mix, model #MX48, $42.

Tea-Time Plastic Dishes, molded, hard plastic, Columbia, USA 40.00

Toy Dishes

Holly Hobbie, boxed set 30.00
Mini Party Set, Tupperware, boxed set, 1980 . . . . .20.00
Spice O' Life Set, Corningware replica, plastic, boxed set 30.00

Toys

Baby Jeanette Ice Cream Maker, metal, 5-1/2" h, 5-1/5" d, c1920-30 . . . .100.00
Begging Scottie, 6-1/4" h, windup, Japan, c1950 . . . . .30.00
Drummer Bear, 6" h, Japan, c1950. .35.00
Musical Top, 6" l, litho tin, Ohio Art, c1960 . . . . .12.00
Rabbit Cart, 9-1/2" h, 10" l, pull toy, Fisher Price, c1960 . . . . .75.00
Typewriter, 8-1/2" l, push type, Simplex, c1950-60 . . . . .30.00

Other

Baby Record Book, C. Burd illus on each page 32.00
Baptism Set, dress and bonnet 65.00
Bed, 29" by 48" by 30-1/2", turned posts and legs, four rails with lattice slats, solid board bottom, old green paint over red 75.00
Bonnet, baby's, Victorian, white 38.00
Booties, Victorian, leather, blue 30.00
Cape, Victorian, white cotton lace, 5-yr size 45.00
Cereal Set, nursery rhyme, amber, divided plate, Humpty Dumpty on mug and bowl, Tiara 125.00
Christening Dress, 40" l 45.00
Coffee Set, Three Little Kittens, aluminum 65.00
Coin Purse, beadwork, slightly rusted clasp 35.00
Cradle, 35-1/2" l, country, pine, refinished 125.00
Dish, 8" d, baby's, divided, three sections, Patriot China 50.00
Mug, Little Miss Muffet, colorful transfers and verse 45.00
Mug, Victorian, re-silvered, engraved 75.00
Doll Feeding Set, Doll-E-Nurser, 21 pieces, Amsco, 1940, boxed set 150.00
Feeding Dish, bunnies, puppies, Nippon .39.00
Jewelry, bangle bracelet, child size, sterling, three dangling hearts . . .75.00
Plate, 8" d, nursery rhymes, green glass 26.00
Pram Coverlette, quilted silk, satin rosebud dec 55.00

Record, Lullaby Time, Little Golden Record, 45 rpm, GL272, includes Twinkle Twinkle Little Star, Rock a Bye Baby and Now I Lay Me Down To Sleep 4.00
Scale, baby, pink, 1940s 38.00
Silverware Box, wooden, 4-3/4" h, 2-3/8" w, English design, top metal plate . 150.00
Spoon, baby, curved handle, kitten dec, Rogers 35.00
Wash Bowl, blue, Dutch children dec 50.00
Wood Holder with Utensils, red wood handle, Germany, 1900 . . . . . . 100.00

Chintz China

Chintz—or "All-Over Floral," as it is known in England and Australia—looks very like wall paper on a plate, and it was one of the hottest collectibles of 1996. Chintz was first made in the early 1800s and continued in production until the mid 1960s. Although copied by the Germans, Czechs and Japanese, the chintz made in various Staffordshire factories is the most sought after. The Victorian chintz is widely collected in England, but in North America it is the 1930-1960 chintz which is commanding increasingly high prices. Factories such as James Kent, Crown Ducal and Lord Nelson produced a number of chintz patterns, but Grimwades' Royal Winton was the pre-eminent producer and is considered by most collectors today to be the "Cadillac" of chintz.

Although Grimwades produced more than 65 different chintz patterns and the other companies far fewer, some of the patterns are much more collectible than others, and new collec-

Grimwades, Royal Winton, dish, Hazel, 8" l, $195.

Lefton, Rose Chintz, tidbit tray, two-tier, 9-1/2" d, $55.

tors should spend some time learning which patterns are considered most desirable. Most of the Royal Winton, James Kent and Elijah Cotton pieces have the pattern name in the backstamp, making identification easier.

When the chintz was sold originally, it was cheap and cheerful. It can turn up anywhere, since it was sold in great quantity throughout North America. Although a breakfast set which retailed for $4.50 in 1951 may be selling for anything up to $1,500 today, a new California collector managed to pick up an Evesham breakfast set for $40 at a local flea market! If the English chintz is too expensive, look for the Japanese and Czechoslovakian copies, which are much cheaper.

Advisors: Linda Eberle, P.O. Box 6126, Folsom, CA 95630, (916) 985-6732; Susan Scott, 882 Queen St. West, Toronto, Ontario M6J 1G3 Canada, (416) 657-8278.

Club: The Chintz Collectors Club, P.O. Box 6126, Folsom, CA 95630.

A.G. Richardson & Co. Ltd.

Bowl, Blue Chintz, lily with black int. 125.00
Bowl, Florida, 8" w, octagonal 450.00
Jug, 7", straight-sided, Ivory Chintz 350.00
Plate, 19", octagonal, Purple Chintz 195.00
Vase, 6", trumpet, Ascot 175.00

Elijah Cotton, Lord Nelson

Bud Vase, Rosetime 135.00
Cup and Saucer, Heather 75.00

Creamer and Sugar on Tray
Beauty 250.00
Jug, 5" d, Marina 200.00
Jam pot with Liner, Royal Brocade . .75.00
Teapot, 6-cup, Skylark 395.00

Grimwades, Royal Winton
Breakfast Set, teapot, creamer and sugar,
toast rack, cup and tray,
Balmoral 1,250.00
Bud Vase, Nantwich 140.00
Cake Plate, open handles, Royalty .250.00
Compote, ftd, all-over pattern,
Peony .100.00
Condiment Set, salt, pepper, cov mustard
and tray, Hazel 275.00
Cup and Saucer, Spring Glory 60.00
Dish, Beeston, canoe-shaped 325.00
Dish, Hazel, 8" 195.00
Jam pot, ceramic lid and liner,
Julia 350.00
Nut Dish, 3-1/2", Joyce-Lynn 65.00
Plate, 9" sq, June Roses 195.00
Sandwich Tray, 12" by 7",
Somerset 195.00
Teapot, Chelsea, Albans-shape,
4-cup .800.00
Teapot, Summertime, stacking 950.00

James Kent Ltd.
Bonbon Dish, 5", ruffled edge, Apple
Blossom 95.00
Bud Vase, Apple Blossom 125.00
Butter Dish, cov, rect, Dubarry 175.00
Coffee Pot, Florita 900.00
Creamer and Sugar on Tray, White
Hydrangea 250.00
Jam pot, ceramic lid, Mille Fleurs . .175.00

W.R. Midwinter, Ltd.
Cake Plate, three-tier, Brama 175.00
Cake Stand, chrome base, Coral . .125.00
Sugar Shaker, chrome top, Lorna Doon
(a.k.a. Bird Chintz) 250.00

Christmas

Of all holiday collectibles, Christmas is the most popular. It has grown so large as a category that many collectors specialize in only one area, e.g., Santa Claus figures or tree ornaments. Anything Victorian is "hot." The Victorians popularized Christmas. Many collectors love to recapture that spirit. However, prices for Victorian items, from feather trees to ornaments, are quickly moving out of sight.

This is a field where knowledgeable individuals can find bargains. Learn to tell a late 19th/early 20th century ornament from a modern example. A surprising number of dealers cannot. If a dealer thinks a historic ornament is modern and prices it accordingly, he is actually playing Santa Claus by giving you a present. Ho, Ho, Ho!

Club: Golden Glow of Christmas Past, 6401 Winsdale St., Minneapolis, MN 55427.

Newsletter: *I Love Christmas*, P.O. Box 5708, Coralville, IA 52241.

Candy Containers
Ball, silver foil with bow,
West Germany 14.00
Elf, cylinder type, wire neck, 8" 25.00
House, cardboard, cotton Santa
on roof 75.00
Santa, Cardboard, 13" h, spring head,
West Germany 60.00
Santa, Fur beard, felt robe, holding feather
tree, separates at waist,
Germany 575.00
Santa Face, hanging tree ornament,
3" d 35.00
Snowman, 7-1/2" h, papier-mâché, West
Germany, 1950s 22.00

Figures
Boot, 5-1/2" h 24.00
Santa, 4-1/4" h, sitting on
wood sleigh 95.00

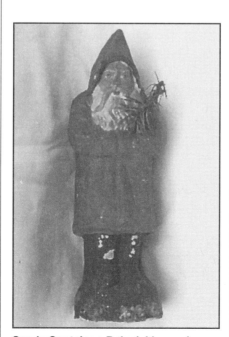

Candy Container, Belsnickle, papier-mâché, red robe, holding feather tree, Germany, $450.

Postcard, emb, divided back, c1920, $3.

Santa, 6-1/4" h, fur beard and hair,
chime hat 70.00
Santa, 7" h, papier-mâché, red coat, fur
beard, squeaks 55.00
Santa, 8-1/2" h, felt, press me voice. 95.00
Santa, 9-1/2" h, Santa with tree,
blue 85.00
Santa, 16" h, red coat, fur beard,
Germany 185.00
Snowman, Carrot nose, 7" h 28.00
Snowman, papier-mâché, set of six,
MIB 225.00

Greeting Cards
"Christmas Blessing," leather type, S.
Hildersheimer & Co. 5.00
"Merry Christmas From Our House,"
American, 1930s 2.50
"Wishing You A Happy Christmas," sepia
tones, Raphael Tuck & Sons,
London 3.00

Ornaments
Ball, miniature, boxed set of 12 . . . . 12.00
Barton Cross, Reed, 1974 . . . . .38.00
Cat in Shoe, glass 38.00
Clown, glass, painted face,
Germany 38.00
Flamingo, blue mercury glass 40.00
French Hens, Towle, 1973 . . . . .34.00
Kugel, cobalt blue 55.00
Santa, figural, honeycomb 8.00
Snake 32.00

Putz Items

Animal, Cow, 3" h, celluloid, brown, USA 7.00
Animal, Dog, 1" h, celluloid, brown, marked "Japan" 5.00
Animal, Horse, 3-1/2" h, brown and tan, rubber, USA 7.00
Animal, Sheep, 1-3/4" h, composition, wool coat, wood legs 20.00
Bank, 3" h, chalk, white, marked "Made in Japan" .10.00
Church, 6" h, cardboard, litho, frosted roof 8.00
Fence, 2-1/2" h, eight 6" sections, wood, red and green 30.00
House, 2-1/2" h, cardboard, frosted roof, marked "Japan" 4.50
House, 3" h, log type, frosted roof, marked "Germany" 10.00
Wagon, wood, driver and horses, Germany 38.00

Tree

5-1/2" h, wire base, glass balls 18.00
6" h, Japan 14.00
9" h, brush, green, glass bead dec, red base 15.00
15" h, cellophane 15.00
18" h, feather, green, white base, Germany, 1920s 150.00
60" h, feather, Germany 295.00
Utensil Set, spoon and fork, A Michelsen, large tablespoon size, sterling silver, heavy gold plate, Cloisonné handles
1925, filigreed poinsettia 90.00
1946, holly leaves and berries 85.00
1949, Christmas wreath and candles 85.00
1953, white angels, blue and gold. . .85.00
1955, green and red spots 75.00
1966, Madonna riding on donkey . . .75.00
1967, gold sunburst pattern 80.00
1968, modern Madonna and Child . .80.00

Other

Bell, honeycomb, red, unused, set of four .19.00
Book, *A Northern Christmas*, Kent Rockwell, American Artists Group Inc., 1941 . . . . .7.00
Card Book, flocked, 1950s 20.00
Creche, paper, 3D, American, 1942 . . . . .15.00
Doll, Santa Claus 32.00
Light Bulb, Chinese Lantern, milk glass, Japan 10.00
Light Bulb, House, milk glass, pink and white, Japan 10.00
Light Set, Noma Bubble Lite, boxed set .27.00
Nativity Scene, plastic, 3-3/4" by 4-3/4", Hong Kong 12.00

Pinback Button, 1-1/4" d, Santa Claus, celluloid, multicolored, steering auto, c1911 . . . . 40.00
Planter, sleeping Santa sitting in chair, 5" by 6-1/2" by 4-3/4" 18.00
Punch Bowl Set, Santa, includes eight cups 50.00
Postcard, hold to light type 35.00
Reflectors, copper foil, Germany, set of 10 . . . . 20.00
Snow Globe, chimney, red brick, water-filled fireplace, Santa, gifts, tree 20.00
Toy, squeaker, Santa, fur beard, 7-1/2" h, Germany 45.00
Tree Stand, revolving 20.00
Tree Topper, angel, lighted, orig box 18.00

Christmas and Easter Seals

Collecting Christmas and Easter Seals is one of the most inexpensive "stamp" hobbies. Sheets usually sell for between 50 cents and $1. Most collectors do not buy single stamps, except for the very earliest Christmas seals.

Club: Christmas Seal and Charity Stamp Society, P.O. Box 39696, Minneapolis, MN 55439.

Cigarette and Cigar

Cigarette products contain a warning that they might be hazardous to your health. Cigarette and cigar memorabilia should contain a warning that they may be hazardous to your pocketbook. With each passing year, the price for cigarette and cigar-related material goes higher and higher. If it ever stabilizes and then drops, a number of collectors are going to see their collections go up in smoke.

The vast majority of cigarette and cigar material is two-dimensional, from advertising trade cards to posters. Seek out three-dimensional pieces. There are some great cigarette and cigar tins.

Clubs: Cigarette Pack Collectors Association, 61 Searle St., Georgetown,

MA 01833; International Seal, Label & Cigar Band Society, 8915 East Bellevue St., Tucson, AZ 85715.

Box Labels

Acristo Cigars, inner lid, roses flanked by children 9.00
Alexander The Great Cigars, inner lid .16.00
Baffin Cigars, inner lid, Arctic explorer and ship 15.00
Bella De Cuba Cigars, inner lid, woman playing guitar 22.00
William Tell Cigars, 5" by 5" 10.00

Cigar Boxes

King Carlos Cigars 12.00
Marksman Cigars, cardboard, two men shooting guns 25.00
Old Virginia Cheroots Tobacco 25.00
Two Orphans Cigars 10.00

Playing Cards

Harley Davidson Cigarettes, two packs cigarettes with free playing cards 10.00
Kool Milds 8.00
Marlboro Cigarettes, logo, red and white 9.00
Newport 3.00

Signs

All Jacks Cigarettes, tin, 1940s 35.00
Avalon Cigarettes, 15" by 10", paper 10.00
Black Cat Cigarettes 150.00
Cabinet Cigar Co., 18" by 22", cardboard, Washington and cabinet illus. 60.00
Call Again, 5 Cent Cigar, 7" by 16", red, white and blue, cardboard 14.00
Camel Cigarettes 10.00

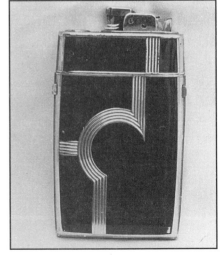

Cigarette Case and Lighter, Art Deco, green enamel and chrome, Evans, 2-1/2" w, 4-1/4" h, $20.

Cigarette Holder, glass, etched roses, Depression era, $45.

Chancellor Cigar, 12" by 36", porcelain 140.00

El Dallo Cigars, 14" by 18", paper. . .30.00

Eventual 5 Cent Cigar, 7" by 20", red and green, cardboard, 1920s 14.00

Lucky Strike, 21" by 10", litho cardboard, framed 120.00

Omar Cigarettes, cardboard 20.00

Red Man Cigars, 10" by 6", litho paper 40.00

Reinken's Havana Cigars, tin, 14" d .40.00

RG Sullivan's 7-20-4 Cigars, porcelain, red, white and yellow on black . . .70.00

Zira Cigarettes, 17" by 14", paper, 1912 . . . . .90.00

Thermometers

Dry Slitz Cigars, 38" by 8", enameled 155.00

El Belmont Havana Cigars, 9" d, dial, paper face 10.00

Marvels Cigarettes 90.00

Portuondo Cigars, wood, black and red 10.00

Tins

Bayuk Cigars, emb 25.00

Edwin Cigars, paper label, round, 1920s 20.00

Home Run Tubac A Cigarettes, slip lid, 1950 . . . . .30.00

Red Dot Cigars, square. 50.00

Robert Fulton Cigars, 6" by 6" by 4"155.00

Sir Haig Cigars, 5" by 6" 125.00

Sunset Trail Cigars 175.00

Two Orphans Cigars 50.00

Other

Apron, Chesterfield Cigarettes, cotton canvas 25.00

Ashtray, Chesterfield Cigarettes, tin, 6" l. 20.00

Ashtray, Player's Navy Cut Tobacco, ceramic, sailor illus, c1940 . . . . . 23.00

Bottle Holder, Camel, 3-D, Camel Joe, vinyl head 10.00

Bubble Gum Cigars, Win With Dick, Presidential Favorites 30.00

Candy Cigarettes, Lucky Strike 5.00

Chair, Cross-Cut Cigarettes, folding, wood 125.00

Cigar, Buster Brown. 7.00

Cigar Cutter, Harvard Cigars, windup, Harvard boy on front 120.00

Cigar Cutter, Master Cigar, cast iron, key wind 150.00

Cigarette Case, Elgin, white finish, enamel front, horse head illus 40.00

Cigarette Case, Havone, sterling silver, signet shield, push spring opener. 65.00

Cigarette Holder, with mouth piece, sterling silver 25.00

Cigarette Pack, Fatima Turkish Cigarettes, empty 2.00

Cigar Holder, sterling silver, gold-lined receiver. 30.00

Display, Helmar Cigarettes, cardboard, die-cut, cowgirl lighting cowboy's cigarette 125.00

Key Chain, Muriel Cigars 10.00

Lunch Box, Green Turtle Cigars, tin 275.00

Magazine Ad, Pall Mall, 1919 . . . . . . 5.00

Match Book Cover, Marlboro 7.50

Match Safe, United Cigar, book-shape 55.00

Mirror, Rajah Cigars, 10" by 26" . . . 20.00

Note Pad, Francie Wilson Havana Cigars, black-and-white portrait, cigar text inside cov, early 1900s 15.00

Pamphlet, Kool, Presidential Election, 1964 . . . . 15.00

Pinback Button, Bill Dugan Cigar, multicolored, 1900 . . . . 8.00

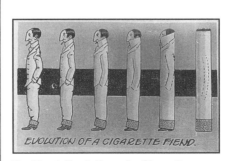

Postcard, Evolution of a Cigarette Fiend, $9.

Pin Cushion, Pinzon All Havana Cigar 61.00

Roulette Game, Sarony Cigarettes, tin, man illus, spinner missing 20.00

Ruler, Philip Morris, plastic, color, bellboy illus, 1940s 22.00

Sheet Music, Cigarettes, Whiskey & Wild, Wild Women 15.00

Sheet Music, Smoke Gets In Your Eyes 10.00

Tip Tray, El Ricardo Havana Cigars, 4" d, colorful illus, 1910 . . . . . . .125.00

Toy, Lark, windup 40.00

Cigarette Lighters

Cigarette lighters come in all shapes and sizes. Collections could be assembled focusing on several different categories, i.e., flat advertising lighters, figural lighters or even figural advertising lighters. The possibilities are endless. Buy lighters in good condition only. Scratches and/or missing parts greatly detract from a lighter's value. Remember, cigarette lighters were mass-produced and therefore plentiful.

Clubs: International Lighter Collectors, 136 Circle Dr., Quitman, TX 75783; Pocket Lighter Preservation Guild & Historical Society, Inc., P.O. Box 1054, Addison, IL 60101.

Advertising

Denver Police Union, butane, red, with holder, Bic Pen Corp., c1978 . . . .5.00

Dodge Trucks, bakelite, figural oil drum, red, c1940 . . . . .15.00

Commemorative, 1939 New York World's Fair, $250.

Kool, metal, figural penguin, c1930. .75.00
Lucky Strike, chromium, painted,
   c1950 . . . . .10.00
Marlboro, butane, black and red,
   c1993 . . . . .15.00
Salem, chromium, slim, Zippo, c1991,
   orig box 15.00
Varga Girl, 1935, pewter, chromium finish,
   tin gift box, c1993 . . . . .20.00
Yellow Pages, Zippo 150.00
Zippo 60th Anniversary, chromium, tin gift
   box, c1992 . . . . .20.00

Art Deco
Electro-Match, plastic, black, gold trim,
   Korex Co. 10.00
Grecian, chromium, tortoise enamel .30.00

Electric
Solar, with instructions, Lyman Meta
   Products, c1980 . . . . .5.00
Table model, glass, jockey on horse,
   figural top 35.00

Figural
Camel, metal, c1930 . . . . .25.00
Book, plastic, uses batteries, butane lighter
   center 15.00
Cowboy Boot, Evans 20.00
Elephant, metal, c1935 . . . . .25.00
Golf Clubs and Bag, brass, Negbaur,
   c1939 . . . . .40.00
Horse, chromium, butane, c1988 . . .15.00
Knight, Occupied Japan 50.00
Lion, silvered brass, April 12, 1912 patent
   date 50.00
Penguin, silver-plated, c1960 . . . . .40.00
Poodle, metal, poodle dog handle,
   c1960 . . . . .10.00
Saxophone, butane, 1990 . . . . .10.00
Stove, brass, c1950 . . . . .10.00
Swan, chromium, c1960 . . . . .10.00
Telegraph, battery, butane, plastic,
   brass and wood 20.00
Telephone, chromium,
   Occupied Japan 80.00
Television, Swank, c1960 . . . . .15.00
Tiger, metal, 2-1/8" h, 3" w, c1935 . .25.00
Torpedo, plastic, green 15.00
Wooden Shoe, hp, Holland, c1940 . .15.00

Miniature
Leather, attached key chain 20.00
Mother of Pearl 25.00

Other
Pocket Lighter/Flashlight, chromium,
   leather, Aurora, c1960 . . . . .15.00
Penciliter, chromium, bakelite, Occupied
   Japan, 1949 . . . . .40.00

Circus

Traveling tent circuses were an exciting event in rural towns across the country—evidence the large amount of memorabilia left behind.

I keep threatening to take my son to see the great annual circus parade in Milwaukee, featuring the equipment from the Circus World Museum in Baraboo, Wis. I need him to be my traveling companion because my wife, Connie, wants nothing to do with my circus fantasies. She insists that living with me is all the circus she needs.

Clubs: Circus Fans Association of America, P.O. Box 59710, Potomac, MD 20859; Circus Historical Society, 3477 Vienna Court, Westerville, OH 43081.

Calendar, "Season's Greetings, Helen and
   Karl Wallenda," multicolor, 1977, 7-1/4"
   by 12-1/4" 10.00
Greeting Card, "1925-1926 Greetings
   From Ringling Bros. and Barnum &
   Bailey Combined Shows," multicolor,
   heavy paper 40.00
Magazine, Cole Bros. Circus, America's
   Favorite Show, 1942, multicolor cov,
   34 pgs, 8-1/4" by 11" 30.00
Map, U.S., shows circus route, black and
   white, 7" by 5" 25.00
Mechanical Drawing, Ringling Bros. and
   Barnum & Bailey Circus big top, two
   plan views, 45" by 30" 65.00
Menu, "Fourth of July, Ringling Bros. and
   Barnum & Bailey Combined, The
   World's Largest Amusement Institution
   at Home on the Nation's Birthday,
   Bridgeport, CT, 1920," 6-1/4" by
   9-1/2" 20.00

Booklet, Barker's "Komic" Picture Souvenir, Part 2, Barker's Liniment adv, black-and-white illus, color-litho covers, 52 pgs, 9-1/2" by 6", $35.

Newspaper, *Sarasota Herald-Tribune*,
   circus edition, Sarasota, FL, Friday,
   March 24, 1944, "Circus Comes to
   Town," eight pgs 30.00
Photograph, Bird's eye view of circus
   grounds, including big top, black and
   white, 10-1/4" by 13", creased
   and torn 7.00
Photograph, Ringling Brothers Barnum &
   Bailey Combined Circus group shot,
   sepia tone, 12" by 20",
   several creases 45.00
Poster, Clyde Beatty-Cole Bros. Combined
   Circus, The World's Largest Circus,
   Clyde Beatty in Person, Roland Butler,
   lion tamer, multicolor, 19" by 26". 85.00
Poster, Hoxie Bros. Old Time Circus Land,
   One Mile West of Walt Disney World,
   multicolor view of circus grounds and
   big top, 20" by 27" 60.00
Program, Ringling Bros. and Barnum &
   Bailey Combined Shows, 1923 season,
   14 pgs, illus, black and white, 6-3/4"
   by 10" .30.00
Route Card, Barnum & Bailey, Greatest
   Show on Earth, 1918 season,
   permanent address and winter
   quarters, Bridgeport, CT, lists dates,
   towns, states, R.R. and miles,
   multicolor, 9" by 15-1/2" 75.00
Tickets, Clyde Beatty-Cole Bros.
   Combined Circus, 1960 season, issued
   by FFR Brown, black and red, 5-1/2" by
   2", price for pair 65.00

Clickers

If you need a clicker, you would probably spend hours trying to locate a modern one. I am certain they exist. You can find a clicker at a flea market in a matter of minutes. As an experiment, I tried looking up the word in a dictionary. It was not there. Times change. Clickers made noise, a slight sharp sound. I believe their principal purpose was to drive parents crazy. I understand they played a major role at parochial school, but cannot attest to the fact, since I attended public school.

Advertising
Blank, tin, gold luster flashing, young boy
   holding display board designed for
   advertising insert, c1930s 15.00
Buster Brown Shoes, litho tin, multicolored
   Buster and Tige image, 1930s . . .45.00
Castles Ice Cream, litho tin, blue and white,
   Kirchof Co., 1930s 25.00

Advertising, Fort Pitt Br'g Company, Sharpsburg, PA, litho tin, green and red, yellow ground, $15.

Phoenix Socks, litho tin, red, white and
blue 8.00
Poll Parrot Shoes, litho tin, traditional red,
green and yellow, Kirchof Co.,
1930s 20.00
Reading Bone Fertilizer, celluloid 8.00
Twinkie Shoes, litho tin, multicolored
image of Twinkie elf standing on
mushroom, green ground, tiny added
inscription "Made by Hamilton-Brown
Shoe Co," FL Rand Co., 1930s . .20.00
VG Prezels, litho tin, blue, white and yellow
image of clown playing musical
instrument resembling tuba but formed
from large pretzel, pale blue ground,
sponsored by "VG Prezels," Kirchof
Co., 1930s 15.00
Weather Bird Shoes, litho tin, yellow, black
and red, Kirchof Co., 1930s 22.50

Western Theme, full-color art, Kirchof Co., 1950s, 2-1/2" l

Bronco rider. 12.00
Cowboy and spurs, yellow ground . .18.00
Cowboy on fence rail. 15.00
Cowboy portrait, guns drawn, yellow
ground .15.00
Cowgirl portrait, three scattered ranch
brand symbols, blue ground. 22.50
Galloping horse. 15.00
Indian portrait, red ground. 20.00
Indian seated, holding bow, tribal design
pattern, blue ground. 27.50
Indian spear fisherman in canoe. . . .25.00
Rodeo rider on bucking bull 20.00

Other

Halloween, litho tin, black and white jack
o'lantern and witch tending bonfire illus,
orange ground, Kirchof Co.,
1950s-60s. 12.00
Little Orphan Annie, Mysto-Snapper
Membership Badge, litho tin, red, white
and blue, issued in 1941 as part of
Secret Guard membership kit. . . 65.00
Political, "Click with Dick (Nixon)," litho tin,
blue and white, 2-1/2" l 15.00

Clocks

Look for clocks that are fun (have motion actions) or that are terrific in a decorating scheme (a school house clock in a country setting). Clocks are bought to be seen and used.

Avoid buying any clock that does not work. You do not know whether it is going to cost $5, $50 or $500 to repair. Are you prepared to risk the higher numbers? Likewise, avoid clocks with extensively damaged cases. There are plenty of clocks in fine condition awaiting purchase.

Club: National Association of Watch and Clock Collectors, Inc., 514 Poplar St., Columbia, PA 17512.

Advertising

AC Fire Ring Spark Plugs, plastic, round,
black, orange, yellow and cream,
"Change Now," 16" d 150.00

Character, Mickey Mouse, Ingersoll, wind-up, 1934, 2-1/4" h, 1-1/2" sq face, $950.

Calumet Baking Powder, wood case, molded top, glazed front, gold lettering "Time To Buy Calumet Baking Powder "Best by Test," shaped and bracketed base, minor soiling, 38" h, 18" w 350.00
Coca-Cola, wood case, cove molded top, glazed front, gold hands and lettering "Coca-Cola In Bottles," shaped and bracketed base, worn keyhole, new gold lettering, 34-1/2" h, 18" w. . 275.00
Duquesne Pilsener Beer, round, reverse glass face, man holding glass of beer, red, gold and blue, missing one cover on back, minor rust around rim, paint flaking from face, c1955, 14-1/2" d 50.00
Wetherill's Atlas Paints, "Estab 1807," electric, octagonal case, neon light-up, black and yellow, soiling and scratches, cracked and repaired plastic cover behind glass, 18" d 375.00
WNAI Dial 1810 KC, Betty Lee Restaurant, electric, round, neon, green illumination, black and white lettering, paint loss around rim, 21" d. . . .325.00

Character, alarm

Cinderella, 2-1/2" by 4-1/2" by 4", windup, white metal case, orig box, Westclox 50.00
Donald Duck, 2" by 4-1/2" by 4-1/2", metal case, light blue, orig box, Bayard. 250.00
Mickey Mouse, 2" by 4" by 4-1/2", plastic case, Ingersoll, 1949 . . . . .250.00
Popeye and Swee' Pea, ivory enameled steel case, color illus on dial, Smiths, c1968. . . . . .100.00
Roy Rogers, windup, metal case, animated, Ingraham, c1951. . . .300.00
Strawberry Shortcake, orig box 25.00

Other

Alarm, metal case, 10-1/4" h, Seth Thomas, 1910-1920 . . . . .50.00
Banjo, 17 5/8" h, inlaid mahogany case, eagle finial, New Haven Clock Co., c1920. . . . . .150.00
Beehive, 5-1/4" h, brass, porcelain dial, Chelsea, c1900 . . . . .50.00
Cuckoo, 5" by 4" by 1-3/4", pressed log design, leaves, flowers, nest of birds, brass spring pendulum, Keebler Clock Co., Philadelphia 90.00
Electric, chrome, 5" by 5", General Electric, 1920s. .80.00
Figural, Refrigerator, 8-1/2" h, white metal, GE label, Warren Telechron Co., Ashland, MA 185.00
Figural, Ship, walnut hull, chrome-plated sails and rigs, lighted portholes, United Clock Co., 1955. . . . . .90.00

Kitchen, Russel Wright, gray and
     white 45.00
Mantel, Fruitwood, Chelsea, c1910. .80.00
Mantel, Rosewood, 10-1/2" h, veneered
     case, Seth Thomas, c1880 . . . . .75.00
School House, Mahogany, 24" h, veneered
     case, Waterbury Clock Co.,
     c1890 . . . . .200.00
School House, Oak, 19-1/2" h,
     orig label, Sessions Clock Co.,
     1915-1920 . . . . .300.00

Clothes Sprinklers

Before steam irons, clothes requiring ironing had to be manually damp-
ened with water. Some housewives
used soda-pop bottles or other common bottles, with sprinkler caps attached, while others owned more
decorative figural bottles made especially for this purpose. These are the
bottles that are now sought after by
collectors willing to pay $10 and up for
the more common examples and as
much as several hundred dollars for
the extremely rare bottles. It is estimated that close to 100 different sprinkle
bottles were manufactured.

The sprinkle bottle had a cap with
several holes (on rarer bottles, the
head was the cap) to allow controlled
dampening. In addition to the sprinkle
bottle, the well-equipped laundry room
had a wetter-downer, which had a single hole for moistening large pieces of
laundry. The Dutch Boy sprinkler and
the Dutch Girl wetter-downer were
sold as a set.

Most sprinkler bottles are ceramic
or glass, but a few are plastic, such as
the ladies known as "Merry Maids."
There are many variations of sprinkle
bottles, the most common being the
green and yellow "Sprinkle Plenty"
Chinaman, the gray elephant and sadirons. Others are much harder to find,
such as the Kitchen Prayer Lady, the
Dachshund and the Fireman.

Advisors: Loretta Anderson, 1208
Lakeshore Dr., Rockwall, TX 75087,
(214) 771-9636; Al Little, 151 Hwy.
173, P.O. Box 288, Antioch, IL 60002,
(847) 395-7700.

Cats
Black, 7-1/2" 115.00

Rooster, metal and cork stopper, $100.

Siamese, Various colors, marble eyes,
     Cardinal Co. 175.00
Siamese, Various shades of cream and
     tan, Cardinal Co. 100.00
Stray 75.00

Chinaman
Emperor. 75.00
Sprinkle Plenty, Common, yellow and
     green. 35.00
Sprinkle Plenty, Head is sprinkler . 125.00
Sprinkle Plenty, Holding iron,
     brown pants 125.00
White with blue trim, Cleminson Co. 45.00

Elephants
Common, gray and pink, trunk up . . 55.00
Happy Face, fat and squatty, trunk curled
     up for handle, rare 200.00
Shamrock on tummy, white and pink,
     trunk up. 75.00

Sadirons
Ceramic, Blue Flowers. 50.00
Ceramic, Ivy. 40.00
Ceramic, Souvenir, theme park adv 75.00
Ceramic, Woman ironing 50.00
Plastic, green. 20.00

Other
Bottle, plastic, advertising 40.00
Bottle, plastic, plain, various styles . 20.00
Clothespin, various colors 125.00
Dachshund, green coat, red bow tie,
     very rare 300.00
Dearie is Weary, yellow dress, holding iron,
     head is sprinkler, rare 225.00
Dutch Boy 125.00
Dutch Girl, Plastic 55.00
Dutch Girl, Wetter-Downer. 125.00
Fireman, holding hose with sprinkler
     cap in front, rare 300.00
Kitchen Prayer Lady, Enesco Co.,
     rare 275.00
Mammy, white dress with red trim . 200.00

Mary Poppins, clear glass, holding
     umbrella and purse 80.00
Mary Poppins, wearing hat and dress with
     striped skirt, Cleminson 250.00
Merry Maid, glass, various colors,
     new 100.00
Merry Maid, plastic, 6-1/2", six colors,
     Reliance Products 20.00
Myrtle, white dress with polka-dot top,
     sprinkler in back of head,
     Pfaltzgraff Co. 175.00
Poodle, standing on hind legs, pink or
     gray 190.00
Rooster, long neck, plastic cap,
     10" h 100.00

Clothing and Accessories

Decide from the outset if you are
buying clothing and accessories for
use or display. If you are buying for
use, apply very strict standards with
respect to condition and long-term survival prospects. If you only want the
items for display, you can be a little
less fussy about condition. Vintage
clothing was a hot collectible craze in
the 1980s. Things have cooled off a
bit. Emphasis in the 1990s seems to
be on accessories, with plastic purses
from the 1950s leading the parade.

Club: The Costume Society of America, P.O. Box 73, Earleville, MD 21919.

Newsletters: *Lilli's Vintage Clothing
Newsletter*, 19 Jamestown Dr., Cincinnati, OH 45241; *The Vintage Connection*, 904 N. 65th St., Springfield, OR
97478; *Vintage Clothing Newsletter*,
P.O. Box 88892, Seattle, WA 92138.

Periodical: *Lady's Gallery*, P.O. Box
1761, Independence, MO 64055.

Apron, handmade, c1950, $5.

Blouses

Rayon, yellow, padded shoulders, button
    back, 1935-45 . . . . .30.00
Silk velvet, purple, enameled
    buttons 45.00
Wool, midi, navy, "Robert Evans Marine
    Togs" label, c WWI 25.00

Dresses

Baby, cotton, tucked, eyelet trimmed yoke,
    sleeves, skirt, 3-1/2" open work,
    scalloped hem, 38" l 20.00
Girls, cotton, belted, scalloped hem, sleeve
    edge, 1898 . . . . .190.00
Ladies, cotton and rayon, V-back, satin
    bow at waist, back zipper, 1950s .45.00

Gloves

Cotton, wrist length, hand stitched accent,
    1940 . . . . .10.00
Silk, black, shirred 15.00
Suede, black, elbow length 25.00

Neckties

Designer, Foreman and Clark 25.00
Wide, blue, bird and foliage illus,
    1951 . . . . .18.00
Wide, red and green, snowflakes,
    1951 . . . . .10.00

Purses

Beaded, white, red and turquoise beads,
    Indian motif, 1920-25 . . . . .60.00
Crocheted, black, cut steel beads,
    1910-20 .30.00
Leather, hand-tooled, Art Deco-style 50.00

Scarves

Lizard skin, brown, 1950-60 . . . . . . .25.00
Long, ladies, 1931 . . . . .35.00
Mesh, gold wash, 1925-35 . . . . .30.00

Shoes

Child's, leather, ankle strap,
    1912-14 .40.00
Men's, leather, black, felt top with buttons,
    1900 . . . . .125.00
Women's, Canvas, white, hi tops, spool
    heel, cotton laces, 1900 . . . . . . .100.00
Women's, Cobra skin 20.00
Women's, Lizard, brown, high heel . .25.00

Other

Apron, full, cotton, 1940 . . . . .15.00
Apron, half, cotton, red, checked,
    1950 . . . . .5.00
Ball Gown, black chiffon, lilac satin,
    two-piece, "H Grazer, 106 Main Street,
    NY" label 170.00
Barrette, celluloid, black, white
    rhinestones, hand painted 15.00
Bathing Suit, skirted, white with green print,
    1940 . . . . .30.00
Bathing Suit, wool, orig tags and box,
    Jantzen, 1931 . . . . .65.00

Belt, 1" w, jet beads 40.00
Bonnet, child's, tie, ruffles, velvet center,
    1890s 55.00
Camisole, cotton, 1924 . . . . 60.00
Cape, fur, blue fox 65.00
Coat, short, collarless, polyester, cotton,
    large pockets, 1960 . . . . 70.00
Collar, satin, black, five-panel, 1" jet
    beads 65.00
Corset 40.00
Duster, cotton, checks, 45" l,
    lace trim 30.00
Evening Gown, Chiffon, aquamarine over
    green, narrow silver braid trim,
    c1910 . . . . 75.00
Evening Gown, Voile, salmon and white
    flowers, Hawaiian-style, V neck,
    3/4-length sleeves, 5' train
    with ruffle 60.00
Fan, silk, white, wooden sticks,
    hand-painted 50.00
Handbag, white, linen, hand-embroidered,
    drawstring 20.00
Handkerchief, English coronation
    commemorative, silk 20.00
Handkerchief, Victorian, wedding,
    silk 35.00
Hat, man's, gray, open crown, fur blend,
    1959 . . . . 30.00
Headband, plastic, black, 1950-60 . . 8.00
Housecoat, taffeta, embroidered collar,
    pockets, 3/4 sleeves, 1940s . . . 120.00
Knickers, men's, wool, 1926-32 . . . . 60.00
Parasol, silk, black, 14k gold handle,
    mother-of-pearl inlay,
    1880-1900 . . . . 80.00
Petticoat, bustle back, lace trimmed ruffles,
    size 8-10 . . . . 50.00
Raincoat, hooded, cotton gabardine,
    double-breasted 90.00
Shawl, Egyptian, white net, embroidered
    with brass, rect, 1920-30 . . . . . . 90.00
Shirt, men's, multicolored, short sleeve,
    1960s 45.00
Skirt, wool flannel, back-kick pleat, front
    pocket, green, 1950s 15.00
Slip, cotton, full, crocheted, tucked . 35.00
Slip, cotton, half, string waist, lace
    bottom 35.00
Sundress, waffle pique, scoop neck,
    spaghetti straps, 1950s 20.00
Tennis outfit, pleated skirt, loose top,
    1930s 50.00

Clothing, Paper

Paper clothing was an innovation of
the 1960s that never quite caught on.
What could be more convenient than
disposable clothing? Perhaps the drawbacks were only evident after the article

**Dress, Holly Paper Party Dress, Hall-
mark, $17.**

was worn. A paper bikini hardly seems
practical.

Bikini, yellow, with hat and pouch. . . 10.00
Dress, Advertising, Campbell's Soup,
    sleeveless 200.00
Dress, Shift, A-line, Capri, floral design,
    yellow yarn, Flower Fantasy,
    Hallmark 40.00
Dress, Shift, A-line, Sierra, ties at back of
    neck, floral print, yellow yarn, Flower
    Fantasy, Hallmark 40.00

Shirt, $15.

Dress, Muumuu, sleeveless, Island
  Paradise, Hallmark. 20.00
Paperdelic, Style A, sleeveless, black and
  white, floral design, Hallmark. . . .10.00
Paperdelic, Style B, ruffled hem,
  sleeveless, tie-dyed, Hallmark . . .10.00
Smock Coat, Hobby-Jobber, long sleeved,
  four buttons, floral textured design,
  pocket, Hallmark 10.00

Coca Cola Collectibles

John Pemberton, a pharmacist from Atlanta, is credited with creating the formula for Coca-Cola. Less than two years later, he sold out to Asa G. Chandler. Chandler improved the formula and began advertising. By the 1890s, America was Coca-Cola conscious.

Coke, a term first used in 1941, is now recognized worldwide. American collectors still focus primarily on Coca-Cola material designed for the American market. Although it would take a little effort to obtain, a collection of foreign Coke advertising would make a terrific display. What a perfect excuse to fly to the Orient.

Club: The Coca-Cola Collectors Club, P.O. Box 49166, Atlanta, GA 30359.

Blotters
1903 . . . . .30.00
1942, girl sitting on blanket and beach
  scene 8.00
1947 . . . . .35.00
1952 . . . . .15.00

Playing Cards
Autumn girl, MIB, 1943 . . . . .200.00
Party girl, complete deck, 1951. . . .135.00
Santa Claus, complete deck 12.00

World War II girl, MIB, 1943. . . . . 225.00

Signs
19" by 54", tin, "Ice Cold Coca-Cola,"
  bottle-shape. 400.00
30" h, figural, bottle-shaped. 250.00
45" d, round, porcelain, bottle illus. 200.00

Toys
Frisbee. 20.00
Pop Gun. 4.00
Truck, Buddy L, 1960s, MIB 200.00

Trays
Barefoot boy with dog, 1931 . . . . . 425.00
Betty, 1914. . . . . 235.00
Cheese and snacks, 1956 . . . . 20.00
Girl in afternoon, 1938 . . . . 125.00
Girl in menu, 1955 . . . . 40.00
Ice Skater, 1940. . . . . 200.00
Pansy Garden, 1961 . . . . 20.00
Picnic Basket, 1958. . . . . 25.00
Santa, 1973 . . . . 15.00
Thanksgiving TV, 1961 . . . . 20.00

Other
Annual Report, 1935 . . . . 5.00
Banner, 1" by 3', plastic, 100th
  Anniversary. 26.00
Belt Buckle/Cigar Cutter, heavy brass, nun
  on outside, naked lady inside,
  c1915 . . . . 50.00
Booklet, The Truth About Coca-Cola,
  1912 . . . . 30.00
Bottle, brown, Huntington, WV,
  1918 . . . . 35.00
Bottle Opener, hand. 10.00
Bridge Score Pad. 5.00
Bubble Bath, bottle-shape 10.00
Can, diamond with bottle center dec,
  c1960 . . . . 15.00
Carrier, cardboard 12.00
Cassette Player 25.00
Charm Bracelet, 6-1/2" l, brass, NFL, four
  miniature charms, punter, football, NFL
  logo, Coke logo, enamel accents,
  c1970 . . . . 20.00

Toy Truck, Metalcraft, tin, miniature glass Coca-Cola bottles, 1932, $525.

Check, Coca-Cola Bottling Co.,
  1948 . . . . .6.00
Clock, round, metal, silver and red,
  c1950. . . . . 150.00
Clothing, bell-bottom pants, 1970s. . 40.00
Cribbage Game, MIB 55.00
Dish, souvenir 1964 New York World's
  Fair 65.00
Fan, cardboard, 1940s 22.00
Festoon, sports car, 1958. . . . . 400.00
Fly Swatter 9.00
Hat, beanie type, c1960 . . . . .7.00
Ice Scraper 8.00
KeyChain, fish-shape 4.00
KeyChain, miniature bottle, c1950 . . .6.00
Marbles, bag, 1950s. 25.00
Matchbook, c1930 . . . . .5.00
Menu, girl holding serving tray,
  unused .30.00
Pencil, bullet-shape 4.00
Pinback Button, 1-1/8" d, red and white,
  "Drink Coca-Cola," c1950 . . . . . .10.00
Pinback Button, 1-1/4" d, red and white,
  "Coca-Cola Big Wheels Club,"
  Cleveland Press newspaper, ship's
  wheel center, c1930s 50.00
Plate, luncheon, china, 1931 . . . . .220.00
Pocket Watch, E. Ingraham, patented
  1907 . . . . .250.00
Postcard, c1940 Coke truck 18.00
Punch Board, small 8.00
Radiator Plate, 1920s. 175.00
Radio, bottle-shape, MIB 35.00
Syrup Jug, 1 gal, paper label, 1950s 18.00
Telephone. 35.00
Thermometer, 12" d, round 100.00
Thermometer, 17" l, bottle-shape. . .90.00
Timer, hourglass. 10.00
Umbrella .25.00
Whistle, 1960s 7.00

Coins, American

Just because a coin is old does not mean that it is valuable. Value often depends more on condition than on age. This being the case, the first step

Cut-Out Picture, litho cardboard, color, 1927, $100.

in deciding if any of your coins are valuable is to grade them. Coins are graded on a scale of 70, with 70 being the best and 4 being good. Start your research by acquiring Marc Hudgeons's *The Official 1996 Blackbook Price Guide To United States Coins*, 34th Edition (House of Collectibles, 1995). Resist the temptation to look up your coins immediately. Read the 100-page introduction, over half of which deals with the question of grading.

Do not overlook the melt (weight) value of silver content coins. In many cases, weight value will be far greater than collectible value. If only we'd have sold when the industry was paying 20 times face value in the midst of the 1980s silver craze!

Club: American Numismatic Association, 818 North Cascade Ave., Colorado Springs, CO 80903.

Periodicals: Krause Publications has several coin-related magazines. Contact the company at 700 E. State St., Iola, WI 54990.

Coins, Foreign

The foreign coins that you are most likely to find at a flea market are the leftover change that someone brought back with them from their travels. Since the coins were in circulation, they are common and of a low grade. In some countries, they have been withdrawn from circulation and cannot even be redeemed for face value.

If you are a dreamer and think you have uncovered hidden wealth, use Chester L. Krause and Clifford Mishler's *Standard Catalog of World Coins* (Krause Publications). This book covers world coinage from 1701 to the present.

Avoid any ancient coinage. There are excellent fakes on the market. You need to be an expert to tell the good from the bad. Coins are one of those categories where it pays to walk away when the deal is too good. Honest coin dealers work on very small margins. They cannot afford to give away anything of value.

College Collectibles

Rah, rah, rah, sis-boom-bah! The Yuppies made a college education respectable again. They tout their old alma mater. They usually have a souvenir of their college days in their office at home or work. You will not find a Harvard graduate with a room full of Yale memorabilia and vice versa. These items have value only to someone who attended the school. The exception is sport-related college memorabilia. This has a much broader appeal, either to a conference collector or a general sports collector.

Periodical: *Sports Collectors Digest*, 700 East State St., Iola, WI 54990.

Advertising Trade Card, Princeton University, die-cut baseball player 40.00
Class Pass, Harvard University, pathological anatomy, 1862 . . . . 25.00
Coin, Basketball, 1990, Duke, Final Four. 30.00
Coin, Basketball, 1991, North Carolina, Final Four. 30.00
Comic Book, Colorado University, Amazing Sports, Colorado University football team, four sports cards . . 4.00
Directory, The Signet, National College Directory Phi Sigma Kappa, 1911, 128 pgs. 5.00
Magazine, College Humor, Vol. 1, 1931 . . . . 2.00
Pinback Button, Rose Bowl, 1-3/4", stadium illus top, football player, majorette and roses bottom, 1960s 15.00
Pinback Button, Sugar Bowl, 1-3/4", two handled sugar bowl illus, 1960s . 15.00

Silk, Rutgers, $8.

Ticket, Pittsburgh vs. Syracuse football game, Oct. 18, 1930, $15.

Program, 1863, Amherst College Class Day 8.00
Program, 1978, Bowl Game, Notre Dame 38, Texas 10 . . . . 10.00
Ticket, Harvard Class Day, lettering superimposed over Memorial Hall image, 1886, price for pair 25.00
Ticket Stub, Football, 1974, Orange Bowl, Penn State/LSU. 5.00
Ticket Stub, Football, 1977, Sugar Bowl, Pittsburgh/Georgia 5.00
Tobacco Silk, Lehigh University, Richmond Straight Cut Cigarettes 15.00
Trading Cards, Football, Notre Dame, 1988, 60-card set 20.00
Trading Cards, Football, Texas A&M, 100-card set 9.00

College Plates

Ah, college! For most of us, it is a treasured memory of new experiences, new friends, new ideas and enough studying to justify our being there. That is what makes the appeal of a college plate almost universal. We can look at it and be transformed in time and distance to an earlier moment in our lives.

The heyday of college plates seems to have been from 1926 to 1950, with the majority of plates being made in the 1930s. Wedgwood, Spode, Lamberton, Balfour and Lenox all made plates with Wedgwood having the lion's share of the market. Some schools commissioned only one plate while others wanted a full set of 12-16. The average number made was eight, and each plate had a different scene on it representing a building or site on campus that was meaningful to all. The colors of the plates represent the rainbow—white, brown, purple, green, pink, mauve, blue, black and burgundy—with all shades in between.

The designs range from very stark with a single building in the center to plates that are entirely filled in with flowers, fruits, animals, buildings, geometric designs and one of my favorites, squirrels. Prices vary. Most average $15 to $25 at flea markets, although they can be had for as little as $3 or as high as $45 for a hard-to-find school. Prices in the northeast are generally 30-percent to 50-percent higher than those listed.

Advisor: Pat Klein, P.O. Box 262, East Berlin, CT 06023 (860) 828-3973.

Berkeley, CA, 1932, mulberry,
   Bowles Hall 25.00
Boston University, Wedgwood, pink,
   Liberal Arts Building 17.50
Brandeis University, MA, 1952,
   Wedgwood, black, The Castle 5.00
Brown University, RI, Wedgwood, brown,
   John Nichols Brown Gate. 20.00
City College of New York, 1947, mulberry,
   The Gymnasium. 25.00
Columbia University, Lenox, blue, Kings
   College. 18.00
Connecticut College, Wedgwood, black,
   Harkness Chapel 20.00
Dartmouth College, Spode, black, Baker
   Library .15.00
Kent State, OH, 1960, Wedgwood, blue,
   Administration Building. 10.00
Lafayette College, NY, Lamberton, Statue
   of Lafayette 17.00
Mass Institute of Technology, 1939,
   Wedgwood, blue, Administration
   Building 28.00
Miss Porters School, Wedgwood, black,
   Headmasters House 20.00
Mount Holyoke College, 1931, Wedgwood,
   pink, Mary Lyon 20.00
New York University, 1932, Wedgwood,
   blue, School of Education 20.00
North Carolina State College, 1946,
   Lamberton, pink 20.00
Notre Dame University, Balfour, gray
   border. 8.00
Ohio State University, 1931, Shenango
   China, green, The Stadium 23.00
Princeton University, NJ, Wedgwood, blue,
   Stanhope Hall. 45.00
Radcliffe College, Wedgwood, pink, Fay
   House. .12.50
Smith College, Wedgwood, blue, Sage
   Hall. 17.50
St. Marks School, Syracuse China, blue,
   seal in center 3.00

Swarthmore College, Wedgwood, pink,
   Parrish Hall 13.00
Texas A&M, Wedgwood, mulberry,
   Gothright Hall 22.00
Tufts University, MA 1950, Wedgwood,
   pink, Ballou Hall 15.00
U.S. Coast Guard Academy, Wedgwood
   Presentation, Memorial Chapel . 36.00
U.S. Military Academy, Wedgwood, pink,
   Cadet Chapel 11.00
University of Chicago, 1931, Spode, black,
   University Chapel 20.00
University of Iowa, 1933, Wedgwood, blue,
   Hall of Liberal Arts 16.00
University of Michigan, 1928, Wedgwood,
   blue, University Library 22.50
University of Pennsylvania, 1929,
   Wedgwood, blue, Law School . . 33.00
Vassar College, NY, 1929, Wedgwood,
   pink, Taylor Hall 20.00
Washington & Lee, Wedgwood, mulberry,
   Washington College 18.00
Wellesley College, MA, Wedgwood, green,
   Tupelo Point 12.50
Wesleyan University, CT, 1931,
   Wedgwood, blue, Memorial
   Chapel 16.00
Yale University, CT, 1931, Wedgwood,
   blue, Old Chapel. 25.00

Coloring Books

The key is to find these gems uncolored. Some collectors will accept a few pages colored, but the coloring had better be neat. If it is scribbled, forget it.

Most of the value rests on the outside cover. The closer the image is to the actual character or personality featured, the higher the value. The inside pages of most coloring books consist of cheap newsprint. It yellows and becomes brittle over time. However, resist buying only the cover. Collectors prefer to have the entire book.

Betsy McCall, Saalfield, #4585, 1964, 64
   unused pgs 25.00
Brady Bunch, Whitman, 1973, family
   portrait cov, camping trip story, nine
   neatly colored pgs. 25.00
Bullwinkle, Whitman, 1971, Bullwinkle in
   sports car cov, includes Moon Men,
   Boris and Natasha, Peabody and
   Sherman and others, some
   coloring. 15.00
Droopy, Whitman, 1957, Droopy on almost
   every pg, half colored, 7" by 7". . 20.00
Family Affair, Whitman, 1968, cov photos,
   some messy coloring 10.00

Felix the Cat, Saalfield, 1956, Felix on
   cardboard cov, missing first pg, two pgs
   neatly colored 25.00
Gumby and Pokey, Whitman, 1970,
   connect the dots, minor coloring . 15.00
Lady and the Tramp, Whitman, 1954, Lady
   and Tramp on cov, other film characters
   inside, some coloring. 25.00
Mickey Mouse Explorer's Club, Western
   Printing, 1965, one pg colored, back
   cov with Explorer's Club membership
   card and adv for Disneyland Trip
   Contest 20.00
Mister Magoo, 1,001 Arabian nights,
   Whitman, 1959, based on Magoo's
   feature film, holes poked through inside
   pgs, some pgs colored or cut out,
   nice cov 45.00
Nanny and the Professor, Saalfield, 1970,
   unused. 12.00
New York World's Fair, Spertus Publishing,
   1964, jumbo edition, Fair attractions as
   viewed by World's Fair Twins,
   unused .25.00
Rin Tin Tin, Whitman, 1956, some pgs
   neatly colored 15.00
Rocky Jones, Space Ranger, Whitman,
   1951, 32 pgs, stiff cov, unused . .25.00
Roy Rogers' Trigger and Bullet, Whitman,
   1956, Trigger, Bullet, Roy, Dale and Pat
   Brady pictures, single Brady pg neatly
   colored, otherwise unused, cov art
   repeated on back. 18.00
The Addams Family, Saalfield, 1965,
   includes puzzles, games and cutout
   figures, cov photo repeated on back,
   unused. 35.00

Howdy Doody, **Whitman, 1950, 80 pgs, unused, 8-1/2" by 11", $35.**

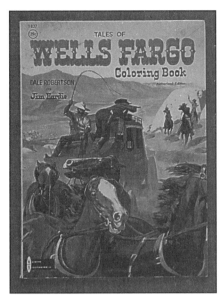

Tales of Wells Fargo, **Authorized Edition, Martian, $25.**

Tom and Jerry, Whitman, 1968, some
    coloring, light watermark along bottom
    edge 12.00
Uncle Wiggily, "Granddaddy Longlegs,"
    1943, story and coloring book, 10 illus
    stories. 8.00
Underdog, Whitman, 1972, Underdog,
    Shoeshine Boy, Sweet Polly, Simon,
    Riff Raff and other characters, nine pgs
    colored 18.00
Walt Disney's Christmas Coloring Book,
    Dell, 1953, cov art repeated on back,
    unused 35.00
Wizard of Oz, 1960s-70s, reprint of earlier
    coloring book, two pgs neatly
    colored 4.00
Woody Woodpecker, Watkins Strathmore,
    1956, Chilly Willy cov, Woody, Oswald,
    Chilly and others inside, few pgs
    colored 15.00

Combs

The form is pretty basic. Value rests in how and in what material the comb is presented. Some hair combs are elaborate and actually should be considered as jewelry accessories. Beware of combs being sold separately that were originally part of larger dresser sets. Their value is less than combs that were meant to stand alone.

You can build an interesting collection inexpensively by collecting giveaway combs. You will be amazed to

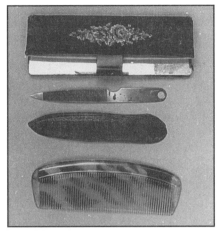

Imitation Tortoiseshell, fabric cov cardboard case with floral petit-point dec, with mirror and fingernail file, 4-3/4" l, $10.

see how many individuals and businesses used this advertising media, from politicians to funeral parlors.

Club: Antique Fancy Comb Collectors Club, 3291 N. River Rd., Libertyville, Il 60048.

Celluloid

Black enamel on yellow 35.00
Butterscotch, rhinestones, c1900 . . 10.00
Green, green glass stones, c1900. . 75.00
Imitation tortoiseshell, pierced
    design 45.00
Imitation tortoiseshell, with Rhinestones,
    c1900-15. . . . . 40.00
Pink, red rhinestones 50.00
Pompadour, white, 1915-30. . . . . . . 30.00
Rhinestone, amber, 5-1/2" w, 6-7/8" h,
    cutout scroll design,
    green outline 100.00

Other

Brass, Hair straightening comb,
    10-1/2" l. 15.00
Tortoiseshell, blue rhinestones 80.00
Tortoiseshell and cut steel, late Victorian,
    stud-set crown motif riveted to metal
    backing, mounted on two-prong
    tortoiseshell comb. 185.00

Comedian Collectibles

Laughter is said to be the best medicine. If this is true, why does it hurt so much when Abbot & Costello meet the Mummy? Comedians of all eras have bestowed upon the public the gift of

laughter. In return the public has made them stars.

Comedian collectibles range throughout the known mediums of radio, vaudeville, television, standup and cinema. The plight of Charlie Chaplin echoes in the antics of Whoopie Goldberg. Comedian collectibles also reflect the diversity of those mediums. So feel free to laugh out loud the next time you find a Groucho Marx eyeglass and mustache mask—I do.

Clubs: Three Stooges Fan Club, P.O. Box 747, Gwynedd Valley, PA 19437; We Love Lucy, The Int'l Lucille Ball Fan Club, P.O. Box 56234, Sherman Oaks, CA 91413.

Don Adams, Coloring Book, Get Smart!
    (Maxwell Smart, That Is), 8" by 11",
    1965 . . . . 60.00
Don Adams, Lunch Box, Get Smart, steel,
    6-1/2" metal thermos, 1966 . . . . . 75.00
Don Adams, Model, car, plastic,
    1967 . . . . 60.00
Steve Allen, balloon, 6-1/2", yellow, blue
    inscription and sketch. 10.00
Lucille Ball, Coloring Book, 80 pgs, Dell
    Publications, 1955 . . . . 30.00
Lucille Ball, Finger Puppet, Ricky Jr., 8",
    soft vinyl head, flannel pajamas, 10" by
    13" flannel blanket, Zany Toys,
    1953 . . . . 50.00
Jack Benny, bank, combination safe,
    plastic, tan, TV set figural, color Benny
    photo, 1950s 75.00
Milton Berle, Pinback Button, Milton Berle
    Make-Up Club 50.00
Milton Berle, Toy, car, lithographed tin,
    windup, 1950s, Marx 300.00
Johnny Carson, tablet, 8" by 10", color
    photo, blue ground, silver stars dec,
    1960s. 10.00
Bill Cosby, Book, *I Spy: Message From
    Moscow*, hardcover, 210 pgs, Whitman,
    1966 . . . . 8.00

Danny Thomas and Jack Carson, Paper Cut-Out Faces, set of four, $50.

Phyllis Diller, pseudo autographed black-and-white publicity photo, $5.

Bill Cosby, Game, I Spy, 10" by 19", orig
    box, Ideal, 1965 . . . . .20.00
Jackie Gleason, Cocktail Napkins, box with
    50 napkins, cartoon Honeymooners
    illus, 1955 . . . . .40.00
Jackie Gleason, Coloring Book,
    8" by 11". 50.00
Laurel & Hardy, game, Game of Monkey
    Business, Transogram, 1962 . . . .20.00
Pinky Lee, serving tray, litho tin,
    multicolored, 1954 . . . . .20.00
Groucho Marx, Game, Groucho TV Quiz
    Game, Pressman 75.00
Groucho Marx, Goggles and Cigar, plastic
    cigar, die-cut plastic face, 1955 . .40.00
Jack Parr, container, cardboard,
    Beech-Nut Gum, three black-and-white
    illus, 1950s 20.00
Rowan & Martin, Laugh-In, Game,
    Knock-Knock Jokes, Romart,
    1969 . . . . .25.00
Rowan & Martin, Laugh-In, Lunch Box,
    emb steel, Aladdin, 1970 . . . . . . .35.00
Soupy Sales, Game, Soupy Sales Sez
    Go-Go-Go!, 1960 . . . . .30.00
Soupy Sales, Pencil Case, vinyl, blue,
    zipper, black illus, 1960 . . . . . . .15.00
Phil Silvers, Fan, I'm A Bilko Fan,
    cardboard, black, white and green,
    Amana Air Conditioner adv 20.00
Phil Silvers, Game, You'll Never Get Rich,
    Gardner Games, 1955 . . . . .50.00
Jimmie Walker, Doll, J.J., Shindana,
    1975 . . . . .35.00
Jimmie Walker, Record, Dyn-O-Mite,
    1975 . . . . .12.00
Robin Williams, Alarm Clock, talking,
    Concept 2000, figural Mork sitting on
    side, 1980. . . . . .35.00

Robin Williams, Gumball Bank, figural
    Mork sitting on top, Hasbro,
    1980 . . . . 20.00
Robin Williams, Mork & Mindy Four-Wheel
    Drive Jeep, Mattel, 1979. . . . . . . 45.00

Comic Books

Comic books come in all shapes and sizes. The number that have survived is almost endless. Although there were reprint books of cartoon strips in the 1910s, 1920s and 1930s, the modern comic book originated in June 1938 when DC issued Action Comics No. 1, marking the first appearance of Superman.

Comics are divided into Golden Age, Silver Age and Contemporary titles. Before you begin buying, read John Hegenberger's *Collector's Guide To Comic* (Wallace-Homestead, 1990) and D.W. Howard's *Investing In Comics* (The World of Yesterday, 1988).

The dominant price guide for comics is Robert Overstreet's *The Overstreet Comic Price Guide.* However, more and more you see obsolete comics being offered in shops and at conventions for 10 percent to 25 percent less than Overstreet's prices. The

V, Number 1, Detective Comics, Feb. 1985, $3.50.

comic book market may be facing a re-evaluation crisis, similar to what happened in the stamp market several years ago when the editors of the Scott catalog lowered the value significantly for many stamps.

Note that most comics, due to condition, are not worth more than 50 cents to a couple of dollars. Very strict grading standards are applied to comics less than 10 years old. The following list shows the potential in the market. You need to check each comic book separately.

Periodicals: *Comic Buyer's Guide*, 700 E. State St., Iola, WI 54990; *Overstreet's Comic Book Marketplace*, 1996 Greenspring Dr., Ste 405, Lutherville-Timonium, MD 21093.

Adventures on the Planet of the Apes, Fury
    In The Forbidden Zone, #5,
    Oct, 1975 . . . . .2.50
ALF, Alf's Summer Camp, Marvel, #31,
    March, 1988 . . . . .1.00
Amazing Spiderman, Kingpin, Marvel 8.00
Aquaman, Return of the Alien, DC,
    #55 . . . . .8.00
Avengers, Living Laser, #34, Marvel 30.00
Batman, Robin Trapped, #466, DC . .2.00
Bullwinkle & Rocky, Boris and Natasha,
    #4, Marvel 2.00
Chamber of Chills, Captains Return,
    #26, June, 1951, Golden Age . . .40.00
Chilly Willy, #1074, Golden Age 10.00
Conan The Barbarian, Curse of the Golden
    Skull, #37, Marvel 8.00
Dick Tracy, Strange Case of Shoulders,
    #143, Golden Age 50.00
Disney Afternoon, Darkwing Duck,
    #7, Marvel 1.50
Doctor Who, The Collector, #8, Oct, 1984,
    Marvel .3.00
Dr. Kildare, #1337, Golden Age 35.00
Elvira, special black and white, movie
    adaptation, Oct, 1988, Marvel 2.00
Flash Gordon, Dale Kidnapped by Voltan,
    #4, DC .1.50
Flintstones, Feb, 1979, #7, Marvel . . .1.25
Generation X, Banshee & White Queen,
    #1, Marvel 5.00
G.I. Joe, Swampfire, #28, Marvel 2.50
Howard the Duck, Circus of Crime,
    #25, Marvel 1.25
Incredible Hulk, Living Shadow, #184,
    Marvel .5.00
Indiana Jones, The Summit Meeting,
    #31 . . . . .1.50
Ironman, Daredevil, #60, Marvel . . .10.00
Mighty Mouse, #1, Dark Mite Returns, Oct,
    1990 . . . . .3.00

Omega Men, Nimbus, #23,
 Dec, 1982, DC 1.50
Popeye, Sweet Pea, #46. . . . . .65.00
Ripley's Believe It Or Not!, #20,
 April, 1967 . . . . .10.00
Star Wars, Luke & Chewbacca, #7,
 July, 1977, Marvel 7.00
Superboy, The Kent's First Super Son,
 #108, March, 1949, DC 12.00
Tales From The Crypt, The Maestro's
 Hand, second series 2.00
Talespin, Khan Job, #3 . . . . .2.00
The New Mutants, #10, Magma,
 March, 1983. . . . . .5.00
Transformers, Autobots vs. Decepticons,
 #33, Marvel 1.25
Underdog, Simon Sez/The Molemen, #2,
 July, 1970. . . . . .20.00

Commemorative Glasses

Before there were modern promotional drinking glasses (the kind you get from a fast food restaurant, gas station or by eating the contents of a glass food container) people bought glasses as souvenirs. The earliest examples have acid-etched decorations. Although these are tough to find, they are not all that expensive. One collector I know specializes in advertising spirit glasses. Her collection numbers in the hundreds.

Advertising and Ale

Black Label Beer, tumbler, 6", black, white
 and red. 14.00
Coors, chaser, clear, red logo, 6 oz,
 set of six. 60.00
Pabst Blue Ribbon, 8 oz 4.00
Water Brothers Brewing Co., etched
 factory scene 30.00

Other

Bicentennial Celebration, A&P Ann Page
 peanut butter, 1976, set of four . .12.00
Bunker Hill, The Revolution, series 2, Don
 Hewitt design 5.00
Eagle, Have It Your Way Bicentennial
 Series, Burger King, 1976 . . . . . . .5.00
Endangered Species, Tiger,
 Burger Chef, 1978 . . . . .6.00
First Stars & Stripes, National Flag
 Foundation, 1976. . . . . .5.00
Gemini IV, Space Spectacular 7.00
Indianapolis 500, Tony Hulman Official,
 Race Winners, 1961, 3-1/4",
 gold rim .6.00
Kentucky Derby, 1989. . . . . .5.00

New York World's Fair, 1939, Flight Around
 the World, Libbey 15.00
Norman Rockwell, Americana series,
 Coke, 1976, set of four 16.00
Preaknesss, 1980, 105th Running, 1973
 issue 25.00
Presidential Series, gold rim, 1940-50,
 Libbey 7.00
Star Spangled Banner, Pittsburgh Press
 logo on back, 1974 . . . . 8.00
Patriots Of The American Revolution,
 1976, four different patriots issued,
 Coca-Cola. 5.00
Post World War II victory glasses, cocktail,
 red, white and blue V illus,
 price each 9.00
Seattle World's Fair, 1962, frosted iced tea
 tumbler, set of eight, price each . . 5.00
Spirit 1776, Coca-Cola Heritage Collector
 Series, set of four 24.00
The Akron Beacon Journal Headlines, The
 Titanic Sinks, highball glass 3.00
The Wonderful World of Ohio, iced tea
 glass, set of 10, different scenes, price
 each 4.00

Commemorative Medals

From the late 19th century through the 1930s, commemorative medals were highly prized possessions. The U.S. Mint and other mints still carry on the tradition today, but to a far lesser degree. Distinguish between medals issued in mass and those struck for a limited purpose, in some cases in issues of one for presentation. An old medal should have a surface patina that has developed over the years causing it to have a very mellow appearance. Never, never clean a medal. Collectors like the patina.

In most medals, the metal content has little value. However, medals were struck in both silver and gold. If you are not certain, have the metal tested.

Club: Token and Medal Society, Inc., P.O. Box 951988, Lake Mary, FL 32795.

Adams & McKinley, establishment of
 capital in D.C., busts on obverse,
 Capitol buildings on reverse, round,
 bronze, 40mm, loop added. 55.00
Apollo II, rocket and astronaut busts on
 obverse, moon landing on reverse,
 round silver or silver-plated,
 50mm 35.00

Baptist Mission Jubilee, 1842, allegorical
 scene on obverse, inscription on
 reverse, round, white metal, 44mm5.00
Battle of Tippecanoe, 1961,
 Sesquicentennial, fight scene and
 Indians, round, silver, 30mm 7.00
California Admission Day, goddess and
 bear on obverse, "Souvenir of
 Admission Day, Sept. 9th" in wreath on
 reverse, round, bronze, 37mm . . 45.00
Columbus, Columbus with chart on
 obverse, bust of youth with torch
 on reverse, round, silver, 30mm . 18.00
Fireman's Day, Dauphin County,
 Harrisburg, PA, 1885, fireman's hat, ax,
 ladder and siren on obverse, inscription
 about county's centennial on reverse,
 round, white metal, 35mm 24.00
Football Hall of Fame, John "Paddy"
 Driscoll, round, sterling silver,
 40mm .10.00
Hawaii Statehood, orig box with papers,
 round, bronze, 63mm 15.00
Pony Express Centennial, 1960, rider on
 obverse, saddle and distance from
 Sacramento to St. Joseph on revere,
 round, silver, 31mm. 15.00
San Buenaventura Mission, Mission on
 obverse, bell on reverse, orig box and
 papers, round, bronze, 41mm 5.00
South Dakota Corn Belt Exposition,
 Mitchell, SD, 1892, castle-like building
 on obverse, "South Dakota's Invitation"
 on reverse, round, aluminum,
 37mm .35.00
United Nations' 25th Anniversary, logo on
 obverse, statue and building on reverse, round, silver, 32mm 8.00
Victoria Anniversary, bust of Queen
 encircled by Latin inscription on
 obverse, "Commemorate The 60th Year
 and Longest Reign" on reverse, round,
 white metal, 44mm 12.50

Compacts

The jewelry market is now so sophisticated that you have to look to its components to find out what is hot and what is not. Compacts are hot. They increased significantly in price in the 1980s. They are still rising in value.

Look for compacts that are major design statements or have gadget mechanisms. Many compacts came with elaborate boxes and pouches. These must be present if the compact is going to be viewed as complete.

Cat, brass, with lipstick, red velvet case, $65.

Club: Compact Collectors Club, P.O. Box 40, Lynbrook, NY 11563.

Coppertone, enameled lid, black cat and blue stars, 2-3/4" by 2-3/8".......50.00

Dorothy Gray, silvertone vanity, blue enameled lid, int. metal mirror separates powder and rouge/lipstick compartments, powder grinder under back lid, 1-3/4" by 2".........50.00

Elgin American, round goldtone compact, lid dec with multicolored enameled Eastern Star emblem, 3" d......50.00

Evans, presentation, goldtone compact and cigarette lighter, both dec with scenic transfer, tap-sift model compact, 2" d, tan suede fitted box, 5" by 3" by 1-1/2".......................80.00

Fillkwik Co., Art Deco silvertone step pyramid-shaped black and red striped vanity, int. metal mirror separates powder and rouge compartments, small triangular fraternal emblem applied to lid, 1-1/2" by 1-3/4"...........90.00

Art Deco, bird, enameled white metal, white metal chain, $150.

K&K, brass colored basket-shaped compact, engine tooled, satin finish lid, emb swinging handle, metal int., 2-1/8" d...................100.00

Richard Hudnut, Le Debut octagonal dark green enameled tango chain vanity, green and gold enameled lid and lipstick tube, int. mirror separates powder and rouge compartments, 2" d, fitted presentation box 200.00

Unknown Maker, Art Deco, goldtone, oblong vanity, blue and gold Art Deco design on lid, int. mirror, side-by-side rouge and powder compartments 2-3/4" by 1-1/2"............... 8.00

Unknown Maker, book-shaped vanity, goldtone and mother-of-pearl, lipstick tube slides out from spine, int. beveled mirror, powder and rouge compartments, 2" by 2-1/2" by 1/2"..................... 80.00

Unknown Maker, Buick Eight, silvertone and maroon, round, logo applied to lid, 3" d...................... 75.00

Unknown Maker, Souvenir, black enameled compact, goldtone Paris scenes on lid, made in France, 3-1/2" by 2-3/4"............ 150.00

Unknown Maker, U.S. Navy hat, plastic, blue and black, lid dec with goldtone Navy insignia, 3" by 1-1/4" 80.00

Wadsworth, Ball & Chain compact, goldtone, lipstick tube attached by chain to round compact, plastic int., 2" d..................... 165.00

Wadsworth, Mini Hatbox vanity, two-sided, tan leather, polished goldtone lid either side, powder/mirror compartment one side, rouge/locket compartment other side, leather finger carrying handle, 1-1/2" d.................... 65.00

Ziegfeld Creation, Lucite photo compact, scalloped edges, photo slides into slot behind int. mirror, 1940s, 4" by 4".................. 100.00

Construction Sets

Children love to build things. Building block sets originated in the 19th century. They exist in modern form as Legos and Lego imitators.

Construction toys also are popular, especially with young boys who aspire to be engineers. The best known is the Erector Set, but it also had plenty of imitators. Alfred Carlton Gilbert, Jr. began his business by producing magic sets as the Mysto Manufacturing Co. With the help of his father, he bought

J. L. Wright, Lincoln Logs from double set, 1930, $90.

out his partner and created the A.C. Gilbert Co., located on Erector Square in New Haven, Conn.

Clubs: A.C. Gilbert Heritage Society, 594 Front St., Marion, MA 02738; Anchor Block Foundation, 980 Plymouth St., Pelham, NY 10803; Girder and Panel Collectors Club, Box 494, Bolton, MA 01470.

A.C. Gilbert
Erector Set, 1913, Mysto Erector, No. 1, cardboard.................100.00
Erector Set, 1914-16, Mysto, No. 4, with motor, wood box............175.00
Erector Set, 1927-28, No. 7, steam shovel...............200.00
Erector Set, 1933, Super 6, 110 V motor 175.00
Erector Set, 1957, 5-1/2", motorized....................60.00
Erector Set, 1957, 8-1/2", electric Ferris wheel.....................90.00
Erector Set, 1958, Musical Ferris Wheel, No. 10072.................200.00
Erector Set, 1963, Lunar Vehicle Set, No. 10127....................50.00
P-51, motor and gearbox, 115 volt AC.................90.00
P-58 motor, 6-12 volt, AC/DC, basket case.......................10.00
Whistle Kit, 7-15 volt AC.........100.00

Richter & Co.
Fortress Set, #402, H3...........90.00
No. E3.......................45.00
No. 3A.......................50.00

Tinker Toy
Double Tinker Toy..............40.00
Easy Tinker Toy, complete set, instructions.................20.00
Spring Motor Tinker Toy.........25.00

Other
American Paper Toy, Bild-A-Set Construction Set, No. 85, erector-type set, cardboard...............18.00

Auburn, Flexi-Blocks, No. 949. . . . . .45.00
Auburn, Plexi Bricks 60.00
Elgo, American Plastic Bricks, No. 715,
    1950s 30.00
Halsam American Skyline 42.00
Ideal, Super City, No. 3361-3 . . . . . .30.00
J.L. Wright, Lincoln Logs, dbl set,
    1930 . . . . .90.00
Kenner, Girder & Panel Set, 1970s. .25.00
Schoenhut, Skyline Builder Set, No. 654,
    engine house 25.00
S.F. Fisher, Gothic Structures,
    Germany 80.00
Wankel Rotary Engine 16.00

Cookbooks

There are 18th and 19th century cookbooks. But, they are expensive, very expensive. It pays to look through old piles of books in hopes that a dealer has overlooked one of these gems. But, in truth, you are going to go unrewarded 99 percent or more of the time.

The cookbooks you are most likely to find date from the 20th century. Most were promotional giveaways. A fair number came with appliances. Some were associated with famous authors. A few years ago, you could buy them from 50 cents to $1 and had

a large selection from which to choose. No longer. These later cookbooks have been discovered. Now you are going to pay between $5 and $20 for most of them.

Cover art does affect price. Most are bought for display purposes. Seek out the ones that feature a recognizable personality on the cover.

Club: Cookbook Collectors Club of America, Inc., P.O. Box 56, St. James, MO 65559.

Periodical: *Cookbook Collectors' Exchange*, P.O. Box 32369, San Jose, CA 95152.

American Feasts, illus, Sallie Williams, 288
    pgs, 1985 . . . . 12.50
Amy Vanderbilt's Complete Cookbook,
    Doubleday, 811 pgs, 1961 . . . . . 14.00
Aphrodisiacs and Love Stimulants, John
    Davenport, illus, 254 pgs 12.00
Appendix To The I Hate to Cook Book, Peg
    Bracken, 178 pgs, 1966, first ed . 12.50
Army Food and Messing, Military Service
    Publishing Co., illus, 418 pgs,
    1942 . . . . 22.50
Better Homes and Gardens Junior Cook
    Book, illus, 77 pgs, 1955. . . . . . . 15.00
Betty Crocker's Kitchen Garden, M.
    Campbell, illus, 170 pgs, 1971 . . 12.50
Blue Ribbon Recipes: Country Fair
    Winners, 384 pgs, 1968 . . . . 12.50
Blue Sea Cookbook, Sarah Alberson,
    290 pgs, 1968. . . . . 10.00
Cape Cod Cook Book, Suzanne Gruver,
    214 pgs, 1936. . . . . 50.00
Come Into the Kitchen, 32 pgs,
    1930 . . . . 4.00
Complete Home Book of Baking, 386 pgs,
    1950 . . . . 20.00
Cooking Out of Doors, Girl Scouts of the
    USA, spiral, 216 pgs, 1960. . . . . 11.00
Cooking with Love, Alice Hall, illus, sgnd,
    222 pgs, 1972. . . . . 15.00
Father Was A Gourmet, Carol Traux, 160
    pgs, 1965, dust jacket, sgnd. . . . 15.00
Food is a Four Letter Word, Eliot Elisofon &
    Gypsy Rose Lee, 176 pgs,
    1948 . . . . 12.50
Gala Day Luncheons, Caroline B. Burrell,
    illus, 221 pgs, 1901. . . . . 35.00
Gold Medal Home Service Recipes, Betty
    Crocker, recipes cards in box,
    c1925 . . . . 15.00
Herbs, Spices and Specialties, spiral, 163
    pgs, 1960 . . . . 6.00
Homemade is Better, Tupperware Home
    Parties, illus, 144 pgs, 1981 . . . . . 9.00
Kate Smith's Favorite Recipes, 8-1/2" by
    11", illus, 47 pgs, 1939 . . . . 15.00

La Cuisine Creole, Lafcadio Hearn, 268
    pgs, 1885, second ed 35.00
Kitchen Kinks, James McEvoy, Mass
    Mutual Life Insurance Co., spiral,
    1956 . . . . 7.00
Macy's Salad, Dessert Book, Mabel Claire,
    illus, 304 pgs, 1933 . . . . 12.50
Maytag Cookbook, pilgrim illus cov, 120
    pgs, 1949. . . . . 5.00
Mrs. Lincoln's Boston Cook Book, Mrs.
    D.A. Lincoln, 536 pgs,
    1884, first ed 200.00
101 Prize Recipes, Postum Cereal Co.,
    40 pgs, 1924 . . . . 4.00
Princess Cook Book, Jenny Akerstrom,
    illus, 315 pgs, 1936, first ed 45.00
Russian Cook Book for American Homes,
    Gaynor Maddox, 92 pgs, 1942 . . 10.00
The Book of Butter, L.H. Bailey, illus,
    270 pgs, 1918 . . . . 12.50
The Enterprising Housekeeper, Helen
    Louise Johnson, illus, 97 pgs,
    1906 . . . . 10.00
The International Institute Cook Book,
    Campbell Soup Co., illus,
    303 pgs, 1980 . . . . 9.00
The White House Cook Book, Ziemann &
    Gillette, illus, 570 pgs, 1897 . . . . 35.00
Your Kitchen and You, Lois Wyse, 32 pgs,
    1925 . . . . 12.50

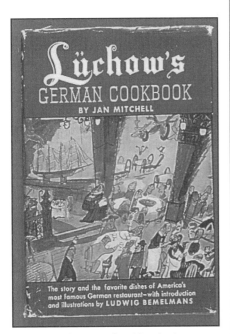

Luchow's German Cookbook, Jan Mitchell, $9.

Cookie Cutters

When most think of cookie cutters, they envision the metal cutters, often mass-produced, that were popular during the 19th century and first third of the 20th century. This is too narrow a view. Do not overlook the plastic cutters of recent years. Not only are they detailed and colorful, they also come in a variety of shapes quite different from their metal counterparts.

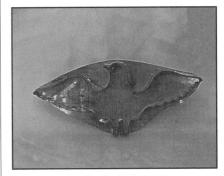

American Eagle, tin, $50.

Horse, tin, 7-1/2" by 5-1/2", $45.

If you want to build a great specialized collection, look for cutters that were giveaway premiums by flour and baking related business. Most of these cutters are valued from $10 to $40.

Club: Cookie Cutter Club, 1167 Teal Road SW, Dellroy, OH 44620.

Newsletter: *Cookies*, 5426 27th St. NW, Washington, DC 20015.

Bisquick, round, plastic, yellow 50
Candy Cane, plastic, red, handle,
    Wilton 1.00
Cat, tin, 3" h, 2-1/2" w 8.00
Cookie Monster, plastic, blue, Pillsbury
    Alphabet Set. 50
Distelfink, tin, 3" l, flatback 10.00
Eagle, tin, 5-1/4" h, crimped wings and
    tail. 40.00
Egg Baking Powder Co., 1-1/2" d,
    1902. . . . . .40.00
Fish, tin, flatback 22.00
Gingerbread Boy, aluminum, 5-3/4" h,
    1940s 5.00
Heart, tin, 4", crimped diamond. 30.00
Horse, tin, rough/trimmed back,
    c1895 . . . . .10.00
Jack O'Lantern, plastic, white, inner
    design, Regal. 1.00
Lady, tin, 5-1/4" h, strap handle, rolled
    edges 35.00
Peacock, tin, 4-1/2" h 60.00
Puss in Boots, tin 2.00
Robin Hood Flour, set of six 25.00
Santa, 4" h, 2-3/4" w 15.00
Turkey, plastic, blue, Stanley Rome
    Products. 2.00
Wilma Witch, plastic, orange, Kiddy
    Kreatures Set. 1.00
Wreath, plastic, red, Educational
    Products. 50

Cookie Jars

Talk about categories that have gone nuts over the past years. Thanks to the Andy Warhol sale, cookie jars became the talk of the town. Unfortunately, the prices reported for the Warhol cookie jars were so far removed from reality that many individuals were deceived into believing their cookie jars are far more valuable than they really are.

The market seems to be having trouble finding the right pricing structure. A recent cookie jar price guide low-balled a large number of jar prices. Big city dealers are trying to sell cookie jars as art objects at high prices instead of the kitsch they really are. You have to be the judge. Remember, all you are buying is a place to store your cookies.

Club: The Cookie Jar Collector's Club, 595 Cross River Rd., Katonah, NY 10536.

Newsletter: *Cookie Jarrin'*, RR 2, Box 504, Walterboro, SC 29488.

Bear, Maddux 150.00
Bird House, Deforrest 100.00
Clown, American Bisque, full figure . 85.00
Clown, Metlox, black and white . . . 145.00
Dutch Boy, Pottery Guild 95.00
Grandfather's Clock, McCoy 50.00
Granny, American Bisque 125.00
Gunfighter Rabbit, Twin Winton. . . . 75.00
Humpty Dumpty, Regal China 275.00

**Hopalong Cassidy, unmkd, 11-1/2",
$350.**

Juggling Clown, California Originals. 75.00
Keystone Cop, Twin Winton 85.00
Little Red Riding Hood,
    Pottery Guild 125.00
Money Bag, white, Abingdon 65.00
Oscar the Doughboy, Robinson-
    Ransbottom. 125.00
Owl, McCoy 45.00
Owl, Metlox. 40.00
Owl, Shawnee, green eyes. 245.00
Quaker Oats, Regal China 95.00
Rabbit in Hat, Deforrest 125.00
Raggedy Andy, Metlox 150.00
Raggedy Ann, California Originals,
    #859 . . . . .60.00
Raggedy Ann, Maddux, colors under
    glaze .150.00
Sailor Jack, Robinson-Ransbottom 195.00
Squash, Metlox. 145.00
Winking Pig, McCoy 265.00

**Hen, Doranne of California, CJ 100,
$75.**

Copper Paintings

Copper paintings, actually pictures stamped out of copper or copper foil, deserve a prize as one of the finest tacky collectibles ever created. I remember getting a four-picture set from a bank as a premium in the late 1950s or early 1960s. It is one of the few things that I have no regrets about throwing out.

However, to each his or her own—somewhere out there are individuals who like this unique form of mass-produced art. Their treasures generally cost them in the $15 to $50 range, depending on subject.

Giants of the Forest, Greetings from Colorado, blue and purple mountains, black trees, red flowers in foreground, 5-3/8" by 4-1/8", $15.

Costumes

Remember how much fun it was to play dress-up as a kid? Seems silly to only do it once a year at Halloween. Down South and in Europe, Mardis Gras provides an excuse; but, in my area, we eat doughnuts instead. Collectors are beginning to discover children's Halloween costumes. While you may be staggered by some of the prices listed below, I see costumes traded at these prices all the time.

There doesn't seem to be much market in adult costumes, those used in the theater and for theme parties. Costume rental shops are used to picking them up for a few dollars each.

Costumes
Ace Freeley, KISS, Aucion, 1978 .. 50.00
Beatnik, Collegeville, 1961 .... 50.00
Bunny, Collegeville 85.00
Cat and moon illus, black and yellow, long
    sleeves, 1938 .... 40.00
Caveman, Ben Cooper, 1963 ..... 45.00
Devil, Masquerade, 1960......... 40.00
Drac, Groovie Ghoulies, Ben Cooper,
    1971 .... 90.00
Dress, homemade, sleeveless, black,
    orange pumpkin dec, 1940 ..... 65.00
Fonzie, Ben Cooper, 1976........ 20.00
Greg Brady, Collegeville, 1970s ... 45.00
Jaime Sommers, The Bionic Woman, Ben
    Cooper, 1975 .... 15.00
Klinger, MASH, Ben Cooper, 1981 . 75.00
Kotter, Welcome Back Kotter, Collegeville,
    1976 .... 20.00
Lamb Chop, 1958 .... 50.00
Laura Ingalls, Little House on the Prairie,
    Ben Cooper, 1970s........... 20.00
Laverne, Laverne & Shirley,
    Collegeville, 1977 .... 30.00
Man from Mars, Halco, 1950s 60.00
Rat Patrol, Ben Cooper, 1967 ..... 55.00
Rosie the Robot, The Jetsons, Ben
    Cooper, 1963 .... 225.00
Tattoo, Fantasy Island, Ben Cooper,
    1978 .... 25.00
Uncle Fester, Addams Family, Ben
    Cooper, 1965 .... 150.00
Yogi Bear, 1974................ 20.00
Zebra, Ben Cooper, 1960s 30.00

Country Store

There is something special about country stores. My favorite is Bergstresser's in Wassergass, Pa. There is probably one near you that you feel as strongly about. Perhaps the appeal is that they continue to deny the present. I am always amazed at what a country store owner can dig out of the backroom, basement or barn.

Country store collectibles focuses heavily on front-counter and back-counter material from the last quarter of the 19th century and first quarter of the 20th century. The look is tied in closely with Country. It also has a strong small town, rural emphasis.

Tin, Towle Log Cabin Syrup, sample size, 1-1/2 oz, $375.

Drop in and prop your feet up on the potbelly stove. Don't visit a country store if you are in a hurry.

Counter Displays
Beech-Nut Gum, tin 90.00
Better Made Cigarette Holders..... 40.00
Chief Watta Pop, lollipop, bust of
    Indian.................... 130.00
Clark's Teaberry Gum, plastic 65.00

Signs
Arm & Hammer Brand Soda, 12" by 16",
    color litho on paperboard,
    black ground 25.00
Campbell's Tomato Soup, sheet metal,
    figural soup can, red, black, yellow and
    white 85.00
Drink Rochelle Club, 12" by 24",
    tin, emb 90.00
Enjoy Orange Crush, 9" by 11", plastic,
    emb, painted, orange and white, blue
    ground.................... 35.00
Otto F. Ernst Saddles, 9" by 20", litho tin,
    emb, black lettering,
    yellow ground 75.00
Tulip Soap, paper, woman surrounded by
    tulips and various other vignettes,
    framed.................... 55.00
Viceroy, tin, door............... 20.00

Thermometers
Clown Cigarettes, 9" d, litho paper dial,
    black and yellow illus,
    white ground 60.00
Joan of Arc Red Kidney Beans, 15" h,
    wood, painted and stenciled, black
    lettering, white ground........ 45.00
Wesson Oil & Snowdrift, 9" d, paper dial,
    black and red illus, white ground . 55.00

Other

Bag Rack, wooden, with cast iron string
    holder 100.00
Bell, rect, soldered spring, tempered metal
    shaft 32.50
Broom Rack, Gold Medal Flour adv 135.00
Butter Churn, wood 150.00
Canister, cov, La Paloma 5 cents Cigar,
    glass. 30.00
Carrier, soda, wood, A-Treat, holds
    24 bottles 20.00
Coffee Bean Dispenser, wall mount,
    16-1/2" w, 41" h, half-round cylinder,
    brass case, glass window, measuring
    spout attached 180.00
Coffee Grinder, Arcade No. 25, wall
    mount 115.00
Container, Jack Spratt Powdered
    Sugar 85.00
Crate, Oswego Silver Gloss Starch,
    wood. 75.00
Crate, Snow Boy Washing Powder,
    wood. 90.00
Gasoline Can, Never-Fail, five gallon, J.A.
    Harps Mfg. Co. 35.00
Gum Dispenser, Wrigley's Gum, 8" w, 14"
    h, revolving cylinder, iron base. .110.00
Jar, glass, clear, Planters Salted Peanuts,
    6-1/2" h, glass cov with finial, flattened
    front and back, emb lettering,
    c1950 . . . . .65.00
Scale, Jacobs, Brooklyn, hardware, 8" dial,
    20 lbs, scoop-type weighing pan,
    suspension chains 48.00
Scoop, tin .15.00
Spittoon, brass 40.00
String Holder, cast iron, c1900 . . . . .65.00
Tobacco Cutter, H.D. Mercantile Co.,
    Wholesale Grocers. 85.00
Trade Card, Barbours Irish
    Flax Thread 10.00
Tray, The Levy & Mercantile Co.. . .125.00
Wrapping Paper Dispenser, Double,
    wood, iron. 35.00
Wrapping Paper Dispenser, Single,
    oak, iron .30.00

Country Western Collectibles

You don't have to be a "rhinestone cowboy" to enjoy Country Western music, and you don't have to travel to Nashville to find its memorabilia. With a large assortment of items available, such as sheet music, signed photographs and record albums, Country Western collectibles won't bring ya back home empty handed. So go

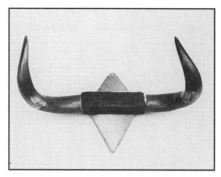

Hat Rack, steer horns, wood plaque, $15.

ahead and enjoy yourselves and "Ya'll come back now, ya' here?"

Newsletter: *Disc Collector*, P.O. Box 315, Cheswold, DE 19936.

Periodical: *American Cowboy*, P.O. Box 12830, Wichita, KS 67277.

Autographs

Anderson, Lynn, photo, sgd 12.00
Atkins, Chet, 6" by 7", sgd and dated
    1956 . . . . 20.00
Carter, Mother Maybelle, photo, sgd 80.00
Fargo, Donna, sgd letter 6.00
Haggard, Merle, photo, sgd 18.00
Jones, Grandpa, photo, sgd 12.00
Mandrell, Barbara, photo, sgd 15.00
Miller, Roger, sgd letter 7.00
Pride, Charlie, photo, sgd 12.00
Rodgers, Jimmie, holding banjo, 8" by 10",
    sgd, c1932 . . . . 300.00
West, Dottie, sgd letter 5.00

Posters

Coal Miner's Daughter, 1979,
    Universal. 9.00
Cowboy From Sundown, Tex Ritter,
    1940 . . . . 20.00
Nine To Five, 1980, 20th Century . . 10.00

Records

Acuff, Roy, Wabash Cannonball,
    78 rpm. 12.00
Cash, Johnny, Don't Take Your Guns to
    Town, Columbia, 45 rpm. 12.00
Flatt & Scruggs, Pearl Pearl Pearl, 33 rpm,
    Columbia. 12.00
Foley, Red, Peace in the Valley, 45 rpm,
    Decca 10.00
Haggard, Merle, Same Train, A Different
    Time, Capitol. 25.00
Jones, George, Hold Everything, 45 rpm,
    Starday 12.00
Jones, Grandpa, Grandpa Jones-Strictly
    Country Tunes, LP, King. 25.00
Lynn, Loretta, Don't Come Home a Drinkin,
    LP, Decca 25.00

Owens, Buck, Sweet Thing, 45 rpm,
    Capitol 20.00
Parton, Dolly, Puppy Love, 45 rpm,
    Goldband. 50.00
Ritter, Tex, Daddy's Last Letter, 78 rpm,
    Capitol 10.00
Tillis, Mel, Walk on Boy, 45 rpm,
    Columbia 10.00
Tubb, Ernest, It's Been So Long, Darlin',
    78 rpm, Decca 10.00

Sheet Music

Dream River, Billy Hill. 3.00
I Like Mountain Music, Weldon. 4.00
You're Only A Star, Gene Autry 4.00

Other

Map, Nashville, TN, sgd by Roy Acuff and
    others, c1948. . . . . 125.00
Necktie, Ernest Tubb likeness, facsimile
    signature 15.00
Paper Dolls, Hee Haw, punch-out,
    Saalfield, #5139, Gunilla, Lulu, Kathy
    and Jeannie dolls, uncut, 1971 . . 12.00
Paper Dolls, Hootenanny, punch-out,
    Saalfield, #4440, four dolls,
    uncut, 1964 . . . . 18.00
Ticket Stub, Willie Nelson concert,
    c1977. . . . . 15.00

Cowan Pottery

R. Guy Cowan founded the Cowan Pottery in 1913 in Cleveland. It remained in almost continuous operation until financial difficulties forced it to close in 1931. Initially, utilitarian redware was produced. Cowan began experimenting with glazes, resulting in a unique lusterware glaze.

Bowls

2" h, 7-1/2" d, shape #587-A, metallic
    glaze 60.00
2-1/4" h, 11" l, 8" w, irregular rect, shape
    #641, yellow ext., green int.,
    c1925. . . . . 60.00
3-1/8" h, 7-1/4" d, shape #733-A, mark # 8,
    white ext., pink int. 50.00
4" h, 9-1/2" d, shape #773-A, ivory ext.,
    green int. 50.00

Compotes

2" h, 6" d, shape #838, mark #8, short, ivory
    ext., green int. 30.00
5", shape #848X, lime 75.00
8", pedestal, shape #779, scroll feet, lemon
    ext., turquoise int. 95.00

Vases

6" h, Logan, shape #649-A, orange
    luster 100.00

7" h, fan, seahorse standard, white. .45.00
8" h, blue luster 45.00
8-1/4" h, Logan, shape #649-B, blue
    luster 190.00
10-3/4" h, blue luster, Art Deco 145.00

Other
Bud Vase, 7" h, shape #554, pearl
    luster 60.00
Candlesticks, pr, 3" h, ivory, shape #782,
    mark #8 . . . . .65.00
Centerpiece Bowl, 9" h, 13-1/2" d, mark #8,
    side scallops extend into slight handles,
    ivory ext., raspberry int. 80.00
Paperweight, 4-5/8" h, shape #D-3,
    elephant, mark #9, c1930, blue .295.00

Cowboy Heroes

The cowboy heroes in this category rode the range in movies and on television. In a way, they were larger than their real-life counterparts, shaping the image of how the West was won in the minds of several generations. Contemporary Westerns may be historically correct, but they do not measure up in sense of rightness.

The movie and television cowboy heroes were pioneers in merchandise licensing. If you were a child in the 1949 to 1951 period and did not own a Hopalong Cassidy item, you were deprived.

Gene Autry, book, *Gene Autry and The Ghost Riders*, $25.

Gene Autry, arcade card, $15.

Club: Westerns & Serials Fan Club, Rt. 1, Box 103, Vernon Center, MN 56090.

Periodicals: *Collecting Hollywood, American Collectors Exchange*, 2401 Broad St., Chattanooga, TN 37408; *Spur*, 4700 Western Heritage Way, Los Angeles, CA 90027.

Annie Oakley
Book, *Annie Oakley in Double Trouble*, 6"
    by 8", Whitman 15.00
Coloring Book, 11" by 13", Whitman,
    1957 . . . . 25.00
Patch, 5" h, fabric, 1955 . . . . 15.00
Record, Annie Oakley Sings, 78 rpm,
    envelope, Little Golden Record,
    c1950s 15.00

Bonanza
Action Figure, Hoss, 8" h, American
    Character series, 1966, boxed . 150.00
Cup, tin, 2-3/4" h, ranch house illus,
    1966 . . . . 30.00
Lunch Box, steel, Aladdin, 1968 . . 125.00
Thermos, steel 50.00
Photo, Little Joe/Michael Landon, 8" by
    10", color, 1960 . . . . 25.00

Buffalo Bill
Comic Book, 7-3/4" by 10", issue No. 1,
    June 1965, Gold Key 7.00

Jigsaw Puzzle, 6-1/2" by 8" by 2", Buffalo
    Bill and Calamity illus, boxed,
    1956 . . . . 20.00
Outfit, child's, two-piece, flannel, plastic
    fringe, simulated fur trim, 1950s . 75.00

Dale Evans
Bath Mitt, 7" by 8", terry cloth 35.00
Book, *Christmas is Always*, 1963 . . . 15.00
Comic Book, No. 5, May-June 1949,
    DC 65.00
Photo, 8" by 10", color, sgd, 1950s . 30.00

Gene Autry
Book, *Golden Stallion*, 6" by 8", Whitman,
    1954 . . . . 20.00
Coloring Book, 11" by 15", Whitman,
    1949 . . . . 30.00
Holster, leather, brown, 1946 . . . . . . 50.00
Lid, Dixie Ice Cream Cup 10.00
Marionette, stringless, 14-1/2" h, fabric and
    rubber, 1951, boxed 125.00
Pinback Button, celluloid, 1987 Film
    Caravan convention 10.00
Postcard, black and white, European,
    1950s 12.00
Poster, Trail To San Antone, 27" by 41",
    1947 . . . . 100.00
Record, Rudolph, The Red-Nosed
    Reindeer, 78 rpm, Columbia,
    1949 . . . . 20.00
Wallet, simulated leather, emb,
    zipper 40.00

Hopalong Cassidy
Bank, plastic, 4" h, removable hat,
    1951 . . . . 35.00
Belt, leather, Yale Belt Corp. 100.00
Book, *Hopalong Cassidy returns*, 4" by 6",
    paperback, Mulford, 1946 . . . . . . 20.00
Book Cover, 12" by 18", paper, Bond Bread
    adv. 30.00
Cap, wool, 6-1/2" h, Pedigree Sportswear,
    1950 . . . . 75.00
Coloring Book, Doubleday, 1950 . . . 50.00
Game, Chinese Checkers, sheriff badge
    illus cov, Milton Bradley, 1950 . . . 75.00
Glass, 4-3/4" h, Western Series, color illus,
    set of four, price each 50.00
Gloves, black leather, white name and
    illus 100.00
Hair Bow, carded 85.00
Handkerchief, 12" by 12", Hoppy and
    Topper illus, tin steer head slide 125.00
Magazine, *Life*, June 12, 1950 . . . . 20.00
Magazine, *Quick*, May 1, 1950 . . . . 35.00
Magazine, *TV Digest*, Nov. 29, 1952 75.00
Necktie, child's, 13" l, Hoppy and Topper
    illus 75.00
Pen, 6" l, ball-point 75.00
Pencil Case, cardboard, 1950 . . . . 125.00
Pistol, paper, 7", die-cut, 1951 . . . . . 35.00

Pocket Knife, steel, black and white
illus.........................75.00
Pogo Stick, 46-1/2" h, steel rod and
spring.....................250.00
Postcard, black and white, sgd 150.00
Poster, The Dead Don't Dream, 22" by 28",
1947.......................75.00
Pressbook, Publicity and Exploitation
Manual, 1940s..............50.00
Puzzle, frame tray..............40.00
Sheet Music, 9" by 12", Hopalong Cassidy
March, 1951.................75.00
Throw Rug, 24" by 60", chenille ...100.00
Toy, Topper, 18" by 19", inflatable, vinyl,
1950s.....................125.00

John Wayne
Badge, celluloid, 3-1/2", red, white, blue
and black, in memoriam, 1979...10.00
Book, *The Shepherd of the Hills*, Grosset &
Dunlap, 1941 ....20.00
Coloring Book, 11" by 14", Saalfield,
1951......................100.00
Magazine, *TV Western and Movie*, June,
1959.......................50.00
Record, The Alamo, 45 rpm 25.00

Lone Ranger
Bandanna, red, white and blue, Cheerios
premium, 1949-50 ....60.00
Book Bag, 9" by 14", canvas, plastic
handle, 1950 ....100.00
Cap Gun, set, metal, 11" l, Fanner 50,
plastic grip, black rubber belt,
Mattel......................75.00
Coloring Book, Whitman, 1955, boxed set
of six.......................40.00
Comic Strip, original, Dec 19,
1959......................125.00
Drum, Tonto, metal and rubber, wood
drumsticks 75.00
Game, 2" by 10" by 19", Parker Brothers,
1938.......................50.00
Hand Puppet, 11" h, 1966.........25.00
Harmonica, plastic..............20.00
Lunch Box, emb steel, Aladdin,
1980.......................30.00
Photo, Clayton Moore, 8" by 10", black and
white, sgd, 1970s.............40.00
Puzzle, frame tray, 1970s, Whitman .20.00
Spoon, 6" l, silver-plated brass, 193850.00
Tattoo Transfer, 1970s 8.00
Thermos, 6-1/2" h, Aladdin, 1980 ...15.00
Wallet, brown vinyl, color illus cov,
1953.......................85.00

Red Ryder
Catalog, Daisy Gun Book, Daisy Mfg. Co.,
1955.......................75.00
Fabric, 15" by 30", brown, red, white and
blue, Red Ryder, Little Beaver and
Yaqui Joe illus, 1950s 50.00

Flashlight, metal, 1949..........40.00

Rifleman
Boxed Board Game, Milton Bradley,
1959 ....50.00
Magazine, *Children's Playmate Magazine*,
Sept. 1958 ....20.00
Photo, Chuck Conners, 4" by 5", black and
white 35.00

Roy Rogers
Badge, tin....................20.00
Coloring Book, Roy & Dale, 8" by 11",
Whitman, 1954 ....40.00
Pencil case, vinyl 50.00

Cow Collectibles

Holy cow! This is a moovelous category, as entrenched collectors already know.

Newsletter: *The MOOsletter*, 240 Wahl Ave., Evans City, PA 16033.

Activity Book, Elsie, 1950s........ 20.00
Bank, Press My Tail Moo Cow, tin,
c1940 ....35.00
Butter Print, round, 5-1/4" d, cow, tree and
flower, scrubbed white, one-pc turned
handle...................150.00
Coloring Book, Elsie, 1950s....... 20.00
Cookie Jar, purple cow with butterfly,
"Poppytrail Calif".............70.00
Creamer, Elsie, figural 35.00
Doll, Elsie, 12" h, plush 40.00
Game, Elsie, Selchow Righter,
1941 ....68.00
Glass, Elsie the Cow, 5-1/2" h, Elsie
portrait, brown and yellow......35.00
Greeting Card, Elsie the Cow,
birthday....................65.00
Ink Blotter, Cow Brand Baking Soda,
cardboard, blue and white,
c1920 ....10.00
Milkbox, metal, Borden's, Elsie illus. 80.00

Creamer, spongeware, $325.

Pinback Button, Horlick's Malted Milk adv, $65.

Mug, Pillsbury Cookies & Cow, 3-3/4" h,
Therm Ware, color............10.00
Pinback Button, Ayrshires, 1-1/4" d,
standing cow, U.S. outline background,
maroon and white, c1940s 15.00
Pinback Button, Guernsey's Rich
Inheritance, cow illus, yellow, brown
and white, 1930-40 ....18.00
Poster, Evaporated Milk-Pure Cow's Milk,
black and white cows illus, green
ground....................15.00
Sheet Music, Cow Cow Boogie,
1942 ....10.00
Sheet Music, Cowbelles, 1922......5.00
Sign, Sharples Tubular Cream Separators,
12" by 19", paper, milkmaid with cows in
field, matted and framed 200.00
Standup, 6" l, Holstein, tin, cow-shape,
black and white 75.00
Sugar Bowl, Elmer, figural, china,
1930-40 ....40.00
Thermometer, Socony Vacuum Sanilac
Cattle Spray adv, 19" h, wood,
1920s.....................100.00
Toy, ramp walker, 3-1/2" l, plastic, brown
and white, orig sealed cellophane bag,
marked "Made In Hong Kong,"
1950s.....................25.00

Cracker Jack Collectibles

You can still buy Cracker Jack with a prize in every box. The only problem is that when you compare today's prizes with those from decades ago, you feel cheated. Modern prizes simply do not measure up. For this reason, collectors tend to focus on prizes put in the box prior to 1960.

Book, miniature, *Cracker Jack Riddles*, 1912, 2-3/4" by 5", $20.

Most Cracker Jack prizes were not marked. As a result, many dealers have Cracker Jack prizes without even knowing it. This allows an experienced collector to get some terrific bargains at flea markets. Alex Jaramillo's *Cracker Jack Prizes* (Abbeville Press, 1989) provides a wonderful survey of what prizes were available.

Club: Cracker Jack Collectors Association, 72 Charles St., Rochester, NH 03867.

Badge, cast metal, 1", six-point star, silver color, 1931 . . . . .35.00
Baseball Card, 2-1/2" by 3-1/2", set of two, full color photo, #6 Mickey Mantle, #13 Willie Mays, Borden Inc. and Topps Chewing Gum copyright, 1982. . .20.00
Baseball Score Counter, 4" l 85.00
Bird, plastic, green, c1950. . . . . .7.00
Book, *Birds We Know*, miniature, 1928 . . . . .45.00
Box, Jack and Bingo, 1919 . . . . .48.00
Cart, two movable wheels, wood dowel tongue 33.00
Decal, nursery rhyme figure 26.00
Decoder, Jack the Sailor 22.00

Disguise Glasses, paper, hinged, with eyeballs, 1933. . . . . 6.00
Game, golf, paper, wooden stick in center 35.00
Iron-On Transfer, patriotic figure, 1939 . . . . 32.00
Pinback Button, 1-1/4" d, lady, multicolored, black hair, pink ribbon, green ground, red and white "Cracker Jack 5 cents/Candied Popcorn & Roasted Peanuts" on back paper, copyright 1910 . . . . 60.00
Puzzle, 7" by 10" 35.00
Postcard, bear illus, 1907 . . . . 22.00
Rocking Horse, 1", cast metal, figural 9.00
Sand Picture, paper, 1967 . . . . 9.00
Sign, 7" by 11", cardboard, c1930 . . 45.00
Squeaker, 2-1/2" by 3-1/2", cardboard, accordion-shape 35.00
Train Set, two pcs 22.00
Wheelbarrow, 2-1/4" l, silvered tin . . 32.00

Crackle Glass

If crackle glass catches your fancy, beware! It is still being produced by Blenko Glass Co., and in Taiwan and China. Examine prospective purchases carefully. "Cracks" are often hard to distinguish from the decorative "crackles."

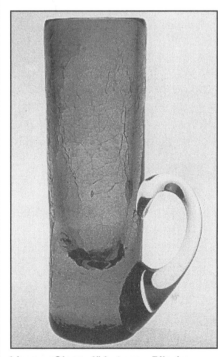

Liqueur Glass, 4" h, topaz, Pilgrim Glass Co., 1949-69, $40.

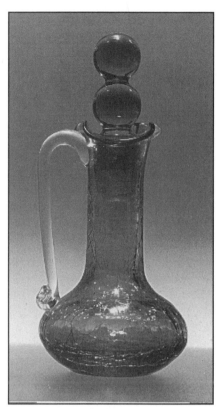

Pitcher, miniature, 5-1/2" h, blue, applied clear handle, double-ball stopper, Pilgrim Glass Co., 1949-69, $27.

Club: Crackle Glass Club, P.O. Box 1186, North Massapequa, NY 11758.

Decanters
6" h, lemon lime, Pilgrim 100.00
6-1/4" h, topaz, ribbed, crystal drop-over handle, Pilgrim. 100.00
7-3/4" h, amberina, crackled top, Rainbow 85.00
8-1/2" h, amberina, Blenko, 1970, price for pair 150.00
11-3/4" h, charcoal, blue tint, Blenko .75.00

Glasses
4" h, topaz, drop-over handle, Pilgrim .40.00
5-1/2" h, cream, drop-over handle . . 35.00
5-3/4" h, sea green, Blenko 50.00
6" h, ruby, pinched, Hamon 60.00

Pitchers
3-1/4" h, Amethyst, drop-over handle, Pilgrim .35.00
3-1/4" h, Ruby, drop-over handle, Kanawha 30.00
3-1/4" h, Topaz, pulled back handle, Hamon. 25.00

3-1/2" h, green, drop-over handle,
Pilgrim 35.00
3-3/4" h, tangerine, pulled back handle,
Pilgrim 30.00
4" h, blue 40.00
5" h, dark amber, drop-over handle,
Pilgrim 25.00
17" h, dark amber, drop-over handle,
Blenko .100.00

Vases
4" h, Amethyst, Pilgrim 60.00
4" h, Olive Green, double-neck,
Blenko 50.00
5-1/4" h, tangerine, Rainbow. 60.00
7" h, crystal, blue rosettes, Blenko . .75.00
7-1/4" h, jonquil, ftd, crimped top,
Blenko .100.00
8" h, crystal, blue, Blenko 100.00

Other
Ashtray, amberina, 7-1/4" h 35.00
Candleholder, pale sea green, 5-1/4" h,
Blenko 50.00
Candy Dish, dark topaz, 5-1/2" by 2-1/4",
ribbed drop-over handle, Hamon .75.00
Creamer and Sugar, gold, 3-1/2" h,
Kanawha 50.00
Cruet, Amber, pulled back handle,
Rainbow. 70.00
Cruet, Sea Green, Pilgrim 40.00
Cup, 2-1/4" h, amberina, drop-over handle,
Kanawha 25.00
Figure, miniature hat, amberina, 2" h,
Kanawha 35.00
Fruit, Apple, 3-1/4" h, crystal pink,
Blenko 50.00
Fruit, Pear, 5" h, sea green, Blenko .50.00
Jug, 4" h, blue, drop-over handle,
Pilgrim 30.00
Jug, 8-1/4" h, amberina, gold drop-over
handle, Blenko 75.00
Mug, amber, 6-1/4" h, drop-over
handle 25.00

Enameled Metal, ladybugs, pink wings, black bodies, silver feet and antennae, Swank, 3/4" l, $15.

Cuff Links

Many people consider cuff links to be the ideal collectible. Besides being available, affordable and easy to display and store, cuff links are educational and offer windows to history. They have been around for centuries and have always reflected the styles, economics and technologies of their era. Cuff link collecting can be profitable. Rare or unusual finds can be worth substantial dollars. Most serious collectors have had the thrill of buying a pair for "pennies" that turned out to be worth a great deal.

Many cuff link collectors specialize in their collections. Some areas of specialization are size, shape and closure type. Other collectors specialize by subject. Examples of this are cuff links that show animals, sports, advertising logos, cars, boats and so on.

Club: National Cuff Link Society, P.O. Box 346, Prospect Heights, IL 60070.

Gold, 14k, Mickey Mouse, $125.

Victorian
Bird, round, sculptured bird and flower
design, gold filled, c1883 . . . . . . .75.00
Flower, sq, gold-filled, engraved. . . .55.00
Knot, gold filled, c1895 . . . . .65.00
Leaf, gold filled 55.00
Squirrel, oval, emb, gold filled,
c1880. . . . . .75.00

Art Nouveau
Elk, oval, emb elk, 9k yg, c1900. . . .90.00
Lady, emb, brass 50.00
Vine, oval, emb, gold filled 65.00

Contemporary
Linear design, red and green enamel, gold
filled, c1970 . . . . .75.00
Silk Knots, c1980 . . . . .5.00
Thoroughbred, gold-plated, figural horse,
c1945. . . . . .65.00

Other
Art Deco, Concentric design, enamel,
yellow and blue, silver base 75.00
Art Deco, Flower motif, etched design, gold
plate. 40.00
Avon, enameled, gilded brass, antique
automobile dec, 1970 . . . . .15.00
Coral, oval, pearl center, Hawaii,
c1950. . . . . .75.00
Milk Glass, flower motif, gold filled,
c1880. . . . . .65.00
Pewter, bulldog head, garnet eyes,
c1895. . . . . .85.00
Souvenir, California State Cable RR Co.,
c1960. . . . . .25.00
Souvenir, State of Texas, star
center 20.00
Walrus Tusk Ivory, hand-carved, gold
nugget center, with tie tack 90.00

Cupids

Be suspicious of naked infants bearing bows and arrows. It is not clear if their arrows are tipped with passion or poison.

Club: Cupid Collectors Club, 2116 Lincoln St., Cedar Falls, IA 50613.

Postcards
Cupid on swing of roses, red hearts and
gold scrollwork border, mkd
"E Nash" 1.25
"February 14th," heart with cupids shooting
hearts and arrows at lovers, green ivy
trim, Germany, 1910 . . . . .1.50
"To My Valentine," two cupids holding garland of hearts, mkd "London,"
1910 . . . . .1.50

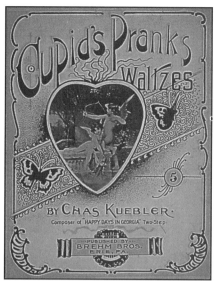

Sheet Music, Cupid's Pranks Waltzes, Chas. Kuebler, $20.

Valentines

Cupid kneeling on daisy, bow and arrow,
two hearts, ribbon easel back,
envelope. 50.00
Cupid with golden wheelbarrow of roses,
quilted heart motif, three-dimensional,
Hallmark. 25.00
Wishing-well center, cupids and trees,
Hallmark, c1960 . . . . .25.00

Other

Candy Basket, C.A. Reed Co., 3" by 4",
c1930-40 . . . . .10.00
Candy Box, two cupids, three-dimensional,
1925 . . . . .25.00
Card, Cupid selling hearts, flat, easel back,
5-1/2" h, 3-1/2" w 5.00
Card Holder, celluloid, 2" by 4",
embellished gold Dresdens,
c1880-1900 . . . . .65.00
Centerpiece, fold-out, honeycomb tissue,
cardboard base 25.00
Cup, paper, red and white, printed cupids,
ribbon swags, package 5.00
Gift Box, cardboard, hearts and cherubs
dec, handkerchief size 3.00
Honeycomb, paper puff, two cupids,
pedestal 50.00
Pocket Knife, 7-1/4" l, flat, mechanical,
Beistle 35.00
Puzzle, To My Valentine, 3-1/2" by 5-1/2",
30 pcs, hand cut, plywood, cardboard
box, c1909 . . . . .14.00
Stickers, Dennison, c1920-30 . . . . . .10.00
Tablecloth, paper, stenciled, cupids and
hearts dec, 1920 . . . . .25.00
Tie, silk, hp cupid with heart, 1930 . .35.00

Cuspidors

After examining the interiors of some of the cuspidors for sale at flea markets, I am glad I have never been in a bar where people "spit." Most collectors are enamored by the brass cuspidor. The form came in many other varieties as well. You could build a marvelous collection focusing on pottery cuspidors.

Within the past year, a large number of fake cuspidors have entered the market. I have seen them at flea markets across the United States. Double-check any cuspidor with a railroad marking and totally discount any with a Wells Fargo marking.

Bennington Pottery, 8" d, molded
flint-enamel glazed yellowware, imp
maker's mark, c1849-58 . . . . . . 350.00
Majolica, 6" h, polychrome-glazed, white
earthenware, emb floral pattern, paper
label, c1894-1900 . . . . 100.00
Majolica, 8-1/2" sq, polychrome-glazed,
white earthenware, emb floral pattern,
c1880-1900 . . . . 90.00
Porcelain, 7-1/2" d, molded,
polychrome-glazed, emb floral dec,
New England Pottery 150.00
Redware, 4" d, lead-glazed, coggled rim
and ear handle 155.00
Rockingham, 8-1/2" d, molded stoneware,
c1860-80 . . . . 40.00
Rockingham, 10" d, glazed yellowware,
molded shell form, c1850-80 . . . 80.00
Stoneware, 8" d, molded, Bristol-glazed,
blue shading, scalloped rim, Western
Stoneware Co., c1920-40 . . . . . . 40.00
Stoneware, 9" d, olive-brown, Meyer
Pottery, c1890-1900 . . . . 175.00
Stoneware, 10" d, salt-glazed, blue bands,
incised ribbon work, Red Wing Union
Stoneware Co., c1906-36 . . . . . 170.00

Cut Glass

Collectors have placed so much emphasis on American Brilliant Cut (1880 to 1917) that they completely overlook some of the finer cut glass of the post-World War I period. Admittedly, much cut glass in this later period was mass-produced and rather ordinary. But if you look hard enough, you will find some great pieces.

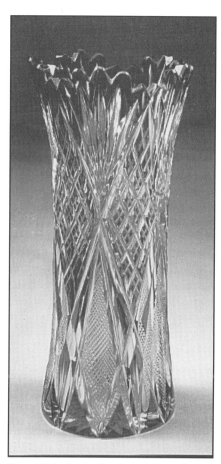

Vase, 8" h, flashed red and clear, $100.

The big news in the cut glass market at the end of the 1980s was the revelation that many of the rare pieces that had been uncovered in the 1980s were of recent origin. Reproductions, copycats and fakes abound. This is one category where you had better read a great deal and look at hundreds of pieces before you start buying.

Condition is also critical. Do not pay high prices for damaged pieces. Look for chips, dings, fractures and knife marks. Sometimes these defects can be removed, but consider the cost of the repair when purchasing a damaged piece. Of course, signed pieces command a higher dollar value. The antiques and collectibles market is governed by caveat emptor (let the buyer beware).

Club: American Cut Glass Association, P.O. Box 482, Ramona, CA 92065.

Bowls

7" d, 2" h, figured blank, hobstars and
fans 75.00
8" d, 2" h, cross-cut diamond and
fan 60.00
8-1/4" d, border of hobstars with floral
panels. 110.00

Knife Rests

3-1/2" l, dumbbell-shape, all over cutting,
Brilliant Period 25.00
4" l, notched prism ball ends and bar 38.00
5" l, faceted ball ends, panel cut bar .45.00

Other

Atomizer, 4" h, 2-1/2" sq, Harvard pattern,
gold washed top 125.00
Bishop's Hat Bowl, 12" d, 5" h, intaglio
diamond point cut. 275.00
Butter, Pat, Cypress, Laurel 32.00
Butter, Pat, Hobstars, well cut. 30.00
Candy Basket, 3-3/4" h, engraved florals,
Hawkes, sterling silver rim and
handle .85.00
Canoe, 2" l, Harvard pattern 70.00
Celery Tray, 11/2" l, 5" w, hobstars, cross
hatch and notched prisms on figured
blank. 60.00
Fernery, 8" d, hobstar and fan,
three ftd 80.00
Hair Receiver, 4" d, 3" h, floral and leaves,
rayed base, engraved sterling silver
top 75.00
Jar, cov, 1-3/4" sq, prism and cane, rayed
base, sterling silver repousse lid, mkd
"Unger Bros." 75.00
Napkin Ring, hobstars and bow-tie
fans 85.00
Pastry Tray, 9" d, 7" h, floral, handle.90.00
Plate, 6" d, Gothic pattern, Baker . . .65.00
Relish, 8" l, 3-1/2" w, hobstars 35.00
Salt Shaker, 4" h, green, sterling silver lid,
Garland pattern 55.00

Czechoslovakian

Czechoslovakia was created at the
end of World War I out of the area of
Bohemia, Moravia and Austrian Sile-
sia. Although best known for glass
products, Czechoslovakia also produced a large number of pottery and
porcelain wares for export.

Czechoslovakia objects do not enjoy a great reputation for quality, but I
think they deserve a second look.
They certainly reflect what was found
in the average American's home from
the 1920s through the 1950s.

**Rose Bowl, mauve ext., white int., scal-
loped gold-rimmed neck, 3-1/4" h, 2-1/4"
d opening, $35.**

Bank, 4-5/8", black Scottie,
white accent 50.00
Basket, 6-1/2", red, jet rim, handle,
cased 75.00
Book, 8" by 10-3/8", double, *Jack and the
Beanstalk* and *Hop O' My Thumb*,
pop-up, Artia Praque, 1962. . . . . 45.00
Bowl, 4-1/2", mottled color, cased . . 55.00
Calendar Holder, 10" by 10", cardboard,
enamel, gold painted design. . . . 35.00
Candlestick, 3", mottled color, cased 50.00
Card Holder, 12" by 7-1/2", hanging
basket, glass beads 75.00
Cruet, 6-1/4", crystal bottom, stopper 55.00
Doll, 11-1/2", girl, native costume with
kerchief, stuffed cloth body, painted
papier-mâché head, mohair wig . 80.00
Dresser Set, three pcs, enameled floral
design 30.00

**Vase, cased glass, six-sided, blue and
yellow mottled colors, $35.**

Figurine, 8-1/2", white ceramic, mother
holding child 50.00
Honey Pot, cov, 5", blue base, enameled
design 75.00
Linen Towel, 16" by 29", blue, green and
orange stripes 13.00
Necklace, 14", red and clear beads, metal
clasp closure 40.00
Pitcher, 11-3/4", red with black base,
cased. 100.00
Pocket Knife, 2-1/4" closed size, celluloid,
three pcs, tortoise shell case, snuff
spoon, ivory toothpick 35.00
Spoon, 5", decorated handle and bowl
edge, Blue Delft porcelain windmill illus
center 45.00
Toothpick Holder, 2-1/4", orange ground,
black and green design, cased . . 30.00
Vase, 6", red, jet rim, serpentine,
cased. 75.00

Dairy Collectibles

For decades, the dairy industry has
been doing a good job of encouraging
us to drink our milk and eat only real
butter. The objects used to get this
message across, as well as the packaging for dairy products, have long
been favorites with collectors.

Concentrate on the material associated with a single dairy, region or
national firm. If you tried to collect one
example of every milk bottle used,
you simply would not succeed. The
amount of dairy collectibles is staggering.

**Milk Bottle, Clover Dale Milk, pyro-
glazed Hopalong Cassidy, fantasy item,
$10.**

Clubs: Creamer Separator Association, Rt. 3, P.O. Box 189, Arcadia, WI 54612; National Association of Milk Bottle Collectors Inc., 4 Ox Bow Rd., Westport, CT 06800.

Newsletters: *Creamers*, P.O. Box 11, Lake Villa, IL 60046; *The Udder Collectibles*, HC 73 Box 1, Smithville Flats, NY 13841.

Award, Borden's, metal, gold,
    Elsie center 95.00
Bank, Land O' Lakes Butter, wood . .25.00
Belt Buckle, brass, 2" by 3", Elsie . . .40.00
Birthday Card, Borden's, Elsie illus. .65.00
Blotter, Hood's Milk, 6" by 3-1/2",
    multicolored 20.00
Book, *Elsie & the Looking Club*, hard cov,
    1946 . . . . .25.00
Booklet, Borden's Eagle Brand Book of
    Recipes, 32 pgs, c1920 . . . . .15.00
Box, Land O' Lakes Pasteurized Process
    Cheese, 2-1/2" by 8", wood, red and
    black 8.50
Calendar, Hood's Milk, 14" by 10", baby
    with bottle illus, Oct 1940 . . . . . .35.00
Container, Borden's Malted Milk, glass,
    paper diamond-shaped label, metal lid,
    emb letters 350.00
Container, Carnation Malted Milk, milk
    glass, aluminum lid 145.00
Game, Elsie's Milkman Game, 1963 .87.00
Glass, Elsie illus, 1776 design 25.00
Pinback Button, Sharples Tubular Cream
    Separators 25.00
Placemat, 11" by 16-3/4", Elsie illus .12.00
Playing Cards, Kempley Ice Cream Co.,
    geometric border 5.00
Pocket Mirror, Ice Cream Dairy Co. .45.00
Pocket Mirror, Sharples Tubular Cream
    Separators, oval 50.00
Postcard, Carnation Ice Cream, billboard
    illus 20.00

Creamer, porcelain, U.S. Navy Commissary, Sterling, East Liverpool, OH, 2-1/2" h, $10.

Recipe Book, Borden, 70 Magic Recipes,
    24 pgs, 1952 . . . . 6.00
Recipe Book, Carnation Milk, Teen Time
    Cooking with Carnation, 16 pgs,
    1959 . . . . 6.00
Salt & Pepper Shakers, pr, Borden's, baby
    Beulah & Beauregard, figural . . . 65.00
Sewing Needle Book, Elsie illus, several
    needles mounted inside 6.50
Sign, Breyer's Ice Cream, neon,
    leaf logo 20.00
Sign, Sealtest Ice Cream, 32", tin, color,
    metal frame, bottom logo 35.00
Sign, Select Brand Milk, 11" by 21", two
    red-haired girls illus, c1920 . . . . . 65.00
Spoon, Breyer's Ice Cream 48.00
Thermometer, Baker's Hygrade Ice
    Cream, 14", wood, black and gold,
    round top and bottom 40.00
Thermometer, Roha's Milk, 7-1/4", wood,
    brown lettering, white bottle illus,
    diamond logo 35.00
Tin, Luter's Pure Lard, mammy illus, red
    and yellow 40.00
Trade Card, Lactart Milk Acid, milkmaid
    with cows illus 4.00
Watch, white plastic, Elsie illus,
    1950 . . . . 18.00

Dakin Figures

The term "Dakin" refers to a type of hollow, vinyl figure produced by the R. Dakin Co. These figures are found with a number of variations—molded or cloth costumed, jointed or nonjointed—and range in height from 5 inches to 10 inches.

As with any popular and profitable product, Dakin figures were copied. There are a number of Dakin-like figures found on the market. Produced by Sutton & Son Inc., Knickerbocker Toy Co., and a production company for Hanna-Barbera, these figures are also collectible and are often mistaken for the original Dakin products. Be careful when purchasing.

Bambi, Disney, 1960 . . . . 35.00
Barney Rubble, orange shirt, yellow hair,
    1970 . . . . 50.00
Big Boy, adv, red-and-white checkered
    overalls, brown hair, holding
    hamburger 200.00
Daffy Duck, 8-1/2" h, 1968 . . . . 11.00
Deputy Dawg, 6" h, 1977 . . . . 40.00
Dewey Duck, red shirt, bent leg,
    Disney 30.00

Dino, squeaky head, blue body, brown
    face, white collar, 1970 . . . . 60.00
Donald Duck, Disney, 1960 . . . . 20.00
Dumbo, cloth collar, Disney, 1960 . . 25.00
Fang, 7" h, 1970 . . . . 25.00
Fred Flintstone, 1970 . . . . 35.00
Gigolo Giraffe, top hat, tux collar with
    tie 19.00
Glamour Kitty, white, gold crown,
    1977 . . . . 150.00
Goofy Grams, brown, 1971 . . . . 30.00
Hobo Joe, bank, 1977 . . . . 80.00
Huckleberry Hound, bank, 5" h, seated,
    1980 . . . . 20.00
Huckleberry Hound, figure, blue body, red
    bow tie, 1970 . . . . 90.00
Jack-in-the-Box, bank, 1971 . . . . 25.00
Lion in a Cage, bank, 1971 . . . . 25.00
Louie Duck, blue shirt, straight legs,
    Disney 30.00
Merlin the Magic Mouse, 1970 . . . . . 35.00
Mighty Mouse, 1977 . . . . 100.00
Miss Liberty Bell, with hat, 1975 . . . . 75.00
Monkey on a Barrel, bank, 1971 . . . . 25.00
Pepe Le Pew, 8" h, 1971 . . . . 25.00
Pink Panther, 8" h, legs apart, 1971 . 15.00
Popeye, nodding head, cloth clothes,
    1974 . . . . 50.00
Ren Hoek, water squirter, Nickelodeon,
    1993 . . . . 10.00
Road Runner, squeaky head, blue body,
    orange legs, yellow beak, 1968 . . 30.00
Sambo's Tiger, 10", sitting, 1977 . . . 14.00
Scooby Doo, 1982 . . . . 75.00
Seal on a Box, bank, 1971 . . . . 25.00
Second Banana, 6" h, 1970 . . . . 15.00
Snagglepuss, 1970 . . . . 30.00
Stan Laurel, 8" h, 1974 . . . . 20.00
Stimpy, water squirter, Nickelodeon,
    1993 . . . . 10.00
Tiger in a Cage, bank, 1971 . . . . 25.00

Dearly Departed

I know this category is a little morbid, but the stuff is collected. Several museums have staged special exhibitions devoted to mourning art and jewelry. Funeral parlors need to advertise for business. I did not put one in the listing, but do you know what makes a great coffee table? A coffin carrier or coffin stand. Just put a piece of glass over the top. It's the right size, has leg room underneath and makes one heck of a conversation piece.

Bottles

Poison Tincture Iodine, skull and
    crossbones, amber,
    rubber stopper 30.00

Skeleton in Cloak, figural, ceramic, brown
and tan, 1880-1920 . . . . .110.00
Skull, figural, cobalt blue, c1972 . . . .60.00
Sure Death Poison, flypaper 5.00
Undertaker's Supply Co., embalming
fluid. 60.00

Catalog

Caskets & Funeral Supplies, Sunbury, PA,
188 pgs, leather cov. 45.00
Cemetery Pillars, Mausoleums, Statues,
Headstones, etc., Flint Granite Co.,
Albany, NY, 49 pgs, 1900s. 20.00
Springfield Metallic Casket Co., 24 pgs,
wrappers, folding casket carriages and
pedestals 30.00

Mourning Jewelry

Brooch, cross-shape, engraved, gold-filled
end caps, C-catch, tube hinge . . .65.00
Necklace, black glass, ribbon, glass beads,
wire, open lacy scalloped-edge pattern,
c1890-1900 . . . . .95.00
Pendant, black onyx, gold, seed pearls,
teardrop shapes, grape motif, chain,
c1880 .125.00

Other

Blotter, Magical 999 Embalmer Formula,
c1900 . . . . .5.00
Book, *Champion Expanding Encyclopedia
of Embalming*, Champion Chemical
Co., 9" by 12", monthly additions,
30 pgs, 1923-28 . . . . .32.00
Cabinet Cards, Corpse lying in open coffin
under evergreen trees, boat-shaped
coffin, c1890. . . . . .50.00
Cabinet Cards, Deceased child in mother's
arms. 20.00
Calendar, A.G. Lundberg, Artistic
Memorials in Granite & Marble,
Westford, MA, 10" by 14", 1926. .20.00
Case, coffin-shape, 2-1/8" l, brass top,
wood sides, int. fitted with erotic
mummy .95.00
Funeral Notice, black-bordered card,
envelope, Farmersville, OK, funeral,
1914. . . . . .8.50

**Love Token Coin, memorial to child,
Great Britain 1/2 crown, 1-5/16" d, $55.**

Painting, mourning, 8-3/8" by 10-3/8",
watercolor, matted, framed, 1810 65.00
Playing Cards, The Campfield-Hickman
Funeral Home, Barberton, OH, funeral
home illus, yellow ground, 1954 . 15.00
Post Mortem, album photo, child in
flower-filled coffin, eyes open,
mounted 25.00
Register, undertaker's, lists information
and costs of funerals from 1891-95,
Toledo, OH 10.00
Tobacco Jar, skull figural, X handle on lid,
ceramic 190.00

Deed and Documents

A document is any printed paper
that shows evidence or proof of something. Subject matter ranges from bap-
tismal certificates to scholastic awards
to stocks and bonds. Flea markets are
loaded with old documents. Though
they generally have minimal value and
are usually copies of the original
forms, it makes good sense to check
before discarding. It may be of value to
its original owner or to a paper-ephem-
era collector.

Many 18th- and early 19th century
deeds are on parchment. In most cases, value is minimal, ranging from a few
dollars to a high of $10. First, check to
see if the deed is the original document.
Most deeds on the market are copies;
the actual document is often on file in
the courthouse. Second, check the signatures. Benjamin Franklin signed a
number of Pennsylvania deeds. These
are worth a great deal more than $10.
Third, check the location of the deed. If
it is a city deed, the current property
owner may like to acquire it. If it is for a
country farm, forget it.

Finally, a number of early deeds
have an elaborate wax seal at the bottom. When framed, these make wonderful display pieces in attorneys'
offices.

Receipts

A.E. Miller, Manufacturers & Jobbers of
Confectionery, Brattleboro, VT . . 10.00
Myers Cox Co., Dubuque, IA, 1918,
notification to customers that receipts
will not be sent 5.00
The Independent Newspaper, Salmon
Falls, 1901, receipt for one-year
subscription. 6.50

**Indenture, deed, note and deposited
check, dated Dec. 21, 1926, $2.**

Stock Certificates

ABC Brewing Corporation, 1934, green, or-
namental engraving. 10.00
Babcock & Wilcox Co., Nuclear Plant
Designers, 1959-71, green border, two
men and logo vignette 4.00
Lincoln Printing Co., 1962-65, engraved
Abe Lincoln vignette 6.00
Northampton Brewing Corporation, 1934,
orange, engraved 20.00

Other

Check, Sedalis, S.P. Johns & Sons, 1909,
ornate, canceled 8.50
Court Martial, Headquarters Dept. of the
East, New York City, Feb. 20, 1865, Spl
Order 44, Court Marshall in Burlington,
VT, by Command of Maj. Gen. Dix, two
attached travel expenses 12.00
Deed, Pike County, IL, 1856, attached
receipt, emb seals, dated
July 9, 1856. . . . . 18.00
Honorable Discharge, Vicksburg Muster-
Out Roll, Aug. 1, 1863, Lt. Joseph
Treadway, 23rd WI Volunteers, sgd by
officers. 30.00
Letter, Office of the Minority Leader, House
of Representatives, Dec. 30, 1949, sgd
Joseph W. Martin, Jr. 9.00
Pay and Allowance, Civil War officer, 11"
by 17", 1864 . . . . 15.00

Degenhart Glass

Degenhart pressed-glass novelties
are collected by mold, by individual

color or by group of colors. Hundreds of colors, some nearly identical, were produced between 1947 and 1978. Prior to 1972, most pieces were un-marked. After that date a "D" or "D" in a heart was used.

Do not confuse Kanawha's bird salt and bow slipper or L.G. Wright's mini-slipper, daisy and button salt and 5" robin-covered dish with Degenhart pieces. They are similar, but there are differences. See Gene Florence's *Degenhart Glass and Paperweights: A Collector's Guide to Colors and Values* (Degenhart Paperweight and Glass Museum, 1982) for a detailed list of Degenhart patterns.

Club: The Friends of Degenhart, Degenhart Paperweight and Glass Museum, 65323 Highland Hills Rd., P.O. Box 186, Cambridge, OH 43725.

Animal Dish, cov
Hen, 3" h, pigeon blood 48.00
Lamb, emerald green 35.00
Robin, taffeta 50.00
Turkey, amber 35.00

Owl
Canary 35.00
Crown Tuscan 40.00
Ivory 30.00
Misty Green 40.00
Seafoam .35.00

Paperweight
Hand-painted plate 75.00
Multicolored 75.00
Red flower 65.00

Toothpick Holders
Baby, gold .8.00
Bird, persimmon 15.00
Elephant Head, amber 20.00

Other
Bicentennial Bell, amethyst 50.00

Slipper, Kat, pink, $25.

Bicentennial Bell, seafoam 10.00
Boot, Texas, peach 12.00
Candy Dish, cov, Wildflower,
   twilight blue 25.00
Child's Mug, stork and peacock pattern,
   green 20.00
Cup Plate, Seal of Ohio, sunset . . . 10.00
Hat, Daisy and Button pattern, blue milk
   glass 12.00
Hat, Daisy and Button pattern,
   vaseline 15.00
Jewelry Box, heliotrope 35.00
Pitcher, mini, jade 20.00
Portrait Plate, crystal, 1974 . . . . 35.00
Priscilla, amber 75.00
Salt, bird, 1-1/2", amber 12.00
Slipper, Daisy and Button, taffeta . . 20.00
Tray, hand-shape, Bittersweet 15.00
Wine, Taffeta 40.00

Depression Era Glassware

Depression-era glassware refers to glassware made between the 1920s and 1940s. It was mass-produced by a number of different companies. It was sold cheaply and often given away as a purchasing premium. Specialize in one pattern or color. Once again, there is no way that you can own every piece made. Also, because Depression-Era Glass was produced in vast quantities, buy only pieces in excellent or better condition.

A number of patterns have been re-produced. See Gene Florence's *The Collector's Encyclopedia of Depression Glass* (Collector Books, revised annually) for a complete list of repro-ductions.

Clubs: The National Depression Glass Association, P.O. Box 8264, Wichita, KS 67209; 20-30-40 Society, Inc., P.O. Box 856, La Grange, IL 60525.

Newspaper: *The Daze*, P.O. Box 57, Otisville, MI 48463.

Adam
Ashtray, 4-5/8", green 25.00
Bowl, 4-3/4", dessert, green 15.00
Bowl, 4-3/4", dessert, pink 15.00
Bowl, 7-3/4", vegetable, green 25.00
Bowl, 9", cov, pink 65.00
Butter, missing lid, pink 35.00
Cake Plate, 10", ftd, green 25.00

Cake Plate, 10", ftd, pink 28.00
Candlestick, green 50.00
Candlestick, pink 48.00
Coaster, green 18.00
Creamer, pink 25.00
Cup, pink 24.00
Iced Tea Glass, green 65.00
Pitcher, sq base, pink 50.00
Plate, 7-3/4", salad, green 15.00
Plate, 7-3/4", salad, pink 17.50
Plate, 9", dinner, green 28.00
Plate, 9", dinner, pink 30.00
Platter, oval, 11-3/4", green 27.00
Platter, oval, 11-3/4", pink 27.00
Platter, rectangular, 11-3/4", green . 30.00
Relish, 8", divided, green 28.00
Relish, 8", divided, pink 30.00
Salt and Pepper Shakers, pr, pink . . 75.00
Saucer, pink 8.00
Sherbet, 6", ftd, pink 28.00
Sugar, cov, pink 45.00
Tumbler, 4-1/2", green 28.00
Tumbler, 4-1/2", pink 28.00

American Sweetheart
Bowl, 9" d, monax 70.00
Bowl, 9" d, pink 50.00
Cereal Bowl, pink 15.00
Cream Soup, 4-1/2" d, monax 140.00
Cup and Saucer, monax 12.00
Cup and Saucer, pink 20.00
Flat Soup, monax 75.00
Plate, 6" d, bread and butter, monax .5.00
Plate, 6" d, bread and butter, pink . . .5.00
Plate, 9-3/4" d, dinner, monax 24.00
Plate, 12" d, salver, pink 25.00
Platter, 13" l, oval, monax 65.00
Platter, 13" l, oval, pink 50.00
Vegetable Bowl, 11" l, oval, Monax . 75.00
Block Optic
Cereal Bowl, 5-1/4" d, green 12.00
Creamer, flat, green 10.00
Creamer, footed, yellow 15.00
Cup, green .5.00
Plate, 6" d, bread and butter, green . .3.00
Plate, 6" d, bread and butter, pink . . .3.00
Plate, 6" d, bread and butter, yellow. .2.50
Plate, 8" d, luncheon, green 4.00
Plate, 8" d, luncheon, pink 4.00
Plate, 8" d, luncheon, yellow 4.00
Plate, 9" d, dinner, green 20.00
Plate, 9" d, dinner, yellow 40.00
Sugar, flat, green 10.00
Sugar, footed, yellow 12.00
Tumbler, 9 oz, flat, pink 15.00
Tumbler, 9 oz, footed, pink 17.50
Tumbler, 9 oz, footed, yellow 22.00
Tumbler, 11 oz, 5" h, flat, pink 18.00

Cameo
Butter, cov, green 225.00
Cake Plate, ftd, green 20.00
Candy, green 65.00

Depression Era
Glassware Patterns

American Sweetheart

Dogwood

Florentine

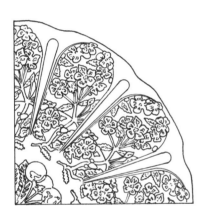

Cherry Blossom

Mayfair Open Rose

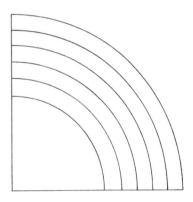

Moderntone

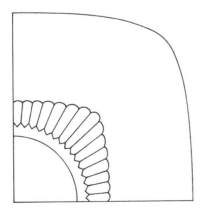

Forest Green

Princess

Cereal Bowl, yellow. 30.00
Cream Soup, green. 75.00
Creamer, 3-1/4", green 18.00
Cup, plain, green. 13.00
Cup, plain, yellow 8.00
Decanter, stopper, green 175.00
Domino Tray, green 185.00
Goblet, water, green 50.00
Goblet, wine, green. 60.00
Flat Soup, green 60.00
Pitcher, 56 oz, green. 50.00
Plate, 6" d, green. 4.00
Plate, 6" d, yellow 4.00
Plate, 7" d, green. 7.00
Plate, 8" d, green. 10.00
Plate, 9-1/2" d, green 17.50
Plate, 9-1/2" d, yellow 9.00
Plate, 10-1/2" d, green 8.00
Platter, oval, green 24.00
Relish, 3 part, green 25.00
Sandwich Plate, 10-1/2", closed handles,
    green 12.00
Sherbet, 3-1/8", green. 12.00
Sherbet, 4-1/4", green. 30.00
Sugar, 3-1/4", green 17.50
Sugar, 3-1/4", yellow 12.00
Tumbler, 5 oz, green. 28.00
Tumbler, 9 oz, ftd, yellow 14.00
Tumbler, 11 oz, green. 30.00
Tumbler, 11 oz, yellow, ftd 60.00
Tumbler, 15 oz, 5-1/4", green 95.00
Vase, 5-3/4", green. 215.00
Vase, 8", green 40.00
Vegetable Bowl, green 30.00

Cherry Blossom
Berry Bowl, individual, 4-3/4" d,
    green 16.00
Berry Bowl, individual, 4-3/4" d,
    pink. 15.00
Berry Bowl, master, 8-1/2" d, green .40.00
Berry Bowl, master, 8-1/2" d, pink. . .42.50
Bowl, 9" d, handled, pink. 45.00
Cake Plate, ftd, green 25.00
Cake Plate, ftd, pink 28.00
Creamer and cov Sugar, green. 50.00
Creamer and cov Sugar, pink 50.00
Cup and Saucer, pink 25.00
Pitcher, 42 oz, flat, green 60.00
Pitcher, 42 oz, flat, pink. 58.00
Plate, 6" d, bread and butter, green . .6.00
Plate, 7" d, salad, green 20.00
Plate, 9" d, dinner, pink. 22.00
Platter, oval, 11" l, green. 40.00
Platter, oval, 11" l, pink 45.00
Platter, oval, 13" l, green. 60.00
Sherbet, green 17.00
Sherbet, pink. 15.00

Dogwood
Berry Bowl, 8-1/2" d, pink 60.00
Cake Plate, 13", green 125.00
Cake Plate, 13", pink. 135.00

Cereal Bowl, 5-1/2" d, pink 28.00
Creamer, 3-1/4", green 50.00
Creamer, 3-1/4", pink. 15.00
Cup, monax 36.00
Cup, pink 15.00
Cup and Saucer, green 45.00
Bowl, 10-1/4" d, green 265.00
Pitcher, dec, pink 180.00
Plate, 6" d, pink 9.00
Plate, 8" d, green. 9.00
Plate, 8" d, pink 7.50
Plate, 9" d, pink 35.00
Salver, monax 20.00
Saucer, green 10.00
Saucer, pink. 5.00
Sherbet, pink 35.00
Sugar, pink. 15.00
Tumbler, 10 oz, 4", green 85.00
Tumbler, 10 oz, 4", pink 40.00
Tumbler, 12 oz, 5", pink 60.00

Florentine #2
Ashtray, 3-3/4" d, green 18.00
Ashtray, 5-1/2" d, green 15.00
Berry Bowl, 5" d, crystal 16.00
Berry Bowl, 5" d, green 10.00
Berry Bowl, 5" d, yellow 25.00
Berry Bowl, 8" d, crystal 18.00
Berry Bowl, 8" d, yellow 30.00
Butter, cov, crystal 100.00
Butter, cov, yellow 145.00
Candleholder, green 28.00
Candlesticks, pr, green 60.00
Candlesticks, pr, yellow 55.00
Candy Dish, green. 110.00
Candy Dish, yellow 150.00
Compote, ruffled, 3-1/2" d, crystal . . 12.00
Creamer, flat, crystal 7.50
Creamer, flat, yellow 8.00
Creamer, footed, crystal 8.00
Creamer, footed, green 12.00
Creamer, footed, yellow 12.00
Cream Soup, green 12.00
Cup and Saucer, yellow 12.00
Custard Cup, crystal 50.00
Custard Cup, yellow 75.00
Gravy Boat, yellow 38.00
Gravy Boat, with underplate, yellow 80.00
Parfait, 6" h, ftd, yellow 60.00
Pitcher, cone, crystal 20.00
Pitcher, cone, green 60.00
Pitcher, cone, yellow 30.00
Pitcher, footed, 28 oz, crystal 28.00
Pitcher, footed, 28 oz, green 45.00
Pitcher, footed, 28 oz, yellow 30.00
Plate, 8-1/2" d, salad, crystal 8.00
Plate, 8-1/2" d, salad, yellow 15.00
Plate, 10" d, dinner, crystal 8.00
Plate, 10" d, dinner, green 15.00
Platter, 11" l, oval, green 16.00
Platter, 11" l, oval, yellow. 20.00
Relish, 10" l, 3 part, yellow 30.00
Salt and Pepper Shakers, pr, yellow 50.00

Sherbet, green 7.00
Sherbet, yellow 12.00
Sugar, ftd, crystal 8.00
Sugar, ftd, green 10.00
Tumbler, 3-1/4" h, ftd, crystal 13.00
Tumbler, 4" h, green. 8.00
Tumbler, 4-1/2" h, green. 25.00
Tumbler, 5" h, green 18.00
Vegetable Bowl, cov, 9" l, yellow . . . 60.00

Forest Green
Bowl, 4-1/4" sq 5.50
Bowl, 4-3/4" sq 5.00
Bowl, 5-1/4" d, gold rim 8.50
Bowl, 7-3/8" sq 18.00
Creamer and Sugar 12.00
Cup and Saucer 5.50
Pitcher, 3 quart 30.00
Plate, 6-1/2" sq 6.00
Plate, 8-3/8" d, luncheon 6.00
Platter, 11" l, rect 24.00
Popcorn Set, one large bowl and six
    smaller bowls 75.00
Punch Bowl, gold rim 25.00
Punch Cup 2.00
Salad Bowl, 7-3/8" sq 18.00
Soup Bowl, 6" sq 17.00
Tumbler, 5 oz 3.00
Tumbler, 10 oz, ftd 5.00
Tumbler, 15 oz 7.50
Vase, 6-3/8" h 5.00
Vase, 9" h 7.00

Mayfair (Open Rose)
Bowl, 12" d, low, blue 75.00
Bowl, 12" d, low, green 35.00
Bowl, 12" d, low, pink 55.00
Butter, cov, blue 275.00
Celery, divided, blue 60.00
Creamer, blue. 75.00
Cup and Saucer, blue. 25.00
Cup and Saucer, pink 30.00
Pitcher, 6" h, blue 140.00
Pitcher, 6" h, pink 50.00
Pitcher, 8" h, 60 oz, blue 160.00
Pitcher, 8" h, 60 oz, pink 50.00
Plate, dinner, pink. 45.00
Platter, oval, blue 70.00
Platter, oval, pink 30.00
Relish, four-part, green. 25.00
Relish, four-part, pink 35.00
Sandwich Server, center handle,
    blue 75.00
Sandwich Server, center handle,
    green 30.00
Sandwich Server, center handle,
    pink 40.00
Vegetable Bowl, 7" d, blue 45.00

Moderntone
Berry Bowl, 8" d, master,
    cobalt blue 55.00
Bowl, 5" d, amethyst 18.00

Creamer and Sugar, amethyst 18.00
Creamer and Sugar, cobalt blue 30.00
Cup and Saucer, amethyst 10.00
Cup and Saucer, cobalt blue. 16.00
Plate, 5-3/4" d, cobalt blue 6.00
Plate, 6-3/4" d, cobalt blue 10.00
Plate, 8" d, cobalt blue 12.50
Plate, 9" d, amethyst. 12.00
Plate, 9" d, cobalt blue 18.00
Platter, 11" l, oval, cobalt blue. 40.00
Platter, 12" d, round, amethyst 38.00
Salt and Pepper Shakers, amethyst .40.00
Salt and Pepper Shakers,
    cobalt blue 40.00
Sugar, amethyst 10.00
Sherbet, cobalt blue 15.00

Princess
Bowl, 9" d, green. 36.00
Bowl, 9" d, yellow 125.00
Cake Stand, 10" d, ftd, green 25.00
Cereal Bowl, 5" d, green 25.00
Cereal Bowl, 5" d, yellow. 25.00
Creamer, yellow 18.00
Plate, 5-1/2" d, green 10.00
Plate, 8" d, green. 15.00
Plate, 8" d, yellow 10.00
Plate, 9" d, green. 22.00
Plate, 9" d, yellow 12.50
Salt and Pepper Shakers, pr, green .50.00
Sherbet, ftd, green 20.00
Sherbet, ftd, yellow 32.00
Vegetable Bowl, 10" l, oval, green . .24.00
Vegetable Bowl, 10" l, oval, yellow . .55.00

Royal Ruby
Ashtray 8.50
Bowl, 4-1/2" d 10.00
Bowl, 4-3/4" sq 7.50
Bowl, 8-1/2" d 30.00
Creamer and Sugar. 12.00
Cup and Saucer 8.00
Leaf Dish, 6-1/2" l 8.00
Marmalade, clear base 15.00
Pitcher, 3 quart 35.00
Plate, 6" d .7.50
Plate, 7-3/4" d 4.50
Plate, 8" d .7.50
Plate, 9" d .15.00
Plate, 13-3/4" d 25.00
Punch Bowl Set, punch bowl, base and
    twelve cups 100.00
Salad Bowl, 11-3/4" d 35.00
Soup Bowl. 12.00
Tumbler, 13 oz 10.00
Vase, 9" h .18.00

Dinnerware

There is a growing appreciation for the thousands of dinnerware patterns that graced the tables of low-, middle-, and some upper-income families during the first three-quarters of the 20th century. Some of America's leading industrial designers were responsible for forms and decorative motifs.

Collectors fall into three groups: those who collect the wares of a specific factory or factories, often with a strong regional emphasis; individuals who are reassembling the set they grew up with; and those who are fascinated by certain forms and motifs. The bulk of the books on the subject appeared in the early 1980s.

Several of the companies have become established collecting categories in their own right. This is why you will find companies such as Blue Ridge and Hall elsewhere in this book.

Club: Porcelier Collectors Club, 21 Tamarac Swamp Rd., Wallingford, CT 06492.

Newsletter: *Coors Pottery Newsletter*, 3808 Carr Place N, Seattle, WA 98103.

Periodicals: *The Daze*, P.O. Box 57, Otisville, MI 48463; *Purinton Pastimes*, P.O. Box 9394, Arlington, VA 22219; *The Pottery Collectors Express*, P.O. Box 221, Mayview, MO 64071.

Coors: Coors Pottery was manufactured in Golden, Colo., from 1920 to 1939

Rosebud
Apple Baker, 14 oz 28.00
Baking Pan, 10-3/4" by 6-3/4" 38.00
Cake Server, 10" 65.00
Casserole, Dutch, 3 3/4 pint 55.00
Eggcup, 3" d 28.00
Jug, 14 oz 95.00
Plate, 6" d 12.00
Saucer. 8.00
Sugar Shaker. 35.00

Crooksville: The Crooksville China Co., Crooksville, Ohio, was founded in 1902 for the manufacture of artware, including vases, flowerpots and novelties. Dinnerware soon became its stock and trade. Manufacturing continued until 1959.

Quadro
Bowl, vegetable 10.00
Creamer. 5.00
Gravy Liner 6.00
Plate, 5-3/4" d 2.00
Plate, 9-1/2" d 6.00
Platter. 10.00
Saucer 2.00
Sugar 10.00

Limoges: American Limoges was made in Ohio in 1897 by the Sebring Brothers. Most pieces have only one backstamp. The Limoges China Co., closed in April 1958.

Chateau France
Bowl, 8" w, gold edge. 8.00
Cup, scenic decal inside, gold lace edge,
    maroon border, Triumph-shape. . . 5.00
Platter, 14" l, scenic decal center, gold lace
    edge 20.00

Good Housekeeping
Creamer 12.00
Plate, 10" d, multicolored, floral design
    center, gold edge, 22k gold,
    1940 . . . . 10.00
Salt and Pepper Shakers, pr, white, floral
    design top, gold-band base. 12.00

Lamour
Dish, cov, red floral-wreath
    design top 35.00
Platter, 11" l, red floral wreath design
    center 10.00

Prince Charles
Cereal Bowl, 6" d, orange floral center,
    beige and gold trim 10.00
Cup and Saucer, orange floral decal,
    beige, orange and gold trim. 10.00
Plate, 10" d, orange floral decal, beige,
    orange and gold trim 10.00

Porcelier: The Porcelier Manufacturing Co., began in East Liverpool, Ohio, in 1927. Porcelier sold its building and seven acres of land to Pittsburgh Plate Glass Industries of Pittsburgh in 1954.

Barock-Colonial
Cookie Jar 95.00
Sugar Shaker 15.00
Teapot 40.00
Waffle Iron 150.00

Geometric Cattails
Creamer 12.00
Sugar Bowl. 12.00

Geometric Wheat
Coffeepot, 6 cup 30.00
Creamer, notched handle. 12.00
Sugar Bowl 12.00

Rose and Wheat
Coffeepot, 2-cup. 30.00
Coffeepot, 6-cup. 25.00

Coffeepot, 8-cup 30.00
Creamer 10.00
Sugar Bowl 10.00

Dionne Quintuplets

On May 28, 1934, on a small farm in Callander, Ontario, Canada, five baby girls, the Dionne Quintuplets (weighing a total of 10 pounds, 1-1/4 ounces) were delivered into this world with the help of Dr. DaFoe and two midwives.

Due to their parents' poor financial circumstances and the public's curiosity, the quintuplets were put on display. For a small fee, the world was invited to come and see the quints at play in their custom-built home or to buy a souvenir to mark their birth. The field of collectibles for Dionne Quintuplets memorabilia is a very fertile one!

Book, *Dionne Years*, 232 pgs 10.00
Box, candy, Baby Ruth, 2" by 8" by 11", cardboard, "Baby Ruth: First and Only Candy Served the Dionne Quints" 75.00
Box, candy, Dionne Pops, 4" by 10-1/2" by 1", Vitamin Candy Co., Providence, RI, 1936 . . . . .125.00
Cake Plate, 11-1/2" d, china, white, gold maple leaf at top, red rim, center color portraits titled "Dionne Quintuplets, Born May 28, 1934, Callander, Ontario, Canada" 135.00
Calendar, 1935, multicolored, 8" by 11-1/4", Dairy Distributors, Inc. . .18.00

Magazine, *Look*, Oct. 11, 1938, $30.

Calendar, 1938, color, 8" by 11-3/4", Brown & Bigelow Co., unused 30.00
Calendar, 1955 . . . . 20.00
Cereal Bowl, 5-7/8" d, chrome-plated metal, Quaker Oats premium, late 1935 . . . . 25.00
Doll, 8" h, swivel head, jointed hips and shoulders, molded hair, painted eyes 250.00
Fan, Plymouth-Dodge adv back, cardboard, flat, color-portrait front, wood stick, 1936. . . . . 40.00
Fan, Stonington Furniture Co adv back, cardboard, multicolored, 1936 . . 15.00
Key Chain, 3" l, celluloid, dark green, gold lettering, "Souvenir of Quint Land, Callander, Canada". 30.00
Lobby Card, 11" by 14", "Five Of A Kind," color, girls playing piano, 1938 . . 70.00
Magazine, Women's World, Feb 1937 . . . . 10.00
Palm Puzzle, steel balls, glass cov, place quints in buggy 35.00
Paper Doll Book, 1930, 6" dolls, 90 pcs 100.00
Paper Doll Book, 1936, 10" by 17". . 45.00
Paper Doll Book, 1937, Palmolive premium 36.00

Disneyana

"Steamboat Willie" introduced Mickey Mouse to the world in 1928. Walt and Roy Disney, brothers, worked together to create an entertainment empire filled with a myriad of memorable characters ranging from Donald Duck to Zorro.

Early Disney items are getting very expensive. No problem. Disney continues to license material. In 30 years the stuff from the 1960s and 1970s will be scarce and eagerly sought. Now is the time to buy it.

Clubs: National Fantasy Fan Club for Disneyana Collectors & Enthusiasts, P.O. Box 19212, Irvine, CA 92713; The Mouse Club, 2056 Cirone Way, San Jose, CA 95124.

Periodicals: *Storyboard Magazine Collectors*, 2512 Artesia Blvd., Redondo Beach, CA 90278; *Tomart's Disneyana Digest*, 3300 Encrete Ln., Dayton, OH 45439; *Toy Shop*, Krause Publications, 700 E. State St., Iola, WI 54990.

Books, Whitman Publishing Co.
Clarabelle Cow, 1938 . . . . 30.00

Night Light, Mickey Mouse, plastic, WDP, 2-1/2" w, 2-1/2" h, $5.

Mickey Mouse and Mother Goose . . 25.00
Snow White & the Seven Dwarfs . . . 16.00
The Wise Little Hen 45.00

Cookie Jars
Eeyore 140.00
Mickey and Pluto, decal, cylinder, 1980 . . . . 20.00
Mickey's Cookie Bus, Sears, Roebuck & Co., 1978. . . . . 90.00

Games
Disneyland Monorail, Parker Bros., 1950 . . . . 20.00
Donald Duck's Tidily Winx, Jay Mar . 30.00
Pin the Nose on Pinocchio, Parker Bros., 1939 . . . . 100.00
Pitfalls of Pinocchio, marble and dice, Whitman, 1940 . . . . 60.00

Paper Dolls
Hayley Mills in That Darn Cat, Whitman, 1965 . . . . 14.00
Mary Poppins, four dolls, Whitman, 1964 . . . . 10.00
Pollyanna, 1960 . . . . 12.00

Planters, ceramic
Donald Duck, 5-1/2" h, figural, sitting atop ABC blocks, Leeds, c1940 . . . . . 35.00
Dopey, Leeds China Co. 50.00
Minnie. 55.00
Thumper. 35.00

Other
Ashtray, Mickey, Bavaria 100.00
Bank, Donald Duck, ceramic, Leeds China Co. 60.00
Button, Pluto, Hollywood Co. 40.00
Button, Snow White and the Seven Dwarfs, yellow 40.00

Camera, Donald Duck, Herbert George
Co. 50.00
Charm, celluloid, various Disney
characters, 1930 . . . . .30.00
Christmas Card, Mickey Mouse, Hall Bros.,
1930. . . . . .35.00
Clock, Donald Duck, quartz, wall . . .70.00
Clock, Dopey, wood,
moveable eyes. 25.00
Colorform Set, Mickey Mouse. 15.00
Coloring Book, Lady and the Tramp,
1954. . . . . .6.00
Coloring Book, Mickey Mouse Explorers
Club Coloring Book, Kroger, 64 pgs,
1965 . . . . .15.00
Cup and Saucer, lusterware, Mickey with
microphone, 1930 . . . . .50.00
Dish, Snow White and Doc, 6" d, ceramic,
1938. . . . . .60.00
Disney Dollar, Disneyland, $1 bill,
1987. . . . . .1.50
Disney Dollar, Walt Disney World, $5 bill,
1987. . . . . .6.00
Doctor Kit, Donald Duck, 1940 . . . .30.00
Doll, Bambi, stuffed, orig tag, button and
label 40.00
Figure, Donald Duck, celluloid,
jointed. 100.00
Figure, Gepetto, wood. 65.00
Game Board, Who's Afraid of the Big Bad
Wolf, Marx Bros.. . . . . .50.00
Glass, Cleo the Fish, juice glass,
1940. . . . . .10.00
Glass, Pinocchio, Libby. 30.00
Guitar, 21" l, plastic, yellow front, large
paper label, six plastic strings, Walt
Disney copyright, c1970 . . . . . . .15.00
Handkerchief, 8" by 8-1/2", fabric, red,
yellow, green, blue and pink,
c1950 . . . . .20.00
Hand Puppet, Tinker Belle, Gund . . .60.00
Hat, Mickey Mouse, paper, cookie
give-away, 1930. . . . . .75.00
Knife Rest, Mickey and Minnie,
ceramic. 150.00

**Rug, Snow White and the Seven Dwarfs,
Alexander Smith & Co., NY, 45" by 60",
$450.**

Mirror, Snow White and the
Seven Dwarfs 35.00
Mousketeer Ears, snap on,
Kohner Bros.. . . . . 60.00
Orange Juice Can, Donald Duck,
1940 . . . . 20.00
Paint Book, The Blue Fairy, Whitman,
1939 . . . . 20.00
Paint Box, Donald Duck, tin, 1930. . 50.00
Party Horn, cardboard, wooden
mouthpiece, Marx Bros. 75.00
Pitcher, Dumbo, ceramic, Leeds
China 40.00
Playing Cards, Dopey, 1938 . . . . . . 40.00
Puzzle, frame tray, Mickey Mouse, 8" by
10", Marx Bros., 1933. . . . . 65.00
Ruler, wood, Yoo Hoo Ice Cream Cone
adv 50.00
Salt and Pepper Shakers, pr, Dumbo,
Leeds China, 1940 . . . . 20.00
Scissors, Donald Duck, electric, box,
c1950 . . . . 75.00
Sheet Music, Give a Little Whistle . . 15.00
Sheet Music, Mickey Mouse's Birthday
Party, Irving Berlin 75.00
Sign, School Sale, Mickey illus, Dixon
pencil box adv. 50.00
Soaky, Pinocchio, Colgate-
Palmolive 30.00
Soap, Jiminy Cricket, treasure-chest
box 85.00
Soap, Snow White and the Seven Dwarfs,
figures, boxed, c1938 . . . . 50.00
Tape Measure, Donald Duck, celluloid,
1930 . . . . 250.00
Teapot and Plate Set, Mickey and Minnie in
a boat illus, Lusterware, Japan,
1930 . . . . 75.00
Tea Set, Pinocchio, Ohio Art Co.,
1930 . . . . 100.00
Tie Clasp, Winnie the Pooh 10.00
Toothbrush, Mickey Mouse, celluloid,
Bakelite, 1930. . . . . 75.00
Toy, Lady and the Tramp, platform,
1955 . . . . 75.00
Toy, Ludwig Von Drake, vinyl, squeeze,
1960 . . . . 10.00
Tray, tin, Mickey and Minnie in boat illus,
red border, Ohio Art 75.00
Watch, Scrooge McDuck 40.00
Watch Stand, Cinderella, plastic, figural,
1960s 12.00
Watering Can, 3-1/2" h, green, red and
yellow can, black and white Mickey and
Minnie illus, Ohio Art, 1930. . . . . 75.00

Dog Collectibles

The easiest way to curb your dog
collection is to concentrate on the representations of a single breed. Many

Perfume Bottle, hp porcelain, $85.

collectors focus only on three-dimensional figures. Whatever approach you
take, buy pieces because you love
them. Try to develop some restraint
and taste and not buy every piece you
see. Easy to say, hard to do!

Club: Wee Scots, Inc., P.O. Box 1512,
Columbus, IN 47202.

Newsletters: *Canine Collectibles
Newsletter*, 736 N. Western Ave., Ste.
314, Lake Forest, IL 60045; *Colliec-
tively Speaking!*, 428 Philadelphia Rd.,
Joppa, MD 21085.

Doorstops, cast iron
Boston Terrier, two-pc
construction. 75.00
German Shepherd, standing 40.00
Three Puppies in a Barrel, 5" by
5-1/4". .50.00

Figure
Chihuahua, 3-1/4" h 4.00
English Bulldog, 3-1/8" h, porcelain . .7.00
Poodle, 9-1/2" by 9-1/2", porcelain. .75.00
Scottie, 8-1/2" by 10-1/2",
composition 30.00
Springer Spaniel, 3-3/4" by 5-3/4",
earthenware, hp nose and eyes,
airbrushed 6.00

Signs
10" by 14", Old Vitality Dog Food . . .85.00
23" by 23", Old Boston Beer, cardboard,
dog illus. 25.00
25" by 17", Sensation Cut Plug, cardboard,
man restraining dogs, framed . . .85.00

Rocker Blotter, Scottie, green opaque glass, $18.

Other

Bank, cast iron, German Shepherd. .38.00
Bank, cast iron, Retriever, 3-3/8" h, traces
    of black paint 50.00
Bookends, pr, cast iron, Scottie at fence,
    6-1/2" by 4-1/2", Kenco, c1940 .150.00
Bookends, pr, cast iron Wirehaired Terrier,
    3-3/4" by 4-1/2" 150.00
Candy Container, bulldog, 4-1/4" h, screw
    closure .60.00
Canister Set, poodle, black, Ransburg,
    Indianapolis 35.00
Cookie Jar, Dalmatian, McCoy 425.00
Cookie Jar, Scottie 25.00
Door Knocker, Scottie 48.00
Letter Holder, 4" by 4-3/4", cast iron .70.00
Napkin Ring, dog pulling sled 250.00
Paperweight, Dachshund, 1-1/2" by 2-1/2",
    cast iron 50.00
Planter, 5" by 6", Scottie, chalkware .10.00
Platter, egg-shape, poodle illus. 15.00
Pin, Scottie, Bakelite, black. 75.00
Planter, Scottie, 5" by 6", chalkware . .9.00

Corkscrew, carved-bone dog handle, sterling-silver band and end cap, glass eyes, 5-3/4" w, 5-3/4" h, $200.

Postcard, wood burned, dog with baby
    bottle 8.00
Puppet, poodle, white plush. 6.00
Record, Train Your Dog, Lee Duncan,
    12-1/4" sq cardboard album, 33-1/3
    rpm, 1961, Carlton Record Corp. 15.00
Ring, hard stone, yg, late Victorian, oval
    cameo of dog, white on black, high
    relief, set in plain yg bezel 250.00
Tape Measure, Armco Steel, red and
    white, collie and company slogan on
    one side, logo on other, inscribed "Lyle
    Culvert and Road Equipment Co.,
    Minneapolis" 18.00
Tie Tack, brass, Mack bulldog,
    1950s 12.50
Tobacco Jar, pug. 75.00
Toy, beagle, cast iron, tail up, blue, red
    eyes 18.00

Dolls

People buy dolls primarily on the basis of sentiment and condition. Most begin by buying back the dolls they remember playing with as a child. Speculating in dolls is risky business. The doll market is subject to crazes. The doll that is in today may be out tomorrow.

Place great emphasis on originality. Make certain that every doll you buy has the complete original costume. Ideally, the box or packaging also should be present. Remember, you are not buying these dolls to play with. You are buying them for display.

Note: The dolls listed date from the 1930s through the present. For information about antique dolls, see Jan Foulke's 12th *Blue Book Dolls and Values* (Hobby House Press: 1995) and R. Lane Herron's, *Herron's Price Guide to Dolls* (Wallace-Homestead: 1990).

Clubs: Chatty Cathy Collectors Club, P.O. Box 140, Readington, NJ 08870; Ideal Toy Co. Collector's Club, P.O. Box 623, Lexington, MA 02173; Madame Alexander Fan Club, P.O. Box 330, Mundeline, IL 60060; United Federation of Doll Clubs, P.O. Box 14146, Parkville, MO 64152.

Periodical: *Doll Reader*, 6405 Flank Dr., Harrisburg, PA 17112.

Advertising

Blue Bonnet Sue, 12" h, cloth 25.00

Tear Bell, vinyl head and body, open nurser mouth, rooted brown hair, 15-1/2" h, $35.

Ceresota Flour, 13" h, cloth 135.00
Chicken of the Sea, mermaid 12.00
Chiquita Banana. 20.00
Del Monte, Shoo Shoo Trudy 15.00
Del Monte, Sweet Pea, 12" h 10.00
Green Giant, 6-1/2" h, Little Sprout,
    vinyl. 20.00
Jack Frost, 19" h. 12.00
Simplicity, 12" h, complete with pattern
    book, measuring tape 70.00

Deluxe Toys

Ann Shirley, 22" h, composition, sleep
    eyes, orig wig 60.00
Baby Catch a Ball, 18" h, vinyl head, plastic
    body, battery operated, throws ball,
    1969 . . . . 30.00
Dawn, 6" h, blond hair, vinyl body . . 15.00

Effanbee

Mae Star, 30" h, composition head and
    limbs, cloth body, tin sleep eyes, orig
    wig and clothing. 400.00
Patsy, 14" h, composition, painted eyes,
    orig clothing. 75.00
Rosemary, 18" h, composition head and
    limbs, cloth body, tin sleep eyes, orig
    mohair wig and clothing. 250.00

Horsman

Floppy, 18" h, foam body,
    rooted hair 30.00

Ballerina, vinyl head with rooted blonde Saran hair, jointed hard-plastic body, 20" h, $45.

Pretty Betty, 16" h, nurser, rooted hair, sleep eyes 25.00
Teensie Baby, 12" h, nurser, plastic, vinyl 15.00

Ideal
Baby Belly Button, 9" h, plastic, vinyl, rooted blond hair 25.00
Baby Big Eyes, 20" h, vinyl, blanket and nightie. 50.00
Baby Crissy, 24" h, vinyl, rooted auburn hair. 40.00
Baby Giggles, 18" h, vinyl 120.00
Betsy Wetsy, plastic, vinyl. 55.00
Bizzie Lizzie, 18" h, vinyl, rooted hair, battery operated. 40.00
Cuddly Kissy, 17" h, vinyl, cloth 60.00
Lazy Dazy, 12" h, vinyl, cloth, rooted blond hair, sleep eyes 20.00
My Baby Bottle, 14" h, cloth, vinyl, pull string .25.00
Tippy Tumbles, 16-1/2" h, vinyl, plastic, rooted hair, stands on head, flips over, battery operated. 40.00

Madame Alexander
Baby Huggams, 9" h, soft stuffed body. 20.00
Elise, 17" h, vinyl face, rooted hair, orig tagged clothes 125.00

Kathy Tears, 15" h, vinyl, closed mouth 70.00
Sound of Music, Gretl, 8" h, hard plastic, vinyl, synthetic wig, sleep eyes, orig tagged clothes 175.00

Mattel
Baby Beans, 11" h, vinyl, beanbag body 20.00
Baby Secret, 18" h, vinyl, foam, red hair, pull-string talker 45.00
Sister Small Talk, 10" h, plastic, vinyl, painted eyes and teeth 25.00
Tiny Baby Tenderlove, vinyl hair piece, vinyl head, painted eyes 20.00

Other
American Character, Betsy McCall, 8" h, hard plastic, jointed knees, rooted hair, sleep eyes. 165.00
American Character, Sweet Sue, 14-1/2" h. 40.00
Arranbee, Nancy, 12" h, composition, jointed at neck, molded hair, painted eyes, orig clothes 225.00
Arranbee, Nannette, 14" h, hard plastic 225.00
Cameo, Kewpie, 12" h, composition, flowered sundress and bonnet, c1940 . . . . 125.00
Cameo, Miss Peeps, 19" h, vinyl, brown skin, 1973 . . . . 35.00
Coleco, Cabbage Patch, 16" h, cowgirl, vinyl head, cowgirl outfit 85.00
Hasbro, Aimee, 18" h, plastic, vinyl, rooted hair 55.00
Jolly Toys, Playpen Doll, 14" h, nurser, plastic, vinyl 12.00
Kenner, Gabbigale, 18" h, vinyl, plastic, blond hair 45.00
LaMotte, 9" h, girl, bisque, googly eyes, Bessie Kerney clothing 85.00
LaMotte, 9" h, Kewpie, bisque, 1978 . . . . 20.00
Remco, Baby Laugh Alot, 16" h, plastic, vinyl. 25.00
Remco, Tumbling Tomboy, 16" h, plastic, vinyl. 25.00
Sayco, Carrie Cries, 19" h, plastic, vinyl. 10.00
Uneeda, Magic Meg, 16" h, plastic, vinyl. 35.00

Doorstops

Cast-iron doorstops have gone through a number of collecting crazes over the past 20 years. The last craze occurred just a few years ago raising the prices to such a level that door-stops are more likely to be found at antiques shows than at flea markets.

Reproductions abound. A few helpful clues are: check size (many reproductions are slightly smaller than the period piece); check detail (the less detail, the more suspicious you need to be); and check rust (bright orange rust indicates a new piece).

Club: Doorstop Collectors of America, 2413 Madison Ave., Vineland, NJ 08630.

Aunt Jemima, Hubley, 12" h 165.00
Basket of Tulips, Hubley, tall slender basket, 13" h 550.00
Boy wearing top hat and bow tie, holding basket of fruit, sq base, 9-1/2" h 400.00
Crying Baby, fists clenched at shoulders, 8-3/4" h 85.00
Geisha Girl, Hubley, kneeling on pillow, playing stringed instrument, 6" h 225.00
Hen, laying, 5" h, 8" l 195.00
Horse, Hubley, 10" h, 12" l 135.00
Major Domo, standing at attention 8-1/2" h 195.00
Owl on Stump, marked "J Co," 10-1/2" h 495.00
Penguin, standing upright, wearing bow tie, 10-1/2" h 165.00
Punch, leaning against stack of books, dog sitting at side, 12-1/4" h 225.00
Sea Dragon, head resting at base, upraised scaly body and tail, 14" h 85.00
Spanish Flamenco Dancer, 9-1/2" h 325.00

Cat, cast iron, painted, American, c1910, 9" h, $125.

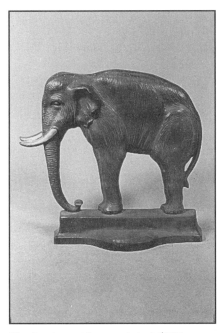

Elephant, cast iron, painted, $300.

Three Boston Terrier Puppies in Tub,
    7-3/8" h, 7" w 450.00
Two Cats, dressed as girl and boy,
    standing upright, 7-3/4" h 325.00
White Cat, glass eyes, oval base,
    11-3/4" h. 325.00

Drag Racing

Drag racing is an acceleration contest between two cars racing in a straight line for a quarter of a mile. The first drag race probably took place shortly after the invention of the wheel. However, drag racing as we know it began in the late 1940s in Southern California. By the early 1950s drag strips were popping up nationwide.

The formation of the National Hot Rod Association in 1951 brought organization to drag racing. The NHRA promoted safety in racing and began to sanction drag strips across the country. The promotion of these races and the ephemera generated as a result of conducting the races provides the source for the drag racing collectibles that are sought today. The drag racing items listed in this section are representative of what is available.

The prices are actual selling prices for the objects listed.

Advisors: Michael and Cheryl Goyda, P.O. Box 192, East Petersburg, PA 17520; (717) 569-7149.

Newsletter: *Quarter Milestones*, Oxhaven Apartments, Apt C-38, Oxford, PA 19363.

Hand-Out Photos

Occasionally privately printed but most often provided by sponsors, these 8" by 10" color photos are handed out by racers at drag racing events. The most collectible and valuable are those from before 1980. Cards printed after that date generally sell for 50-cents to $3. Cards in this list date prior to 1980.

Amalie Oil, Gene Snow's
    Rambunctious 15.00
Amalie Oil, Ray Godman's Tennessee
    Boll Weevil 12.00
Pennzoil, Superstar Jeb Allen
    Dragster 12.00
Pennzoil, Superstar Tom McEwen Coors
    Funny Car 10.00
Quaker State, Al Segrini Super Brut . 8.00
Quaker State, Roland Leong Hawaiian
    Punch Funny Car 6.00
U.S. Army, Don Prudhomme Army Funny
    Car 16.00

Jackets

Both sold and won at drag races, jackets prior to 1975 are difficult to find.

Muncie Dragway, red cotton, embroidered
    front-engine dragster 175.00

Peterson Drag Way, white cotton,
    embroidered red lettering 100.00
York US 30, red nylon, York US 30 and
    Superstock patch. 75.00

Magazines

Beginning in 1964, various slick magazines came into existence catering to drag racing enthusiasts. Some early issues and very special issues will command a premium, but an average magazine in clean condition sells for $3 to $5.

Model Kits

Numerous model kits have been produced featuring well-known drag racers and their cars. Vintage kits in unbuilt condition command a premium.

AMT, Don Garlit's Wynn's Jammer
    Front-Engine Dragster. 85.00
MPC, Dyno Don Nicholson's Pro Stock
    Pinto 65.00
Revell, Ed "The Ace" McCullough
    Revellution Funny Car. 75.00

Posters

Event posters are relatively hard to find, because they are usually destroyed after the race.

Ventura, Funny Car & AA Fuel Dragster
    Meet, 11" by 17" 75.00
Winternationals, 1971, 14" by 20" . .95.00
York, 1972 Super Stock Nationals,
    13" by 20" 45.00

Press Kits

Issued by both racers and sponsors, press kits provide biographical

Checkered Flag, $125.

information, photos, etc. The best frequently have artwork covers.

Grumpy Jenkins, Grumpy's Toy Pro Stock
Vega. 50.00
Jeb Allen, Praying Mantis Dragster. .35.00
Tony Nancy, The Loner Front-Engine
Dragster .45.00

Programs

Programs are traditionally printed for most events and the best are done for the major races.

1955, first NHRA Nationals 100.00
1965, NHRA U.S. Nationals 28.00
1969, Superstock Nationals 18.00
1972, NHRA Nationals 22.00

Trophies

Trophies vary in price based on age and the type of car that tops the trophy. A front-engine dragster on top will command more than a generic four-door sedan.

Indianapolis, NHRA Race, 1961,
8" h. 45.00
Vargo Dragway, 1962 Roadster top,
6" h. 40.00
York US 30, 1960 Dragster top,
9" h. 65.00

Drinking Glasses, Promotional

It is time to start dealing seriously with promotional glasses given away by fast-food restaurants, gas stations and other merchants. This category also includes drinking glasses that start out life as product containers.

Most glasses are issued in a series. If you collect one, you better plan on keeping at it until you have the complete series. Also, many of the promotions are regional. A collector in Denver is not likely to find a Philadelphia Eagles glass at his favorite restaurant.

Just a few washings in a dishwasher can cause a major change in the color on promotional drinking glasses. Collectors insist on unused, unwashed glasses whenever possible. Get the glass, drink your drink out of a paper cup.

Newsletter: *Collector Glass News*, P.O. Box 308, Slippery Rock, PA 16057.

Dudley Do-Right, Canadian Mountie, Rocky & Bullwinkle Show, Pepsi, $10.

Archie Bunker, green goblet, 1972, all four
Bunker characters in yellow with
campaign slogans. 3.00
Batman, with Robin the Boy Wonder, "Zok!
Crack, Whack!," gray and blue . . 15.00
Belmont Stakes, 125th Running,
1993 . . . . 14.00
Bullwinkle, Brockway, Holly Farms, 1975,
Collectors Series, 16 oz 40.00
Burger King, "Where Kids are King," set of
four, Liberty Bell, Patriots, Flags, Eagle
& Shield 24.00
Coca-Cola, stained glass, kites flying,
button bottom 5.00
Country Time Lemonade Flavor Drink,
yellow, 6-1/4" h. 3.00
Derby Day Contest Winner Awarded by
Kentucky Club, late 1950s, etching on
clear glass, 5-1/2" h 3.00
Dopey, Snow White and the Seven Dwarfs,
Walt Disney, 4-3/4" h 33.00
Dr Pepper, hot-air balloon in clouds . 2.00
Flintstones, Hanna-Barbera, Bedrock U,
Phi Boulder Kappa, Bedrock City,
Grand Canyon, Arizona, mug, yellow
and red, 5-3/8" h. 4.00
Gulliver's Travels, 1939 Paramount,
Princess Glory, green, 4-3/4" h. . 73.00
Indianapolis 500, 1961 Official Tony
Hullman rocks glass, gold rim,
3-1/4" h 7.00
Kellogg's Dig 'Em, 1977, Collector
Series 9.00
Pinocchio and Jiminy Cricket, Walt Disney,
4-9/16" h 26.00

1982 Knoxville World's Fair, McDonald's, $5.

Tom Sawyer, Libbey Classics, short . 6.00
Unwashable Jones, Al Capp, 1949, blue,
4-3/4" h 22.00
Wyatt Earp, OK Corral, black, gold and
green, 4-7/8" h. 24.00

Drugstores Collectibles

Corner drugstores, especially those with a soda fountain, were major hangouts in almost every small town in the United States. Almost all of them dispensed much more than medically related products. They were the 7-11s of their era. This category documents the wide variety of material that you could acquire in a drugstore. It barely scratches the surface. This is a new collecting approach that has real promise.

Tins

Bayer's Aspirin, 7" d 100.00
Century Tobacco, factory graphics, flat,
pocket .110.00
Dearso Respicoal Ointment 15.00
Golden Pheasant Condom 88.00
Hope Denture Powder 35.00
Hygenol Violet Talcum, litho image,
chartreuse, green and red,
1920s. .25.00
Lauxes Tablets 15.00
Mentholatum, 1-1/2" d, litho, young nurse
illus, 1920-30 . . . . .25.00
Ramsey's Condoms, 1929 . . . . .60.00

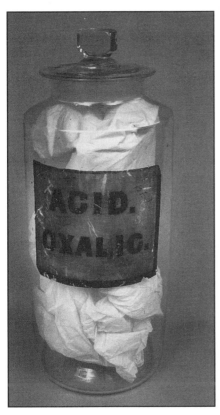

Apothecary Jar, blown glass, stenciled label, blown-glass stopper, 14" h, 5-7/8" d, $25.

Rexall Foot Powder, blue 15.00
Smith's Rosebud Salve 20.00
Three Merry Widows, condoms 25.00

Other
After Shave, Colgate-Palmolive Co., 5 oz,
 clear, glass bottle, red plastic lid,
 red and white label, black and white
 letters 7.00
After Shave, Sir After Shave Lotion,
 1.69 oz, clear, glass bottle, blue and
 white plastic lid, blue and black label,
 black and white letters 7.25
Bath Set, Spring Morning Shower Mitt Set,
 3 pcs. 14.00
Book, *American Drug Index, Lippincott*
 Co., 650 pgs, 1957 . . . . .10.00
Book, *Dispensatory of the United States of
 America*, 25th edition, 2,379 pgs,
 1960 . . . . .9.00
Bookmark, Climax Catarrh Cure, woman
 wearing fur coat 10.00
Bottle, Eli Lilley & Co., Gentian,
 1 pt 16.00
Bottle, Wallace Laboratories, Brunswick,
 NJ, Soma Carisoprodol 6.50
Bottle Opener, Dr. Brown's Celery
 Tonic 20.00

Calendar, McKesson's First Aid and Good
 Health Almanac, 1946 . . . . 15.00
Cold Tablets, St. Joseph, 36 tablets, brown
 and white cardboard box,
 Plough Inc. 6.00
Cold Tablets, Surety, 12 tablets, yellow
 metal box, guard at open safe illus,
 Wallace Brands Co. 6.50
Container, Band-Aid Charmers, tin, white,
 red, blue, yellow and green,
 flip-top lid 2.75
Cookbook, Dr. Ward's Medical Co. Cook
 Book, tonics and patent medicines,
 c1920 . . . . 3.00
Counter Card, Dr. Carman's Dentalaid,
 full-color illus, late 19th C 15.00
Display, Peter Rabbit Safety Pins, colorful
 cartoon 25.00
Jar, Tinactin, 8" by 2-3/4" h, round, clear,
 glass, red and silver label,
 red letters 15.00
Laxative, Cascara-Lax, 2 oz, brown, glass
 bottle, black plastic lid, blue, red and
 white label, blue and white
 letters 2.75
Mirror, Nature's Remedy Tablets, 2-1/2" d,
 white lettering, red rim 55.00
Mirror, People's Drug, birthstones,
 pocket 20.00
Mirror, Star Soap, pocket 20.00
Prophylactic, Ramses Rolled Rubber
 Prophylactics, three pack, yellow and
 black cardboard box, Schmid . . . 10.00
Prophylactic, Sheik Rubber Prophylactics,
 three pack, brown-cellophane wrapped,
 full box, Schmid 9.00
Scale, Rexall Drugs, metal 165.00
Shampoo, Old Gibraltar Opal Shampoo,
 clear, glass bottle, cork lid, brown
 cardboard box, blue letters,
 woman washing hair illus,
 Kiefer-Stewart Co. 10.00
Shampoo, White Rain Lotion Shampoo,
 clear, glass bottle, blue plastic lid, blue
 and white label, blue letters, 3/4 full
 bottle, Toni, Gillette Co. 8.00

Cylinder, Oil of Pine, Leach Chemical Co., Cincinnati, 1/2 oz, 3-1/4" by 1", paper label, $18.

Sign, Electric Prescription Sign, white
 metal, plastic sign, blue letters, Ohio
 Advertising Display 50.00
Sign, Pepto Bismol, standup, 16" by 24",
 brown, yellow and red, red and black
 letters, turkey-head illus 30.00
Scoop, tin, curved handle, soldered to flat
 back, rounded scoop 7.00
Vitamins, Children's Vitamin Capsules,
 100 caps, Kiger's Drug Store 7.00
Vitamins, Squibb Viosterol in Oil, octagonal
 blue bottle, gold metal cap,
 dropper, cap 7.00

Easter Collectibles

Now that Christmas and Halloween collectibles have been collected to death, holiday collectors are finally turning their attentions to Easter. The old Easter bonnet still hangs in the Clothing Collectibles closet, but chicken and rabbit collectors now have to contend with Easter enthusiasts for their favorite animal collectible.

Baskets
Chenille, miniature, chicks 55.00
Paper, woven, grass, candy eggs,
 1940 . . . . .35.00
Wicker, oval, colored band, 1940s . .25.00

Candy Containers
Basket, cardboard, rect, two chicks on
 each end, marked "Ertel Bros
 Wmspt, PA" 18.00
Duck, 4" h, yellow composition, ribbon
 around neck, standing on 3" d
 cardboard box, opens at base,
 Germany 35.00
Egg-shape, papier-mâché, litho of little girl
 and St. Bernard, marked
 "Germany" 40.00

Chocolate Mold, tin, bunnies on an egg boat, $65.

Postcard, "A Joyful Easter," $8.

Rabbit, 8" h, potbellied, white, head and
    ears on wire spring, white glass-beaded
    trim, separates at belt line, marked
    "U.S. Zone, Germany" 15.00
Chicken on Nest, molded cardboard,
    candy eggs inside, 1940 . . . . . .100.00
Cookie Cutter, egg-shape, tin 5.00

Postcards
Chick coming out of shell 10.00
Girl with dog on leash, Drayton 25.00

Eggs
Ceramic, pink marbled, gold stripe . .30.00
Porcelain, daisies, gold dec,
    Dresden 35.00

Other
Banner, cotton, chicks, bunnies,
    embroidered, 1930 . . . . .45.00
Bell, ceramic, rabbit handle,
    "Happy Easter 1979" 15.00
Book, *The Tale of Peter Rabbit*, Edna M.
    Aldredge and Jessie F. McKee, Harter
    Publishing Co., 1931 . . . . .18.00
Egg-Dye Packet, PAAS, 1930-40 . . .10.00
Gift Box, litho cardboard, bunnies,
    eggs 5.00
Invitation, cardboard, flower basket illus,
    dated May 1 . . . . .7.00
Lunch Pail, Peter Rabbit, 1920s 75.00
Mug, Germany, 1900 . . . . .20.00
Nut Cup, figural basket, crepe paper, card-
    board, cut-out chick emerging from egg,
    1930 . . . . .10.00
Potholder, white and red, embroidered,
    1940s 8.00
Rabbit, 6" l, composition, painted . . .75.00
Sheet Music, Easter Parade 10.00
Tablecloth, paper, lilies and
    ribbon swags 10.00

Eggbeaters

America has borne a grudge
against eggs for decades—evidence
the innumerable gadgets invented for
beating them. There were well over
1,000 patents issued for eggbeaters
since 1856. Any collector should be
able to assemble a large collection of
eggbeaters without any duplication.

Archimedes Type
11" h, Keystone Egg and Cream Beater,
    emb jar 80.00
11-1/2" h, Ashley 500.00
13" h, Clipper 150.00
15" h, Ashley 525.00

Dover
9" h, steel handle 45.00
10" h, beveled wheel, 1870 . . . . 65.00
10" h, cast iron, Earle, 1863 . . . . . . 450.00
10" h, flat wheel, 1870 . . . . 75.00
12", cast iron 75.00

EKCO
9-3/4" h 5.00
11" h 6.00
11-1/4" h, Mary Ann 10.00
12-3/4" h 7.00

Holt-Lyon
8-1/2" h, side handle 200.00
10" h, Cream Whip, 1897 . . . . 120.00
10-1/2" h, 1900 . . . . 45.00
11-1/2" h, Jar Cream Whip and
    Mayonnaise Mixer, qt jar,
    1900 . . . . 300.00
14-1/2" h, Holt's Butter Merger, paper
    label, qt jar 250.00

Ladd
9-3/4" h 20.00
10" h 25.00
10-1/2" h, Saturn 25.00

**Edlund Co., Burlington, VT, stainless-
steel blades, red-painted wood handle
and knob, $8.**

12-1/2" h 25.00

Taplin
5-1/2" h, loop handle 15.00
5-1/2" h, wooden handle 15.00
6" h, clear plastic cup 60.00
6" h, red plastic cup 50.00
10-1/2" h, wooden handle 25.00
11" h, 1924 . . . . 10.00
11-1/2" h, wooden handle 30.00
12-1/2" h, Light Running 50.00
16-1/2" h, Mammoth, No. 300, with shelf
    mount 250.00

Turner & Seymour
9-1/2" h, Triumph, 1876 . . . . 200.00
10", family eggbeater, 1876 . . . . . . 300.00
11-1/2" h, Super Whirl,
    Bakelite handle 20.00
11-1/2" h, Super Whirl,
    plastic handle 15.00
12" h, Merry Whirl 40.00

Elephant Collectibles

Public television's unending series
of documentaries on African wildlife
has destroyed the fascination with wild
animals. By the time parents take their
children to the zoo or circus, elephants
are old-hat. Things were different for
the pre-television generations. The elephant held a fascination that is difficult for us to comprehend. When
Barnum brought Jumbo from England
to America, English children (and a fair
number of adults) wept.

There are a few elephant-related
political collectibles listed. It is hard to
escape the GOP standard bearer.
However, real elephant collectors focus on the magnificent beasts themselves or cartoon representations that
range from Dumbo to Colonel Hathi.

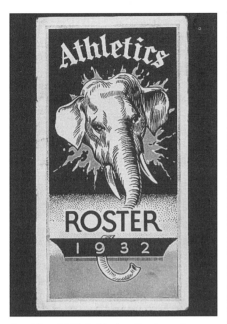

Booklet, 1932 Athletics Roster, elephant mascot, $35.

Club: The National Elephant Collector's Society, 380 Medford St., Somerville, MA 02145.

Periodical: *Jumbo Jargon*, 1002 W. 25th St., Erie, PA 16502.

Banks
Ceramic, pink glaze, Rosemeade . . .95.00
Chalkware, Dumbo, 8-3/4" h 20.00
Metal, still, seated elephant. 35.00
Razor-Blade bank, figural 15.00

Figures
Chalkware .20.00
Glass, red .50.00
Pottery, green, Zsolnay 60.00

Other
ABC Plate, Wild Animals: The Elephant, ceramic, dark brown transfer, green enameled highlights, alphabet border, Staffordshire, 7-1/2" d 75.00
Ashtray, Occupied Japan. 12.00
Automaton, Mumbo the Drumming Elephant 130.00
Baby Bottle, glass, emb elephant, wide mouth, 1930s, 8 oz 30.00
Bottle Opener, cast iron, seated, flat, pink 135.00
Brooch, Bakelite, multicolor, movable legs, 1930s, 1-3/4" by 2-1/2" 25.00
Chocolate Mold, standing elephant . 65.00
Cookie Jar, figural, McCoy. 45.00
Creamer, Shawnee 25.00
Doily, crocheted, elephant in center, 8-1/2" w 25.00
Hairbrush, baby's, celluloid 15.00
Hand Puppet, Dumbo, Gund 30.00
Jar, peanut butter, emb Jumbo, 4 oz 25.00
Lamp, ceramic, Dumbo 55.00
Letter Opener, celluloid, painted details, elephant head, raised trunk 30.00
Mug, Nixon and Agnew, sand-white glaze, Frankoma, 1968 . . . . 55.00
Napkin, Win With Wilkie!, elephant logo, red, white and blue 15.00
Nodder, Alex Ceramics 20.00
Paper Dolls, Dumbo, uncut 45.00
Pin Tray, elephant holding shell, Bavarian 18.00
Planter, blue, Rosemeade, 5" h 60.00
Plate, I Like Ike!, elephant 20.00
Powder Jar, cov, double elephant, green frosted. 35.00
Pull Toy, wood 20.00
Rocker Blotter, amethyst glass, figural 85.00
Salt and Pepper Shakers, pr, Ceramic Arts Studio 35.00
Soap, Elmer Elephant, Castle Soap 30.00

Tape Measure, figural. 30.00
Toothpick Holder, amber glass. 15.00
Vase, elephant handles, Austrian . . . 25.00
Whiskey Bottle, Jim Beam, 1956 . . . 30.00

Elongated Coins

Although the elongation of coinage first began in 1893 at the Columbian Exposition in Chicago as souvenirs of that event, the revival of producing and collecting elongated coins began in earnest in the early 1960s. Initially available to hobbyists and souvenir collectors from a few private roller/producers, the elongation of coins advanced by way of commercial enterprises beginning in 1976 during the Bicentennial celebration. Automated vending rolling machines producing souvenirs are all over the United States and abroad, from historical sites to national parks and amusement areas. For further information on elongated coins, old and modern, contact the advisor listed below.

Advisor: Angelo A. Rosato, 70 Grove St., New Milford, CT 06776, (860) 354-5684.

Club: The Elongated Collectors, 70 Grove St., New Milford, CT 06776.

Match Safe, silver-plated, ivory tusk, English, 2-1/4", $170.

Political, Theodore Roosevelt for President, U.S. penny, $12.

Elvis

Elvis was hot, is hot and promises to be hot well into the future. Elvis collectibles are bought from the heart, not the head. A great deal of totally tacky material has been forgiven by his devoted fans. Elvis material breaks down into two groups: items licensed while Elvis was alive and items licensed after his death. The latter are known as "fantasy" items. Fantasy Elvis is collectible, but real value lies in the material licensed during his lifetime.

Beware of any limited-edition Elvis items. They were manufactured in such large numbers that the long-term prospects for appreciation in value are very poor. If you love an item, fine. If you expect it to pay for your retirement, forget it.

Club: Elvis Forever TCB Fan Club, P.O. Box 1066, Pinellas, FL 34665.

Magazines
Aquarian Weekly, #225, Elvis: One Year Later, 1978....................5.00
Elvis Years, #1, 1979 ....5.00
Filmland, June, 1957.............15.00
TV Guide, Nov. 10-16, 1973.......8.00
TV Star Parade, December 1956 ...15.00

Pinback Buttons
Concert photo, 3-3/8" d..........12.00
Elvis Presley for President, Lou Monte, Campaign Manager, 1-3/4" d, blue and white, metal tab, celluloid 15.00
I Hate Elvis, 1-3/4" d, red and white, celluloid.................... 15.00
I Want Elvis For XMAS, 3-3/8" d, red and green, celluloid 30.00

Postcards
3-1/2" by 5-1/2", color, Easter Greetings, 1969 .... 10.00
5" by 6-3/4", black and white, Elvis in Las Vegas 8.00

Sheet Music
Frankie and Johnny 12.00
Hound Dog.................... 20.00
Love Me Tender................ 25.00

Stuffed Animals
Hound Dog, 10" h, Elvis Presley Enterprises 100.00
Teddy Bear, 24" h, Elvis Presley Enterprises, 1957 .... 100.00

Other
Ashtray, 3-1/2" d, black and white, Elvis photo center 65.00
Belt, leather 350.00
Book, *The Elvis Presley Story*, 160 pgs, 32 black-and-white photo pgs, Hillman Books, 1960 .... 25.00
Bracelet, silver, blue imprinted picture, inscribed "Follow That Dream, Elvis Presley," Elvis Presley Enterprises 15.00
Brush, guitar, figural, 1970s....... 40.00

Catalog, Elvis RCA Victor Records, lists of albums and 45 rpm singles 18.00
Game, Elvis Welcomes You to His World, Duff, 1978 ....80.00
Glass, gold-overlay images, Elvis playing guitar front, gold records back, 1956 ....75.00
Handkerchief, black, white, pink and blue, 1956 ....125.00
Hat, woven material, blue and white, Elvis-design fabric 30.00
Mug, plastic, multicolored, marked "Elvis the King Lives On, 1935-1977" ...5.00
Ornament, Hallmark, 1992 ....40.00
Pen, souvenir, marked "From Elvis and the Colonel"....................15.00
Pennant, 11-1/2" by 5", felt, blue and black, marked "American Knitwear and Emblem Mgrs," 1970s 6.00
Perfume, "Teddy Bear," 1957......75.00
Photo, 5" by 7", color, gold and white plastic frame, 1956 ....75.00
Pillow, 10" by 10", blue, white and red......................100.00
Pocket Watch 45.00
Spoon, commemorative, gold, with envelope, marked "Presley Palladium Concert Reserved Seat Holders Only-Not For Resale," England, c1960......................35.00
Sweater Clip, dog-tag style, Elvis Presley Enterprises 50.00

Employee Badges

Although in use long before the Civil War, employee identification badges achieved widespread use during World War I with the addition of photos and signatures for greater security. Often called "pay buttons," they had to be shown to the company paymaster for the worker to collect his wages, similar to the "pay checks" used by the coal companies. America's entry into World War II triggered an even greater security challenge.

All primary and most secondary war-production badges were coded by color, letter and/or number for one or more of such items as security clearance, job, specific task, crew, responsibility, shift, specific areas of shipyard, flight line, steel mill, etc.

Badges were made of steel, brass, copper, aluminum and Lucite in many

Sheet Music, I Want You, I Need You, I Love You, $10.

U.S. Naval Training Station Annex, Navy Inspector, Great Lakes, IL, oval, 1-7/8" by 2-5/8", plated-metal frame, white ground, employee photo and number, $30.

sizes and shapes, including round, oval, square and triangular. They ranged in length from less than 1 inch to 3 inches. Manufacturing methods varied from sand and die-cast to molded, stamped and coin-struck. Some were ornately figured with eagles, flags, crests, coats of arms, planes, ships and tanks, providing a crossover with art-metal collectors.

Although many companies made identification badges and buttons, Whitehead & Hoag of Newark, N.J., was by far the most prolific manufac-turer, followed by Bastian Brothers of Rochester, N.Y., and Robbins Co., of Attleboro, Mass.

Avoid badges with cloudy or wrinkled Lucite, faded photos, broken pins/clips or bent, corroded, heavily scratched, gouged or deformed frames.

Advisor: Douglas W. Tietze, 4909 Harter Rd., Slatington, PA 18080.

A.C. Lawrence Leather Co., round, 1-3/4", plated-steel frame, yellow ground, employee photo and number . . . 20.00

Army Air Base, Walla Walla, WA, round, 1-7/8", plated-steel frame, pink ground, employee photo and number. . . . 25.00

Army Air Field, Great Bend, KS, 2-1/4", plastic, steel back, black ground, employee photo and number. . . . 25.00

Bethlehem Steel Co., Bethlehem Plant, rect, 2-3/8" by 2-1/2", plated steel, employee photo and number, department code 25.00

Bethlehem Steel Co., Industrial Police, shield, 2-3/8" by 2-1/2", plated brass, raised letters, brass number 45.00

B.F. Goodrich Co., round, 1-7/8", plated-steel frame, yellow ground, employee photo and number. . . . 20.00

Brooklyn Union Gas Co., round, 1-7/8", plastic, employee photo, name and number 20.00

Chrysler Plymouth, Main Plant, Ord Mech, Edward Bachman, Executive, rect, 1-5/8" by 2-5/16", plated-steel frame, employee photo and signature . . 30.00

Colt's, rect, 1-5/8" by 2-3/8", plated-steel frame, white enamel, employee photo and number 50.00

Conmar Products Corp., Newark, NJ, round, 1-3/4", plated-brass frame, black enamel letters, employee photo and number, black woman 30.00

Eastman Kodak Co., round, 2-1/8", celluloid, steel back, red ground, employee photo and number. . . . 20.00

Federal Telephone and Radio Corp., square, 1-7/8", plastic, employee photo and number 20.00

Franklin Sugar Refining Co., round, 2", plated-steel frame, employee photo 20.00

Freedomland, oval, 2-1/2" by 1-5/8", brass-plated pot metal, enamel letters and mat, employee number. 45.00

Fiyr-Fiter Co., Contracting Officer, U.S. Army, round, 2", copper-plated steel, red enamel letters 25.00

Hall Electric, Muskegon, round, 1-3/4", plated brass, black enamel letters, employee number 15.00

Ingersoll-Rand, Phillipsburg, oval, 1-3/8" by 1-3/4", plated brass, red enamel plant strip, black enamel employee number, employee photo. 20.00

Lone Star Ordnance Plant, rect, 1-1/2" by 2-1/4", plated-brass frame, employee photo and number 40.00

Naval Supply Depot Guard, round 1-7/8", white enamel on brass, blue enamel employee number 20.00

Norfolk Naval, Virginia, round, 1-3/4", celluloid with steel back, employee photo and number 20.00

Ingersoll-Rand, Phillipsburg, oval, 1-3/8" by 1-3/4", plated brass, red-enamel plant strip, black-enamel employee number, employee photo, $20.

Pennsylvania Railroad, round, 1-7/8",
plated-steel frame, red ground,
employee photo and number 25.00
Philadelphia Bureau of Water Inspector,
shield, 1-1/2" by 2", plated brass, blue
enamel ring, city seal 20.00
Proctor & Schwartz, Inc., War Plant,
Philadelphia area, round, 1-1/2",
plastic, red ground, employee photo
and number 25.00
Proximity Cotton Mills, round, 1-3/4",
plated-metal frame, yellow ground,
employee photo and number 20.00
Public Service (Bus), NJ, shield,
3" by 2-1/4", plated brass, blue enamel
circle, red enamel triangle, employee
number 25.00
Reading Fair, round, 2-1/4", celluloid,
metal back, light green ground, black
lettering, employee number 10.00
Royal Mfg. Co. of Duquesne, round 1-5/8",
plated-steel frame, plastic cover, red
ground, employee photo 22.00
Socony Vacuum, round, 2", plated-steel
frame, red enamel letters and flying
horse, employee photo and
number 35.00
Southern California Edison Co.,
oval 2-5/8", by 1-7/8", tin-plated steel
frame, text and number 20.00
Southern California Telephone Co.,
bell-shape, 2-1/8" by 2-3/8", blue
enamel on brass, silver highlights,
employee number, made by G.G.
Braxmar Co. 75.00
Standard Aircraft Corp., round, 2" plated
brass, black enamel letters, employee
photo and number 25.00
Steelton & Highspire Railroad, oval,
2" by 2-1/2", steel, relief
"S&H/RR/STEELTON/PA,"
employee photo and number 45.00
Stokely Brothers and Co., round, 1-1/2",
celluloid, "Food Is Ammunition,"
employee number, red border, blue
ground, white shield 15.00
Susquehanna Power Co., Watchman,
shield, 2-1/8" by 1-3/4", plated brass,
black enamel letters 25.00
Tampa Shipbuilding Co., Inc., rect, 1-5/8"
by 2-1/4", plated-steel frame, black
enamel lettering, employee photo and
number 25.00
Todd Shipyards Corp., Hoboken,
octagonal, 2-1/8" by 2-1/8", plated-steel
frame, green enamel outer ring, black
ground, employee number 25.00
U.S. Steel Corporation, Fairless Works,
oval, 2" by 3-1/8", plated-steel frame,
employee photo and number, black
man 25.00

U.S. Army Hawaiian Dept., round, 1-7/8",
white enamel on brass, blue enamel
employee number 20.00
U.S. Naval Air Station, Jacksonville, FL,
round, 2", plated-brass frame, black
enamel letters, employee photo . 30.00
U.S. Naval Hospital, Great Lakes, IL, oval,
1-7/8" by 2-5/8", plated-metal frame,
white ground, red cross, employee
photo and number. 30.00
U.S.S. Wasp, Mater at Arms, shield, 1-3/4"
by 2-3/4", plated brass, black enamel
letters, employee number 45.00
Walter Kidde & Co., Engineers &
Constructors, NY, round, 1-3/4",
celluloid, employee number,
black lettering on tan ground . . . 20.00
Willys Overland Motors, guard, shield,
1-7/8" by 3", plated brass,
brass center 40.00
Yellow Cab, shield, 2-3/8" by 2-1/2", plated
brass, emb with yellow enamel body,
black enamel fenders 40.00

Ertl Banks

This is another of those highly
speculative areas that are addressed
as the need arises. The 1980s and
1990s saw a surge in the number of
cast-iron banks produced by several
companies, Ertl being the most dominant. These banks were often made to
commemorate special events or used
as promotions or fundraising efforts for
local charities.

Most of the Ertl banks were recently
manufactured in Hong Kong. They
should only be purchased if in fine
condition or better and only if the originally packaging is included. All of the
banks are marked and numbered.
Avoid any that are not marked. The serial numbers and series numbers are
important in cataloging and pricing
these items.

Club: Ertl Collectors Club, P.O. Box
500, Dyersville, IA 52040.

A&W Root Beer, Ford, 1905, delivery van,
#9827 . . . . 35.00
Ace Hardware, #5 in series, Ford, 1905,
delivery van, #9431. . . . . 25.00
American Store, Ford Model T, 1913,
#9478 . . . . 20.00
Amstel Light Beer, Hawkeye, 1931,
#9358 . . . . 24.00
Arm & Hammer, Ford Runabout, 1918,
#B052 . . . . 39.00

Atlantic City Show, Hawkeye Wrecker,
1931, #9634 . . . . .19.00
Baltimore Gas & Electric, #6 in series,
Hawkeye, 1931, #9848 . . . . .25.00
Baseball II, California Angels, Ford,
1917, #B371 . . . . .18.00
Big A, Ford Runabout, 1918, limited
edition, #1324 . . . . .20.00
Bit-O'-Honey, Chevy Van, 1923,
#1317 .23.00
Chiquita Bananas, Hawkeye Crate Truck,
1931, #9343 . . . . .19.00
Country Time Lemonade, Ford Model T,
1913, #1640 . . . . .28.00
Diamond Motor Oil, International, 1931,
#4078 .22.00
Enchanted Forest, Chevy Van, 1923,
#9044 .19.00
Esso Imperial, #2 in series, Diamond T
Tanker, 1930, #B124 . . . . .32.00
Happy Birthday, Ford, 1905, delivery van,
#9685 .14.00
Harley-Davidson, motorcycle sidecar,
#1993 .80.00
Heatcraft, Mack truck, 1926,
#7562 .20.00
Hershey's Transit, trolley car,
#B310 .20.00
Hills Dept. Store, Ford Model T, 1913,
#9768 .23.00
Humble Oil, Stearman Plane,
#37509 . . . . .59.00
J.C. Whitney, Chevy Van, 1923,
#B234 .32.00
Jimmy's Auto Parts, Fram Filter,
#2951 .27.50
John Deere, Cameo Pickup, 1955,
#5614 .18.00
John Deere, Seagraves Fire Engine, #1 in
series, #5710. . . . . .21.00
Kendall Oil, Hawkeye Tanker, 1931,
#4073 .30.00
Kraft Dairy Group, Ford Model T, 1917,
#9675 .35.00
Lea & Perrins, Model T, 1913,
#9170B 32.00
Missouri Tourism, Ford, 1905,
#2143 .24.00
Slice, Step Van, #9709. . . . . .24.00
Sunoco, Tanker, #2 in series, 1931,
#3791 .28.00
Terminix, Ford, 1905, #9086 . . . . . .20.00
Texaco, Dodge, #10 in series, 1939,
#9500 .18.00
Texaco, Horse and Wagon, #8 in series,
#9390 .25.00
Texas World Speedway, Ford, 1920,
#3092 .65.00
United Airlines, Model T, 1913,
#9223 .27.00

Fans, Electric

Electric table fans fall into the same general category as toasters and waffle irons: household appliances. Fans were manufactured by many companies in a wide range of designs. Most collectors concentrate on fans made from the 1880s until about 1920, although models manufactured up until the 1940s are often included. Fans are abundantly available, many in working condition. Most were mass-produced and have four blades, a black finish, trumpet-style base and sliding switch at the bottom.

Fan collectors should look for unusual shapes or innovations. Earlier models often had exposed coils with connectors on the back. Power sources varied from batteries, DC and variable AC to water, alcohol and even self-air generation. Prices rise in direct proportion to the amount of brass used in the fan's manufacture. Many fans have brass blades but some older models also have brass guards, support arms, nuts and/or other hardware. Unusual oscillating mechanisms can also add value.

Breakdowns in older fans often were caused by damaged electrical cords (easily fixed), bent or twisted blades and broken casings. Don't

Polar Cub, Gilbert Fan Co., 6" steel blades and guard, cast base, center logo depicts a bear sitting in front of a fan, 1920s, $50.

throw away those older broken fans—their parts are worth something to collectors who restore old fans to their original glory. Even name tags from Edison, Meston, Crocker and Holtzer-Cabot are worth a few dollars.

Advisor: Mike Roberts, 4416 Foxfire Way, Ft. Worth, TX 76133 (817) 294-2133.

Club: American Fan Collectors Association, P.O. Box 804, So Bend, IN 46624.

Emerson

12646, 12" brass blades, ornate ribbed base, oscillator on rear with external double arm, 1910 . . . . 250.00
71666, six steel blades, steel cage, painted black, oscillates, mass produced 45.00
FI-1, 1898, four brass blades, cast-iron hub, tripod ftd base, rear-mounted switch 400.00
Jr., 9" steel blades, steel base, oscillates, 1930s. 15.00
Seagull, unusual design, thin metal, Art Deco-style, 8" blades, 1930s. . . . 10.00
Silver Swan, fat aluminum blades, non-trumpet-shaped base, "quiet blader" 75.00
Whirlwind, 8" pressed-steel one-pc blade, tin construction, last of S-wire cages. 10.00

General Electric

Coin-operated, 12" brass blades, steel cage, one speed, operates one-hour-per-nickel, 1905 . . . . 250.00
Ornate base, yoke motor support, flat/pancake-shaped motor, five-speed switch at center rear 200.00
Oscillator, 16" brass blades, steel cage, handle on top of motor 45.00
Tin case, 8" pressed-steel blades, dark "GE" green paint 10.00
Vortalex blades, three blades, steel, 10" and 12" models, various colors, 1947 . . . . 35.00

Polar Cub, Gilbert Fan Co.

6" blades, open cage, no front bars, nickel-plated motor 60.00

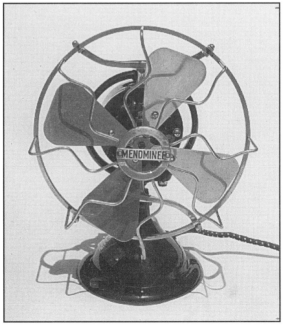

Menominee, 8" brass blades and guard, large rear oscillating mechanism, 1906-18, $150.

6" pressed blade, simple fan,
     silver button 20.00
8" pressed blades, oscillating, tin/steel
     housing. 25.00

Westinghouse
12" fiber blade, steel cage, tapered base,
     sliding switch 40.00
Wind-oscillator "vane" fan, brass plates in
front of fan cage serve as oscillating
mechanism, no gears 300.00

Other
Adams-Bagnall Gyro Fan, ceiling mount,
     two table-type fan units suspended by
     T-shaped bracket, ball-shaped
     motors .400.00
Barber-Coleman, desk model, Bakelite, 8"
     blades. 25.00
Colonial Oscillating Fan, 12" brass blades,
     unusual oscillator on front of motor, tab
     ftd, 1916 . . . . .150.00
Diehl, 12" brass blades, steel cage,
     common rear oscillator, black . . .45.00
Eck Hurricane, 12" brass blades, two front
     legs with rear tab feet on base, exposed
     rear oscillating gears 300.00
Edison, battery-operated, exposed coils,
     six blades, tripod legs, 1892. . . .700.00
Eskimo, 12" aluminum blades, steel case,
     rotating switch, 1940s 10.00
Hunter, 12" brass blades, steel cage, light
     green, oscillates 20.00
Jandus, round ball motor, 12" brass blades
     and cage, ornate tab ftd base . .400.00
Knapp-Monarch, 12" overlapping
     steel/aluminum blades, straight-wire
     cage, tin .15.00
Menomonee Electric, 12" brass blades and
     cage, unusual cage, brass arms 200.00
Peerless, 12" brass blades, steel cage,
     non-oscillating, heavy cast base .40.00
Western Electric, bi-polar motor, brass
     blades and cage, ftd base, exposed
     coils, star in front cage, 1898 . . .400.00

Farm Collectibles

The agrarian myth of the rugged individual pitting his or her mental and
physical talents against the elements
remains a strong part of the American
character in the 1990s. There is something pure about returning to the soil.

The country look heavily utilizes the
objects of rural life, from cast-iron
seats to wooden rakes. This is one collectible area in which collectors want
an aged or well-worn, appearance. Although most of the items were factory-
made, they have a hand-crafted look.
The key is to find objects that have
character—a look that gives them a
sense of individuality.

Clubs: Antique Engine, Tractor & Toy
Club, 5731 Paradise Rd., Slatington,
PA 18080; Cast Iron Seat Collectors
Association, RFD #2, P.O. Box 40, Le
Center, MN 56057.

Periodical: *Farm Antique News*, 812
N. 3rd St., Tarkio, MO 64491.

Calendar
1899, Listers Fertilizers, woman with
     sheaves of wheat, farm
     background. 125.00
1914, McCormick Machinery 175.00
1920s, John Deere 35.00
1929, Minnesota Binders, DeLaval
     Separators, Oliver Implements,
     flapper-girl illus 28.00

Catalogs
International Harvester, 1934, 112 pgs,
     6-3/4" by 9-1/2" 25.00
Kraus Farm Cultivators, 1911,
     62 pgs. 20.00
Leroy Plow Co., 1913, 20 pgs,
     3-1/2" by 6" 28.00
Oliver Chilled Plow Works, 1924, 18 pgs, 4"
     by 8-1/2" 24.00
Walter A. Wood, M&RM Co., 1923, 16 pgs,
     6" by 9" 45.00

Milk Cans
Marked, 10 gal, brass nameplate showing
     name of shipper 20.00
Repainted, gold dec decal 10.00
Unmarked, 10 gal 15.00

Pinback Buttons
Deering Harvester Co., multicolored,
     farmer on horse-drawn mower, black
     inscriptions 50.00
Frick Co., red, white, gold and lavender,
     Eclipse farm tractor. 15.00
Globe Poultry Feed, color image . . . 75.00
International Harvester Co., yellow, black
     and white, February 1938 issue . 12.50

Tape Measures
Blue Seal Grain Products, blue and white,
     1950s 20.00
Bone Fertilizers, multicolored illus of
     Griffith & Boyd's fertilizer bag, blue
     text on other side 25.00

Watch Fobs
Allis Chalmers, tractor 28.00
Gardner Denver Jackhammer 25.00
Lima Shovels, Draglines 22.00

Weather Vanes
Chicken, 51" h, primitive, sheet metal,
     cutout silhouette, old worn red, white
     and black paint, directional arrows,
     wear and rust. 125.00
Horse, 31" l, copper, repaired,
     polished 95.00

Other
Apple Picker, wire cage, long wooden
     handle 25.00
Bow Saw, primitive, ash, old working
     repairs 25.00
Branding Iron, 21" l, wrought iron,
     "D" 25.00
Chicken Feeder, tin 15.00
Chisel, 2" w, 16" l, primitive, hardwood
     handle 17.50
Corn Dryer, wrought iron 15.00
Goat Yoke, single, wood, bentwood
     bow 10.00
Grain Cradle, 41" l, four fingers 65.00
Grain Shock Tyer, wood and iron. . .65.00
Hay Rake, 76" l. 30.00
Husking Tool, leather palm guard,
     shoestring laces 10.00
Ice Tongs, 26" l, wrought iron, double
     handles .45.00
Incubator, 39" h, wooden cabinet . . .75.00
Leather Punch, 9" l, hollow pins, brass
     base. 15.00
Medallion, John Deere Centennial,
     1937 . . . . .10.00
Milking Pail, 8 qt, tin, wire handle . . .60.00
Milking Stool, 12" h, primitive,
     three legs. 30.00
Nesting Box, 14-1/2" h, wood. 15.00
Post-Hole Digger, clamshell shovels,
     double wooden handles 40.00
Pump, cast iron, c1900. . . . . .55.00
Sap Spout, wood, carved 7.50
Scale, butcher, standard computing,
     enamel. .75.00
Shovel, cast-iron blade, wooden
     handle 25.00
Sickle, iron blade, wooden handle . .20.00
Sign, Goodyear Farm Tires, porcelain, two
     sided, die-cut. 225.00
Thermometer, John Deere, 150th
     Anniversary Commemorative . . .45.00
Windmill Weight, Crescent, 10-1/2" l,
     Fairbanks Morse and Co., Chicago,
     marked "Eclipse A13" 95.00

Farm Toys

The average age of those who play
with farm toys is probably well over 30.
Farm toys are adult toys. Collectors
number in the tens of thousands. The

Tractor, litho tin, windup, rubber treads, green, red and white, mkd "Marx, Made in USA," $95.

Wagon, litho tin, wind-up, Marx, 1930s, 4-1/4" h, 9-1/2" l, $150.

annual farm toy show in Dyersville, Iowa, draws a crowd in excess of 15,000.

Beware of recent "limited" and "special edition" farm toys. The number of each toy being produced hardly qualifies them as limited. If you buy them other than for enjoyment, you are speculating. No strong resale market has been established. Collectors who are not careful are going to be plowed under.

Clubs: Ertl Collectors' Club, P.O. Box 500, Dyersville, IA 52040; Farm Toy Collectors Club, P.O. Box 38, Boxholm, IA 50040.

Newsletters: *Spec-Tacular News*, P.O. Box 368, Dyersville, IA 52040; *Turtle River Toy News & Oliver Collector's News*, RR1, P.O. Box 44, Manvel, ND 58256.

Periodicals: *The Toy Tractor Times*, RR3 Box 112-A, Osage, IA 50461; *Toy Farmer*, 7496 106th Ave. SE, LaMoure, ND 58458; *Tractor Classics*, P.O. Box 489, Rocanville, Saskatchewan SOA 3LO Canada.

Ertl Tractors
Case 800, #2616	6.00
Deutz-Allis 6620 All Wheel, #2332	3.00
Fordson Super Major, 1:16 scale, #0307	19.00
IH Farmall Int'l. Cub Tractor, #0653	19.00
John Deere, 1:64 scale, #5606	6.00
Massey #3070, #1107	4.00
McCormick Farmall Super-A, #0250	9.00

Other
Corn Picker, Tru-Scale, pressed steel, 1/16 scale, Carter, 1971	70.00
Disc Harrow, Dinky, #27-H, 1951	25.00
Furrow Plow, Corgi, #56-A1, four furrows, 1961-63	20.00
Hen Pulling Cart, tin, 9-1/4" l, polychrome painted, chick passenger, windup, squeak box not working	50.00
Horse Transporter, Corgi, #1105-B, 1976-80	50.00
Livestock Trailer Truck, Dodge, Corgi, #484-A, 1967-72	50.00
Livestock Trailer Truck, Indian-Head Trademark, Japan, friction, litho tin, black rubber tires, rear door opens, 9-1/2" l, 1960s	90.00
Marx, 8-1/2" l, windup, tin, orig box, Climbing Tractor, white rubber treads	115.00
Marx, 8-1/2" l, windup, tin, orig box, Mechanical Tractor, rubber reads	60.00
Manure Spreader, Dinky, #27-C, 1949	45.00
Pip Squeak, 12" h, rooster, composition, cloth, fur and feather coat, painted wooden base with colorful plaid paper litho cov, head bobs, lever-activated voice box, some tail feathers replaced	50.00
Tandem Disc Harrow, Corgi, #71-A, 1967-72	18.00
Triple Gang Mower, Dinky, #27-J, 1952	60.00

Play Set, Judy's Farm, Judy Toys, Minneapolis, #100, flat wood playing pcs, four family members, car, tractor, truck, animals, cardboard fencing and barn, instructions, $15.

Fast Food Collectibles

If you haunt fast food restaurants for the food, you are a true fast-food

Puzzle, frame tray, Burger King, $20.

Stuffed Doll, Zippy, Tony's Pizza, $8.

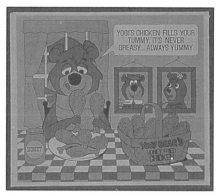

Puzzle, frame tray, Yogi Bear's Honey Fried Chicken, 1969, $35.

junkie. Most collectors haunt them for the giveaways. If you stop and think about it, fast food collectibles are the radio and cereal premiums of the second half of the 20th century. Look at what you have to eat to get them. Whenever possible, try to preserve the original packaging of the premiums. Also, save those things which are most likely to be thrown out. I see a great many Happy Meals toys and few Happy Meals boxes.

Club: McDonald's Collectors Club, 424 White Rd., Fremont, OH 43420.

Newsletters: *Collecting Tips Newsletter*, P.O. Box 633, Joplin, MO 64802; *Fast Food Collectors Express*, P.O. Box 221, Mayview, MO 64071; *The Fast Food Premium Press*, P.O. Box 488, Stony Brook, NY 11790.

Cloth Dolls

Burger King, red, yellow, flesh, black and
white, 16" h 7.50
Chuck E. Cheese, plush, 13" 15.00
Noid, plush, 19", Dominos Pizza. . . .25.00
Wendy's, 11-1/2" h 5.00

Figures

Big Boy, soft rubber. 10.00
Chuck E. Cheese, bendable 10.00
Colonel Sanders, Kentucky Fried Chicken,
12" h. 20.00
Lion King characters, Burger King,
1994 . . . . .3.50
Noid, rubber, 7" h, bendable, Domino's
Pizza, 1988 . . . . .10.00

Pinback Buttons

Dominos Pizza 2.00
McDonald's, Michael Jordan. 1.00
Pizza Hut, Book It 3.00

Other

Bookmark, Dominos Pizza, 1989. . . . 8.00
Bucket, Aladdin, Burger King. 3.00
Bucket, Halloween, Roy Rogers,
glow-in-the-dark 2.00
Calendar, 20 Magical Years, Burger King,
1992 . . . . 4.00
Chalk, four colors, Big Boy 4.00
Coloring Book, Keep Your World Beautiful,
Burger King. 2.00
Cookie Cutter, McDonald's, plastic, Fry Kid
on unicycle, 1987 . . . . 5.00
Cookie Cutter, Pizza Hut, plastic, figural
pizza 3.00
Decals, sheet, iron-on, A&W, Root Beer
Bear and A&W logo, 1977 . . . . . . 2.50
Frisbee, plastic, emb Burger King
character, 3-3/4" d 6.50
Glass, Big Mac, Captain Crook, Grimace,
Hamburglar, Mayor McCheese and
Ronald McDonald, Collector Series,
mid-1970s, 5-5/8" h, set of six . . 25.00
Glass, Domino's Pizza, frosted design and
logo, 4-1/8" h. 2.00
Magnet, Be A Sport, Roy Rogers, set of
four 22.00
Night-Light, Big Boy 95.00
Nodder, Colonel Sanders, Kentucky Fried
Chicken. 135.00
Pencil Topper, Looney Toons, six different
characters, 1988, Arby's, ea. 5.00
Pin, metal, enameled, egg-shaped, yellow
arches on red center band,
"We Hatched Egg McMuffin, Santa
Barbara California," McDonald's,
1980s 20.00
Pogs, McPogs, 24 pcs,
Universal Studios 12.00
Poster, McDonaldland, 18" by 25". . 20.00
Puppet, rubber, Eureka's Castle,
Pizza Hut 5.00
Record, One Million Dollar Menu,
McDonald's, 1988 . . . . 5.00
Ruler, Ronald McDonald, 6" l 2.00
T-shirt, Batman Returns,
McDonald's 10.00
Wallet, Chuck E. Cheese 5.00
Watch, quartz, Ronald face,
McDonald's 55.00
Whistle, McDonald's, Tootler 2.00
Wristpak, Babar, Arby's, set of 3 . . . .8.00

Fenton Glass

Frank L. Fenton founded the Fenton Art Glass Co., as a glass-cutting operation in Martins Ferry, Ohio, in 1905. In 1906, construction began on a plant in Williamstown, W.V. Production began in 1907 and has continued since. The list of Fenton glass products is endless. Early production included carnival, chocolate, custard, pressed and opalescent glass. In the 1920s, stretch glass, Fenton dolphins and art glass were added. Hobnail, opalescent and two-color overlay pieces were popular in the 1940s. In the 1950s, Fenton began reproducing Burmese and other early glass types.

Throughout its production period, Fenton has made reproductions and copycats of famous glass types and patterns. Today, these reproductions and copycats are collectible in their own right. Check out Dorothy Hammond's *Confusing Collectibles: A Guide to the Identification of Contemporary Objects* (Wallace-Homestead: 1979, revised edition) for clues to spotting the reproductions and copycats of Fenton and other glass manufacturers of the 1950s and 1960s.

Vase, Burmese, mkd "Hand Painted by B. Montgomery," 3-1/2" d, 7-1/2" h, $50.

Clubs: Fenton Art Glass Collectors of America, Inc., P.O. Box 384, Williamstown, WV 26187; National Fenton Glass Society, P.O. Box 4008, Marietta, OH 45750.

Basket
4" h, Hobnail handle	55.00
7" h, Hobnail handle	57.00
12-1/2" h, Silvercrest	47.50

Bonbon
5" d, Hobnail, French opalescent, handle	17.00
5" d, Lincoln Inn, green	8.00
8" d, Silver Crest	11.00

Bowl
Oval, pink ring	75.00
Round, 8" d, Thistle, carnival, marigold, ruffled edge	90.00
Round, 11" d, Silver Crest	48.00

Candlesticks, pr
Hobnail, blue opalescent, 3-1/2" h, cornucopia	42.00
Silver Crest, low, ruffled	20.00

Hat
3-1/2" h, Hobnail, blue opalescent	22.00
4" h, Polka Dot, French opalescent	95.00
4-1/2" h, Spiral Snow Crest, emerald green	80.00

Tumbler
Hobnail, Blue opalescent	24.00
Hobnail, Yellow opalescent	30.00
Lincoln Inn, red	25.00

Compote, Silver Crest, $14.

Vase
3-3/4" h, fan, Hobnail, French opalescent	30.00
4" h, Apple Blossom Crest, dec	40.00
4-1/4" h, Silver Crest, fan	12.00
4-1/4" h, Waffle, green opalescent	40.00
6-1/4" h, Jade, ebony vase, hand dec	425.00
8" h, Emerald Crest, bulbous	60.00
8" h, Polka Dot	95.00

Other
Ashtray, 5-1/2", fan, Hobnail, yellow opalescent	35.00
Candy Box, cov, ftd, Silver Crest	125.00
Champagne, Hobnail, French opalescent	18.00
Compote, Silver Crest	14.00
Epergne Set, Silver Crest, bowl and three horn vases	120.00
Figure, Happiness Bird, black satin	25.00
Flowerpot, Emerald Crest, attached saucer	70.00
Fruit Bowl, sq, ftd, Silver Crest	70.00
Juice Set, 5-1/4" h squatty jug, six 5-oz juice tumblers, Hobnail, French opalescent	110.00
Juice Tumbler, Hobnail, blue opalescent	13.00
Lamp Base, 9" h, Dancing Lady, Mongolian green	375.00
Mustard, cov, Emerald Crest, orig spoon	75.00
Pitcher, 4-1/2" h, Hobnail	60.00
Plate, 6-1/2" d, bread and butter, Aqua Crest	15.00
Relish, 9-1/2", divided, Silver Crest	57.00
Shaker, sugar, ruby overlay	75.00
Sherbet, Silver Crest	18.00

Fiesta Ware

Fiesta was the Melmac of the mid 1930s. The Homer Laughlin China Co., introduced Fiesta dinnerware in

Fruit Bowl, 11-3/4" d, 2-3/4" h, cobalt blue, $125.

January 1936 at the Pottery and Glass Show in Pittsburgh. It was a huge success. The original five colors were red, dark blue, light green (with a trace of blue), brilliant yellow and ivory. Other colors were added later. Fiesta was redesigned in 1960, discontinued about 1972 and reintroduced in 1986. It appears destined to go on forever.

Values rest in form and color. Forget the rumors about the uranium content of early red-colored Fiesta. No one died of radiation poisoning from using Fiesta. However, rumor has it that they glowed in the dark when they went to bed at night.

Clubs: Fiesta Club of America, P.O. Box 15383, Loves Park, IL 61115; Fiesta Collectors Club, P.O. Box 361280, Strongsville, Oh 44136.

Cups and Saucers
Cobalt Blue	30.00
Green	20.00
Yellow	22.00

Juice Tumblers
Cobalt Blue	45.00
Green	30.00
Ivory	45.00

Mixing Bowls
#1, Green	200.00
#1, Red	235.00
#1, Turquoise	225.00
#2, cobalt blue	165.00
#3, green	115.00
#4, Cobalt Blue	185.00
#4, Green	125.00
#4, Ivory	195.00
#4, Yellow	125.00
#5, Green	175.00

#5, Turquoise 175.00

Nappy, 5-1/2"
Chartreuse 32.00
Dark Green 32.00
Medium Green 110.00
Red 30.00
Rose 32.00
Turquoise 28.00

Onion Soup, cov
Ivory 750.00
Red 750.00
Yellow 615.00

Plates, 10" d
Cobalt Blue 35.00
Green 25.00
Ivory 32.00
Turquoise .32.00
Yellow 18.00

Vases
8" h, ivory 600.00
10" h, Green 750.00
10" h, Ivory 800.00
10" h, Yellow 750.00
12" h, cobalt blue. 1,200.00

Water Tumbler
Cobalt Blue 65.00
Ivory 75.00
Turquoise .65.00

Other
Candlesticks, pr, tripod,
    cobalt blue 850.00
Carafe, turquoise. 325.00
Chop Plate, 13" d, Cobalt Blue 65.00
Chop Plate, 13" d, Medium Green .275.00
Cream Soup, red. 75.00
Creamer, medium green 75.00
Demitasse Pot, red 495.00
Eggcup, yellow 45.00
Fruit Bowl, 4-3/4" d,
    medium green 500.00
Fruit Bowl, 11-3/4" d, yellow 325.00
Mug, ivory 70.00
Platter, medium green. 110.00
Salt Shaker, ivory 45.00
Teapot, large, Cobalt Blue 195.00
Teapot, large, Red 195.00

Figurines

Looking for a "small" with character? Try collecting ceramic figurines. Collecting interest in the colorful figurines produced by firms such as Ceramic Arts Studio, Florence Ceramics, Vernon Kilns and others has grown considerably during the past 10 years.

Pieces are starting to become pricey. However, there are still bargains to be found. A surprising number of these figurines are found at garage sales and flea markets for less than $10.

Clubs: Abingdon Pottery Club, 210 Knox Hwy. 5, Abingdon, IL 61410; Arkansas Pottery Collectors Society, P.O. Box 7617, Little Rock, AR 72217; Ceramic Arts Studio Collectors Association, P.O. Box 46, Madison, WI 53701; Florence Collector's Club, P.O. Box 122, Richland, WA 99352.

Newsletter: *Vernon Views*, P.O. Box 945, Scottsdale, AZ 85252.

Ceramic Arts Studio
Archibald the Dragon. 70.00
Dutch Girl. 33.00
Lamb 10.00

Florence Ceramics
Abigail, 8-1/2" h, green,
    blue and tan 140.00
Adeline, 8-1/2" h, gray 165.00
Amelia, 9-1/4" h 160.00
Belle. 125.00
Douglas, white 225.00
Gary, Green. 225.00
Gary, Pink 260.00
Haru and Misha, 11" h, red, pr. . . . 260.00
Jeanette. 160.00
Jim, 6 1/2 h, gray and green, pr. . . . 65.00
Joyce, pink. 280.00
Lillian, gray. 110.00
Matilda, tan and blue 125.00
Mickey, blue 150.00
Sara, gray 105.00
Southern Belle, white. 240.00

Gonder
Cowboy on Bronco, black, gold dec, 7-1/2"
    h, 1940-1944. . . . . 25.00
Horse's Head, bluish green, 13" h . . 35.00

Cat, playing with ball of yarn, ceramic, unmkd, $10.

Mandolin Player, porcelain, gold dress and highlights, $75.

Oriental Coolie, pink and green glaze,
    8" h 18.00
Panther, jade green, 18-1/4" l. 90.00

Midwest Potteries
Bear, brown spray glaze, 10" h,
    1940-44 . . . . .30.00
Goose, long neck, white, yellow dec, 5-3/4"
    h, 1940-44 . . . . .8.00
Parrot, perched on stump, blue, yellow and
    white, brown spray glaze on white,
    4-1/2" h, 1940-44. . . . . .12.00
Stallion, rearing, gold, 10-3/4" h,
    1940-44 . . . . .25.00

Morton Potteries
Kangaroo, burgundy, 2-1/2" h 6.50
Swordfish, yellow, 5" h 8.00
Whippet, c1940. . . . . .80.00

Other
Brayton Laguna, Arthur, boy with
    chicken .35.00
Cliftwood Art Potteries, elephant standing
    on log, ginger jar on back, chocolate
    drip glaze, 6-1/2" h 60.00
Hagen Renaker, donkey, 2" h, 1986 10.00
Hedi Schoop, girl with poodle. 85.00
Japan, white kitten on brown shoe,
    3" l 9.00
McCarley, CA, Oriental boy and girl, 7-1/4"
    h boy with large hat and baskets, 6-1/2"
    h girl with parasol and baskets,
    price for pair 15.00
Niloak, Frog 20.00

Niloak, Polar Bear, white matte
glaze. 35.00
Shaw, Dumbo, Disney elephant, seated,
wearing yellow bonnet, 5-1/2" h . .60.00
Vernon Kilns, Sprite 135.00
Vernon Kilns, Unicorn, black, Disney movie
"Fantasia". 200.00

Fire King

Remember those great coffee mugs you used to find at diners? Those nice big warm cups filled to the brim by a smiling waitress, not the Styrofoam of this decade. Chances are they were Fire-King mugs. Fire-King dinnerware and ovenware was sold in sets from the 1940s through the 1970s. The company guaranteed to replace broken pieces and their colorful wares were quite popular with housewives. While Fire-King has been around for many years, collectors are now discovering quantities at flea markets and many are enjoying this new collecting area.

Club: Fire-King Collectors Club, 1161 Woodrow St., Apt. 3, Redwood City, CA 94061.

Black Dots
Mixing Bowl, 6-1/2" 15.00
Mixing Bowl, 7-1/2" 15.00
Mixing Bowl, 8-1/2" 20.00

Charm Square, azurite
Cup and Saucer 3.00
Plate, Bread and Butter, 6-5/8" d 5.00
Plate, Dinner 20.00

Coupe Shape, white, silver border
Cup 3.00
Mixing Bowl, Colonial, 6" d 7.50
Refrigerator Jar, cov, 4-1/8" sq 8.50
Refrigerator Jar, cov, 4-1/4" by 8-1/4",
rect. 14.00

Fleurette
Creamer. 4.00
Cup 3.50
Plate, 9" d 5.00
Sugar, cov 7.50

Fruits, hp, white
Box, cov, sq. 8.50
Casserole, 1 qt, missing cov 9.00
Meat Loaf, 5" by 9", 1 qt. 10.00
Snack Set 7.00

Golden Shell
Cup 3.00
Plate, dinner. 4.00
Saucer 50

Ivory Swirl
Plate, 7-1/4" d 12.50
Plate, 10" d 9.00
Platter, oval, 12" l. 12.50

Jadite, emb dec
Coffee Mug 7.00
Refrigerator Jar, cov, 4-1/2" by 5" . . 28.00
Refrigerator Jar, cov, 5-1/8" by
9 1/8". 40.00
Shaving Mug 27.00

Jane Ray, Jadite
Bowl, Cereal 7.00
Bowl, Dessert. 3.50
Creamer and cov Sugar. 16.00
Cup and Saucer. 4.00

Pink Dogwood, hp
Casserole, cov, 1 Pint 10.00

Casserole, cov, 1 1/2 Quart 18.00
Coffee Mug. 6.50

Primrose
Dessert Bowl 2.50
Platter. 12.00
Snack Set. 6.00

Restaurant Ware, jadite
Mug, thin style 6.00
Plate, 9" d, luncheon 14.00

Sapphire Blue
Casserole, individual, 10 oz,
tab handle 13.00
Custard, 5 oz 3.00
Juice Saver. 130.00
Lid, 7-1/4" d, knob handle. 10.00
Loaf Pan, 9-1/8" by 5-1/8" 18.00
Measuring Cup, 8 oz, one spout. . . . 20.00
Measuring Cup, 8 oz, three spout . . 25.00
Mug. 25.00
Nurser, 4 oz 9.00
Pie Baker, 7" d, cov 9.00
Pie Baker, 9" d 8.50
Roaster, 10-3/8" l 65.00
Utility Bowl, 8-3/8" d 16.00
Utility Bowl, 10-1/8" d 20.00
Utility Pan, 10-1/2" by 2". 20.00

Swirl Golden Anniversary
Creamer and Sugar 6.00
Plate, 9" 3.00

Swirl Lustre
Cup and Saucer 4.00
Mixing Bowl 8.00

Swirl Pink
Bowl 3.75
Chop Plate 13.00
Cream and Sugar, cov 15.00
Plate, 9" 3.50
Saucer 1.00
Soup Bowl 8.00

Turquoise Blue
Bowl, 8" d 14.00
Snack Set. 9.00
Plate, 9" d 9.00
Sugar 5.00

Wheat
Bowl, 4-1/2" 4.00
Cake Pan, 8" sq 10.00
Chili Bowl, 5" d 7.00
Snack Tray 3.00

Fisher Price Toys

In 1930, Herman Guy Fisher, Helen Schelle and Irving R. Price founded the Fisher-Price Toy Co., in Birmingham, N.Y. From that year forward,

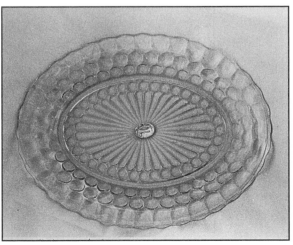

Bubble, platter, 12" l, blue, $14.

Tailspin Tabby, #400, Pop-Up Kritters, c1931, $90.

Fisher-Price toys were built with a five-point creed: intrinsic play value, ingenuity, strong construction, good value for the money and action. With these principles and manufacturing contributions, the Fisher-Price has successfully maintained quality and creativity in the toy market. The collectibility of Fisher-Price toys is a direct reflection upon their desirability, due to their unique characteristics and subject matter.

Club: Fisher-Price Collectors Club, 1442 N. Ogden, Mesa, AZ 85205.

Bossy Bell, #0656, 1961 . . . . .50.00
Bunny Truck, #0015, 1941 . . . . .75.00
Circus Train, three figures, two animals,
    #0991 . . . . .18.00
Cry-Baby Bear, #0711, 1967 . . . . . . .40.00
Cuddly Cub, #0719, 1973 . . . . .20.00
Doggy Racer, #0005, 1942 . . . . . . .200.00
Jolly Jalopy, #0724, 1965 . . . . .15.00
Moo-oo Cow, #155, 1958 . . . . .150.00
Music Box Teaching Clock, #0998 . .25.00
Musical Sweeper, #225, 1953 . . . . .85.00
Musical Tick-Tock Clock, #997,
    1962 . . . . .75.00

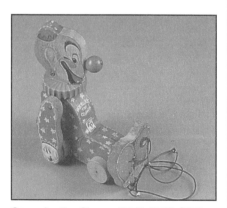

Squeaky the Clown, #777, 1958, $275.

Nosey Pup, #445, 1956 . . . . 175.00
Peek-a-Boo Block, #0760, 1970 . . . 30.00
Picture Disc Camera, five picture discs,
    #0112, 1968 . . . . 30.00
Play Family Patio Set, four figures and
    accessories, #0726, 1970 . . . . . . 20.00
Playland Express, #192, 1962 . . . . . 85.00
Pocket Radio, It's a Small World, #0746,
    1977 . . . . 20.00
Pudgy Pig, #478, 1962 . . . . 50.00
Pull-a-Tune Xylophone, #0870, 1978 6.00
Push Bunny Cart, #401, 1942 . . . . 225.00
Puzzle Puppy, eight pc, #0659,
    1976 . . . . 15.00
Rainbow Stack, #446, 1960 . . . . . . 15.00
Roller Chime, green, #124, 1961 . . . 55.00
Scottie Dog, 2" by 6" by 5-1/2", wood,
    red wood wheels, 1950s 75.00
Sesame Street Music Box TV,
    People in Your Neighborhood,
    #0114, 1984 . . . . 10.00
Shaggy Zilo, #738, 1960 . . . . 150.00
Snap-Lock Beads, #760, 1957 . . . . 12.00
Stake Truck, #0649, 1960 . . . . 50.00
Suzie Seal, with ball, #460, 1961 . . 50.00
Tailspin Tabby, 455, 1939 . . . . 85.00
Talky Parrot, #698, 1963 . . . . 125.00
Tote-a-Tune-Radio, Toyland,
    #0795, 1984 . . . . 10.00
Tuggy Tooter, #0139, 1967 . . . . . . 40.00
Woodsy's Airport, figures and
    accessories, 32-pg book,
    #0962, 1980 . . . . 40.00

Fishing Collectibles

There has been a lot written recently about the increasing value of fishing tackle of all types. What has not been said is that high-ticket items are very limited in number. The vast majority of items sell for less than $5. Fishing collectors emphasize condition. If a rod, reel, lure or accessory shows heavy use, chances are that its value is minimal. The original box and packaging are also important, often doubling value.

You will make a good catch if you find wooden plugs made before 1920 (most that survive were made long after that date), split bamboo fly rods made by master craftsmen (not much value for commercial rods) and reels constructed of German silver with special details and unique mechanical action. Fishing collectors also like to supplement their collection with advertising and other paper ephemera. Find

a pile of this material and you have a lucky strike.

Clubs: National Fishing Lure Collectors Club, 22325 B Drive South, Marshall, MI 49068; Old Reel Collectors Association, 849 NE 70th Ave., Portland, OR 97213.

Newsletter: *The Fisherman's Trader*, P.O. Box 203, Gillette, NJ 07933.

Periodical: *Fishing Collectibles Magazine*, P.O. Box 2797, Kennebunkport, ME 04046.

Creels

Brady, trout size, whole willow,
    leather harness and shoulder strap,
    canvas cov, large front pocket, two
    pouches 150.00
Ed Cumings, Flint, MI, fly-fisher's
    landlocked salmon creel, whole willow,
    orig sliding wooden latch mkd with J.F.
    Anderson's 1937 patent #2,085,564,
    curved back, leather and web
    harness, 13" l 100.00
Unmarked, brook trout, split willow, 6" ruler
    attached to top, orig leather latch strap
    and hinges, classic shape, damage
    along rear of lid 60.00

Lures

Calkin, minnow tube, glass, sgd "L.B.C.,"
    bulbous midsection, raised rings at front
    and back to retain wire line tie and
    rear-hook hangers, holes for corks at
    each end, 2-5/8" l 300.00
CCBC, sucker, wood, natural blue sucker
    scales, glass eyes, belly age lines,
    minor chips, c1932 . . . . .335.00
Hastings, frog, hollow rubber, hp, thick line
    tie wire follows body into external belly
    weight, two tail hooks and weed guard
    wires enter rear end of belly weight,
    c1895, 3-1/2" l 175.00
Heddon, #170 SOS Wounded Minnow,
    L-rigs, early shiner finish with red color,
    glass eyes, finish age lines, tiny chip at
    tail end, minor chips at one hook rig,
    4-1/2" l .90.00

Lure, Creek Chub Bait Co., Garrett, IN, Dingbat, two treble-hooks, glass eyes, hair tuffs, frog colors, red lips, 1-1/2" l, $150.

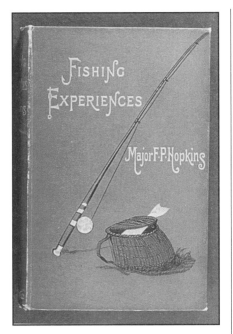

Book, *Fishing Experiences*, Major F.P. Hopkins, $10.

North Coast Minnow, green back with
 age-yellowed body, round end tail prop
 mkd "Pat. Pen," glass eyes, single
 trailing hook, three belly weights,
 c1909, 3" l 125.00
Pfleuger, five hook, polished nickel
 minnow, glass eyes, never-fail hangers,
 front prop mkd "Pfleuger" in straight
 line, crack along right side, few
 hairlines, 3-5/8" l 225.00
Shakespeare, Revolution, hollow
 aluminum, prop mkd "Pat. Appl'd For,"
 trailing feathered double hook,
 3-1/8" l .90.00
Stump Dodger, name stenciled in red on
 top of back, wood, tacked eye, green
 back, red lateral stripe, white belly, two
 treble hooks, 3-3/4" l 80.00

Rods
Constable, Fine Fly, trout, 8', two pc, one
 tip, #7 weight line, ferrule plug, orig bag,
 no tube 125.00
Edwards Quadrate, Special Luxor, medium
 freshwater action spinning rod, 7', two
 pc, full length, no bag or tube. . . .55.00
E.F. Roberts, trout, 7', 2 pc, 2 tips,
 #5 weight line, orig bag and labeled
 tube 275.00
The Green Mountain Special "Back
 Packer," 7', #4/5, Vivian R. Shoker,
 maker, impregnated trout rod, four pc,
 one tip, #4/5 line, 21" one sections,
 agate-striped guide, orig bag
 and tube 350.00

Other
Book, *Fishing for Fun and to Wash Your
 Soul*, Random House, 1963, 86 pgs,
 hard cov, dj 12.00
Calendar, Bristol Steel Rod Co., 1935,
 14" by 18" 55.00
Catalog, South Bend Fishing Tackle,
 1934 . . . . 37.50
License, pinback button, 1948,
 Pennsylvania, resident fishing license,
 maroon and white ground, black serial
 number 15.00
Pin, silvered brass, replica speckled fish,
 inscribed "Illinois" 10.00
Reels, Takapart, No. 480, A.F.
 Meisselbach Mfg., patent
 1904-09. . . . . 40.00
Reels, Winchester, Model #1135, fly, black
 finish 60.00
Sign, South Bend Co., boy holding stringer
 of fish 65.00
Store Display, Spiral Wind Fishing Reels,
 "Gets Double Results," two 1-1/2-lb yellow perch stuffed and suspended on
 painted background of man fishing in
 backwoods stream, hand-blown glass
 dome covers fish, painted frame,
 30-1/4" w, 22" h 500.00

Flags and Flag Collectibles

There certainly was a great deal of flag waving as a result of Operations Desert Shield and Desert Storm. Many collectors salted away "yellow ribbon" flags. Unfortunately, they forgot a basic rule of collecting—the more made, the lower the future value. Ask anyone who owns a 48-star flag.

Flags themselves are difficult to display. Old flags are quite fragile. Hanging them often leads to deterioration. If you own flags, you should be aware of flag etiquette as outlined in Public Law 829, 7th Congress, approved Dec. 22, 1942. Many collectors do not collect flags themselves, but items that display the flag as a decorative motif. A flag-related sheet music collection is one example.

Club: North American Vexilological Association, 1977 N. Olden Ave., Ste. 225, Trenton, NJ 08618.

Flags
18 Stars, Navajo, hand woven, carded with
 natural dyes, mid-1930s, 33" sq 400.00
36 Stars, souvenir of 1876 Philadelphia
 Centennial, "America & France, Union
 Forever, 1776". 250.00
38 Stars, "20th Reunion—New Hampshire
 Volunteer Gilmanton Iron Works, 1885"
 printed on flag's stripes 275.00
46 Stars, printed coarse cotton material,
 attached to stick, all-over slight fading,
 no grommets for flying, 30-1/2" by
 44-1/2" .65.00
48 Stars, "This flag enthusiastically waved
 to greet President Herbert Hoover, Nov.
 2, 1928" printed on stripes,
 9-1/4" by 6" 55.00

Other
Advertising Cover, St. Louis Catering Co.,
 devil waving American flag over
 lobster pot and Indian, red, blue and
 gray 475.00
Advertising Trade Card, "Buy The United
 States Playing Cards, Manufactured by
 the Russell & Morgan Printing Co.,
 Cincinnati, O," American flag back-

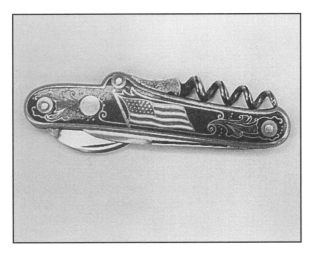

Pocket Knife, cloisonné flag on grips, Kastor, $100.

Flag, tin automobile mount, Universal Fixture Corp., NY, $10.

ground, field of stars contains central large white star with red "U.S." surrounded by smaller white stars .5.00

Automobile Ornament, litho tin, Universal Fixture Corp., NY, red, white and blue flag on white ground, 3-3/4" h 5.00

Bandanna, silk, souvenir of 1893 Chicago World's Fair, brown and gray buildings on red, white and blue flag ground, 16" by 17-3/4" 100.00

Banner, Commemorative, cotton sailcloth, William McKinley portrait, red ground, red, white and blue draped flags flanking portrait, copyrighted by C Parker, 1900, 22" sq 175.00

Banner, Souvenir, silk embroidered, gold-thread highlights, "In Remembrance of my cruise in China, Japan and Philippine waters," dark blue ground, sepia eagle with glass eyes resting on life preserver flanked by draped American flags 400.00

Calendar, 1905, woven jacquard, silk, Betsy Ross making first U.S. flag, Anderson Brothers, Paterson, NJ, 8" by 4-7/8" .100.00

Drum, toy, emb flag and portrait of Admiral Dewey, orig drum sticks, c1899, 9" d 300.00

Fan, 1876 Philadelphia Centennial souvenir, eagle, flag and "100 years, 1776/1876," Horticultural Hall on reverse, made in Japan 200.00

Pillow Cover, silk, 48-star flag, inscription to Mother and Dad in shield, banner reads "Tennessee Maneuvers, 1944," red and blue flocking on white ground, red silk fringe border, 17-1/2" sq .25.00

Sheet Music, General Grant's Grand March, Mack, C.C. Church & Co., WWI artwork, $6.

Pinback Button, Orange County Fair and Races, waving flag, 1916, 1-1/4" d 20.00

Poster, "History of Old Glory," color litho, Babbitt soap premium, 14" by 19" 150.00

Flamingos

The fabulous flamingo offers a wide range of collectibles, from a lovely art glass vase to those ever-present pink plastic yard birds. The most popular flamingos are the graceful ceramic figurines produced en masse in the late 1940s and early 1950s by such artists and companies as Will George, Brad Keeler, Maddux, Lane and California Pottery. These figurines were sold mostly in pairs with one bird standing upright and the mate standing in a head-down position. Measurements for pairs always refers to the upright flamingo.

The raised wing or in-flight flamingos, TV lamps and planters are more difficult to find. A few white flamingos were produced, but they hold little interest to collectors compared to those birds depicted in dark rose and pink. Also highly prized are both the mirror-framed air-brushed prints produced by Turner and copycats from that period.

Advisor: Lynn Rogers, 1997 Sherman Ave., North Bend, OR 97459, (541) 756-4678.

Figures

1-1/2", bone china, raised wing, set of three 12.00

2-1/2", bone china, raised wing, Kelvin. 15.00

4", elegant, unmkd, price for pr 15.00

5-1/2", elegant, Lefton China, price for pr 45.00

6", Chalkware 12.00

6", Pot Metal, Victorian 35.00

8-1/2", plain, Maddux 20.00

9", mother with two babies, raised wing, unmkd .50.00

9-1/2", elegant, Maddux 35.00

10-1/2", high relief, raised wing 75.00

11", large body, leaf base, unmkd . .65.00

13", cold-painted bird, unmkd. 30.00

18", California Pottery, price for pr .350.00

36", papier-mâché 75.00

Other

Console Set, 10", pr flamingos with bowl and candlesticks, Will George . .395.00

Demitasse Cup and Saucer, two birds .20.00

Mirror, 22" by 34" 75.00

Mirror, 22" by 36", ornate 125.00

Planter, 6", raised wing, Maddux . . .35.00

Planter, 10", Maddux, price for pr . . .95.00

Plate, 8-1/4", two birds and palms, Harker Brothers. 25.00

Print, Turner, orig frame, 5" by 7", two flamingos, rare. 50.00

Print, Turner, orig frame, 16" by 22", two flamingos. 75.00

Print, Turner, orig frame, 22" by 28", four flamingos. 150.00

TV Lamp, 14", Lane 150.00

Vase, 15", art glass, huge leaves and flamingos. 250.00

Flamingos, assorted, $12-$150.

Flashlights

Most people take the flashlight for granted. Flashlights, however, can be so much more than simple tools. There are beautiful, unusual and decorative varieties. The flashlight was invented about 1896. In 1897 Conrad Hubert founded the American Electrical Novelty and Manufacturing Co., which went on to become Eveready (the Eveready name did not exist until 1900 when it appeared as "Ever Ready").

Flashlights were so named because early models could not give a steady stream of light. The batteries were weak and bulbs were inefficient, allowing the flashlight to be flashed only for a few moments at a time. Over time, batteries and bulbs improved. The improvements in design of the flashlight's switch is often what makes one flashlight worth more than another.

What is there to collect in flashlights? Name brands, early lights, unusual lights, lanterns, military lights, comic character or personality lights, gun-shaped lights, penlights, novelty lights, innovative lights and so forth. Most collections grow in a haphazard way. Buy the ones in your price range. Some of the quality names in flashlights include Bond, Bright Star, Burgess, Eveready, Franco, French (Ray-O-Vac), Kwik-Lite, Micro-Lite, USA-Lite and Winchester. Condition counts (subtract for dents, corrosion or damage) and prices are listed for flashlights in working, excellent condition.

Advisor: Stuart Schneider, P.O. Box 64, Teaneck, NJ 07666.

Newsletter: Flashlight Collectors Newsletter, P.O. Box 4095, Tustin, CA 92681.

Burgess
Purse Light, "Snaplite," Art Deco-style,
  1930s 45.00
Tubular Light, metal, 1920s 20.00
Tubular Light, metal, 1930s 15.00

Eveready
Masterlight, chrome and black,
  1930s 80.00
Pistol Light, 1910s 50.00
Pocket Light, SS, 1910s 150.00

Eveready, pistol light, c1914, $50.

Tubular Light, 1910s, black 35.00
Tubular Light, 1920s, black 22.00
Tubular Light, 1930s, metal 18.00
Tubular Light, 1940s, metal 12.00
Tubular Light, 1950s, Metal 10.00
Tubular Light, 1950s, Plastic 4.00

Franco, tubular light
1910s, black. 45.00
1920s, black. 25.00
1920, triple switch 45.00

USA-Lite
Mickey Mouse Light, 1935 . . . . 250.00
Red Head, tubular light, 1936 . . . . . 14.00
Tubular Light, early 1930s 22.00

Winchester, tubular light
1920s 65.00
1930s 50.00
1940s 35.00

Other
Bond, tubular light, 1930s, Black . . . 20.00
Bond, tubular light, 1930s, Metal . . . 15.00
Bright Star, tubular light, black,
  1920s 17.00
Ever Ready, nickel-plated and fiber tubular
  light, pre-1905 . . . . 200.00
French, Bullet-Shell shape, 1918. . . 60.00
French, Tubular (Ray-O-Vac), 1920s 20.00
Homart, tubular light, 1930s. 20.00
Kwik-Lite, tubular light, nickel-plated,
  1920s 35.00
Micro-Lite, novelty light, 1940s 25.00
Ray-O-Vac, tubular light, 1930s. . . . 15.00

Food Molds

Commercial ice cream and chocolate molds appear to be the collectors'

Chocolate Mold, stork, tin, E. & Co., #7032, 6-3/8" by 10-3/8", $50.

favorites. Buying them is now a bit risky because of the large number of reproductions. Beware of all Santa and rabbit molds. Country collectors have long touted the vast array of kitchen food molds, ranging from butter prints to Turk's head cake molds. Look for molds with signs of use and patina.

Do not forget the Jell-O molds. If you grew up in the 1950s or 1960s, you ate Jell-O and plenty of it. The aluminum Jell-O molds came in a tremendous variety of shapes and sizes. Most sell between 10 cents and $1, cheap by any stretch of the imagination.

Chocolate
Chicken, tin, clamp type 20.00
Cowboy, tin, clamp type 48.00
Rabbit, six 3" h cavities, hinged . . .125.00
Turkey, pewter 35.00

Cookie
5" l, cast iron, oval, bird on branch . .75.00
5-1/4" l, 4" w, cast iron, cornucopia 165.00
6" l, 4-1/2" w, pine, primitive, carved-bird
  design both sides 225.00

Ice Cream
Basket, pewter, replaced hinge pins. 20.00
Castle, rook, mkd "S & Co". 60.00
Shoe, lady's, 5-3/4" l, pewter 65.00
Smoking Pipe, pewter. 30.00

Other
Cake, cast iron, two pc, Lamb 55.00

Cake, cast iron, two pc, Santa, Griswold,
  12-1/4" h, base emb
  "Hello Kiddies" 525.00
Maple Candy, wood, fruit and foliage
  design, two parts 28.00
Pudding, tin, melon-shape, flat lid,
  c1890 . . . . .40.00

Football Cards

Football cards are hot. It was bound to happen. The price of baseball cards has reached the point where even some of the common cards are outside the price range of the average collector. If you cannot afford baseball, why not try football?

Football card collecting is not as sophisticated as baseball card collecting. However, it will be. Smart collectors who see a similarity between the two collecting areas are beginning to stress Pro-Bowlers and NFL All-Stars. Stay away from World Football material. The league is a loser among collectors, just as it was in real life. The prices listed below are for cards in good condition.

Periodicals: *Beckett Football Card Magazine*, 15850 Dallas Parkway, Dallas, TX 75248; *Sports Cards* and *Sports Collectors Digest*, 700 E. State St., Iola, WI 54990.

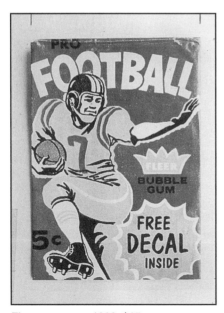

Fleer, wrapper, 1960, $15.

Bowman Gum Co.
1954, Complete Set. 480.00
1954, Common Card 4.25
1954, 7 Kyle Rote 3.50
1954, 57 Chuck Bednarik 7.50
1954, 82 Ken Jackson 4.25
1954, 115 Al Carmichael 1.75
1955, Complete Set. 450.00
1955, Common Card 1.25
1955, 3 John Olszewski. 1.25
1955, 7 Frank Gifford. 27.00
1955, 40 Jim Dooley 1.25
1955, 65 Buddy Young 1.50
1991, Complete Set. 4.00
1991, Common Card 01
1991, 15 Deion Sanders 20
1991, 30 Andre Reed. 04
1991, 45 Thurman Thomas 20
1991, 71 Chris Zorich 10
1991, 122 Alvin Harper 20

Fleer Gum Co.
1961, Complete Set. 480.00
1961, Common Card 1.75
1961, 1 Ed Brown 3.25
1961, 18 Walt Michaels 1.00
1961, 28 Leo Sugar. 1.00
1961, 30 John Unitas. 21.00
1961, 41 Don Meredith 49.00
1962, Complete Set. 240.00
1962, Common Card 1.75
1962, 4 Babe Parilli 2.00
1962, 17 Ken Rice 1.75
1962, 59 Don Maynard 10.50
1962, 74 Fred Williamson 6.00

Philadelphia Gum Co.
1965, Complete Set. 230.00
1965, Common Card 45
1965, 8 Lenny Moore. 1.75
1965, 14 Don Shula 4.25
1965, 31 Jim Brown 18.00
1966, Complete Set. 260.00
1966, Common Card 45
1966, 15 Raymond Berry 2.00
1966, 32 Mike Ditka 6.00
1966, 47 John Morrow 45

Pinnacle
1992, Complete Set. 8.75
1992, Common Card 02
1992, 25 Tony Tolbert 02
1992, 40 Mark Rypien 04
1992, 58 Emmitt Smith 2.00
1992, 88 Keith Jackson 04

Topps Chewing Gum
1956, Complete Set. 210.00
1956, Common Card 60
1956, 9 Lou Groza 3.10
1956, 11 George Blanda 6.25
1958, Complete Set. 160.00
1958, Common Card 40
1958, 22 John Unitas 19.00

Topps, 1960, #51, Bart Starr, good condition, $4.

1958, 73 Frank Gifford 8.25
1960, Complete Set 85.00
1960, Common Card 25
1960, 23 Jim Brown 12.50
1960, 56 Forrest Gregg 4.00
1964, Complete Set 160.00
1964, Common Card 40
1964, 30 Jack Kemp. 20.00
1964, 96 Len Dawson. 9.50
1966, Complete Set 160.00
1966, Common Card 40
1966, 48 George Blanda 5.00
1966, 96 Joe Namath 38.00
1969, Complete Set 70.00
1969, Common Card 15
1969, 26 Brian Piccolo 8.25
1969, 120 Larry Csonka 10.00
1969, 161 Bob Griese. 3.40
1973, Complete Set 52.50
1973, Common Card 05

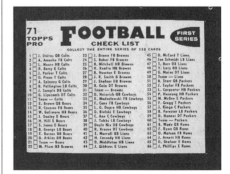

Topps, 1960, #71, Los Angeles Rams Team Card, checklist 1-66, back, good condition, 50 cents.

1973, 60 Fran Tarkenton. 1.90
1973, 89 Franco Harris 7.50
1973, 475 Roger Staubach 4.00
1976, Complete Set 47.50
1976, Common Card. 03
1976, 75 Terry Bradshaw 1.00
1976, 148 Walter Payton. 25.00
1993, Complete Set 10.00
1993, Common Card. 02
1993, 22 Troy Drayton 14
1993, 40 Reggie White 05

Football Collectibles

At the moment, this category is heavily weighted toward professional football. Do not overlook some great college memorabilia. Local pride dominates most collecting. Taking an item back to its hometown often doubles its value. Because of their limited production and the tendency of most individuals to discard them within a short time, some of the hardest things to find are game promotional giveaways. Also check the Breweriana collectors. A surprising number of beer companies sponsor football broadcasts. Go Bud Light!

Coins, Salada
Don Webb 4.00
Jimmy Brown. 50.00

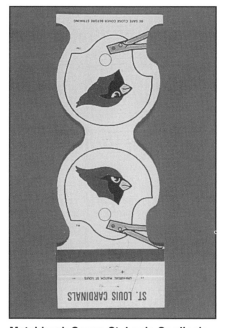

Matchbook Cover, St. Louis Cardinals, $3.

Ticket, 1944, Lehigh Valley Transit Co., Allentown, PA, $2.50.

John Unitas 100.00
Tommy McDonald 5.00

Programs
AFC Division, Baltimore vs. Cincinnati,
    1970 . . . . 28.00
Iowa vs. Notre Dame, 1951 . . . . 50.00
Lincoln University vs. Howard University,
    1949 . . . . 15.00
Notre Dame vs. Navy, 1940s-1950s 12.00

Other
Autograph, Terry Bradshaw,
    sgd football . . . . ・. . . 30.00
Beer Can, 5" h, 1975 Steelers
    Commemorative, aluminum, Iron City
    Beer, 12 oz 15.00
Book, *King Football: The Vulgarization of
    American Colleges*, R. Harris,
    Vanguard Press, 254 pgs, first ed 6.50
Catalog, "A.J. Reach Fall & Winter
    Catalogue," Philadelphia, 1912-13, 32
    pgs, football and other sporting
    equipment 25.00
Cigarette Lighter, Baltimore Colts, musical,
    MIB 75.00
Comic Book, Football Thrills, Approved
    Comics, Red Grange Story,
    1952 . . . . 150.00
Game, Vince Lombardi's Game, Research
    Games Inc., 1960s 40.00
Jug, "Who Will Win," made for
    Michigan-Minnesota Football Game,
    Red Wing 195.00
Magazine, *Football Digest*, 1952 . . . 60.00
Nodder, SAM's, Dan Marino 40.00
Nodder, SAM's, Emmitt Smith 40.00
Pennant, felt, Los Angeles Rams, 29-1/2" l,
    blue and white, NFL logo and
    1967 date 20.00
Pennant, felt, St. Louis Cardinals, red and
    white, c1967 . . . . 15.00
Poster, Dick Butkus, 68-71 . . . . 65.00
Poster, O.J. Simpson, 68-71 . . . . . . 85.00
Stadium Cushion, 11" by 16", vinyl, stuffed,
    red, NFL team names and mascot illus,
    orig tag, unused, 1950s 18.00
Yearbook, NFL, autographed handbook,
    1968 . . . . 25.00

Fostoria Glass

The Fostoria Glass Co., was founded in Fostoria, Ohio, in 1887 and moved to Moundsville, W.V., in 1891. In 1983, Lancaster Colony purchased the company, but produced glass under the Fostoria trademark.

Fostoria is collected by pattern, with the American pattern the most common and sought-after. Other patterns include Baroque, Georgian, Holly, Midnight Rose, Navarre, Rhapsody and Wister. Hazel Weatherman's *Fostoria: Its First Fifty Years*, published by the author about 1972, helps identify patterns.

Clubs: Fostoria Glass Collectors, 10221 Slater Ave. #103-396, Fountain Valley, CA 92708; Fostoria Glass Society of America, P.O. Box 826, Moundsville, WV 26041.

American Pattern
Almond, individual, oval 12.00
Beer Mug, 4-1/2" h 50.00
Bitters Bottle 50.00
Boat, 9" l 14.00
Bowl, 10" d, ftd 45.00
Box, cov, 2" sq 450.00
Box, 3" sq 250.00
Candlesticks, pr, tall, hexagonal
    base. 38.00
Candy Dish, cov, hexagonal, ftd. . . .35.00
Celery Tray, 10" l, oblong 16.00
Celery Vase, 6" h 40.00
Cheese and Cracker. 50.00
Coasters, set of four 30.00
Cracker Jar, cov 275.00
Creamer and Sugar, large, handles . 45.00
Cruet, 7 oz .30.00
Ice Tub, 6-1/2" h 52.00
Jelly, 5" h, flared. 10.00
Jug, 1 qt, 7-1/4" h 65.00
Jug, 2 qt, 8" h, ice lip 12.00
Marmalade, cov, glass spoon. 65.00
Mayonnaise, ftd 25.00
Mustard, cov. 30.00
Nappy, 5" w, tri-corner 12.00
Oyster, 4-1/2" h, ftd 18.00
Platter, 12" l, oval 60.00
Relish, oval, 10-1/2" l, three-part . . .38.00
Salt and Pepper Shakers, pr,
    individual 28.00
Salt and Pepper Shakers, pr,
    regular 20.00
Tumbler, water, 8 oz, flared 45.00

Century Pattern
Basket, 10" l, oval. 100.00
Bonbon, 7" d, round 20.00

Bowl, 10-1/2" d, three ft, rolled 55.00
Candy Dish, cov, ftd 50.00
Celery, 3 part, 9-1/4" l 34.00
Cheese Compote, bouquet dec . . .27.00
Compote 22.00
Creamer and Sugar. 30.00
Cruet, orig stopper 50.00
Cup and Saucer 18.50
Float Bowl, 9" d. 37.00
Ice Bucket, missing handle 60.00
Pickle, 8-1/4" l 21.00
Platter, 12" l. 85.00
Relish, three-part, 11" d 34.00
Salt and Pepper Shakers, pr 20.00
Sherbet 14.00
Tidbit Tray, bouquet dec 18.00
Tumbler, 6" h, ftd. 30.00
Urn Vase, bouquet dec 85.00

Chintz Pattern

Bonbon, ftd 35.00
Bowl, 10" d, handled 50.00
Bowl, 11-1/2" d, flared rim. 70.00
Cake Plate, 10" d, three handles. . . .45.00
Candlesticks, pr, Double Socket 70.00
Candlesticks, pr, Single Socket. 20.00
Celery Dish, 11" l. 45.00
Cheese and Cracker Plate 75.00
Compote, 5-1/2" d 38.00
Cordial, pr .35.00
Creamer and Sugar, individual,
    undertray 55.00
Creamer and Sugar, large. 48.00
Cruet, 3 1/2 oz. 100.00
Cup and Saucer 12.50
Jelly, cov 95.00
Mayonnaise Set, three pcs 58.00
Nappy, center handle, 5" d 24.00
Oyster Plate 6.00
Plate, 7-1/2" d 14.00
Relish, three-part, 10-1/2" d 40.00
Relish, five-part, #2419 . . . . .90.00
Salt and Pepper Shakers, pr 90.00
Server, center handle 48.00
Sherbet 20.00

Franciscan

Charles Gladding, Peter McBean and George Chambers organized the Gladding, McBean and Co., pottery in 1875. Located in California, the firm's early products included sewer pipes and architectural items. In 1934, the company began producing dinnerware under the Franciscan trademark. The earliest forms consisted of plain shapes and bright colors. Later, the company developed molded, underglaze patterns such as Desert Rose, Apple and Ivy.

Franciscan ware can be found with a great variety of marks—more than 80 were used. Many of the marks include the pattern name and patent dates and numbers.

Newsletter: *Franciscan Newsletter*, 8412 5th Ave. NE, Seattle, WA 98115.

Apple

Bowl, 8" d, low 60.00
Candlesticks, pr 100.00
Coffeepot 100.00
Cookie Jar 250.00
Creamer and Sugar, jumbo 75.00
Cup and Saucer. 15.00
Flat Soup 20.00
Gravy 45.00
Jam Jar, cov 85.00
Mug, 10 oz. 125.00
Mug, 12 oz. 40.00
Platter, 12-1/2" l 30.00
Platter, 14" l 50.00
Platter, Turkey 250.00
Salad Bowl, 10" d. 95.00
Salt and Pepper Shakers, pr,
    bulbous. 225.00
Sherbet 30.00
Tumbler, 10 oz. 35.00
Tureen, ftd 595.00
Vegetable Bowl, 7-1/2" d 35.00
Vegetable Bowl, divided 60.00

Desert Rose

Butter Pat. 18.00
Cereal Bowl, 6" d 14.00
Coffeepot, cov 95.00
Cup and Saucer. 10.00
Demitasse Cup and Saucer. 50.00
Eggcup, single 25.00
Gravy, liner 45.00
Milk Pitcher, 1 quart. 85.00
Plate, 6-1/2" d 7.00
Plate, 8-1/2" d 12.00
Plate, 9-1/2" d 15.00
Plate, 10-1/2" d 16.00
Plate, 14" d, chop. 75.00

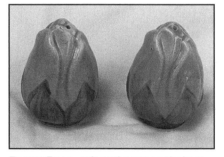

Desert Rose, salt and pepper shakers, pr, small, 2-3/4" h, $20.

Platter, 14-1/2" l 40.00
Salt and Pepper Shakers, pr, large . 35.00
Salt and Pepper Shakers, pr, small,
    rosebud 20.00
Vegetable Bowl, 10" d, divided. 45.00
Water Pitcher 125.00

Duet Rose

Ashtray, individual 10.00
Ashtray, large 35.00
Berry Bowl 6.00
Canister, small 95.00
Cup and Saucer 10.00
Gravy 15.00
Pepper Mill 65.00
Pitcher, large 55.00
Plate, Dinner. 10.00
Plate, Salad 8.00
Teapot 95.00
Vegetable, oval. 18.00

Frankart

Every time there is an Art Deco revival, Frankart gets rediscovered. Frankart was founded in the mid 1920s by Arthur Von Frankenberg, a sculptor and artist. The key is to remember that his pieces were mass-produced. Frankart figures are identified through form and style, not specific features. Do I have to tell you that the nudes are the most collectible? Probably not. Nudes are always collectible. Do not overlook other human figures or animals.

Almost every Frankart piece is marked with the company name followed by a patent number or "pat. appl. for." Avoid unmarked pieces that dealers are trying to pass as Frankart. Frankenberg's wares were frequently copied during the late 1920s and early 1930s.

Ashtray, 7" h, 3" d, caricature monkey,
    glass ash receiver in tail 85.00
Bookends, pr, Angel Fish, stylized,
    exaggerated fins 90.00
Bookends, pr, Bears, 6 h. 70.00
Bookends, pr, Scotties 135.00
Candlesticks, pr, 12-1/2" h, nude figures
    standing on tiptoes, holding candle cup
    overhead 365.00
Cigarette Box, 8" h, figural nude, green
    glass 425.00
Figure, Elk, 6-1/4" h, bronze patina
    finish 120.00
Figure, Mexican riding donkey, ceramic
    hat, dated 1928 . . . . 295.00

Bookends, pr, nudes, white metal, 6-1/2" by 5-1/2", $175.

Incense Burner, cov, 10" h, draped figure
    holds burner 250.00
Lamp, figural nude, 8" h, 4" crystal bubble
    ball 585.00
Lamp, figural nude, 12" h, wrought iron,
    metal .285.00

Frankoma

This is one of those potteries, such as Gonder and Hull, that runs hot and cold. Last edition, I suggested it was freezing. There has been a mild thaw, especially in the Midwest. Frankoma is great 1950s. It's just that collectors and dealers have not yet discovered it as such.

In 1933, John N. Frank, a ceramic art instructor at Oklahoma University, founded Frankoma, Oklahoma's first commercial pottery. Originally located in Norman, it eventually moved to

Limited Edition Collector's Plate, Christmas, 1969, $40.

Sapulpa, Okla., in 1938. A series of disastrous fires, the last in 1983, struck the plant. Look for pieces bearing a pacing leopard mark. These pieces are earlier than pieces marked "FRANKOMA."

Club: Frankoma Family Collectors Association, P.O. Box 32571, Oklahoma City, OK 73123.

Figures
English Setter, 5" h 48.00
Gardener Girl, 5-3/4" h, #701 . . . . . . 95.00
Panther, 7-1/2" l, green, sgd, early . 40.00
Swan, 9" h, open tail, brown glaze. . 20.00

Wall Pockets
Biliken 75.00
Leaf 65.00
Phoebe 75.00

Other
Bell, 6" h, brown satin 10.00
Bookend, Boot, 7" h, price for pr . . . 35.00
Bookend, Mountain Girl, 5-3/4" h. . . 95.00
Candleholder, Wagon Wheel,
    6-1/2" d 20.00
Chip and Dip Set 20.00
Christmas Card, 1948 . . . . 75.00
Christmas Card, 1984, Grace Lee & Milton
    Smith. 35.00
Compote, Gracetone, pine cone,
    #85 . . . . 20.00
Dish, leaf-shape, Gracetone 15.00
Match Holder, 1-3/4" h, #89-A 15.00
Mug, Donkey, red and white, 1976 . 18.00
Pitcher, miniature, 2" h, Desert Gold,
    Ada Clay 10.00
Planter, swan, 7-1/2" h, Wisteria . . . 12.00
Salt and Pepper Shakers, pr, figural
    elephant, 3" h 65.00
Vase, ram's head, 6" h. 25.00

Fraternal Order Collectibles

In the 1990s, few individuals understand the dominant societal role played by fraternal orders and benevolent societies between 1850 and 1950. Because many had membership qualifications that were prejudicial, these "secret" societies often were targets for the social activists of the 1960s.

As the 20th century ends, America as a nation of joiners also seems to be ending. Many fraternal and benevolent organizations have disbanded. A surprising amount of their material has worked its way into the market. Lodge-hall material is often given a "folk art" label and correspondingly high price. The symbolism is fun. Some of the convention souvenir objects are downright funky. Costumes are great for dress-up. Do not pay big money for them. Same goes for ornamental swords.

Benevolent & Protective Order of the Elks (BPOE)
Beaker, 5" h, cream, black elk head, mkd
    "Mettlach, Villeroy & Boch" 100.00
Book, *National Memorial*, color illus,
    1931 . . . . 30.00
Cigar Box Label, Elks Temple,
    multicolored, emb gold trim 25.00
Shaving Mug, pink and white, gold elk's
    head, crossed American flags and floral
    dec, mkd "Germany" 70.00
Silk, 10" l, relief elk's head 40.00
Tie Tack, SS, jeweled dec 28.00

Independent Order of Odd Fellows (IOOF)
Cane, 34-1/4" l, 3" handle, all-over carving,
    ox's head, relief-carved hand in sleeve,
    snake (head missing), two alligators
    (one missing tail) and leaves, old nail
    repairs, 1900 . . . . 110.00
Watch Fob, 94th Anniversary, April 12,
    1913 . . . . 25.00

International Order of Odd Fellows, catalog, Henderson-Ames Company, $50.

Masonic, Golden Peacock, Monongahela Valley Shrine #9, ceramic, monogrammed, 6-1/2" by 10-1/2" l, $125.

Masonic

Apron, painted satin, applied faded blue
ribbon edging, wear and damage,
framed .40.00
Creamer, Ruby Thumbprint pattern,
engraved "Masonic Temple
1893" .30.00
Shelf, 15-1/2" h, folding, walnut, old varnish
finish, good carved detail, incomplete
bottom bracket 55.00

Shrine

Cup and Saucer, china, Los Angeles,
1906 . . . . .70.00
Fez Hat, brass scarab 22.00
Ice Cream Mold, 4-1/4" l, pewter, crescent
with Egyptian head, marked
"E & Co., NY" 25.00
Letter Opener, 32nd emblem, c1920 20.00
Mug, Syria Temple, Pittsburgh 1895,
Nantasket Beach, gold figures . .120.00

Other

Eastern Star, demitasse cup and saucer,
porcelain. 18.00
Grand Army of the Republic, (GAR),
badge, Wisconsin State Encampment
at Trenton, NJ, June 22 and 23, 1905,
cork closure 150.00
Fraternal Order of Eagles (FOE),
Ashtray. 12.00
Knights of Columbus, matchbook holder,
1919 . . . . .24.00

Frog Collectibles

A frog collector I know keeps her collection in the guest bathroom. All the fixtures are green also. How long do you think it took me to find the toilet? In fairy tales, frogs usually received good press. Not true for their cousin, the toad. Television introduced us to Kermit the Frog, thus putting to rest the villainous frog image of Froggy the Gremlin.

Club: The Frog Pond, P.O. Box 193, Beech Grove, IN 46107.

Bank, cast iron, 4-1/2" h, green, red and
yellow 500.00
Cane Handle, 5-1/2" h, figural, silvered
white metal, inset glass eyes, early
1900s 50.00
Clicker, yellow, green and red 2.00
Colorforms, Kermit the Frog, 8" by 12-1/2"
by 1", 1980 Henson Associates . 10.00
Cookie Jar, ceramic, California
Originals 35.00
Doorstop, 3" h, full figure, sitting, yellow
and green 50.00
Figure, reclining, wearing jacket . . . 15.00
Game, Frog Pond, 1895-97 . . . . 45.00
Key Chain, 1" d, metal, frog riding bicycle,
c1940 . . . . 8.00
Mug, ceramic, white, small green frog
sitting in bottom, c1972. . . . . 5.00
Napkin Ring, figural frog holding
drumstick 300.00
Paperweight, 5-1/4" l, green, polychrome
dec, "I Croak for the
Jackson Wagon" 275.00
Sign, 35-1/2" h, Buckeye Camp, frog illus,
plywood, polychrome paint 185.00
Tin, frogs playing leapfrog illus, 8" d, emb
alphabet border. 125.00

Cookie Cutter, red transparent plastic, 50 cents.

Fruit Jars

Most fruit jars that you find are worth less than $1. Their value rests in reuse for canning rather than in the collectors' market. Do not be fooled by patent dates that appear on the jar. Over 50 different types of jars bear a patent date of 1858 and many were made as long as 50 years later.

However, there are some expensive fruit jars. A good price guide is Douglas M. Leybourne, Jr.'s *The Collector's Guide to Old Fruit Jars: Red Book No. 7*, published privately by the author in 1993.

Clubs: Ball Collectors Club, 22203 Doncaster, Wyandotte, MI 48192; Federation of Historical Bottle Collectors, 88 Sweetbriar Branch, Longwood, FL 32750.

Newsletter: *Fruit Jar Newsletter*, 364 Gregory Ave., West Orange, NJ 07052.

Allen's Pat. June 1871, qt, aqua, sq with
beveled corners, ground mouth, emb
base, reproduction metal clamp . 90.00
All Right, qt, aqua, cylindrical, ground
mouth, smooth base, glass lid,
wire bail 60.00
Ball, qt, light green, profuse amber
striations, swirled coloring, cylindrical,
smooth mouth, zinc cap 80.00
Ball Perfect Mason, 1/2 gal, yellow-green,
cylindrical, smooth base, zinc lid . 30.00
Banner, qt, aqua, cylindrical, ground
mouth, smooth base 60.00
Economy, pt, amber, cylindrical, metal lid,
spring clip 5.00
Flaccus Bros., pt, clear, cylindrical,
steer's head, ground mouth,
glass lid 50.00
Franklin Fruit Jar, 1/2 gal, aqua, cylindrical,
ground mouth, glass lid,
zinc band 30.00
G. Dillon Co., Fairmount, IN, 1/2 gal, light
green, cylindrical, applied wax sealer
mouth 30.00
Glassboro Trade Mark Improved, qt, pale
yellow-green, cylindrical, ground mouth,
glass lid, zinc screw band 20.00
Independence Jar, qt, clear, cylindrical,
ground mouth, glass lid 40.00
John M. Moore & Co., Manufacturers,
Fislerville, NJ, 1/2 gal, aqua, cylindrical,
applied mouth, smooth base, glass lid,
iron clamp, small manufacturer's mouth
fissures 160.00

Atlas E-Z seal, qt, aqua, $2.

Lyon Jar, qt, clear, cylindrical, emb "Patented Apr 10 1900," ground mouth 2.50

Mason, qt, golden amber, emb "Mason's (cross) Patent Nov 30th 1858," cylindrical, ground mouth, zinc lid .135.00

Sun Trade Mark, pt, aqua, cylindrical, clear glass lid, ground mouth, metal yoke clamp 80.00

The Vacuum Seal, qt, sun-colored amethyst, cylindrical, light haze . .60.00

The Van Vliet Jar Of 1881, qt, aqua, cylindrical, ground mouth, smooth base, metal yoke clamp, wire bail, no lid, reproduction clamp and wire 325.00

Trade Mark, The Dandy, qt, light yellow-amber, cylindrical, ground mouth, wire bail 105.00

Woodbury Improved (monogram), qt, aqua, cylindrical, ground mouth . .35.00

Furniture

Much of the furniture found at flea markets is of the second-hand variety. If you want to learn more about antique or collectible furniture, consult *Warman's Furniture*, one of the many volumes in the *Warman's Encyclopedia of Antiques and Collectibles.*

Beds
Birch and Pine, 53" w, 74" d, 48" h 250.00
Maple, 24" w, 73" d, 28" h 250.00
Poplar, 42" w, 57" d, 32-1/2" h. . . . 150.00

Blanket Chests
Cherry, maple and walnut rect blocks, dovetailed, handmade from RCA cabinet scraps, brass side handles, c1920, refinished 165.00
Walnut veneer, cedar-lined, diamond-shaped molding on front, Lane, 1930s 150.00
Bookcase, oak, stacking, four sections, glass sliding doors, drawer in base, orig paper labels 425.00

Chairs
Child's, Sunday School type, rounded back, spindles, plank seat, worn dark finish 30.00
Dining, Windsor type, painted floral dec and striping, worn stretchers and feet. 90.00
Ladder Back, armchair, maple, acorn finials, four slats, woven splint seat, 44" h 75.00

Dining Tables
Drop Leaf, Sheraton-style, cherry, rect top, six turned- and rope-carved legs, 23" w leaves 275.00
Duncan Phyfe-style, mahogany, drop leaves, brass caps and castors, 42" w, 1940s 225.00
Extension, walnut veneer, molded apron, six legs, U-shaped stretchers, 60" w, 1925 . . . . 175.00
Pedestal, oak veneer, circular top, gargoyle feet, two leaves, 1920s 325.00

Ice Boxes
Acme, ash, extra high, brass locks. 750.00
Economy, elm, golden finish, galvanized steel lining, brass hinges, 45-lb ice capacity, 41-1/4" h 500.00
Lapland Monitor, Ramey Refrigerator Co., Greenville, MI, oak, three paneled doors, paneled ends, square feet, metal name plate, 35" w, 20" d, 48" h 575.00
Northey Duplex, oak, four doors, 74-1/2" h 425.00
North Pole, oak, applied dec on two paneled doors, paneled ends, bracket feet, zinc lined, orig hardware, metal name plate, 25" w, 19" d, 55" h . 475.00
Victor, Challenge Refrigerator Co., Grand Haven, MI, oak, single raised panel door, paneled ends, zinc lined, orig hardware, metal name plate, 22" w, 15" d, 40" h 500.00

Other
Bedroom Suite, maple, twin bed, chest of drawers, matching wall mirror, night stand with one drawer 125.00
Bench, pine, simple apron, rounded ends, old red paint, Amish 110.00
Candlestand, country Chippendale, sq top, turned column, tripod base, dark finish 650.00
Chest of Drawers, mahogany, line-inlaid drawers, two short drawers and two long drawers, 42" w, 38" h, 1920s. 275.00
China Cabinet, oak, bow front, convex glass side panels, four shelves, mirrored back, 38" w, 60" h, 1920s. 575.00
Coffee Table, kidney-shape, blue glass top, walnut frame. 175.00

Work Table, cherry, fitted drawers, 17-1/2" w, 28-1/2" h, $250.

Curio Cabinet, oak, hanging, glass door,
   six shelves, 38" h 150.00
Desk, child's, oak, roll top, three drawers,
   matching chair 125.00
Dry Sink, pine, shallow well, two paneled
   doors, feet missing, 36" w 350.00
File Cabinet, oak, two drawers 85.00
Footstool, hardwood, oval top, splayed
   legs. 75.00
Hutch, oak, Empire-style, oblong top, pillar
   base, scroll feet, 1920 . . . . . . .400.00
Kitchen Table, black and white porcelain
   top, painted legs. 75.00
Parlor Table, oak, square top,
   spiral-turned legs, base shelf,
   claw and ball feet 175.00
Piano Bench, oak, rect top, square legs,
   40" w 125.00
Plant Stand, oak, 12" square top, cutout
   keyhole design in legs 90.00
Porch Rocker, woven splint back and seat,
   wide arms. 95.00
Potty Chair, child's, rocking, pine, cutout
   carrying handle in back, arms . .125.00
Rocker, oak, pressed back, minor split in
   seat, worn finish 150.00
Sewing Stand, Priscilla type, painted red,
   dark trim, floral decal, rod carrying
   handle, 25" h, 1930s 28.00
Smoking Stand, walnut veneer, brass
   gallery on top, figured veneer on door,
   base shelf, zinc lined 85.00
Washstand, mahogany, Country
   Hepplewhite, 17" sq, 18-1/2" h,
   lift lid, sq tapered legs, chamber
   pot missing. 135.00

Gambling Collectibles

Casinos and other types of gambling are spreading across the country, just as they did more than a century ago. Gaming devices, gaming accessories and souvenirs from gambling establishments—from hotels to riverboats—are all collectible.

Gambling collectors compete with Western collectors for the same material. Sometimes the gunfight gets bloody. With the price of old—late 19th- and early 20th century—gambling material skyrocketing, many new collectors are focusing on more modern material dating from the speakeasies of the 1920s and the glitz of Las Vegas in the 1950s and 1960s.

Playing Cards, Harrah's, Reno and Lake Tahoe, Diamond Back, U.S. Playing Card Co., $15.

You might as well pick up modern examples when you can. Some places last only slightly longer than a throw of the dice. Atlantic City has already seen the Atlantis and Playboy disappear.

Club: Casino Chip & Gaming Token Collectors Club, P.O. Box 490, Altamont, NY 12009.

Ashtrays
Flamingo Hilton, smoked glass, round, red
   imprint, bird logo 5.00
Harrah's, glass, round, amber, blue
   imprint. 3.00
Trump Taj Mahal, glass, round, red
   imprint. 3.00

Poker Chips
Etched, playing cards, horses, eagles and
   animals design, 66 chips 95.00
Inlaid, four crosses. 4.00
Ivory, scrimshaw, eagle 30.00

Slot Machines, Mills
1-cent, QT, diamond front, 12-1/2" by
   18-1/2" by 13" 550.00
5-cent, Operators Bell, cast iron,
   gooseneck, orig tin strips and award
   card, 1915, 16" by 25" by
   16-1/2" 1,450.00
25-cent, high top, watermelon feature,
   two/five payout, 16" by 26" by 16",
   1940s 1,425.00

Other
Card Counter, plated, imitation-ivory face,
   black lettering 18.00
Card Press, 9-1/2" by 4-1/2" by 3",
   dovetailed, holds ten decks,
   handle. 140.00
Cigarette Lighter, figural gun 50.00
Dice, Poker, celluloid, set of five . . . 24.00
Dice, Weighted, always total 12,
   set of three 35.00
Gaming Box, tin, 10" d, oblong,
   roulette-wheel illus 65.00

Slot Machine, Watling Rol-A-Top, 25 cents, twin jackpots, three-slot, c1941, $3,000.

Poker Chip Box, celluloid, rect, four aces
   on lid, pearlized center, red, blue and
   black, emb base, sides and top edges,
   satin lining, c1900 . . . . .175.00
Poker Chip Rack, 11-1/2" by 4", revolving,
   wood, holds four decks of cards and
   400 chips. 35.00
Roulette Ball, set of three, one metal, two
   composition. 15.00
Roulette Wheel, wood, inlaid dec, F.
   Denzler, Denver, 31-1/2" d 75.00
Shot Glass, ribbed dec, porcelain
   dice in bottom 24.00
Table Cover, 30" sq, dice, chips,
   score pad and poker hands. 130.00
Watch Fob, gold-plated, enameled
   suit signs 125.00

Games

Many game collectors make distinctions between classic games—those made between 1840 and 1940—and modern games—those dating after 1940. This is the type of snobbishness that gives collecting a bad name. In time, 1990s games will be 100 years old. I can just imagine a collector in 2090 asking dealers at a toy show for a copy of the Morton Downey "Loudmouth" game. I am one of the few who have a mint-condition example put aside.

Barney Miller, Parker Brothers, 1977, $10.

Condition is everything. Games that have been taped or have price tags stuck to their covers should be avoided. Beware of games at flea markets where exposure to sunlight and dirt causes fading, warping and decay. Also, avoid common games, such as "Go to the Head of the Class," "Monopoly" and "Rook." They were produced in such vast quantities that they hold little attraction for collectors.

Most boxed board games found are in heavily used condition. Box lids have excessive wear, tears and are warped. Pieces are missing. In this condition, most games fall in the $2 to $10 range. However, the minute a game is in fine condition or better, value jumps considerably.

Club: American Game Collectors Association, 49 Brooks Ave., Lewiston, ME 04240.

Aero-Chute Target Game, eight playing pieces, sky and target game board, American Toy Airship Co. 35.00

Batman vs. Joker, electronic, Blue Box, 1989 .... 115.00
Bionic Woman, Parker Bros., 1976 . 38.00
Bottoms Up, dice, nine round domino-type counters, 1934 .... 15.00
Bugaloos, Milton Bradley, 1971, piece of tape and slight water spotting on box 30.00
Camelot, Parker Bros., 1931, small tear in box................. 20.00
Careers, Parker Bros., 1957 ...... 32.00
Casper the Friendly Ghost, Milton Bradley, 1959 .... 15.00
Chutes and Ladders, Milton Bradley, 1943, first ed............... 30.00
Combat, Ideal, 1963, tape and tears to box, worn pieces................ 32.00
Comic Conversation Cards, instruction sheet, question and answer cards, J. Ottmann Lith. Co., c1905 .... 40.00
Concentration, Milton Bradley, 1959, orig ed, one missing piece......... 55.00
Dark Shadows, Whitman, 1968 .... 50.00
Dig, Parker Bros., 1959 .... 15.00
Disney, card game, set of three, 1950 .... 15.00
Dogfight, Milton Bradley, 1962..... 35.00
Emily Post Popularity Game, Selchow & Righter, 1970 .... 45.00
Ernie Banks Ball 'n' Strike Batting Game, 1970s 45.00
Escape from the Casaba, Selchow & Righter, 1975 .... 32.00
Eye Guess, Milton Bradley, 1966 .. 20.00
The Fall Guy, Milton Bradley, 1982 . 22.00
Family Game, Hasbro, 1967 ...... 38.00
Felix the Cat, Milton Bradley, 1960 . 35.00
Fireball Island, Milton Bradley, 1986 24.00
Flying Nun, Milton Bradley, 1968... 72.00
Fond, Milton Bradley, 1976 .... 30.00
Ginasta, Kohner Bros., 1954 ..... 15.00
Gremlins, card game 30.00
Hats Off, Transogram, 1941 ...... 30.00

I Dream of Jeannie, Milton Bradley, 1960s.....................45.00
India, Milton Bradley, 1910........30.00
Knight Rider Pinball Game, 1982...10.00
Popeye Card Game, Parker Bros., 1983 ....18.00
Put & Take, Schaper, 1956 ....15.00
Rack-O, Milton Bradley, 1961......10.00
Rat Patrol, Transogram, 1966 .....30.00
Supercar to the Rescue, Milton Bradley, box and board only 55.00
Tabit, John Norton Co., 1954 ......40.00
Wicket the Ewok, Parker, 1983 ....16.00
Wildlife, E.S. Lowe, 1971 ....60.00
Yahtzee, E.S. Lowe, 1956 ....20.00
Yertle, Dr. Seuss 75.00

Gas Station Collectibles

Approach this from two perspectives: items associated with gas stations and gasoline company giveaways. Competition for this material is fierce. Advertising collectors want the advertising; automobile collectors want material to supplement their collections.

Beware of reproductions, ranging from advertising signs to pump globes. Do not accept too much restoration and repair. There were hundreds of thousands of gasoline stations across America. Not all their back rooms have been exhausted.

Club: International Petroliana Collectors Association, P.O. Box 937, Powell, OH 43065.

Periodical: *Petroleum Collectibles Monthly*, 411 Forest St., LaGrange, OH 44050.

The Waltons Game, Milton Bradley, 1974, $30.

Hess Truck, plastic, American Hess Corp., Hong Kong, 1975, 14" l, 2-1/2" w, $300.

Cans

1 qt, Bison Oil, bison illus, 5-1/2" h .130.00
1 qt, Red Indian Aviation Motor Oil
    Imperial, Indian head with headdress,
    6-1/2" h....................450.00
1 qt, Thermo Antifreeze, snowman image,
    5-1/2" h....................50.00
1 qt, Tydol Motor Oil, winged "A" logo,
    5-1/2" h....................10.00
1 gal, Americo Motor Oil, winged
    "A" logo, 10" h..............45.00
1 gal, Blue Ribbon Cream Metal Polish,
    early race-car image, 10-1/4" h ..35.00
1 gal, Monogram Oils & Lubricants "Stand
    Up!," caricature soldiers standing in
    line, 9-1/2" h................100.00
1 gal, Texaco Marine Motor Oil, ocean
    liner and boats illus, 9-1/2" h ...350.00
2 gal, Bureau Penn Motor Oil 45.00
2 gal, Capitol Motor Oil, Capitol dome
    illus........................10.00
2 gal, Penn Airliner Motor Oil, propeller-
    plane image.................175.00
2 gal, Zeppelin Motor Oil, Zeppelin flying
    over ocean..................120.00
5 Gal, Polarine Motor Oil, vignette with
    early touring car............110.00
5 Gal, Trop-Arctic, arctic and tropical
    scenes with open-air car illus...875.00

Pump Globes

Aeropel Gas, wings and propeller logo,
    single lens, clear Gill rippled body,
    13-1/2" d................2,150.00
Mobilgas Special, winged-horse logo, red
    metal body, 16-1/2" d........325.00
Musgo, Indian-chief image, "Michigan's
    Mile Maker," one pc, dated Sept 1928,
    13-1/2" d................5,250.00
Sky Chief, logo, Gill body, gray,
    13-1/2" d...................500.00
Texaco Diesel Chief, Capcolite body,
    13-1/2" d...................875.00

Signs

Mobiloil Pegasus, emb porcelain,
    die-cut, figural flying horse, red and
    white....................2,100.00
Pennzoil, painted metal, two-sided, "Sound
    Your Z—100% Pure Pennsylvania
    Pennzoil Safe Lubrication"
    superimposed over Liberty Bell image,
    16-1/2" w, 11-3/4" h.........100.00
Safety First, porcelain, dark blue ground,
    white lettering "No Cars Filled While
    Motor Is Running, Or Occupants
    Smoking, Thank You," Standard Oil
    Company, IN, 12" w, 17-5/8" h. .275.00

Other

Clock, Auto-Lite, Original Service Parts,
    reverse-painted glass, white and red
    ground, blue numbers, 18" d ...175.00

Display, Kanotex Oil, hanging dirigible,
    flexible electrical fan mounted
    underneath, 58" w, 12" h 600.00
License Attachment, Tydol Man and Flying
    Horse....................35.00
Motor Oil Rack, wire, four emb glass
    bottles with metal spouts, 9" w . 225.00
Paperweight, Richfield Gasoline, figural,
    airplane engine and propellers-shape,
    "The Gasoline of Power," 5-1/4" w,
    6-1/2" h...................300.00
Pump Sign, Sky Chief Supreme, painted
    metal, mkd "Made in USA 3-10-60," 18"
    h, 12" w...................110.00
Radio, Champion Spark Plug, figural
    spark plug, plastic, Japan, 5" w,
    14-1/2" h..................100.00
Thermometer, Bowes Seal Fast Radiator
    Chemicals, "The Famous '500' Line,"
    painted metal, black, red and white,
    38-1/2" h..................110.00

Geisha Girl

Geisha Girl porcelain is a Japanese export ware whose production began in the last quarter of the 19th century and still continues today. Manufacturing came to a standstill during World War II. Collectors have identified more than 150 different patterns from over 100 manufacturers. When buying a set, check the pattern of the pieces carefully. Dealers will mix and match in an effort to achieve a complete set.

Beware of reproductions that have a very white porcelain, minimal background washes, sparse detail coloring, no gold or very bright gold enameling. Some of the reproductions came from Czechoslovakia.

Biscuit Jar, Vantines Blue, pale blue,
    Vantines stamp mark.........55.00
Candlestick, 6-1/2" h, Lantern A, Kutani
    mark.......................75.00
Cocoa Pot, 6-1/2" h, Basket A,
    light green..................45.00
Creamer, Long-Stemmed Peony, slender,
    fluted, blue and gold, mkd "Made in
    Japan".....................10.00
Cup and Saucer, Bamboo Tree, mkd
    "Made in Japan"..............8.50
Cup and Saucer, Kite A, brown and
    gold.......................15.00
Cup and Saucer, Tea, child reaching for
    butterfly, red................4.00

Teacup and Saucer, Parasol Lesson variant, mkd "Japan," gold line through scalloped blue border, $10.

Demitasse Cup and Saucer, Carp A, green
    and red....................15.00
Eggcup, Long-Stemmed Peony,
    orange......................5.00
Figure, cherub, 3" h, playing violin ...6.00
Hair Receiver, Garden Bench C,
    green......................25.00
Match Holder, hanging, Parasol C,
    red........................35.00
Salt and Pepper Shakers, pr, Ikebana in
    Rickshaw, grass green........15.00
Salt and Pepper Shakers, pr, Visiting with
    Baby, blue and gold..........20.00
Teapot, Bamboo Tree............12.00
Wall Pocket, brown, red, flower
    dec........................12.00

G.I. Joe

The first G.I. Joe 12-inch tall posable action figures for boys were produced in 1964 by the Hasbro Manufacturing Co. The original line was made up of one male action figure for each branch of the military. Their outfits were styled after World War II, Korean Conflict and Vietnam Conflict military uniforms.

In 1965 the first black figure was introduced. The year 1967 saw two additions to the line—a female nurse and Talking G.I. Joe. To stay abreast of the changing times, Joe was given flocked hair and beard in 1970. The creation of the G.I. Joe Adventure Team made Joe the marveled explorer, hunter, deep-sea diver and astronaut, rather than just an American serviceman. Due to the Arab oil embargo in 1976, the figure was reduced in height to 8 inches and was renamed the Super Joe. In 1977, production stopped.

It wasn't until 1982 that G.I. Joe made his comeback, with a few changes to the character line and to the way in which the Joe team was viewed. "The Great American Hero" is now a posable 3-3/4-inch tall plastic figure with code names corresponding to the various costumes. The new Joe must deal with both current and futuristic villains and issues.

Clubs: G.I. Joe Collectors Club, 12513 Birchfalls Dr., Raleigh, NC 27614; G.I. Joe: Steel Brigade Club, 8362 Lomay Ave., Westminster, CA 92683.

Newsletter: *Headquarters Quarterly*, 62 McKinley Ave., Kenmore, NY 14217.

Action Figures

Atomic Man, camp shirt, brown
    shorts 45.00
British Commando, #8104, complete, all
    accessories, mint 395.00
Copter Rescue, flight suit, boots,
    camera 75.00
Demolition, complete, all accessories,
    mint 175.00
Eight Ropes of Danger, complete, all
    accessories, mint 275.00
French Resistance, #8103, complete, all
    accessories, mint 350.00
Frogman, #7602, complete scuba outfit, all
    accessories, painted hair, mint. .395.00
German Soldier, #8100, complete, all
    accessories, mint 395.00

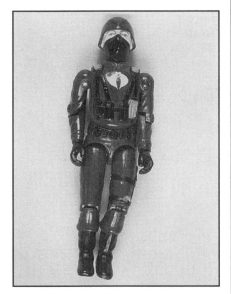

Action Figure, Cobra Officer, swivel arm, $10.

GI Joe, Hasbro, mark 1, 1964, no
    clothes 52.00
Scuba Diver, complete, all
    accessories. 175.00
Talking Action Soldier, complete, all
    accessories. 150.00

Clothing and Accessories

Adventure Foot Locker 40.00
Air Force Academy Trousers 45.00
Air Vest, plastic, orange. 11.00
Aqua Footlocker. 50.00
Australian Entrenching Tool. 5.00
Bazooka Shell 4.00

Figures, 3-3/4" h, near mint, orig file card

Airborne, 1983 . . . . 15.00
Blowtorch, 1984 . . . . 9.00
Cobra Commander, 1982, mail
    premium 50.00
Doc, 1983 . . . . 15.00
Duke, 1984 . . . . 9.00
Firefly, 1984 . . . . 14.00
Flash, 1982 . . . . 20.00
Grunt, 1982 . . . . 18.00
Gung Ho, 1983 . . . . 14.00
Recondo, 1984 . . . . 9.00

Playset

GI Joe Training Center,
    incomplete 100.00
Special Training Center, Sears,
    MIB 300.00
White Tiger Hunt, MIB 195.00

Puzzle, 221 pcs, Mural

Scene #2, 1985 . . . . 3.00
Scene #2, 1988 . . . . 5.00
Scene #3, 1985 . . . . 3.00
Scene #4, 1988 . . . . 5.00

Vehicles

APC, complete, MIB 30.00
Armadillo 15.00
Buggy, 1970s. 20.00
Cobra Hiss, complete, orig box 60.00
Crew Fire truck 35.00
Desert Patrol Jeep, MIB. 900.00
Helicopter, includes orig accessories,
    1970s 68.00
Mamba, complete, orig box 30.00
Mobile Command Vehicle, MIB . . . 195.00
Motorcycle, side car. 135.00
Night Raven, complete, orig box . . . 45.00
Parasite, complete, MIB. 15.00
Rattler, complete, orig box. 60.00
Slugger, complete, orig box 35.00
Snow Cat, complete, MIB 20.00
Thunderclap, complete, MIB 25.00
Tomahawk 50.00
Vector Vet, Battle Force 2000, 1987 25.00

Other

Lunch Box, metal, 1967 . . . . 26.00
Playing Cards, mint 95.00
Table Centerpiece, honeycomb, 1986,
    sealed 4.00
TV Commercial, #4, The Adventures of G.I.
    Joe Eight Ropes of Danger/Mouth of
    Doom, fair picture quality. 30.00

Girl Scouts

Adults make up the bulk of collectors in this category, just as with Boy Scout collectibles. There are still a lot of great bargains out there for Girl Scout items. Don't wait too long, though—sooner or later the girls are bound to catch up.

Beret, green, patch. 3.00
Book, The Girl Scouts Rally, Katherine
    Keene Galt, 1921 . . . . 15.00
Book, Juliette Lowe and the Girl Scouts,
    Choate & Ferris, 1928 . . . . 10.00
Calendar, 1953, color cover photo,
    unused. 20.00
Calendar, 1954, color photo, penciled
    notes 15.00
Certificate, Daisy Girl Scout, floral border,
    birds and butterflies, Girl Scout
    emblem 5.00
Coin, gold, commemorative, 50th
    Anniversary, 1962 . . . . 5.00
Comic Book, Daisy Lowe of the Girl
    Scouts, color, history text, 16 pgs,
    1954 . . . . 15.00

Compass, pocket watch-style, metal and glass, U.S. Gauge Co., NY, 2" d, $10.

Compass, six-sided, green 10.00
Cup, eagle in trefoil image,
    collapsible 10.00
Diary, orange cov, black silhouette,
    1929 . . . . .12.00
Doll, Ginger Brownie Scout, brown uniform
    and hat, gold socks 75.00
Figurine, copper, metal, striding Scout,
    5" h 50.00
Handbook, Brownie Scout Handbook,
    8th printing 5.00
Handbook, Girl Scout Handbook, 7th
    edition, 1st printing, 1953 . . . . . . .3.00
Kerchief, Brownie, compass-point motif,
    yellow, turquoise and brown,
    1940-50 .25.00
Letter, Girl Scouts of Houghton, MI,
    letterhead, accepting resignation of
    director, orig envelope 12.00
Magazine, *The American Girl*, June 1934,
    52 pgs 10.00
Pinback Button, Ecology Campaign,
    green, blue lettering, 1980 . . . . . .10.00
Pinback Button, Walkathon, footprint illus,
    Girl Scout symbol, yellow ground, black
    lettering .10.00
Sewing Kit, Brownies, red case,
    1940s 10.00
Sheet Music, Girl Scouts Together, Gladys
    Cornwell Goff, illus cov 6.00
Thermos, metal, white, red and green,
    striped, white logo, plastic cup, 6-1/2" h,
    Aladdin, 1960 . . . . .50.00

Gold

Twenty-four-karat gold is pure gold. Twelve-karat gold is half gold and half other elements. Many gold items have more weight value than antique or collectible value. The gold-weight scale is different from our regular English pounds scale. Learn the proper con-

Pin, 1910 World Series, World Champions, 20k, diamonds, pin back with clasp, $3,500.

version procedure. Review the value of an ounce of gold once a week and practice keeping that figure in your mind. Pieces with gold wash, gold gilding and gold bands have no weight value. Value rests in other areas. In many cases the gold is applied on the surface. Washing and handling leads to its removal.

Take time to research and learn the difference between gold and gold-plating before starting your collection. This is not an area in which to speculate. How many times have you heard that an old pocket watch has to be worth a lot of money because it has a gold case? Many people cannot tell the difference between gold and gold plating. In most cases, the gold value is much less than you think.

Gold coinage is a whole other story. Every coin suspected of being gold should first be checked by a jeweler and then in coin price guides.

Golf Collectibles

Golf was first played in Scotland in the 15th century. The game achieved popularity in the late 1840s when the "gutty" ball was introduced. Although golf was played in America before the Revolution, it gained a strong foothold in the recreational area only after 1890.

The problem with most golf collectibles is that they are common, while their owners think they are rare. This is an area where homework pays, especially when trying to determine the value of clubs. Do not limit yourself to items used on the course. Books about golf, decorative accessories with a golf motif and clubhouse collectibles are eagerly sought by collectors. This is a great sports collectible to tee-off on (no pun intended!).

Clubs: Golf Collectors' Society, P.O. Box 491, Shawnee Mission, KS 66201; Logo Golf Ball Collector's Association, 4552 Barclay Fairway, Lake Worth, FL 33467; The Golf Club Collectors Association, 640 E. Liberty St., Girard, OH 44420.

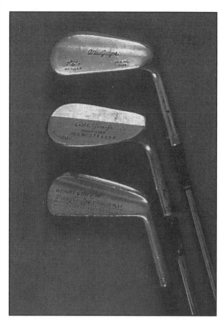

Clubs: (top) MacGregor, Junior Member, Reg. No. 3162; (middle) Robert Jones Jr., Reg No. 376435A; (bottom) Wright & Ditson, Harry Cooper, Straight Play, open iron; price each, $10-15.

Newsletter: *US Golf Classics & Heritage Hickories*, 5407 Pennock Point Rd., Jupiter, FL 33458.

Balls
Bramble Ball, The Crown 15.00
Chemico Bob, yellow dot 35.00
Dino's Brand, Pro-Tel 36.00
Gutty, Mitchell, Manchester 35.00
Mickey Mouse 2.00

Clubs
Brass, steel shaft 35.00
J&B Scotch, figural 10.00
Wood, Spalding Autograph A40 . . . .35.00

Tees, price per dozen
Brass 8.00
Plastic 2.00
Wooden 2.00

Other
Ashtray, wood, brass, glass,
    "Butts-N-Putts" 18.00
Autograph, Ben Hogan, Sports Illustrated
    photo, 1955 . . . . .200.00
Bookends, pr, golfer in relief,
    4" by 6" .55.00
Bottle Opener, figural golf ball, green
    shamrock dec, pot metal, Scott
    Products 29.00
Cigarette Box, bronze, Art Deco, Silver
    Crest 130.00

Puzzle, die-cut cardboard, Goofy Golf Puzzle No. 1, A Swiss-ituation, Richfield Gasoline, 1930s, 9" by 7", $15.

Cigarette Lighter, figural golf bag . . .45.00
Club Cover, leather 20.00
Coaster, Tin, Forest Hills Country Club illus 3.00
Cookie Jar, porcelain, 6" h, figural golf ball 10.00
Decanter, Ceramic, musical, figural golfer, plays "How Dry I Am," Japan, 1960-70 . . . . .35.00
Decanter, Glass, SS, 9" h, golfer illus, missing stopper 150.00
Doorstop, golfer swinging club 375.00
Figure, die-cut celluloid, lady golfer in back swing position, yellow cap, red sweater, green and white checkered skirt, black shoes, brown club, tube attached to back, 1930s, 3" h 35.00
Flask, pocket, figural, golfer on green with two ladies, nickel silver, 5-1/2" by 4". 195.00
Game, Golf-O-Matics, Royal London 18.00
Nut Dish, brass, china, golfer illus center, Bavaria, 1890-1900 . . . . .95.00
Pitcher, Bob Hope Desert Classic, 7" h, Tanqueray Gin, 1972 . . . . .25.00
Plate, cobalt blue, Morgantown Glass Co., 7-1/2" d. .18.00
Powder Box, SP, figural lady golfer handle, 1920 . . . . .175.00
Press Badge, Chicago Area Golf Tournament, 1950-60. . . . . .12.00
Record, Arnold Palmer, golf instructions, two-record album, instruction booklet .40.00
Spike Wrench, Phillips, 1940 . . . . . .18.00
Tray, brass, 10" d, golfer illus center, Wallace Trophy, 1920s 45.00
Tray, silver-plated, 12-1/2" d, Bob Hope Desert Classic, 1974 . . . . .45.00

Gonder Pottery

In 1941, Lawton Gonder established Gonder Ceramic Arts, Inc., at Zanesville, Ohio. The company is

Gonder Pottery mark.

known for its glazes, such as Chinese crackle, gold crackle and flambe. Pieces are clearly marked. Gonder manufactured lamp bases at a second plant and marketed them under the trademark "Eglee." Gonder ceased production in 1957.

Club: Gonder Collectors Club, P.O. Box 21, Crooksville, OH 43731.

Newsletter: *Gonder Collector Newsletter*, P.O. Box 4263, North Myrtle Beach, SC 29597.

Figurines

Collie, 9" l, gray 15.00
Deer, 11" h. 25.00
Elephant, 10-1/2" h, raised trunk, gray and rose. 40.00
Gay Nineties water bearer 80.00
Horse Head, 13" h 75.00
Madonna, full figure 15.00
Oriental Coolie, 8" h, pink and green glaze 20.00
Panther, 15" h, resting 75.00

Other

Basket, 9" by 13" 30.00
Bowl, 7" d, blue and brown, swirl . . . 15.00
Candlesticks, pr, 4-3/4" h, turquoise, pink coral int., mkd "E-14 Gonder" . . . 20.00
Console Set, Crescent Moon 25.00
Cookie Jar, round, swirl, plain lid . . . 40.00
Jar, cov, round, dragon illus. 50.00
Jug, ice lip 20.00
Pitcher, 7" h, blue and wine, high pointed handle and spout 12.00
Planter, 7" h, swan, shaded blue, pink int. 14.00
Vase, 8" h, cornucopia. 18.00

Goofus Glass

Goofus glass is a patterned glass on which the reverse of the principal

portion of the pattern is colored in red or green and covered with a metallic gold ground. It was distributed at carnivals between 1890 and 1920. There are no records of it being manufactured after that date. Crescent Glass Co., Imperial Glass Corp., LaBelle Glass Works and Northwood Glass Co., are some of the companies who made Goofus glass.

Value rests with pieces that have both the main color and ground color still intact. The reverse painting often wore off. It is not uncommon to find the clear pattern glass blank with no painting on it whatsoever. Goofus glass is also known as Mexican Ware, Hooligan Glass and Pickle Glass. Says a lot, doesn't it?

Newsletter: *Goofus Glass Gazette*, 9 Lindenwood Ct., Sterling, VA 20165.

Basket, 5" h, strawberry dec. 45.00
Bonbon, 4" d, red and green strawberry dec, gold ground 35.00
Bowl, 5-1/2" d, La Belle Rose pattern, sq. 30.00
Bowl, 7" d, Iris pattern, gold and red 25.00
Cake Plate, 11" d, Dahlia and Fan pattern, red dec, gold ground 32.00
Coaster, 3" d, red floral dec, gold ground 8.00
Decanter, single red rose dec, gold basketweave-type ground, emb rose stopper 48.00
Dish, 7-1/4" l, fluted, green, floral dec. 12.00

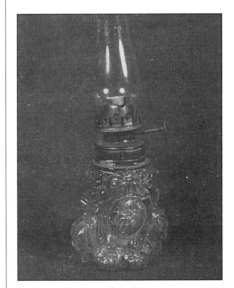

Miniature Lamp, 3" h, $35.

Jewel Box, cov, single red rose dec, gold
    ground 45.00
Mug, Cabbage Rose, gold ground . .30.00
Plate, 7-3/4" d, red carnations, gold
    ground .18.00
Plate, 10-3/4" d, red flowers,
    gold ground 12.00
Platter, 18" l, red rose dec,
    gold ground 65.00
Vase, 7-1/4" h, purple and green grape
    dec, gold ground 25.00
Vase, 8" h, Grapes pattern, purple
    dec 20.00

Graniteware

Graniteware, also known as ag-ateware, is the name commonly given to iron or steel kitchenware covered with an enamel coating. American production began in the 1860s and is still going on today. White and gray are the most common colors. However, wares can be found in shades of blue, brown, cream, green, red and violet. Mottled pieces, those combining swirls of color, are especially desirable.

For several years, there was a deliberate attempt by some dealers to drive prices upward. This scheme was quite successful until the 1990 recession. Never lose sight of the fact that graniteware was inexpensive utilitarian kitchen and household ware. Modern prices should reflect this humble origin.

Soap Dish, wall mount, gray mottled, $30.

Club: National Graniteware Society, P.O. Box 10013, Cedar Rapids, IA 52410.

Bed Pan, gray mottled 30.00
Bowl, blue and white mottled, 7" d. . 25.00
Bowl, creamware, green trim 12.50
Bread Loaf Pan, gray 15.00
Coffeepot, black and white speckled,
    large 30.00
Colander, 12" d, gray, pedestal base 20.00
Cup, child's, green, cat on side 22.00
Dipper, gray and white 20.00
Dipper, red and white 15.00
Double Boiler, white, red trim 20.00
Dry Measure, light blue and white . . 35.00
Funnel, gray mottled, wide mouth . . 45.00
Lunch Pail, cov, gray mottled, tin lid 40.00
Milk Pail, blue and white 35.00
Milk Pan, blue and white swirl 45.00
Mixing Bowl, brown swirl 85.00
Muffin Pan, 8" by 15", gray 35.00
Mug, cream, green trim 6.50
Pie Pan, 6" d, cobalt blue and white
    marbleized 25.00

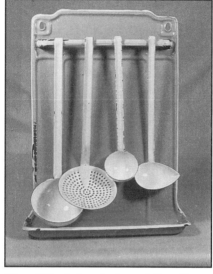

Utensil Rack, four ladles, white with cobalt blue trim, 18" h, 13-3/4" w, $50.

Pitcher, 6" h, green shaded 20.00
Platter, white, blue trim 25.00
Roaster, cobalt blue, white mottled . 20.00
Skimmer, 10" l, gray mottled 25.00
Soap Dish, blue and white swirl,
    hanging 110.00
Soup Ladle, red and white 22.00
Spittoon, blue 35.00
Strainer Insert, 8-1/2" d, wire bail,
    brown and white, large mottle,
    straight sides 55.00
Tea Kettle, red, 1960s 50.00
Teapot, gray, gooseneck 90.00
Tray, red and white mottled, dark blue trim,
    1960s. 85.00
Tube Pan, gray mottled, octagonal. . 40.00
Tumbler, azure blue, orig label. 35.00

Grapette

Grapette was first bottled in Camden, Ark., in 1939 by B.T. Fooks. It was a delicious and inexpensive (wholesale cost for a 30-bottle case was $1) drink in a 6-ounce bottle. During the 1950s, Grapette was one of the top 10 national brands, with bottlers stretching from New York to California. Eventually, flavors other than grape were added, including Lemonette, Orangette, Lymette, Botl'o and Mr. Cola.

While Grapette collectibles can be found nationwide at malls, soda-pop shows and from dealers/collectors,

Basin, dark green and white swirled ext., white int., cobalt blue rim and riveted handles, 20" w, 5" h, $85.

Sign, die-cut cardboard, standup, $125.

they are most abundant in the South and Southeast. Cardboard signs, clocks, calendars and thermometers are of special interest to collectors, with prices ranging from $2 to more than $1,000!

Advisor: Van Stueart, 2240 Hwy. 27N, Nashville, AR 71852, (501) 845-4864.

Signs

Cardboard, "Thirsty—Or Not, Enjoy Grapette Soda," pretty girl wearing straw hat, holding bottle, multicolored, 1940s, 22" by 32" 125.00

Glass, "Drink Grapette Soda, Thirst's Best Bet," reverse painted, 1940s, 9" by 13" 225.00
Porcelain, two pcs, "Enjoy" on one pc, "Grapette" on other, 1940s, 7-1/2" by 18" and 7-1/2" by 22" 300.00
Tin, Flange, "Enjoy Grapette Soda, Thirsty Or Not" in oval, green arrow behind oval, 1940s, 16" by 20" 450.00
Tin, Outdoor, "Enjoy Grapette Soda, Thirsty Or Not," bottle illus, 1949, 36" by 72" 300.00

Other

Calendar, pretty girl illus, "New Flavor Enriched, Grapette Soda," 1952, December sheet, 16" by 32" . . . 155.00
Clock, electric, round, glass cov, illuminated, Grapette bottle in center, Telechron, 1950s, 15" d 550.00

Greeting Cards

Greeting cards still fall largely under the wing of postcard collectors and dealers. They deserve a collector group of their own. At the moment, high-ticket greeting cards are character-related. But someday, collectors will discover Hallmark and other greeting cards as social barometers of their era. Meanwhile, enjoy picking them up for 25 cents or less.

Christmas

"Best Wishes," cherub holding dove, raised message, ribbon on top, c1900 . . 1.50

Birthday, children's ages 1-9, Mia Cards, England, heavy gauge paper, 1930s, price for set, $22.

Clint Eastwood, 1959 . . . . .20.00
Elvis, wearing Army uniform, 1959. . 15.00
Flash Gordon, 1951, unused 12.00
"Hail, Day of Joy," angel kneeling, dove on finger, L. Prang and Co, 1870s . . 15.00
Lady and the Tramp, 4" by 5-1/2", stiff paper, beaver carrying basket of Christmas ornaments illus, Lady and Tramp and beaver dec tree int., unused, orig envelope, Gibson, 1950s . . . 15.00
Mechanical, bird and birdhouse, litho, late 19th C .25.00
Santa Claus, fold-out 12.00
Nativity Scene, fold-out, c1820. . . . . .8.00

Sign, tin, flange, 1940s, 16" by 20", $450.

Valentine, die-cut foldout, emb, Germany, 4-7/8" h, $10.

"With a Thousand Good Wishes, May Christmas Bring Happiness and Sweet Content," country churchyard and women wearing colonial dress, c1900 . . . . 1.50

"With Best Christmas Wishes," girl holding flowers, Raphael Tuck and Sons, late 1800s 15.00

Easter

Birds, Bible verses, late 19th C 4.00

Girl climbing out of egg, shell, fringed, German, 19th C 12.00

"Joyous Easter," angel in oval, daisies and emb decoration, c1910 . . . . 2.00

"Loving Wishes for Easter," cherub on emb ground, crucifix motif, emb flowers on edges, 1890-1900 . . . . 3.00

Victorian, message surrounded by paper lace, C1800 . . . . 12.00

Other

Birthday, Children illus, 19th C 4.00

Birthday, Floral design, blue fringe, c1880 . . . . 20.00

Chanukah, emb paper, gilt dec, box, mid-20th C 10.00

Mother's Day, Cracker Jack, die-cut, full color, puppy, c1940 . . . . 40.00

New Year's, Girl holding bird, palm tree, 19th C 5.00

New Year's, "Wishing You a Happy New Year," girl on front, man on back, fringed, tasseled cord, L. Prang and Co., c1884 . . . . 25.00

Thanksgiving, Family seated at table, mid 20th C 3.00

Thanksgiving, "Happy Thanksgiving," turkey dec, mid 20th C 5.00

Hall China

In 1903, Robert Hall founded the Hall China Co., in East Liverpool, Ohio. Upon his death in 1904, Robert T. Hall, his son, succeeded him. Hall produced refrigerator sets and a large selection of kitchenware and dinnerware in a variety of patterns. The company was a major supplier of institutional (hotel and restaurant) ware.

Hall also manufactured some patterns on an exclusive basis: Autumn Leaf for Jewel Tea, Blue Bouquet for the Standard Coffee Co., of New Orleans and Red Poppy for the Grand Union Tea Co. Hall teapots are a favorite among teapot collectors.

Pitcher, Wildfire, pink roses, blue ribbon, $30.

For the past several years, Hall has been reissuing a number of its solid-color pieces as the "Americana" line. Items featuring a decal or gold decoration have not been reproduced. Because of the difficulty in distinguishing old from new solid-color pieces, prices on many older pieces have dropped.

Periodical: *The Hall China Encore*, 317 N. Pleasant St., Oberlin, OH 44074.

Crocus Dinnerware

Cereal Bowl, 6" d 12.00

Cup 12.00

Gravy 25.00

Plate, 7-1/4" d 6.00

Saucer 1.50

Homewood Dinnerware

Coffeepot, Terrace 45.00

Cup 6.00

Drip Jar, Radiance 20.00

Salt Shaker, handled 16.00

Mums Dinnerware

Casserole, Medallion 35.00

Creamer 14.00

Pie Baker 25.00

Salad Bowl, 9" d 18.00

Teapot, Medallion 90.00

Orange Poppy Dinnerware

Fruit Bowl, 5-1/2" d 6.00

Cup 14.00

Plate, 6" d 5.00

Platter, oval, 11-1/4" l 20.00

Saucer 2.50

Red Poppy Dinnerware

Fruit Bowl, 5-1/2" d 4.50

Cup 11.00

Cereal Bowl, 6" d 15.00

Gravy 25.00

Pie Baker 38.00

Plate, 9" d 11.50

Plate, 10" d 30.00

Saucer 2.00

Serenade Dinnerware

Cereal Bowl, 6" d 4.50

Creamer, Art Deco 14.00

Cup 8.00

Gravy 20.00

Plate, 6" d 3.00

Plate, 9" d 6.00

Platter, 11-1/4" l 16.00

Pretzel Jar 80.00

Silhouette Dinnerware

Cereal Bowl, 6" d 9.00

Coffeepot, Medallion 90.00

Gravy 25.00

Mug 37.00

Springtime Dinnerware

Bowl, 9-1/4" d 18.00

Cake Plate 14.00

Coffeepot 30.00

Cup 6.00

Drip-O-Lators

Ball, Bird of Paradise 35.00

Banded Ball, Tulips 42.00

Bricks and Ivy, plain 20.00

Cathedral, large, orange ground, gray and blue floral decal 17.50

Crest, Minuet decal 35.00

Drape, floral decal, aluminum insert . 25.00

Lattice, floral decal 35.00

Medallion, Crocus 75.00

Meldown, ivory and red, platinum trim 25.00

Monarch, floral lattice design 45.00

Perk, Shaggy Tulip 55.00

Rounded Terrace, small, plain 12.00

Sash, white with blue sash and white stars 65.00

Scoop, floral decal, aluminum insert 17.50

Sweep, blue and orange tulips, aluminum insert 28.00

Target, Dutch decal 28.00

Terrace, light blue, gold flowers 20.00

Trellis, green, with tile 50.00

Viking, Flamingo decal 40.00

Teapot, Aladdin, cobalt blue, gold trim, three pc, $50.

Teapots

Airflow, cobalt, gold dec 75.00
Aladdin, burgundy, gold dec 55.00
Albany, brown, gold dec 70.00
Baltimore, yellow. 50.00
Basketball, red 750.00
Boston, Dresden, gold dec 40.00
Cleveland, green. 65.00
Donut, red .550.00
Globe, Delphinium. 90.00
Hollywood, pink, gold dec 35.00
Melody, Orange Poppy pattern 275.00
Moderne, marine, gold dec 45.00
New York, Red Poppy pattern,
    platinum dec. 75.00
Newport, pink, floral decal. 50.00
Parade, canary yellow, gold dec 45.00
Star, cobalt, gold dec 125.00
Starlight, canary yellow 25.00
Streamline, red 100.00
Twinspout, forest green. 80.00
Windshield, Gold Dot 55.00

Hallmark Ornaments

Hallmark Cards, Inc., was founded by Joyce C. Hall. Hallmark Keepsakes were first marketed in 1973, and these first-year ornaments are avidly sought by collectors. Handcrafted Keepsakes were added to the line in 1975, followed the next year by Baby's First Christmas and Bicentennial ornaments.

1980, Elfin Santa, 6" h, $20.

1987, Santa in Automobile, 3-1/2" h, $15.

Collecting Hallmark Keepsake Ornaments became a popular hobby in 1987, leading to the creation of The Keepsake Ornament Collector's Club, whose membership roles now exceed 250,000. As with any contemporary collectible, keep in mind that secondary market values can be speculative.

Clubs: Hallmark Collectors Club Connection, P.O. Box 110, Fenton, MI 48430; The Keepsake Collector's Club, P.O. Box 412734, Kansas City, MO 64141.

Periodical: *The Ornament Collector*, RR1, Canton, IL 61520.

1974, Keepsake Yarn Ornament
Angel 28.00
Mrs. Santa 23.00
Snowman. 23.00

1976, Yarn Ornament
Caroler. 28.00
Raggedy Andy 40.00
Santa 24.00

1977, Beauty of America
Desert 25.00
Mountains 15.00
Wharf. 40.00

1979, Commemorative
Baby's First Christmas. 22.00
Friendship 18.00
Grandmother 10.00
Mother 10.00
Teacher 15.00

1979, Property Ornament
Joan Walsh Anglund 25.00
Mary Hamilton 20.00
Winnie the Pooh 35.00

1980, Decorative Ball Ornament
Christmas Cardinals 35.00
Christmas Time 30.00
Santa's Workshop 25.00

1981, Commemorative
Baby's First Christmas 15.00
The Gift of Love 20.00
Grandson 15.00
Mother and Dad 17.00

1982, Brass Ornament
Bell 20.00
Santa's Sleigh. 25.00

1983, Handcrafted Ornament
Bell Wreath. 35.00
Brass Santa 23.00
Christmas Koala. 20.00
Holiday Puppy 15.00
Santa's Many Faces. 30.00

1984, Magic Moments
All Are Precious 15.00
City Lights. 50.00
Stained Glass 19.00

1990, New Attractions Ornament
Baby Unicorn 15.00
Billboard Bunny 18.00
Cozy Goose 14.00
Home for the Owlidays 13.00
Stocking Kitten 7.00

Halloween

Halloween collectibles deserve a category of their own. There is such a wealth of material out there, it nearly rivals Christmas as the most decorated

Postcard, Ellen Clapsaddle illus, Inter-Art Series 1301, Series 1301, $85.

Rattle, litho tin, wood handle, $12.

holiday season. (Note: See "Costume" listing for Halloween costumes.)

Newsletters: *Boo News*, P.O. Box 143, Brookfield, IL 60513; *Trick or Treat Trader*, P.O. Box 499, Winchester, NH 03470.

Candy Containers
Black Cat, plastic, orange trim 5.00
Jack-O'-Lantern, composition, orange, black trim, early 20th C 75.00
Witch, papier-mâché, cone-shape, West Germany 30.00

Clickers
Litho tin, black and white Halloween art on orange ground, 1950-60s Smiling Jack-O'-Lantern, leaves and two black cats, Kirchof Co., Newark, NJ ...12.00
Two silhouette witches flying across full moon, two bats below, T. Conn Inc., Brooklyn....................15.00

Trick or Treat Bag, White Castle Kid's Meal giveaway, $10.

Witch, broom and black cat, Kirchof Co., Newark, NJ 10.00

Decorations
Bat, crepe paper, 21" l, Beistle 30.00
Cat on Moon, die-cut, H.E. Lehrs copyright, 14" h 35.00
Owl, die-cut, emb paper, 9" by 13-1/2" 30.00
Skeleton, wall hanging, die-cut cardboard, 1950s, 60" h 35.00
Witch, honeycomb, orange and black, 1928 .... 30.00

Postcards
American Post Card Co., witch and pumpkin scene, 1909 .... 14.00
Photo, girl in costume, 1915 ...... 20.00
Tuck, children and pumpkin scene, 1910 .... 15.00

Trick-or-Treat Bags
Dancing skeletons illus, glow-in-the-dark, 13" h, Applause, 1990 .... 12.00
McDonald's, vinyl, glow-in-the-dark, 12" h, 1990, set of three 6.00
Pumpkin Head, "Happy Halloween," litho paper, 1940................. 20.00

Other
Apron, crepe paper, cats on pumpkin illus, 22" l, Dennison, 1918 .... 75.00
Candle, figural, skeleton, 8-1/2" h, Gurley, 1965 .... 15.00
Candy Box, Babe Ruth, Halloween motif 40.00
Candy Cups, set of three, cat, owl and pumpkin, 4" d 15.00
Earrings, "Trick or Treat," black and orange, 3/4" w................ 6.00
Fan, black cat, orange tissue, Germany, 1920.............. 25.00
Favor, witch with broom, composition head, pipe-cleaner body, 3" h, 1950 .... 6.00
Game, Cat and Witch, Whitman, 1940s 50.00
Hat, Bat illus, litho paper, Germany, 1915 .... 45.00
Hat, Rats on pumpkin illus, crepe paper, cat's-head dec top, 1918 ...... 20.00
Horn, Litho Paper, 8" h, Germany, 1930 .... 50.00
Horn, Metal, USA.............. 20.00
Invitation, skeleton and clock illus, Beistle, 1934 .... 15.00
Lantern, devil's head, papier-mâché, two-tone red, paper insert behind cutout eyes and mouth, wire bail handle, Germany, 7" h............. 100.00
Mask, gauze, luminous 30.00
Party Kit, Peggy's Halloween Box, lamp-shade covers, coasters, place cards, invitations, 1915........ 80.00

Pez, Witch "A". 165.00
Rattle, crepe paper, stick handle, Halloween motif, 4" d 45.00
Shot Glass, black cats, black and orange............. 15.00
Sign, S.N. Burt Co. adv, pumpkin and cat lanterns, devil's horns and other Halloween illus 195.00
Squeaker, litho cardboard, Halloween motif, 2-3/4" h 40.00
Tambourine, litho tin, kids and jack-o'-lantern design, 7" h, Chein.................. 30.00

Hanna Barbera

How much is that gorilla in the window? If it's Magilla Gorilla, it could be pricey. Merchandise associated with Hanna-Barbera cartoon characters is becoming increasingly popular as Baby Boomers rediscover their childhood. Keep in mind that these items were mass-produced. Condition is a key element in determining value.

Atom Ant
Costume, one pc, fabric, with mask, Ben Cooper, 1965............25.00
Lunch Box, metal, 1966 ....35.00
Magic Slate, cardboard, wood stylus, 1967 ....25.00
Soakie, plastic, removable head, Purex, 1965 ....15.00

Flintstones, bank, Dino and Pebbles, molded vinyl, $35.

Jetsons, game, The Jetsons Fun Pad Game, Milton Bradley, $85.

Flintstones
Bank, Barney and Bamm-Bamm, figural, vinyl, 19" h, 1971 . . . . .25.00
Flintstone Circus, Kohner, 1963 . . . .50.00
Mug, Bamm-Bamm's head, molded hard plastic, Flintstone Vitamins premium, 1972. . . . . .7.50
Pillowcase, cotton, Fred playing piano, Wilma, Betty and Barney singing, 1960. . . . . .10.00

Huckleberry Hound
Game, Huckleberry Hound "Bumps," Transogram, 1960 . . . . .25.00
Pencil Case, cardboard, lid, drawer, illus, decal, Hasbro, 1960. . . . . .15.00
Tray, tin, 16" by 12", painted scene . .20.00
Xylophone, litho, multicolored, 1960 .20.00

Jonny Quest
Activity Set, Crayon by number, six sketches, 16 crayons, Transogram, 1965. . . . . .100.00
Activity Set, Pencil by number, eight sketches, six colored pencils, sharpener, 1965. . . . . .75.00

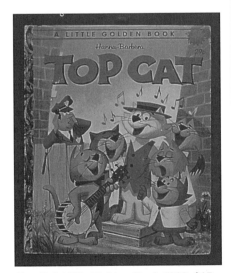

Top Cat, **Little Golden Book #296, $15.**

Coloring Book, Whitman, 1965 . . . . 25.00

Top Cat
Coloring Book, 100 pgs, Whitman, 1961 . . . . 15.00
Figure, plastic, painted, hollow, Ideal, 1965 . . . . 10.00
Record, Robin Hood, multicolored cov, 45 rpm, four songs, 1962. . . . . 10.00

Yogi Bear
Bank, Yogi, figural, plastic, 10" h, Knickerbocker, 1959. . . . . 15.00
Number & Stencil Set, eight sketches, 24 crayons, sharpener, Transogram, 1963 . . . . 35.00
Stamp Set, stamps, pad, Lido, 1961 20.00

Other
Jetsons, puzzle, frame tray, George and Elroy, Whitman, 1962, 11" by 14" 25.00
Jetsons, toy, Astro, windup, tin litho, Marx, 1963 . . . . 250.00
Magilla Gorilla, doll, "Twistables," stuffed, vinyl, posable, 8" h, Ideal, 1964 . 35.00
Magilla Gorilla, hand puppet, vinyl head, fabric body, 10" h, Knickerbocker, 1965 . . . . 20.00
Quick Draw McGraw, gloves, pr, Western-style, cloth, Quick Draw image on fringed cuffs, 1960 . . . . 15.00
Quick Draw McGraw, wall plaque, Quick Draw playing cello, molded hard plastic, painted, 1960, 11" h 10.00
Ruff & Reddy, doll, Reddy, stuffed plush, Knickerbocker, 1960, 15" h. 85.00
Ruff & Reddy, record, 45 rpm, illus sleeve, 1959 . . . . 12.00
Scooby Doo, doll, stuffed, orange and brown, tag, 14" h, 1970. . . . . 25.00
Scooby Doo, View-Master Reel, talking, 8" by 8", boxed set, reels, accessories, GAF, 1970 . . . . 8.00
Space Ghost, costume, one pc, fabric, mask, illus front, Ben Cooper, 1965 . . . . 50.00
Space Ghost, Jigsaw Puzzle, 100 pc, 8" by 10" box, Whitman, 1967 . . . . . . 20.00
Wally Gator, puppet, plastic, mechanical, 3" h, Kohner, 1964 . . . . 15.00

Hangers

Clothing hangers come in an imaginative variety of forms depending upon their specific function. Hangers have been fashioned to hold shirts, suits, skirts, pants, belts, ties and any combination of these garments. There are even hangers made for shoes.

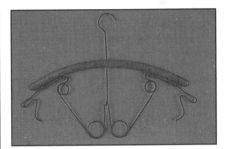

Coat and Skirt, $35.

Hangers designed for traveling purposes have employed folding sides, telescoping arms and accordion extensions. Hangers for drying may use a framework with clothespins or take the contoured shape of a glove, stocking, sweater or pants.

Many hangers have patent dates from the 1890s through the 1920s. The most common type of hanger has a single loop of steel wire which fits in each shoulder of the garment. Prices tend to rise as the construction and shape become more elaborate. Though not commonly found, antique hangers are interesting because of their variations in design—often beautiful works of art. They are generally inexpensive, easy to store and may still be used for their intended purpose.

Advisors: Cheryl and Roger Brinker, 1051 Fullerton Ave., Allentown, PA 18102, (610) 432-8393.

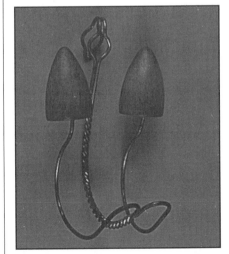

Shoes, bent wire, wood toe supports, $30.

Acme Hanger, pants hanger, vertical sliding center ring pinches wooden slats, patented June 5, 1900 . . . .10.00
Belmar, patented May 18 and Nov. 2, 1897 . . . . .25.00
Butterfly Wing, basic hanger, wire loop through shoulders, folding 10.00
Butterfly Wing, basic hanger, wire loop through shoulders, offset hooks . . .8.00
Midget, folding travel hanger, patented Jan. 7, 1913 . . . . .35.00
Shoe Hanger, holds pair, bent wire, wooden toe supports 30.00
Stay-Fast, wooden shoulder supports with metal band spring action for garment straps 15.00
Travel Hanger, folding, accordion-style 30.00
Union, folding hanger, wood block with folding wire extensions 10.00

Hardware

The first thing one should realize about computer systems...Sorry, wrong kind of hardware. Here we're talking about architectural and carpentry hardware. Any self-respecting flea market will have an abundance of assorted items capable of pleasing any collector.

Club: The Antique Doorknob Collectors of America, P.O. Box 126, Eola, IL 60519.

Door Knockers

Basket of Flowers, 3-3/4" l, cast iron, orig polychrome paint 30.00
Dog's Head, figural, 7" h, brass. 65.00
Eagle, figural, brass 55.00
English Setter, 4" by 5", bronzed metal 20.00
Fox Head, figural, 5-1/2" h, cast iron, ring hanging from mouth 85.00
Lion's Head, figural, bronze, ring hanging from mouth. 50.00
Rooster, figural, cast iron 155.00

Other

Coat Hook, cast iron, bronze finish, acorn finial 8.00
Curtain Tieback, cast iron, 3" d, painted, bouquet of flowers dec, 19th C, set of six .45.00
Doorbell, brass, spheres hanging from metal netting, mounting bracket. .85.00
Doorknob, faceted crystal, 2-1/2" d, brass hardware 2.00
Door Latch, butterfly-shape, iron. . . .75.00
Flagpole Finial, 7" w, spread-wing eagle, brass 25.00

Garden Stake, 30" h, sunburst and scrolls, wrought iron 250.00
Hook, cast iron, ornate. 12.00
Lock, 4" by 6", iron, turn handle with key, c1840 . . . . 100.00
Padlock, wrought iron, key and fastening spikes 75.00
Shelf Brackets, pr, 5-1/2" h, iron, swivel 18.00
Shutter Dogs, 8-1/2" l, cast iron, mkd "Brevete SGDG" with anchor, set of four 150.00
Snowbirds, pr, 5-1/4" h, eagles, figural, cast iron 125.00

Harker Pottery

In 1840, Benjamin Harker of East Liverpool, Ohio, built a kiln and produced yellowware products. During the Civil War, David Boyce managed the firm. Harker and Boyce played important roles in the management of the firm through much of its history. In 1931, the company moved to Chester, W.V. Eventually, Jeannette Glass Co., purchased Harker, closing the plant in March 1972.

Much of Harker's wares were utilitarian. The company introduced Cameo ware in 1945 and a Rockingham ware line in 1960. A wide range of backstamps and names were used.

Newspaper: *The Daze*, P.O. Box 57, Otisville, MI 48463.

Cameoware

Drip Jar, round 15.00
Fork 20.00
Jug, 1/2 pt. 15.00
Plate, 10" d, dinner. 10.00
Rolling Pin 65.00
Salt and Pepper Shaker, pr, round. . 15.00

Colonial Lady

Cereal Bowl 10.00
Cup and Saucer 12.00
Fork 25.00
Plate, 7" d, salad 6.00
Spoon. 25.00
Vegetable Bowl. 22.00

Embassy

Creamer 4.00
Vegetable Bowl, 9" l, oval. 10.00

Gadroon

Cup. 4.00
Plate, 6-1/4" d. 1.00
Saucer 1.00
Sugar 8.00

Modern Age

Cake Tray, 11-1/2" d 15.00
Cookie Jar, oval 30.00
Creamer, oval. 4.00

Utility Plates: (top left) utility plate, Red Apple 1, 12" w, $15; **(top right)** utility plate, Red Apple 2, 12" w, $15; **(bottom left)** spoon, Red Apple 1, $20; **(bottom center)** tea tile, Red Apple 1, $18; **(bottom right)** server, Red Apple 1, $25.

White Rose

Jug, sq, 2 qt. 30.00
Pie Baker, 9" d 12.00
Rolling Pin. 45.00
Tea Tile, 6-1/2" w, octagonal. 18.00

Harmonicas and Related Items

Harmonica collecting has caught on. One indication is the unrealistically high prices being asked for common models in flea markets. What makes collecting harmonicas such an appealing hobby? Some important reasons include the endless variety of models—some quite bizarre—their small size, ease of playing and low cost compared to many collectibles. A major collector has estimated that some 20,000 different models have been produced since the late 1800s. Yet, harmonica collecting has relatively few serious participants as yet—too few to even have a club or newsletter. One organization which may appeal to collectors is SPAH, a worldwide association whose members are primarily harmonica players. They publish a quarterly newsletter (SPAH, Inc., P.O. Box 865, Troy, MI 48099).

The following prices are based on harmonicas (or related items) in nice playable (or usable) condition with minimal dents, rust spots or other defects and with the original box (unless indicated). Hohner's "star in trademark" is found on the side opposite the model name and consists of a star in a circle held by two hands.

Advisors: Alan G. Bates, 495 Dogwood Dr., Hockessin, DE 19707, (302) 239-4296; Buzzie Nightingale, P.O. Box 447, Madison, NH 03849, (603) 367-4459.

Harmonicas

Aeroband, Hohner, 14 holes, brass cover plates shaped like Zeppelin, litho bust of Gen. Zeppelin on one side, Matthias Hohner on other, no box 300.00
Alpina, Koch, double-sided, 24 holes each side, unusual holes on covers, 9-3/8" l 75.00

American Ace, Hohner, 10 holes, World War I biplanes or jet fighter shown on box 20.00
Atta Boy, Hotz, 10 holes, two boys from 1930 pictured on box 20.00
Chimes, Hohner, double-sided, 12 holes per side, 4-1/4" l, cathedral on box cov 75.00
Chromatic Harmonica, Hohner, No. 260, 10 holes, first commercial model with outside spring, c1925, 4-7/8" l, "First and Only Practical One" on black hinged box 65.00
Chromatic No. 265 Bass, Hohner, two harmonicas hinged together, 29 holes, 8-3/4" l, star in trademark, sturdy felt-lined wooden box 275.00
Chromonica II Deluxe, Hohner, 12 holes, rounded lever instead of slide button, streamlined, fully encased in nickel steel, 6-1/2" l 125.00
Color Harmonica, Thorens, Switzerland, 10 holes, ivory and green 35.00
Doerfel's International, sliding celluloid wraparound cover, 10 holes, pre-1900, no box. 65.00
Echo Luxe, Hohner, double-sided, 24 holes each side, enameled Art Deco designs, 6-3/4" l 120.00
Echo Luxe, Hohner, single-sided, 14 holes, enameled Art Deco designs, 4-1/2" l, "Century of Progress" on box cov 65.00
Echophone, Hohner, maroon plastic resonator, 10 holes, 4-3/4" l 95.00
44 Chromatic, Borrah Minevitch, 10 holes, slide with external spring, c1935, 4-7/8" l, Minevitch picture on box 75.00
Goliath, Hohner, 24 holes, 7-1/2" l, no star. 45.00
Harmonette, Hohner, harp-shape, 14 holes, 4-3/4" l, telescoping box. 100.00
Harmonophone, Clover, 10 holes, funnel-shaped tin resonator stamped with name and U.S. patent numbers, 4" l, no box 200.00

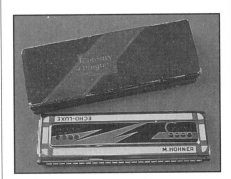

Echo-Luxe, Hohner, single-sided, 14 holes, enameled Art Deco designs, 4-1/2" l, "Century of Progress" on box cov, $65.

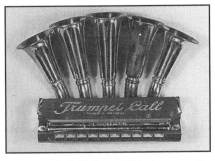

Trumpet Call, Hohner, 10 holes, wood covers with five brass horns projecting from back, 4-7/8" l, simple cardboard box, $375.

Harmonotone, Harmonic Reed Corp., 10 holes, plastic, sliding mouthpiece, 4-1/8" l 20.00
Herb Shriner's Hoosier Boy, Hohner, 10 holes, gold covers, 4" l 40.00
Hit Parade, Wm. Kratt Co., 10 holes, 4" l 25.00
Hohner Miniature, four holes, 1-3/8" l, plastic box 15.00
Marine Band, Echo Tremolo, Hohner, double-sided, 48 holes each side, 4 keys, 15-5/8" l, wooden box with brass catches, "No. 683" on cover, early-style printing on labels 150.00
Marine Band, Model 1896, Hohner, 10 holes, with star in trademark, pre-1940 . . . . .25.00
Marine Band, Model 1896, Hohner, 10 holes, without star in trademark, cardboard box 20.00
Marine Band, Model 1896, Hohner Tremolo, Hohner, single-sided, 20 holes, 7-3/4" l 55.00
1,000,000 $ Baby, Japan, miniature, four holes, cardboard box. 20.00
Old Standby, Hohner, 10 holes, 4" l, star in trademark 25.00
Opera, "Made in U.S. Zone Germany," 16 holes, 6-1/4" l, tin box with opera performers. 55.00
Playasax, Plarola, small sax with harmonica inside which plays music rolls by turning crank and blowing through mouthpiece, three playable rolls, no box. 175.00
Rascal, Borrah Minevitch, 10 holes, 4" l, box cover with photo of Borrah and his 10 Rascals on stage 40.00
Rolmonica, 4" sq brown Bakelite case with orange flecks, special harmonica inside plays music rolls by turning crank and blowing through mouthpiece, five playable rolls, no box. 125.00
Rolmonica-Chromatic, 4-5/8" brown Bakelite case, special chromatic harmonica inside plays music rolls by

turning crank and blowing through mouthpiece, three playable rolls, no box 160.00

Tremolo Quartet, Hohner, four harmonicas in different keys on spindle mount, 20 holes each side, 7-3/4" l, star in trademark, sturdy cardboard box 175.00

Tremolo Sextet, Hohner, six harmonicas in different keys on spindle mount, 20 holes each side, 7-3/4" l, star in trademark, sturdy cardboard box 250.00

Trumpet Call, Hohner, 10 holes, wooden covers with five brass horns projecting from back, 4-7/8" l, simple cardboard box 375.00

Trumpet Call, Hohner, 16 holes each side, double-sided, brass covers depicting nude wooden nymphs playing horns, flared trumpets either end, 7" l, dec box 250.00

Tuckaway, Hohner, clamshell covers close down to protect harmonica, 10 holes, 4" l, no box 75.00

University Chimes, Beaver Brand, double-sided, two bells mounted on top under metal arch, 24 holes each side, 9-1/4" l, sturdy cardboard box . .225.00

Violin King, Bohm, double-sided, 16 holes per side, 5" l, tin box. 75.00

Related Items

Display Case, "M. Hohner" on cover, three tiers of trays fold back, label inside cover shows costumed harmonica players from around the world and "Over 7 Million Sold". 200.00

Sign, Marine Band harmonica-shape, silver-colored celluloid and cardboard, 24" l 125.00

Hatpin Holders and Hatpins

Women used hatpins to keep their hats in place. The ends of the pins were decorated in a wide variety of materials—ranging from gemstones to china—and the pins themselves became a fashion accessory. Since a woman was likely to own many hatpins and they were rather large, special holders were developed for them.

Clubs: American Hatpin Society, 20 Monticello Dr., Palos Verdes Peninsula, CA 90274; International Club for Collectors of Hatpins and Hatpin Holders, 15237 Chanera Ave., Gardena, CA 90249.

Holders

Belleek, floral dec, gold top 55.00
China, black bear standing beside tree stump, heart-shaped base, Germany. 90.00
Limoges, gold emb border, cream. . 30.00
Royal Bayreuth, courting couple, cutout base with gold dec, blue mark . 395.00
Royal Doulton, 6" h, earth tone, Dickensware, Sam Weller. 110.00
Royal Rudolstadt, lavender and roses dec 25.00
Schafer & Vater, 5" h, Jasperware medallion, woman's profile 125.00
Schlegelmilch, RS Germany, 4-1/2" h, poppy pattern 110.00
Schlegelmilch, RS Prussia, floral and scroll dec, gold accents, ftd 170.00
Silver, etched, engraved, sixteen holes. 120.00

Pins

Advertising, 10" l, Economy Stoves and Ranges 45.00
Art Deco, 8-1/2" l, brass, knob design 95.00
Art Deco, 10-1/2" l, plastic, amber. . 15.00
Art Nouveau, 8" l, silver-tone head, female profile 110.00
Art Nouveau, 12" l, SS, four sided . . 85.00
Bakelite, black fluted disc, rhinestone dec, silver accents 35.00
Brass and Glass, two-sided, iris and leaf motif 100.00
Carnival Glass, figural rooster, marigold 35.00
Crystal, hand cut, blown teardrop-shape 125.00
Ivory, ball-shape, carved dec. 65.00
Mother-of-Pearl, snake motif, ruby head, gold top, USA 175.00
Peking Glass, 3/4" oval head, roses and gold dec, turquoise ground. . . . 135.00
Porcelain, scenic design, ornate mounting 35.00

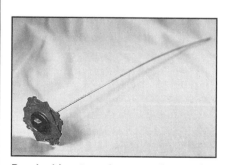

Purple rhinestone, brass setting, 1-1/4" d, $20.

Sterling, die-stamped flower head in relief, flat backing 110.00

Hats, Lady's Vintage

Hats galore and more! Most of these beautiful items of fashion have been stuffed into trunks, drawers and closets. Hats are treasured possessions of the past. Due to changing hairstyles, fashions and lifestyles, they have evolved into many shapes, sizes, colors and forms. They have been used for dress-up by children throughout the years. Hats can be bought for a few dollars or can cost hundreds, according to age, condition, fabric, decoration and uniqueness. Due to the increased interest in vintage clothing, hats are getting more respect and their values are increasing.

Remember, if you are buying to resell, don't overpay. Check your closets and attics for these beautiful treasures, but keep your hats on!

Advisor: Danielle Ware, 1199 S. Main Rd., Vineland, NJ 08360, (609) 794-8300.

Felt

Fedora, black, John Wanamaker, 1930s, good condition. 45.00
Powder blue borsalino, 1960s, fair condition 15.00
Tam, black with black feathers on side at front, 1930s, fair condition. 45.00
Taupe, pink sequin and gray bead dec, taupe netting, 1945, good condition. 30.00
Woven multicolored with one feather curling across front, E. Chard Doerr, 1940s, MIB 65.00

Cotton, bonnet, calico print, Pennsylvania Dutch, $18.

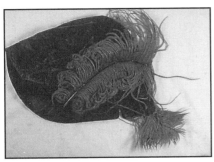

Velour, wedding hat, brown, quilted, red ostrich feathers, $20.

Straw

Jockey-type cap, purple, purple grosgrain ribbon and cloth violets dec, Hale Original, 1940s, good condition . .45.00
Plain, tan, silk-lining cloche, 1920s, fair condition. 65.00
Red velvet piping and plastic pearls around base, 1940s, good condition 25.00
Small brim, navy blue, white cloth magnolias and leaves dec, blue grosgrain chin straps, early 1900s, good condition 55.00
Wide brim, red with red chiffon wrapped around base and over brim, Margaret Longfellow, 1940s, fair condition .35.00

Velvet

Black with black glass bead dec, made in France, 1940s, good condition. . .55.00
Burgundy with burgundy ostrich feather in front, Marshall Field & Co., 1940s, fair condition. 20.00
Cap, pink, two points over one side tipped with rhinestones, 1940s, fair condition. 25.00
Turban-style, turquoise, 1960s, fair condition. 10.00

Other

Cloth, Poke Bonnet, hand-stitched cotton, gray and black, late 1800s, fair condition. 65.00
Cloth, Tennis Hat, brown and cream hound's tooth, 1940s, fair condition. 20.00
Feather, black ostrich, all feather, John Wanamaker, 1950s, good condition 55.00
Feather, turquoise and cobalt blue, all feather with tuft of feathers at crown, 1950s, MIB. 40.00
Fur, pillbox, mink, brown netting, brown brocade at crown, 1960s, good condition 25.00
Horsehair, off-white, floppy wide brim, white silk ribbon and white cloth magnolia on brim, 1910, good condition 75.00

Lace, black with black silk rim over wire base, pink velvet rose dec, 1880, good condition 125.00
Silk, taupe silk over wire base, wide brim narrowing in front and back, off-white fabric with rose dec, early 1900s, good condition 225.00

Heisey Glass

A.H. Heisey Co., of Newark, Ohio, began operations in 1896. Quickly, it was one of the major suppliers of glass to Middle America. Its many blown and molded patterns were produced in crystal, colored, milk (opalescent) and Ivorina Verde (custard). Pieces also featured cutting, etching and silver-deposit decoration. Glass figurines were made between 1933 and 1957. Not all Heisey glass is marked. Marked pieces have an "H" within a diamond. However, I have seen some non-Heisey pieces with this same marking at several flea markets.

It is important to identify the pattern of Heisey pieces. Neila Brederhoft's *The Collector's Encyclopedia of Heisey Glass: 1925-1938* (Collector Books: 1986) is helpful for early items. The best help for post-World War II patterns is old Heisey catalogs.

Club: Heisey Collectors of America, 169 W. Church St., Newark, OH 43055.

Newsletter: *The Newscaster*, P.O. Box 102, Plymouth, OH 44865.

Cocktail

Arctic, #4002 Aqua Caliente, diamond H 15.00
Fox Chase, #3405 Alibi, 3 oz, set of three 50.00
Fox Chase, #4002 Aqua Caliente, set of four 130.00
Minuet, #5010 Symphone, set of 11 . . . . 175.00

Plate

Formal Chintz, #1401 Empress, 7" sq, diamond H, set of seven 55.00
Landon Silhouette, #1183 Revere, 7" 70.00
Normandie etch #480, #1184 Yeoman, 10-1/2" d, set of six 75.00
Old Colony, #1401 Empress, sahara, 7-1/2" d, set of eight, some wear 65.00

Sherbet

Diana etch #442, #3357 King Arthur, diamond H 10.00
Frontenac etch #440, #3350 Wabash, Hawthorne, diamond H, set of six 90.00
Plantation Ivy etch #516, #5086 Plantation Ivy, diamond H 15.00

Soda

Fox Chase, #2401 Oakwood, 12 oz . 25.00
Lancaster, #2401 Oakwood, 12 oz . . 45.00
Polo Player etch #495, #2401 Oakwood, 8 oz, price for pr 65.00

Other

Champagne, Renaissance, #3333 Old Glory, diamond H, set of four . . . 20.00
Champagne, Rose, #5072 Rose Stem, price for pr 40.00
Claret Wine, Pied Piper, #3350 Wabash, 4 oz, diamond H 15.00
Claret Wine, Rose, #5072 Rose Stem, price for pr 160.00
Cordial, Empress, #3380 Old Dominion, flamingo, 1 oz, diamond H. 150.00
Creamer and Sugar, individual, Orchid, #1519 Waverly, diamond H, price for pr 50.00
Goblet, Cassandra, #3315 Polanaise 25.00
Goblet, Elizabeth etch #412, #3330 Hanover, 8 oz, diamond H. 25.00
Grapefruit, Chintz, #3389 Duquesne, Sahara. 45.00
Mug, Fisherman, #4163 Whaley, 16 oz, diamond H. 150.00
Sandwich Plate, Orchid, #1509 Queen Anne, 16" d 80.00
Torte Plate, Ivy, #1567 Plantation, 14". 60.00
Water Goblet, Belvedere etch #500, #4090 Coventry, 10 oz 30.00
Wine, Chintz, #3389 Duquesne, 2 1/2 oz 7.50
Wine, Minuet, #5010 Symphone, set of seven. 225.00

Hi-Fi Equipment

Remember your "hi-fi" from the 1950s and 1960s? The equipment used those glowing little bulbs called vacuum tubes and music came from black vinyl discs called records, not CDs. Now it's the 1990s, and some of that old hi-fi gear is now collectible. Items that are in demand are U.S.-made vacuum-tube-type amplifiers, pre-amplifiers, AM/FM tuners and receivers. Also desirable are certain brands of speakers and record turntables from the United States and England. Certain vacuum tubes, if new and in their original boxes, also have value.

The key to ascertaining an item's value is to know the manufacturer or brand and the model number. Some of the amplifiers to look for include those made by McIntosh, Marantz, Western Electric, Fisher, Altec, Eico, Acrosound, H.H. Scott, Gott and Harmon Kardon. Record-turntable names include Thorens and Garrard.

WARNING: Never plug old hi-fi gear into an AC outlet with the power on! Tube equipment used high-voltage circuits and old power cords are almost always deteriorated—creating a potential hazard of shock or electrocution!

Advisor: Jeffrey Viola, 784 Eltone Rd., Jackson, NJ 08527, (908); 928-0666.

Fisher
80AZ, amplifier, mono, 30 watts, 6L6GC
    tubes, narrow-style chassis 50.00
800C, receiver, stereo, AM/FM, 50 watts,
    walnut case 75.00
FM1000, tuner, stereo, FM only, wooden
    case 75.00

Marantz
2, amplifier, mono, 40 watts, EL34 output
    tubes, meter 200.00
5, amplifier, mono, 30 watts, EL34 output
    tubes, meter 200.00
7-C, pre-amplifier, stereo, tubes, wood
    case, metal knobs 250.00
8-B, amplifier, stereo, 70 watts, EL34
    output tubes 400.00
10-B, tuner, stereo, tubes, AM/FM,
    oscilloscope display 300.00

McIntosh
C-20, pre-amplifier, stereo, tubes,
    wooden case 250.00
MC-60, amplifier, mono, 60 watts, 6550
    output tubes 100.00
MC-240, amplifier, stereo, chrome chassis,
    80 watts, 6L6GC tubes 300.00
MC-275, amplifier, stereo, chrome chassis,
    150 watts, 6550 tubes 500.00

Other
Acrosound UL-II, amplifier, Ultra Linear,
    stereo, 60 watts,
    EL34 output tubes 120.00
Amperex EL34, vacuum tube, output,
    made in France or Holland, new . .3.00

Eico, HF-60, amplifier, mono, 60 watts,
    EL34 output tubes 100.00
Eico, HF-87, amplifier, stereo, 70 watts,
    EL34 output tubes 75.00
Harmon Kardon, Citation I, pre-amplifier,
    stereo, tubes, wood case 50.00
Harmon Kardon, Citation II, amplifier,
    stereo, 120 watts, KT88 output tubes . .
    100.00
Telefunken 12AX7, vacuum tube, dual
    triode, flat plates, made in Germany,
    new in box 3.00
Thorens TD124, record turntable, four
    speeds, belt drive, wooden base 25.00
Western Electric, 91, amplifier, mono, 15
    watts, 300-B tubes,
    two large chassis 100.00
Western Electric, 300B, vacuum tube,
    output, triode, new 12.50

Holiday Collectibles

Holidays play an important part in American life. Besides providing a break from work, they allow time for patriotism, religious renewal and fun. Because of America's size and ethnic diversity, there are many holiday events of a regional nature. Attend some of them and pick up their collectibles. I have started a Fastnacht Day collection.

This listing is confined to national holidays. If I included special days, from Secretary's Day to Public Speaker's Day, I would fill this book with holiday collectibles alone. Besides, in 50 years is anyone going to care about Public Speaker's Day? No one does now.

Club: National Valentine Collectors Association, P.O. Box 1404, Santa Ana, CA 92702.

Fourth of July, postcard, $5.

Newsletter: *Toy Cannon News* (Big-Bang Cannons), P.O. Box 2052-N, Norcross, GA 30071.

Periodical: *Pyrofax Magazine*, P.O. Box 2010, Saratoga, CA 95070.

Fourth of July
Bank, carnival glass,
    figural Liberty Bell 10.00
Candy Container, milk glass,
    figural Uncle Sam's hat,
    painted stars and stripes 85.00
Flag, 10" h, 48 stars, wooden stick. . .2.00
Flask, figural Uncle Sam. 32.00
Noisemaker, horn, litho tin, flags and bells
    dec, 1920. . . . . .10.00
Pinback Button, July 4th, multicolored Miss
    Liberty, 1906-07 . . . . .30.00
Pinback Button, Safe and Sane 4th of July,
    multicolored, red lettering 25.00
Postcard, "4th of July Greeting," red, white
    and blue, gold ground, Germany,
    1910 . . . . .2.00
Postcard, Yankee Doodle,
    emb cardboard 10.00

President's Day
Bank, Abraham Lincoln, glass,
    bottle-shape, tin closure 25.00
Bookends, pr, bronze-colored plaster,
    Lincoln sitting on bench. 35.00
Bottle, figural Lincoln 10.00
Postcard, Lincoln Centennial Souvenir,
    Lincoln's Birthday Series 1, emb, gilt
    highlights, 1908 . 6.00Postcard, "Three

Groundhog Day, postcard, $200.

**Sheet Music, "Patrick's Day Parade,"
Harrigan & Hart, NY, $20.**

Cheers for George Washington," children waving flag
beneath Washington's portrait,
1909 . . . . .1.75
Postcard, "Washington The Father of His
Country," 1912 . . . . .2.00

St. Patrick's Day
Banner, cloth, stenciled, 1930s 75.00
Die-cut, 3" h, gold harp entwined with
shamrocks and green ribbon,
Germany .1.50
Nut Cup, crepe paper, green and white,
double frill, cardboard shamrock . .5.00
Party Hat, cardboard and foil,
shamrock dec. 20.00

**Thanksgiving, candy container, turkey,
painted papier-mâché body, lead feet,
3-3/4" h, $45.**

Pinback Button, green shamrock with red,
white and blue American flag,
1930s 15.00
Place Card, name tag and leprechaun with
pot of gold dec 5.00
Postcard, "Ireland Forever," shamrock with
view of Ireland in each leaf, mkd
"Germany". 1.00
Postcard, "To My Little Colleen," girl
dressed in green, large shamrock for
hair bow, mkd "London" 1.50
Sheet Music, Danny Boy, 1940s 5.00

Thanksgiving
Book, *Thanksgiving*, Dennison, 193010.00
Chocolate Mold, 8" h, turkey,
Germany 30.00
Figure, 4" h, Pilgrim Couple, composition,
man and woman, mkd "Germany"45.00
Figure, 4" h, Turkey, celluloid, white, pink
and blue, weighted bottom,
mkd "Irwin, USA". 25.00
Greeting Card, turkey with feather tail illus,
1930s 8.00
Platter, 10-1/2" l, multicolored transfer
scene, Johnson Brothers,
England. 50.00
Postcard, "A Thanksgiving Greeting," large
harvest pumpkin in background, three
turkeys eating from dish outside a
home, 1910. . . . . 1.00
Postcard, "Thanksgiving Greetings," children playing with turkeys, 1909 . . 2.50
Postcard, "With Thanksgiving Greeting,"
turkey and maiden,
John Winsch, 1911 . . . . 25.00
Tablecloth, paper, Pilgrims and Indians
feast, matching napkins 25.00

Valentine's Day
Cookie Cutter, plastic heart 3.00
Gift Box, litho cardboard, heart motif 10.00
Greeting Card, "Best Wishes," folding,
shades of blue, picture of bird in center,
poem beneath, blank inside,
4-1/2" h 5.00
Greeting Card, "To My Sweetheart," folding, small girl wearing green dress and
hat, red wild-rose border,
verse inside, 6-1/2" h 10.00
Greeting Card, "To My Sweetheart,"
standup, white dog holding envelope in
mouth, 6" h, mkd "Germany". 3.50
Napkin Ring, SS, band
with heart center 35.00
Postcard, Cupid on swing of roses,
bordered by red hearts and gold scroll
work, small verse, mkd "E Nash" . 1.25
Postcard, "February 14th," trimmed in
green ivy, cupids shooting hearts and
arrows at two lovers, enclosed in heart,
mkd "Germany, 1910". 1.50

Postcard, Hearts with arrows, cupid and
flowers, early 20th C 10.00
Postcard, "To My Dear Valentine," monk
child with wings 8.00
Sheet Music, My Funny Valentine . . . 4.00

Home Front Collectibles

Home-front collectibles emerged as
a separate collecting category about
three years ago. The fact that it took so
long is surprising. However, many
home-front collectibles have been sold
for years in crossover categories; e.g.,
post cards and magazines. See the
Anti-Axis listing for related items.

Club: Society of Ration Token Collectors, 3583 Everett Rd., Richfield, OH
44286.

Badge, American Boy Junior Pilot, metal
wings, gold colored, red, white and blue
paper insert, "Keep 'Em Flying". . 25.00
Blackout Kit, Vernon Co., Newton, IA,
1942, unused. 200.00
Blotter, "The Schmidt Family Has Gone to
War," New Bedford, MA, business,
unused. 13.00
Gardening Set, Plant for Victory,
Vaughan's Seed Store seed packets
attached, unused. 200.00
Glow Button, Air Raid Warden, celluloid,
red, white and blue, "Buy War Bonds at
Minnesota Federal Savings & Loan
Association" on back 35.00
Map, World-Wide News Map, Richfield Oil
Co., Europe and North Africa one side,
small world, South Pacific and Polar
maps on other, lists major war events
from 1931 through early 1943 . . .25.00
Model Airplane, "Allied Sport" aircraft,
Victory Series, American Modelcraft,
Chicago, balsa wood, mid-1940s 32.00
Patch, American War Mothers, red, white
and blue stiff felt, 4" d 25.00

**Pillow Cover, dark-blue silk, red-orange
fringe, $25.**

Pillow Cove, glossy fabric, single-star
service flag above inscription "Berlin or
Bust, in God We Trust, Serving in U.S.
Army," fringed edges 35.00
Pin, GOC U.S. Air Force Observer,
Assistant Chief, wings, blue and white
enameled symbol for Ground Observer
Corps volunteer worker, SS 12.00
Pinback Button, "I'm Housing a War Hero,"
Hospitality House building with
"Welcome" awning, red,
white and blue 12.00
Postcard, Victory Series, #V1, soldier,
civilian worker and sailor, Tichnor Bros.,
1941, unused 20.00
Poster, Third War Loan, #542950, 1943,
green and white $100 savings bond
above diagonal inscriptions,
20" by 28". 55.00
Punchboard, "Remember Pearl Harbor,
Hula Jackpot, Coconut Jackpot," war
bond purchase symbols, unused,
11-1/2" by 8". 175.00
Sheet Music, A Yank and a Tank, 1943,
Armored Divisions symbol on red, white
and blue cover, Carl Fischer Co., New
York City, Everett Bentley 25.00
Stamp Album, Sky Heroes, Sinclair Oil
premium, 24 pgs, unused,
4" by 8-3/4". 110.00
Valentine, Army Sweetheart, folder, emb
eagle, flag and heart design, red, white
and blue, sentimental verse to soldier
inside, Gibson Greeting Card Co.,
unused, 5" by 6". 10.00

Homer Laughlin

Homer Laughlin and his brother,
Shakespeare, built two pottery kilns in
East Liverpool, Ohio, in 1871. Laughlin
became one of the first firms in America to produce whiteware. In 1896, William Wills and a Pittsburgh group led
by Marcus Aaron bought the Laughlin
firm. New plants were built in Laughlin
Station, Ohio and Newall, W.V. Plant
advances included continuous tunnel
kilns, spray glazing and mechanical
jiggering.

The original trademark used from
1871 to 1890 merely identified the
products as "Laughlin Brothers." The
next trademark featured the American
eagle astride the prostrate British lion.
The third mark featured a monogram
of "HLC" which has appeared, with
slight variations, on all dinnerware produced since about 1900. The 1900

Virginia Rose, 9-1/4" d, $5.

trademark contained a number that
identified month, year and plant at
which the product was made. Letter
codes were used in later periods.

Prices for Homer Laughlin china
(with the possible exception of Virginia
Rose pieces) are still moderate. Some
of the patterns from the 1930 to 1940
period have contemporary designs
that are very artistic. Also, see Fiesta
listing.

REPRODUCTION ALERT: Harle-
quin and Fiesta lines were reissued in
1978 and marked accordingly.

Newsletter: *The Laughlin Eagle*, 1270
63rd Ter. South, St. Petersburg, FL
33705.

Newspaper: *The Daze*, P.O. Box 57,
Otisville, MI 48463.

Americana
Bread and Butter Plate 2.00
Creamer. 20.00
Cup and Saucer. 12.00
Gravy Boat. 45.00
Plate, 9" 12.00
Soup Bowl 20.00

Blue Willow
Cup and Saucer. 3.00
Plate, 9" d 9.00
Soup Bowl 8.00

Harlequin
Ashtray, spruce 50.00
Ball Jug, forest. 110.00
Ball Jug, maroon 55.00
Ball Jug, turquoise 40.00
Bowl, 9" d, spruce 25.00
Casserole, oval, maroon 30.00
Cereal, forest. 15.00
Creamer, mauve 10.00
Creamer, red, novelty 30.00
Cream Soup, turquoise 10.00
Eggcup, double, forest green. 17.00
Eggcup, double, maroon 22.00
Gravy, rose 18.00

Gravy, yellow 15.00
Marmalade, mauve. 225.00
Oatmeal Bowl, forest green 18.00
Oatmeal Bowl, gray 20.00
Oatmeal Bowl, medium green 25.00
Platter, oval, large, maroon 40.00
Platter, oval, small, yellow 15.00
Relish, 5 part, multicolors 210.00
Salad, individual, maroon 45.00
Salt and Pepper Shakers, pr, gray . .20.00
Saucer, after dinner, red. 20.00
Sugar, cov, mauve 15.00
Syrup, cov, red 175.00
Teacup, chartreuse. 6.00
Teacup, dark green 6.00
Teacup, red .6.00
Teacup, spruce. 6.00
Teacup, turquoise 5.00
Teacup, yellow 5.00
Teapot, mauve 60.00
Teapot Lid, gray 50.00
Teapot Lid, turquoise 40.00
Tumbler, maroon 45.00
Tumbler, mauve 35.00
Tumbler, red. 38.00

Rhythm Rose
Berry Bowl, Kitchen Kraft 1.00
Bread and Butter, Kitchen Kraft 2.00
Casserole, cov, 9" d, Kitchen Kraft. . .9.00
Creamer, Kitchen Kraft. 2.00
Mixing Bowl, 6-1/4" d 4.00
Platter, 13" l 13.00
Salad Plate, Kitchen Kraft. 2.00
Water Pitcher, 5-3/4" h, Kitchen Kraft. 8.00

Riviera
Batter Jug, open, mauve 95.00
Batter Jug, open, Yellow. 75.00
Berry Bowl, 5" d, yellow 8.00
Butter Dish, 1/4 lb, turquoise 345.00
Casserole, cov, blue. 60.00
Casserole, cov, ivory 125.00
Dinner Service, 20-pc set, red, yellow,
green and mauve, four each cups and
saucers, 4-1/2" bowls, 7" plates and 9"
plates, orig box 170.00
Pitcher, juice, yellow. 185.00
Plate, 6" d, bread and butter, yellow. . 6.00
Salt and Pepper Shakers, pr, ivory. .20.00
Saucer, green. 2.00
Teapot, ivory. 180.00
Tumbler, juice, green 95.00
Tumbler, juice, mauve 85.00
Tumbler, juice, turquoise 95.00

Royal Harvest
Cup and Saucer 3.00
Dinner Plate .6.00

Serenade
Chop Plate, pink20.00
Creamer, pink. 15.00
Gravy Boat, green 20.00

Plate, 7" d, pink 9.00
Teapot, blue 110.00

Turquoise
Cereal Bowl .5.00
Platter, 11" l 12.00
Sugar Bowl, cov 12.00

Horse Collectibles

This is one of those collectible categories where you can collect the real thing—riding equipment, ranging from bridles to wagons, and/or representational items. It is also a category in which the predominant number of collectors are women. The figurine is the most-favored collectible. However, horse-related items can be found in almost every collectible category from Western movie posters to souvenir spoons. As long as there is a horse on it, it is collectible.

A neglected area among collectors is the rodeo. I am amazed at how much rodeo material I find at East Coast flea markets. I never realized how big the Eastern rodeo circuit was.

Club: Equine Collectors Club, P.O. Box 42822, Phoenix, AZ 85080.

Newsletter: *The Model Horse Trader*, 143 Mercer Way, Upland, CA 91786.

Periodicals: *Hobby Horse News*, 5492 Tallapoosa Rd., Tallahassee, FL 32303; *Just About Horses*, 14 Industrial Rd., Pequannock, NJ 07440; *TRR Pony Express*, 71 Aloha Cir., North Little Rock, AR, 72120.

Books
Black Fury and the White Mare, Albert
  Miller 4.00

Fruit Crate Label, Polo Brand, $5.

Misty of Chincoteague,
  Rand McNally 10.00
The Original Mr. Ed, Bantam, 1963 . 14.00

Figures
Horse jumping fence, Breyer 45.00
Prancing horse, plastic, Hartland . . . 10.00
Roughneck, palomino, ceramic, Hagen
  Renaker 100.00
Zillo, Arabian foal, Hagen Renaker 100.00

Pinback Buttons
Horse portrait, black and white, blue
  ground, white border, c1940 . . . . . 8.00
Rochester, NH, fair, triple horse's-head
  illus, black and white, 1909 . . . . . 30.00
Rodeo Souvenir, Let 'er Buck, 1-1/4" d,
  bucking bronco illus, red and black,
  white ground, 1930s 5.00

Other
Calendar, Pratts Veterinary Remedies,
  1911 . . . . 225.00
Catalog, Ames Plow Co., Boston, 72 pgs,
  tools and implements, 1900 . . . . 60.00
Christmas Ornament, hobby horse,
  Dresden 80.00
Cigarette Lighter, Dale Evans,
  horse head 15.00
Comb, mane and tail, mkd "Oliver Slant
  Tooth," 1940s 15.00
Comic Book, Quick Draw McGraw,
  #3, Dell, 1960 . . . . 13.00
Decanter, Appaloosa, Jim Beam, Regal
  China, 1974 . . . . 25.00
Doorstop, 5" l, cast iron, figural,
  Hubley 175.00
Farrier's Nail Box, wood,
  metal base and handle 40.00

Manual, All About Horse Brasses, H.S. Richards, $6.

Game, Derby Day, board folds out to 72",
  six wooden horses and hurdles, Parker
  Brothers, 1959 . . . . 40.00
Game, My Little Pony,
  Milton Bradley, 1988 . . . . .7.00
Hoof trimmer, Butteris, forged iron, wooden
  shoulder brace, c1850 . . . . 35.00
Horseshoe, Hopalong Cassidy, "Good
  Luck," orig insert card, 1950 . . . . 20.00
Lunch Box, Trigger 45.00
Medal, Ohio horseshoer's, ribbon,
  1917 . . . . 57.50
Photo, rancher on horse,
  mountain scene 15.00
Pincushion, metal, horseshoe-shape 10.00
Saddle, Rocky Mountain cross-tree type,
  pack saddle, weathered wooden
  supports 75.00
Saddle Ring, SS 35.00
Sleigh Bells, 29 graduated brass bells,
  leather strap 150.00
Souvenir Spoon, Cheyenne, WY, bucking
  horse, SS 22.00
Spurs, pr, 5" l, steel chains 120.00
Toothpick Holder, wooden,
  pony with cart 3.00
Toy, My Little Pony, Hasbro, pink,
  spots on rear 3.00

Horse Racing Collectibles

The history of horse racing dates back to the domestication of the horse itself. Prehistoric cave drawings show horse racing. The Greeks engaged in chariot racing as early as 600 B.C. As civilization spread, so did the racing of horses. Each ethnic group and culture added its own unique slant. The British developed the thoroughbred breed from a group of horses that were descendants of three great Arabian stallions: Carley Arabian, Byerley Turk and Goldolphin Arabian. Receiving royal sponsorship, horse racing became the Sport of Kings.

Horse racing reached America during the colonial period. By the 1800s four-mile match races between regional champions were common. In 1863, Saratoga Race Track was built. The first Belmont Stakes was run at Jerome Park in 1867. As the 19th century ended, more than 300 race tracks operated a seasonal card. By 1908, society's strong reaction against gambling reduced the number of American race tracks to 25.

Of course, the premier American horse race is the Kentucky Derby. Programs date back to 1924; glasses, a favorite with collectors, to the late 1930s. There are so many horse racing collectibles that one needs to specialize from the beginning. Collector focuses include a particular horse-racing type or a specific horse race, a breed or specific horse or racing prints and images. Each year, there are a number of specialized auctions devoted to horse racing, ranging from sporting prints sales at the major New York auction houses to benefit auctions for the Thoroughbred Retirement Foundation.

Club: Sport of Kings Society, 1406 Annen Ln., Madison, WI 53711.

Kentucky Derby Glasses
1959 . . . . .32.50
1961 . . . . .45.00
1964 . . . . .25.00
1972 . . . . .30.00
1973 . . . . .25.00
1986, 5-1/4" h, clear, frosted white panel, red roses and green leaf accents, red and green inscription 10.00

Pinback Buttons
Bergen, jockey, yellow polka dotted shirt, "Celebrated American Jockey," American Pepsin Gum adv on back, c1900, 7/8" d 15.00
Dan Patch, harness racing, portrait, International Stock Food adv, multicolored, c1905, 1-1/2" d . . .125.00
Foolish Pleasure, brown photo portrait, green lettering, "The Great Match," New York Racing Association, 1965, 2-1/4" d 20.00
Him, Race Horse Special Event, NY Racing Association, 1975. . . . . . .12.00

Game, Kentucky Derby Racing Game, Whitman, No. 2956-29, 1938, $35.

Plate, Dan Patch, Champion Harness Horse of the World, photo print, tinted, East Liverpool Potteries, $60.

Joe Joker, harness racing, black and white portrait, tin rim, early 1900s, 1-3/4" d 65.00

Other
Ashtray, 5-1/4" h, china, race-horse portrait, Kentucky Derby and Belmont Stakes winner 15.00
Badge, 3" d, Budweiser Million, full-color illus, August 1982 . . . . 8.00
Game, Kentucky Derby Racing Game, 11" by 7" 35.00
Glass, Pimlico, 1974 Preakness, frosted white, black portraits of famous Triple Crown winners, lists winners from 1873 through 1973, 5-1/4" h 15.00
Hartland Statue, horse and jockey, dark brown horse with wrapped ankles and bobbed tail, jockey wearing red jacket, white cap, trousers and black boots. 85.00
Pass, Florida Jockey Club, 1926 . . . 25.00
Pennant, 18" l, Derby Day, felt, red, white lettering, red and white design with pink accents, 1939 . . . . 15.00
Program, 4" by 9", Kentucky Derby, May 4, 1963 . . . . 18.00
Ticket, Kentucky Derby, Saturday, May 2, 1936 . . . . 8.00
Tray, 13-1/4" by 21-1/2", 100th Running Kentucky Derby, litho tin, color illus, black rim, gold rose-design rim. . 55.00

Hot Wheels

In 1968, Mattel introduced a line of two-inch long plastic and die-cast metal cars. Dubbed "Hot Wheels," there were originally 16 cars, eight play sets and two collector sets.

Hot Wheels are identified by the name of the model and its year that are cast on the bottom of each vehicle.

The most desirable Hot Wheels cars have red striping on the tires. These early vehicles are the toughest to find and were produced from 1968 to 1978. In 1979, blackwall tires became standard on all models. The most valuable Hot Wheel vehicles are usually those with production runs limited to a single year or those in a rare color. Hop in your own set of wheels and race to your nearest flea market to find your own hot collectibles.

Club: Hot Wheels Collector Club, 2263 Graham Dr., Santa Rosa, CA 95404.

Newsletter: *Hot Wheels Newsletter*, 26 Madera Ave., San Carlos, CA 94070.

Accessories
Belt Buckle, red and black, Lee, 1984 . . . . .16.00
Button, plastic, Jet Threat 7.50
Case, Collectors Case, missing handle, 1981 . . . . .4.00
Lap Counter, 1970 . . . . .11.50

Vehicles
Custom Corvette, metallic blue. 54.00
Custom Eldorado, brown 50.00
Custom Mustang, red 60.00
Datsun 200SX, gold, 1983 . . . . .10.00
Demon, metallic orange, 1969 . . . . . .5.00
Dodge Viper, red, MBP. 2.00
Driven to the Max Dragster, orange, MBP 4.00
Fangster, green, MBP 9.00
Ferrari 512-S, metallic red 50.00
Fleetside, custom, green 35.00
Grass Hopper, magenta 30.00
Gremlin Grinder, green. 30.00
Grim Gripper, MBP 10.00
Inferno, yellow 35.00
Jet Threat, light green. 40.00
Kenworth Big Rig, black, MBP 2.00
Lamborghini Countach, white, MBP . .5.00
Light My Firebird, blue, 1970, MOC .45.00
Lola GT70, dark green enamel, 1969, MOB .35.00
Mod Quad, metallic green 28.00
Monster Vette, black walls, yellow with flames, European 1.50
Mustang Boss Hoss, chrome, club car 50.00
Neet Streeter, red, 1983 . . . . .15.00
Noodle Head, metallic blue. 59.00
Paddy Wagon, black, 1969. . . . . .5.00
Porsche 959, black walls, red, MBP . .2.00
Python, gold 25.00
Rodzilla, purple, MBP 2.00
Roll Patrol, tan 3.00

Sheriff Patrol, black and white,
black-wall tires 10.00
Silhouette, metallic brown 19.00
Splittin' Image, metallic red 10.00
Spoiler Sport, green, MBP 13.50
Sugar Caddy, metallic purple 34.00
Supervan, white with flames 19.00
Tall Ryder, metallic silver, MBP 4.00
Thunderstreak, Hot Wheels #1, black-wall
tires, black and green, MBP. 5.00
Vampyra, black, MBP 3.00
Warpath, red, 1973 . . . . .10.00
Xploder, black, red-line tires 100.00

Promotional-Issued Cars

Deep Purple, Nomad, white-wall tires,
MBP 10.00
Getty Oil, custom Corvette,
black body 10.00
Gulf Gasoline,
set of four different cars 40.00
Jack Baldwin Camaro, certificate,
MBP 15.00
Kool Aid, '63 split-window Corvette,
white body 10.00
Osh Kosh Snowplow,
black and orange 3.00

Howdy Doody

The Howdy Doody show is the most famous of early television's children's programs. Created by "Buffalo" Bob Smith, the show ran for 2,343 performances between Dec. 27, 1947 and Sept. 30, 1960. Among the puppet characters were Howdy Doody, Mr. Bluster, Flub-A-Dub and Dilly-Dally. Princess Summerfall-Winterspring and Clarabelle, the clown, were played by humans.

There is a whole generation out there who knows there is only one answer to the question: "What time is it?"

Film, "Howdy Doody's Christmas," No. 824, Castle Films, 8mm, 3" sq box, $25.

Club: Howdy Doody Memorabilia Collectors Club, 8 Hunt Ct., Flemington, NJ 08822.

Games

Bean Bag 125.00
Bowling, flip over, Howdy
and four characters 145.00
Flub-A-Dub Flip a Ring, orig pkg . . . 95.00
Howdy Doody's TV Game, Milton Bradley,
playing board, Howdy-shaped spinner,
six cardboard figures, Kagran copyright,
1951-56 . . . . 75.00
Howdy Doody's 3-Ring Circus,
Harett-Gilmar, orig box, Kagran
copyright, 1951-56 . . . . 75.00

Other

Album, photo, 8-1/2" by 11", 8 pgs, Poll
Parrot Shoes premium, c1950 . 100.00
Badge, 3-1/2" d, Howdy Doody's 40th
Birthday, red, white and blue,
1987 . . . . 20.00
Bag, 4" by 5-1/4", Howdy Doody Fudge
Bar, red, white and blue, waxed paper,
premium offer on back, unused . 18.00
Bank, figural, head, Vandor 75.00
Belt Buckle, 1950s 8.00

Bubble Pipe Set, Howdy
and Clarabelle 95.00
Clock, figural, Howdy sitting on Clarabelle,
Bob Smith wake-up voice, MIB . 135.00
Decorations, 9" by 9", birthday cake image,
die-cut, red, white and blue, six pink
plastic character candleholders,
Kagran, 1951-56 . . . . 75.00
Detective Disguises, cutouts, uncut, Poll
Parrot Shoes premium, mint 70.00
Dinner Set, three pcs, plate, mug and bowl,
porcelain, mint 155.00
Doll, 12-1/2" h, wood, jointed, painted
composition head, Bob Smith copyright,
1948-51 . . . . 400.00
Football, white 75.00
Hand Puppet 45.00
Handkerchief 30.00
Ice Cream Spoon, 3" l wooden paddle-type
spoon, waxed paper wrapper, Howdy
Doody Ice Cream, Kagran copyright,
1951-56 . . . . 15.00
Iron-On Transfer, unused 30.00
Little Golden Book, Howdy Doody and the
Princess, 28 pgs, 1952,
6-1/2" by 8" 15.00
Magazine, *Jack and Jill*, January 1960,
full-color cover, six-pg article 25.00
Marionette, orig box 275.00
Model Clay Kit, three red, white and blue
die-cut cardboard figures, thin
plastic-mold sheet 25.00
Mug, 3-1/4" h, plastic, red, full-color decal,
Ovaltine premium 50.00
Night Lamp, figural 145.00
Plaque, 14" d, Howdy with Santa,
orig box, 1950 . . . . 95.00
Puzzle, 9-1/4" by 11-1/2", Whitman, Howdy
and Clarabelle, full color, titled "Skiing
With Clarabelle," Kagran copyright
1951-56 . . . . 25.00
Record Album, 78 rpm, Howdy Doody and
the Air-O-Doodle,
glossy paper sleeve 50.00
Shoe Polish, orig box 45.00
Sticker Book 22.00
Tin, Howdy Doody Cookie-Go-Round,
1950s 130.00
Towel, bath, Howdy on horse illus . 125.00
Toy, Pinball, Ja-Ru, #2312, 1987 . . . 15.00

Hull Pottery

Hull Pottery traces its beginnings to the 1905 purchase of the Acme Pottery Co., of Crooksville, Ohio, by Addis E. Hull. By 1917, a line of art pottery designed specifically for flower and gift

Game, Howdy Doody's TV Game, Milton Bradley, 1950s, $75.

shops was added to Hull's standard fare of novelties, kitchenware and stoneware. A flood and fire destroyed the plant in 1950. When the plant reopened in 1952, Hull products had a new glossy finish.

Hull is collected by pattern. A favorite with collectors is the Little Red Riding Hood kitchenware line, made between 1943 and 1957. Most Hull pieces are marked. Pre-1950 pieces have a numbering system to identify pattern and height. Post-1950 pieces have "hull" or "Hull" in large script letters.

Newsletters: *Hull Pottery News*, 466 Foreston Place, St. Louis, MO 63119; *Hull Pottery Newsletter*, 11023 Tunnell Hill NE, New Lexington, OH 43764.

Baskets
Iris 225.00
Parchment and Pine 70.00
Sunglow 65.00

Candleholders
Camelia, doves, 117, 6-1/2" h . . .90.00
Parchment and Pine, 2-3/4" h . . .50.00
Water Lily, L-22, pr 50.00
Wildflower, double, #69, 4" h. 75.00

Ewers
Bowknot, turquoise to blue,
 B-1, 5-1/2" h. 100.00
Magnolia, #5, 7" h 130.00
Poppy, 4-3/4" h 100.00
Rosella 40.00
Tokay, pink, tall 150.00
Wildflower, pink and blue, W-11,
 8-1/2" h. 100.00

Pitchers
Blossom Flite, 8-1/2" h 100.00
Camelia, #128, 4-3/4" h. 35.00
Rosella, R, 6-1/2" h 45.00
Wildflower, W-2, 5-1/2" h. 55.00

Vases
Art Ware, 8" h 70.00
Blossom Flite, sq, 10-1/2" h 85.00
Thistle, 6-1/2" h. 150.00
Wildflower, 4-1/2" h 95.00

Other
Ashtray, Continental, 8" d 35.00
Ashtray, Ebbtide 150.00
Bean Pot, House and Garden, 2 qt . .20.00
Bell, Sunglow, rope handle, #87 . . . .75.00
Bowl, Iris, oval, #409, 12" d. 95.00

Planter, Twin Geese, #95, 1951, 7-1/4" h, $50.

Bowl, Poppy, boat-shape, #604, 8" d 75.00
Bud Vase, Woodland, double,
 W-15, 8-1/2" h. 50.00
Candy Dish, Continental, 8-1/2" h . . 50.00
Casserole, Sunglow, 7-1/2" d 50.00
Coffeepot, Parchment and Pine. . . 125.00
Cookie Jar, House and Garden 15.00
Cornucopia, Wildflower 75.00
Creamer, Camellia. 85.00
Creamer, Little Red Riding Hood. . 150.00
Figure, Love Birds 40.00
Figure, Swan 40.00
Flowerpot, Tulip, #116-33, 6" h 75.00
Jar, Camelia, ram handles, 8-1/2" h 285.00
Jardiniere, Orchid 75.00
Jardiniere, Tulip 95.00
Planter, Continental, ftd, rect 25.00
Planter, Tokay 50.00
Planter, Sunglow 65.00
Salt and Pepper Shakers, pr, Little Red
 Riding Hood 170.00
Serving Dish, Cinderella, sq 15.00
Spice Jar, Wheat 65.00
Tea Set, Water Lily 275.00
Teapot, Blossom Flite, #T14 . . . . . . 85.00
Wall Pocket, Rosella, heart-shape. . 85.00
Window Box, Dogwood 150.00

Hummels

Hummel items are the original creations of Berta Hummel, a German artist. At 18, she enrolled in the Academy of Fine Arts in Munich. In 1934, Hummel entered the Convent of Siessen and became Sister Maria Innocentia. She continued to draw. In 1935, W. Goebel Co., of Rodental, Germany, used some of her sketches as the basis for three-dimensional figures. American distribution was handled by the Schmid Brothers of Randolph, Mass. In 1967, a controversy developed between the two companies involving the Hummel family and the convent. The German courts decided The Convent had the rights to Berta Hummel's sketches made between 1934 and her death in 1964. Schmid Bros., could deal directly with the family for reproduction rights to any sketches made before 1934.

All authentic Hummels bear both the M.I. Hummel signature and a Goebel trademark. Various trademarks were used to identify the year of production. The Crown Mark (trademark 1) was used from 1935-1949; Full Bee (trademark 2) 1950-1959; Stylized Bee (trademark 3) 1957-1972; Three Line Mark (trademark 4) 1964-1972; Last Bee Mark (trademark 5) 1972-1980; Missing Bee Mark (trademark 6) 1979-1990; and the Current Mark or New Crown Mark (trademark 7) from 1991 to the present.

Hummel lovers are emotional collectors. They do not like to read or hear anything negative about their treasures. At the moment, they are very unhappy campers. The Hummel market for ordinary pieces is flat, with little signs of recovery in the years ahead.

Hummel material was copied widely. These copycats also are attracting interest among collectors. For more information about them, see Lawrence L. *Wonsch's Hummel Copycats With Values* (Wallace-Homestead: 1987).

Clubs: Hummel Collector's Club, Inc., P.O. Box 257, Yardley, PA 19067; M.I. Hummel Club, Goebel Plaza, Rt. 31, P.O. Box 11, Pennington, NJ 08534.

Angel Trio, 238/B, TM 4 . . . . .40.00
Bird Duet, 169, TM 5 . . . . .90.00
Bookworm, 8, TM 6 . . . . .140.00
Boy with Horse, 117, TM 5, crazed . 15.00

Chimney Sweep, 12/2/0, TM 3 . . . . .80.00
Close Harmony, 336, TM 5 . . . . . . .200.00
Congratulations, 17/0, TM 5, crazed .40.00
Crossroads, 331, TM 5,
    severe crazing 90.00
Culprits, 56/A, TM 3, crazed 90.00
Doctor, 127, TM 3 . . . . .110.00
Flower Vendor, 381, TM 5 . . . . . . .115.00
For Father, 87, TM 3, crazed 70.00
Friends, 136/1, TM 5, crazed 75.00
Friends Together, 662/1, TM 7,
    limited ed, orig box 285.00
A Gentle Fellowship, 628, TM 7 . . .345.00
Girl with Fir Tree, 116, TM 5, crazed.25.00
Girl with Sheet Music, 389, TM 5 . . .60.00
Girl with Trumpet, 391, TM 5. . . . . .60.00
Grandma's Girl, 461, TM 7,
    first issue 100.00
Going to Grandma's, 52/0, TM 6. . .145.00
Happy Traveler, 109, TM 5,
    plain number 90.00
Harmony in Four Parts, 471, TM 6,
    orig box 1,200.00
Hear Ye Hear Ye, 15/0, TM 2, chip on
    base, all-over crazing 60.00
I Brought You a Gift, 479, TM 6,
    orig box 70.00
I Didn't Do It, 626, TM 7, orig box . .125.00
I Wonder, 486, TM 7, orig box. 100.00
Kiss Me, 311, TM 4, crazed 210.00
Knitting Lesson, 256, TM 4 . . . . . .425.00
Letter to Santa, 340, TM 5 . . . . . .225.00
Little Cellist, 89/1, TM 2. . . . . .215.00
Little Fiddler, 4, TM 3, small base-rim chip,
    all-over crazing. 60.00

Little Goat Herder, 200/0, TM 4 . . . 115.00
Little Sweeper, 171, TM 3, crazed . . 70.00
Lost Sheep, 68/2/0, TM 5 . . . . 90.00
Madonna, 46/0, TM 5, red stars around
    halo, color, crazed 25.00
Mail Coach, 226, TM 5,
    small nick on coat, crazed 150.00
March Winds, 43, TM 2, pencil-point chip
    on rear of base 110.00
Merry Wanderer, 11/2/0, TM 3. . . . . 75.00
Nativity—We Congratulate, 260/F,
    TM 6 . . . . 235.00
Parade of Lights, 616, TM 7 . . . . . 170.00
Retreat to Safety, 201/2/0, TM 2 . . 120.00
She Loves Me Not, 174,
    TM 6, crazed. 75.00
Smart Little Sister, 346, TM 4 . . . . 170.00
Star Gazer, 132, TM 5 . . . . 130.00
Strolling Along, 5, TM 6, orig box. . 115.00
Soloist, 135, TM 3, crazed 60.00
Sweet Music, 186, TM 3, crazed . . . 85.00
Telling Her Secret, 196/0, TM 2. . . 335.00
Volunteers, 50/2/0, TM 5 . . . . 135.00
Wash Day, 321, TM 4, crazed 70.00
Wayside Harmony, 111/3/0, TM 4 . . 75.00
Weary Wanderer, 204, TM 4 . . . . . 140.00
Whitsuntide, 163, TM 6, crazed,
    no candle 65.00
With Loving Greetings, 309, TM 6,
    blue inkwell 180.00

Hummel Look Alikes, Erich Stauffer Figures

These childlike figures from Arnat Imports of New York, were imported from Japan from the late 1950 to the 1980s. These are not Hummels, but they are often referred to as Hummel lookalikes because of their distinct similarities. When studied closely, it is evident that the children's activities are not quite the same as those of the Hummel figurines. In addition, the quality of the decoration is inferior to Hummels. Not all Stauffer figures were created equal—the larger examples are superior in quality to the smaller versions.

Each Stauffer figure is marked with a style number and the words "Designed by Erich Stauffer." In addition, a paper label was placed on the front edge to designate the figure's title, e.g., Life on the Farm, April Showers, etc. Variation in marks include

crossed arrows, a crown, the letter "S" or "U" before the style number or an Arnart sticker. There is no known significance to these variations. Confusion often occurs regarding style numbers. Occasionally, different figures will carry the same style number or two of the same figures, differing only in size, will have different style numbers. Value depends on a figure's activity and props, condition and the presence or absence of its title label.

Advisor: Joan Oates, 685 S. Washington, Constantine, MI 49042.
44/169, Farm Chores, boy with watering
    can, 4-3/4" h 14.00
55/972, Picnic, boy with basket, fence at
    side, 4-1/4" h 12.00
55/972, Picnic, girl with purse, fence at
    side, 4-1/4" h 12.00
55/1059, School Time, girl with books on
    back, rooster, 4-1/2" h 18.00
55/1550, Sore Thumb, boy with hammer,
    Band-Aid on knee, 5-3/4" h 18.00
55/1556, Dancing Time, boy and girl on
    same base, 5-1/2" h 35.00
8213, Harvest Time, girl with sheaf of
    wheat, rooster and chick, 5" h . . .25.00
8218, Winter Time, girl with snow shovel,
    trees with snow, 5" h 20.00
8248, Sandy Shoes, seated boy shaking
    out boot, large figure, round 4-5/8" d
    base, 6-3/8" 30.00
8268, Farm Chores, boy holding ladder
    and orange, goose beside him, missing
    title label, 5-1/4" h 22.00
8394, Life on the Farm, girl with sandwich
    and orange, two geese at her side,
    missing title label, 4-1/2" h 15.00
S8515, Young Folks, girl sitting on log,
    spade in hand, 6" h 20.00
S8543, Junior Doctor, seated boy holding
    boy doll, wearing stethoscope,
    6-1/4" h 25.00
U8536, Little Mender, seated girl mending
    sock, holding needle in hand,
    7-1/2" h 30.00
U8561, April Shower, boy with black
    umbrella under arm, 6-3/4" h. 22.00
U8561, Play Time, boy with toy horse,
    tail in hand, 7" h. 28.00
U8564, Little Gardener, girl with sprinkling
    can and flower, orig Arnart hang tag,
    6-5/8" h 28.00
U8588, Boy Skier, boy on skis, wearing hat
    and earmuffs, 6" h 24.00
U8588, Junior Doctor, standing boy with
    doll at feet, 6-1/2" h 25.00

Catalog, M.I. Hummel Figurines by Goebel, Goebel-Hummelworks, West Germany, 1978, $17.50.

Hunting Collectibles

The hunt is on, and the only foxes are good flea market shoppers. It is time to take back the fields and exhibit those beautiful trophies and hunting displays. I do not care what the animal activists say. I love it. Old ammunition boxes, clothes, signs, stuffed beasts, photographs of the old hunting cabins or trips and the great array of animal-calling devices. Oh yeah, this is the stuff that adventures and memories are made from.

Care and condition are the prime considerations when collecting hunting-related items. Weapons should always be securely displayed, insect deterrents and padded hangers are best for clothing or accessories and humidity-controlled areas are suggested for paper ephemera. Good luck and happy hunting!

Ammunition Box
American Cartridge Co.,
    American eagle, 12
    gauge, XL grade, buff and red . .45.00
Dominion Cartridge Co., .22 gauge, long,
    yellow and blue, partial box 10.00
Monark, 20 gauge, skeet shot, green
    ground, man dressed in red,
    empty 20.00

Magazine Tear Sheet, Savage-Stevens rifles, *The Saturday Evening Post*, Sept. 27, 1924, black and white, 10-3/4" by 14", $10.

Remington Arrow Express, 12 gauge,
    white banner, red arrow, dark green and
    orange label, empty 110.00
Superior, Fast Flight, .22 gauge, long, red
    and blue, partial box 20.00
Whiz Bang, .22 gauge, long, yellow, red
    and blue, full box. 25.00

Catalogs
Hunter Arms Co., 1907, 30 pgs, features L
    C Smith Guns, string bound,
    8" by 9" 190.00
Marlin Fire Arms Co., 1888, 56 pgs, rifles,
    revolvers, ammo, tools,
    sights, etc.. . . . . 450.00
Parker Guns, 1930, 32 pgs, green cov with
    flying geese. 80.00
Remington Arms Co., 1906, 48 pgs. 55.00
Spencer Arms Co., Windsor, CT,
    1887, 20 pgs. 150.00

Rifles
Marlin, Model 1889, Deluxe, 32-20 caliber,
    lever action, checkered pistol-grip
    stock, blued crescent butt plate, 24"
    barrel. 500.00
Parker, Trojan, 16 gauge, double barrel,
    28" barrel 400.00
Parker, VH Grade, 20 gauge, double
    barrel, 28" barrel 2,000.00
Remington, Model 121 Fieldmaster, .22
    caliber, slide action, 24" barrel . 175.00

Other
Box, tin, contains Winchester reloading
    tool, roll crimper mkd "Paragon," three
    cappers and six brass
    12-gauge shells 25.00
Calendar, 1930, Philip R Goodwin illus,
    man on horse shooting elk,
    oak frame 70.00
Calendar Holder, Western, brass, missing
    brass screw, 21" by 11" 95.00
Counter Mat, felt, Union Metallic Cartridge
    Co., red, yellow and gray, reverse
    stamped "C.E. Akins, Mfgs, Feltmats,
    New York". 160.00
Display, Mossberg, cardboard, standup,
    advertises .22 rifles and scopes,
    multicolored, c1953, 8" by 11" . . 25.00
Display, Remington UMC, die-cut, pretty
    girl holding rifle, easel back . . . 275.00
Poster, Hercules Powder Co., paper, two
    quail hunters with dogs, sepia,
    15" by 24" 160.00
Poster, Remington for Shooting Right,
    boys and men target shooting,
    top band, 26" by 20. . . . . 250.00
Shotgun Cleaning Kit, Marbles, steel box,
    unused, 4-1/2" by 14-1/2" 35.00
Target Ball, glass, amber,
    2-3/4" d, pr 125.00

Target Ball, glass, cobalt blue,
    window-pane type 75.00

Ice Skating

I hope that I am not skating on thin ice by adding this category to the book, but the staff has found many skating-related items and they were hard to ignore. Since ice skating has been around for centuries and is something I have never gotten the knack of, I can only hope that this is better than letting all these goodies go unnoticed.

Autographs
Brian Boitano, 8" by 10" photo 30.00
Peggy Fleming, document, sgd 55.00
Sonja Henje, 8" by 10" photo 50.00

Doll, Victorian Elegance Barbie, ice skater, Hallmark, #12579, $175.

Skates, pr

Clarke's, Syracuse, NY, child's, curved prow, bell-shaped stanchions, wood footplate, 1860s 225.00

Douglas Rogers & Co., Norwich, CT, Blondin skate, wooden footplate, 1860 . . . . .600.00

Dutch, Child's, plain blade, wooden footplate, leather straps, 1950s . .40.00

Dutch, Touring skate, long-heeled, wooden footplate, early 1800s. 185.00

German, Jackson Haines-era, clamp attachment, c1848 . . . . .250.00

Raymond Skate Co., Boston, torpedo skate, small cast toe and heel plates, leather straps, blade stamped "Warranted Tool Steel," 1800s . .250.00

Samuel Winslow, Worcester, MA, plain flat blade, wooden footplate, 1886. .175.00

Union Hardware, Torrington, CT, child's, clamp-on, tighten with key, all metal, metal toe and heel plates, c1900 .45.00

Union Hardware, Donoghue Racing Skate, painted red, 1860s 195.00

Union Hardware, Hockey Skate, clamp-on, early 1900s. 95.00

Union Hardware, Thick extended prow, curly-maple footplate, toe and heel with brass trim, mid 1800s. 250.00

Union Hardware, Torpedo racing skate, small toe and heel plates, holes punched in blade for weight reduction, 1800s 210.00

Whelpley, Boston, racing skate, wooden footplate, mid-1800s. 350.00

Wm. Hawkins, Derby, CT, clamp-on, metal, ornate, c1860 . . . . .275.00

Wright & Ditson, shoe skate, tuxedo model, blade marked "Synthite Steel Tempered," early 1900s. 60.00

Other

Book, *Wings on My Feet*, Sonja Henie, 1940 . . . . .35.00

Box, Sonja Henie Knitwear, winter cap, c1940, 9" by 10" by 2" 15.00

Coloring Book, features Sonja Henie, Merrill Publishing Co., 1941 . . . . .50.00

Doll, Sonja Henie, The Skating Doll, 17" h, composition, sleep eyes, marked "R&B" 350.00

Paper Dolls, Sonja Henie, Merrill Publishing Co., No. 3418, 1941, uncut .50.00

Pinback Button, Ice Capades, Donna Atwood photo portrait, yellow ground, black lettering, late 1950s 12.00

Program, Fifth Transcontinental Tour, Sonja Henie, Presented by Hollywood Ice Productions, Chicago, 1941-42 . . . . .25.00

Sheet Music, Let's Bring New Glory to Old Glory, from movie "Iceland," 194215.00

Tobacco Card, Sonja Henie, Drapkin Cigarettes, black and white photo, 1930 . . . . 8.00

Imperial Glass

The history of Imperial Glass dates back to 1901. Initially the company produced pattern and carnival glass. In 1916 an art-glass line, "Free-Hand," was introduced. However, Imperial's reputation rests on a wide variety of household glassware products. Imperial was responsible for some neat Depression-era glassware patterns. They were practical, plentiful and very affordable. Today their bright colors delight collectors.

The company made a practice of acquiring molds from firms that went out of business, e.g., Central, Cambridge and Heisey. Imperial used a variety of marks over time. Beware of an interlaced "I" and "G" mark on carnival glass. This is an Imperial reproduction.

Club: National Imperial Glass Collectors Society, P.O. Box 534, Bellaire, OH 43906.

Figures

Baby Rabbit, Sunshine Yellow, head down, 1982 . . . . 75.00

Duckling, Sunshine Yellow, standing, 2-5/8" h, 1983 . . . . 20.00

Vase, Free-Hand, art glass, Drag Loop, cobalt blue and yellow, 6-1/2" h, $575.

Duckling, Ultra Blue, floating, 2" h, 1983 . . . . .35.00

Filly, #1, etched crystal, head forward, 8-1/2" h, 1982 . . . . .70.00

Marmota Sentinel, woodchuck, amber, 4-1/2" h .55.00

Piglets, pr, 1" h sitting and 7/8" h standing, pink, 1983 . . . . .40.00

Other

Ashtray, 6" sq, purple slag 25.00

Bowl, Beaded Block, 5-1/2" sq, amber7.50

Bowl, Beaded Block, 6-3/4" d, milk white. 16.00

Butter Dish, cov, Cape Cod, crystal . 30.00

Cake Plate, Molly, opalescent green 45.00

Cocktail Shaker, Big Shot, red 75.00

Dish, cov, hen on nest, amethyst slag 115.00

Iced Tea Tumbler, Cape Cod, crystal .12.00

Mayonnaise Set, Laced Edge, opalescent, three-pc set 130.00

Plate, 10" d, Laced Edge, opalescent. 80.00

Sherbet, Victorian, yellow. 10.00

Ink Bottles

In the 18th and early 19th centuries, people mixed their own ink. The individual ink bottle became prevalent after the untippable bottle was developed in the middle of the 19th century. Ink bottles are found in a variety of shapes, ranging from umbrella style to turtles. When the fountain pen arrived on the scene, ink bottles became increasingly plain.

Periodical: *Antique Bottle and Glass Collector*, P.O. Box 187, East Greenville, PA 18041.

Blackwood & Co., 2-1/2" h, pottery, rect base. 50.00

Carter's Ink, amethyst, mold blown, applied lip 4.00

Drapers Improved Patent, clear, 3" by 4" .100.00

Dunbars Black Ink, 6-3/4" h, aqua, open pontil 50.00

Eells Writing Fluid, Mansfield, pottery, 4-3/8" h .55.00

Greenwood's, clear, sheared top 8.00

Harrison's, cylindrical, sapphire blue. 300.00

House Ink Bottle, figural house, opaque milk glass 150.00

Paul's, aqua 12.00

Sanford, clear, round, crown top 2.00

Waterman's Ideal Ink, ink bottle and wood case, 4-1/2", $30.

Shaw & Co., Chinese, black ink, cylindrical,
  olive amber 75.00
Signet Ink, cobalt blue 18.00
Thaddeus Davids & Co. Steel Pen Ink,
  6" h, blue-green 70.00
Todd, WB, green 6.00
Umbrella Ink, octagonal,
  golden amber 125.00
Winslow's Improved Chemical Indelible
  Ink, 5" h, olive amber, label 330.00

Inkwells

Inkwells enjoyed a "golden age" between 1870 and 1920. They were a sign of wealth and office. The common man dipped his ink directly from the bottle. The arrival of the fountain pen and ball-point pen led to their demise. Inkwells were made from a wide variety of materials. Collectors seem to have the most fun collecting figural inkwells—but beware, there are some modern reproductions.

Silver, mother-of-pearl panels, traveling desk set, two ink bottles, powder bottle, assorted pen nibs and crystal stand, $150.

Club: The Society of Inkwell Collectors, 5136 Thomas Ave. South, Minneapolis, MN 55410.

Brass
Art Nouveau, glass insert, hinged lid 80.00
Bradley & Hubbard 45.00
Egyptian Bust, glass insert,
  hinged lid 60.00
Glass
1-1/2" by 2-1/2", ringed, deep olive, open
  pontil 150.00
1-7/8" h, funnel-shape, olive amber, open
  pontil 60.00
1-7/8" by 3-3/4", turtle-shape, clear 145.00

Brass, felt-lined, glass bottle with silver stopper, 1889 Paris Expo, $225.

2-7/8" by 3", boot-shape,
  turquoise blue 100.00
6" by 7", two screw-in hexagonal inkwells,
  attached cast metal
  George Washington statuette standing
  beside horse, wooden stand . . . 125.00
Porcelain
Domed, multicolored floral dec, white
  glaze, metal cap 30.00
Figural, two children playing,
  Germany 85.00
Floral design, red, green and blue,
  3-1/8" h 50.00
Other
Blown Three Mold, cylindrical, disk mouth,
  1-1/2" h, 2-1/2" d,
  dark olive amber 140.00
Cast Iron, double well,
  storks on sides 50.00
Cast Metal, camel, painted 275.00
Cut Glass, 4-3/4" h, brass collar, glass
  stopper 95.00
Metal, tree-stump figural, whippet, painted
  white, orig insert 125.00
Pewter, pen rest with cherub dec,
  glass insert, floral dec on cov . . . 65.00
Stone, 2-1/2" d, tan, marbleized, curling,
  hinged lid 75.00

Insulators

Insulators were a trendy collectible of the 1960s and prices have been stable since the 1970s. Insulators are sold by "CD" numbers and color. Check N.R. Woodward's *The Glass Insulator in America* (privately printed, 1973) to determine the correct CD number. Beware of "rare" colors. Unfortunately, some collectors and dealers have altered the color of pieces by using heat and chemicals to increase the rarity value. The National Insulators Association is leading the movement to identify and stop this practice. They are one of the few clubs in the field that take their policing role seriously.

Club: National Insulator Association, 1315 Old Mill Path, Broadview Heights, OH 44147.

Periodical: *Crown Jewels of the Wire*, P.O. Box 1003, St. Charles, IL 60174.

102, Bar/Bar, dark purple 18.00
102, Diamond, royal purple 25.00
102, Star, aqua 2.00
106.1, Duquesne, cornflower 75.00
112, Star, blue 4.00
115, McLaughlin #10, light green 7.00
115, Whitall Tatum #3, peach 4.00
121, Agee, amethyst 25.00
121, AM Tel & Tel, jade milk 8.00
121, CD&P Tel Co., light blue 20.00
121, McLaughlin 16, dark green 12.00
121, WFG Denver, steel/cornflower 125.00
122, McLaughlin 16, light citron . . .100.00
124, Hemingray 4, aqua-jade swirl .135.00
126.4, WE Mfg. Co., lime green 45.00
133, BGM Co.,
    sun-colored amethyst 75.00
133, No name #20, green 3.00
133.1, Electric Supply Chicago,
    aqua 25.00
134, WGM, sun-colored amethyst . . .65.00
142, Hemingray TS-2, carnival 25.00
145, American, light grass green . . .60.00
145, HG Co., petticoat, emerald . . .175.00
147, Patent Oct. 8, 1907, aqua 5.00
152, Diamond, light green 8.00
154, Whitall Tatum, purple 20.00
154, Whitall Tatum, straw 3.00
160, McLaughlin 14, dark olive 25.00
161, California, light yellow 125.00
162, Hamilton Glass Co.,
    light blue-aqua 25.00
162.4, No name, dark purple 75.00
164, HG Co., green milk 30.00
164, McLaughlin, emerald, with drips .8.00
164, Star, aqua 3.00
165.1, Whitall Tatum, aqua 5.00
168, Hemingray D510, gold carnival .30.00
168, Hemingray D510, ice blue 5.00
168, Hemingray D510, olive amber. .15.00
168, Hemingray D510, red amber. . .25.00

168, Hemingray D510,
    silver carnival 20.00
178, Cal Santa Ana, purple 110.00
190/191, B, blue 35.00
208, Brookfield, aqua,
    large olive streak. 20.00
214, Nacionales, red amber. 75.00
218, Hemingray 660, clear. 7.00
280, Prism, aqua 30.00
296, #20, dark aqua 6.00
326, Pyrex #453, dark carnival . . . 125.00
326, Pyrex #453, light carnival. 75.00
422, Agee, dark amethyst 30.00
575, L'Electro Verre, emerald 125.00
734, McMicking, aqua 50.00
735, Mulford, bright aqua,
    no UPRR. 275.00

Irons

Country and kitchen collectors have kept non-electric iron collecting alive. The form changed little for centuries. Some types were produced for decades. Age is not as important as appearance—the more unusual or decorative the iron, the more likely its value will be high. There are still bargains to be found, but cast-iron and brass irons are becoming expensive. Electric irons are the iron collectible of the future.

Clubs: Club of the Friends of Ancient Smoothing Irons, P.O. Box 215 Carlsbad, CA 92008; Midwest Sad Iron Collectors Club, 754 34th Pl., West Des Moines, IA 50265.

Newsletter: *Iron Talk*, P.O. Box 68, Waelder, TX 78959.

Charcoal
Bless, Drake, 1852 . . . . 100.00
Eclipse, single damper, two-tier top with
    handle, patent 1903 . . . . 35.00
Edna, turned chimney, European,
    1892 . . . . 100.00

Flat Iron or Sad Iron
Carver, Racine, WI, combination flat and
    reversible fluter, pointed ends, patent
    1898 . . . . 50.00
Mexican, wrought, expanded hollow
    handle, various sizes and shapes,
    Berney #21 A-B 50.00

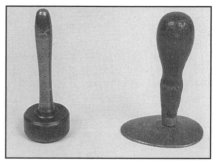

Vertical Polishers: (left) brass handle, late 1800s, 5-3/8" l, $175; (right) wood handle, late 1800s, 5-3/8" l, $150.

Nelson Streeter, Sensible, various sizes,
    Glissman Fig. 179 . . . . 20.00
Weida, iron handle disengages at one end,
    1870, Berney #32A-B 110.00

Fluter
English Boxwood Pleater, fluted rolling pin
    and board, 4-1/2" by 3" base, Berney
    #37A 250.00
Geneva 75.00
Hewitt Revolving Iron,
    fluter attachment 170.00
New Geneva, rocker-style 50.00
The Best, rocker-style. 65.00

Natural Gas
Clefton Plumbing & Heating Co., spout on
    front, Berney #166A 120.00
Imperial, hose coupling at rear, five holes
    on each side of base 55.00
Vulcan, Wm. Crane Co. 115.00

Other
Alcohol, Manning, Bowman & Co., tank
    missing, c1900 . . . . 150.00
Electric, Wolverine 10.00
Gasoline, Coleman, round rear tank,
    pressure pump, plastic handle . .25.00
Gasoline, Montgomery Ward, pump in
    handle, triangular tank in rear . . .70.00
Sleeve, Grand Union Tea Co., 8" l, charcoal, detachable bentwood
    handle 45.00
Sleeve, Ober, detachable handle . . .85.00
Slug, Bless and Drake, combination fluter
    and flat iron 55.00
Slug, LF Dean's, 6-3/4" l,
    removable top 175.00

Ironstone Pottery

This was the common household china of the last half of the 19th century and first two decades of the 20th

Plate, multicolor floral and vine dec, gilt highlights, c1875, England, $45.

century. This ceramic ware was supposed to wear like iron—hence the name "ironstone." Many different manufacturers used the term ironstone when marking their pieces. However, the vast majority of pieces do not bear the ironstone mark. Pieces that are all white, including the pattern, are known as White Patterned Ironstone. A more decorative appearance was achieved by using the transfer process.

Club: White Ironstone China Association, Inc., RD #1 Box 23, Howes Cave, NY 12092.

Cake Plate, Cable and Ring, reticulated handles, 12" l, Anthony Shaw & Son, England. 10.00
Chamber Pot, cov, Wheat and Blackberry, Meakin 35.00
Coffeepot, Wheat and Blackberry, Clementson Bros. 100.00
Creamer, Fig, Davenport 60.00
Creamer, Wheat and Clover, Turner & Tomkinson 60.00
Cup and Saucer, Acorn and Tiny Oak, Pankhurst 25.00
Cup and Saucer, Ceres, Elsmore & Forster, handleless 48.00
Cup and Saucer, Grape and Medallion, Challinor 35.00
Pitcher, red transfer, rooster, iris and leaves, 5" h, Regout & Co., Haan 65.00

Teapot, hp, pink band, gold and black stripes, gold trim, unmkd, 5-1/4" h, 5-1/4" w, $60.

Pitcher, Wheat, ribbed, 8-1/2" h 30.00
Plate, Ceres, 8-1/2" d, Elsmore and Forster 12.00
Plate, Mulberry Transfer, polychrome enamel, 9-1/4" d, Maastricht 20.00
Platter, Ceres, 16" l, Elsmore & Forster 55.00
Sauce Tureen, Ribbed Bud, oval, 6-5/8" h, 1860s 220.00
Soup Plate, blue transfer, 9" d, Adams 20.00
Toothbrush Holder, cov, Hyacinth, Wedgwood 60.00
Tureen, cov, oval, bamboo finial and handles, orig ladle and underplate 95.00

Ivory

Ivory is a yellowish-white organic material that comes from the teeth and tusks of animals. In many cases, it is protected under the Endangered Species Act of 1973, amended in 1978, which limited the importation and sale of antique ivory and tortoiseshell items. Make certain that any ivory you buy is being sold within the provisions of this law.

Vegetable ivory, bone, stag horn and plastic are ivory substitutes. Do not be fooled. Most plastic substitutes do not approach the density of ivory nor do they have crosshatched patterns. Once you learn the grain patterns of ivory, tusk, teeth and bone, a good magnifying glass will quickly tell you if you have the real thing.

Newsletter: *Netsuke & Ivory Carving Newsletter*, 3203 Adams Way, Ambler, PA 19002.

Figures
Apple, 3" h, carved scene inside . . 120.00
Buddha, 3" h, sitting 95.00
Elephant, 1-3/4" h 40.00
Guanyin, 9" h, standing, pouring water from vase, Chinese, 18th C 300.00

Other
Cane, 33-1/2" l, inlaid geometric dec, incised pattern 50.00
Ceremonial Drum, oval, carved, cords with stone beads 220.00
Chess Set, American, wooden box 275.00
Cigarette Holder, 2" l, ivory, 14k gold ferrule, black hinged case 30.00
Crochet Hook, carved 12.50

Ship, brown cotton-string rigging, $850.

Darning Egg, 1-1/4" l, miniature,
  mushroom-shape 12.00
Frame, 5-1/4" h, oval, easel-style, carved
  dragon, scroll and heart 60.00
Knitting Needles, pr, 14" l,
  black heads 25.00
Mask, 5" h, carved, man and woman, j
  eweled headdresses, Chinese,
  price for pair 100.00
Memo Pad, 1-1/2" by 2-3/4",
  silver fittings 25.00
Napkin Ring, 2" d, relief-carved bird .12.00
Needle Case, cylinder, carved
  basketweave pattern 85.00
Netsuke, 1-1/4" h, musician with stringed
  instrument, sgd, Japan,
  early 20th C 175.00
Pendant, 1" by 1-1/2" by 2-1/4", double
  dragon design, orig silk chord . .150.00
Pen Holder, 4" h, three carved monkeys
  and tree 180.00
Pie Crimper, 6-1/4" l, pewter wheel, wood
  handle 30.00
Pincushion, 2" h, red velvet cushion,
  pedestal base 40.00
Ruler, carved demarcations 150.00
Sewing Box, cov, small 65.00
Shoehorn, 8-1/2" l, maiden and child
  illus 150.00
Snuff Bottle, 2-1/4" h, floral and figural
  carved sides, stone stopper,
  Chinese 130.00

Jewelry

All jewelry is collectible. Check the prices on costume jewelry from as late as the 1980s. You will be amazed. In the current market, antique jewelry refers to pieces that are 100 years old or older, although an awful lot of jewelry from the 1920s and 1930s is passed as "antique." *Heirloom/estate* jewelry normally refers to pieces between 25 and 100 years old. *Costume* refers to quality and type, not age. Costume jewelry exists for every historical period.

The first step to determine value is to identify the classification of jewelry. Have stones and settings checked by a jeweler or gemologist. If a piece is unmarked, do not create hope where none deserves to be. Finally, never buy from an individual that you cannot find six months later. The market is flooded with reproductions, copycats, fakes and newly made pieces. Get a receipt that clearly spells out what you believe you bought. Do not hesitate to have it checked. If it is not what it is supposed to be, insist that the seller refund your money.

Club: American Society of Jewelry Historians, P.O. Box 103, 1B Quaker Ridge Rd., New Rochelle, NY 10804.

Newsletter: *Old Jewelry News*, P.O. Box 272, Evanston, IL 60204.

Bar Pin, copper, landscape design, etched,
  c1900 .85.00
Bar Pin, silver, glass, cutout center
  sections, curve rounded end, marked
  "800 silver" back 100.00
Bar Pin, sterling, glass, rect, sq blue glass
  cab bezel center, marked "M" and
  "sterling" on back 95.00
Bracelet, Bangle, gold filled, etched band
  dec 75.00
Bracelet, glass, brass, rhinestones, enamel, rope twist frame, black enamel scroll
  and floral design, spring clasp, mkd
  "Czechoslovakia" on back 85.00
Brooch, porcelain, portrait, gold-filled
  frame .250.00
Brooch, sash-type, Victorian. 90.00
Brooch/Pendant, bakelite, yellow, blue
  vinyl cord, safety catch, c1935 . .95.00
Cuff Links, sterling, rounded, abstract face
  design, mkd "sterling Mexico"
  #151 . . . . .85.00
Earrings, sterling, pierced, cutout profile of
  face, mkd "sterling Salvador". . .100.00
Locket, Sterling, oval, die stamped relief,
  profile of woman with flowers in hair
  design .125.00
Locket, yg, oval painted miniature, half
  pearl floral frame 225.00
Necklace, brass, 10 faux-seed pearls,
  beaded-scroll design, profile of woman
  with flowing hair. 150.00
Pendant, figural, carved lava,
  gold fittings 250.00
Pins, Art Deco, antelope motif, SS . .55.00

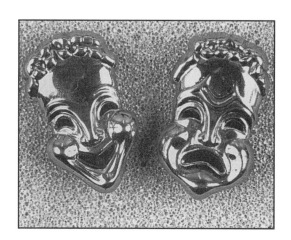

Earrings, pr, copper, Curtain Call, mkd "Renoir," $85.

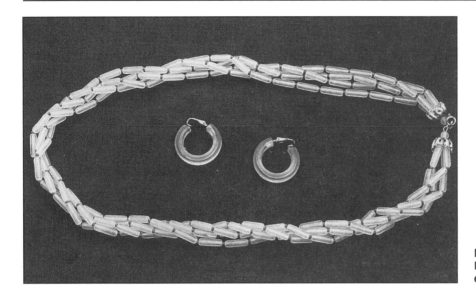

Necklace and Earrings, frosted plastic links, lime green spacer beads, gold-plated clasps, $10.

Pins, brass, shield-shape, green glass center, die-stamped scroll work, sash ornament, c1910 . . . . .60.00

Pins, Marcasites, enamel, rect open work, geometric design, blue enamel corners, c1930 . . . . .45.00

Ring, Bakelite, dome-shape, blue-green, laminated black-dot center, c1940 . . . . .55.00

Ring, German Silver, arrowhead-shaped head, bezel set, engraved swastika motif 85.00

Stick Pin, six-pointed star-shape, copper bordered with silver overlay, cut-out silver lozenge center, Heintz Art Metal Shop 95.00

Jewelry, Costume

Diamonds might be a girl's best friend, but costume jewelry is what most women own. Costume jewelry is design and form gone mad. There is a piece for everyone's taste—good, bad or indifferent.

Collect it by period or design—highbrow or lowbrow. Remember that it is mass-produced. If you do not like the price the first time you see a piece, shop around. Most sellers put a high price on the pieces that appeal to them and a lower price on those that do not. Since people's tastes differ, so do the prices on identical pieces.

Club: Vintage Fashion/Costume Jewelry Club, P.O. Box 265, Glen Oaks, NY 11004.

Brooches

Carnegie, Hattie, gold-plated white metal, plastic, Chinese junk, molded green sail, boat bottom and ocean waves, c1960 . . . . 125.00

Matisse/Renoir, copper, "Starburst" with inset oval mottled blue-turquoise enameled plaque, 3" by 1-3/4", c1955 . . . . 85.00

Necklace and Earrings, copper, "Genuine Copper" paper label, $15.

Trifari, gold-plated metal, dragonfly, cast brushed finish, red glass eyes, c1960 . . . . .45.00

Unknown maker, Bakelite, red heart with dangling berries on red stems, 2-1/2" w, c1935 .265.00

Unknown maker, Brass, stamped, seal balancing colorless Lucite ball on nose 20.00

Other

Bracelet, Haskell, Miriam, faux pearls, hinged brass bangle encircled with a row of applied faux baroque pearls, c1950 . . . . .125.00

Bracelet, unknown maker, Bakelite, red bangle with laminated black polka-dots, 1/2" w, c1930 . . . . .275.00

Charm Bracelet, Bakelite, five dark amber-colored carved charms including horse head, horseshoes and boots suspended from gilded link chain, c1940 . . . . .250.00

Charm Bracelet, Sterling Silver, military motif, 20 assorted, some with moving parts, c1940 . . . . .150.00

Clip, Eisenberg Original, sterling silver, multicolored rhinestones, starburst, c1940 . . . . .500.00

Clip, Trifari, rhodium-plated white metal, painted enamel, five-petaled flower, small rhinestone accents, c1940 . . . . .125.00

Cuff Links, pr, sterling silver, six-guns with mother-of-pearl handles, revolving barrels, c1945 . . . . .100.00

Earrings, pr, KJL, gold-plated white metal, faux pearls and rhinestones, elaborate pendant drops, 4" l, clips, c1965 . 50.00

Earrings, pr, Rosenstein, Nettie, gold-plated white metal, five-petal flowerheads with colorless and green rhinestones, clips 15.00
Necklace, Haskell, Miriam, faceted black glass beads, 60" l, c1950 . . . . . .80.00
Necklace, unknown maker, faceted lead crystal, 15" l necklace of prong set square, baguette and round colorless stones with a 3-1/4" geometric pendant and a 3-1/2" back drop, Art Deco, c1925 . . . . .175.00
Suite, unknown maker, off-white plastic hinged bangle, front half pave-set with black rhinestones, matching hoop earrings, clips, c1955 . . . . .100.00

Johnson Brothers Dinnerware

The Johnson Brothers, Alfred, Frederick and Henry, acquired the J.W. Pankhurst pottery, located in the Staffordshire District of England in 1882, and began manufacturing dinnerware the following year. Another brother, Robert, joined the company in 1896 and took charge of American distribution.

Over the years, the company produced hundreds of variations of patterns, shapes and colors. One of the most popular and readily found patterns is blue and white Coaching Scenes, first introduced in 1963. Although is was also made in green and white, pink and white and brown multicolored, only blue and white was

shipped to the United States. Other popular patterns include Old Britain Castles and Friendly Village.

Coaching Scenes, blue and white
Berry Bowl 7.50
Cereal Bowl 15.00
Cup and Saucer. 15.00
Flat Soup 25.00
Plate, 6" d, bread and butter 5.00
Plate, 10" d, dinner 15.00
Platter, 14" l, oval. 55.00
Vegetable Bowl, open, round. 35.00

Friendly Village
Butter, cov 25.00
Cup and Saucer. 6.00
Milk Pitcher, 5-1/2" h 30.00
Plate, 6" d, bread and butter 3.00
Plate, 10" d 8.00
Platter, 11" l 18.00
Vegetable Bowl, round. 18.00

Old Britain Castles, pink and white
Bowl, 5" d, berry. 9.00
Cream and Sugar 12.00
Cup and Saucer. 16.00
Plate, 6" d, bread and butter 7.00
Plate, 7-1/2" d 16.00
Plate, 8-3/4" d 17.00
Plate, 10" d, dinner 16.00
Platter, 12" l, oval. 40.00
Serving Tray, center handle. 60.00
Vegetable Bowl, 8-1/2" sq 40.00

Josef Figurines

Muriel Josef George began producing Birthday Girls figurines in 1946 in Arcadia, Calif. It wasn't long that cheap imitations from Japan, Korea

and Taiwan were finding their way onto the market. To compete, George relocated to Japan in 1955 and expanded her line to include Christmas items, animals and other utilitarian ceramics. Items produced in Arcadia between 1946 and 1955 are marked "California." Those produced in Japan are marked "Josef Originals."

Animals
Bull, 2-3/4" 18.00
Camel, 2-1/2" h. 25.00
Cat, peering into fishbowl 18.00
Dog, Boxer 18.00
Dog, German Shepherd 22.00
Hippo, 2-1/2" l. 20.00
Horse 40.00
Kitten with yarn. 18.00
Mouse, Blowing bubble 16.00
Mouse, Christmas. 18.00
Mouse, Graduate 18.00
Mouse, Holding Candle 18.00
Mouse, Planter 40.00
Penguin .20.00
Skunk 18.00

Figures
Africa, Little Internationals, 3-1/2" h .30.00
Birthday, with number. 25.00
Bongo. 50.00
Bon Voyage 30.00
First Formal, 5-1/4" h 45.00
Girl with tea cup 25.00
Graduation Angel, blue. 25.00
Holiday, 4-1/4" h. 50.00
Joy of Spring, blue 55.00
Morning, Noon and Night, green, 5-3/4" h 45.00
Mama, rose, 7-1/2" h 85.00
March, Dolls of the Month, 3-1/4" h .30.00
Miss America 25.00
Pisces. 30.00
Puppy Love. 25.00
Saturday, Days of the Week. 35.00
The Little Pets, with Pekinese, 5-1/4" h 35.00
Wedding Belle 35.00

Music Boxes
Amazing Grace. 40.00
Anniversary Waltz. 80.00
Bridal March 40.00
Come to the Cabaret 80.00
Happy Birthday. 30.00
Love Story 80.00
My Darling Clementine 70.00
Santa Claus 70.00
Swan Lake 70.00

Coaching Scenes, cup and saucer, $15.

Platter, 12-3/4" l, orange glaze, $50.

Jugtown

Jugtown is the pottery that refused to die. Founded in 1920 in Moore County, N.C., by Jacques and Julianna Busbee, the pottery continued under Julianna and Ben Owens when Jacques died in 1947. It closed in 1958 only to reopen in 1960. It is now run by Country Roads, Inc., a nonprofit organization.

The principal difficulty in identifying Jugtown pottery is that the same type of wares and glazes are used on modern pieces as were used decades ago. Even the mark is the same. Since it takes an expert to distinguish between the new and old, this is one category that novices should avoid until they have done a fair amount of study.

Carolina pottery is developing a dedicated core group of collectors. For more information read Charles G. Zug III's *Turners and Burners: The Folk Potters of North Carolina* (University of North Carolina Press: 1986).

Bowl, 3" h, 5" d, green
    frog-skin glaze 45.00
Bowl, 5-1/2" d, tea bowl figural, mottled
    ochre glaze. 75.00
Cookie Jar, cov, 12" h, ovoid, strap
    handles. 95.00
Creamer, 3-1/3" h, linear design, salt glaze
    finish, cobalt accents at handle and rim,
    imp "Jugtown Ware" mark 60.00

Creamer, 4-3/4" h, cov, yellow, mkd 45.00
Jar, cov, 6" h, green glaze 95.00
Mug, brown glaze 25.00
Pie Plate, 9-1/2" d, orange ground, black
    concentric circles dec 70.00
Pitcher, 6-1/2" h, incised dec 90.00
Plate, 6" d, orange glaze 40.00
Rose Jar, cov, 4-1/2" h, blended olive
    green glaze. 50.00
Sugar, cov, 3-3/4" h, Tobacco Spit glaze,
    mkd 35.00
Vase, 3-3/4" h, brown glaze,
    two handles. 35.00
Vase, 4" h, Chinese White
    flowing glaze. 70.00

Juicers

Finding juicers (or reamers as they're often called) in mint condition is next to impossible. The variety of materials from which they were made is staggering, ranging from wood to sterling silver. As in many other categories, the fun examples are figural. Scholarly collectors might enjoy focusing on mechanical examples, although I am not certain that I would mention on the cocktail circuit or the church social hall that I collect "mechanical reamers."

Reamers are identified by a number system developed by Ken and Linda Ricketts in 1974. This cataloging system was continued by Mary Walker in

Glass, transparent green, slick handle, graduated measurements, U.S. Glass Co., $30.

her two books on reamers. Edna Barnes has reproduced a number of reamers in limited editions. These are marked with a "B" in a circle.

Club: National Reamer Collectors Association, 47 Midline Ct., Gaithersburg, MD 20878.

Aluminum
Gem Squeezer, two pc, crank handle, table
    model. .100.00
Knapp's, crank at top, hand-held, patent
    1930 . . . . .10.00
Mason's Sealed Sweet Juicer, wall
    mounted, 1930s. 10.00
Pearl, cast iron, wood insert,
    long handled 18.00
Presto Juicer, porcelain, metal stand 60.00

China
Orange-shape, Bavaria, two pc, 4" h,
    yellow, green leaves and handle,
    white top 18.00

China, pear shape, three pc, 5", mkd "L-39," $32.

China, Grape Arbor, reamer, pitcher and five tumblers, mkd "Made in Japan," $75.

Doll, 4-1/4" h, porcelain, "Rose O'Neill" label on back, $100.

Orange Luster, Czechoslovakia, two pc,
    3-3/4" h, pink flowers,
    green leaves. 30.00
Duck, Japan, 2-1/4" h,
    white and yellow. 20.00
Happy Face, Japan, two pc, lemon-rind
    textured surface, yellow spots, green
    leaves and handle, painted face, white
    ground, 1950 . . . . .50.00
Pear, three pc, 4-1/2" by 5", yellow and
    orange, green leaves 32.00

Glass
Amber, Federal, ribbed, loop handle.20.00
Black, Anchor Hocking, fired on,
    ribbed, tab handle 12.00
Clambroth, Hocking, tab handle 90.00
Clear, Easley Mfg. Co., baby, one pc, four
    blades, basket pattern, rope border,
    c1902 .35.00
Clear, Fenton, elephant dec,
    two handles 95.00
Clear, Ideal, baby, patent 1888 . . . . .25.00
Clear, Westmoreland, baby, two pc,
    painted flowers and "Baby's Orange"
    inscription on base, c1900 . . . . .30.00
Cobalt Blue, Hazel Atlas,
    tab handle 225.00
Delphite, Jeannette, loop handle,
    small. 60.00
Green, Federal, pointed cone,
    tab handle 30.00
Green, Fry, one pc, tab handle 25.00
Light Jadite, Jeannette, loop handle,
    large. 20.00
Milk Glass, Hazel Atlas, two pc,
    blue dots. 35.00
Milk Glass, McKee, "Sunkist" in block
    letters .20.00
Pink, Hazel Atlas, tab handle, large .30.00
Pink, U.S. Glass, two-cup pitcher set35.00

Kewpies

Kewpies are the creation of Rose Cecil O'Neill (1876-1944), artist, novelist, illustrator, poet and sculptor. The Kewpie first appeared in the December 1909 issue of *Ladies Home Journal*. The first Kewpie doll followed in 1913.

Many early Kewpie items were made in Germany. An attached label enhances value. Kewpie items also were made in the United States and Japan. While Kewpies aren't being collected as they once were, O'Neill's memory and products are being kept alive by a small but dedicated group of collectors.

Club: International Rose O'Neill Club, P.O. Box 688, Branson, MO 65616.

Newsletter: *Traveler*, P.O. Box 4032, Portland, OR 97208.

Dolls
5" h, bisque, O'Neill 60.00
6" h, bisque, Rose O'Neill. 200.00
8" h, Ragsy, MIB. 45.00
11" h, composition, red heart, orig clothes
    and shoes 130.00
12" h, plastic, sleep eyes 250.00

Other
Bank, still, chalkware, black 50.00

Figure, 1-5/8" h, Kewpie Doodle Dog, hp porcelain, German, $600.

Book, *The Kewpies & Dotty Darling*, Rose
    O'Neill, 88 pgs, 1912 . . . . .275.00
Cake Decorations, 2-1/2" h, bride and
    groom, celluloid 45.00
Candy Container, 3" h, glass, painted,
    no closure. 110.00
Clock, Jasperware, green 625.00
Display, 12" h, counter, Santa, sgd "Rose
    O'Neill," 1913 . . . . .45.00
Display, 13" h, Royal Society, Christmas,
    easel back, 1913 . . . . .150.00
Flour Sifter, child's, tin 45.00
Paper Dolls, Kewpies in Kewpieland,
    uncut book 20.00
Pin, 2" d, cameo 50.00
Postcard, Christmas, 1923 . . . . . . .38.00
Recipe Book, Jell-O 30.00
Salt and Pepper Shakers, pr 125.00
Soap, orig box, 1917 . . . . .95.00
Sugar and Creamer, hp china 95.00

Key Chains

Talk about an inexpensive collecting category. Most examples sell for
less than $10. If you are really cheap,
you can pick up plenty of modern examples for free. Why not? They are
going to be collectible in 30 years and
antiques in a 100 years. Who knows,
maybe you will live that long! One of
the favorite charity fundraising gim-
micks in the 1940s and 1950s was the
license plate key chain tag. There is a

**Advertising, Duquesne Pilsener Beer,
aluminum, penny center, $10.**

collectors' club devoted to this single
topic.

Club: License Plate Key Chain & Mini
License Plate Collectors, 888 Eighth
Ave., New York, NY 10019.

Automobile, Chrysler, 7/8" by 1-3/4", emb
    copper, Airflow model, inscription on
    back to return to owner, 1934 . . . 20.00
Automobile, Packard, metal key holder,
    attached metal ring, shades of gold and
    silver, blue, white and black enameled
    convertible titled "Packard Panther,"
    brass Packard logo, late 1950s . 20.00
Bayonne Motors, with tube to hold license,
    c1940 . . . . 16.00
Chevrolet, brass, 50th Anniversary
    commemorative 15.00
Dodge, enameled logo, leather 12.00
Ford, tubular, blue and white, oval script
    logo. 20.00
Gasoline, Esso, 1-3/8" d, gold-finished
    metal, raised tiger head symbol, Esso
    logo under slogan "Put A Tiger In Your
    Tank," 1960s, serial number on back for
    Happy Motoring Club 8.00
Good Luck, 1-1/2" h, aluminum, 1946
    penny insert, inscribed "Keep Me And
    Never Go Broke," back "Parts Boys,
    Auto Specialty Co.". 10.00
Motorcycle, American Motorcycle
    Association, 1940 Gypsy Tour, 1-1/2"
    by 1-1/2", brass, raised image of cycle
    rider, worn enamel, mail drop guarantee
    on back 45.00
Political, John F. Kennedy, metal, brass
    finish, die-cut initials, brass chain 15.00
Political, Richard Nixon, brass case, two
    knife blades, white plastic grips, red and
    blue lettering reads "President Nixon.
    Now more than ever." 15.00

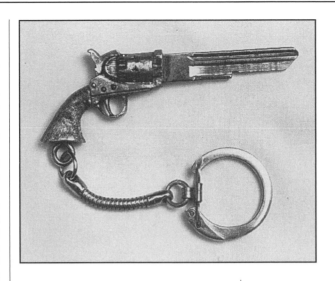

**Automobile Key, GM
Cars, 2-3/4", Colt '45
shape, 1968, $15.**

Premium, P.F. Sneakers, 3" l, ivory plastic,
    large animal tooth-shape, logo and
    antelope head dec, built-in siren
    whistle, sun dial and alphabet code,
    1960s. 25.00
Swift Premium Hams, enamel 12.00
World's Fair, New York, 1939, Micro-Lite
    pen flashlight, orange barrel, circular
    blue symbol, silver and blue design
    bands, orig bulb. 50.00
World's Fair, New York, 1964, domed
    acrylic over silver and black unisphere,
    title, dates, flat silvered metal back,
    worn. 15.00

Keys

There are millions of keys. Focus
on a special type of key, e.g., automobile, railroad switch, etc. Few keys are
rare; prices above $10 are unusual.

**Cabinet: (left) silver-plated, 2-3/4", lyre
design, $15; (center) sterling silver, 1-
3/8", $18; (right) nickel-plated, 3", $1.**

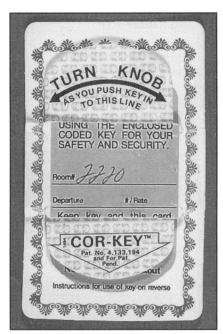

Card Key, motel, 50 cents.

Collect keys with a strong decorative motif. Examples include keys with advertising logos to cast keys with animal or interlocking scroll decorations. Be suspicious if someone offers you a key to King Tut's Tomb, Newgate Prison or the Tower of London.

Club: Key Collectors International, 1427 Lincoln Blvd., Santa Monica, CA 90401.

Cabinet, barrel type

Brass, bow, steel shank and bit 35.00
Bronze, dolphin design, 2-1/2" l 12.00
Gold-plated, 2-5/8" 16.00
Iron, 3-1/8", chest key, 1880s 35.00
Nickel-plated, Art Deco bow, 2-1/2" l. .5.00
Steel, Art Deco, 2" l. 6.00
Steel, standard bow and bit, 3" l 75

Car

Auto Dealer Presentation Keys,
    gold-plated 1.50
Crest Key, common cars 1.50
Chrysler "Omega," brass, five-piece set,
    Yale, 1933. . . . . 15.00
Edsel, any maker. 2.50
Nash, Ilco #132 . . . . 5.00
Studebaker, Eagle Lock Co., logo key 1.50

Door

Brass, 5-1/4" 20.00
Bronze, special logo bow, 6" l 15.00
Steel, standard bow and bit 3.50

Jail

Bronze, 4-1/2", bit-type with cuts, barrel
    type. 28.00
Spike Key, 5-1/2", steel-plated bow, serial
    number, Yale 40.00
Steel, flat, lever tumbler, Folger-Adams,
    cut. 18.00

Railroad

B&M RR, Boston & Maine 20.00
CM&ST P SIGNAL Chicago Milwaukee
    & St. Paul 10.00
LM RR Little Miami Railroad 55.00
SPCO&CS Southern Pacific 9.00
TT RR Toledo Terminal Railroad. . . 18.00

Other

Casting Plate, bronze, 3". 18.00
Clock, 2", brass, Ingraham & Co.. . . 22.00
Clock, 2-1/4", steel, iron,
    Waterbury Clock Co.. . . . . 16.00
Folding, jackknife, bronze and steel, bit
    cuts, maker's name, 5" l 18.00
Folding, jackknife, steel, bit cuts, Graham,
    5-1/2" l. 6.50
Gate, iron, bit-type, 6" l 4.00
Hotel, bronze, bit-type, 3", name and room
    number on bow. 4.50
Hotel, steel, bronze tag 3.00
Keys to the City, presentation, 10",
    Chicago World's Fair, copper,
    thermometer 8.50

Pocket Door, bow folds sideways,
    nickel-plated, Art Nouveau,
    oval bow 15.00
Ship, bit-type, bronze,
    foreign ship tag 6.00
Ship, pin tumbler-type, USN Tag 2.00
Watch, Advertising, brass, shield . . . 10.00
Watch, Art Nouveau, brass, loop bow 9.00

Kitchen Collectibles

Kitchen collectibles are closely linked to Country, in which the concentration is on the 1860-1900 period. This approach is far too narrow. There are a lot of great kitchen utensils and gadgets from the 1900 to 1940 period. Do not overlook them.

Kitchen collectibles were used. While collectors appreciate the used look, they also want an item in very good or better condition. It is a difficult balancing act in many cases. The field is broad, so it pays to specialize. Tomato slicers are not for me; I am more of a chopping-knife person.

Clubs: International Society for Apple Parer Enthusiasts, 3911 Morgan Center Rd., Utica, OH 43080; Jelly Jammers, 110 White Oak Dr., Butler, PA 16001; Kollectors of Old Kitchen Stuff, 501 Market St., Mifflinburg, PA 17844.

Newsletters: *Kettles 'n Cookware*, Drawer B, Perrysville, NY 14129;

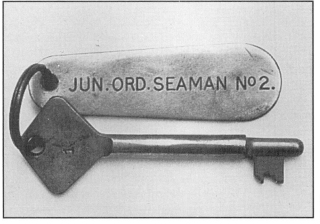

Ship, brass, factory tag, 6-1/2", $8.

Flour Sifter, Bromwell's Bee, tin, wood crank handle, $18.

Trivets, cast metal, price each, $10.

Kitchen Antiques & Collectibles News, 4645 Laurel Ridge Dr., Harrisburg, PA 17110.

Basting Spoon, granite,
    cobalt handle 12.00
Bread Mixer, Landers Frary, tin. 40.00
Breakfast Skillet, sq. 40.00
Butter Churn, table top type, stave
    construction, handle. 110.00
Butter Dish, Criss Cross, 1/2 lb. 15.00
Cake Mold, Griswold, lamb 125.00
Can Opener, cast iron, Universal Dazey,
    pat pend 87.00

Cleanser Shaker, Kleanser Kate, figural
    girl 18.00
Coffee Canister, glass, clear, emb zipper
    pattern 22.00
Coffee Grinder, counter top, 11" h, cast
    iron, crank handle, orig paint,
    Landers 120.00
Coffee Grinder, lap-type, wood 20.00
Coffee Grinder, wall, windmill design, blue
    and white 75.00
Corn Stick Pan, Griswold #273, red and
    white, 13" l 50.00
Cream Can, cov, aluminum, wood bail
    handle 10.00

Cutlery Tray, tin, center handle 25.00
Dish Towels, embroidered days of week,
    set of six 15.00
Dutch Oven, Wagnerware No. 9. . . . 40.00
Eggbeater, red Bakelite trim,
    Androck 25.00
Flour Sifter, wood, mechanical, Blood's
    Pat, Sept. 17, 1861,
    partial label 325.00
Food Chopper, Universal 6.00
Food Mold, cov, tin,
    tapered pail-shape, corn center, seven
    cavities 55.00
Frying Pan, Griswold #12,
    emblem. 50.00
Griddle, Griswold, handled 35.00
Kettle, graniteware, light blue swirl, marked
    "Wrought Iron Range" 235.00
Meat Fork, marked "Vintage" 18.00
Muffin Pan, Griswold #10 . . . . 35.00
Onion Chopper, glass jar,
    paper label. 10.00
Pea Sheller, iron, crank handle 27.50
Popover Pan, Griswold #10 . . . . 75.00
Recipe Box, metal, blue,
    includes recipes. 10.00
Refrigerator Dish, cov,
    rect, green glass 12.00
Tea Canister, glass, white,
    Anchor Hocking 20.00

Knowles Dinnerware

In 1900, Edwin M. Knowles established the Edwin M. Knowles China Co., in Chester, W.V. Company offices were located in East Liverpool, Ohio. The company made semi-porcelain dinnerware, kitchenware, specialties and toilet wares and was known for its commitment to having the most modern and best equipped plants in the industry. In 1913, a second plant in Newell, W.V., was opened. The company operated at Chester until 1931, at which time the plant was sold to the Harker Pottery Co. Production continued at Newell. Knowles ceased operations in 1963.

Knowles dinnerware lines enjoyed modest sales success. No one line dominated. Some of the more popular lines with collectors are Deanna (a solid color line occasionally found with decals—introduced in 1938), Esquire (designed by Russel Wright and manufactured between 1956 and 1962) and Yorktown (a

Scale, Columbia Family Scale, Landers, Frary & Clark, New Britain, CT, metal, $25.

Platter, floral decal, $12.

f4modernistic line introduced in 1936). Yorktown can be found in a variety of decal patterns such as Bar Harbor, Golden Wheat, Penthouse and Water Lily, in addition to solid colors.

When collecting decal pieces, buy only pieces whose decals are complete and still retain their vivid colors. Knowles also made a Utility Ware line that is gaining favor with collectors. Do not confuse Edwin M. Knowles China Co., with Knowles, Taylor and Knowles, also a manufacturer of fine dinnerware. They are two separate companies. The only Edwin M. Knowles China Co., mark that might be confusing is "Knowles" spelled with a large "K."

In the 1970s, the Knowles entered into a special relationship with the Bradford Exchange to produce limited edition collector plates, with titles such as "Gone With the Wind" and "The Wizard of Oz," in addition to Norman Rockwell subjects.

Alice Ann
Bowl, 8", oval...................10.00

Platter, rose decal, $8.

Butter Dish...................20.00
Cup 4.00
Jug.........................15.00
Plate, 8" d 5.00
Platter, 15" l 15.00
Saucer......................5.00

Beverly
Butter Dish, open..............15.00
Cup 4.00

Deanna
Creamer and Sugar, light blue.....25.00
Cup and Saucer, yellow..........10.00
Lug Soup, yellow 5.00
Plate, 10" d, dinner, dark blue 10.00
Platter, daisies decal 8.00
Shaker, plaid 8.00

Tia Juana
Bowl, 9" d....................12.00
Mixing Bowl 30.00
Plate, 6" d 3.00
Plate, 9-1/2" d 6.00
Platter 12.00
Serving Tray, Utility Ware 20.00
Shaker......................8.00
Soup, flat, 8" d 15.00
Stack Set, Utility Ware, set of 3 ....15.00

Tulip
Cookie Jar, Utility Ware..........35.00
Pie Plate, Utility Ware 15.00

Tuliptime
Platter, octagonal..............10.00
Vegetable Bowl, octagonal 12.00

Yorktown
Casserole....................25.00
Chop Plate, 10-3/4" d, burgundy ...18.00
Creamer.....................6.00
Cup and Saucer, orange-red.......8.00
Gravy Boat, Penthouse 10.00
Plate, 10" d, dinner, Picket Fence ..10.00

Williamsburg
Creamer 4.00
Plate, 6" 1.00

Labels

Labels that advertise anything from cigars and citrus fruits to soaps and tobacco make great make great decorative accents. Properly framed and displayed, they become attractive works of art.

The first fruit crate art was created by California fruit growers about 1880. The labels became very colorful and covered many subjects. Most depict the type of fruit held in the box. The advent of cardboard boxes in the 1940s marked the end of fruit crate art and the beginning of a new collecting category. When collecting paper labels, condition is important. Damaged, trimmed or torn labels are significantly less valuable than labels in mint condition.

Clubs: Cigar Label Collectors International, 14761 Pearl Rd. #154, Strongsville, OH 44136; The Citrus Label Society, 131 Miramonte Dr., Newberry Springs, CA 92365; Florida Citrus Label Collectors Association, P.O. Box 547636, Orlando, FL 32854; International Seal, Label & Cigar Band Soci-

Fireworks, Big Bear, $4.

Fruit Crate, Doe Brand Carrots, 7" by 10", $1.

ety, 8915 E. Bellevue St., Tucson, AZ 85715.

Newsletter: *Please Stop Snickering*, 4113 Paint Rock Dr., Austin, TX 78731.

Beverage

Bellows Club Bourbon, green, black and
cream 75
Chief Beer, Indian chief, pine trees, deer
and lake 50
Orange-O-3 Soda, three oranges and
leaves illus 25

Cigar

Booker T. Washington, litho, raised,
multicolored 175.00
Emilia Garcia, lady in pink, standing on
globe, ships in bay 2.00
La Miretta, lady and plantation 3.00
Sunny Boy, 2-1/4" by 6-1/2",
father and son 25

Soda Bottle, Ritz Lemon Soda, 3-1/2" by 4-1/4", $1.

Uncle Jake's Nickel Seegar, comical man
with beard and cat, c1925. . . . . . . 3.00

Food

Butterfly Golden Sweet Corn,
bowl of corn 1.00
Electric Sweet Corn, gilt dec 2.00
Preston Lima Beans, pods, leaves, black
and red ground 1.00

Fruit Crate

American Beauty, big red rose, dark green
ground. 2.00
Bronco, cowboy swinging lariat, riding
galloping brown horse, western desert
scene, Redlands 2.00
Blue Parrot, green and blue parrot on
flowering pear branch 75
Cascade, smiling boy holding partially
eaten apple, blue ground 50
Don't Worry, little boy holding apple, black
ground. 1.00
Eat One, arrow pointing to juicy orange,
aqua ground, Lindsay 2.00
Forever First, red holly berries, greens and
plump juicy pears, blue ground. . . 2.00
Great Valley, scenic, orange orchard,
Orange Cove 1.00
L-Z, smiling boy holding green grapes. .50
Old Mission, Spanish Mission scene,
mission bells, green grapes, 1920s .50
Red Diamond, red and yellow apples, red
diamond, blue ground 1.00
Sea Coast, two lemons, blue triangle,
brown ground, Ventura 2.00
Sunkist California Lemons, lemon, yellow
letters, black ground 1.00
Wilko, red apple, red border, yellow
ground. 1.00

Other

Carpet, Bibb Manufacturing Co., 5" by 15",
"carpet warp, 20 cuts, long reel," Beatty
& Co. Lith., NY 20.00
Medicine, Dr. B.D. Eldridge's Forest Leaf
Compound, Indian maiden, gold trim,
black and white 10.00
Tobacco, Arline, lady wearing low-cut
dress, garden background 37.50
Tobacco, Gypsy, lady wearing gypsy
dress, woodland background . . . 18.00
Travel, American Airlines, color 6.00

Lace

While there are collectors of lace, most old lace is still bought for use. Those buying lace for reuse are not willing to pay high prices. A general rule is the larger the amount or piece in a single pattern, the higher the price is likely to be. In this instance, price is directly related to supply and demand.

On the other hand, items decorated with lace that can be used in their existing forms, e.g., costumes and tablecloths, have value that transcends the lace itself. Value for these pieces rests on the item as a whole, not the lace. Learn to differentiate between handmade and machine-made lace.

Club: International Old Lacers, Inc., P.O. Box 481223, Denver, CO 80248.

Periodical: *The Lace Collector*, P.O. Box 222, Plainwell, MI 49080.

Lady Head Vases

Heart-shaped lips and dark eyelashes mark the charm of the typical lady head vase. Manufactured in the early 1950s, these semi-porcelain glazed or matte finished vases were produced in Japan and the United States. The sizes of lady head vases range from 4-1/2 inches to 7 inches high. The decoration is thoughtfully done with a flare for the modeled feminine form. Many of the vases have the character shown from the shoulders up with elaborate jewelry, delicate gloves and a stylized hair-do or decorated hat. A majority of the head vases are marked on the base with the company and place of manufacture.

Club: Head Vase Society, P.O. Box 83H, Scarsdale, NY 10583.

Inarco

3-1/2" h, #774, 1963, earrings, hand under
chin, lavender, marked 22.50
5-1/2" h, E–779, 1962, Cleveland, OH,
earrings, marked 25.00
5-7/8" h, E–1852, Jackie Kennedy,
marked, paper label. 275.00
6-3/4" h, #4611, 1964, Eskimo with
earrings, mitten by cheek, marked,
paper label. 325.00
7-7/8" h, #2321, earrings, necklace, gloved
hand by cheek, bow, pierced hat,
marked, paper label. 165.00

Relpo, K1696, 5-1/2" h, purple hair bow and dress, pearl earrings and necklace, $35.

Japan

4-1/2" h, turned head, closed eyes, marked .17.50

4-3/4" h, child, pigtails, impressed and stamped "NC," Japan paper label 27.50

6" h, 1458, plastic flower in hair, painted earrings, RB Japan paper label . .30.00

6-1/8" h, young woman, ringlets, red ink "Japan" .80.00

Napco

5" h, C32872A, 1958, painted earrings, bracelet, fingers on chin, marked, paper label 60.00

5-1/2" h, 3M2544, all white, black brows and lashes, turned head, paper label, Japan sticker 12.50

5-7/8" h, C5037C, 1960, child, earrings, inset jewel for ring, ponytail, marked, impressed "CW Napco," paper label 70.00

Rubens

4-3/8" h, 4125, ponytail, impressed mark 40.00

5-1/2" h, 4135, earrings, braided hair, impressed mark, paper label 70.00

5-5/8" h, 495, earrings, gloved crossed hands under chin, marked 50.00

Unknown Maker

5" h, S569A, gloved hand by chin, pierced brim of hat 35.00

5-3/8" h, unmarked, white, black lashes and brows, red lips, flowers, turned head 15.00

5-3/4" h, 3140B, pierced brim hat with applied flowers, hand by cheek, marked .60.00

6-1/2" h, impressed "N" in circle, painted earrings, applied rose, turban-style hat 45.00

Other

Ardco, 5-3/8" h, necklace, raised gloved hand, gold highlights, paper label 25.00

Ardco, 5-3/4" h, earrings, necklace, applied flowers on dress, paper label . . . 70.00

ArtMark, 5-7/8" h, pierced ears, necklace, hand by face, paper label 20.00

Exclusive Lark Brand, Japan, 7" h, JN–4113, earrings, necklace, bow in hair, paper label 175.00

Glamour Girls USA, 6-1/4" h, turned head, gold highlights, impressed mark . 20.00

Lefton, 5-1/2" h, 1736, arm crossing chest, other resting near face, painted necklace with inset jewel, marked, paper label 35.00

Lefton, 6-3/4" h, 1499, Christmas girl, marked 105.00

Napcoware, 6" h, C7472, pearled brooch, earrings, marked, paper label . . . 45.00

Napcoware, 6" h, C794, earrings, necklace, marked, paper label . . 30.00

National Potteries, Bedford, OH, 6" h, C5675, necklace, marked 35.00

Our Own Import, 5-1/8" h, necklace, paper label on shoulder 25.00

Relpo, 7" h, 2005, earrings, necklace, marked, paper label 210.00

Robens Original, 6" h, 501, 1959, earrings, necklace, coronet braid, marked, paper label 50.00

Sons Co., 5" h, pierced ears, necklace, applied flowers, paper label 15.00

Topline Imports, 5-1/2" h, 50/427, hand by chin, marked, paper label 25.00

UCAGCO, 5-3/4" h, winking, open mouth, holding fan 110.00

Lamps

Collecting lamps can be considered an *illuminating* hobby. Not only is the collection practical, versatile and decorative, but it keeps you out of the dark. Whether you prefer a particular lamp style, color or theme, you will find a wonderful and enlightening assortment at any flea market.

Figural

Cockatoo, glass, red, U.S. Glass. . 750.00

Draped Maiden, leaning against lamp post, bronzed white metal, white glass globe, rectangular stepped base 95.00

Boudoir, custard glass shade, metal base, 16" h, $85.

Fish, ceramic, brown, leaping out of waves, brown and ivory circular paper shade 25.00

Flowers, stylized, three flaring wrought-iron stems with curlicue leaves, plastic globular shades, circular brass base, 1930s. 45.00

Hula Girl, white metal, wearing grass skirt, motorized hip movement, circular base, late 1940s 75.00

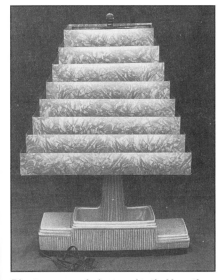

Planter, ceramic base, plastic Venetian blind shade, mkd "Modern...&...Co., Cleveland 5 Ohio," 21-1/2" h, $65.

Table, white-glass dome shade, bronze-color base, $10.

Native Man, ceramic, two bulbs, Shawnee Pottery 42.00

Oriental Figures, pr, ceramic, two figures each lamp, Shawnee Pottery 20.00

Rooster, ceramic, red, black and white, crowing, circular paper shade with hex sign dec, 1950s 12.00

Saturn, blue depression glass, circular stepped base, 1930s 60.00

Telephone, plaster, turquoise, black and white speckled, desk-type phone with clock face replacing dial, removable receiver with built-in cigarette lighter, matching rect venetian-blind shade 35.00

Western Theme, ceramic, cowboy and cowgirl flanking inverted horseshoe surrounding clock face, white, gold trim, rect white plastic venetian blind shade, 1950s 25.00

Miner's

Candlestick type, unmarked 150.00

George Anton, brass, teapot type . .145.00

Justrite, nickel-plated, 1913 . . . . . . .70.00

Wolf, safety, miniature 400.00

Novelty

Artillery Shell, brass, metal dome shade 40.00

Deer Trophy, tripod base made from three deer legs, photo transfer shade with grazing animals dec 30.00

Fish Bowl Stand, ceramic, green double-tree stump base, black cat sitting on one stump, glass fish bowl on other 35.00

Lava, bottle-shaped, Lava Simplex Corp., Chicago 50.00

Motion, illustrated plastic cylinder, Econolite, 11" h, Niagara Falls, 1957 . . . . 35.00

Motion, illustrated plastic cylinder, Econolite, 11" h, Vintage Cars, some damage to inside 90.00

Motion, illustrated plastic cylinder, Econolite, 11" h, Water-skiers, 1958 . . . . 55.00

Table

Candlestick Type, brass, ribbed and fluted column, circular dished base, orange paper shade 15.00

Painted, glass dome-shaped shade with mountain landscape, bronzed-metal vasiform column, circular base . 325.00

Tiffany Type, six caramel slag glass panels in dome-shaped shade, floral and foliate dec framework, cylindrical illuminated base with caramel slag glass panels, three bulbs 325.00

Other

Banquet, figural glass font, Jenny Lind, black iron pedestal and base . . 255.00

Banquet, miniature, 17" h, bronze pedestal, brass font, base with four ornate feet, milk-glass globe . . . 220.00

Betty, tin, simple design, hook hanger 60.00

Boudoir, Art Deco-style, ribbed cone-shaped green Depression Glass shade flanked by pair of metal stylized rearing horses, stepped black glass base, 1930s 125.00

Boudoir, Art Nouveau-style, tall tubular octagonal pink Depression Glass shade with emb nudes on four sides, square black metal base 85.00

Character, Popeye, spinach can with raised figures, ceramic, 1975 King Features 150.00

Character, Strawberry Shortcake . . 65.00

Country Store, 29" h, 20 " d, nickel-plated brass font, wire frame, orig waffle tin shade, Aladdin 395.00

Desk, Sheaffer pen, adv 250.00

Hanging, brass 95.00

Miniature, milk glass, shade, marked "Improved Banner" 85.00

Silhouette, Harem Girl, plaster, green, red and gold accents, circular frame with central harem girl carrying lantern, blue glass panel, PGH Statuary Co. . . 50.00

Silhouette, nude, figural, pot metal, painted green, standing before shield-shaped frosted glass panel, 1930s 110.00

Sparking, 3-1/2" h, camphene, pewter, single tube, cap burner, side handle 150.00

Law Enforcement Collectibles

Do not sell this category short. Collecting is largely confined to the law enforcement community, but within that group, collecting badges, patches and other police paraphernalia is big. Most collections are based upon items from a specific locality. As a result, prices are regionalized.

There are some crooks afoot. Reproduction and fake badges, especially railroad police badges, are prevalent. Blow the whistle on them when you see them.

Newsletter: *Police Collectors News*, RR1, Box 14, Baldwin, WI 54002.

Badge

Special Police, 1922, Kansas City, Hallmark 75.00

Special Police, 1930s, 2-1/2" h, sunburst-shape, silvered brass, black inscription 25.00

Trenton Police, 2-1/4" by 2-1/2", star-shape, silvered brass, black inscription, raised "70" in center, 1930s .25.00

Handcuffs

Alcyon, chrome-plated, swivel chain, 20 locking positions, c1971 . . . . . . .75.00

Handcuffs, metal, $20.

Clejuso, lightweight, chrome-plate, adjustable, oval, single lock, 12 lock positions, Germany, c1970 . . . . .65.00

Takeda, model 660, steel and aluminum, pinwheel, exposed stop lever, three-link chain, steel and brass, Japan . . .90.00

Other

Billy Club, turned mahogany, carved handle, cord and tassel, San Francisco Police Department, c1900 . . . . . .75.00

Book, *Knots Untied: Or Ways and Byways in the Hidden Life of American Detectives by Officer George S. McWatters, Late of the Metropolitan Police*, NY, 665 pgs, 1871 . . . . . .35.00

Booklet, "The ABCs of Practical Pistol Instruction For Home Guards," Police Auxiliary, c1920, 27 pgs, NRA of America 4.25

Brochure, The New 1953 Ford Police Car, police badge-shape outline, policemen riding in police car on front cov . .12.00

Buckle, New York City, c1900. . . . .75.00

Cigar Box, Yellow Cab, policeman and yellow taxi cab, 2" by 5-1/2" 5.00

Cracker Jack Prize, 1-1/2" l,-1/2" h, litho tin paddy wagon, blue, white and yellow. 12.00

Game, Rival Policeman, McLoughlin Bros., 1896, policeman chasing man on box cov 275.00

Helmet, New York City, riot type, leather 200.00

Magazine, *Police Gazette*, January 1959 . . . . .40.00

Medallion, Texas Ranger, bronze, dinner banquet commemorative, 1958 .200.00

Lefton China

Lefton China was founded by George Zoltan Lefton in Chicago in 1941. The company markets porcelain giftware from suppliers in Japan, Taiwan, Malaysia and China, with the bulk imported from Japan.

Club: National Society of Lefton Collectors, 1101 Polk St., Bedford, IA 50833.

Busts, 5-1/2" h

Charles Dickens, #2301 . . . . .18.00
Chopin, #1166. . . . . .18.00
George Washington, #1121 . . . . . . .18.00

Figures

Angel of the Month, 4" h 25.00
Angel of the Month, 5-1/2" h 25.00
Angel of the Week, framed, 3-1/4" by 4" h 28.00

Angel of the Week, unframed, 4" h . 30.00
Bobwhite, 4" h 20.00
Butterfly on flowers, 3-3/4" h 15.00
Kewpie, bisque, #228 . . . . 35.00
Owl, bisque, 6-1/2" h 21.00
Pig, pearl luster, 5-1/2" h 16.00
Roosters, pr, 6" h 60.00

Teapots

Green Heritage, #792, 6-cup 75.00
Heirloom Violet, #1075 . . . . 90.00
Rose Chintz, #660, 8-3/4" h. 80.00

Vases

Bisque, pink, applied flowers, #1847 13.00
Milk China, fan, #840, 6-1/4" h. . . . 70.00
Porcelain, fluted, gold sandy edge, forget-me-not trim, pastel, #7290 32.00

Wall Plaques

Angel, #2371, 7-1/4" h 30.00
Floral, #2780, 8" h, set of 4 . . . . 42.00
Home Sweet Home, #219, 7" h 15.00

Other

Candy Dish, cov, egg-shape, 2-1/2" h 13.00
Canister Set, Fiesta, four pc, #5254 80.00
Cigarette Holder and Ashtray, Fleur de Lis, #1028 . . . . 14.00
Coffee Pot, #4383, Poinsettia, 5-cup, 8-1/2" h 80.00
Compote, Pink, #2027, latticed, 8". . 15.00
Compote, Roses on white, #109, reticulated, 7" 25.00
Cookie Jar, grapes, #3319, 7" h . . . 80.00
Cup and Saucer, French Rose, #3450 8.00
Dish, divided, Holly, red, white and green, #31 . . . . 30.00
Jam Jar, Holly, #2039 . . . . 40.00
Jewelry Box, #2748 . . . . 55.00
Lamp, kerosene, Rose Chintz, #686, 5-1/2" h 18.00
Pin Box, with baby, 3" h 10.00
Planter, Violin, #1734, 7-1/4" h 15.00
Planter, Wheelbarrow, white, #071, 3-1/2" h 12.00
Plate, Dogwood, #2818, 7-1/2" d . . . 18.00
Powder Box, 4" h 40.00
Ring Holder, hand figural, 3-3/4" h. . 18.00
Salt & Pepper Shakers, pr, Mr. and Mrs. Claus, #73. . . . . 18.00
Sugar and Creamer, Golden Tree, #1880 . . . . 35.00
Tidbit Tray, Green Heritage, #1153, 2 tier 40.00

Lenox

Johnathan Cox and Walter Scott Lenox founded the Ceramic Art Co., Trenton, N.J., in 1889. In 1906, Lenox

established his own company. Much of Lenox's products resemble Belleek, not unexpectedly, since Lenox lured several Belleek potters to New Jersey.

Lenox has an upscale reputation. China service sets sell, but within a narrow price range, e.g., $600 to $1,200 for an ordinary service of eight. The key is Lenox gift and accessory items. Prices are still reasonable. The category has not yet been truly discovered. Lenox produces limited-edition items. Potential for long-term value is limited.

Sculptures

American Goldfinch, 1987 . . . . .45.00

Blue Jay, 1986 . . . . .45.00

Peace Rose, 1988 . . . . .125.00

Wood Duck, 1991. . . . . .45.00

Other

Chocolate Set, cov chocolate pot, six cups and saucers, Golden Wheat pattern, cobalt blue ground, 13 pcs 275.00

Chop Plate, 12-3/4" d, Flirtation 45.00

Platter, 13" d, Temple Blossom 90.00

Shoe, white, bow trim 185.00

Vase, 6-3/4" h, two handles, green mark 85.00

Letter Openers

Isn't it amazing what can be done to a basic form? I have seen letter openers that are so large that one does not have a ghost's chance of slipping them under the flap of a No. 10 envelope. As they say in Eastern Pennsylvania, these letter openers are "just for nice."

Advertising letter openers are the crowd pleaser in this category. However, you can build an equally great collection based on material (brass, plastic, wood, etc.) or theme (animal shapes, swords, etc.)

Advertising, Lincoln, Nebraska Telephone/Telegraph, Silver Anniversary, phone logo on handle 75.00

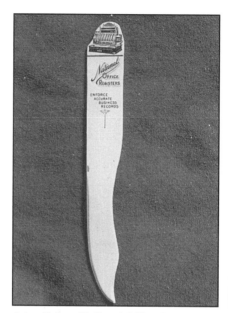

Advertising, National Office Registers, 5-3/4" l, $50.

Advertising, Purity Brand Salt, International Salt Co. of NY, celluloid, made by Whitehead and Hoag, Newark, NJ, 7-3/4" l 20.00
Alligator, beige, black and white eyes, Germany, c1900. . . . . .75.00
Art Deco, rooster 25.00
Dragon, brass 40.00
Elephant, celluloid, elephant head, trunk raised, painted detail 30.00
Horse, rearing, brass, cutout floral blade, 7-1/4" l 18.00
Indian, beige, black accents 60.00
Ivory, three-layer handle, mother-of-pearl insets, ornate 125.00
Owl, celluloid 65.00
Pacific Railroad, brass 40.00
World's Fair, New York, 1939 . . . . . .15.00

License Plates

License plate collecting is a fast growing hobby. Just now breaking out of its infancy, "tag" collecting may one day equal stamps and coins in widespread popularity and appeal.

The trend toward use of colorful graphics and optional or "specialty" issues in the 1980s and 1990s has contributed greatly to interest in plates. The majority of the modern general issue plates can be obtained inexpensively, usually for $5 or less. Remember, millions are produced

each year! Limited-production special organization, commemorative or environmental issues can circulate on the collectors' market for 10 or 20 times the price of a common issue from the same state, but prices typically fall off after the optional issues have been in production awhile. A good example is the Florida Challenger plate, which commanded $100 or more from collectors shortly after its introduction. Today, nice examples can readily be found for $20 or less.

Values of older metal issues dating back to the early teens and the colorful porcelain plates in use mainly in the pre-1920 era are arbitrary and difficult for a novice to accurately determine. Condition is key. Badly chipped or rusted plates or those with only traces of original paint remaining are of little value, no matter what their vintage. Repainting of rare items is acceptable to some collectors, but in most cases the resulting value is a fraction of what the item would be worth in original condition. In the old days of annual issues, it was common for runs of plates from the family car to be tacked up in the garage or barn. This poor form of preservation of fragile plates was better than none at all, but today's advanced collectors seek out those choice specimens that were kept indoors, away from destructive humidity. Plates from the industrialized North and East are most easily found, while issues from the South and West are much less common.

Advisor: Dave Lincoln, P.O. Box 331, Yorklyn, DE 19736, (610) 444-4144.

Clubs: Automobile License Plate Collectors Association, P.O. Box 77, Horner, WV 26372; Nevada International License Plate Society, P.O. Box 61771, Boulder City, NV 89006.

Newsletter: *The Plate Trader*, 10-M Ridge Run, Marietta, GA 30067.

Periodical: *PL8S, The License Plate Collector's Hobby Paper*, P.O. Box 222, East Texas, PA 18046.

Pennsylvania, 1935, $15.

Alabama, undated, porcelain, white and green, four digit, glossy, no chips in lettering .500.00
Alaska, 1976 Bicentennial, standing bear. 15.00
Arizona, current multicolor environmental issue with lizards 15.00
Arkansas, Land of Opportunity or Natural State 2.00
California, 1914, porcelain, white and red, minor chips 75.00
Colorado, 1958, green and white, skier design, price for pair, excellent condition 30.00
Connecticut, porcelain, any color but black and white, chipped 30.00
Delaware, porcelain, white and black, tab slots, five digit, very good displayable condition 35.00
District of Columbia, inaugural, 1937 .350.00
District of Columbia, inaugural, 1957 .150.00
Florida, current issues including manatee, panther, challenger 17.50
Georgia, current Olympics special issue 15.00
Hawaii, current issue rainbow design 10.00
Idaho, 1928, potato, professional repaint 100.00
Illinois, 1943-48, fiberboard composition, not soybean. 10.00
Indiana, 1913, porcelain, black and yellow, minor chips 110.00
Iowa, 1930s-60s, average displayable condition .5.00
Kansas, 1942, sunflower decals intact 25.00
Kentucky, undated, porcelain, white and black, with letter code B, L, M or G, few chips .400.00
Louisiana, 1930s-50s, pelican design 100.00
Maine, 1948, solid brass, polished, most paint missing 10.00
Maryland, 1920-60s, price for matched pair 75.00
Massachusetts, 1910-15, porcelain, blue and white, some chips. 25.00

Michigan, 1976, red, white and blue
 Bicentennial, mint condition 7.50
Minnesota, 1920-60s. 6.00
Mississippi, 1920s, rusty, some paint60.00
Missouri, 1904-11, porcelain,
 St. Louis. 1250.00
Montana, 1920-40s, original paint. . .30.00
Nebraska, metal numbers on leather pad,
 marked "NEB," pre-state 175.00
Nevada, miner,
 graphic optional issue 35.00
New Hampshire, 1914-18, porcelain,
 few chips 50.00
New Jersey, 1911-15, porcelain, some
 chips, medallion intact 30.00
New Mexico, 1930-40s, zia symbol. .30.00
New York, 1938-40, World's Fair slogan,
 single plate of pair 20.00
North Carolina, 1920-30s,
 displayable. 50.00
North Carolina, 1940-60s, excellent .25.00
North Dakota, 1920-50s except 1943,
 excellent. 17.50
Ohio, 1910 or 1911, excellent. 120.00
Ohio, undated, porcelain,
 white and blue 250.00
Oklahoma, 1930-50s. 15.00
Oregon, Oregon Trail graphic 15.00
Oregon, Pine tree graphic. 3.00
Pennsylvania, 1906-1909,
 porcelain. 300.00
Pennsylvania, 1910-15, medallion . .75.00
Rhode Island, 1980-90s, non-graphic.7.00
South Carolina, 1989-90, green, gold and
 aqua, personalized. 35.00
South Dakota, 1952-56, Mt. Rushmore
 decal. .15.00
Tennessee, 1936-56, map, state-shaped .
 25.00
Texas, 1920-30s, matched pair. . . .110.00
Utah, Centennial arch graphic. 20.00
Vermont, 1912-15, porcelain,
 some chips. 50.00
Virginia, 1950-60s, matched pair . . .35.00
Washington, 1939, yellow and green,
 Golden Jubilee, matched pair . . .65.00
West Virginia, 1910-16, porcelain, various
 colors, some chips 250.00
Wisconsin, 1920-30s, very good original
 condition. 10.00
Wyoming, 1936-40s, bronco rider. . .22.00
Wyoming, 1950-90s, bronco rider. . .10.00

Liddle Kiddles

The Mattel Co., broke from tradition when it introduced its Liddle Kiddles line of dolls in 1965. Previously, most dolls were fashion dolls or baby dolls, with an average height of 8-1/2 inches. Liddle Kiddles ranged in size from a

tiny 7/8-inch to 4 inches in height and had oversized heads with rooted hair that could be combed and styled.

Liddle Kiddles are easily distinguished from rival imitators. All dolls are marked with either Mattel or MI, a date and Japan, Hong Kong or Taiwan.

Club: Liddle Kiddles Klub, 3639 Fourth Ave., La Crescenta, CA 91214.

Dolls
Freezy Sliddle, 3-1/2" h, blue sled, Mattel,
 1967 . . . . 40.00
Heather Hiddlehorse, 4" h, pink plastic
 horse, Mattel, 1969. . . . . 65.00
Lenore Limousine, 1969 . . . . 45.00
Louise Locket, 1968. . . . . 15.00
Telly Viddle, 3-1/2" h, miniature yellow and
 orange TV set, cardboard box of
 pretzels, Mattel, 1968 . . . . 50.00

Other
Book, *Liddle Kiddles, A Counting Book*,
 Whitman, 1966 . . . . 15.00
Book, *The Liddle Kiddles Book*, Golden
 Press, 1968. . . . . 20.00
Case, Liddle Kiddles Club, 12" by 6" by 9",
 vinyl, house-shape, yellow plastic
 handle, metal closure 15.00
Colorforms, 34 pcs, vinyl clothes,
 instruction book, 1968. . . . . 25.00
Coloring Book, Whitman, 1967 . . . . 25.00
Game, Liddle Kiddle Baby Animals Game,
 plastic, blue case, cards, 1965 . . 50.00
Hat Box Case, round, vinyl, zipper, white
 plastic handle, 1966 . . . . 15.00
Jewelry, Lucky Locket Kiddles, Wee-Three
 set, window box 85.00
Lunch Box, vinyl, blue, white plastic
 handle, metal closure top, King-Seeley
 Thermos Co., 1968. . . . . 125.00
Magic Slate, vinyl, cardboard, plastic
 pencil, Western Pub
 Watkins/Strathmore, 1968 . . . . . 50.00
Paper Dolls, Skediddle Kiddles, three dolls
 and plastic stands, eight fold-out pages
 of clothing, 1968 . . . . 20.00
Pop-Up Boutique, vinyl, book-shape, metal
 closure, Mattel 1968 . . . . 20.00
Postcard, Expo '70, Kiddles dressed in
 costumes from other countries, plastic
 coated, 3-D 15.00
Puzzle, frame tray, Beddy-Bye and her bed
 scene, 14-1/2" by 11-1/2", Whitman,
 1968 . . . . 45.00
Snap-Happy Furniture, three-room set, two
 pcs, Mattel, 1970 . . . . 35.00
Tote Bag, oblong, vinyl, pink, zipper, hard
 plastic handle, 1968 . . . . 15.00

HYLO, cased filament, $25-30.

Light Bulbs and Sockets

Bulb collecting is a growing hobby, due in part to the important role the bulb has played in history. The fact that many of these fragile hand made glass spheres have survived more than 100 years adds to their appeal. Not all bulbs are valuable. Pre-1900 examples bring the highest prices, starting at around $10 and increasing to $17,000. Post-1900 bulb prices may be as low as 10 cents, although some will fetch higher prices. The prices listed below are average prices; price ranges can be extreme.

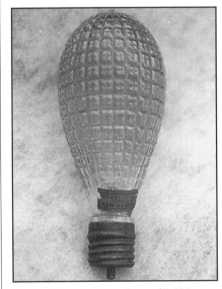
Sawyer-Man, stopper lamp, $3,000.

Here are the keys to determining a bulb's value: the base, what type and the material from which it is made; the filament, its shape and material; and the envelope (whether it is hand-blown or machine-made). Unless a bulb is very rare, the condition of its filament is very important. A common $20 bulb may decrease in value to $1 if its filament is open. A rare bulb worth $1,500 with a good filament will still bring $750 with an open filament.

Sockets can be as inexpensive as a dime a dozen or worth as much as $200 or more, depending on their manufacturer and composition.

Advisor: Rob M. Simon, 245 N. Stewart, Lombard, IL 60148, (708) 620-4770.

Bulbs

Edison, 1879	5,000.00+
Edison, 1900	15.00
Heisler, 1883	400.00
Thompson-Houston, 1883	250.00
Thompson-Houston, 1900	25.00
Westinghouse, 1885	125.00
Westinghouse, 1900	25.00

Sockets

Edison, 1880, wood	750.00
Edison, 1900	1.00
Thompson, 1883	125.00
Thompson, 1900	25.00

Lightning Rod Balls

Lightning rod balls are the ornamental portion of lightning rod systems, typically found on the roofs of barns and rural houses from the 1840s to 1930s. The glass balls served only aesthetic purposes and did not contribute to the operation of the lightning rod system.

Glass balls were made in a rainbow of colors, ranging from common white or blue milk glass to red and clear. Many clear-glass balls turned shades of sun-colored amethyst (SCA) through exposure to the sun. Mercury colored balls were created by silvering the interior surface of balls of different colors to produce silver, gold, cobalt, red and green mercury colors. Lightning rod balls were also colored using flashing and casing techniques. There

D&S, 10-sided, blue milk glass, $25.

are 34 standard shapes or styles of lightning rod balls.

Newsletter: *The Crown Point*, 2615 Echo Ln., Ortonville, MI 48462.

Plain Round

3-1/2", amber	95.00
3-1/2", SCA	85.00
4", amber	40.00
4-1/2", root beer	15.00
4-3/4", blue milk glass	22.50
5", white milk glass, vaseline	12.50
5-1/2", amber	20.00

Other

Chestnut Pattern, green milk glass	60.00
D&S Pattern, SCA	15.00
D&S Pattern, White milk glass	10.00

Hawkeye, white milk glass, $35.

Diddie Pattern, clear	40.00
Doorknobs Pattern, SCA	75.00
Electra Cone Embossed Pattern, clear	75.00
Electra Cone Embossed Pattern, white milk glass	35.00
Electra Round Pattern, amber	
Electra Round Pattern, white milk glass	10.00
Moon & Star Pattern, amber	45.00
Moon & Star Pattern, SCA	95.00
National Belted Round, SCA	70.00
Pumpkin Pattern, blue milk glass	65.00
Quilt Pattern, raised, white milk glass	55.00
"S" Company, medium blue milk glass	50.00
Shinn System Round	20.00
SLR Co., wide collar, not emb, cobalt	65.00
Swirl Pattern, blue milk glass	65.00
Thompson, two-pc, cobalt	70.00
Thompson, two-pc, teal	40.00

Limited Edition Collectibles

Collect limited edition collectibles because you love them, not because you want to invest in them. While a few items sell well above their initial retail price, the vast majority sell between 25 percent and 50 percent of their original cost. The consistent winner is the first issue in any series.

When possible, buy items with their original box and inserts. The box adds another 10 percent to 20 percent to the value of the item. Also, buy only items

Mug, John James Audubon, Cardinal, 4" h, 24k gold trim, $5.

Bing & Grondahl, Christmas Series, 1964, The Fir Tree and Hare, $50.

in excellent or better condition. Very good is not good enough. So many of each issue survive that market price holds only for the top-condition grades.

Clubs: International Plate Collectors Guild, P.O. Box 487, Artesia, CA 90702. In addition, many companies that issue limited-edition collectibles have company-sponsored clubs. Contact the company for further information.

Periodicals: *Collector Editions*, 170 Fifth Ave., 12th Fl., New York, NY 10010; *Collector's Mart Magazine*, 700 E. State St., Iola, WI 54990; *Collectors News*, 506 2nd St., P.O. Box 156, Grundy Center, IA 50638; *Plate World*, 9200 N. Maryland Ave., Niles, IL 60648.

Berlin Design, plate, Christmas Series
1971, Christmas in Rothenburg 40.00

Rockwell Society, Edwin M. Knowles, Mother's Day Series, 1979, Reflections, $15.

1973, Christmas in Wendelstein ... 45.00
1978, Christmas in Berlin......... 75.00
1981, Christmas Eve in Hahnenklee 50.00

Bing & Grondahl
Figurine, Peter, #1696.......... 145.00
Plate, Christmas in America Series, 1989,
    Christmas in New England 60.00
Plate, Christmas in America Series, 1990,
    Christmas Eve At The Capitol... 50.00
Christmas Series, 1961,
    Winter Harmony 75.00
Christmas Series, 1964, The Fir Tree and
    Hare 50.00
Christmas Series, 1967,
    Sharing The Joy 50.00
Christmas Series, 1969,
    Arrival Of Guests 25.00
Christmas Series, 1982,
    Christmas Tree 35.00
Jubilee 5-Year Christmas Series, 1920,
    Church Bells 65.00
Jubilee 5-Year Christmas Series, 1955,
    Dybol Mill 200.00
Jubilee 5-Year Christmas Series, 1970,
    Amalienborg Castle 25.00
Jubilee 5-Year Christmas Series, 1975,
    Horses Enjoying Meal........ 50.00
Mother's Day, 1970,
    Birds And Chicks 45.00
Mother's Day, 1974, Bear And Cubs 15.00
Mother's Day, 1976, Swan Family.. 20.00
Mother's Day, 1988, Lapwing Mother With
    Chicks.................... 55.00
Olympic Games, 1972,
    Olympiad-Munich 20.00
Olympic Games, 1980,
    Moscow By Night 35.00

Cybis, figurine
1964, Rebecca................ 215.00
1966, First in Flight 285.00
1975, Wendy with Doll......... 225.00

Department 56, figurine
1992, North Pole Series, North Pole Post
    Office 50.00
1993, Easter, Duckling, bisque,
    2-3/4" h.................. 15.00
1994, Alpine Village Series, Bakery &
    Chocolate Shop 38.00

Hackett, plate
Endangered Species Series, 1981, Asian
    Pandas, S. Mano 65.00
Special Moments Series, 1982, April, Rudy
    Escalera 35.00
Wondrous Years Series, 1981, After The
    Rains, Rudy Escalera........ 25.00

Hamilton Collection
Ornament, Christmas, 1994, Angel Of
    Charity 20.00

Ornament, Christmas, 1995, Angel Of
    Faith 20.00
Plate, I Love Lucy, 1990, Queen Of The
    Gypsies, J. Kritz 50.00
Plate, Nutcracker Ballet, 1978, Clara, Shell
    Fisher 40.00

Haviland & Parlon, plate
Christmas Madonnas Series, 1972,
    Madonna And Child........... 80.00
Mother's Day, 1975,
    Mother And Child............. 80.00

Kirk, Stieff, Christmas Ornament
1987, Six Geese A-Laying 10.00
1988, Eight Maids A-Milking....... 10.00

Knowles, Edwin M.
Aesop's Fables, 1988, The Goose That
    Laid The Golden Egg 25.00
Aesop's Fables, 1989, The Milk Maid And
    Her Pail 20.00
Frances Hook Legacy Series, 1985,
    Daydreaming............... 20.00
Frances Hook Legacy Series, 1985,
    Discovery................. 20.00
It's A Dog's Life, 1992, We've Been
    Spotted 30.00
It's A Dog's Life, 1993, Playing Ball . 35.00
Oklahoma Series, 1985, Oh What a
    Beautiful Mornin' 15.00
The Sound Of Music, 1986, My Favorite
    Things 20.00
The Sound Of Music, 1987,
    Edelweiss 20.00
The Sound Of Music, 1987, Climb Ev'ry
    Mountain 15.00

Lenox
Ornament, Christmas, 1989, Cat ... 20.00
Ornament, Christmas, 1990, Medieval
    Horse..................... 20.00
Plate, Boehm Bird Series, 1972, Mountain
    Bluebird.................. 45.00
Plate, Boehm Bird Series, 1980,
    Black-Throated Blue Warbler ... 95.00

Lladro, Ornament, Christmas
1992, Christmas Ball 55.00
1995, Landing Dove 49.00

Noritake, Easter Egg
1975........................ 18.00
1982........................ 18.00

Porsgrund, plate
Christmas, 1974, The Shepherds... 35.00
Christmas, 1977,
    Drought Of The Fish 45.00
Father's Day, 1971, Fishing 15.00
Father's Day, 1972, Cookout 15.00
Traditional Norwegian Christmas, 1978,
    Guests Are Coming........... 25.00
Traditional Norwegian Christmas, 1981,
    Christmas Skating........... 35.00

Rosenthal, plate, Christmas
1915, Walking to Church 180.00
1916, Christmas During War 240.00
1931, Path of the Magi 225.00
1957, Christmas by the Sea 195.00
1971, Christmas in Garmisch 100.00

Royal Copenhagen
Figurine, Boy with Gourd, #4539. . .225.00
Figurine, Two Children, #1761 . . . .625.00
Figurine, Milkmaid, #899 . . . . .425.00
Plate, Christmas, 1977,
    Immervad Bridge 20.00
Plate, Christmas, 1980, Bringing Home the
    Tree 35.00

Royal Doulton, plate
Beswick Christmas, 1972, Christmas in
    England .30.00
Beswick Christmas, 1973, Christmas In
    Mexico 30.00
Beswick Christmas, 1978, Christmas In
    America .45.00
Commedia Dell' Arte, 1974, Harlequin . . .
    80.00
Commedia Dell' Arte, 1975, Pierrot. .75.00
Victorian Childhood, 1991, the Original
    "In Disgrace". 55.00
Victorian Childhood, 1991,
    Breakfast In Bed. 70.00

Royal Worcester, plate, Kitten Encounters
1987, Fishful Thinking. 45.00
1988, Stablemates 50.00

Schmid
Germany, plate, Davis Red Oak Sampler,
    1986, General Store. 85.00
Germany, plate, Davis Red Oak Sampler,
    1987, Country Wedding 75.00
Japan, plate, Peanuts Special Edition,
    1976, Bicentennial 30.00
Japan, plate, Peanuts, Valentine's Day,
    1977, Home Is Where
    The Heart Is 35.00
Japan, plate, Peanuts World's Greatest
    Athlete, 1983, Go Deep 25.00

Spode, plate, Christmas
1971, Angels Singing 30.00
1977, Holly And Ivy 35.00

U.S. Historical Society, plate
Buffalo Bill's Wild West Series, 1984,
    Congress of Rough Riders. 35.00
Buffalo Bill's Wild West Series, 1984, Pony
    Express .45.00
Stained Glass Cathedral Christmas, 1978,
    Canterbury Cathedral. 95.00

Waterford-Wedgwood, plate
Children's Story, 1971,
    The Sandman. 25.00

Children's Story, 1978,
    The Frog Prince 25.00

Child's Birthday, 1981, Peter Rabbit 20.00

Child's Birthday, 1988,
    Oakapple Wood 20.00

My Memories, 1983, Our Garden . . 50.00

My Memories, 1985,
    Mother's Treasures. 35.00

Little Golden Books

Read me a story! For millions of children that story came from a Little Golden Book. Colorful, inexpensive and readily available, these wonderful books are a hot collectible. You see them everywhere. Be careful, you may be subject to a nostalgia attack, because sooner or later you are going to spot your favorite. Relive your childhood. Buy the book. You won't be sorry.

Club: Golden Book Club, 19626 Ricardo Ave., Hayward, CA 94541.

*Alice in Wonderland Meets the White
    Rabbit*, Jane Werner, 1951 . . . . . 12.00

The Black Hole, 1979 . . . . 6.00

Buffalo Bill Jr., Gladys Wyatt, c1956 . 5.50

The Bunny Book 9.00

Captain Kangaroo and Panda, 1st ed,
    average condition 9.00

Davy Crockett's Keelboat Race,
    Irwin Shapiro, 1955 . . . . 18.00

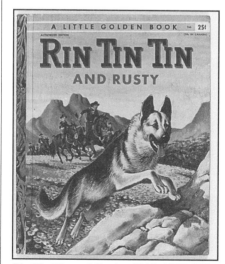
Rin Tin Tin and Rusty, #246, 1955, $15.

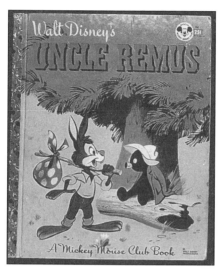
Walt Disney's Uncle Remus, Joel Chandler Harris, 1947, #D6, $20.

Doctor Dan at the Circus, Pauline Wilkins,
    c1960. .17.50
Grandpa Bunny, Jane Werner, illus Walt
    Disney Studios, c1951. . . . . .15.00
Heidi 8.00
Houses, Elsa Jane Werner, 1955. . . .7.00
I'm an Indian Today, 1st ed 9.00
It's Howdy Doody Time, 1st ed. 20.00
Lassie Shows the Way, fair 9.00
Little Boy With a Big Horn,
    Jack Bezchdolt, 1950 . . . . .10.00
Ludwig Von Drake, 1st ed 14.00
*Mr. Rogers Neighborhood: Henrietta
    Meets Someone New*, Fred M. Rogers,
    1974 . . . . .4.00
My First Book of Sounds, Melanie Bellah,
    1963 . . . . .1.00
Pink Panther and Sons Fun at the Picnic,
    Sandra Baris, 1985 . . . . .3.00
Rusty Goes to School, Pierre Probst,
    c1962. . . . . .5.00
Saggy Baggy Elephant. 9.00
Santa's Toy Shop, 1950, 1st ed,
    very good condition 20.00
Snow White 9.00
*The Tawny Scrawny Lion and the Clever
    Monkey*,1974. . . . . .5.00
The Three Bears, 1948. . . . . .8.00
Uncle Remus, Walt Disney Studios,
    1947 . . . . .2.00
What's Next Elephant?, 1949 . . . . . . .1.00

Little Orphan Annie

Little Orphan Annie is one of those characters that pops up everywhere— radio, newspapers, movies, etc. In the early 1930s, "Radio Orphan Annie" was syndicated regionally. It went network in 1933. The show's only sponsor was Ovaltine. Many Little Orphan Annie collectibles were Ovaltine premiums.

Actually, Little Orphan Annie resulted from a sex-change operation. Harold Gray, an assistant on the "Gumps" strip, changed the sex of the leading character and submitted the same basic strip concept as a proposal to the *New York News.* The 1924 operation was a success.

Annie's early companions were Sandy, her dog and Emily Marie, her doll. Daddy Warbucks replaced the doll and the strip went big time. Gray died in 1968. The strip was farmed out to a succession of artists and writers. The result was disastrous. Radio and cartoon strip Little Orphan Annie material is becoming expensive. Try the more recent movie- and stage-related items if you are looking for something a bit more affordable.

Application, Secret Guard Captain's Commission, 3" by 5", 1941 Quaker Puffed Wheat and Rice Sparkies premium, paper, unmkd 15.00
Bandanna, ROA "Flying W," 2" by 18", Ovaltine premium, c1934, red, white and brown fabric. 35.00
Book, *Little Orphan Annie and the Gila Monster Gang*, 5-1/2" by 8" Whitman, c1933, 248 pages. 20.00
Decoder, ROA, 1-3/4" h, 1936, secret compartment 15.00
Doll, 14" h, stuffed cloth, yarn hair, stitched oilcloth shoes, 1930s 175.00

Mug, ceramic, back view, front with Annie holding same mug and "Didja Ever Taste Anything So Good As Ovaltine? And It's Good For Yuh, Too," c1932, $35.

Folder, ROA "Code Captain Secrets," Ovaltine premium, 3" by 6-1/2" closed size, 1939 . . . . 85.00
Game, Little Orphan Annie's Treasure Hunt, Ovaltine premium, c1933, cardboard folder, 11" by 16-1/2" open size 40.00
Handbook, Orphan Annie's Secret Guard, 8-1/2" by 11" closed size, 1941 Quaker Puffed Wheat and Rice Sparkies premium 60.00
Manual, ROA "Secret Society," first manual, 5" by 7-1/2", Ovaltine premium, 1934, 12 pgs 75.00
Map, ROA Simmons Corners, 19" by 24" open size, c1937, Ovaltine premium, community "Where Radio's Little Orphan Annie Has Had So Many Thrilling Adventures" 75.00
Mask, Einson-Freeman Co., 7-1/2" by 9", die-cut stiff paper, Ovaltine premium, c1933 . . . . 60.00
Membership Pin, ROA Secret Society, 1" h, bronze luster, first Annie premium, 1934 . . . . 20.00
Mug, Orphan Annie's Cold Ovaltine Shake-up Mug, 4-1/2" h, white Beetleware, orange lid, 1930-31 . 50.00
Pez Dispenser, 4" h, plastic, red stem, brown hair 15.00
Penny Books, *Little Orphan Annie at Happy Home* and *Little Orphan Annie and the Pinchpennys*, 3" by 3-1/2", c1964, Ovaltine premium, Whitman, price for pair 35.00
Salt and Pepper Shakers, pr, 3" h, painted plaster, Annie and Sandy, 1940s 65.00
Sheet Music, Little Orphan Annie's Song, 8-3/4" by 11-1/4", 1929, Ovaltine premium 18.00

Little Red Riding Hood

On June 29, 1943, the U.S. Patent Office issued design patent #135,889 to Louise Elizabeth Bauer, Zanesville, Ohio, assignor to the A.E. Hull Pottery Co., for a "Design for a Cookie Jar." Thus was born Hull's Little Red Riding Hood line. It was produced and distributed between 1943 and 1957.

Early cookie jars and the dresser jars with a large bow in the front can be identified by their creamy off-white color. The majority of the later pieces have very white pottery, a body attributed to The Royal China and Novelty Co., a division of Regal China. Given the similarity in form to items in Royal China and Novelty Company's "Old

Cookie Jar, gold trim, 13" h, $350.

McDonald's Farm" line, Hull possibly contracted with Royal China and Novelty for production, as well as decoration.

Great hand-painted and decal variation is encountered in pieces, e.g., the wolf jar is found with bases in black, brown, red or yellow. Prices for many pieces are in the hundreds of dollars. Prices for the advertising plaque and baby dish are in the thousands.

Attempts at determining production levels have been unsuccessful. This category has the potential for an eventual market flooding, especially for the most commonly found pieces. New collectors are advised to proceed with caution. Undecorated blanks are commonly found. Value them between 25 percent and 50 percent less than decorated examples.

REPRODUCTION ALERT: Be alert for a Mexican produced cookie jar that closely resembles Hull's Little Red Riding Hood piece. The Mexican example is slightly shorter. Hull's examples measure 13 inches high.

Butter Dish, cov 350.00
Canister, flour 650.00
Cookie Jar, red shoes, open basket, gold star apron 275.00
Creamer, pantaloons 400.00
Creamer, side pour. 115.00
Dresser Jar, 9" h. 260.00
Dinner Plate, 10" d 7.00

Lamp, base, 12" h 60.00
Milk Pitcher, standing, 8" h 275.00
Salt and Pepper Shakers, pr, large .140.00
Salt and Pepper Shakers, pr, small. .60.00
Spice Jar, allspice, cinnamon, cloves,
    nutmeg or pepper, price each . .625.00
String Holder 1,850.00
Sugar, crawling 65.00
Teapot, cov 285.00
Wall Pocket, iron figural 35.00

Lladro Porcelains

Lladro porcelains are Spain's contribution to the world of collectible figures. Some figures are released on a limited-edition basis; others remain in production for an extended period of time. Learn what kinds of production numbers are involved.

Lladro porcelains are sold through jewelry and gift shops. However, they are the type of item you either love or hate. As a result, Lladro porcelains from estates or from individuals tired of dusting that thing that Aunt Millie gave for Christmas in 1985 do show up at flea markets.

Club: Lladro Collectors Society, 1 Lladro Dr., Moonachie, NJ 07074.

Attentive Polar Bear, white 75.00
Baby Jesus, L-4670 . . . . .55.00
Curiosity, L-5393 . . . . .40.00
Dog playing bongo drums, L-1156 .500.00
Dog Singing, L-1155 . . . . .500.00
Ducklings, L-1307 . . . . .130.00
Feed Me, L-5113 . . . . .80.00
Graceful Swan, L-5230 . . . . .90.00
Heavenly Sounds, L-2195-M 170.00
Japanese Camelia, L-5181 . . . . .90.00
Pastoral Couple, flower basket,
    L-4669 .850.00

Rabbit, 4-1/2" l, $100.

Play With Me, L-5112 . . . . 80.00
Rag Doll, L-1501 . . . . 195.00
Sharpening the Cutlery, L-5204 . . . 450.00
Sleeping Bunny, L-5904 . . . . 75.00

Locks and Padlocks

Padlocks are the most desirable lock collectible. While examples date back to the 1600s, the mass production of identifiable padlocks was pioneered in America in the mid 1800s. Padlocks are categorized primarily according to tradition or use: combination, pin tumbler, Scandinavian, etc. Cast, brass and iron are among the more sought-after types.

Reproductions, copycats and fakes are a big problem. Among the trouble spots are screw key, trick, iron-lever and brass-lever locks from the Middle East, railroad switch locks from Taiwan and switch lock keys from the Midwest United States. All components of an old lock must have exactly the same color and finish. Authentic railroad, express and logo locks will have only one user name or set of initials.

Clubs: American Lock Collectors Association, 36076 Grennada, Livonia, MI 48154; Key Collectors International, 1427 Lincoln Blvd., Santa Monica, CA 90401.

Combination

Canton Combination Lock Co., Canton O.,
    1-3/4", nickel-plated brass 200.00
Karco, 3-1/4", steel, three dials 55.00
Uneek U.S. & Foreign Pats. Pending,
    2-1/2", nickel-plated steel 65.00

Padlocks, variety of American locks including Master, U.S. and G&J Products, price each, $5-10.

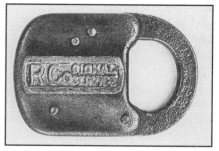

Railroad, R. Co., brass, signal, Fraim, $25.

Pin Tumbler

Brass, Best, Phil Fuels Co., logo lock,
    key-hole cov, 1-1/2" h\18.00
Brass, Fraim, 2 15/16" h 15.00
Brass, Hibbard, Spencer & Bartlett & Co.,
    Chicago, 3", "OVB-Our Very Best,
    Chicago" 150.00
Brass, Reese US, 1-3/4" h 5.00
Brass, USA Ordinance Dep., Corbin,
    2" h, logo lock 18.00
Brass, Yale, push key 15.00
Iron, Eagle, 2" h, push key,
    brass hasp 30.00
Iron, Pritzlaff, 2-1/16" h, push key, brass
    hasp and chain 35.00
Iron, Yale, 2" h, push key,
    brass hasp 10.00

Push Key

Three lever, Eagle Lock Co., 1-5/8" d,
    brass, round 120.00
Four lever, Champion, 2" d, brass,
    round 60.00
Six lever, Cyclone, 2-1/2" d, brass,
    round 70.00
Eight lever, SB Co., 2-3/8" d, brass,
    round 160.00

Railroad

C&EI RY, 2" h, brass, signal, XCLR,
    Corbin 28.00
C&NW RY, 3-1/2" h, steel, Eagle . . .25.00
CMSTP & P, 3-1/8" h, iron, brass hasp,
    Adlake 32.00

Scandinavian, iron, sloping shoulders, 3-1/2" h, $30.

CSTPM & O, 2-1/4" h, iron, Fraim. . .20.00
L&N RR, 2-1/2" h, switch, steel,
    Slaymaker 40.00
Milwaukee, 2-1/2" h, brass, Leoffelhotz &
    Prier 100.00

Other

1904 St. Louis World's Fair, 2-1/2", "Worlds
    Fair", brass body, iron shackle. .250.00
Four lever, Ajax, Corbin, 2" h, iron . .12.00
Trunk Latch Lock, Eagle Lock Co. . .20.00

Luggage

Until recently luggage collectors focused primarily on old steamship and railroad trunks. Unrestored, they sell in the $50 to $150 range. Dealers have the exterior refinished and the interior relined with new paper and then promptly sell them to decorators who charge up to $400. A restored trunk works well in both a Country or Victorian bedroom. This is why decorators love them so much.

Within the past three years, there is a growing collector interest in old leather luggage. It is not uncommon to find early 20th century leather overnight bags priced at $150 to $300, in good condition. Leather suitcases sell in the $75 to $150 range.

Lunch Boxes

Lunch kits, consisting of a lunch box and matching thermos, were the most price-manipulated collectibles category of the 1980s. Prices in excess of $2,500 were achieved for some of the early Disney examples. What everyone seemed to forget is that lunch boxes were mass-produced. The lunch kit bubble has burst. Prices dropped for commonly found examples. If you are buying, it will pay to shop around for the best price.

Buy lunch kits. Resist the temptation to buy the lunch box and thermos separately. I know this is a flea market price guide, but lunch kits can get pricey by the time they arrive at a flea market. The best buys remain at garage sales where the kits first hit the market and sellers are glad to get rid of them at any price.

Club: Step Into the Ring, 829 Jackson St. Ext, Sandusky, OH 44870.

Periodical: *Paileontologist's Retort*, P.O. Box 3255, Burbank, CA 91508.

Adam-12, plastic thermos, Aladdin,
    1973-74. . . . . 30.00
A-Team, steel, plastic thermos,
    King-Seeley, 1985 . . . . 25.00
Auto Race, steel,
    King-Seeley, 1969 . . . . 35.00
Banana Splits, vinyl, 1970 . . . . 130.00
Battlestar Galactica, plastic thermos,
    Aladdin, 1963-65. . . . . 75.00
Bobby Sherman, steel, King-Seeley,
    1972 . . . . 50.00
Captain Kangaroo, vinyl, thermos,
    King-Seeley, 1964-66 . . . . 95.00
Charlie's Angels, steel, Aladdin,
    1978 . . . . 35.00
Dawn, vinyl, plastic thermos, Aladdin,
    1971 . . . . 50.00
Deputy Dawg, vinyl, thermos, Aladdin,
    1979-80. . . . . 30.00
Dick Tracy, 1967 . . . . 95.00
Disco, steel, plastic thermos, Aladdin,
    1979-80. . . . . 30.00
Disney School Bus, steel dome type, Aladdin, 1961-73 . . . . 35.00
Dr. Seuss, steel, plastic thermos, Aladdin,
    1970 . . . . 50.00
Ellie Mae Clampett. 15.00
E.T., steel, plastic thermos,
    Aladdin, 1983 . . . . 25.00
Flintstones, steel, Aladdin, 1962-63 145.00
Glamour Girl, vinyl, Aladdin, 1960 . . 20.00
Gone With The Wind, 1940 . . . . . . 450.00
Have Gun Will Travel, steel,
    Aladdin, 1960. . . . . 125.00
Holly Hobbie, steel,
    Aladdin, 1973-74. . . . . 16.00
Joe Palooka, 1948. . . . . 120.00

Dukes of Hazzard, $10.

Space: 1999, orig thermos, King-Seely, $30.

Julia, steel, thermos, King-Seeley,
    1969 .110.00
Jungle Book, steel, plastic thermos,
    Aladdin, 1968-69 . . . . .65.00
Knight Rider, steel, plastic thermos,
    King-Seeley, 1984-85 . . . . .25.00
Laugh-In, steel, plastic thermos,
    Aladdin, 1970 . . . . .70.00
Lawman 50.00
Little House on the Prairie, steel, plastic
    thermos, 1976 . . . . .55.00
Masters of the Universe, steel, plastic
    thermos, Aladdin, 1983-84 . . . . .35.00
Nancy Drew, steel, plastic thermos,
    King-Seeley, 1978. . . . . .35.00
New Zoo Review, vinyl, plastic thermos,
    Aladdin, 1975 . . . . .65.00
Peter Pan, steel, plastic thermos, Aladdin,
    1969 . . . . .65.00
Pigs In Space, steel, plastic thermos,
    King-Seeley, 1979-80 . . . . .35.00
Pink Panther, steel, 1984 . . . . .30.00
Pony Express, steel, plastic thermos,
    Ohio Art, 1982-84 . . . . .22.00
Rat Patrol, steel, Aladdin, 1967 . . .120.00
Scotch Plaid, steel, Ohio Art,
    1957-59 . . . . .12.00
Sesame Street, steel, Aladdin,
    1980-82 . . . . .16.00
Space Cadet, 1952. . . . . .120.00
Star Trek I, steel, 1979 . . . . .30.00
Superman, steel, thermos, King-Seeley,
    1967 .125.00
The Osmonds, steel, Aladdin, 1973 . 60.00
Thundercats, steel, plastic thermos,
    Aladdin, 1985-86 . . . . .25.00
Twiggy, vinyl, thermos, King-Seeley,
    1967-68 . . . . .190.00
Universal Hi-Way Markers, steel, Ohio Art,
    1972-75 . . . . .40.00
Wagon Train, steel, thermos, King-Seeley,
    1964 .140.00
Welcome Back Kotter, steel, plastic
    thermos, Aladdin, 1977 . . . . .30.00
Yogi Bear and Friends, steel,
    Aladdin, 1963 . . . . .85.00

Yosemite Sam, vinyl, thermos,
King-Seeley, 1971-72........100.00
Ziggy's Brunch Bag, vinyl, plastic thermos,
Aladdin, 1979...............40.00

MAD Collectibles

What kid from the 1960s on doesn't remember Alfred E. Neuman and his zany, somewhat irreverent humor? Alfred is getting older, as are many of his fans, but items adorned with his unforgettable face are very collectible.

Action Figure, Alfred E. Neuman, rubber,
bendable, Concepts Plus, 1988..15.00
Balloon, yellow, red print,
"What, Me Worry"?............5.00
Bank, tin, Chelsea Marketing Group,
1976......................15.00
Beach Towel, A La Carte/Sayde,
1988......................25.00
Book, *Completely Mad*, 10" by 10",
hardback, first printing, dj, 1991..40.00
Book, *Mad For Keeps*, 8" by 11", 128 pgs,
hardback, 1958..............20.00
Calendar, 1976, Warner Books....10.00
Calendar, 1993, Prehysterical Calendar,
Character Imprints...........10.00
Costume, Collegeville, 1960, MIB..350.00
Figure, Alfred E. Neuman, bisque,
5-1/2" h...................350.00
Game, Mad Magazine Card Game, Parker
Brothers, 1980..............20.00
Game, Spy vs. Spy, Milton Bradley,
1986......................15.00
Game, What, Me Worry?,
Parker Brothers, 1979........25.00

Plaque, plastic, Swedish, $40.

Magazine, *Life*, Mad Show photos, Batman
cov, March 11, 1966..........25.00
Magazine, MAD, #122, recalled, Robert
Kennedy cov, October 1968...100.00
Matchbook Cover, Dick's Coffeehouse,
Ashland, NE.................15.00
Model, Aurora, 1965, MIB......225.00
Mug, Alfred E. Neuman, 1988, MIB.20.00
Pen, black or white, Spy vs. Spy,
Applause, 1988..............10.00
Pin, logo, yellow and blue, 1991...25.00
Pinback Button, Up The Academy,
3-3/4" d...................25.00
Poster, 29" by 23", color, Uncle Sam image
of Alfred E. Neuman, Pandora
Productions, 1969...........100.00
Record, A Mad Record, 33-1/3 rpm,
6" by 6", 1960s.............18.00
Record, Up The Academy, 33-1/3 rpm,
Capitol, 1980...............12.00
Sign, 8" by 26", logo, plastic,
mirrored..................25.00
Skateboard, small, Nash, 1987....40.00
Stationery, 485 MADison Ave.,
no watermark, 1980-90........5.00
Watch, analog, orig box,
Applause, 1988..............25.00

Magazines

The vast majority of magazines, especially if they are less than 30 years old, are worth between 10 cents and 25 cents. A fair number of pre-1960 magazines fall within this price range as well. There are three ways in which a magazine can have value: the cover artist, the cover personality and frameable interior advertising. In three instances, value rests not with the magazine collector, but with the specialty collectors.

At almost any flea market, you will find a seller of matted magazine advertisements. Remember that the value being asked almost always rests in the matting and not the individual magazine page.

Newsletter: *The Illustrator Collector's News*, P.O. Box 1958, Sequim, WA 98382.

Periodicals: *Collecting Cult Magazines*, 449 12th St., #2-R, Brooklyn, NY 11215; *Paper Collectors' Marketplace*, P.O. Box 128, Scandinavia, WI 54977.

All Hands, September 1945.......18.00

National Geographic, January, February and July 1974, price each, 25 cents.

American Artist, April 1960.........5.00
American Boy, pre-1940...........5.00
American Home..................2.00
Atlantic Monthly, 1914.............4.00
Atlantic Monthly, 1929............1.50
Better Homes and Gardens, 1933...1.50
Boy's Life, August 1957..........15.00
Building Age National Builder, 1920s.8.00
Capper's Farmer, illus cov,
Twelvetrees.................12.00
Charlie, June 1971,
John Lennon article............4.00
Child's Life, 1930................5.00
Country Home...................75
Delineator, 1918................25.00
Designer, small format...........12.00
Ebony, 1958....................5.00
Esquire, September 1934.........12.00
Etudes, 1940s..................4.00
Farm Mechanics, 1928............8.00
Field and Stream................3.00
Girl's Companion, post-1940.......1.00
Good Housekeeping, 1942.........2.00
Harper's Bazaar................10.00

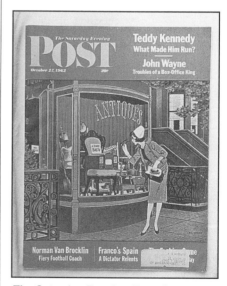

The Saturday Evening Post, Oct. 27, 1962, J. Williamson cov illus, $5.

The Saturday Evening Post, Dec. 14, 1963, JFK memorial edition, $10.

Harper's Monthly, 1922 . . . . .4.00
Harvest World, 1931 . . . . .2.50
Highway Traveler, Greyhound, 1936 .2.50
Hot Rod, post 1960 . . . . .1.00
Judge, Teddy Roosevelt 20.00
Ladies' Home Journal, 1925 . . . . .5.00
Leica & Ziess, 1938 . . . . .10.00
Life, Baseball Stars 25.00
Life, Chaplin, Charlie 10.00
Life, Fred Astaire and son cov,
    Aug. 25, 1941 . . . . .9.00
Life, Manson, Charles 15.00
Life, Political figures 4.00
Life, World War II 8.00
Literary Digest, 1924 . . . . .1.00
Living Church, 1924 . . . . .1.00
Mattel Barbie Magazine,
    Nov-Dec 1963 . . . . .10.00
McCall's, 1932 . . . . .10.00
Metropolitan Magazine, July 1907 . .10.00
Modern Art, 1927, nude poses 30.00
Motorcycling & Bicycling, 1920 . . . . .25.00
Motion Picture, August 1939,
    Gary Cooper cov 6.00
Movie & Theatre News, 1933 . . . . . . .7.00
National Observer, December 1968 . .1.00
Needlecraft, 1927 . . . . .3.00
New Yorker, 1948 . . . . .2.50
People's Home Journal, 1918 . . . . . . .8.00
Pictorial Review, March 1915 . . . . . .12.50
Photoplay, March 1941,
    Ginger Rogers cov 4.00
Playboy, 1958 . . . . .10.00
Popular Homecraft, May 1931 . . . . . .4.00
Prairie Farmer, February 1867 . . . . . .4.00
Radio Mirror, 1936, Fred Astaire cov 30.00
Redbook, April 1925 . . . . .5.00
Saturday Evening Post, 1916, May 20,
    first Rockwell cov 150.00

Saturday Evening Post, 1922, New Year's
    Eve, Leyendecker cov 30.00
Saturday Evening Post, 1964, Dec. 12,
    Johnny Unitas cov 12.00
Scientific American, June 1933 . . . . . 3.50
Silver Screen, December 1945
    Judy Garland cov 4.00
Sports Illustrated, swimsuit issue 4.00
Sunbathing For Health,
    December 1951 . . . . 2.50
The Theater Magazine, 1908 . . . . 5.00
Time, 1939 . . . . 1.00
Time, 1940, Mickey Rooney 10.00
Travel, 1915, Santa cov 25.00
TV Guide, Captain Video cov,
    Feb. 22, 1952 . . . . 50.00
TV Guide, Dark Shadows cov 30.00
TV Guide, post-1970 . . . . 1.00
Vanity Fair 4.00
Vogue, 1928, Lepape illus cov 40.00
Who's Who In Sports, 1st issue,
    1950 . . . . 35.00
Wild West Weekly, 1915 . . . . 7.00
World Today, 1909 . . . . 4.00

Magic Collectibles

Presto, chango—the world of magic has fascinated collectors for centuries. The category is broad; it pays to specialize. Possible approaches include children's magic sets, posters about magicians or sleight-of-hand tricks. When buying a trick, make certain to get instructions—if possible, the original. Without them, you need to be a mystic, rather than a magician to figure out how the trick works.

Magic catalogs are treasure chests of information. Look for company names such as Abbott's, Brema, Douglas Magicland, Felsman, U.F. Grant, Magic Inc., Martinka, National Magic, Nelson Enterprises, Owen Magic Supreme, Petrie-Lewis, D. Robbins, Tannen, Thayer and Willmann. Petrie-Lewis is a favorite among collectors. Look for the interwoven "P&L" on magic props.

Magicians of note include Alexander, Blackstone, Carter The Great, Germain The Wizard, Houdini, Kellar, Stock and Thornston. Anything associ-

ated with these magicians has potentially strong market value.

Club: Magic Collectors Association, P.O. Box 511, Glenwood, IL 60425.

Newsletter: *Magic Set Collector's Newsletter*, P.O. Box 561, Novato, CA 94948.

Booklets

Mysto Magic, 5-1/2" by 7", 48 pgs,
    A.C. Gilbert kit, copyright 1922. . 25.00
Nicola Magician-Illusionist, 8" by 11", 20
    pgs, 1915 . . . . .75.00
Thurston's Book of Magic, 3-1/2" by 6",
    8 pgs, 1920-30 . . . . .15.00

Books

Fred Keating/Magic's Greatest Entertainer,
    16 pgs, c1950 . . . . .25.00
Gilbert Knots & Splices, rope tying tricks,
    66 pgs, 1909 . . . . .40.00
Magic Made Easy, 28 pgs,
    1930 copyright 20.00
Magicdotes, Robert Orben, 44 pgs,
    1948 copyright 15.00
Transcendental Magic, Eliphas Levi. 85.00

Pinback Buttons

14th Annual International Brotherhood of
    Magicians Convention, Battle Creek,
    Michigan, blue and white, 1939 . . . 6.00
Houdini Convention Club of Wisconsin,
    blue and white, 1930s 8.00
The International Brotherhood of
    Magicians, orange, 1930s 12.00

Other

Activity Set, Mysto Magic Exhibition Set,
    complete with instructions, Gilbert,
    1938 . . . . .87.00
Activity Set, Mysto Magic Set #2, complete
    with instruction book 270.00
Broadside, 5" by 24", De La Mano, magic
    acts vignettes, c1880 . . . . .85.00
Catalog, Heaney Co., 1924 . . . . . . .20.00
Catalog, Learn to Entertain with Super
    Magic Tricks & Puzzles 20.00

Cups and Ball Set, turned mahogany, $75.

Flyer, De La Mano's, double-sided, c1880, 5" by 14", Magic Show adv 60.00

Flyer, De La Mano's, double-sided, c1880, 6" by 10", blue stock. 25.00

Magazine, *Linking Ring, Magicians of the World*, 1939 . . . . .15.00

Magic Box, 5-1/2" sq, orig sealed carton, 1960s 18.00

Magic Kit, PF Fliers Blackstone Magic Wedge Kit, sealed bag with Balance Magic, Disappearing Coin Trick and Defy Gravity, box with Blackstone Jr. illus, 1970s 15.00

Magic Kit, Scarecrow Magic Kit, Ralston Purina Co. premium, 1960s 25.00

Magic Trick, Fun, Magic and Mystery, 4" by 9 " red and white envelope with Phantom Card Trick and Pick-It-Out Card Trick, 1930s 20.00

Magnifying Glasses

Most magnifying glasses offered for sale at flea markets are "fantasy" examples. Their handles come from old umbrellas, dresser sets and even knives. They look old and are highly decorative—a deadly combination for someone who thinks they are getting a 100-year-old-plus example. There are few collectors of magnifying glasses. Therefore, prices are low, often a few dollars or less, even for unusual examples. The most collectible magnifying glasses are the Sherlock Holmes type and examples from upscale desk-accessory sets. These often exceed $25.

Marbles

Marbles divide into handmade glass marbles and machine-made glass, clay and mineral marbles. Marble identification is serious business. Read and re-read these books before buying your first marble: Paul Baumann, *Collecting Antique Marbles*, Second Edition (Wallace-Homestead, 1991); and Mark E. Randall and Dennis Webb, *Greenberg's Guide to Marbles* (Greenberg Publishing, 1988).

Children played with marbles. A large number are found in a damaged state. Avoid these. There are plenty of examples in excellent condition. Beware of reproductions and modern

Ribbon Swirl, 2-1/2" d, red, white and blue ribbon, yellow swirl ext., $150.

copycats and fakes. Comic marbles is just one of the types that is now being reproduced.

Clubs: Marble Collectors' Unlimited, P.O. Box 206, Northborough, MA 01532; Marble Collectors Society of America, P.O. Box 222, Trumbull, CT 06611; National Marble Club of America, 440 Eaton Rd., Drexel Hill, PA 19026.

Comic Strip, glass

Bimbo. 100.00
Emma 60.00
Herbie 100.00
Koko. 30.00
Sandy. 100.00
Skeezix 45.00
Tom Mix. 55.00
Smitty. 100.00

Games

Chen Check Chinese Checkers, American Toy Works. 150.00
Melican Checkee King Fuu Checkee, cardboard, wood frame, checkerboard on reverse,
Straits Manufacturing Co. 25.00
Ting Tong Tan,
Alox Manufacturing Co. 35.00

Sulphide

1-1/4" d, pig 60.00
1-5/8" d, woman. 150.00
1-3/4" d, Chow dog 75.00

Sulphides: (left) 1-1/2" lamb; (right) 1-3/4" duck; price each, $65.

Transparent Swirl, 5/8" d

Divided Core Swirl 15.00
Latticino Core Swirl. 10.00
Solid Core Swirl 20.00

Other

Advertising, Morton's Salt, mesh bag containing rainbow marbles 30.00
Onionskin, 1/2" d, blue and white swirls 25.00
Onionskin, 2" d, red and yellow swirls 275.00
Opaque Swirl, 5/8" d. 35.00
Swirl, 1" d, blue, orange and green .55.00
Translucent, single color, 3/4" 20.00

Marilyn Monroe

In the 1940s, a blonde bombshell exploded across the American movie screen. Born Norma Jean Mortonson in 1926, she made her debut in several magazines in the mid 1940s and appeared in the Twentieth Century Fox movie "Scudda Hoo! Scudda Hey!" in 1948. Now known as Marilyn Monroe, she captured the public eye with her flamboyant nature and hourglass figure. Her roles in such films as "The Dangerous Years" in 1948, "Bus Stop" in 1956, "Some Like It Hot" in 1959 and "The Misfits" in 1961 brought much attention to this glamour queen.

Her marriages to baseball hero Joe DiMaggio and playwright Arthur Miller,

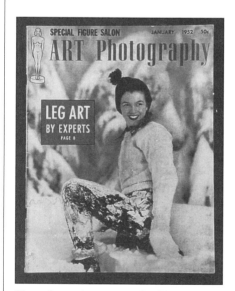

Magazine, cover story, *Art Photography*, January 1952, $40.

not to mention her assorted illicit affairs with other famous gentlemen, served to keep Marilyn's personal life on the front burner. It is commonly believed that the pressures of her personal life contributed to her untimely death on Aug. 5, 1962.

Club: All About Marilyn, P.O. Box 291176, Los Angeles, CA 90029.

Books

Norma Jean: The Life of Marilyn Monroe, dj, 1969 . . . . .25.00

Marilyn, Norman Mailer, hard cov, dj, 270 glossy pgs, black-and-white and color photos, library copy 10.00

Seven Year Itch, paperback, 1955 . .28.00

Magazine Covers

Life, April 7, 1952 issue, cover article, 172 pgs, 10-1/2" by 14". 25.00

That Girl Marilyn!, 56 pgs, black and white photos, 4" by 6", c1955 . . . . . . .18.00

TV Guide, Vol. 6, #4, Jan. 23-29, 1953. . . . . .35.00

Other

Calendar, 1954, spiral bound, October Monroe portrait, nude on red background, added lace overprint, various models other months, 8" by 11". 65.00

Calendar, 1954, "Golden Dreams," nude on red background portrait, glossy, full pad, 11" by 24". 175.00

Lamp, figural, orig Vandor label 80.00

Lobby Card, "The Seven Year Itch," No. 8, 11" by 14", 1955. . . . . .35.00

Magazine, cover story, memorial, *Life*, Aug. 17, 1962, $35.

Newspaper, Aug. 6, 1962, Marilyn Monroe Dies. 19.00

Photo, 8" by 10", color, wearing yellow two pc outfit, A Sheer copyright, late 1950s 25.00

Playing CardsPhoto Art, nude on red background portrait illus on card backs and box, c1955 . . . . 75.00

Poster, "Bus Stop," 20th Century Fox, 1956 . . . . 300.00

Script, "Bus Stop," 123 pgs, 1956 . 120.00

Sheet Music, When Love Goes Wrong, "Gentlemen Prefer Blondes," Jane Russell and Marilyn Monroe color photo cov, 1953 . . . . 35.00

Marx Toy Collectibles

My favorite days as a child were filled with the adventures of cowboys and Indians in their constant struggle for control of Fort Apache. I have only Louis Marx to thank for those hours of imagination and adventure, for I was a proud owner of a Marx playset.

The Marx Toy Co., was founded after World War I, when Louis and David Marx purchased a series of dies and molds from the bankrupt Strauss Toy Co. In the following years, the Marx produced a huge assortment of tin and plastic toys, including 60 to 80 playsets with hundreds of variations. These playsets, some with litho-

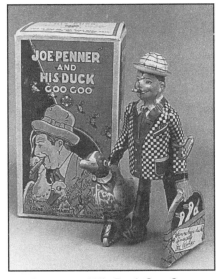

Joe Penner and His Duck Goo Goo, litho tin, windup, 1930s, 9" h, orig box, $850.

graphed tin structures, are very collectible if complete. Marx also manufactured a number of windup and action toys, such as Rock-em Sock-em Robots and the very popular Big Wheel tricycle.

The company was bought and sold a number of times before finally filing for bankruptcy in 1980. The Quaker Oats Co., owned Marx from the late 1950s until 1978, at which time it was sold to its final owner, the British toy company, Dunbee-Combex.

Playsets, MIB

Captain Blood & The Buccaneers . . 50.00

Desert Storm Air Wars LTD 55.00

Gold Rush. 85.00

Prehistoric Times, #1000 . . . . 155.00

Prehistoric Times, #3398, orig booklet, animals, men, trees, mountains, 1961 . . . . 135.00

Superior Barn, livestock 30.00

Superior Gas Station, tin 75.00

Other

Aircraft Carrier, 21" l, missing two missiles and airplane. 265.00

Army Play Set. 30.00

Butterfly, 8" l 25.00

Captain America, 5-1/2" l, Marvel Comics, 1968, MIB 95.00

Catfish Tug Boat, 15" l, c1960 . . . . 154.00

Circle X Ranch, 21" by 15" by 5", die-cut cardboard, punch-out pieces, MIB 150.00

Climbing Sailor, litho tin, 7" h, pull cord. 25.00

Dump Truck, #1013, 18" l, plastic, c1950. . . . . 150.00

Fighter Plane, 5" wingspan, litho tin, windup, two engines, wooden wheels, stars and bars decal on wings and fuselage, 1940s 75.00

Flashy Flickers Picture Gun, tin, plastic 95.00

G-Man Pursuit Car, #7000, 14-1/2" l, litho tin, windup, sparking mechanism, red and navy blue body, cream trim, aluminum rear bumper, 1935 . . 500.00

Hey Hey the Chicken Snatcher, 8-1/2" h, litho tin, windup, 1926 . . . . 250.00

International Agent Car, litho tin, 4" l, vinyl headed driver 150.00

Midget Tractor, 5-1/4" l, litho tin, red, green, yellow and black, curved radiator, 1940 . . . . 65.00

Mystery Car, 9" l, steel, tin radiator, red, 1936 . . . . 175.00

Mystic Motorcycle, 4-1/4" l, litho tin, windup, blue, yellow and white, 1936 . . . . 175.00

North American Van Lines Tractor Trailer,
13" l, litho tin, windup 200.00
Old Jalopy, 5-3/4" l, litho tin, windup, crazy
car, driver wearing glasses,
1950. . . . . .250.00
Popeye Pirate Click Pistol, 10" l, litho tin,
1930s .115.00
Racer, windup 35.00
Road Grader 40.00
Space Creature, cone-shaped body,
5-1/2" h, black antennae, rubber ears,
sound 75.00
Tricky Taxi, 4-1/2" l, litho steel, clockwork
motor, 1935 . . . . .75.00
Trunk, holds Royal Bus 125.00
Tumbling Monkey, 4-1/2" h, litho tin,
windup, 1942 . . . . .110.00
Turnover Tank, 9" l, litho tin, windup,
1930. . . . . .250.00
Twirling Tail Donald, plastic, 6-1/2" h 85.00
Willy's Jeep, lights, horn 45.00

Mary Gregory Glass

Who was Mary Gregory? Her stuff
certainly is expensive. Beware of objects that seem like too much of a bargain. They may have been painted by
Mary Gregory's great-great grand-
daughter in the 1950s rather than in
the 1880s. Also, watch the eyes. The
original Mary Gregory did not paint
children with slanted eyes.

Barber Bottle, 7-3/4" h, bulbous, amethyst,
white enamel boy
and flying birds dec 230.00
Box, 5"d, 3-3/8" h, lime green ground, white
enamel, young boy with hat on hinged
lid dec, white enameled sprays around
sides. 200.00
Cologne Bottle, 7" h, amber, girl and foliage
dec, white trim, bulbous, amber ball
stopper. .175.00
Cordial, 2-1/2" h, cylindrical, cranberry,
colorless stem and base, white
enameled Victorian girl on one, boy on
other, facing pr 220.00
Creamer, 2-1/2" d, 3-3/4" h, green, inverted
thumbprint pattern,
green handle 145.00
Ewer, 10" h, 3-1/8" d, cranberry, girl in
garden setting dec, clear handle 220.00
Miniature, pitcher, 2" h, sapphire blue,
white enameled dec 225.00
Mug, 3" h, 2-1/8" d, cranberry, boy,
clear handle 80.00
Perfume Bottle, 4-5/8" h, cranberry, little
girl, clear ball stopper. 165.00

Tumblers, honey amber, cobalt blue
pedestal base, boy and girl dec, price
for pair, $165.

Pitcher, 9-1/2" h, medium green, boy and
girl dec .250.0010-1/2" h, clear, man in
sailboat, ruffled top 125.00
Plate, 6-1/4" d, cobalt blue, white enamel
girl with butterfly net 125.00
Plate, 11" d, black amethyst,
running stag 285.00
Stein, 4" h, smoky amber, boy and girl,
pewter and glass lids, pr 110.00
Toothpick Holder, cranberry, girl and floral
sprays 55.00
Tumbler, 2-1/4" h, cranberry, boy on one,
girl on other, price for pair. 100.00
Tumbler, 4-1/2" h, blue, boy, ribbed. 65.00
Vase, 4" h, cranberry, boy and girl reading
books, price for pair 110.00
Vase, 5" h, robin's egg blue, girl running
through flower field dec. 125.00
Vase, 12-1/2" h, green, woman holding
hoop around her, birds perched on
hoop dec 330.00
Wine Bottle, 9" h, 3-1/8" d, cranberry, girl
holding floral spray dec,
clear stopper 165.00

Matchbooks

Don't play with matches. Save their
covers instead. A great collection can
be built for a relatively small sum of
money. Matchcover collectors gain a
fair amount of their new material
through swapping. A few collectors
specialize in covers that include figur-
al-shaped or decorated matches. If
you get into this, make certain you
keep them stored in a covered tin container and in a cool location. If you

Dakota Motor Hotel, girlies, $2.

don't, your collection may catch fire
and go up in smoke.

Clubs: Casino Matchcover Collectors
Club, 5001 Albridge Way, Mount Lau-
rel, NJ 08054; Rathkamp Matchcover
Society, 25 Huntsman's Horn, The
Woodlands, TX 77380; The American
Matchcover Collecting Club, P.O. Box
18481, Asheville, NC 28814. Note:
There are more than 30 regional clubs
throughout the United States and Can-
ada.

Newsletters: *Matchcover Classified*,
16425 Dam Rd. #31, Clearlake, CA
95422; *The Match Hunter*, 740 Poplar,
Boulder, Co. 80304.

Abbott's Bitters Tones the Stomach . . 2.00
Ascot Aromatic Pipe Mixture 8.00
Auto Allied Mutual Association 3.50
Banks 02
Big Joe Sells Best Because It Is Best,
diamond quality 2.00
Billiards 05
Black Angus Motel 2.25
Bob's Tavern, Brewster, NE 2.00
Casinos. 05
Chevrolet, 1952 . . . . 3.00
Chesty Morgan 14.00
Court of the Moon Gardens 3.50
Eagle Star Insurance 8.00
Feuer's Restaurant, Chicago, diamond
quality 2.00

Gem Blades, $1.50.

For Safety, Buy War Bonds-Stamps . .4.00
Gardena Bowl, bowling ball striker . . .7.00
Girlies, non stock. 40
Griffith's Sinclair Station,
    Danielsville, GA 2.00
Holiday Inns, stock design 10
Hotel Detroiter, Your Headquarters. .12.00
Hotel La Fayette, Lexington, KY 3.00
Joe Louis/Max Schmeling Championship
    Fight, Kolb's Restaurant,
    New Orleans 3.00
King's Fare Cocktails, Kenosha WI. . .8.00
Lone Star Beer, stock cov 2.50
Lou's Diner, Mill Plain, CT. 3.00
Matchtones, Universal trademark 10
Medford Cafe, Mystic 6010,
    diamond quality 2.25
New York Telephone Co. 3.50
Nile Hilton, Cairo, Egypt 5.00
Odd Strikers, Lion Match Co. 15.00
Patriotic. 05
Playboy Club, Atlanta 2.00
Pontiac Motor Division 3.50
Presidential Yacht, Patricia. 10.00
Pull for Willkie, Pullquick Match 28.00
Remember Pearl Harbor, red, white and
    blue, anti-Japan slogan on cover, Uncle
    Sam on back, early 1940s 10.00
Revelation Tooth Powder, 1930s 6.00
San Diego Zoo, c1970 . . . . .1.00
Shurfire Coffee, 1930s 1.50
Standex Egyptian Blend Cigarettes . .5.00
Texas Centennial, Dallas, 1936 . . . . .2.50

The United Merchant Seaman's Service
    Club 5.00
Twenty One, Bermuda. 22.00
Vote For Governor Brown, photo. . . . 2.00
Washington Bicentennial, 1932 . . . . . 5.00

Matchbox Toys

Leslie Rodney Smith founded Lesney Products, an English company, in 1947. They produced the first Matchbox toys. In 1953, the trade name "Matchbox" was registered and the first die-cast cars were made on a 1:75 scale. In 1979 Lesney produced more than 5.5 million cars per week. In 1982, Universal International bought Lesney.

Clubs: American-International Matchbox Collectors & Exchange Club, 532 Chestnut Street, Lynn, MA 01904; Matchbox Collectors Club, P.O. Box 977, Newfield, NJ 08344; The Matchbox International Collectors Association, P.O. Box 28072, Waterloo, 6JB Canada; Matchbox U.S.A., 62 Saw Mill Rd., Durham, CT 06422.

Allis-Chalmers Earth Scraper, 1961 25.00
1920 Aveling Porter Steam Roller, Models
    of Yesteryear, 1959 . . . . 65.00
Baja Dune Buggy. 10.00
14-C Bedford Ambulance, 1962 . . . 18.00
Bedford Car Transporter, 1957,
    blue body 65.00
Bedford Car Transporter, 1957, Red cab,
    gray trailer. 150.00
BMW Sport Coupe, orange, 1980 . . . 2.00
Boss Mustang, 1972 . . . . 12.00
Cadillac, 1965 . . . . 6.00
Caterpillar DW20 Earth Scraper,
    1957 . . . . 45.00

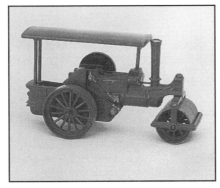

Road Roller #11, green body, red wheels, $95.

Playset, Action Central, $25.

1957 Chevrolet Belair Sport
    Convertible 25.00
Comm Lyons Maid Ice Cream Truck,
    1963 . . . . .35.00
Double Decker London Bus, 1954 . .60.00
59-B Ford Fairlane Fire Chief Car,
    1963 . . . . .20.00
9-C Merryweather Marquis Fire Engine,
    1959 . . . . .15.00
Ford Galaxy Police Car, 1966 . . . . .30.00
Ford Model A Van,
    Champion Spark Plug, 1982 . . . .10.00
Ford Model A Van, Kellogg's Corn Flakes
    Advertising, 1982. . . . . .10.00
1912 Ford Model T Tanker, 1982. . .18.00
1912 Ford Model T Truck, issued
    1979, 1982 . . . . .25.00
Ford Thames Singer Van, 1958 . . . .40.00
Ford Thunderbird, 1959 . . . . .45.00
Fowler "Big Lion" Showman's Engine,
    Models of Yesteryear, 1958 . . . .80.00
1936 GMC Van, Goblin Electric Cleaners
    logo, 1988 . . . . .18.00
1936 Jaguar SS 100, Models of
    Yesteryear, 1977 . . . . .30.00
Jeep Hot Rod, 1971 . . . . .20.00
Lamborghini Miura, 1970 . . . . .15.00
Leyland Site Office Truck, 1970 . . . .15.00
Lincoln Continental, 1970. . . . . .5.00
1899 London Double Decker Horse-Drawn
    Bus, Models of Yesteryear, red,
    1959 . . . . .75.00
1907 London E Class Tram Car, Models of
    Yesteryear, 1956. . . . . .60.00
Mack Dump Truck, 1968 . . . . .30.00
Massey Harris Tractor,
    4-A, with fenders 65.00
Massey Harris Tractor, 4-B, without
    fenders 60.00
Mercedes 500 SL Convertible, 1991 .5.00
Midnight Magic, 1972 . . . . .6.00
1926 Morris Cowley Bullnose, Models of
    Yesteryear, 1954. . . . . .80.00
1906 Rolls Royce Silver Ghost, Models of
    Yesteryear, issued 1969, 1982 . .35.00
Orange Peel, 1971 . . . . .8.00
Swamp Rat, 1976. . . . . .8.00
Weasel, 1974 . . . . .10.00

Mixing Bowls: Nelson McCoy Sanitary Stoneware Co., shield in circle mark, 1926; (left) #4, yellow, 11-1/2" d, $20; (right) mkd "4," green, 9-5/8" d, $15.

McCoy Pottery

Like Abingdon Pottery, this attractive pottery is sought by those no longer able to afford Roseville and Weller pottery. Commemorative cookie jars and planters seem to be rapidly increasing in price, like the Apollo Spaceship cookie jar at $1,000. These specialty items bring more from secondary collectors than from McCoy collectors, who realize the vast quantity of material available in the market.

Beware of reproductions. The Nelson McCoy Pottery Co., is making modern copies of their period pieces. New collectors are often confused by them.

Newsletters: *The NM Express*, 3081 Rock Creek Dr., Broomfield, Co. 80020; *Our McCoy Matters*, P.O. Box 14255, Parkville, MO 64152.

Cookie Jars
Asparagus 50.00
Cabin 50.00
Cookie Kettle 22.00
Forbidden Fruit 65.00
Granny 47.00

Urn, Brown Onyx, 7" h, $50.

Milk Can 25.00
Oaken Bucket 35.00

Other
Basket, basketweave design, green and
   white ext, white int, 1957 . . . . . . 25.00
Bean Pot, cov, brown 8.00
Bowl, 6" d, matte green 25.00
Bud Vase, Lily 55.00
Console Bowl, 8-3/4" d, blue,
   tulip dec 7.50
Cornucopia, Bittersweet, 4-1/2" by
   11-1/2", double 18.00
Decanter, Astronaut 45.00
Fern Box, blue 14.00
Jardiniere, 9" h, brown 50.00
Mug, Suburbia pattern, yellow 7.50
Pitcher, elephant, white, 1940s 45.00
Planter, Baby Birds, green 20.00
Planter, Sprinkling Can, white,
   rose decal 6.50
Salt and Pepper Shakers, pr,
   cabbage 10.00

Vase, 8-1/4" h, chrysanthemums, late 1940s, paper label, $25.

Soap Dish, Lucile 100.00
Strawberry Jar, stoneware, blue 24.00
Teapot, Grecian pattern 25.00
Teapot, Pine Cone 75.00
Vase, 7-1/2" h, mottled green, mkd "Brush,
   #709" 18.00
Wall Pocket, Sunflower, orange 18.00

Medical Items

Anything medical is collectible. Doctors often discard instruments, never realizing that the minute an object becomes obsolete, it also becomes collectible. Many a flea market treasure begins life in a garbage can behind the doctor's office. Stress condition and completeness. Specialize in one area. Remember some instruments do not display well. My wife will not let me keep my rectal examiners in the living room.

Club: Medical Collectors Association, 1300 Morris Park Ave., Bronx, NY 10461.

Newsletter: *Scientific, Medical & Mechanical Antiques*, P.O. Box 412, Taneytown, MD 21787.

Books
McClellan's Regional Anatomy, Vol. 2,
   1894 . . . . 18.00
Obstetrics, Manual for Students & Practitioners, 1903 . . . . 6.00
People's Medical Lighthouse, Dr. Harmon
   Knox, New York, 1854 . . . . 20.00

Bottles, glass
Atlas Medicine Co., 9-1/4" h, amber . 15.00
Dr. Nywall's Family Medicine,
   7-1/2" h, amber 15.00
Elliman's Embrocation,
   yellowish aqua 20.00
Himalya The Kola Compound Natures,
   7-1/4" h, yellow amber 40.00
J. Paul Liebe, golden yellow 15.00
Phillip's Emulsion Cod Liver Oil,
   amber 10.00
Box, Dr. Green's Nervura Nerve Tonic,
   wood, black print, stenciled 60.00

Signs
Dr. D. Jaynes Family Medicines, glass,
   emb silver and gold foil lettering, gold
   border, black ground, framed . . 110.00
Marvine for Headache & Neuralgia, tin,
   ivory lettering on green 22.50
Pepto Bismol, figural, bottle, die-cut
   cardboard, red and
   black lettering 50.00

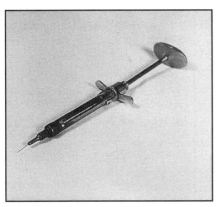

Dental Syringe, $25.

Other

Advertising Trade Card, Lydia E.
  Pinkham's Vegetable Compound,
  scenic, color, text on back 10.00
Almanac, Dr. D. Jayne's Medicine,
  1915 . . . . .4.00
Blotter, Smith Brothers Cough Drops 30.00
Catalog, Brewer & Co., pharmaceutical,
  1939 . . . . .20.00
Cookbook, Dr. Ward's Medical Co. Cook
  Book, illus, c1920 . . . . .3.00
Coupon, Dr. Blumer's products premiums,
  floral dinnerware. 25
Door Push, Foley Kidney Pills, 6-1/2" by 3",
  yellow and black. 75.00
Display, Smith Brothers Cough Drops, die-
  cut cardboard 150.00
Forceps, dental, silver-plated, handle
  design. .50.00
Matchbook Cover, Tums, set of 12, front
  strike, colorful. 11.50
Mortar and Pestle, 9" h, ash burl,
  turned. 125.00
Pill Maker, brass, iron and wood, 12" l,
  American, c1900 . . . . .130.00
Pliers, dental, nerve canal. 15.00
Pocket Mirror, Nature's Remedy Tablets,
  2-1/8" d. 40.00
Ruler, Tums, 12" l, wood. 5.00

Bleeding Knife, brass case, $45.

Stethoscope, monaural, metal 110.00
Thermometer, Ramon's pills, 21" l,
    wood, stenciled 130.00

Melmac

Durable Melmac dinnerware was all
the rage in the late 1960s and early
1970s. Children could finally be as-
signed the chore of washing the dishes without fear of loss and breakage.
Despite its claims of being indestructi-
ble, continued dishwasher washing
will take its toll. If you plan to collect
Melmac and use it, you'll have to re-
vert to hand washing.

Durawear/Capac
Cup 5.00
Plate, charcoal, 10" d 7.00
Platter, salmon red, 14" l 8.00
Serving Bowl, pink 6.00

Marcrest
Bowl, turquoise, 6" d 2.00
Creamer, brown 3.00
Cup and Saucer, pastel 3.00
Serving Bowl, divided, 11-1/2" l 4.00

Miramar
Cup and Saucer, pink and white 3.00
Serving Bowl, brown, 8" d 4.00
Sugar Bowl, avocado 2.00

Monteray
Bowl, yellow, 5" d 3.00
Cup and Saucer, light blue 4.50
Plate, red, 10" d 4.00
Platter, yellow, 11" l 5.00

Prolon
Plate, red, 10" d, Florence 8.00
Platter, yellow, 14" d, mkd "Grant Crest by
    Prolon" 5.00
Cup and Saucer, turquoise 5.00
Serving Bowl, oval, turquoise, 11" d . 8.00

Riviera-Ware
Bowl, blue, 5-1/2" d 3.00
Cup and Saucer. 4.00
Plate, yellow, 10" d 5.00

Royalon
Cup and Saucer, red and white 3.00
Saucer, red 1.50
Serving Bowl, divided, red, 10" d 4.50

Stetson
Butter Dish, pink 7.00
Cup and Saucer, pink 4.00
Gravy Boat, pink 5.00
Mug, salmon 3.00

Plate, turquoise, 9" d 3.00
Platter, brown, 12" d 5.00
Sugar Bowl, pink. 5.00

Windsor
Cup and Saucer, turquoise. 3.50
Serving Bowl, divided, white, 9" d . . . 5.00
Sugar and Creamer, turquoise,
    missing lid 6.50

Metlox

In 1921 T C. Prouty and Willis, his
son, founded Proutyline Products, a
company designed to develop
Prouty's various inventions. Metlox (a
contraction of metallic oxide) was established in 1927. The company began producing a line of solid-color
dinnerware similar to that produced by
Bauer. In 1934, the line was fully developed and sold under the Poppytrail
trademark. Other dinnerware lines
produced in the 1930s include Mission
Bell, Pintoria and Yorkshire. In the late
1930s, Metlox introduced a line called
Modern Masterpieces, featuring bookends, busts, figural vases, figures and
wall pockets.

The California Ivy pattern was introduced in 1946, California Provincial
and Homestead Provincial in 1950,
Red Rooster in 1955, California Strawberry in 1961, Sculptured Grape in
1963 and Della Robbia in 1965. A
number of new shapes and lines came
out in the 1950s, among which are Aztec, California Contempora, California
Free Form, California Mobile and Navajo.

When Vernon Kilns ceased operation in 1958, Metlox bought the trade
name and select dinnerware molds,
establishing a separate Vernon Ware
branch. This line soon rivaled the Poppytrail patterns. Between 1946 and
1956 Metlox made a series of ceramic
cartoon characters, under license from
Walt Disney. A line of planters and
Poppets were marketed in the 1960s
and 1970s. Recent production includes novelty cookie jars and Colorstax, a revival solid color dinnerware
pattern. The company ceased operations in 1989.

Periodical: *The Pottery Collectors Express*, P.O. Box 221, Mayview, MO 64071.

California Ivy

Creamer	.22.00
Cup and Saucer	.14.00
Gravy Boat, minor chip on base	.30.00
Plate, 6-1/2" d	.8.00
Plate, 9-1/2" d	.16.00
Platter, 13" l, oval	.50.00
Serving Bowl, 9" d, cone-shape	.40.00
Serving Bowl, round	.40.00
Sugar Bowl, cov	.25.00
Vegetable Bowl, divided	.45.00

Homestead Provincial Blue

Cruet Set, with stand, #519	.100.00
Marmalade, cov.	.80.00
Oil Cruet, orig stopper	.45.00
Salt and Pepper Shakers, pr, cone-shape	.35.00

Provincial Blue

Batter Pitcher	.75.00
Coaster	.15.00
Cup and Saucer	.18.00
Fruit Bowl	.15.00
Gravy	.50.00
Plate, bread and butter	.8.00
Plate, dinner	.20.00
Plate, salad	.12.00
Platter	.40.00
Salt and Pepper Shakers, pr	.24.00
Vegetable Bowl, covered	.80.00
Vegetable Bowl, open, round	.40.00

Red Rooster, figural

Bread Basket	.50.00
Casserole, small	.75.00
Coffee Carafe	.100.00
Cup and Saucer	.20.00
Eggcup	.20.00
Plate, bread and butter	.5.00
Plate, dinner	.14.00
Salad	.20.00
Salt and Pepper Shakers, pr	.56.00
Vegetable Bowl, divided	.50.00
Vegetable Bowl, round	.40.00

Other

Colorstax, fern green, 15 pcs, four dinner and salad plates, four mugs and three cereal bowls 100.00
Poppytrail Aztec, platter, 13" l, oval. .45.00

Mexican Collectibles

When you live on the East Coast and do not roam west of Chicago, you are not going to see south-of-the-border collectibles, except for the tourist souvenirs brought home by visitors to Central and South America. However, the growing Hispanic population is looking back to its roots and starting to proudly display family and other items acquired in Mexico.

Within the past year there has been a growing interest in Mexican jewelry. In fact, several new books have been published about the subject. Mexican pottery and textiles are also attracting collector attention. At the moment, buy only high-quality, handmade products. Because of their brilliant colors, Mexican collectibles accent almost any room setting. This is an area to watch.

Vase, 6-1/4" h, Texas Centennial 1836-1936, brown, blue and green, $60.

Microscopes

Microscopes are the best collectible to epitomize the history of science. High quality, signed, all-brass instruments are hard to find but easy to sell. Signatures are important, although turn-of-the-century microscopes signed "Bausch & Lomb" or "Spencer" are quite common. American-made microscopes are generally more valuable than imported instruments.

Do not polish instruments you plan to resell. Collectors hate this! Be wary of missing or replaced parts, especially the mirror. Having a large antique microscope's original case can increase its value by $50 to $100. Most serious microscope and toy collectors are uninterested in toy microscopes, although exceptions do exist.

Advisor: Randy D. Watson, MD, 545 SE Oak, Ste. D, Hillsboro, OR 97123.

Club: Maryland Microscopical Society, 8621 Polk St., McLean, VA 22102.

Bausch & Lomb, Brass, monocular, case	.150.00
Bausch & Lomb, Little Gem	.75.00
Bockett, oil microscope lamp, c1880	.125.00
Continental, unsgd, all brass, 13" h	.175.00
Culpepper, unsgd, c1800	.750.00
Dissecting Microscope, single eyepiece	.55.00
Drum, student set, brass, unsgd, case	.65.00
English, unsgd, Bar-Limb, c1860	.275.00
French, unsgd, pillar-style	.125.00
Gilbert, toy set, #10, green wood case	.25.00
Gilbert, toy set, metal box	.15.00
Gundlach, case-mounted, c1905	.175.00
Hensoldt, portable, field microscope	.150.00
Junior, portable, tripod legs	.60.00
Ken-A-Vision, projection microscope, highly polished aluminum	.75.00
Meccano, cardboard case	.25.00
Microcraft #277, student set, blue wood box	.15.00
Microtome, slide-making machine	.75.00
Olympus, monocular, modern	.125.00

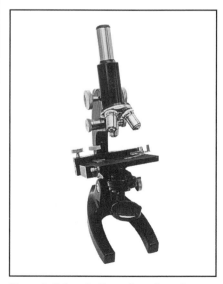

Bausch & Lomb, three-lens turret mechanical stage, clips, $250.

Porter, student set, metal case 15.00

R&J Beck, binocular, c1870 . . . . . .850.00

Ring, toy set, c1935, cardboard case15.00

Ring, toy set, c1935, wood case 35.00

Skil Craft, student set, metal case. . .12.50

Spencer, professional quality 175.00

Tasco, student set, 750-power,
    wood box 15.00

Tasco, student set, 1200-power,
    wood box 20.00

Zeiss, research microscope,
    black and brass 300.00

Militaria

Soldiers have returned home with the spoils of war as long as there have been soldiers and wars. Look at the Desert Storm material that is starting to arrive on the market. Many collectors tend to collect material relating to wars taking place in their young adulthood or related to re-enactment groups to which they belong. It pays to specialize. The two obvious choices are a specific war or piece of equipment. Never underestimate the enemy. Nazi material remains the strongest segment of the market. Reproduct-ions abound. Be especially careful of any Civil War and Nazi material.

Clubs: American Society of Military Insignia Collectors, 526 Lafayette Ave., Palmerton, PA 18071; Association of American Military Uniform Collectors, P.O. Box 1876, Elyria, OH 44036; Company of Military Historians, North Main St., Westbrook, CT 06498; Imperial German Military Collectors Association, 82 Atlantic St., Keyport, NJ 07735; Military Collectors Society, 137

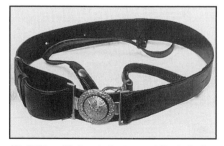

Civil War, Union infantry soldier's belt, 1863, $450.

Civil War, prisoner's bone jewelry, 10-1/2" I, $225.

S. Almar Dr., Fort Lauderdale, FL 33334.

Periodicals: *Military Collectors' News*, P.O. Box 702073, Tulsa, OK 74170; *Military Magazine*, P.O. Box 2925, Framingham Center, MA 01701; *Military Trader*, P.O. Box 1050, Dubuque, IA 52004; *North South Trader*, P.O. Drawer 631, Orange, VA 22960.

Civil War

Bayonet, U.S. musket 50.00

Bottle, ink, umbrella-style, aqua,
    open pontil 20.00

Bullet, Sharps carbine, four raised rings,
    .54 caliber 20.00

Bullet Mold, picket pattern bullet . . . 45.00

Cartridge Box, Weston 300.00

Button, Louisiana state seal, two pc,
    rope edging 115.00

Field Glasses, 7-1/2" I, brass, Lemaire
    Fabt, Paris 125.00

Helmet Badge, brass shield and eagle,
    company number in center 45.00

Insignia, brass, lieutenant 25.00

World War II, AAF M-3 flak helmet, modified M-1 design, flocked green finish, OD web liner, leather neck strap, pivoting ear flaps, worn by B-24 pilots, $45.

Leg Irons, old barrel key 85.00

Mess Gear, knife, fork, spoon, two pc
    combination, "Richards patent of July
    23, 1861" 125.00

Mess Kit, bone handles,
    orig leather case 175.00

Plate, 8" d, 50th Anniversary Battle of
    Gettysburg, W. Adams & Co. 50.00

Pocketknife, Sheffield 75.00

Ribbon, blue-gray, Lincoln's head
    surrounded by "With Malice Toward
    None, With Charity For All,"
    1861-65 . . . . .90.00

Shell Jacket, Union cavalry, buttons, lining
    and inspector's marks 425.00

Sword, NCO, dated 1863 . . . . .275.00

Tintype, full length, unidentified
    Confederate Cavalry man, gear, sword
    and carbine 450.00

World War I

Ammunition Belt, olive web, rimless eagle
    snap on pocket flap, brass, Mills . 75.00

Blanket Strap, leather, brown, buckles,
    strap, center hook 36.00

Blouse, summer, Army, cotton, tan, bronze
    removable buttons 20.00

Dog Tag, Navy, oval, man's name, USN
    mark on front, thumbprint reverse side,
    1917 . . . . .28.00

First Aid Kit, canvas, bi-fold, snap lid,
    contents 55.00

Gas Mask, carrying can, shoulder strap,
    canister attached to bottom,
    German 75.00

Grenade Pouch, canvas, tan,
    web strap 20.00

Helmet, Army 50.00

Helmet, Doughboy, mini, Nashville,
    1934 . . . . .59.00

Medal, Iron Cross 35.00

Patch, Army Medical Chevrons, 1902,
    maroon, felt, branch design on rect
    white cotton base 19.00

Periscope, wood,
    used in trench warfare 75.00

Pinback Button, 7/8" d, Western Electric
    Soldier's Comfort Club, black and
    white 8.00

Pinback Button, 1-3/4" d, Welcome Home
    Soldiers of York County, PA 20.00

Poster, "Lend the Way They Fight, Buy
    Bonds to Your Utmost," full color action
    scene, red and black lettering,
    green border 50.00

Uniform, U.S. Army, engineer, coat, belt,
    pants, cap, canvas leggings, wood
    puttees, leather gaiters, canteen300.00

Visor Cap, wool, navy blue, crown top,
    black mohair band, stamped wreath
    with lyre in center, gold wire chin-strap,
    size 7-1/8" 25.00

Water Bag, canvas, portable, strap,
crossed ropes bottom,
dated 1918 . . . . .20.00

World War II

Ammunition Bag, canvas, web straps, mkd
"US," 1945 . . . . .20.00
Aviator Sunglasses, AAF, green tint
lenses, bridge and forehead pads, wire
frame, leather case, snap flap . . .50.00
Badge, Nazi, General Assault, silver,
c1940 . . . . .30.00
Binoculars, Army, M-17, field type, 7-1/2" l,
olive drab, 7-by-50 power,
fixed optics 100.00
Book, A. Hitler, *Mein Kampf*, 1933, 407
pgs, dj. .15.00
Cigarette Case, plastic, yellow,
lift-off lid 12.00
Envelope, Iwo Jima flag raising, 8/29/45,
GF Hadley artist 15.00
Flag, 2" by 3", Nazi 40.00
Flashlight, Army, plastic,
metal belt clip 28.00
Knife, black finish blade, "USN" and "Mark
S Sheath" mkd on guard, gray web belt,
gray-fiber scabbard 50.00
Magazine, *Time*, 1942, Nazi cov, Gen.
Field Marshall Fedor Von Bock . .34.00
Manual, Recognition Pictorial Manual,
Bureau of Aeronautics, Navy
Department, Washington, DC, June
1943, contains silhouettes and
technical information on Allied and Axis
aircraft, 6" by 10", 80 pgs, black and
white 45.00
Oxygen Mask, AAF, rubber, web-strap,
ribbed-hose 47.00
Patch, pilot's wings, leather, AAF, emb,
standard design, flying jacket
attachment type 30.00
Pencil Holder, 3-1/2" h, plastic, red, white
and blue, marked "Victory" 10.00
Periscope, 30" l, steel tube 56.00
Pistol Holster, U.S., leather, brown, emb,
mkd Boyt/44 . . . . .84.00
Poster, 22" by 28", "Fill It! Harvest War
Crops," full color 45.00
Sea Bag, USMC, canvas, tan 20.00
Sewing Kit, AAF, cotton, roll-up, thread and
safety pins 26.00
Telescope, metal tube, 1943 . . . . . .25.00
Wallet, Japanese, woven and leather,
Rising Sun 45.00

Vietnam

Aviator Flare Pen, 4" l, aluminum,
spring-loaded firing pin 16.00
Book, *Frontline: The Commands of Wm.
Chase*, 1975, autographed 1st edition,
228 pgs .38.00
Bracelet, POW, names 25.00

Dog Muzzle, leather, tan, multi-piece,
1968 . . . . 22.00
Helmet, U.S. tanker, Fiberglas, dark green,
intercom system on side 50.00
Medal, Air Force Commendation, parade
ribbon and lapel bar, orig case . . 20.00
Medal, Vietnam Service 15.00
Medical Kit, pouch, nylon, plastic, contents,
belt-clip back 40.00
Walkie-Talkie, metal,
web-wrist strap 28.00

Milk Bottles

There is an entire generation of
young adults to whom the concept of
milk in a bottle is a foreign idea. In another 15 years, a book like this will
have to contain a chapter on plastic
milk cartons. I hope you are saving
some.

When buying a bottle, make certain
the glass is clear of defects from manufacture and wear and the label and/or
wording in fine or better condition. Buy
odd-sized bottles and bottles with special features. Don't forget the caps.
They are collectible too.

Club: National Association of Milk Bottle Collectors, Inc., 4 Ox Bow Rd.,
Westport, CT 06880.

Periodical: *The Udder Collectibles*,
HC 73 Box 1, Smithville Flats, NY
13841.

Bellow's Falls Creamery,
John T. O'Connor, VT, qt 35.00
Brenner's Coop, qt, round,
red pyroglaze 35.00
Bringhams Dairy, Burlington, VT, qt, round,
orange pyroglaze 38.00
The Dairy Farm Ice & Cold Storage Co.,
Ltd. Hong Kong, 1/2-pint,
red pyroglaze 5.00
Dublin Coop Dairies,
pint, war slogan 30.00
Ethan Allen Creamery, Essex Jet, VT, qt,
round, orange pyroglaze 35.00
Farmers Dairy Co., Inc., pint, picture of
baby, black pyroglaze 17.50
Frain's Dairies, Wilmington, DE, qt, Minute
Man on back with war slogan "Buy
United States War Bonds," brown
pyroglaze 100.00
Gray's Harbor Dairy Products,
1/2-pint .7.00
Gridley Dairy Co., pint, amethyst, base
mkd "TMFGCO". 17.50
Hastings Springfield, VT, qt, emb . . .25.00
Meadow Gold, qt, cream top 25.00
Meadow Gold, 1/2-gal, sq. 12.50
Merrils Dairy, Keesville, NY, qt, war slogan
"Think, Act, Work for Victory" on back,
orange pyroglaze 86.00
Morse's Dairy, Morrisville, VT, qt, sq, green
pyroglaze 25.00
Monterey Bay Milk Distributors, Inc.,
1/4-pint 20.00
Mount Mansfield, VT, qt, sq, cow skiing,
green pyroglaze 150.00
Proctor Creamer, Proctor, VT,
qt, emb 35.00
RJ Mercure, Dairy Winooski, VT, qt, round,
orange pyroglaze 55.00

Borden's, miniature creamer, 2" h, py-roglaze, $7.

Producer's Milk Co., quart, 9-1/2" h, emb label, $12.

Royal Perfectly Pasteurized It's The
  Cream 10.00
Spokane Bottle Exchange, Inc., qt, round,
  blue pyroglaze 15.00
Sunrise Farm Dairy Baltic, CT, 1/2-pint,
  two-color pyroglaze, orange sunrise on
  front, red "Good Morning and Good
  Health" on back 7.00
Sunset Farm Dairy, Woodstock, VT, qt, sq,
  orange pyroglaze 20.00
Sweets Dairy, Bennington, VT, qt, round,
  black pyroglaze 65.00
This bottle property of West Coast Dairy,
  Everett, WA, qt. 12.00
UVM, Burlington, VT, qt, round, amber
  pyroglaze 65.00

Milk Glass

Milk glass is an opaque white glass that became popular during the Victorian era. A scientist will tell you that it is made by adding oxide of tin to a batch of clear glass. Most collect it because it's pretty. Companies such as Atterbury, McKee and Westmoreland have all produced fine examples in novelties, often of the souvenir variety, as well as household items. Old-timers focus heavily on milk glass made before 1920. However, there are some great pieces from the post-1920 period that you would be wise not to overlook.

Sugar Castor, Paneled Sprig, 4-1/2" h, $40.

Milk glass has remained in continuous production since it was first invented. Many firms reproduce old patterns. Be careful. Old-timers will tell you that if a piece has straw marks, it is probably correct. Some modern manufacturers who want to fool you might have also added them in the mold. Watch out for a "K" in a diamond. This is the mark on milk glass reproductions from the 1960s made by the Kemple Glass Co.

Club: National Milk Glass Collectors Society, 46 Almond Dr., Hershey, PA 17033.

Avon, figural
Capitol Decanter 10.00
Cornucopia 8.00
Poodle Cologne 8.00

Bottles
5-1/2" h, emb flower, Fostoria,
  #2519 . . . . 50.00
10" h, leaf and scroll design,
  brown roses 45.00
11" h, scroll ftd, crown topper 40.00
11-1/2" h, decanter, grape pattern,
  Imperial Glass. 45.00

Bowls
3" h, 4-3/4" d, seashell, ftd,
  Cambridge 45.00
8" h, 4-3/4" d, handled,
  Daisy Ray design 20.00
8-1/2" w, 12" l, daisy and button panel,
  wing-like handles 25.00
10-1/4" d, open lacy edge,
  Atterbury 35.00

Compotes
Bird, pedestal base, Guernsey Glass 40.00
Blue, swirled split-rib,
  Porteiux-Vallerystahl. 50.00
Doric border, three-column stem,
  Westmoreland. 40.00

Covered Dish
Cat on Lacy Base, Westmoreland . . 95.00
Civil War Cannon on Snare Drum,
  Westmoreland. 100.00
Dove, milk glass base, crystal lid,
  Imperial. 95.00
Fish 50.00
Lion, scroll base. 85.00
Love Birds, Westmoreland. 70.00
Resting Camel, Westmoreland . . . 110.00
Santa on Sleigh, Westmoreland . . . 80.00
Swan, raised wing, red glass eyes 175.00

Plates
7-1/2" d, beaded edge, iris motif,
  Westmoreland. 15.00

8" d, Petalware, ribbon edge, MacBeth
  Evans Glass 12.00
12" d, Souvenir of Detroit, gold, painted
  roses 20.00
15" d, Eagle and Shield, Mar Cor . . . 45.00
16" d, medallion center, hp man and
  woman in garden scene 50.00

Vases
3-3/4" h, hat-shape, amber crest, hp
  flowers, gold, Fenton 30.00
9" h, Scroll and Daisy 20.00
10" h, Bristol type, hp foliage, black edge
  and base band. 40.00

Other
Barber Bottle, 7" h, "Witch Hazel". . . 80.00
Candlestick, 4" h, satin finish,
  emb roses 30.00
Candlestick, 6-1/4" h, double, English
  Hobnail, Westmoreland,
  price for pair 70.00
Cake Stand, 6" h, 9-1/8" d, floral trim,
  multicolored ring base, Challinor,
  Taylor 45.00
Collar Box, 8" d, convex domed top, bow tie
  base, patented April 10, 1894 . . . 75.00
Dresser Box, 3-7/8" d, emb girl and doll
  on lid 20.00
Goblet, Dewberry, Kemple Glass . . . 15.00
Goblet, Jewel & Dewdrop,
  Kemple Glass 15.00
Handkerchief Box, 5-3/4 w, 5" d,
  three kittens. 70.00
Ladle, curved handle, ice lip 40.00
Lamp, electric, 7-5/8" h,
  dancing couple figural 40.00
Lamp, electric, 8-3/4" h, Violets in the
  Snow, Fenton Art. 125.00
Rolling Pin, wood handles,
  Cambridge. 50.00
Toothpick Holder, boy with basket, blue,
  Vallerysthal 65.00

Miniatures

If you want to find miniatures at flea markets, look in cases, because the size that you are most likely to find is "doll house." The other two sizes are child's and salesman's sample. These rarely show up at flea markets. Beware. Miniatures have been sold for years. Modern crafts people continue to make great examples. Alas, their handiwork can be easily aged so that it will fool most buyers. Also Cracker Jack giveaways, charms, etc., should not be confused with miniatures.

Sofa, china, hp floral dec, gold trim, Continental, late 19th C, $75.

Clubs: International Guild of Miniature Artisans, P.O. Box 71, Bridgeport, NY 18080; National Association of Miniature Enthusiasts, P.O. Box 69, Carmel, IN 46032.

Periodicals: *Doll Castle News*, P.O. Box 247, Washington, NJ 07882; *Miniature Collector*, 30595 Eight Mile Rd., Livonia, MI 48152; *Nutshell News*, 21027 Crossroads Cir., P.O. Box 1612, Waukesha, WI 53187.

Child's

Chair, Windsor, 26" h, bamboo, yellow striping and stenciled flowers on crest dec 250.00

Cradle, 37" l, walnut, dovetailed, shaped sides, hand holds, cut-out rockers 225.00

Measuring Cup, Pyrex. 10.00

Piano, Falconer, 22 keys, stool. . . .225.00

Rocker, 9-1/4" h, arms, painted blue 165.00

Wash Bowl, Dutch children dec 60.00

Doll House Furniture, Nancy Forbes Dream House Furniture, Set #171, American Toy & Furniture Co., wood, seven pcs, $50.

Doll House

Bed, Petite Princess 18.00

Candelabra, Petite Princess 20.00

Cradle, wood 25.00

Desk, 5-1/2" h, lady's, chair, c1875 . 90.00

Dining Room Set, table, two benches, cast iron, white lacquer finish, Arcade, price for three-pc set 50.00

Fireplace Set, cast metal, includes mantel, gas insert, screen and tools, T&B, England 65.00

Ironing Board, cast iron, folding, Kilgore, c1930 . . . . 20.00

Kitchen Set, cast metal, partial set, orig box, Tootsie Toy 50.00

Range, Roper, 6" h, painted cast iron, Arcade 100.00

Stool, metal, Tootsietoy 12.00

Stove, metal, Tootsietoy, c1920 . . . 25.00

Tea Set, porcelain, cov teapot, creamer, cov sugar and tray 50.00

Vanity, Renwal. 8.00

Salesman's Sample

Chair, 9" by 4", shoe store 55.00

Cash Register, RC Allen, dated 1958 . . . . 25.00

Food Grinder, 3" h, JP Co.. . . . . 35.00

Gate, 18" l, 10-1/2" h, wood and metal 200.00

Harrow, 7-1/2" l, iron and wood, horse-drawn 95.00

Loom, 9-1/2" w, 15-1/2" d, 12-1/2" h, "Miniature Loom" paper label, NRA ink stamp 25.00

Lunch Pail, 4" h, metal, nickel-plated, cup, two liners, Lisk 275.00

Model Kits

A plastic model kit is a world of fun and fantasy for people of all ages. Model kit manufacturers, such as Revell/Monogram, Aurora and Horizon, create and produce detailed kits that let the builders imagination run wild. Creative kits give movie monsters a creepy stare, F16 fighter planes a sense of movement and hot rod roadsters that race on a dragstrip across a table top.

Most model kits were packed in a decorated cardboard box with an image of the model on the surface. It contained the requisite pieces and a set of assembly instructions. Model kits are snapped together or glued together. Painting and decoration is up to the assembler. Model kits are pro-

Batman, Aurora, No. 467-149, 1964, unassembled, $175.

duced from plastic, resin or vinyl, often requiring a bit of dexterity and patience to assemble.

Buying model kits at flea markets should be done with a degree of caution. An open box spells trouble. Look for missing pieces or lost instructions. Sealed boxes are your best bet, but even these should be questioned because of the availability of home shrink wrap kits. Don't be afraid—inquire about a model's completeness before purchasing it.

Clubs: Kit Collectors International, P.O. Box 38, Stanton, CA 90680; Society for the Preservation and Encouragement of Scale Model Kit Collecting, 3213 Hardy Dr., Edmond, OK 73013.

Periodical: *Kit Builders and Glue Sniffers*, P.O. Box 201, Sharon Center, OH 44274.

American Astronaut, Aurora, 1967 . 114.00

Anzio Beach, Aurora, 1968. . . . . . . .75.00

Apollo-Saturn, Monogram, 1968. . . .55.00

Attack Trak, Masters of the Universe, Monogram, 1984 . . . . .15.00

Batmobile, Ertl, 1989, MIB 20.00

Billy Carter's Redneck Power, Revell, 1978 . . . . .16.00

Black Belt Firebird Funny Car, MPC, 1981 . . . . .30.00

Black Hole, Vincent, MPC, 1979,
  complete, unsealed 12.00
Boeing F4B4, Aurora, 1959. . . . . . .45.00
Bounty, Revell, 1960. . . . . .35.00
Cave, Prehistoric Scenes, Aurora,
  1971 . . . . .32.00
Cornfield Roundup Diarama, Planet of the
  Apes, Addar, 1975 . . . . .45.00
Corvette, Model Builders Club,
  Revell, 1966. . . . . .25.00
Dick Tracy's Getaway Car, Ertl,
  1990. . . . . .20.00
Dragula, Blueprinters series, AMT/ERTL,
  1991. . . . . .20.00
Duke's Digger, Dukes of Hazzard,
  MPC, 1980. . . . . .25.00
Elegant Farmer Wild Wheelbarrow Show
  Rod, MPC. 55.00
Elvira's Macabre Mobile,
  Monogram, 1988 . . . . .20.00
Enterprise & Space Lab, Revell,
  1978. . . . . .28.00
Evil Kneivel's Sky Cycle X2,
  Addar, 1974 . . . . .25.00
Farrah's Foxy Vette, AMT 30.00
FBU Crusader Jet #548, Lindberg . . .8.00
First Lunar Landing, Monogram,
  1979. . . . . .34.00
Flag Raising on Iwo Jima, Esci 9.00
Frantics Steel Pluckers, Hawk,
  box only 35.00
Freddy Krueger, Horizon, 18" h. 85.00
Gruesome Goodies, Aurora, 1971 . .85.00
HMS Bounty, Mutiny on the Bounty, Revell,
  1961. .100.00
Hot Dogger Hangin' Ten, Silly Surfers,
  Hawk, 1964 . . . . .45.00
Human Brain, Lindberg, 1972 . . . . .20.00
Indian Warrior, Pyro, 1960 . . . . . . .60.00
Invaders Flying Saucer, Monogram .45.00
Invisible Man, Horizon, 1988. . . . . .29.00
Jaguar XJS, Return of the Saint, Revell,
  1979. . . . . .45.00
Jaws of Doom, Six Million Dollar Man,
  MPC, 1975. . . . . .30.00
Jeckyl as Hyde, Aurora Glow,
  orig box 50.00
Joker's Goon Car/Gotham City Police Car,
  AMT/ERTL, 1990 . . . . .15.00
John F. Kennedy, Aurora, 1965 . . .125.00
Lone Ranger, Aurora, 1972, MIB . . .60.00
Ma Barker's Getaway Car, Bloody Mama,
  MPC, 1970. . . . . .65.00
Masters of the Universe, Monogram,
  1983. . . . . .25.00
Mazinga, Shogun Warriors, Monogram,
  1977. . . . . .30.00
Metaluna Mutant, Jumbo Kit, Tskuda,
  1986. . . . . .80.00
Mexican Senorita, Aurora, 1957 . . . .45.00
Miami Vice, Daytona Spider, Monogram,
  1986. . . . . .25.00

Mummy, Aurora, 1972, England,
  MISB. 50.00
My Mother the Car, AMT, 1965 . . . . 75.00
1914 Stutz Bearcat, Bearcats, MPC,
  1971 . . . . 55.00
Northern White Rhino, Revell, 1974 16.00
Pilgrim Space Station Model, #9001, MPC,
  1970, sealed, slight box warp . . . 25.00
Pink Panther Custom Car, Eldon,
  1969 . . . . 90.00
Rawhide, Gil Favor, Pyro, 1958. . . . 60.00
Red Knight of Vienna, Aurora, 1961,
  MISB. 25.00
Roadster, Mannix, MPC, 1968. . . . . 75.00
Rocketeer, Screamin' 60.00
Roto the Assault Vehicle, Masters of the
  Universe, Monogram, 1984 . . . . 15.00
Sand Worm, Dune, Revell, 1985 . . . 20.00
Signaling Device for Shipwrecked Sailors,
  Multiple Toymakers, 1965. . . . . . 50.00
Snoopy and His Motorcycle, Monogram,
  1971 . . . . 40.00
Space Shuttle Challenger, Monogram,
  1979 . . . . 12.00
Sta-Puft Marshmallow Man, Jumbo Kit,
  Tskuda, 1986 . . . . 45.00
Steel Plunkers, Frantics, Hawk,
  1965 . . . . 45.00
Strange Change Time Machine, MPC,
  1974 . . . . 65.00
Stroker McGurk and His Surf/Rod, MPC,
  1964 . . . . 125.00
Superman, Monogram, 1974. . . . . . 18.00
Sweathogs Car, Welcome Back Kotter,
  MPC, 1976 . . . . 40.00
Tarpit, Prehistoric Scenes, Aurora,
  1972 . . . . 45.00
Tarzan, Aurora, 1972, MISB 45.00

Godzilla, Aurora, No. 469-149, 1964, un-assembled, $425.

The Bride of Frankenstein, Horizon,
  1988 . . . . 45.00
The Mummy, Luminators Series,
  Monogram, 1991 . . . . .7.00
Tranquillity Base #8604, Revell,
  1982 . . . . 20.00
20 Mule Team, Death Valley Days,
  Borax premium 45.00
Vampire Glow Heads, MPC, 1975 . . 35.00
Volkswagen Beetle, Pyro 30.00
White-Tail Deer, Palmer Plastics,
  1950 . . . . 24.00
Wolfman, Aurora, 1972, England,
  MIB 30.00

Monsters

Collecting monster-related material began in the late 1980s as a generation looked back nostalgically on the monster television shows of the 1960s, e.g., "The Addams Family," "Dark Shadows" and "The Munsters," along with the spectacular monster and horror movies of the 1960s and 1970s. Fueling the fire was a group of Japanese collectors who were raiding the American market for material relating to Japanese monster epics featuring reptile monsters such as Godzilla, Rodan and Mothra. It did not take long for collectors to seek the historic roots for their post World War II monsters. A collecting revival started for Franken-

Action Figure, Gorilla Alien, Kenner, 1986, includes Dark Horse Comic Book, $10.

Magazine Tear Sheet, Aurora monster models adv, *Boys' Life*, 1962, $5.

stein, King Kong and Mummy material. Contemporary items featuring these characters also appeared.

This is a category rampant with speculative fever. Prices rise and fall rapidly, depending on the momentary popularity of a figure or family group. Study the market and its prices carefully before becoming a participant. Stress condition and completeness. Do not buy any item in less than fine condition. Check carefully to make certain that all parts or elements are present for whatever you buy. Since the material in this category is of recent origin, no one is certain how much has survived. Hoards are not uncommon. It is possible to find examples at garage sales. It pays to shop around before paying a high price.

While an excellent collection of two-dimensional material, e.g., comic books, magazines, posters, etc., can be assembled, stress three-dimensional material. Several other crazes, e.g., model kit collecting, cross over into monster collecting, thus adding to price confusion.

Clubs: Club 13, P.O. Box 733, Bellefonte, PA 16823; Count Dracula Fan Club, 29 Washington Sq. West, New York, NY 10011; Dark Shadows Fan Club, P.O. Box 69A04, West Hollywood, CA 90069; Munsters & The Ad-

dams Family Fan Club, P.O. Box 69A04, West Hollywood, CA 90069.

Newsletters: *Dark Shadows Collectables Classifieds*, 6173 Iroquois Trail, Mentor, OH 44060; *Future News*, 5619 Pilgrim Rd., Baltimore, MD 21214; *Japanese Giants*, 5727 N. Oketo, Chicago, IL 60631; *Questnews*, 12440 Moorpark St., Ste. 150, Studio City, CA 91604.

Books
The Addams Family, Paperback Library, 176 pgs, 1965 . . . . 5.00
The Outer Limits Annual, hardcover, color illus, 96 pgs 50.00
Rod Serling's The Twilight Zone, hardcover, 208 pgs, Grossett & Dunlap, 1963 . . . . 20.00

Games
Boris Karloff's Monster Game, die-cut figures, tiles, board, Gems, 1965 50.00
Creature of the Black Lagoon, die-cut figures, board, Hasbro, 1963 . . 150.00
Dracula Mystery Game, cardboard figures, spinner, board, Hasbro, 1963 . . . 75.00
Monster Old Maid Card Game, Milton Bradley, 1963 . . . . 35.00
The Munsters Card Game, box, cards, paper board, plastic markers, Milton Bradley, 1964 . . . . 25.00
The Outer Limits, Milton Bradley, 1964 . . . . 90.00

Jigsaw Puzzles
Frankenstein, Frankenstein fighting Wolfman scene, 7" by 10", Jaymar, 1963 . . . . 50.00
The Munsters, color, Whitman, 1965 . . . . 30.00
The Outer Limits, 100 pc, Milton Bradley, 1964 . . . . 45.00

Model Kits
Gigantic Tarantula, plastic, orig box, unassembled, Fundimensions, 1975 . . . . 25.00
Godzilla, assembled, Aurora 80.00
My Name Is Glob, plastic, Lindbery, 1965 . . . . 40.00
The Outer Limits, The Sixth Finger, Golden Era Models 50.00

Posters
Creature From The Haunted Sea, 1961 . . . . 40.00
Dracula vs. Frankenstein, 1971 . . . . 40.00
Godzilla vs. The Smog Monster, 1972 . . . . 40.00
King Kong vs. Godzilla, 1963 . . . . . 150.00
Monster Zero, 1966 . . . . 50.00

Twilight Zone, The Movie, 1983 . . . . 15.00

Other
Bank, Grandpa Munster, figural, vinyl, Remco, 1964 . . . . 75.00
Coloring Book, The Addams Family, Saalfield, 1965 . . . . 25.00
Comic Book, The Outer Limits, Dell, 1964 . . . . 10.00
Costume, The Outer Limits, polyester, monster illus, mask, Collegeville, 1964 . . . . 75.00
Magazine, *TV Time*, 16 pgs, June 6, 1965 . . . . 10.00
Jewelry Box, Munsters, musical, MIB 35.00
Paper Dolls, The Munsters, cardboard folder, five paper figures, six costume sheets, Whitman, 1966 . . . . 60.00
Pez Container, Creature of the Black Lagoon, plastic, molded creature head 50.00
Pinback Button, Creature of the Black Lagoon, 3-1/2" d, litho metal, color illus, Elwar Ltd., 193 . . . . 35.00
Pinback Button, Creepy Magazine Fan Club, 2-1/2" d, litho metal, color illus of Uncle Creepy, Warren Publishing Co., 1968 . . . . 15.00
Postcard, Dark Shadows, color, 5" by 7", set of 12, 1969 . . . . 50.00
Record, Dark Shadows, 33-1/3 rpm, black-and-white poster, Philips, 1969 . . . . 25.00
Record, The Addams Family, 45 rpm, RCA, c1964 . . . . 20.00
Shopping Bag, 15" by 15", Famous Monsters 1974 Convention, plastic, red, yellow, white and black 20.00
Snowdome, Creature of the Black Lagoon, MIB 15.00
Thermos, The Munsters, steel, King-Seeley Thermos, 1965 . . . . 35.00

Morton Potteries

Morton is an example of a regional pottery that has a national collecting base. Actually, there were several potteries in Morton, Ill.: Morton Pottery Works and Morton Earthenware Co., 1897-1917; Cliftwood Art Potteries, 1920-1940; Midwest Potteries, 1940-1944; and Morton Pottery Co., 1922-1976.

Prior to 1940 local clay was used and fired to a golden ecru. After 1940, clay was imported and fired white. Few pieces are marked. The key to identifying Morton pieces is through the company's catalogs and Doris and Burdell Hall's book *Morton's Potteries: 99 Years* (published by the authors, 1982).

American Art Potteries: 1947-1961
Demitasse Cup and Saucer, stylized flower dec on cup, gray, pink spray glaze 14.00
Figure, Hen and Rooster, 8" and 6-1/2", black spray glaze, pr 30.00
Figure, Squirrel, 6" h, brown spray glaze 35.00
Planter, Fish, 5" h 14.00
Television Lamp, 7" by 10", conch shell, purple, pink spray glaze 18.00
Vase, 10-1/2" h, cornucopia, gold, white int 10.00

Cliftwood Art Potteries, Inc., 1920-1940
Candlesticks, pr, 11" h, sq base, chocolate drip glaze 50.00
Figure, Police Dog, 5" h, 8-1/2" l, chocolate brown drip 55.00
Figure, Reclining Cat, 4-1/2" l, cobalt blue glaze. 25.00
Lamp 7-1/2" h, owl on log, yellow . . .35.00
Pretzel Jar, cov, barrel-shape, green 60.00
Sweetmeat Bowl, sq, green lid, yellow drip 50.00

Midwest Potteries, Inc., 1940-1944
Figure, Afghan Hound, 7" h, white, gold dec 35.00
Figure, Female Dancer, 8-1/2" h, stylized, white, gold dec 25.00
Figure, Pony, 3-1/2" h, yellow, gold dec .18.00
Flower Bowl, 10" d, 5-1/2" h, circular, brown, yellow drip glaze, two pcs.16.00
Planter, Lion, 3-1/4" by 6-1/2", yellow 12.00
Planter, Lioness, 3" by 6-1/2" 12.00
Wall Mask, 5" by 3-1/4", smiling, curly hair. 16.00

Morton Pottery Co., 1922-1976
Bank, Bulldog, brown 16.00
Bank, Pig, wall hanger, blue 25.00
Bookends, pr, Eagles, natural color .40.00

Morton Pottery Co., 1922-76, planter, $18.

Figure, Cat, reclining, white, gray spots 18.00
Figure, Seeing Eye Dog, mkd "Leader Dog," black 20.00
Lamp, Teddy Bear 25.00
Pie Bird, 5" h, white, multicolored wings and back 22.00
Planter, 9-1/2" h, rabbit, female holding umbrella, egg-shape planter 12.00
Wall Pocket, 6-1/2" h, teapot-shape, white, red apple dec 12.00

Morton Pottery Works and Morton Earthenware Co., 1877-1917
Baker, 5-1/2" d, brown Rockingham mottled glaze 35.00
Crock, 1 gal, Rockingham 50.00
Mixing Bowl, 12-1/2" h, yellow ware, white band, narrow blue stripes top and bottom. 45.00
Paperweight, buffalo, Rockingham . 40.00
Pitcher, 1-1/4" h, miniature, bulbous body, green glaze. 25.00

Mother's Day Collectibles

It's not fair. The amount of Mother's Day memorabilia is about 10 times that of Father's Day memorabilia. It has something to do with apple pie. A great deal of the Mother's Day memorabilia seen at flea markets is "limited edition." The fact that you see so much is an indication that few of these issues were truly limited. Insist on excellent or better condition and the original box when buying.

Since so many collectors are focusing on limited edition material, why not direct your efforts in another direction, for example, greeting cards or pinback buttons. Your costs will be lower and your collection will be out of the ordinary, just like your mother.

Bells, limited edition
1976, Devotion for Mothers, Hummel 55.00
1985, Mother's Little Lamb, Everson 35.00
1991, Mother's Watchful Eye, Reynolds. 35.00

Figurines
1983-84, Avon, Little Things, 3-3/4" h, porcelain boy, hp, MIB 18.00
1987, Artaffects, limited edition, musical, Motherhood. 65.00
1988, Byers' Choice Ltd., Mother's Day, daughter 175.00

Pinback Buttons, 1920s
3/4" d, bust of woman in center, carnation on either side, "Mothers Day" on banner below, multicolored 3.50
3/4" d, carnation, "Anna Jarvis Founder Philadelphia, Mother's Day," multicolored 3.00
1-1/4" d, carnation behind heart inscribed "Mother, May, 2nd Sunday, Mothers Day," red and white 5.00

Plates
1973, Anri, Mother's Day Series, Alpine Mother and Children 55.00
1983, Madre, Motherhood Series. . .75.00
1990, Pride & Joy, Mother's Love Series, Perillo .50.00
1991, Michele & Anna, Mother's Day Annual, Hibel. 65.00
1995, Remembrance, A Mother's Love, Anderson. 30.00

Motorcycles

Some of these beauties are getting as expensive as classic and antique cars. Motorcycles are generational. My father would identify with an Indian, my son with the Japanese imports and I with a BMW or Harley Davidson. I suspect that most users of this book are not likely to buy an older motorcycle. However, just in case you see a 1916 Indian Power Plus with sidecar for $1,000 or less, pick it up. It books at around $15,000.

Club: *Antique Motorcycle Club of America*, P.O. Box 300, Sweetser, IN 46987.

Periodicals: *Motorcycle Shopper Magazine*, 1353 Herndon Ave., Deltona, FL 32725; *Old Bike Journal*, 6 Prowitt St., Norwalk, CT 06855.

Movie Memorabilia

The stars of the silver screen have fascinated audiences for over three-quarters of a century. In many cases, this fascination had as much to do with their private lives as their on-screen performances. This is a category in which individuals focus on their favorites. There are superstars in the collectibles area. Two examples are Charlie Chaplin and Marilyn Monroe.

Posters are expensive. However, there are plenty of other categories in which a major collection can be built for

Lobby Card, "A Very Special Favor," Rock Hudson, Leslie Caron, Charles Boyer, color, 11" by 14", $25.

less than $25 per object. Also, do not overlook present-day material. If it's cheap, pick it up. Movie material will always be collectible.

Club: The Manuscript Society, 350 N. Niagara St., Burbank, CA 91505.

Periodicals: *Big Reel*, P.O. Box 1050, Dubuque, IA 52004; *Collecting Hollywood Magazine*, 2401 Broad St., Chattanooga, TN 37408; *Movie Collector's World*, 17230 13 Mile Rd., Roseville, MI 48066; *The Movie Poster Update*, 2401 Broad St., Chattanooga, TN 37408.

Comic Books

How the West Was Won, Gold Key,
   1963 . . . . .6.00
Moby Dick, Dell, 1956 . . . . .10.00
The Creature, Dell, 1964 . . . . .12.00

Magazines

Clark Gable and Lana Turner, *Life*, Oct. 13,
   1941, Honky Tonk cov photo 24.00
Donna Reed, *Life*, Aug. 31, 1953, From
   Here to Eternity feature article . . .15.00
Elizabeth Taylor, *Quick*, Dec. 31, 1951,
   cov photo .7.00
Gregory Peck, *Quick*, Sept. 22, 1952,
   cov photo .4.00
Ingrid Bergman, *Life*, Nov. 12, 1945,
   cov photo, feature story 25.00
John Wayne, *Look*, Aug. 2, 1960, cov pho-
   to and six-pg article 8.00

Other

Arcade Card, 3" by 5", Connie Stevens,
   1950s 5.00
Bubble Gum Card, Close Encounters, 66
   cards, color photos, 1978 . . . . . .20.00
Bubble Gum Card, Raiders of the Lost Ark,
   88 cards, color photos, 1981 . . . .20.00
Card Game, James Bond, Milton Bradley,
   1966, orig box 44.00
Game, Thunderball, James Bond, Milton
   Bradley, 1965 . . . . .70.00

Jigsaw Puzzle, Oliver Twist, 100 pcs,
   orig box with movie scenes, Jaymar,
   1968 . . . . 24.00
Lobby Cards, set of eight, James Bond,
   The Spy Who Loved Me, 11" by 13",
   color photos 48.00
Model Kit, Aurora, Dracula, plastic,
   unassembled, orig box with Bela Lugosi
   photo, 1962 . . . . 250.00
Model Kit, Aurora, Phantom of The Opera,
   molded black plastic, unassembled,
   orig box with Lon Chaney photo,
   1963 . . . . 280.00
Paperback book, *Vincent Price, Masque of
the Red Death*, movie edition, five film
   photos on front and back covers,
   1964 . . . . 14.00
Pressbook, Don't Raise the Bridge...Lower
   the River, Jerry Lewis, 1968 . . . . 24.00
Pressbook, The Spy Who Loved Me,
   James Bond, 1977 . . . . 20.00
Record, soundtrack, 33-1\3 rpm, Guys and
   Dolls, Decca, 1950s, orig sleeve . 8.00
Record, soundtrack, 33-1\3 rpm, Pepe,
   Colpix, orig fold-open sleeve features
   35 stars from movie, 1960 . . . . . 12.00
Record Sleeve, Jayne Mansfield, posed on
   bed wearing negligee, 1950s . . . 18.00
Sheet Music, James Bond, song book,
   movie theme songs, 13 photos,
   8" by 11", 1964 . . . . 24.00
Sheet Music, Wait and See, Judy Garland
   photo cov, 1945 . . . . 5.00

Mugs

The problem with every general price guide is that it does not cover the broad sweeping form categories, e.g., wash pitchers and bowls, any longer. A surprising number of individuals still collect this way. If you stay away from beer mugs, you can find a lot of examples in this category for less than $10.

Look for the unusual, either in form or labeling. Don't forget to fill one now and then and toast your cleverness in collecting these treasures.

Club: Advertising Cup and Mug Collectors of America, P.O. Box 182, Solon, IA 52333.

Advertising

Buckeye Root Beer, stoneware, logo cen-
   ter, figural handle 40.00
Busch Bavarian Beer, metal, can figural,
   1970 . . . . .10.00
Carter Carburetor, stoneware 15.00
Esso, milk glass, tiger's face illus, orange,
   white and brown, Anchor Hocking . 8.00
Keebler, plastic 18.00
Lipton Tea, ceramic, logo,
   yellow and red 4.00
Morton Salt, Morton salt girl illus, set of
   four, 1968, MIB 25.00
Nestle's Quik, 4" h, plastic, bear,
   figural 18.00
O'Keefe Beer, ceramic, logo,
   twist handle 15.00
Post Toasties, ceramic, car mug 8.00

Other

Batman and Robin, pr, 3" h, milk glass,
   black Batman illus on one, other with
   orange Robin illus, Westfield copyright
   1966, National Periodical
   Publications Inc. 25.00
Beatles, 3" h, white glass, black images,
   "Yea!, Yea!, Yea!, Yea!," unauthorized,
   1960s 25.00
Care Bear, days of week, American
   Greeting Corp 2.00
Charlie's Angels, Thermo-Serv,
   1977 . . . . .10.00
Dukes of Hazzard, 3-1/2" h, plastic, white,
   red, white and blue design, color
   photos, Irwin copyright 1981 . . . .15.00
Grog, BC Comics 3.00

Souvenir, City Hall, Philadelphia, gold lustre, Germany, $15.

Gulliver's Travels, 3-1/4" h, china, gold accent, Hammersley & Co., England, c1939 . . . . .125.00
Hopalong Cassidy, 3" h, milk glass, red Hoppy illus and name on front, western scene on back 25.00
Howdy Doody, 3-1/4", h, plastic, red, full color decal, Ovaltine premium, 1948-51 . . . . .50.00
Jiggs, 5" h, ceramic, yellow cane handle, mkd "Jiggs" and "Puck" on back, 1960s .125.00
Joe 90, 3" h, china, white, color illus, ATV copyright 1968, Washington Pottery Ltd. 25.00
Mickey Mouse, 2-3/4" h, china, color image of Mickey and dog, orange rim and handle, mkd "Made In Japan," 1930 .100.00
Pogo Possum and Beauregard Hound, pr, 4-1/4" h, plastic, blue, full-color decals, Walt Kelly copyright, 1960s 25.00
Welcome Back Kotter, Dawn, 1976 .10.00

Musical Instruments

Didn't you just love music lessons? Still play your clarinet or trumpet? Probably not! Yet, I bet you still have the instrument. Why is it that you can never seem to throw it out?

The number of antique and classic musical instrument collectors is small but growing. Actually, most instruments are sold for reuse. As a result, the key is playability. Check out the cost of renting an instrument or purchasing one new. Now you know why prices on "used" instruments are so high. Fifty dollars for a playable instrument of any quality is a bargain price. Of course, it's a bargain only if someone needs and wants to play it. Otherwise, it is $50 ill-spent. Also, do not overlook music-related items.

Clubs: American Musical Instrument Society, Rd. 3 Box 205-B, Franklin, PA 16323; Automatic Musical Instrument Collectors Association, 919 Lantern Glow Trail, Dayton, OH 45431; Miniature Piano Enthusiast Club, 633 Pennsylvania Ave., Hagerstown, MD 21740.

Periodicals: *Concertina & Squeezebox*, P.O. Box 6706, Ithaca, NY 14851;

Vintage Guitar Classics, P.O. Box 7301, Bismarck, ND 58507.

Instruments and Accessories

Banjo, Dandy, 11" head, 16 hooks, 17 frets, F holes resonator, maple, replaced nut 85.00
Banjo, unknown maker, 10" head, 11 high frets, snake skin head, aluminum hoop, fancy cutouts in aluminum resonator and armrest, c1950 . . . . 50.00
Banjo Ukulele, Pannant, 12 hooks, spruce hoop and resonator, ebony fingerboard, laminated neck 95.00
Banjo Bag, cloth, green, button closure 10.00
Castanets, pr, early 20th C 38.00
Cello, Sears Roebuck, inlaid edges, c1900 . . . . 475.00
Clarinet, Laube, 13 keys, two rings, Grenadilla wood, C, low pitch . . 350.00
Coronet, Carl Fisher Coronet, silver, original mouthpiece, flat spring missing 95.00
Coronet, Conn New Wonder Model, serial #154146 . . . . 65.00
Coronet, The Clippertone, Hawks and Sons, London, serial #50834, silver 125.00
Cymbals, 13" d, pr, leather handles, c1900 . . . . 140.00
Drum, Bass, German, foot pedal, c1860 . . . . 550.00
Drum, Snare, 14" d, Acme Professional, c1900 . . . . 175.00
Glockenspiel, carrying strap and case 65.00
Guitar, Cambridge, rosewood and spruce, ebony fingerboard, nickel-plated head, 1905-10. . . . . 145.00
Guitar, The Marlowe, c1900 . . . . . 160.00
Guitar Case, canvas, brown, leather bound edges, strap, buckle and handles, late 1800s 15.00
Organ Stool, orig needlepoint upholstery 75.00
Piano Stool, metal, circular seat, ornate design, adjustable height, claw and glass ball feet, 1880-1915. . . . . 125.00
Piano Stool, wood, circular seat, plain design, adjustable height, 1880-1915. . . . . 75.00
Pick, oval, gutta percha 4.00
Saxophone, Marceau, B-flat, tenor, brass, polished 150.00
Saxophone, Tourville & Co., tenor, silver 350.00
Tambourine, Mexican, c1900 . . . . . 80.00
Trombone, Marceau, B-flat, bass, brass 250.00
Ukulele, Favilla Tear Drop 125.00
Ukulele, Milton G. Schiller, friction koa wood 85.00

Ukulele, Baritone, Conrad, import . . 65.00
Violin, Hopf brand below button, golden brown, with case and bow 250.00
Violin, Made in Czecho Slovkia label, 1/4" size, 11", l2-pc back, bow and case included 125.00
Violin Case, wood, flannel lining, varnished, nickel-plated lock 40.00
Zither Tuning Hammer, ivory handle, early 1900s 8.00

Music Related

Book, *History of English Music*, Davey, London, 1895 . . . . .12.00
Booklet, How Music Is Made, CG Conn Co., 1927 56 pgs, illus. 5.00
Catalog, Carl Fischer, Inc., c1929, 48 pgs, 4-1/2" by 7-1/2" 40.00
Catalog, Needham Organ & Piano Co., 1900, 16 pgs, 7" by 9-1/4" 30.00
Catalog, Rudolph Wurlitzer Co., 1920, 176 pgs, 8" by 10-1/4" 95.00
Catalog, Simplex School of Music, 1910, 32 pgs, 5-3/4" by 8-3/4" 14.00
Catalog, Thomas A. Edison, Inc., 1919, 12 pgs, 5" by 8" 20.00
Cigar Label, 5" by 5", Huyler Cigars, musician image 4.00
Postcard, Battle Creek military band, Battle Creek, IA, black and white. 10.00
Poster, Roca, 36" by 56", Roca posed with squeezebox illus, c1900 . . . . . .200.00
Poster, Woody Herman, 14" by 22", "America's New Sensation!", Herman with clarinet illus, c1951 . . . . . .185.00
Program, 10" by 13", Johnny Mathis, 1970 . . . . .10.00
Song Book, Songs Scouts Sing, 4-1/4" by 6-3/4", musical note cov 25.00
Toy, Guitar, Tom and Jerry, hard plastic, black, full-color paper illus, Mattel Toys, c1965. .30.00
Toy, Musical Ge-Tar, Mattel, illus of Bugs on guitar, crank handle plays music, 1977 . . . . .20.00

Napkin Rings

If you get lucky, you may find a great Victorian silver-plated figural napkin ring at a flea market. Chances are that you are going to find napkins rings used by the common man. But do not look down your nose at them. Some are pretty spectacular. If you do not specialize from the beginning, you are going to find yourself going around

Cherub and puppy, silver-plated, J.A. Babcock & Co. #322, $235.

in circles. Animal-shaped rings are a favorite.

Bulldog, right paw raised, glass eyes, hammered ring, bronze 50.00
Butterfly and reed design, anchor mark, sterling silver 50.00
Cat, bisque, mkd "Japan" 20.00
Dragon, pewter 20.00
Egyptian scene, Nippon 75.00
Elves, dogs and dragon, brass 25.00
Flowers and butterfly,
    Noritake China 15.00
German scene, silver-plated 35.00
Grapes, figural, celluloid, emb. 12.00
Harvard pattern, cut glass 75.00
Hobstars and diamonds, cut glass . .85.00
Knight, standing beside ring, round base, sterling silver, Babcock & Co. . . .40.00
Lady holding stick, metal, c1942 . . . .15.00
Mickey Mouse, paper face, plastic . . . . . .
    50.00Nursery Rhyme figures,
    sterling silver 25.00
Owl, seated on ring, China 25.00
Parrot, rect base, silver-plated, Rogers
    Mfg. Co. 50.00

Boy carrying ring, silver-plated, Rogers Bros., #223, $235.

Peacock, standing, sterling silver . . 75.00
Rabbit, plastic 25.00
Ring, floral band, 2" w, silver-plated 20.00
Sailboat, yellow, 2" d, bisque 60.00
Scottie Dog, Catalin 25.00
Thistle pattern, cut glass 45.00
Tiger, figural, celluloid 36.00
Turtle, silver-plated 30.00
Wishbone, applied, silver-plated . . . 30.00

Nautical

There is magic in the sea, whether one is reading the novels of Melville, watching Popeye cartoons or standing on a beach staring at the vast expanse of ocean. Anyone who loves water has something nautical around the house. This is one case where the weathered look is a plus. No one wants a piece of nautical material that appears to have never left the dock.

Club: Nautical Research Guild, 62 Marlboro St., Newburyport, MA 01950.

Periodicals: *Nautical Brass*, P.O. Box 3966, North Fort Myers, FL 33918; *Nautical Collector*, P.O. Box 949, New London, CT 06320.

Almanac, Nautical Almanac, Riggs & Brother, Philadelphia, 1910, 154 pgs, nautical instruments, partially used ship's log 125.00

Fishing Float, green glass, Japanese, 12" d, $25.

Hydrometer, Sikes, made by Buss, London, used for proofing liquor and wines for customs purposes, $295.

Book, *American Nautical Art and Antiques*, 248 pgs, black and white illus, Crown Publishers, 1975 . . . . .40.00
Brochure, Cruising With Safety, 1947, 76 pgs, sailboat and motorboat photos, glossy stiff covs 10.00
Business Card, green, black printing, The Island Tool Store, Ship Builders, 171 Lewis St., New York City,
    c1875 . . . . .40.00
Cigar Label, 5" sq, Cutter Cigars, sailing yacht flying U.S. flag, 1887 . . . . .32.00
Crew List, whale ship Montpelier, Sept. 6, 1853, names, positions, number of shares in voyages
    to be received 125.00
Fog Horn, 30" l, brass, 19th C 85.00
Figure, whale, 6-3/8" h 75.00
Lantern, copper, 15" 85.00
Lantern, copper, 19" 55.00
Log Book, bark, Manchester voyage between Boston and New Orleans,
    c1884 .125.00
Magazine Tear Sheet, Sterling Engine Co, "The New Models for 1935," multicolored Donald Douglas yacht paintings, 1935 . . . . .15.00
Model, Seaview Nuclear Submarine, Voyage to the Bottom of the Sea, reissue, Aurora, 1975, MIB 125.00
Model, USS Alabama Battleship, Revell, 1969, MIB 45.00
Model, USS Missouri Battleship, Revell, 1973, MIB 16.00
Rudder, 59" l, orig white paint traces, 19th C .50.00
Photo, 10" by 12-1/2", whaleship under sail, wood frame, tan matting . . .75.00
Sea Chart, 23" by 19", Chart of the North and Baltic Seas, J. Thompson, outline colored, 1816 . . . . .35.00

Signal Horn, 15" l, foot operated, "E A Gill, Gloucester, MA"...........110.00

Newsboy Collectibles

For those of us who heaved newspaper from bike baskets in the rain and snow, then spent hours collecting from subscribers who always seemed to be away, collecting items related to newsboys is a labor of love.

Newsboys and newspaper carriers were given a variety of items to make their jobs easier and retain subscribers. Collectibles range from metal and celluloid newsboy badges, authorizing the sale and delivery of newspapers, to aprons and bags emblazoned with the name of the paper, to awards received for a job well done.

Newsboy collectibles also include the freebies distributed to faithful customers, such as ornate carrier greetings and calendars (most pre-dating World War I), rulers, pocket mirrors, pinback buttons and related memorabilia, all carrying the name of the newspaper or magazine it represented.

Advisor: Tony Lee, P.O. Box 134, Monmouth Junction, NJ 08852, (201) 429-1531.

Badges
Celluloid, Agent, *Saturday Blade and Chicago Ledger*, 2 Papers for 5 cents, 2-1/4" d, red and black lettering, orange ground 25.00

Celluloid, Chicago American Newsboys Association, 1-3/4" d, white lettering, blue ground................ 12.00
Celluloid, Sell the Cleveland News, oval, eye above inscription, black lettering, white ground................ 30.00
Metal, Boston Newsboy, Licensed 1907, School Committee, shield...... 45.00
Metal, Daily News Carrier, shield with star silhouette in center 50.00
Metal, Newsboy, Registered by (name inserted), Board of Education, City of New York, oval 25.00
Metal, 1936, Newsboy, Atlantic City, N.J., octagon shield............... 40.00
Metal, Toledo Newsboys Association, buckeye-shape shield........ 20.00

Other
Advertising Trade Card, newsboy holding copy of *Chicago Daily News*, 2" by 5", 1884 calendar on reverse...... 5.00
Calendar, carrier's greeting, *Buffalo Courier*, 9" by 12", 12 pgs, 1895, each month with famous American illus 25.00
Calendar, carrier's greeting, *Syracuse Herald*, 2" by 6", Aug. 1911 ..... 4.00
Delivery Bag, *The Dallas Times Herald*, canvas, blue lettering, white ground, 1950s 10.00
Membership Card, Toledo Newsboy's Association, 2" by 5", red 6.00
Newsletter, The Hustler, April 1922, *Cleveland Press* 5.00
Pen Stand, Honor Carrier, *Baltimore News-Post American*, 1960, Lucite 10.00
Pennant, *Cleveland Press* Carrier Tour, 6" l, felt, red lettering, white ground............... 15.00
Photograph, newsboy wearing *Syracuse Herald* delivery bag, 3" by 5", black and white............. 15.00
Ribbon, Baltimore Newsboys Reading Room Club, 1897, 4" l, cotton, gold lettering, red ground 10.00

Ribbon, Second Annual Picnic, *Muncie Press* Newsboys, July 20, 1912, 5" l, silk, black lettering, cream ground. 8.00
Sheet Music, Only a Newsboy, published by National Music Co. 18.00
Sign, We Deliver the *Asbury Park Press*, Evening, Sunday, 14" by 60", white lettering, blue ground.......... 75.00
Sign, We Have the Sun Delivered by Auto, 4" by 4", tin, black lettering, white ground 25.00

Newspapers

"Read All About It" is the cry of corner newspaper vendors across the country. Maybe these vendors should be collected. They appear to be a vanishing breed. Some newspapers are collected for their headlines, others because they represent a special day, birthday or anniversary. Everybody saved the newspaper announcing that JFK was shot. Did you save a paper from the day war was declared against Iraq? I did.

Club: Newspaper Collectors Society of America, Box 19134, Lansing, MI 48901.

Periodical: *Paper Collectors' Marketplace*, P.O. Box 128, Scandinavia, WI 54977.

1811, Sept. 21, *Niles Weekly Register*, article on affair of Little Belt, event leading to War of 1812...............10.00
1859, Nov. 5, Harper's Ferry 15.00
1863, Battle of Gettysburg 175.00
1865, Funeral of Abraham Lincoln in NY, *New York Times* 95.00
1898, Feb. 15, sinking of the Maine . 40.00
1900, McKinley/Bryan election......8.00

Tip Trays, *The Boston Herald*, litho tin, price each, $175.

Sept. 16, 1959, comical Khrushchev headline, *Watertown Daily Times*, $10.

July 21, 1969, Man Walks On Moon, *The New York Times*, **$15.**

1906, April 18, San Francisco earthquake,
   Chicago Daily News 110.00
1917, Wilson Calls for Declaration
   of War. .38.00
1919, June 28, Peace Treaty Signed 15.00
1924, Coolidge/Davis Election 5.00
1929, Oct. 28, stock market crash . .65.00
1933, Jan. 30, Hitler Made Chancellor
   of Germany 12.00
1934, July 22, Dillinger Shot
   and Killed 35.00
1937, July 2, Amilia Earhart Vanishes in
   Round the World Flight 14.00
1941, Dec. 8, Lou Gehrig's Death,
   The Morning Post. 31.00
1945, Aug. 6, First Atomic Bomb Dropped
   on Japan 24.00
1954, May 17, school segregation
   decision .10.00
1962, Feb. 20, John Glenn's
   space flight. 15.00
1963, Nov. 22, Kennedy
   assassination 30.00
1973, Vietnam Peace Pacts Signed .10.00
1974, Aug. 9, Nixon resignation 25.00
1977, Aug. 17, Elvis Dies,
   Los Angeles Times. 27.00
1980, John Lennon's Death,
   New York newspaper. 18.00
1986, Jan. 28, Challenger Explodes . .5.00

Niloak Pottery

When you mention Niloak, most people immediately think of swirled brown, red and tan pottery, formally known as Mission Ware. However, Niloak also made items in a host of other designs through 1946. These included utilitarian wares and ceramics

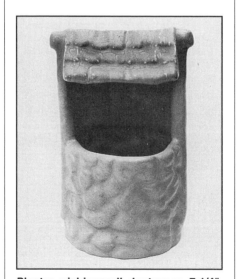

Planter, wishing well, dusty rose, 7-1/4" h, $12.

used by florists that can be bought for a reasonable price. If Niloak prices follow the trend established by Roseville prices, now is the time to buy some of these later pieces.

Club: Arkansas Pottery Collectors Society, P.O. Box 7617, Little Rock, AR 72217.

Planters
Bird, 2-1/4" .10.00
Cat, 4-1/4" .15.00
Duck, 4-1/2", low relief 15.00
Swan, pink, small 5.00
Wishing Well, 7-1/4" h, dusty rose . . 12.00

Vases
1-1/2" h, miniature, swirl,
   Mission Ware. 80.00
6" h, green, wing handles 25.00
6-1/2" h, blue, glossy finish,
   wing handles 25.00

Other
Ashtray, 3-1/4" by 1-1/4", swirl 60.00
Bowl, 4-1/2", swirl, Mission Ware . . . 80.00
Bud Vase, 4" h, blue and pink,
   matte finish 22.00
Candlesticks, pr, 2" h, brown, blue and
   cream, Mission Ware. 65.00
Cornucopia, light pink. 5.00
Creamer, 4", low relief 10.00
Creamer, 4-1/2" cow, figural. 60.00
Match Holder, duck, figural, brown and
   white swirls 15.00
Pitcher, 7" h, glossy finish 25.00
Shot Glass, 2-1/4" h, swirl 75.00

Nippon

Nippon is handpainted Japanese porcelain made between 1891 and 1921. The McKinley tariff of 1891 required goods imported into the United States to be marked with their country of origin. Until 1921, goods from Japan were marked "Made in Nippon."

More than 200 different manufacturer's marks have been discovered for Nippon. The three most popular are the wreath, maple leaf and rising sun. While marks are important, the key is the theme and quality of the decoration. Nippon has become quite expensive. Rumors in the field indicate that Japanese buyers are now actively competing with American buyers.

Club: International Nippon Collectors Club, 112 Oak Ave. North, Owatonna, MN 55060.

Ashtray, Phoenix Bird, 4-1/2" h, blue, gold trim, wreath mark 90.00
Ashtray, Playing Cards, 5" h, colorful, brown ground, wreath mark 135.00
Basket, 3-1/2" h, white ground, blue scenic. 45.00
Basket, 4" h, white ground, garlands of tiny flowers, rising sun mark 95.00
Berry Set, seven pcs, master and six serving bowls, bisque, pastel orange flowers outlined in gold, RC mark 98.00
Biscuit Jar, ruffled, narrow center, pink and red roses, white ground, TEOH mark 125.00
Bouillon Cup, cobalt blue, white and gold, two handled, lid, underplate, wreath mark 120.00
Bowl, 5-1/2" d, bisque, forest scene, maple leaf mark 48.00
Bowl, 5-3/4" l, ftd, pierced handles, gold outlined berries and leaves, RC mark. 50.00
Bowl, 7-1/2" d, pink flowers, green garlands, cherry blossom mark . .25.00
Butter Tub, 7-1/4" d, bisque scenic, lid, insert, underplate, TEOH mark . .85.00
Cake Set, cream ground, cake plate and six serving plates, wreath mark . .95.00
Candlestick, 5-1/2" h, child's, bunnies dec, wreath mark 100.00
Candlestick, 7" h, Gouda type dec . .95.00

Vase, 8-3/4" h, hp lake scene, green M in wreath mark, $75.

Candy Dish, oblong, ftd, pink and white rosebuds on gold medallions, multicolored jewels, gold beaded trim, dark green ground, maple leaf mark 65.00
Celery Dish, 11-1/2" l, bisque, scenic, wreath mark 50.00
Coaster, 3-3/4" d, floral, blue mark . 28.00
Dish, 7-1/2" w, divided, three sections, green mark 90.00
Feeding Dish, child's 8" d, girl and dog illus, blue mark 75.00
Inkwell, 3" sq, horse and rider, green mark 165.00

Mustard, cov, 3-1/2" h, floral, matching underplate and spoon, wreath mark. 65.00
Plaque, pierced to hang, 8" d, hp sunset with sailboat scene, blue maple leaf mark 95.00
Plaque, pierced to hang, 9-5/8" sq, hp landscape, houses, mountains, water, boats, geese and man carrying water vessel, gold rim 135.00
Plaque, pierced to hang, 11" d, basket with nuts, green mark 275.00
Plate, 6-1/2" d, bisque, scenic, wreath mark. 45.00
Plate, 7-1/2" d, floral border, wreath mark 65.00
Plate, 10-1/2" d, floral dec, heavy gold beading and designs, scalloped rim, green "M" in wreath mark 80.00
Shaving Mug, 3-3/4" h, yellow mark . 85.00
Sugar Shaker, white, grape design, gold leaves, blue mark 55.00
Tea Set, 17 pcs, 9" h, cov teapot, six cups, five saucers, four tall cups, paneled hexagonal form, white chrysanthemum blossoms and colored leaves, white ground 75.00
Tidbit Plate, rose panels and Greek key design 30.00
Vase, 5" h, yellow, blue floral, rising sun mark 65.00
Vase, 6" h, pink thorny roses, hexagonal body, handled, six legs 65.00
Vase, 6-1/2" h, Art Deco design, wreath mark 75.00

Noritake Azalea

Noritake china in the Azalea Pattern was first produced in the early 1900s. Several backstamps were

Plaque, 10" d, hp white and yellow floral dec, pierced for hanging, green maple leaf mark, $65.

Vegetable, cov, oval, $375.

used. You will find them listed in *Warman's Americana & Collectibles* (Wallace-Homestead). They will help date your piece.

Azalea Pattern wares were distributed as a premium by the Larkin Co., of Buffalo and sold by Sears, Roebuck & Co. As a result, it is the most commonly found pattern of Noritake china. Each piece is handpainted, adding individuality to the piece. Hard-to-find examples include children's tea sets and salesmen's samples. Do not ignore the handpainted glassware in the Azalea Pattern that was manufactured to accompany the china service.

Bonbon, 6-1/4" w. 50.00
Bread Tray, 12" l 110.00
Candlesticks, pr. 35.00
Cake Plate, two handled 35.00
Condiment Set 75.00
Cup and Saucer 15.00
Fruit Bowl, 8-1/2". 50.00
Gravy Boat 50.00
Mustard, no spoon 50.00
Plate, dinner 20.00
Plate, salad 10.00
Plate, square 50.00
Relish, 8-1/2", oval 18.50
Soup, flat 28.00
Vegetable Bowl, round, large 50.00

Noritake China

Noritake is quality Japanese china imported to the United States by the Noritake China Co. The company, founded by the Morimura Brothers in Nagoya in 1904, is best known for its dinnerware lines. More than 100 different marks were used, which are helpful in dating pieces. The Larkin Co., of Buffalo, N.Y., issued several patterns as premiums, including the Azalea, Briarcliff, Linden, Savory, Sheridan and Tree in the Meadow patterns, which are readily found.

Be careful. Not all Noritake is what it seems. The company also sold blanks to home decorators. Check the artwork before deciding that a piece is genuine.

Club: Noritake Collectors' Society, 1237 Federal Ave. East, Seattle, WA 98102.

Bowl, 8-1/2" d, 2" h, white flowers, orange ground, green rim band, gold edge, red M in wreath mark, $25.

Bread Plate, 14" l, 6-1/4" w, white, pale green and gold floral border, open handles 24.00
Candy Dish, cov, multicolored stylized floral dec 95.00
Celery Dish, 10-1/2" l, red mark 25.00
Chamberstick, 4-3/4" h, green mark 75.00
Chip and Dip Dish, 9" w, green mark 70.00
Coffeepot, cov, Scheherazade pattern 48.00
Condiment Tray, 7" l, rect, gilt dec, white ground. 25.00
Demitasse Cup and Saucer, orange and blue flowers. 18.00
Dish, 8" w, relief molded, nut dec, handled, green mark 120.00
Napkin Rings, pr, Art Deco-style, portrait dec, one with girl wearing red fur trimmed cloak, other with man wearing top hat and cape 100.00
Plaque, 8-1/2" d, silhouette of girl in bouffant dress, looking in hand mirror, green "M" in wreath mark 100.00
Relish Dish, 7-1/2" l, red mark 25.00

Sauce Dish, 7-1/4" w, underplate, green mark 50.00
Serving Tray, 9" w, green mark 40.00
Shaving Mug, 3-3/4" h, hp stalking tiger scene, green "M" in wreath mark. 200.00
Vase, 5" h, oval medallions with scarlet birds and flowers, gold lustre ground, 1930s. 35.00
Waffle Set, handled serving plate, sugar shaker, Art Deco flowers, "M" in wreath mark 45.00
Wall Pocket, 8" h, wooded landscape, house near water, blue lustre ground 75.00
Wall Pocket, 8-1/2" h, red flower dec, red mark .95.00

Noritake Tree in the Meadow

If you ever want to see variation in a dinnerware pattern, collect Tree in the Meadow. You will go nuts trying to match pieces. In the end you will do what everyone else does. Learn to live with the differences. Is there a lesson here? Tree in the Meadow was distributed by the Larkin Co., of Buffalo, N.Y. Importation began in the 1920s, almost 20 years after the arrival of Azalea Pattern wares. Check the backstamp to identify the date of the piece.

Ashtray, 5-1/4" d, green mark. 30.00

Salt and Pepper Shakers, pr, mkd "Made in Japan," $30.

Bowl, 6-1/2" d, green mark 28.00
Cake Plate. .32.00
Celery Tray .40.00
Compote 80.00
Condiment Set, five pcs, mustard pot,
    ladle, salt and pepper shakers
    and tray .40.00
Demitasse Cup and Saucer 35.00
Dish, pierced handles,
    blue lustre border, 6" l 40.00
Gravy Boat .50.00
Jam Jar, underplate, spoon. 65.00
Lemon Dish, center ring handle,
    5-1/2" d. .15.00
Plate, 7-1/2" d 12.00
Plate, 8-1/2" d 15.00
Platter, 12" l .30.00
Relish, divided. 48.00
Salt and Pepper Shakers, pr 30.00
Snack Set, tray and cup 25.00
Sugar, cov. .25.00
Tile, chamfered corners,
    5" w, green mark 25.00
Vegetable Dish, 9-3/4" l, oval,
    Noritake mark. 30.00
Waffle Set, sugar shaker
    and syrup jug 70.00
Waste Bowl .35.00

Nutcrackers

Fast food and time did-in the nut-cracking community. From the mid-19th through the mid-20th century, it was not uncommon to find a bowl of nuts awaiting cracking in the kitchen, livingroom or dining room. Just as there is a never-ending search for a better mousetrap, so was man never content with his nutcracker design. The variety is endless, from cast iron dogs of the turn-of-the-century to brass legs from the Art Deco period.

Many modern collectors like the wooden military and civilian figures

that come from Germany. Have you ever tried cracking a nut with them? Useless, utterly useless.

Alligator, cast iron, mkd "T" 40.00
Clown, cast iron 40.00
Dog, cast iron, bronze finish 45.00
Dog, cast iron, nickel finish, 11" l, mkd "The
    LA Althoff Mfg Co, Chicago". . . . 45.00
Eagle, brass. 25.00
Fish, cast iron, nickel-plated 150.00
Grandfather's clock, brass. 65.00
Jester, brass 75.00
Mermaid, brass 100.00
Punch & Judy, pr, brass. 65.00
Rabbit head, wooden. 125.00
Rooster, brass 25.00
Squirrel, cast iron. 20.00
Wooden Shoe 45.00

Occupied Japan

America occupied Japan from 1945 to 1952. Not all objects made during this period are marked "Occupied Japan." Some were simply marked "Japan" or "Made in Japan." Occupied Japan collectors ignore these two groups. They want to see their favorite words.

Beware of falsely labeled pieces. Rubber-stamp marked pieces have appeared on the market. Apply a little fingernail polish remover. Fake marks will disappear. True marks are under glaze. Of course, if the piece is un-glazed to begin with, ignore this test.

Club: The Occupied Japan Club, 29 Freeborn St., Newport, RI 02840.

Figures
3-3/4" h, cowboy on rearing horse,
    metal. 15.00
5-1/2" h, ballerina. 42.50
5-3/4" h, black shoeshine boy 40.00
8" h, porcelain, lady,
    lavender and yellow dress 20.00

Toys, windup
Boy on Tricycle, celluloid boy 70.00

Car, Baby Pontiac, tin, orig box 65.00
Dancing Couple, 5" h, celluloid. 40.00
South Seas Native, 6" h, celluloid,
    grass skirt 50.00

Vases
5-1/4" h, figural, Hummel-like boy
    reading book 25.00
6-1/2" h, porcelain, fluted rim, brightly
    colored, three maidens
    with flowing skirts 65.00
10" h, bisque, figural, young lady and
    cornucopia. 65.00

Wall Pockets
Colonial Couple, hanging out window
    with baskets. 30.00
Dutch Girl, 7-1/4" h, mkd "Made in
    Occupied Japan". 12.50
Lady with hat, 5" h, porcelain, Art
    Deco-style 35.00

Other
Ashtray, 4-3/4" h, metal, spring loaded,
    head of black boy smoking cigar . 50.00
Ashtray, 5-5/8" d, clear, depicts life-cycle of
    silk worm, dragon motif, marked "Made
    in Occupied Japan" 35.00
Bowl, cov, double-handled, Capodimonte-
    style, enamel cherub dec, mkd
    "Occupied Japan" 20.00
Box, cov, Hen on nest 50.00
Box, cov, Dog motif, inlaid 15.00
Cigarette Dispenser, mechanical, inlaid
    woods, spring-operated sliding drawer
    dispenses cigarette
    into bird's beak 55.00
Clock, bisque, double figure, colonial
    couple, 10-1/2" h, bisque,
    dancing couple, flowers. 250.00
Clock, bisque, double figure, colonial
    couple, 12" h, bisque, cubbyhole scene
    of young maiden and gentleman seated
    at table, enameled bead
    and floral dec. 350.00
Crumber and Brush, emb metal 10.00

Negro, cast iron, painted, 5-1/2" h, $225.

Tea Set, miniature, $25.

Toothpick, 2-3/4" h, white ground, blue rims, brown floral dec, mkd "PICO Made in Occupied Japan," $20.

Demitasse Set, coffeepot, sugar bowl, creamer, saucer and three cups, translated script means "Black like the devil, hot like hell, pure like an angel, sweet like love:
Recipe of Rareecand" 40.00
Finger bowl, 5-3/4", porcelain, winged cherub and raspberry motif 30.00
Flower Frog, underplate, green crown mark 27.50
Lamp, 13-1/2" h, colonial couple, gentleman with guitar, lady holding bouquet, emb floral base. 25.00
Lantern, 4-1/2" h, owl motif 35.00
Nativity Scene, bisque, Baby Jesus, cradle, animals, wise men, complete, original box 195.00
Paperweight, bronze, mkd "Captured Japanese Material" from Yokosuka Naval Air Station, USS Webster, ARV-2 60.00
Planter, figural, bunny rabbit 12.50
Purse, lady's, faux pearl dec 50.00
Rolling Pin, wood 45.00
Salt and Pepper Shakers, pr, cobalt blue glass coffeepots, metal tray, red bakelite handles, orig box 25.00
Tape Measure, 2-3/8", celluloid, pig, stamped "Occupied Japan" in large letters .45.00
Tea Set, teapot, creamer and cov sugar, base mkd "Sango China, made in Occupied Japan" 30.00

Ocean Liner Collectibles

Although the age of the clipper ships technically fits into this category, the period that you are most likely to uncover at flea markets is that of the ocean liner. Don't focus solely on American ships. England, Germany, France and many other countries had transoceanic liners that competed with and bested American vessels. Today is the age of the cruise ship. This aspect of the category is being largely ignored. Climb aboard and sail into the sunset.

Clubs: Steamship Historical Society of America, Inc., 300 Ray Dr., Ste. 4, Providence, RI 02906; Titanic Historical Society, P.O. Box 51053, Indian Orchard, MA 01151; Titanic International, Inc., P.O. Box 7007, Freehold, NJ 07728.

Activity Book, Rigby's Book of Model Ships, 1963, punch-out, unused .50.00
Book, *Wreck of the Titanic*, Everett, 320 pgs 30.00

Creamer, 3" h, White Horse China, c1880, $60.

Booklet, Alcoa Line, Arcadia and Saint John, Bermuda service, March 10, 1941, sailing schedule 8.00
Booklet, Cunard, September 1953, 23 pgs 10.00
Booklet, Royal Interocean Lines, May 1965, 12 pgs, color photos 12.00
Cabinet Card, 1890s steamboat . . . 36.00
Candy Container, litho tin, full color Queen Mary, illus on lid, 1930s 40.00
Check, Old Colony Steamboat Co, July 25, 1881, canceled 6.00
Cup, Lattorff Ocean Liner 20.00
Deck Plan, SS Manhattan, 10 pgs, unfolds to 28" by 9", 1936 . . . . 50.00
Deck Plan, SS Paris, 16 pgs, unfolds to 43" by 8-1/2", decks, cabins and int. views, c1934 . . . . 75.00
Magazine, *Canadian Pacific Princess*, 16 pgs 4.00
Matchbook Cover, Holland-American Lines 1.75
Menu, Matson Line 7.00
Menu, SS City of Omaha, Christmas 1940. . . . . 5.00
Menu, Sun Line cruise ship, Stella Solaris, 1930s, set of seven. 18.00
Passenger List, SS Leviathan, 1924 15.00
Photo, Carnival, color, aerial view . . . 1.50
Playing Cards, SS Milwaukee Clipper, ship in ocean scene 12.50

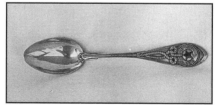

Spoon, 5-1/2" l, Red Star Lines, German silver, $75.

Sheet Music, The Band Played "Nearer My God To Thee" As The Ship Went Down, Morris Music Co., NY, 1912 . . . .60.00
Stock Certificate, Cunard Steamship Co., Ltd. 7.50

Olympic Collectibles

Gallantly marching behind their flags, the best athletes from nations around the world enter the Olympic Coliseum. Whether the first modern Olympic games in 1896 or the recent 1994 Winter Games, the spirit of competition remains the same. The Olympic collector shares this feeling.

It's a contest to see who can garner the most and have the scarcest items. Olympic collectors are adept at leaping hurdles and running miles in pursuit of their oft-elusive gold medal collectibles. A few select collectors focus on objects picturing the games of ancient Greece. Bronze and ceramic figures, decorated pottery and jewelry with an Olympic motif do surface occasionally.

Olympic collectibles run hot and cold. They are more popular in Olympic years than in years when there are no games. American collectors concentrate on the Olympic games held in the United States. The one exception is the 1936 Olympics in Berlin, a game popular with collectors worldwide.

Club: Olympin Collector's Club, 1386 5th St., Schenectady, NY 12303.

Puzzle, jigsaw, 1932 Olympic Games, Toddy premium, color litho, 13" by 10", $45.

Autographs

Evelyn Ashford, photo, 8" by 10"....20.00
Carl Lewis, document, sgd.......16.00
Jesse Owens, document, sgd.....55.00
Joan Benoit, photo, 8" by 10"......25.00
Mark Spitz, document, sgd.......15.00
Shannon Miller, photo, 8" by 10"....12.00

Pins

XI, Berlin, souvenir, white, gold outline, eagle with swastika above colored Olympic rings...............65.00
XIV, London, Great Britain, Olympic rings, 1948...........35.00
XVI, Melbourne, Australia, Romanian, gold, torch-shape, multicolored Olympic rings on white enamel flame, "Romania" on torch, 1956...............30.00
XX, oval, gold, enameled, Olympic rings on white ground, "Munich 1972"....20.00

Programs, Summer Olympics

1948, London, England...........30.00
1960, Rome, Italy...............25.00
1976, Montreal, Quebec.........10.00

Programs, Winter Olympics

1932, Lake Placid, NY............50.00
1956, Cortina d'Ampezzo, Italy....60.00
1984, Sarajevo, Yugoslavia.......10.00
1992, Albertville, France...........2.00

Ticket Stubs, Summer Olympics

1928, Amsterdam, Holland........40.00
1956, Stockholm, Sweden........75.00
1964, Tokyo, Japan..............20.00
1984, Los Angeles..............5.00

Ticket Stubs, Winter Olympics

1952, Oslo, Norway..............35.00
1976, Innsbruck, Austria..........15.00
1992, Albertville, France...........2.00

Other

Badge, Judge's, bronze, Olympic rings above Brandenburg Gate, "XI Olympiade Berlin 1936".....75.00
Badge, Security, 1968, XIX, Mexico City, Mexico, white metal, rect, enameled..............100.00
Coaster, XX, Munich, Germany, 1972, paper, "Munscher Bier," double sided................25.00
Ewer, 12" h, ceramic, nude athlete stringing bow, Olympic logo and "1960".................33.00
Frisbee, 9-1/2" d, Olympic illus and inscriptions in silver and gold, orig box, {c}1979.............25.00
Media Pin, XXIV, Sports Illustrated, cloisonné, rect, white ground, "Seoul 88".................25.00

Media Pin, XXV, NBC, domed, gold colored, multicolored peacock, Olympic rings, "Barcelona 92"..10.00
Press Pin, 1932, Los Angeles, inscribed "Xth Olympiad 1932 Los Angeles"...............100.00
Tickets, pr, XXII, Moscow, USSR, unused, 1980...............8.00
Visor, 1980 Olympics, fabric, elastic headband, full color Winter Games symbol...................25.00

Owl Collectibles

Most people do not give a hoot about this category, but those who do are serious birds. Like all animal collectors, the only thing owl collectors care about is that their bird is represented.

Cookie Jars

Nite Owl, mkd "DeForest of Calif USA 5537"....................40.00
Snow Owl, mkd "Made in Poppytrail Calif"......38.00
Winking Owl, mkd "856 USA".....32.00
Wise Owl, mkd "Japan"..........25.00
Woodsy Owl..................95.00

Figurines

1-1/2", Hagen-Renaker...........8.00
4" h, carnival glass, Mosser.......18.00
5-7/8" h, Kay Finch.............35.00

Limited Edition Collectors Plates

1991, Peek-A-Whoo: Screech Owls, Baby Owls of North America, J. Thornbrugh...............37.00

Andirons, 14-3/4" h, cast iron, glass eyes, mkd "407E," $375.

1992, Whoo's There: Barred Owl, Baby Owls of North America Series, J. Thornbrugh...............50.00
1993, Great Gray Owl Family, Family Circles, R Rust.........30.00
1994, Great Horned Owl Family, Family Circles, R Rust.........30.00

Other

Ashtray, White Owl Cigars, blue, white and brown, 1930s.................8.00
Book, *An Owl Came To Stay*, Clair Rome, Crown Pub, NY, 1980.........65.00
Book, *Woodsy Owl*, #017, 2nd ed...6.00
Bookends, pr, brass, Frankart.....35.00
Cigar Tin, White Owl............20.00
Clock, metal, 2" dial, Bentley, Germany...................25.00
Dakin Figure, Woodsy Owl, 1974...60.00
Doll, 6-1/2" h, Woodsey Owl, plush, "Give A Hoot, Don't Pollute"...........25.00

Matchsafe, 2" w, 1-5/8" h, brass, glass eyes, $250.

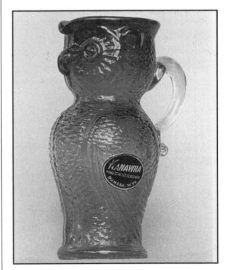

Pitcher, 5" h, Kanawha Glass, vintage color, $6.

Match Holder, 2-1/2" h, dark green,
    Wetzel Glass Co. 5.00
Paperweight, cast iron, owl family, two
    babies, plus baby in papa's arms.35.00
Salt and Pepper Shakers, pr, china, brown
    and white, scholarly expressions, horn
    rim glasses. 6.50
Tape Measure, brass, glass eyes, 1-3/8" h,
    mkd "Germany" 35.00
Vase, 8-1/4" h, Knifewood, Weller. .145.00

Paden City

The Paden City Glass Manufacturing Co., Paden City, W.V., was founded in 1916. The plant closed in 1951, two years after acquiring the American Glass Co. Paden City glass was handmade in molds. There are no known free-blown examples. Most pieces were unmarked. The key is color. Among the most popular are opal (opaque white), dark green (forest) and red. The company did not produce opalescent glass.

Bowl, 8-3/4" d, cobalt blue,
    Orchid pattern 30.00
Bowl, 9" d, amber, ftd,
    Sunset pattern 35.00
Candlesticks, pr, Cheriglo, low 24.00
Cake Plate, pink,
    Black Forest pattern. 35.00
Candy Dish, cov, crystal, gold encrusted
    flowers, Crow's Foot pattern 18.00
Compote, 5" sq, yellow, Crow's Foot
    pattern .20.00
Creamer, green, Orchid pattern 15.00
Cup and Saucer, amber, Crow's Foot
    pattern 7.00
Cup and Saucer, dark green, Largo
    pattern .10.00
Figure, Cottontail Rabbit, crystal. . . .65.00
Figure, Squirrel, log base 45.00
Finger Bowl, green,
    Black Forest pattern. 15.00
Goblet, red, 9 oz, 5-13/16" h, Georgian
    Line 69 .18.00
Mayonnaise Dish, pink, ftd,
    Nora Bird 40.00
Pitcher, cov, green, Party pattern . . .60.00
Plate, 7-1/2" d, amethyst, Penny Line .5.00
Plate, 8" d, ruby, Wotta Line 7.00
Plate, 9" d, amber,
    Crow's Foot pattern 9.00
Salt and Pepper Shakers, pr, orig tops, red,
    Party Line pattern. 45.00
Sandwich Tray, chrome handles
    Amy pattern 20.00
Sherbet, red, Georgian Line 69. . . . .12.50
Sugar, cov, ruby, Wotta Line. 8.00

Tray, 10-1/2" l, green, Popeye and Olive
    pattern. 8.00
Tumbler, 3-1/2" h, ftd, red, V-shape,
    Georgian Line 69 . . . . 10.00
Tumbler, 6" h, red,
    Penny Line pattern 12.00
Vase, 6-1/2" h, pink,
    Black Forest pattern 45.00
Vase, 10" h, yellow, Orchid pattern . 35.00

Paint By Number Sets

Paint-by-number sets are most frequently collected according to subject matter. Crossover collectors are the biggest customers. To date, there is little interest in the category by itself. Perhaps someday a generic animal picture painted on black velvet will be collectible in its own right.

Character

Beatles, John Lennon, 11" by 14" picture,
    paint, thinner, brushes, 14" by 19" box,
    Artistic Creations. 250.00
Fess Parker Oil Paint-by-Number Set,
    Standard Toykraft, 1964 . . . . 35.00
Green Hornet, Hasbro,1966 . . . . . . 90.00
Howdy Doody, acrylic, Art Award,
    1976 . . . . 25.00
Land of the Giants, Hasbro, 1969 . . 50.00
The Rifleman, Standard Toykraft,
    1960 . . . . 70.00
Rin Tin Tin, four 9-1/4" by 12" sheets,
    watercolor tablets, orig box,
    Transogram, 1956 . . . . 60.00
Tom Sawyer. . . . Standard Toykraft, 20.00

Craft Master

New Artist Series, #12, 12 oil paints,
    glass jars, two mounted
    12" by 16" panels, two
    brushes, cleaner, instructions . . 20.00

Tom Sawyer Paint By Numbers Deluxe Watercolor Set, Standard Toykraft, complete, $20.

New Artist Series, #18, 18 oil paints, two
    mounted 16" by 20" panels, three
    brushes, cleaner, instructions . . .20.00
Pann, 22 oil paints, two mounted 10" by 14"
    panels, brush, instructions. 25.00
Space Traveler, eight fluorescent color
    paints, brush, instructions 35.00

Paperback Books

This is a category with millions of titles and billions of copies. Keep this in mind before paying a high price for anything. A great deal of the value of paperbacks rests in the cover art. A risqué lady can raise prices, as well as blood pressure. Great art can make up for a lousy story by an insignificant author. However, nothing can make up for a book's being in poor condition, a fate that has befallen a large number of paperbacks.

For a detailed listing, I recommend consulting Kevin Hancer's *Hancer's Price Guide To Paperback Books*, Third Edition (Wallace-Homestead, 1990) and Jon Warren's *The Official Price Guide to Paperbacks* (House of Collectibles, 1991). Both are organized by company first, and then issue number. Hence, when trying to locate a book, publisher and code number are more important than author and ti-

Moon, Bucklin, *The Darker Brother*, Bantam, $15.

Woodford, Jack, *The Abortive Hussy*, Avon, $5.

tle. The majority of paperbacks sell between 50 cents and $2.50.

Periodical: *Paperback Parade*, P.O. Box 209, Brooklyn, NY 11228.

Paper Dolls

Paper dolls have already been through one craze cycle and appear to be in the midst of another. The publication of Mary Young's *A Collector's Guide To Magazine Paper Dolls: An Identification & Value Guide* (Collector Books, 1990) is one indication of the craze. It also introduces a slightly different approach to the subject than the traditional paper doll book.

The best way to collect paper dolls is in uncut books, sheets and boxed sets. Dolls that have been cut out, but still have all their clothing and accessories, sell for half or less of their uncut value. Paper doll collectors have no desire to play with their dolls. They just want to admire them and enjoy the satisfaction of owning them.

Club: The Original Paper Doll Artists Guild, P.O. Box 14, Kingfield, ME 04947.

Newsletters: *Paper Doll News*, P.O. Box 807, Vivian, LA 71082; *Paperdoll Review*, P.O. Box 485, Princeton, IN 47670; *Yesterday's Paper Dolls*, 808 Lee Ave., Tifton, GA 31794.

Alfie, Lowe, 1956 . . . . 8.00
Archie's Girls, Lowe, 1964 . . . . 35.00
Barbie Doll, Lowe, 1962 . . . . 30.00
Bedknobs and Broomsticks, Whitman, 1971 . . . . 30.00
Betty Hutton and Her Girls, Whitman, 1951 . . . . 70.00
Betty Plays Lady, Jack-in-the-Book Bonnie Book, Lowe, 1953 . . . . 8.00
Buffy and Jody, Whitman, 1970 . . . . 15.00
Career Girls, Lowe, 1950 . . . . 25.00
Carol Lynley, Whitman, 1960 . . . . . . 35.00
Cathy Quick Curl, Whitman, 1975 . . . 9.00
Cecelia My Kissin' Cousin, 30" h, Lowe, 1960 . . . . 35.00
Chatty Baby, Whitman, 1963 . . . . . . 25.00
Cinderella Steps Out, Lowe, 1948 . . 10.00
Gabby Hayes, Lowe, 1954 . . . . 35.00
Here Comes the Bride, Lowe, 1971 . . 6.00
Janet Leigh Cutouts & Coloring, two dolls, Merrill Publishing Co. 45.00
Lennon Sisters, Whitman, copyright 1958, 9" by 12", unpunched 60.00
Little Lulu, Whitman, 1972 . . . . 15.00
Malibu Francie, Lowe, 1973 . . . . 10.00
Miss America Magic Doll, Parker Bros., 1953 . . . . 18.00
Mrs. Beasley, Whitman, 1974 . . . . . . 8.00
Natalie Wood, Whitman, 1958 . . . . . 75.00
Petticoat Junction, Lowe, 1964 . . . . 40.00

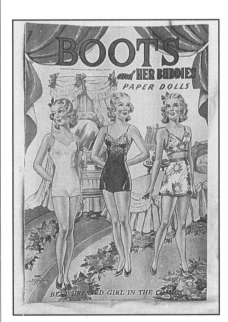

Boots and Her Buddies, Saalfield, #2460, 1943, $35.

Grown-Up Paper Dolls, Merrill, #3408, 1936, uncut, $30.

Shari Lewis, five pgs, Treasure Books 32.00
Shirley Temple, Saalfield, Christmas, uncut 60.00
Sleeping Beauty, Whitman, 1970, 10" by 13" 80.00
Swing Your Partners, Abbott, 1940s, 11" by 13" 40.00
The Brady Bunch, Whitman, 1972 . . . 9.00
The Gingham's, Katie's Country Store, Whitman, 1978 . . . . 6.00
The Waltons, Whitman, 1974 . . . . 8.00
Wishnik Cut-Outs, Lowe, 1954 . . . . . 20.00

Paper Money

People hid money in the strangest places. Occasionally, it turns up at flea markets. Likewise, early paper money came in a variety of forms and sizes quite different from modern paper currency. Essentially, paper money breaks down into three groups—money issued by the federal government, by individual states and by private banks, businesses or individuals. Money from the last group is designated as obsolete bank notes.

As with coins, condition is everything. Paper money that has been heavily circulated is worth only a fraction of the value of a bill in excellent condition. Proper grading rests in the hands of coin dealers. Krause Publica-

U.S. Occupation Currency, price each, $4-6.

tions (700 E. State St., Iola, WI 54990) is a leading publisher in the area of coinage and currency. *Bank Note Reporter*, a Krause newspaper, keeps collectors up-to-date on current developments in the currency field. There is a wealth of information available to identify and price any bill that you find. Before you sell or turn in that old bill for face value, do your homework.

Paperweights

This is a tough category. Learning to tell the difference between modern and antique paperweights takes years. Your best approach at a flea market is to treat each weight as modern. If you get lucky and pay modern paperweight prices for an antique weight, you are ahead. If you pay antique prices for a modern paperweight, you lose and lose big.

Paperweights divide into antique (prior to 1945) and modern. Modern breaks down into early modern (1945 to 1980) and contemporary (1980 and later). There is a great deal of speculation going on in the area of contemporary paperweights. It is not a place for amateurs or those with money they can ill-afford to lose. If you are not certain, do not buy.

Clubs: International Paperweight Society, 761 Chestnut St., Santa Cruz, CA 95060; Paperweight Collectors Association, Inc., P.O. Box 1059, East Hampton, MA 01027.

Advertising

Badger Mutual Fire Insurance Co., cast iron, emb badger figure, oval base 45.00
Chelton Trust Co., 2-1/2" d, celluloid over metal, bright green, red and white design, die-cut celluloid perpetual calendar disk wheel on bottom, orig box, early 1900s 40.00
Chisholm Steel Shovel Works, Cleveland, glass 65.00
Columbia National Bank, glass 10.00
Crane Co., Chicago, 75th Anniversary, brass, 2-3/8" d, round 30.00
General Abrams Cigar 45.00
Hoover Ball & Bearing Co., 1-3/4" d, 2" h, chromed steel, eight ball bearings in channel around one large bearing 35.00
Laco Drawn Wire Quality, ceramic, white ground, black letters, half-lightbulb shape, backstamped "Rosenthal" 60.00
Lehigh Sewer Pipe & Tile Co., Ft. Dodge, IA, glass 12.00
Merchants Awning Co., oval, glass, red, white and black 20.00
Morton's Iodized Salt, blue, white, green and gold 38.00
Northwestern National Life Insurance Co., glass 22.00
Old Crow, hard plastic, 5-1/2" h, figural, crow, inscribed gray base, c1960 75.00
Star Line Goods, 1-3/4" by 2-1/4" by-1/2" h, cast iron, brass colored, figural, turtle, 1" oval celluloid shell, inscription in center of shell, c1904 . . . . 80.00
The Ransbottom Bros. Pottery Co., Roseville, OH, glass, dome type, illus of brothers. 70.00
Universal Block 18.00

Cast Iron, figural

Cowboy, 4-1/4" by 3" h 100.00
Elephant, 1-3/4" by 1-1/2" h. 50.00
German Shepherd, 3" h 50.00
Sea Turtle, 1" by 4-1/2" 100.00

Other

Commemorative, Prince Charles and Lady Diana Spencer, 3" d, etched portraits, purple ground, Caithness 175.00
Confederate Monument, Montgomery, AL, glass 30.00
Franklin Mint, Baccarat 75.00
Political, John F. Kennedy, 2-7/8" d, sulfide, bust, black amethyst ground, Baccarat 90.00
Political, McKinley, 1" by 2-1/2" by 4", glass, rect, sepia photo, inscribed "Pres McKinley, Wife and Home, Canton, O," mkd "Cent Glass & Nov Co" on reverse, 1900s 50.00

Commemorative, United Nations Building, New York, #638, antique brass finish, 3" h, $20.

Souvenir, Mt. St. Helens, iridized, dated 1988 . . . . 25.00
Trans World Airlines, Framed Milestones, Man in Flight, six medallions 65.00
World's Fair, Chicago World's Fair, 1933, Century of Progress, metal, painted gold, Fort Dearborn exhibit-shape, orig box 30.00

Parking Meters

I have seen them for sale. I have even been tempted to buy one. The meter was a lamp base, complete with new lamp wiring and an attractive shade. To make the light work, you put a coin in the meter. I'm not sure why, but they are rather pricey, usually in the $50 to $100 range. Maybe it has something to do with the fine that you will pay if you obtain one illegally. Might be a good idea to stash a few coin-operated meters away. Have you experienced one of the new electronic meters? Isn't progress wonderful?

Patriotic Collectibles

Americans love symbols. We express our patriotism through eagles, flags and shields, the Liberty Bell, Statue of Liberty and Uncle Sam. We even throw in a few patriots, such as Benjamin Franklin.

Activity Set, The American Brilliant Paints, American Crayon Co., 1943 . . . . 60.00
Bank, cast iron, Uncle Sam, c1974 . 15.00
Book, *Uncle Sam's Story Book*, Wilhelmina Harper, 1944 . . . . 35.00

Figure, Statue of Liberty, metal, gold color, 4-1/2" h, $5.

Bumper Sticker, Bush/Quayle 88, red, white and blue 2.00

Figure, 6-1/2" by 4-1/2" h, gnome, Uncle Sam wearing blue hat, white stars, Tom Clark, 1985. . . . . .35.00

Ornament, Uncle Sam Keepsake Ornament, pressed tin, Hallmark, 1984. . . . . .25.00

Paint Book, 10" by 13-1/2", Old Glory, 20 pgs, war scenes, Saalfield, 1917 .30.00

Pin, die-cut silvered metal eagle with shield symbol on chest, holding miniature replica brass alarm clock, c1890 . . . . 30.00

Pinback Button, Carter, red, white and blue, Uncle Sam riding back of eagle, holding yellow oval frame, Carter picture 10.00

Pinback Button, Ford, red, white and blue, star and stripe design, black-and-white photo, Pinback Button, President Ford's Visit to South Dakota, Oct. 16, 1974 . . . . 25.00

Planter, ceramic, top hat, figural, Ruben's Originals, 1974 . . . . 15.00

Plate, bread and butter, clear glass, Constitution signer's names, emb 1776-1876. . . . . 80.00

Puppet, marionette, 36" h, composition, wood, Uncle Sam, metallic thread, red, white and blue, sequined top hat, metallic shoes, Macy & Co. . . . 150.00

Seal, "Patriotic Decorations," die-cut gummed seals, red, white and blue,10 of orig 25, Dennison, c1925 . . . . 15.00

Sheet Music, Yankee Doodle Dandy, George M. Cohan, 1932 . . . . 5.00

Sheet Music, Your Flag And My Flag, Harry Woods, 1918. . . . . 10.00

Stamp Machine, automatic, red, white and blue, Uncle Sam illus front, serial #4819, nickel and dime slots, c1945 . . . . 100.00

Stickpin, brass, emb gold bug, red, white and blue cloth flag. 70.00

Stuffed Doll, Garfield, plush, 8" by 7", red, white and blue hat, holding flag, Dakin, 1978 . . . . 30.00

Tie, red, white and blue flag, 47" l, Wilson/Marshall, black, white embroidered names 50.00

Toy, Bugs Bunny, rubber, 8-5/8" by 3-1/2" by 3", Warner Bros., 1975 . . . . . . 25.00

Peanuts

Peanuts is a newspaper cartoon strip written and illustrated by Charles M. Schulz. The strip started about 1950 and starred a boy named Charlie Brown and his dog Snoopy. Its popularity grew slowly. In 1955, merchandising was begun with the hope of expanding the strip's popularity. By the 1970s, Charlie Brown and the gang were more than just cartoon strip characters. They greeted every holiday with TV specials; their images adorned lunch boxes, pencils, pins, T-shirts and stuffed toys. Macy's Thanksgiving Day Parade wouldn't be complete without a huge Snoopy floating down Seventh Avenue.

Club: Peanuts Collector Club, 539 Sudden Valley, Bellingham, WA 98226.

Bells, Schmid
1977, Woodstock's Christmas 18.00
1978, Mother's Day 15.00
1984, Snoopy and the Beagle Scouts 12.00

Dolls
Lucy, cloth, stuffed, 14" h, 1970 . . . . 22.00

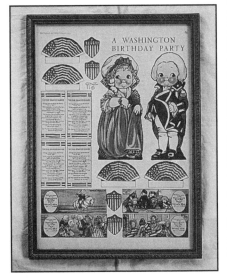

Paper Dolls, Grace Drayton, A Washington Birthday Party, *Pictorial Review Magazine*, **1932, 10-1/2" by 14", $15.**

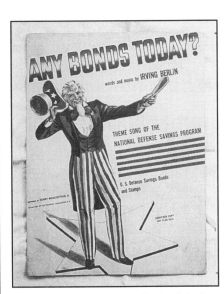

Sheet Music, Any Bonds Today?, Irving Berlin, $8.

Bank, figural Snoopy, 6" h, $12.

Peppermint Patty, cloth, stuffed,
14" h........................18.00
Woodstock, 1972 ....15.00

Figures

Belle, Dress & Play series, Sleepy Time
version, vinyl, 9" h, 1970s 35.00
Charlie Brown and Linus, plastic,
cloth, 7" h..................40.00
Snoopy, Golfer, vinyl, 9" h, 1970....35.00
Snoopy, Red Baron, vinyl,
7" h, 1966..................25.00

Other

Activity Set, Colorforms, Hold That Line
Charlie Brown, 1969..........20.00
Bank, Lucy, 6" h 30.00
Bank, Snoopy, wearing baseball hat and
mitt, ceramic, 1973...........50.00
Bike Horn, Snoopy, 1966 ....10.00
Box, cov, porcelain, heart-shaped,
Snoopy finial.................25.00
Candle Holder, composition, 7-1/2" h,
Linus sucking thumb and holding blan-
ket, brass insert cup,
Hallmark, 1970s.............25.00
Charm Bracelet, Lucy, Snoopy and Charlie
Brown, enamel, Aviva, 1969 ....25.00
Comic Book, Peanuts, Dell, #878, Charlie
Brown and Snoopy watching TV
cov illus, 1958 ....20.00
Cookie Jar, Snoopy, standing......30.00
Game, Peanuts, Selchow & Righter,
1959......................45.00
Lamp, hurricane-style, Snoopy dancing
among flowers illus, key type switch,
white and blue, 1978 ....50.00
Lunch Box, Snoopy, blue, dome top,
1978......................5.00
Magazine, *Newsweek*, cov story,
Dec. 27, 1971................8.00
Mug, Snoopy, "Allergic to Mornings"..5.00
Nodder, Snoopy as Joe Cool, 5" h ..50.00

**Limited Edition Collector Plate, Peanuts
Mother's Day series, 1972, Linus, $10.**

Paper Dolls, Snoopy, 10 outfits,
Determined, #274, 1976...... 25.00
Pencil Holder, Snoopy, ceramic, dog
house, figural, 1975 .... 25.00
Pinback Button, Snoopy as Red Baron,
1-1/2", Millbrook Bread, 1970 .... 2.00
Pillow, Snoopy bowling illus, green and
yellow 10.00
Push Puppet, Snoopy as sheriff,
Ideal 14.00
Radio, Snoopy on doghouse 30.00
Scissors, plastic, red, Joe Cool figure on
front..................... 9.50
Snoopy Tea Set, child's toy, metal,
J. Chein & Co., #276,
orig box, 1970s............ 100.00
Snow Dome, Snoopy,
musical, 1988 .... 40.00
Switchplate, Pigpen, "Cleanliness Is Next
To Impossible," Hallmark, 1970 .. 6.00
Tote Bag, Snoopy, canvas, Butterfly
Originals 6.00
Toy, Jack-in-the-box, Mattel 75.00
Toy, Squeeze toy, Snoopy as golfer . 3.50
Umbrella, Snoopy, 1965 .... 26.00
Watch, Snoopy as Flying Ace, Timex,
#84111, 1979 .... 50.00

Pencil Clips and Paper Clips

Paper clips clip pieces of paper together. Pencil clips hold pencils in
one's pocket. Both were popular; both
were used to advertise products. Neither form is used much today. After
seeing several hundred examples, I
think they should be missed. The listings below are for paper clips with celluloid buttons and metal spring clips,
all dating from the early 1900s. Pencil
clips have celluloid buttons with metal
pencil holders.

Paper Clips

Bickmore's Gall Cure, black and white,
7/8" l 20.00
Bissel Co., multicolored,
red inscription, 1" l 30.00
Edison Portland Cement Co., celluloid,
yellow and black design, Thomas A.
Edison Trademark, 1920s,
1-3/4" d 25.00
Eureka Jewelry Co., sepia photo portrait of
woman wearing pearl necklace, sheer
off-the-shoulder white gown, light green
and white inscription, dark brown
border, 1-1/4" l 40.00
Lane Mfg. Co., Montpelier, VT, black and
white sawmill, c1900, 2-1/2" l ... 25.00

Peacock Condoms, litho metal, yellow,
green and red, c1940, 2" by 2" ..35.00

Pencil Clips

Atherton Coaster Brake, black, white and
red, c1920s 5.00
Carey Salt, black and white, metal clip,
1930s.....................20.00
Coca-Cola, white lettering,
red ground.................15.00
Colonial Salt, black and yellow,
1930s.....................10.00
Dad's Root Beer, yellow, black and red,
1940s.....................12.00
Diamond Crystal Salt, red and white,
litho 12.00
Knights Life Insurance, yellow and black,
silver luster metal clip, 1930s ...25.00
Millbrook Bread, red, white and blue 12.00
Morton Salt, black and white 8.00
Mr. Peanut, yellow, black and white, die-cut
litho tin tab, 1940s 18.00
Pepsi-Cola, red, white and blue,
1940s.....................18.00
7-UP, black, white and red, 1940s ..12.00

Pennants, Felt

Pennants were produced in large
enough quantities for collectors to be
picky. Buy pennants only if they are in
good condition. Images and lettering
should be crisp and the pennant
should show no signs of moth or insect
damage. When storing pennants,
keep them flat or roll them on a cylinder. Do not fold! Creases left from
years of folding can be very difficult to
remove.

Political

Coolidge-Dawes, Lincoln Tour 1924, 11"
by 24" l, blue, white letters......75.00
Thomas E. Dewey For President, 11" l, red,
white letters,
yellow felt streamers 15.00

**Sports, baseball, American League All
Stars, Philadelphia, 1976, $25.**

Souvenir, Pennsylvania Turnpike, yellow and black, 27" l, $20.

Dwight Eisenhower, Eisenhower-Nixon
  Inauguration, 29" l, brown, white illus
  and lettering, white Capitol building
  scene, blue, yellow and green shading,
  1953 . . . . .20.00
Humphrey, Unite With Humphrey, 30" l,
  red, white and blue, 1968 . . . . . . .10.00
Kennedy/Johnson, 30" l, red, white and
  blue, 1960 . . . . .30.00
George Wallace, Stand Up For America,
  28" l, red, white and blue, 1968 . . .8.00
Woodrow Wilson, 17" l, dark purple, tin
  support bar, Wilson portrait and
  inscription "March 4th Inaugura-
  tion/1913 Washington DC" 40.00

Sports
Baseball, Dizzy Dean, Cardinals 35.00
Basketball, Charles Barkley 5.00
Boxing, 26-1/2" l, blue, white letters, Ali and
  Wepner 1975 heavyweight champion-
  ship, March 24, 1975 . . . . .28.00
Derby Day, 18" l, red, white lettering, red
  and white design, pink accents . .15.00
Football, 28" l, green, football player illus,
  yellow lettering, Boston Yanks,
  c1950 . . . . .20.00

Other
Character, Batman, 29" l, black, white
  lettering, color illus, c1966 . . . . . .25.00
Character, Beatles, 22" l, white, red and
  black, Irwing Specialties. 100.00
Ringling Bros. Barnum & Bailey
  Circus, 24" l, brown, white
  lettering, circus scenes,
  yellow trim and streamers, c1940 25.00
Space Flight, Feb. 20, 1962 first U.S.
  orbital space flight commemoration,
  white, red and blue, 3" black and white
  John Glenn photo. 40.00
World War I, 27th Division. 24.00

Pennsbury Pottery

Henry and Lee Below established
Pennsbury Pottery, named for its close
proximity to William Penn's estate
"Pennsbury," three miles west of Morrisville, Pa., in 1950. Henry, a ceramic
engineer and mold maker, and Lee, a
designer and modeler, had previously
worked for Stangl Pottery in Trenton,
N.J. In 1970, the pottery filed for bankruptcy and the contents were auc-
tioned off. In 1971, a fire destroyed the
pottery and support building. Many of
Pennsbury's forms, motifs and manufacturing techniques have Stangl
roots. A line of birds, similar to those
produced by Stangl, were among the
earliest Pennsbury products. While the
carved design technique originated at
Stangl, high bas-relief molds did not.

Pennsbury products are easily
identified by their brown-wash background. The company also made pieces featuring other background colors.
Do not make the mistake of assuming
that a piece is not Pennsbury because
it does not have a brown wash. Pennsbury motifs are heavily nostalgic, farm-
and Pennsylvania/German-oriented.
The pottery made a large number of
commemorative, novelty and special-
order pieces. Marks differ from piece
to piece, depending on the person who
signed the piece or the artist who
sculpted the mold.

Concentrate on one pattern or type.
Since the pieces were hand-carved,
aesthetic quality differs from piece to
piece. Look for pieces with a strong

design sense and a high quality of ex-
ecution. Buy only clearly marked pieces. Look for decorator and designer
initials that can be easily identified.

Many of the company's commemorative and novelty pieces relate to
businesses and events in the Middle
Atlantic States, thus commanding their
highest price within that region.

Look-Alike Alert: The Lewis Brothers
Pottery, Trenton, N.J., purchased 50
of the lesser Pennsbury molds. Although they were supposed to remove
the Pennsbury name from the molds,
some molds were overlooked. Further,
two Pennsbury employees moved to
Lewis Brothers when Pennsbury
closed. Many pieces similar in feel and
design to Pennsbury were produced.
Many of Pennsbury's major lines, including the Harvest and Rooster patterns, plaques, birds and highly
unusual molds, were not reproduced.

Figures
Blue Bird, #103, sgd
  "K Violet Kanivrael" 140.00
Chickadee, #11, 3-1/2" h 100.00
Slick-Bunny, 5-1/2" h, paper label . 100.00

Pitchers
Amish, 2-1/2" h 25.00
Blue Dowry, 5" h 45.00
Delft Toleware, 5" h 45.00
Barbershop Quartet, 7-1/4" h 85.00

Plates
Angel, Christmas, 1970 . . . . .30.00
Boy and Girl, 11" d 40.00
Courting Buggy, 8" d, sgd
  "S" Sue Below 70.00
Kissing Over Cow, 6" d 40.00

**Vegetable Dish, 9-1/2" l, rooster, divid-
ed, $35.**

Dish, 7-7/8" l, oval, Pennsylvania Railroad, 1856 Tiger, $45.

Other

Ashtray, commemorative, Summerseat,
    1804-1954 . . . . .25.00
Bank, Hershey Kiss, figural, 4" h. . . .18.00
Bell, Mother's Day, 1977 . . . . .35.00
Bowl, Hex, 9" d 35.00
Cigarette Box, Eagle 35.00
Mug, Barbershop Quartet 35.00
Mug, Swallow the Insult 35.00
Pie Pan, 9-1/2" d 70.00
Powder Jar, Hex, 6-1/2" d 55.00
Pretzel Bowl, Red Barn, 12" by 8" . .125.00
Salt and Pepper Shakers,
    pr, Amish 45.00
Spice Set, Rooster, five pc,
    3-3/4" h. 125.00
Tile, Harvest, 6" d, sgd "LB" 30.00
Wall Pocket, figural bellows,
    Eagle dec 45.00

Pens and Pencils

Forget the ordinary and look for the unusual. The more unique the object or set is, the more likely it is that it will have a high value. Defects of any kind drop value dramatically. When buying a set, try to get the original box, along with any instruction sheets and guarantee cards (you will be amazed at how many people actually save them).

Clubs: American Pencil Collectors Society, 2222 S. Millwood, Wichita, KS 67213; Pen Collectors of America, P.O. Box 821449, Houston, TX 77282; Pen Fancier's Club, 1169 Overcash Dr., Dunedin, FL 34698.

Newsletter: *Pens*, P.O. Box 64, Teaneck, NJ 07666.

Periodical: *Pen World Magazine*, P.O. Box 6007, Kingwood, TX 77325.

Pens

Amoco, retractable, ball-point, red, white
    and black 20.00
Bell Telephone, Waterbury,
    ball-point, MIB. 25.00
Conklin, Model 30, black hard rubber,
    1903 . . . . 80.00
Dunn, black, red barrel, gold-plated trim,
    1920 . . . . 50.00
Parker, Model 51, maroon, stainless steel
    cap, chrome-plated trim, aeromatic
    filler, 1950 . . . . 95.00
Parker, Model 61, first edition,
    1956 . . . . 100.00
Sheaffer, Strato Writer, ball-point, gold
    filled, metal mounted, 1948 . . . . . 65.00
Sheaffer, White Dot, snorkel, black, 14k
    gold cap and band, plunger filled,
    1948 . . . . 65.00
Swan, Eternal Model, black, gold-filled
    trim, marked "44 E.T.N., Model 4" 70.00
Wahl, ribbon pen, lady's double-narrow
    band on cap, 14k, #2 nib 100.00
Waterman, Lady Patricia, gray mottled
    finish, lever fill, 1936 . . . . 75.00
Waterman, Taperite, black, metal mounted
    cap, gold-filled trim, lever filler,
    1949 . . . . 100.00

Pencils

AC Auto Parts, mechanical, gold-plated,
    floating AC oil filter inside, 1940s 35.00
Amoco American Gas, mechanical, oil
    sample in end,
    red, white and black 25.00
Coca-Cola, 7-1/2" l, Drink Refreshing
    Coca-Cola, 1950s 2.50
Elsie, 5" l, mechanical, Secretary Pen Co.,
    Borden Co., 1930-40 . . . . 60.00
Hudson-Essex, PA dealership, metal
    bullet-shape, "Shoot Straight For
    Triangle Motor Co.," 1930s, 4" l . 30.00

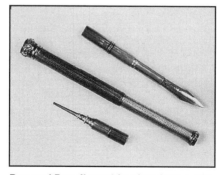

Pen and Pencil combination, brass, nib mkd "B.T. Benton, New York, 1851," telescoping, 7-1/4" l open, $75.

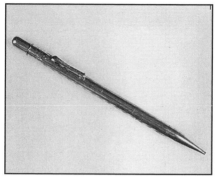

Pencil, Conklin, No. 4V, rolled gold, 5-1/4" l, $45.

Jeep Willys Motors, mechanical, red Jeep
    illus 20.00
Kendall Oil, "The 2000 Mile Oil," mechani-
    cal, metal and plastic, late 1930s,
    5-1/2" l 15.00
Lindbergh, wood, lead, gold colored, blue
    "Plucky Lindy" portrait, red Spirit of St.
    Louis, 7-1/2" l, unsharpened 28.00
Orange-Crush, mechanical, Mexican 20.00
Parker, Fineline 4000, novel point,
    platinum plating 40.00
Pennzoil, mechanical, green, yellow, red
    and black, perpetual calendar . . . 20.00
Popeye, 10-1/2" l, metal, mechanical,
    silver-gray, black and dark red illus and
    text, Eagle Pencil Co., 1930-40. . 25.00
"Remember Pearl Harbor, United We
    Stand, We Will Win," red, white and blue
    plastic, local business sponsor adv,
    5" l 65.00
Wahl-Eversharp, 1919, gold-filled . . 60.00
Wahl-Eversharp, 1923, ring top, gold-filled
    case 50.00

Other

Blotter, Esterbrook Writing Sets, ink sets
    and pen tips illus, multicolored . . . 8.00
Lamp, Parker Pens, wood base, metal
    shade, black 130.00
Pen and Pencil Set, Chevron adv, The
    Heartbeat of America, Parker,
    orig box 15.00

Perfume Bottles

Perfume bottles come in all shapes and sizes. In addition to perfume bottles, there are atomizers (a bottle with a spray mechanism), colognes (large bottles whose stoppers often have an application device), scents (small bottles used to hold a scent or smelling salts) and vinaigrettes (an ornamental box or bottle with a perforated top).

The stopper of a perfume is used for application and is very elongated.

Perfume bottles were one of the hottest collectibles of the 1980s. As a result of market manipulation and speculative buying, prices soared. The wind started to blow in the wrong direction. The field began to stink. Many prices collapsed. But the wind is changing again as new collectors follow the scent. Today's collectors are also interested in commercial bottles They enjoy their pretty shapes and colors as well as those sexy names.

Clubs: International Perfume Bottle Association, P.O. Box 529, Vienna, VA 22180; Mini-Scents, 7 St. John's Rd., West Hollywood, CA 90069.

Newsletter: *Perfume & Scent Bottle Quarterly*, P.O. Box 187, Galena, OH 43021.

Atomizers

3-1/2" h, octagonal, dark amethyst, cone finial, silver-plated neck,
rubber bulb 38.00

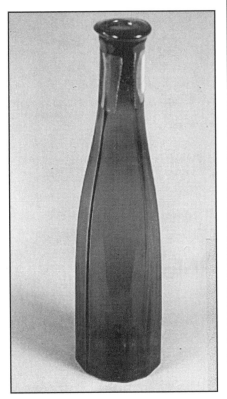

Cologne, 5" h, light amethyst, 12 panel, $90.

4-1/4" h, opaque pink, rubber bulb, gold-plated fittings, paper DeVilbiss sticker, c1925 . . . . 60.00
6" h, opaque, black glass, mkd "DeVilbiss," c1920 . . . . 70.00
6-1/4" h, orchid glass, long glass stopper, c1920 . . . . 75.00

Perfume, Commercial
Ambergris, U.S. Treasury, sample. . 10.00
Avon, 3-1/4" h, California Perfume Co., glass, violet sachet, half full, violet paper label, 1912 . . . . 125.00
Black Satin 8.00
Bourjois, Evening in Paris, blue, long stopper 120.00
Chaine D'Or, encased, beige tasseled cardboard box, imitation shagreen, c1926 . . . . 45.00
Corday, Femme de Jour, frosted . . . 50.00
Forever Amber, mermaid torso, figural 27.50
Florida Water, Stevens & Stevens Co. . . . 10.00
Geisha Girl, Japanese Mfrs., Chicago, c1900 . . . . 25.00
Givenchy, orig red silk box 45.00
Langlois, inner glass stopper, metal cap, c1920 . . . . 45.00
Le Narcisse Bleu, octagonal 75.00
Le Narcisse Noir, 5-1/2" h, 1912 . . . 50.00
Lionettes, frosted glass, brass top, 1923 . . . . 65.00
Mavis, 8-1/2" h, 1915 . . . . 85.00
My Own Jasmine, gold cap, wooden base, Safuran 83.00
Obsession, store display 95.00
Olor de la Noche, 1940s 45.00
Petit Mimosa, c1917 . . . . 30.00

Scent Bottle, violin-shape, amber glass, pewter top, $125.

Saxony 5.00
Scottish Heather 45.00
Sweet Pea, blue stripes, red leather case, brass cap, Renaud 38.00
Tre Lis, plume stopper, paper label . 10.00
Valdome La Marquis 65.00
White Shoulders, lipstick-type 10.00
Wildewood Toilet Water, frosted glass, molded nude, c1920 . . . . 75.00

Perfume, Figural
Acorn, Wild Musk, chain, celluloid box, Max Factor 50.00
Buddha, frosted glass head, c1920 . 85.00
Cat, German, 1910 . . . . 60.00
Dog, green, Sitzendorf Porcelain Manufacturing Co., Germany . . . 60.00
Flapper's Head, lay-down type 60.00
Lady and Parrot, 3-3/8" h, china, blue, white, black, yellow, green and orange, metal and cork stopper 70.00
Little Dutch Girl, Goebel, c1935 . . . . 60.00
Oriental Lady's Head, Schaffer & Vater, Germany, c1896 . . . . 85.00
Queen Elizabeth, Crown Staffordshire, England, c1930s 125.00

Perfume, Scent
Blown glass, green, silver cap, floral and scroll motif, 4-1/2" h, c1875 . . . . 250.00
Glass, hobnail 35.00
Seahorse, opaque white stripes, clear glass, c1700s 100.00
Smelling Salts, amethyst, threaded neck, Sandwich Glass Co., c1850 . . . . 75.00

Perfume, Other
Cranberry Glass, 3-3/4" h, bulbous, enameled blue and gray flowers, blue, orange and white leaves, clear flattened ball stopper 90.00
Cranberry Glass, 5-1/2" h, beveled, clear-cut faceted bubble stopper 110.00
Fenton, Hobnail, cranberry opalescent, flat stopper 90.00
Pairpoint, 5-1/2" h, heavy crystal, controlled bubbles 60.00

Pez Dispensers

The Pez dispenser originated in Germany and was invented by Edvard Haas in 1927. The name "Pez" is an abbreviation of the German word for peppermint—pfefferminz. The peppermint candy was touted as an alternative to smoking. The first Pez container was shaped like a disposable cigarette lighter and is referred to by collectors as the non-headed or regular dispenser.

Tom and Jerry; 4-1/4" h Tom, 4-1/8" h Jerry, price each, $10.

By 1952, Pez arrived in the United States. New fruit flavored candy and novelty dispensers were introduced. Early containers were designed to commemorate holidays or favorite children's characters including Bozo the Clown, Mickey Mouse and other popular Disney, Warner Brothers and Universal personalities.

Collecting Pez containers at flea markets must be done with care. Inspect each dispenser to guarantee it is intact and free from cracks and chips. Also, familiarize yourself with proper color and marking characteristics.

Newsletter: *PEZ Collector's News*, P.O. Box 124, Sea Cliff, NY 11579.

Merry Melody Makers

Clown	6.00
Dog	20.00
Frog	15.00
Koala	20.00
Lamb	15.00
Monkey	20.00
Panda	6.00

Other

Batgirl	65.00
Betsy Ross	60.00
Bouncer Beagle	6.00
Bozo, die-cut, 1960s	100.00
Bunny, fat ears, Easter, 1960s	1.00
Captain America, black, visor	50.00
Captain PEZ	85.00
Casper, die-cut, 1960s	100.00
Cat, derby	40.00

Chick in Egg	12.00
Cockatoo, Kooky Zoo, 1970s	10.00
Cool Cat, Warner Brothers cartoon characters, 1970-89	20.00
Creature from the Black Lagoon, 1960s	175.00
Crocodile, Kooky Zoo, 1970s	30.00
Daffy Duck	15.00
Dead Head Dr. Skull, Halloween, 1960s	1.00
Dino	3.00
Donald Duck	15.00
Droopy Dog	8.00
Dumbo	25.00
Engineer, Pez Pal, 1960-79	30.00
Fat-Ears Rabbit	15.00
Fireman	30.00
Fozzie Bear, licensed character, Sesame Street, 1991	1.00
Garfield, with visor	3.00
Gorilla, circus, 1970s	10.00
Gonzo	3.00
Goofy	3.00
Gorilla	45.00
Hulk, light green	10.00
Jiminy Cricket, Disney, 1960s	15.00
Joker	70.00
Lamb, Easter, 1960s	1.00
Li'l Bad Wolf	25.00
Maharaja, Pez Pal, 1960-79	60.00
Merlin Mouse	10.00
Miss Piggy	10.00
Moo Moo Cow, Kooky Zoo, 1960s	20.00
Mr. Ugly Scrooge, Halloween, 1960s	1.00
Mowgli	30.00
Nermal	3.00
Octopus	40.00
Pebbles Flintstone	3.00
Pineapple, crazy fruit, 1970s	200.00
Popeye, removable pipe	45.00
Rhino	6.00
Ringmaster, circus, 1970s	25.00
Road Runner, MOC	6.00
Rooster	35.00
Santa Claus, painted eyes	5.00
Scrooge McDuck	20.00
Silly Clown, 1970s	25.00
Silver Glow, MOC	10.00
Skull, with feet	3.00
Smurfette	8.00
Snoopy	5.00
Snowman	5.00
Spiderman	3.00
Sylvester, white whiskers	2.00
Thor, Super Heroes, 1970s	60.00
Tiger, whistle head	6.00
Uncle Sam	70.00
Winnie the Pooh	20.00
Witch, three pc, no feet	10.00

Pez-Related

Coloring Book, non-English, Safety #2	15.00
Peter Pez bag, pink	10.00
Puzzle, 500 pcs, Springbrook/Hallmark	10.00
Stand, plastic, with fuzz, holds six non-footed dispensers	9.00

Picture Frames

We have reached the point where the frame is often worth more than the picture in it. Decorators have fallen in love with old frames. If you find one with character and pizzazz at a flea market for a few dollars, pick it up. It will not be hard to resell. Who said picture frames have to be used for pictures? They make great frames for mirrors. Use your imagination.

Art Deco, 14-1/2" by 17", beveled glass, etched floral and leaf design, c1940	85.00
Art Deco, Brass, 6" by 8"	80.00
Art Deco, Wood and Glass	65.00
Curly Maple, 16-3/4" by 20-1/2", refinished	90.00
Gesso, pine framework, oval, acorns and leaves dec, gilded inner edge, beaded outer edge, mahogany stained	48.00
Henitz, 3" by 3-1/4" h, oval center, scrolled openwork	100.00
Henitz, 5-3/4" by 7-3/4" h, silvered bronze, geometric sterling overlay	200.00
Henitz, 8" by 11" h, textured bronze, emb bronze stylized overlay, Silver Crest	85.00
Oak, 7" by 23-1/2" h, dark stain, lilies in vase painting, sgd "R Hill, 1877," wood backing, some wear	155.00

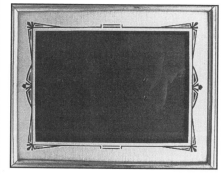

Metal, silver colored, silver and black Art Deco-style cardboard matte, easel back, 7" by 9", $35.

Wood, daguerreotype case, 3-1/4" by 3-3/4" closed size, $45.

Oak, 15-1/2" by 19-1/2" h, oval, dark stain,
    raised beading edge trim 165.00
Oak, 19-3/4" by 26" h, gilt liner,
    no glass 55.00

Pie Birds

Pie birds do not whistle while they work, however, they are hot collectibles and are functional kitchen novelties. A pie bird is a baking aide used to prevent juices from overflowing onto the oven floor and to keep the upper pie crust firm. Basic criteria for a pie bird are: most commonly made from a pottery material, glazed inside and out, 3 inches to 5 inches tall, arches at the base to allow steam to enter and continue out the top hole (usually inside the beak) and most important, shoulders to support the top crust.

The pie bird is centered on the bottom crust and surrounded with filling. A slit is cut in the top crust and slipped over the pie bird's head to rest on its shoulders. The crust is then pinched firmly around the neck. Most of the bird is inside the pie. When served, the pie is sliced around the bird.

English pie funnels can be traced back to the mid 1800s, via patent research. These were functional bell-shaped funnels. It was not until the 1930s that the bird shape was introduced and in the mid 1950s, a pie elephant. Most pie birds produced in the United States were made between 1940 and the 1960s. As a rule, older pie birds were air brushed rather than

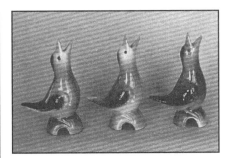

Birds, U.S., mass produced, blue, pink and cinnamon with black details, 1950s-60s, price each, $22.

hand painted. Figural pie vents (leprechauns, pilgrims, Santas, animals with clothes, etc.) were introduced in the 1980s and are still made today by small individual potteries.

Advisor: Lillian Cole, 14 Harmony School Rd., Flemington, NJ 08822, (908) 782-3193.

Newsletter: *Piebirds Unlimited*, 14 Harmony School Rd., Flemington, NJ 08822.

Birds
England, reg numbers on white base30.00
Imported, no eyes, beak not pointed,
    glazed halfway up 5.00
Iron and Lace Pottery, Queen Anne Lace
    flower fired on bird's breast,
    modern 20.00
Morton Pottery, rose, yellow and turquoise
    patches 20.00
Royal Worcester, England, two pc, blue
    and white, no box 65.00
Wide open mouth, 1980s to present 15.00

Other
Benny the Baker, Cardinal
    China Co., holds pie
    crimper and cake tester 75.00
Chef, Taiwan, black face, holding round
    spoon, painted red and yellow, crazed,
    1990, price for pair 10.00
Corn Shock Funnel, England,
    1970s 40.00
Crow, feather detailing, 1970-80s . . 20.00
Duck, U.S., long neck, mass produced,
    blue, rose or yellow with black or brown
    details, 1950-60s 22.00
Elephant, Nutbrown, England,
    gray or cream 50.00
Figural, variety of people, birds and bird in
    pie, mkd "SB, England". 30.00
Funnel, Pyrex Brand, 1970s 35.00
Funnel, Scipio Creek Pottery, sgd,
    pre-1993 . . . . 25.00

Rooster, Cleminson Pottery,
    1940-60s 20.00
Rooster, Pearl China Co., U.S.,
    mass-produced, various color
    combinations 40.00
Swan Head, England, pink-cinnamon
    color. 50.00

Pig Collectibles

This is one animal that does better as a collectible than in real life. Pig collectibles have never been oinkers. Established pig collectors focus on the bisque and porcelain pigs of the late 19th and early 20th centuries. This is a limited view. Try banks in the shape of a pig as a specialized collecting area. If not appealing, look at the use of pigs in advertising. If neither please you, there is always Porky. "That's All, Folks!"

Club: The Happy Pig Collectors Club, P.O. Box 17, Oneida, IL 61467.

Banks
Carnival Chalkware, 7" h, 1950s . . . 45.00
Harley-Davidson, black. 20.00
Porky Pig, plastic 25.00
White clay, seated, clear glaze. 30.00

Cookie Jars
Girl Pig, yellow, blue, unmkd 75.00
Lady Pig, gold trim, unmkd. 75.00

Cookie Jar, Robinson-Ransbottom, Sheriff Pig, mkd "RRP Co, Roseville, OH, #363," 12-1/2" h, $150.

Winnie Pig with Sweet Clover, gold trim,
Shawnee, mkd "USA"........190.00

Figures

Dutch Shoe, pig sitting in shoe 35.00
Porcelain, 4-1/2" h, spongeware....85.00
Spongeware, 5" h, unmkd........55.00

Other

Ashtray, Two pigs hugging, bisque,
stamped "Made in Germany"....80.00
Ashtray, Two pigs looking into old
fashioned Victrola............75.00
Carnival Chalkware, 7" h, 1950s....45.00
Chocolate Mold, figural, tin, two parts....
65.00
Comic Book, Porky Pig, Whitman,
#1408, 1942................25.00
Cutting Board, 19-1/2" by 9-1/2",
pig-shape, black edge within red outer
edge......................40.00
Jar, 2-3/4" h, pig along side,
orange seal 60.00
Matchsafe, bisque, 5" h, pink pig, one
captioned "Scratch My Back," other
reads "Me Too"..............100.00
Pail, 6-1/2" d, 3" h, litho tin, Three Little
Pigs illus, 1930s.............75.00
Paperweight, figural, glass, "Best Pig For-
ceps, compliments J. Reimers,
Davenport, IA" 100.00
Pillow, figural...................15.00
Pinback Button, Blue Ribbon For Hogs
Meat Meal, blue and white, crowned pig
sitting upright on rear haunches,
c1920.....................20.00
Playing Cards, Three Little Pigs, complete
deck, orig box mkd "By Special
Permission Walt Disney Enterprises,"
1930s.....................50.00
Salt and Pepper Shakers, pr, 4" h, figural,
one playing accordion, other playing
saxophone, glazed and painted, mkd
"Japan," c1930..............45.00
Puppet, Porky Pig, hand.........25.00

Postcard, photo card, tinted, divided back, $10.

Puppet, Porky Pig, push 40.00
Soaky, Porky Pig, Colgate-Palmolive25.00
Statue, 7" h, Porky Pig, plaster, painted,
1940-50................... 50.00
Stuffed Toy, mohair, 6-1/2", pink, felt
mouth and tail, cord on neck.... 85.00
Toothpick Holder, 2-3/4" h, two little pigs
in front of egg 50.00
Toothpick Holder, 4" h, three large pigs
in front of water trough 60.00
Vase, two pigs looking out of large shoe,
Germany.................. 60.00

Pinback Buttons

Around 1893, the Whitehead & Hoag Co., filed the first patents for celluloid pinback buttons. By the turn of the century, the celluloid pinback button was used as a promotional tool covering a wide spectrum, ranging from presidential candidates to amusement parks, not that there is much difference between the two.

This category covers advertising pinback buttons. To discover the full range of non-political pinbacks consult Ted Hake and Russ King's *Price Guide To Collectible Pin-back Buttons*

1896-1986 (Hake's Americana & Collectibles Press: 1986).

Aristocrat Milk, red and white, 1930s . 4.00
Ball Brand Trade Mark All Knit, red, black
and white..................10.00
Ballistite Smokeless Powders......15.00
Bartle's & Jaymes, Thank You For Your
Support, multicolored, photo 8.00
Bill Dugan Cigar, multicolored, c1900 8.00
Buick, white on red.............21.00
Blue Ribbon Cake, blue and white,
1930s.....................4.00
Cameo Baking Powder, Purest Best, red,
yellow, black and white,
product illus.................8.00
Dalton Adding Machine, red, black and
white, c1900 ....5.00
Del Monte, black and white, red logo,
1900s.....................5.00
Dixie Boy Shoes, Geo. D. Witt
Shoe Co....................20.00
Dold Foods, red, white and blue,
1920s.....................5.00
Dr. Sweet's Original Root Beer, girl
hugging horse's head, stars and stripes
border, red, white and blue 40.00
Favorite Stoves and Ranges, We
Guarantee, Best In The World,
multicolored..................8.00
Gold Medal Flour, Washburn Crosby Co.,
blue, white and gold 12.00
Hanley's Ale & Lager, red, white and blue,
bulldog illus 37.00
Heckers Flour, red and white, blue serial
number, c1900 ....9.00
Indera Figurfit Swim Suits, black on white,
girl ready to dive illus..........36.00
John Deere, gold and white, blue lettering,
c1900......................18.00
Karl's Bread, green, gold and white, clover-
leaf illus 6.00

Mirror, adv, Newton Collins Short Order Restaurant, St. Joe, MO, 2-1/8" d, $35.

Dupont Powders, The Record Breakers, $15.

Mickey Mouse Globe Trotters Member, Eat Friehofer's Perfect Loaf, black, red and white, 1-1/4" d, $75.

Keeley Stove Co., red and white, black
  serial number, c1900 . . . . .6.00
Kingnut Spread, yellow, blue and white,
  1930s 4.00
Knox Knit Hosiery, multicolored, green
  border, yellow lettering, world globe
  illus, c1900. . . . . .4.00
Libby, McNeill & Libby Corned Beef, red,
  white and blue, 1940 . . . . .5.00
Maltex Breakfast Cereal, red, white and
  blue, 1930s. 4.00
Miller's Soap, blue and white, c1900. .5.00
Mint Julep Products, maroon and green,
  1950s 3.00
Morton's Iodized Salt, yellow dots around
  Morton girl above product name .34.00
Munsing Wear, green and white,
  1930s 5.00
Oliver Typewriter, black and white,
  red border. 12.00
Patton's Sun-Roof Paints,
  yellow and brown 12.00
Pilsener Bread, brown and white,
  1930s 5.00
Quaker Ranges, product name above and
  below illus, red,
  white and green 28.00
Red Cross Macaroni, Little Orphan Annie
  and Red Cross emblem 44.00
Red Seal Lye, multicolored,
  canister illus 8.00
Sabo Coffee, black and white, red logo,
  c1900 . . . . .5.00
Singer Sewing Machines, porcelain, red
  "S" logo, Dec 1939 . . . . .15.00
Standard Safe & Lock Co Manufacturers,
  brown, black and white. 12.00
Starrett Tools, red and white,
  c1900 . . . . .4.00
Van Camp Hard Ware, elongated oval,
  blue, white and gold 6.00

Velvet Molasses Candy, yellow,
  black and white 22.00
Wessel Brothers Cough Drops,
  blue and white. 22.00
Yankiboy Play Clothes,
  Tom Mix, 2" d 42.00

Pin Up Art

The stuff looks so innocent, one has to wonder what all the fuss was about when it first arrived upon the scene. Personally, I like it when a little is left to the imagination.

George Petty and Alberto Vargas (the "s" was dropped at Esquire's request) have received far more attention than they deserve. You would be smart to focus on artwork by Gillete Elvgren, Billy DeVorss, Joyce Ballantyne and Earl Moran. While Charles Dana Gibson's girls are also pinups, they are far too respectable to be considered here.

Newsletters: *Glamour Girls: Then and Now*, P.O. Box 34501, Washington, DC 20043; The *Illustrator Collector's*

Calendar, May 1948, Earl Moran illus, 3-1/4" by 6", $60.

News, P.O. Box 1958, Sequim, WA 98382.

Calendars

Armstrong, Rolf, 1930s, 12" by 18", color
  artwork, Nehi adv 150.00
Armstrong, 1947, See You Soon, 11" by
  23", salesman's sample, September
  pad 45.00
Chippendale Revue, 1988 . . . . .8.00
Elvgren, Gillete, 1952, 8-1/2" by 13",
  glossy, spiral bound, full color art,
  Brown & Bigelow 90.00
Elvgren, 1955, Stepping Out, 16" by 33",
  December pad. 85.00
Moran, Earl, 1939, 15" by 33",
  lithograph. 175.00
Moran, 1944, desk 50.00
Moran, 1945, Starlight, blonde, dark green
  drape, black background 47.00
Moran, 1946, Evening Star, 16" by 33",
  unused. 175.00
Munson, 1947, 12 cheesecake poses,
  orig envelope. 95.00
Petty, George, 1949, Come On Along,
  7-1/2" by 16", full-color art,
  unused. 65.00
Petty, 1955, Esquire, 12 poses. 95.00
Pogony, Willie, 1948, "Gone With The
  Wind," 12" by 19", nude at seaside with
  one foot on inflatable horse, black
  Scottie dog looking on 75.00
Varga, 1944, 12 poses,
  orig envelope. 165.00

Magazine Tear Sheet, *Esquire*, February 1940, George Petty illus, $12.

Matchbook Covers, George Petty illus, price each, $5.

Varga, 1946, pocket folder, 3" by 4-1/2" closed, opens to 4-1/2" by 21-1/2" strip,

Magazines

Hollywood Tales, Vol. 1, #36, full color art, 24 pgs, 1930s. 30.00
Life, Aug 11, 1941, Rita Hayworth in swimming suit on cov. 10.00
Playgirl, 1976 . . . . .10.00

Other

Book, *Art of Steve Woron*, autographed. 15.00
Booklet, World's Smallest Pin-Up Book, 1955-60, 16 fold-out photos of nude nymphs, vinyl bound 5.00
Box, candy, Billy DeVorss, 11" by 16", color image, 1930s. 150.00
Vargas and Esquire copyrights 60.00
Calendar Top, Jayne Mansfield, 1950s. .45.00
Calendar Top, Daisy, DeVorss, nude woman, 22" by 30", no pad 110.00
Christmas Card, 5-1/2" by 8", multicolored, MacPherson. 22.00
Cigarette Lighter, George Petty, chrome, 1950s. .45.00
Date Book, 1945 Esquire, 5" by 7", spiral bound, subtitled "GI Edition, pinup art by Vargas," movie star photos . . .60.00
Exhibit Cards, set of 10, 1930-40 . . .60.00
Fan, adv, flapper, color, 1920s 55.00
Figure, 9-1/2" by 10-1/2", female, Sanzio .25.00
Folder, Sally of Hollywood & Vine, cardboard, sliding insert changes dress to underwear to nude 22.00
Gatefold, Esquire, Dorothy Dandridge. 15.00
Gatefold, Al Moore 10.00

Hairpin, George Petty, orig 4" by 5-1/2", yellow, red, black and white card, artist sgd, 1948 . . . . 20.00
Illusion Glass, 5" h, full color decal of pin-up wearing sheer clothing, clothing disappears when glass sweats, set of five, c1938. . . . . 100.00
Letter Opener, 8-1/2" h, plastic, figural, flat back, standing nude holding adv disk overhead, designed by Gillete Elvgren, 1940-50. . . . . 18.00
Matchbook Cover, Petty girl, "Snug as a Bug," Martins Tavern, Chicago, late 1940s 3.00
Notebook, Earl Moran, 1945 . . . . . . 45.00
Note Pad, 3" by 4-1/2", pastel, 1944 calendar on back 6.00
Photocard, Esquire, Hurrell Girl, set of six in orig envelope, 1940 . . . . 95.00
Playing Cards, Elvgrin, 1950s, MIB . 65.00
Playing Cards, Vargas, Esquire, double deck, alligator case 95.00
Poster, 17" by 33", full color, woman in shorts walking wire-haired terrier, Walt Otto, c1951 . . . . 50.00
Program, Ice Capades, Esquire, Petty illus 32.00
Puzzle, 10-1/4" by 15-1/2", Perfect Double, Winter Queen skier and All American Girl ice skater, 5-1/4" by 7-1/4" black, white and yellow box, cov with half of completed puzzle, Buell, c1942 . 20.00
Sample Calendar, 1941, 16" by 33-1/2" stiff paper, wall type, full color portrait art by Rolf Armstrong, brunette model, clinging red dress, black bodice, white fur stole. 150.00
Sketch Book, Fritz Willis, 1966 . . . . 85.00
Yearbook, 10-1/2" by 14", spiral bound, wall calendar with cardboard cov and backing sheet, 1947, Esquire, Varga 60.00

Planters

No, I am not talking about Planter's Peanuts. I am chronicling those strange and decorative containers that people seem intent to force vegetation to grow from. If I had a "You have to be nuts to own it" category in this book, I might have been tempted to include planters in it. Don't you find it just a bit strange to see English ivy growing out of the top of a ceramic pig's head?

A planter is any container suitable for growing vegetation. It may be constructed of any number of materials, ranging from wooden fruit crates and painted tires found on suburban front

Egyptian Princess, Art Deco, pale green, drilled as lamp base, 10" h, $95.

lawns to ceramic panthers stalking 1950s television sets. If you thought all those planters you got from the florist were junk, read on. Too bad you threw them out or sold them for a dime each at your last garage sale. This category deals with the figural ceramic variety found in abundance at all flea markets.

Baby and pillow, blue, Hull, #92 . . . . 32.00
Baby Scale, McCoy 80.00
Blackamoor, gold trim, Brayton 65.00
Bunny with Carrot, matte white, McCoy 65.00
Canopy Bed, Shawnee, #734. . . . . . 85.00
Clown, riding pig, McCoy 30.00
Cockatoo, Maddux 40.00
Cradle, blue or pink 24.00
Davy Crockett, American Bisque . . . 39.00
Doe and Fawn, Shawnee, #669 . . . . 13.00
Donald Duck, Disney, Leeds 65.00
Duck, Art Deco 40.00
Duckling, Kay Finch 40.00
Elephant, Hull. 35.00
Fawn, Brad Keeler 65.00
Fish, Maddux 30.00
Gazelles, pr, #613 . . . . 14.00
Girl, Kay Finch 100.00
Girl, Holding Kitty, De Lee Art. 90.00
Girl, With bonnet and Basket, Brayton 65.00
Girl, With Wolfhounds, Brayton 95.00
Goose, Patrician Goose, Weller. . . . 45.00
Grist Mill, green, Shawnee, #769 . . . 13.50
Horse Head, 12" h, Maddux 30.00
June, Florence Ceramics 28.00
Kitten and Yarn, yellow, Royal Copley. 28.00

Two birds and tree stump, orange and yellow, unmarked, 9-1/2" h, $20.

Lamb, Hull. 45.00
Lovebirds, Maddux 45.00
Miss Piggy, Sigma. 25.00
Orientals, carrying basket, Shawnee,
    #537 . . . . .5.00
Piano, #528 . . . . .20.00
Pheasant, Brad Keeler 75.00
Puppy in Boat, gold trim, Shawnee,
    #736 . . . . .55.00
Roadster, gold trim, Shawnee,
    #506 . . . . .36.00
Rocking Chair, green, McCoy 22.00
Rocking Horse, pink, Shawnee,
    #526 . . . . .22.00
Stork and Bassinet, aqua, McCoy. . .44.00
Swan, Glossy Black, stylized,
    Maddux 125.00
Swan, Lime Green, Hull, #69 . . . . .35.00
Swan, McCoy 15.00
Twin Shoes, aqua, McCoy 12.00
Wheelbarrow, Brayton. 35.00

Planter's Peanuts

Amedeo Obici and Mario Peruzzi organized the Planter's Nut and Chocolate Co., in Wilkes-Barre, Pa., in 1906. The monocled Mr. Peanut resulted from a trademark contest in 1916. Standard Brands bought Planters only to be bought themselves by Nabisco. Planter's developed a wide range of premiums and promotional items. Beware of reproductions.

Club: Peanut Pals, P.O. Box 4465, Huntsville, AL 35815.

Banner, plastic, 1988 . . . . .25.00
Baseball, yellow, black and white,
    Mr. Peanut illus 4.00
Basket Cooler, wooden, foam insert,
    Mr. Peanut logo on lid 25.00

Bookmark, cardboard, 1939 New York World's Fair souvenir, yellow, black and white, 6-1/2" h, $15.

Beach Ball, blue and yellow,
    Mr. Peanut logo 8.00
Beach Towel, cotton, Heritage logo. 30.00
Boat, vinyl, yellow and blue, motor,
    two oars 60.00
Book, *Mr. Peanut's Book of Magic*,
    1970s 10.00
Book, *Smokey Bear Finds a Friend*,
    1971 . . . . 8.00
Book, *Soup to Nuts*, 1970 . . . . 5.00

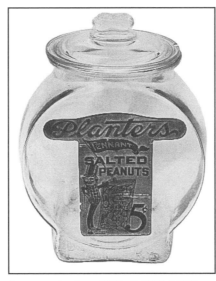

Jar, counter top, 13" h, 9-1/2" d, $95.

Measure, red plastic, 1/4, 1/2 and 1 tsp, 1 tbsp, $3.

Bottle, plastic, Planters Peanut Oil,
    24 oz 4.00
Can Holder, Styrofoam, 1981 . . . . . .5.00
Canister, figural peanut, plastic, reissue,
    11" by 5" by 5" 5.00
Child's Dish Set, Melmac, three pcs,
    1972 . . . . .15.00
Clock, plastic, Mr. Peanut
    logo center. 20.00
Container, 1 gal, plastic, Mr. Peanut illus
    front, yellow lid. 20.00
Coloring Book, Presidents of the United
    States to color, 56 pgs. 15.00
Costume, plastic, cloth,
    Mr. Peanut,
    1974 . . . . .30.00
Cufflinks, pr, gold tone, oval, Mr. Peanut
    figure inside. 45.00
Desk Set, wooden, calculator, note pad
    and pen, 1980s 30.00
Dispenser, plastic,
    Honey Roast, 1986 . . . . .15.00
Frisbee, plastic, white, Heritage logo 15.00
Golf Ball, Mr. Peanut logo. 5.00
Hat, plastic, hard hat type, Mr. Peanut
    emblem front 20.00
Ice Bucket, top hat,
    figural, 8" by 11" h 15.00
Key Chain, brass, Munch 'N Go logo . 4.00
License Plate, plastic, 1970s 15.00
Lighter, Mr. Peanut logo front. 5.00
Mug, plastic, holder, Munch 'N Go Planters
    illus 8.00

Mug, plastic, blue, $5.

Necklace and Earring Set, gold-tone chain,
    black Mr. Peanut figure 10.00
Nut Dish, top hat, figural, plastic,
    4" by 7" h, 1993 . . . . .8.00
Pen 4.00
Oven Mitt, cotton, Mr. Peanut illus,
    1989 . . . . .7.00
Pin, gold tone, enamel, blue, Planters 75th
    Anniversary, 1981 . . . . .15.00
Playing Cards, Munch 'N Go logo 3.00
Puzzle, Between Meals Candy Bar,
    Hallmark/Springbrook, 1977. . . . .15.00
Radio, can, figural, 1978 . . . . .40.00
Rocking Horse, wooden, 27" by 33",
    Planters logo on back leg, 1988. .50.00
Shirt, cotton, Christmas motif, 1994 .25.00
Shopping Bag, paper, white, Mr. Peanut
    illus front, marked "Compliments of
    Planters Peanut Store". 10.00
Tape Measure, Planter's 75th anniversary,
    1906-1981 . . . . .6.00
Thermometer, Lucite,
    Mr. Peanut illus 30.00
Tie Pin, enamel, Mr. Peanut figure . .10.00
Tote Bag, cloth, 18" l,
    blue and yellow 10.00
Toy, riding, peanut, figural, 1960s. . .80.00
Train, five-car set, battery operated,
    HO scale 50.00
Tray, plastic, football field design, Planters
    and Lite beer adv,
    clip-on goal post ends 15.00
Umbrella, red and white,
    Heritage logo 25.00
Watch, Mr. Peanut's 75th Anniversary,
    plastic strap 25.00
Yo-Yo, plastic, yellow, logo front 10.00

Playboy Collectibles

Playboy memorabilia, from magazines to club items is a popular collecting category, especially since the clubs have closed. Hugh Hefner began his empire in 1953 with the debut of the first issue of *Playboy Magazine*. Marilyn Monroe graced its cover and centerfold. Many Playboy collectibles can be found at yard sales, swap meets and antiques malls. Value on many items, such as playing cards and puzzles, will be higher if they are unopened and/or unused.

Advisor: Ronnie Keshishian, P.O. Box 2654, Glendale, AZ 85311, (602) 435-2665.

Club: Playboy Collectors Association, P.O. Box 653, Phillipsburg, MO 65722.

Ashtrays
Round, clear, emb rabbit head 5.00
Square, 3-3/4" w, Femlin, Playboy Club in
    circle, early 1960s, orange 5.00
Square, 3-3/4" w, Femlin,
    smoked or white 8.00
Square, 3-3/4" w, Femlin, Yellow. . . 10.00

Mugs
Aluminum, 5" h, engraved rabbit head,
    glass bottom, early 1960s. 5.00
Black, "Playmate of the Year," heavy,
    1976 . . . . 20.00

Puzzle, jigsaw, Playboy Playmate Puzzle, American Publishing Corp., AP110, 1967, $15.

Magazine, Vol. 18, No. 9, September 1971, $2.50.

Black Glass, 6" h, Femlin in gold, Playboy
    Club in circular, 1960s. 5.00
Clear Glass, 5-1/2" h,
    Playboy Club and city 10.00
Gray Glass, 6" h, emb rabbit head,
    1960s. 5.00
Thermo-Serv, 6-1/4" h, black, white rabbit
    head 5.00

Puzzles, complete
Boxed, Marilyn Monroe, 1973. . . . . .25.00
Boxed, Annie Fanny, 1972. . . . . . . .50.00
Boxed, Vargas, 1971 . . . . .75.00
Coffee can size, open, 1967-73 . . . .10.00

Swizzle Sticks
Black and White 1.00
Solid Color .5.00
Transparent Color. 3.00

Other
Bar Set, stainless steel,
    four pcs, box 25.00
Beach Towel, colorful design,
    early 1960s 20.00
Belt Buckle, round, gold color,
    rabbit head 10.00
Candle, vase-style, red, early 1960s 15.00
Coffee Cup and Saucer,
    early 1960s 20.00
Dinner Plate, china, Femlin with or without
    Playboy Club name 40.00
Dinner Plate, Pewter, 10" d, VIP,
    early 1960s 50.00
Food Pick 50
Frisbee, 1970s. 10.00
Glass, VIP on the Rocks. 5.00
Hand Puppet, 1963. . . . . .100.00

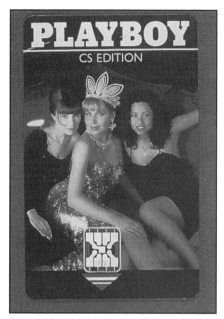

Telephone Card, $15.

Key Card, Playboy Club, plastic or metal,
    gold or white, 1960s 20.00
Key Chain, oval, rabbit head 5.00
Liquor Caddy, 1960 . . . . .100.00
Magazine, 1980-95 . . . . .3.00
Matchbook, unused, 1961 . . . . .5.00
Matchbook, unused, 1980 . . . . .3.00
Matches, wooden, boxed, 1961 . . . . .5.00
Plaque, bunny tail, "Caught Live at the
    Playboy Club," early 1960s 75.00
Playing Cards, Playmate, open and
    complete, 1971-73 . . . . .20.00
Pocket Lighter, black or white,
    1960s 10.00
Poker Chips, box of 100, 1974 . . . . .24.00
Shot Glass, clear, Femlin,
    Playboy Club around 10.00
Silverware, knife, fork or spoon, engraved
    rabbit head, early 1960s,
    price each 10.00
Soap, small bar, from resort hotel 5.00
Wine Glass, long stem, small rabbit head
    logo 10.00

Playing Cards

The key is not the deck, but the design on the deck surface. Souvenir decks are especially desirable. Look for special decks such as Tarot and other fortune-telling items. Always buy complete decks. There are individuals who just collect Jokers and have a bad habit of removing them from a deck

Pin-Up, 52 American Beauties, Elvgren illus, Creative Playing Card Co., Inc., St. Louis, $40.

and then reselling it. Also, if you are buying a playing card game, make certain that the instruction card is included. Prices listed are for complete decks.

Clubs: Chicago Playing Card Collectors, Inc., 1826 Mallard Lake Dr., Marietta, GA 30068; 52 Plus Joker, 204 Gorham Ave., Hamden, CT 06514; International Playing Card Society, 3570 Delaware Common, Indianapolis, IN 46220; Playing Card Collectors Association, Inc., 1203 Meadowbrook, Round Lake Beach, IL 60073.

Advertising

Bumble Bee Tuna 6.00
Champion Spark Plug, red and black logos,
    white border 8.00
Diamond Salt, orig box 18.00
Gold Medal Flour, flour sack for joker, 52
    cards, joker, extra card 60.00

Hertz Rent-A-Car, dark green 8.00
United Founders Life Insurance Co.,
    blue and white 7.50

Airline
American Airlines, DH-4 . . . . .10.00
Ozark Airlines, 1984 World's Fair,
    sealed deck 2.00
Pan American, white logo, light blue
    ground 10.00

Souvenir
Pro Football Hall of Fame,
    Canton, OH 7.50
The Vista Dome, 1950-60 . . . . .15.00
Wild Animal Park, San Diego 6.50

Other
Airship, oval vignette of flying airships, red
    tones, 52 cards, joker,
    extra card 145.00
Hotel Fremont and Casino, Las Vegas, red
    and white, diamond design 5.00
Marilyn Monroe, nude, sealed deck . 30.00
New York City, c1915, Statue of Liberty,
    52 cards, joker 75.00
Niagara Falls, 1901, red-tone vignette of
    Indian hunting buffalo, 52 cards, joker,
    extra card 130.00
Ocean Liner, Holland/America,
    orig box .25.00
Poker Taurino, Mexican, Spanish
    inscription on box, c1950 . . . . . .12.00
Railroad, Union and Pacific Railroad,
    c1910, river scene, two horses with
    riders, 52 cards, joker, extra card,
    booklet .60.00
Railroad, Washington and Pacific
    Northwest, 1900, scenic landscape, 52
    cards, joker and extra card 110.00
Shirley Temple, c1940, bridge deck, red
    box, black and white portrait of Shirley
    wearing bonnet, 52 cards, joker,
    extra card 65.00

Advertising, Prosser's Drug Store, Inc., Hellertown, PA, $5.

Tee-Up, golf cartoon on each card,
   orig box, c1950. . . . . .10.00
World's Fair, 1933 Chicago World's Fair,
   Walgreen building, two complete decks,
   unopened box 45.00
Yale University, university seal and
   pennants, 52 cards and joker. . . .65.00

Political Items

Collect the winners. Time has not treated the losers well, with the exception of the famous Cox-Roosevelt pinback button. This is a good category to apply my 30-Year Rule: For the first 30 years of anything's life, all its value is speculative. Do not pay much for items less than thirty years old. But, do remember that time flies. The Nixon/Kennedy election was more than 30 years ago.

Also concentrate on the non-traditional categories. Everyone collects pinbacks and posters. Try something

Card of Appreciation, JFK funeral, black and white, printed signature, 5-1/2" by 3-3/8", 1963, $18.

unusual. How about political ties, mugs or license plates?

Clubs: American Political Items Collectors, P.O. Box 340339, San Antonio, TX 78234; Third Party & Hopefuls, 503 Kings Canyon Blvd, Galesburg, IL 61401.

Newsletter: *The Political Bandwagon*, P.O. Box 348, Leola, PA 17540.

Periodical: *The Political Collector*, P.O. Box 5171, York, PA 17405.

Compact, "Elect Willkie President," 3" d,
   red, white and blue enameled lid,
   1940 . . . . 40.00

Contribution Certificate, Smith/Robinson,
   4" by 11-1/2", Democratic National
   Committee, 1928 . . . . .25.00
Cup and Saucer, Reagan, 2-1/2" cup, 6" d
   saucer, white china, Reagan portrait in
   cup bottom, blossoming branches,
   Capitol dome and "President '81" on
   saucer 45.00
Fountain Pen, LBJ, Esterbrook Desk Pen,
   plastic, black and clear, white lettering
   "The President-The White House,"
   orig box 20.00
Lapel Stud, Cleveland, c1888, brass figural
   drum and drumstick. 25.00
Lighter, Goldwater, gold finish, black
   outlined elephant wearing glasses,
   caption "Au H20," mkd "Park Lighter,"
   2-1/4" h 45.00
Medalet, Harding/Baker, brass, jugate
   portraits, reverse reads "1822-1922
   Centennial Anniversary Marion, Ohio,"
   red, white and blue ribbon bow . . 15.00
Menu, Ike/Nixon, 1953 inaugural souvenir,
   8-1/2" by 11", cardboard, red, white and
   blue, blue portrait photos,
   The Hotel Raleigh 20.00
Necktie, 47" l, Wilson/Marshall, black,
   white embroidered names, red, white
   and blue flag 50.00
Needle Book, 2-3/4" by 4-3/4", Hoover,
   black-and-white photos, red, white and
   blue cardboard, lists Ohio state
   candidates on inside, 1928 . . . . .18.00
Paperweight, 2-1/2" by 4" by 1", Grant's
   Tomb Dedication, clear glass, sepia
   paper illus of Washington, Lincoln and
   Grant affixed to back, 1897 . . . . .20.00
Pen, 5" l, Eisenhower, brass, black and
   white plastic, slogan "For The Love of
   Ike—Vote Republican" 25.00
Pennant, GOP Republican National
   Convention, elephant head and
   building, Chicago, 1952. . . . . . . .25.00

Box, Kraft Macaroni & Cheese, 1996 Republican convention limited edition, $15.

Bumper Sticker, Richard Nixon, red, white and blue, 9-1/2" by 4", $4.

Pinback Button, Pat for First Lady, 3-1/4" d, pink and black, $15.

Pin, Roosevelt, enameled brass, shield-shape, red, white and blue, threaded post 15.00

Pin, Willkie, 2" by 3-1/2", red, white and blue enameled white metal, ribbon-like design,10 inset rhinestones and center Willkie button 35.00

Plate, 12" d, Franklin D Roosevelt, cobalt border 30.00

Postcard, "The Nation Needs Nixon and Lodge," black and white, Oregon for Nixon Comm, unused. 15.00

Poster, 14" by 22", Nixon Rally, black and white, heavy cardboard, Levittown, PA, 1968 . . . . .40.00

Record, 7" sq, Stevenson Speaks, black-and-white photo overlaid with thin plastic 78 rpm record, issued by AFL-CIO, Philadelphia address on back. 25.00

Ribbon, Taft/Hughes, 7" l, blue lettering, cream ground, "Republican County Committee," V-shaped bottom . . .45.00

Ribbon, For President Gen. W.S. Hancock, 3" by 5-3/4", dark pink ribbon, gold design, 1" sepia paper photo of Hancock 80.00

Sample Ballot, Republican party, 4-1/4" by 12-1/2", 6th Congressional District, Pennsylvania primary, April 26, 1960, Nixon and Republican Congressional candidate portraits 18.00

Sheet Music, Anchors Aweigh, President F.D. Roosevelt portrait cov, 1935 . . . . .20.00

Sheet Music, Dedicated To The GOP/A Victory is Ours/A Rousing Republican Campaign Song, c1904, blue and white, 7" by 11". 15.00

Tray, Bryan/Stevenson, 5" l, aluminum, 12-sided raised edge, patriotic design with candidates' portraits 50.00

Watch Fob, Taft/Sherman, brass, incised letters 25.00

Window Poster, JFK, 8-1/2" by 11", paper, black and white, small Kennedy portrait, American flag and "Win for Kennedy Vote Democratic" 70.00

Wristwatch, Spiro Agnew, caricature Agnew wearing stars and stripes costume on dial, dark blue vinyl band, overwound, 1970s 50.00

Poodle Collectibles

People who collect dog and cat memorabilia are a breed apart. While most cat collectors collect items with any cat image (except Siamese collectors), dog collectors tend to specialize. Poodle collectors are more fortunate than most because the poodle was a popular decorating motif during the 1950s and 60s. Poodles were featured on everything from clothing to lamps.

Figures

Ceramic, 14-1/2" h, Calif. Ceramics. 70.00
Lady walking poodle, Hedi Schoop . 75.00
Pink Poodle Lady, mkd "KB80552 Lefton China Hand Painted" 20.00
Poodle with bow tie, paper label reads "Thames made in Japan" 15.00

Purses

Plastic, white poodle dec 30.00
Wicker, leash handle, mkd "Maybelle Marie Birch California" 40.00
Wooden, sgd "Gary Gails Dallas" . . 15.00
Woven, white, two black poodles dec, "Princess Charming By Atlas Hollywood Fla" label 20.00

Other

Action Figure, Peteena The Pampered Poodle, six outfits, Hasbro, 1966 50.00
Advertising, Magazine Tear Sheet, Old Gold Cigarettes, two poodles sitting at table in front of ashtray and two cigarettes illus 5.00
Advertising, Magazine Tear Sheet, Pepsi, man and woman walking two poodles illus 5.00
Advertising, Magazine, Almond Kisses, Barton's Bonbonniere 4.00
Ashtray, pink poodle design, Lefton. 12.00
Book, Playtime Poodles, Helen Wing 6.00
Brooch, bakelite, poodle figural 35.00
Canister Set, four pc, emb, Ransburg of Indianapolis 40.00
Casserole Dish, cov, Chi Chi poodle pattern, Glidden 167 . . . . 30.00

Container, ceramic, lid, Besshunferl, Goebel, Germany, c1962 . . . . . .25.00
Creamer and Sugar, cov, Enesco . .20.00
Pattern, child's poodle skirt, Simplicity, 1950s. 3.00
Puppet, Marionette, Pelham puppet, England, 1968 . . . . .80.00
Puppet, Plush, vinyl, unmarked 6.00
Salt & Pepper Shakers, pr, mkd "E 2167". 12.00
Serving Tray, mkd "Made in Calif. U.S.A.". 10.00
Skirt, Clown with poodle jumping through hoops dec 25.00
Skirt, Labeled "Len Nay Originals a division of Len Jay Originals," c1950 . . . .65.00
Stuffed Animal, Mimi the Parisian Poodle, C&M Srery Co. 10.00
Stuffed Animal, Snooby, Steiff 30.00
Tea Towel, linen, hand embroidered . 5.00
Toy, Fifi, battery-operated, Japan. . .40.00
Vase, black poodle with pink rose illus, paper label, Josef Original. 18.00
Wall Plaque, pr, plaster, white poodle dec, Miller Studios, 1969 . . . . .10.00

Postcards

This is a category where the average golden age card has gone from 50 cents to several dollars in the last decade. Post cards' golden age is between 1898 and 1918. As the cards have become expensive, new collectors are discovering the white-border

Comic, Mickey Mouse, $25.

Black, tennis player, artist sgd "Arthur Thiele," $15.

cards of the 1920s and 30s, the linens of the 1940s and the early glossy photograph cards of the 1950s and 1960s.

It pays to specialize. This is the only way that you can build a meaningful collection. The literature is extensive and can be very helpful.

Club: Deltiologists of America, P.O. Box 8, Norwood, PA 19074. Note: *Barr's* and *Postcard Collector* list more than 50 U.S. regional clubs.

Periodicals: *Barr's Post Card News*, 70 S. 6th St., Lansing, IA 52151; *Postcard Collector*, P.O. Box 1050, Dubuque, IA 52004.

Advertising
BPD Gunshot, hunting dog and equipment, Italian 50.00

Comic, MWM General Comic Series, color litho, $4.

Cherry Smash, black servant serving George Washington and wife, "Cherry Smash" spelled out on lawn . . . 100.00

Continental Rubber Heels, crow looking at box of heels, German 65.00

Gaumont Chocolates, "Do You Like Chocolate Drops?", image of black man, emb, yellow ground 40.00

Gold Medal Flour, lighthouse scene at Nice, France, advertisement for free cookbook, c1905 . . . . 45.00

Goodrich Tires, "Best in the Long Run," auto racing donkey on dirt road, 1915 . . . . 85.00

Kaiser Wilhelm Spring Water, Art Nouveau design, Germany 85.00

Kempinski Champagne, woman romancing champagne bottle, 1905, Germany 40.00

Prudential Insurance, groceries and grocery receipt illustration 40.00

V. Guarro Durban Co., neckties, colorful necktie image, Barcelona 65.00

Aviation
Amelia Earhart, christening of the Essex Terraplane, 1932 . . . . 85.00

Graf Zeppelin, face formed of balloons and zeppelins, 1909, Germany 60.00

Panair Airlines, plane flying over Rio, Brazil 35.00

The Inquirer Airship, souvenir of Founder's Week, Philadelphia, inset photo of pilot Lincoln Beachey, 1908 . . . . 75.00

Holiday
Christmas, Advertising, Huyler's Chocolates, Santa holding box of chocolates. 50.00

Christmas, hold-to-light type, "A Joyful Christmas," die-cut, girl holding small decorated tree, star background, 1908 . . . . 150.00

Christmas, Santa wearing red silk suit, sleeping child, emb, 1909 . . . . . . 40.00

Easter, hold-to-light type, die-cut, rabbit and girl leaning on tree with colored eggs 60.00

Halloween, "Hallowe'en," witch and verse, HL Woehler. 35.00

Halloween, "With Hallowe'en Wishes," man reading book to two children, ghosts rising from book, emb . . . 85.00

Photographic, #6880, Proud Mother, $4.

St. Patrick's Day, Irish girl in front of shamrock, emb, Winsch publisher, 1911 . . . . 60.00

Oceanliner
Cunard Line, "Cunard Line to Canada" 75.00

Red Star Line, woman playing piano while crowd looks on 40.00

RMS Olympic, White Star Line, British, sgd "Walter Thomas" 45.00

Titanic, White Star triple-screw steamer, real photo, Batchelder Bros., England, used. 150.00

Political
Ohio's seven Presidents, photos of McKinley, Hayes, Harrison, Grant, Garfield, Harding and Taft 85.00

Taft For President, elephant with "GOP" on its side, inset black-and-white photo, 1908 . . . . 85.00

The Prohibition Nominees, Chafin and Watkins, brown and white, 1908 . 85.00

Win With Willkie, real photo, 1940 . . 60.00

Sports
Baseball, Chas. F. Broadwater hardware store, illus sgd "RF Outcault," 1913 . . . . 50.00

Baseball, Air brush design, emb. . . . 35.00

Billiards, Monarch Billiard Tables, Netherlands 85.00

Billiards, "I am advised to take a rest," man
    playing pool, Premier series,
    British 40.00
Golf, Chick Golf Balls, "Don't ask your op-
    ponent where he thinks his ball went,"
    man climbing over fence 60.00
Golf, Chick Golf Balls, "Don't be surprised
    if it's your wife who doctors the greens!",
    woman on golf course 60.00
Golf, Chick Golf Balls, "On The Lynx,"
    animals playing golf, 1907 . . . . . .40.00
Olympics, 1912, Stockholm, real photos,
    Discus, RL Byrd 50.00
Olympics, 1912, real photos, Hammer
    Throw Winners, MacGrath, Gillis and
    Childs .50.00
Olympics, 1912, real photos, High Kump
    Winner, Platt Adams 50.00
Olympics, 1912, real photos, Pole Vault
    Winners, F. Nelson, H. Babcock
    and M. Wright. 50.00
Olympics, 1924, Paris, French, sgd,
    Rugby. .50.00
Olympics, 1924, Paris, French, sgd,
    Speed Race 50.00
Olympics, 1924, Paris, French, sgd,
    Swimming. 50.00

World's Fairs and Expositions

Columbian Exposition, 1893, illus of
    Manufacturers and Liberal Arts,
    Transportation and Federal
    Buildings. 125.00
Ohio-Columbus Centennial, 1912. . .45.00
St. Louis World's Fair, 1904, Palace of Arts
    illus, emb 85.00

Posters

Want a great way to decorate? Use
posters. Buy ones you like. This can
get a bit expensive if your tastes run to
old movie or advertising posters. Prices in the hundred of dollars are not uncommon. When you get to the great
lithography posters of the late 19th
and early 20th century, prices in the
thousands are possible.

Concentrate on one subject, manufacturer, illustrator or period. Remember that print runs of two million copies
and more are not unheard of. Many
collectors have struck deals with their
local video store and movie theater to
get their posters when they are ready
to throw them out. Not a bad idea. But
why not carry it a step further? Talk
with your local merchants about their
advertising posters. These are going

Movie, "Invitation to a Gunfighter,"
United Artists, 1964, $20.

to be far harder to find in the future
than movie posters.

Because so many people save
modern posters, never pay more than
a few dollars for any copy below fine
condition. A modern poster in very
good condition is unlikely to have long-
term value. Its condition will simply not
be acceptable to the serious collector
of the future.

Newsletter: *The Movie Poster Update*, 2401 Broad St., Chattanooga,
TN 37408.

Advertising

Buckwheat Flour, 19" by 10" 25.00
Ceresota Flour, 20" by 24",
    mother and son. 50.00
Holsum Bread, 12" by 20" 8.00
Take Some Home—Independent Brewing
    Co of Pittsburgh, 21" by 11", Maynard
    Williamson 85.00
Van Heusen Century Shirts, Ronald
    Reagan modeling shirt,
    23" by 17" 45.00

Cause

Be Ready! Keep Him Smiling, United War
    Work, 21" by 11". 95.00
Hey Fellows! Your Money Brings The Book
    We Need, JE Sheridan,
    20" by 30" 75.00
NRA/We Do Our Part, 21" by 27", red,
    white and blue, orig folds 90.00

World's Fair, Water Goddess, Louisiana
World Exposition, by Hugh Ricks, multicolor, 1984, 27" by 15", $12.

Movie

Day Mars Invaded Earth,
    three-sheet 75.00
Great Plane Robbery, Columbia, 1940,
    one sheet. 75.00
Haunted House, Monogram, 1940 . . 75.00
The Glory Stompers, 27" by 41", American
    International Picture, black, white and
    red, 1967 . . . . 50.00
Voyage to Bottom of the Sea,
    one sheet. 50.00

Political

Alfred E. Neuman For President, 21" by
    30", glossy, full color, MAD Party mas-
    cot in lower corner, pronounced fold
    creases, c1968 . . . . 20.00
Ford/Dole, 15" by 24", full color glossy,
    statesmen-like image 35.00
Kennedy for President/Leadership For The
    60s, 13" by 21", red, white and blue,
    black-and-white photo, rolled . . 125.00
Mondale/Ferraro, 13-1/2" by 12", stiff
    cardboard, red, white and blue . . 15.00
Students for Reagan, 22" by 28",
    cardboard, bluetone photo
    of Reagan and students, red,
    white and blue type, white
    ground, "Paid for By Citizens
    for Reagan '80: A Special
    Project of the Fund for a
    Conservative Majority" 20.00

Promotional

American Airlines, Arizona,
    40" by 30" 50.00

World War II, Norman Rockwell illus, distributed by Office of War Information, 28" by 20", $40.

Lena Horne, The Lady and Her Music,
    14" by 22"....................35.00
Saturday Evening Post, 28" by 41",
    promoting David O. Selznick's Gone
    With The Wind article, 1942.....85.00
The Steve Miller Band, "Book of Dreams,"
    36" by 36", thick stiff cardboard, Kelly &
    Mouse artists, c1976, small Capitol
    Records logo 60.00
TWA, Las Vegas—Fly TWA,
    25" by 40"..................225.00

World War I
Cheer Up, Let the Hun Have the Grouch,
    He Has Good Reason for It, Gordon
    Grant artist, black, white
    and orange..................40.00
Do Your Duty, Join the Marines,
    20" by 30"..................135.00
Register! Tuesday, June 5th, State of
    Massachusetts draft, 14" by 22"..75.00

World War II
Be a Marine—Free a Marine to Fight,
    woman Marine in uniform,
    28" by 40"..................125.00
Join the WAC, 22" by 28"........100.00
United Nations For Freedom, 28-1/2" by
    40", paper, black and white Statue of
    Liberty, Broder artist, 30 color flags on
    black ground, OWI Poster #19, 1942
    printing number 60.00
Waste Fats, 20" by 28", paper, full color art,
    H. Koerner artist, OWI Poster #63, 1943
    printing number 65.00

We're In The Fight Too!, farm woman, blue,
    red, black and white, 14" by 20" 150.00

Other
Concert, Family Dog, 13-1/2" by 20", stiff
    paper, May 3, 1968,
    Avalon Ballroom 75.00
Concert, GD On The Road, Grateful Dead,
    18-1/2" by 28", stiff paper, color illus of
    skeleton and roses in black, dark purple
    trim, 1968 ....80.00
Disneyland, 18" by 24", Insurance By North
    America, large color photo, titled
    "Happiness Afloat At Disneyland," Mark
    Twain riverboat, c1957 ....150.00

Puppets

No, somebody is not pulling your strings, there really is a category on puppets. This category covers marionettes and related jointed play toys, as well as finger and paper puppets. There are bound to be a few of your favorite character collectibles hanging around this new category.

Periodical: *Puppetry Journal*, 8005 Swallow Dr., Macedonia, OH 44056.

Finger
Crypt Keeper, rubber 12.00
Monkees, Davy Jones, 5" h, vinyl, sticker
    with 1970 Columbia Pictures Inc. 25.00
Raggedy Ann, Knickerbocker, 1972 10.00
Three Stooges, Applause 25.00

Hand
Alf, Cookin' with Alf, plush, 12" h....8.00
Batman, 1966, MIB 100.00
Bozo the Clown, plush...........40.00
Charlie Brown, foam body 25.00
Court Jester...................20.00
Dr. Doolittle, Mattel, 1967 ....55.00

Hand Puppets, Jerry Mahoney and Knucklehead Smiff, plastic heads, vinyl bodies, 1966 by Paul Winchell, price each, $135.

Lucy, Peanuts Magic Catch Puppets, blue
    dress, Synergistics, 1978 ......15.00
Manny Rabbit, Steiff.............95.00
Minnie Mouse, bow in hair, Disney..25.00
Mister Ed, 1962 ....100.00
Pokey, 9" h, fabric and vinyl, Lakeside
    Toys, c1965..................55.00
Popeye, 8" h, blue plush, soft vinyl head,
    "Hygienic Toys Made in England
    by the Chad Valley Co. Ltd."
    tag, 1960s 25.00
Raggedy Ann & Andy, pr,
    Knickerbocker 20.00
Robin, 10" h, vinyl, Ideal, 1966.....80.00
Topo Gigio 50.00
Yogi Bear 55.00
Zorro, Gund 70.00

Marionette
Bengo the Dog, Pelham, MIB.....135.00
Clippo the Clown, Curtis Craft,
    MIB 65.00
Dutch Boy, Pelham..............45.00
Fred Flintstone, 1960s 75.00
Marie Osmond, plastic, orig box, Madison
    Ltd., c1978
    Osbro Productions, Inc.........50.00

Push-Button
Donald Duck, Tricky Trapeze......35.00
Incredible Hulk, Fleetwood, 1979...29.00
Ricochet Rabbit 45.00
Snoopy, sheriff, Ideal 14.00

Purinton Pottery

Bernard Purinton founded Purinton Pottery in 1936 in Wellsville, Ohio. In 1941, the pottery relocated to Shippenville, Pa. Dorothy Purinton and William H. Blair, her brother, were the chief designers for the company. Maywood, Plaid and several Pennsylvania German designs were among the pat-

Apple, plate, salad, $15.

Apple, teapot, 2 cup, $20.

terns attributed to Dorothy Purinton. William Blair designed the Apple and Intaglio patterns.

Purinton did not use decals, as did many of its competitors. Greenware was hand painted and then dipped into glaze. A complete dinnerware line and many accessory pieces were produced for each pattern. The plant ceased operations in 1958, reopened briefly and then closed for good in 1959.

Newsletter: *Purinton Pastimes*, P.O. Box 9394, Arlington, VA 22219.

Apple
Cereal Bowl	15.00
Cup and Saucer	18.00
Kent Jug	15.00
Meat Platter	90.00
Plate, dinner	25.00
Sugar, open	10.00
Vegetable Bowl, open	40.00

Fruit
Canister, oval, sugar, cobalt trim	95.00
Lazy Susan, four canisters, no lids	50.00
Salt and Pepper Shakers, pr, range, red trim	42.00
Teapot, 4-cup	48.00

Intaglio.
Cereal Bowl	8.00
Cruet, oil & vinegar set, jug-shape, sq, handled	60.00
Cup and Saucer	12.00
Fruit Bowl, ftd, 12" h	60.00
Platter, oblong, 12" l	40.00
Tea & Toast Set	45.00
Vegetable, open	20.00

Maywood
Beer Mug, barrel-shape, 16 oz, 5" h	60.00
Casserole, 9" d	55.00
Cup	8.00

Plate, 6-3/4" h	10.00
Saucer	3.00
Teapot, 6-cup	75.00

Normandy Plaid
Bean Pot, cov	35.00
Beer Mug	70.00
Cereal Bowl	12.00
Chop Plate, 12" d	50.00
Cookie Jar	110.00
Cruet, jug-shape, round, handled	75.00
Cup and Saucer	15.00
Plate, 6-3/4" d	10.00
Plate, 9-3/4" d	20.00
Tumbler, 12 oz, 4-3/4" h	30.00
Vegetable, divided	40.00

Purses

It is amazing what people will carry draped over their shoulders! Remember those alligator purses, complete with head and tail? Or how about those little metal mesh bags that held a lady's hankie and a book of matches, at most? As impractical as they were, these are some of the most collectible purses on the market. Where value is concerned—think unusual.

Club: California Purse Collector's Club, P.O. Box572, Campbell, CA 95009.

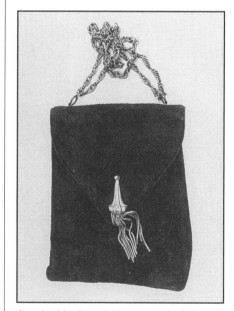

Suede, black, gold tassel and chain, satin lining, $35.

Beaded, box-style
Blue carnival glass, plastic top, metal frame, beaded handle, navy faille lined, inside mirror	125.00
Bronze, plastic frame, lid, braided handle, mkd "Fre-Mor"	125.00
Cut steel, beaded handle, button fastener	12.00
Geometric design, Czechoslovakian, 1930s	65.00
Shaggy bead, wrist, snap closure, silk-lined	150.00

Chatelaine
Black silk, nickel-plated, black, crocheted rings, silver-bead fringe, beehive pattern, c1905	125.00
Crocheted, steel beads, ornate German silver frame, hook, c1900-05	125.00
Cut steel beads, fringe, beige silk-crocheted back, chamois lined, nickel-plated frame	150.00
French jet beads, black velvet, nickel silver emb frame, hook, chamois lined	125.00
German Silver, flat mesh, ornate emb frame mkd "Warranted German Silver"	150.00
Jet bead front, chamois back and lining, nickel-plated flower motif frame	135.00

Mesh
Clutch, envelope-style, Whiting and Davis	75.00
Gun metal, ring mesh, hand engraved frame, chain handle, silk lined, metal tag reads "Real Gunmetal," France	150.00
Silver colored, jeweled frame, Whiting and Davis	150.00
Soldered, cathedral dome-shaped frame, mkd "Whiting and Davis"	120.00

Other
Antelope, ornate silver-plated frame, cupid motif	140.00
Broadcloth, black, molded plastic front, colored glass stones, satin lined, stamped "Guild Creations"	50.00

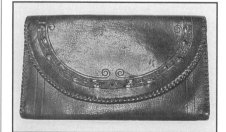

Leather, Roycroft, 10-1/8" by 5-3/4", $75.

Corde, brown, panier handle, imitation
tortoiseshell frame 60.00
Gimp, crocheted, plastic frame 40.00
Lace, zipper closure 30.00
Leather, handwoven, black strap, button
fastener, silk-lined, 1932 . . . . . . .50.00
Lucite, clear, white cloth lining 100.00
Metal, basket weave, plastic top, mkd
"Majestic" 90.00
Metallic Gauze, chenille, floral embroidery,
gilded frame, silk lined, contains shirred
pocket and round mirror 95.00
Plastic, coil zipper pull 40.00
Silk, rhinestone studs, sequins, jeweled lift
lock, chain handle 100.00
Suede, black, zipper, white fur dog motif,
goldtone metal ring 65.00
Tapestry, leather handle, floral dec, nickel
frame, silk-lined 125.00
Velvet, black, steel beads, geometric deco,
silk-lined 100.00
Wooden, box-style, leather trim, beads,
glass stones, gold braid and painted
butterfly dec, contains mirror, Enid Collins, 1966 . . . . .60.00

Puzzles

The keys to jigsaw puzzle value in
order of importance are: *completeness*
(once three or more pieces are missing, forget value); *picture* (no one is
turned on by old mills and mountain
scenery); *surface condition* (missing
tabs or paper or silver fish damage
causes value to drop dramatically);
age (1940 is a major cutting off point);
number of pieces (the more the better
for wood); and *original box and label*
(especially important for wooden puzzles). Because of the limitless number
of themes, jigsaw puzzle collectors
find themselves competing with collectors from virtually every other category.

Jigsaw puzzle collectors want an
assurance of completeness, either a
photograph or a statement by the seller that they actually put the puzzle together. "I bought it as complete"
carries no weight whatsoever. Unassembled cardboard puzzles with no
guarantees sell for $1 or less, wooden
puzzles for $3 or less. One missing
piece lowers price by 20 percent, two
missing pieces by 35 percent and
three missing pieces by 50 percent or
more. Missing packaging (a box or en-

**Advertising, Turkish Trophies Ciga-
rettes, American Tobacco Co., NY, tobacco insert, c1909, 2-1/2" by 3-1/4",
$10.**

velope) deducts 25 percent from the
price. Note: The following retail prices
are for puzzles that are complete, in
very good condition, with their original
box.

Clubs: American Game Collectors As-
sociation, 49 Brooks Ave., Lewiston,
ME 04240; National Puzzler's League,
P.O. Box 82289, Portland, OR 97282.

Advertising Puzzles
Black Cat Hosiery, 60 pcs, c1909 . 100.00
Chevrolet School Bus, 35 pcs,
1932 . . . . 75.00
Cream of Wheat, cowboy's mailbox,
c1909 . . . . 35.00

Folger's Coffee, c1965, cardboard, metal
container .5.00
Hood Farm Puzzle Box, c1905,
set of three 50.00
Jap Rose Soap, Kirk Co., 1910 . . . .75.00
Old Fashioned New England Country Stor,
Chase & Sanborn, c1909 . . . . . .25.00
Sparkalong Burgess, Burgess Battery Co.,
1952 . . . . .18.00
The Everett Piano, 16 pcs,
cardboard folder 60.00
Use Coe's Fertilizer, c1909 . . . . . . .30.00

Animal Puzzles
Boston Terrier, Hobby Jig Saws series,
300 pcs, Jaymar, 1944 . . . . .5.00
Circus Puzzle, Milton Bradley 75.00
Cut Up Animals Spelling Slips, 27 pcs,
McLoughlin Brothers, c1900 . . . .90.00
Domestic Animals, Parker Brothers,
1930 . . . . .40.00
Farm Friends, Zig Zag Puzzle Co.,
1933 . . . . .20.00
Thoroughbred, CC Stevens, 1930 . .30.00

Biblical Puzzles
Temple of Knowledge, 86 pcs,
double-sided, c1890 . . . . .65.00
The Ark Puzzle, c1880 . . . . .175.00
The Tower of Babel, 1870s 50.00

Character
Aladdin and His Lamp, cardboard, metal
canister, c1970 . . . . .3.00
Atom Ant, tile, black and white,
c1960 . . . . .50.00

**Advertising, Standard Oil Co.,
NJ, cardboard, $40.**

Santa Claus Puzzle Box, Milton Bradley, set of three puzzles in orig box, c1925, $325.

Bambi, frame tray, Jaymar, 1950s . .20.00
Barbie & The Rockers, Golden, 1987 .5.00
Bullwinkle, 1971 . . . . .25.00
Captain Kangaroo, frame tray, 1977. .8.00
Dukes of Hazzard, 200 pcs, 1982. . .10.00
Fairy Tales Puzzles, c1963,
    set of four. 8.00
Flipper, frame tray, Whitman, 1966. .12.00
Ghostbusters, 49 pcs, floor puzzle . .20.00
Howdy Doody, 9" by 12", color,
    cardboard, Milton Bradley 75.00
Little Black Sambo, masonite pcs,
    1963. . . . . .10.00
Mickey Mouse, "On the Way," Mickey and
    friends in car, Jaymar, 1962. . . . .15.00
Mother Goose Scroll Puzzles,
    set of two 75.00
Munsters, 1965, Whitman. 60.00
Our Gang, 80 pcs,
    11" by 14" envelope. 100.00
The Wizard Of Oz, Jaymar, 1960 . . .25.00
Wee Willie Winkie, 30 pcs,
    Milton Bradley, 1930s. 14.00

History and Geography Puzzles
Dissected Map of the United States, with
    colored guide map, 1854 . . . . . .100.00
Gen. John J. Pershing,
    420 pcs, 1920s 35.00
Highlander, Girl and Tommy, England,
    1915. . . . . .35.00
John Glenn, plastic envelope, Japan,
    1960s. 5.00
Nelson at Trafalgar, plywood, cardboard
    box 40.00
Our Battleships, Milton Bradley, 1917. . . .
    100.00
Reading of the Declaration, Milton Bradley,
    1930. . . . . .75.00
Spiro Agnew, Friend of the Silent Majority,
    500 pcs, 1970. . . . . .8.00
Tank Busters and Jeeps on The Job,
    Victory series, 365 pcs, J. Pressman &
    Co., c1943-45. . . . . .14.00
The Conquerors, 1933 . . . . .7.00
World's Columbian Exposition Puzzle,
    cardboard, 49 pcs, 1891 . . . . . .125.00

Post Card Puzzles
Custom House, Boston, Mass, c1933 6.00
Head House and Beach City Point, South
    Boston, Mass, c1909 . . . . 8.00
Jig Saw Greetings, girl holding dog,
    Hallmark Cards, c1940. . . . . 8.00

Puzzle Books
Case of the Duplicate Door, Mystery
    Puzzle of the month #2, with 16-pg
    booklet, Pearl Publishing Co.,
    1940s 18.00
Little Golden Book, #101, 28 pgs, frame,
    Simon & Schuster, NY, c1951 . . 25.00
Murder By the Stars, Mystery-Jig series,
    300 pcs, with eight-pg booklet . . 30.00

Pyrex

I'll bet everyone has at least one piece of Pyrex glassware in his/her house. This heat-resistant glass can be found in many forms, including casserole dishes, mixing bowls, sauce pans and measuring cups. Pyrex was manufactured by Corning Glass Works.

Baking Dish, open, 7-3/4" l 5.00
Cake Dish, sq, 8-1/2", handled 9.00
Cake Dish, sq, 9". 9.00
Casserole, oval, 1 qt 7.00
Casserole, round, 1/2-qt 6.00
Chip and Dip Set, golden scroll design,
    1-1/2 pt dip, 4 qt chip bowl,
    1959 . . . . 20.00
Custard Cup, 6-1/2 oz 3.00
Bowl, clear, 1-1/2 pt. 5.00
Bowl, hostess, 2-1/2 qt 15.00
Calendar, Pyrex Ware, 1948 . . . . 7.00
Cookbook, New Facts About Cooking,
    1922 . . . . 12.00
Cookbook, Pyrex Prize Recipes,
    hardcover, 1953 . . . . 6.00

Mixing Bowls, nesting set of four, #401 1-1/2 pint blue, #402 1-1/2 quart red, #403 2-1/2 quart green and #404 4 quart yellow, c1975, price for set, $20.

Cookbook, The Ladies Home Journal-Mrs.
    Rorer's New Cookbook,
    reprint, 1952 . . . . .17.00
Dish, divided, Town & Country,
    1-1/2 qt 15.00
Loaf Pan, 1-1/2 qt. 8.00
Mixing Bowl, clear, 1-1/2 qt 6.00
Nesting Bowl, Americana, set. 25.00
Nesting Bowl, Butterprint, set. 18.00
Nesting Bowl, Clear, 1 qt 4.00
Percolator, 4-cup, Flameware,
    black handle 15.00
Percolator, 6-cup, Pyrex. 20.00
Pie Plate, 6" d, fluted 6.00
Pie Plate, 9" d, hexagonal 8.00
Platter, oval, 12" l 9.00
Saucepan, 2 qt, Flameware 12.00
Serving Bowl with candle warmer,
    2-1/2 qt 20.00
Teapot, squat, 4-cup, engraved, metal tea
    ball and top 70.00
Teapot, squat, 6-cup. 65.00
Tea Kettle, 2-1/2 qt, Flameware. . . .15.00
Utility Dish, oblong, 3 qt 12.00

Radio Characters and Personalities

Radio dominated American life between the 1920s and the early 1950s. Radio characters and personalities enjoyed the same star status as their movie counterparts. Phrases such as "The Shadow Knows" or "Welcome Breakfast Clubbers" quickly date an in-

Charlie McCarthy, windup toy, litho tin, $400.

Horace Heidt, adv tin, Tum's Pot-O-Gold, 2-1/4" l, $15.

dividual. Many collectors focus on radio premiums, objects offered during the course of a radio show and usually received by sending in proof of purchase of the sponsor's product. Make certain an object is a premium before paying extra for it as part of this classification.

Many radio characters also found their way into movies and television. Trying to separate the products related to each medium is time consuming. Why bother? If you enjoyed the character or personality, collect everything that is related to him or her.

Clubs: North American Radio Archives, 134 Vincewood Dr., Nicholasville, KY 40356; Oldtime Radio-Show Collectors Association, 45 Barry St., Sudbury, Ontario P3B 3H6 Canada; Radio Collectors of America, 8 Ardsley Cir, Brockton, MA 02402; Society to Preserve & Encourage Radio Drama, Variety & Comedy, P.O. Box 7177, Van Nuys, CA 91409.

Periodicals: *Friends of Old-Time Radio*, P.O. Box 4321, Hamden, CT 06514; *Old Time Radio Digest*, 10280 Gunpowder Rd., Florence, KY 41042.

Amos 'n' Andy

Figure, cardboard, with folder, 1930 .40.00
Game, Acrobat Ring and Disk,
   1930s 95.00

Paperback Book, Amos & Andy, 4" by 6" vertical format, 16 pgs, dusty, heavily soiled covers, extensive wear, c1930s 150.00
Photo, 8" by 10", black and white, inscribed signature in blue ink 150.00
Puzzle, 1931 . . . . 50.00
Sheet Music, Three Little Words, six pgs, c1930 . . . . 25.00

Charlie McCarthy

Game, Charlie McCarthy Radio Game, 1938 . . . . 10.00
Perfume Bottle, 3-1/2" h, clear glass, removable black plastic hat, late 1930s 40.00
Spoon 5.00

David Harding Counterspy

Badge, Junior Counterspy Agent, photo 25.00
Matchbook, 1-1/2" by 2", red, white and orange, matches removed, adv for Old Nick candy bars, reverse lists times of Counterspy Radio Show, ABC network, c1940 . . . . 15.00
Membership Certificate 15.00

Green Hornet

Book, *The Case of the Disappearing Doctor*, Whitman, 212 pgs 20.00
Fork and Spoon, silvered metal, vertical lettering and Hornet illus on handle, Imperial, c1966 . . . . 25.00
Mug, white, color illus, 1966 . . . . . . 35.00
Record, The Green Hornet Meets The Hornet, Al Hirt, orig jacket. 20.00

Popular Radio Stars, booklet, biographical sketches, 30 pgs, 1942, 5-3/8" by 8-3/8", $8.

Lone Ranger

Blotter, colorful, Bond Bread adv . . . 10.00
Book, *The Lone Ranger*, Little Golden Book, Simon & Schuster, 24 pgs, 1956 .11.00
Game, Legend of The Lone Ranger. 10.00
Pen, Silver Bullet Secret Code Ball Point, 1950 . . . . .75.00
Sheet Music, Hi Yo Silver, The Lone Ranger's Song, 1938. . . . . .80.00

The Shadow

Book, *The Living Shadow*, Maxwell Grant, c1931. .8.00
Matchbook Cover, 1-1/2" by 4" open size, black and red, silhouette illus, die-cut portrait flap inside, 1940s 30.00
Pinback Button, 1-1/4" d, celluloid, yellow and green, "The Shadow of Fu Manchu," 1930s. 75.00

Other

Archie, booklet, Duffy's First Reader by Archie, 5" by 7", 49 pgs, softcover, published by Bristol-Myers, c1943. . . . . .50.00
Archie, Pinback Button, "Meet 'Archie' Thursday Night," 2-3/4" l, white lettering, dark red ground, c1940. . . . . .45.00
Jack Benny, photo, 8" by 10", black and white, sgd "Hello Again, Jack Benny," 1930s. 45.00
Jack Benny, Record Set, four 78 rpm records, comedy sketches, Top Ten Records, orig cov, 1947 . . . . . . .45.00
Burns & Allen, coffee server set, 1950s. 120.00
Captain Midnight, record, "The Years to Remember," 7" d, flexible vinyl, punch out decoder, Longines Symphonette Society, #6 from "The Silver Dagger Strikes" series, 1960s 35.00
Captain Midnight, Sliding Secret Compartment Ring 50.00
Eddie Cantor, book, *Eddie Cantor's Book of Magic*. 16.00
Eddie Cantor, record set, 10" by 12", stiff cardboard cov, set of four 78 rpm records, c1947, distributed by Monitor, minor damage, inked inscriptions, one record broken 30.00
Fibber McGee and Molly, fan card, 8" by 10", black and white, one large photo and six small photos below 50.00
Fibber McGee and Molly, game, Wistful Vista, 1936 . . . . .10.00
Kate Smith, pinback button, 2-1/4" d, photo illus, black and red lettering 25.00
Mitzi Green, pinback button, 1-1/4" d, photo and "I'm on the Air, Mitzi Green, in Happy Landings" in center, "Ward's Soft

Bun Bread, WKAN, Tues & Thurs, 6:00 pm" in white lettering on rim, 1930s 5.00

Red Skelton, postcard, 3-1/2" by 5-1/2", radio show cast photo, matte finish, postmarked 1948 ....20.00

Uncle Don, bank, oval, 2-1/4" h, Uncle Don's Earnest Saver Club, paper label, photo and cartoon illus, Greenwich Savings Bank, New York City, 1930s 35.00

Radios

If a radio does not work, do not buy it unless you need it for parts. If you do, do not pay more than $10. A radio that does not work and is expensive to repair is a useless radio.

The radio market went through a number of collecting crazes in the 1980s and 1990s. It began with Bakelite radios, moved on to figural and novelty radios and now is centered on early transistors and 1940s plastic case radios. These crazes are often created by manipulative dealers. Be suspicious of the prices in any specialized price guide focusing on these limited topics. There are several general guides that do a good job of keeping prices in perspective.

Clubs: Antique Radio Club of America, 300 Washington Trails, Washington, PA 15301; Antique Wireless Association, 59 Main St., Bloomfield, NY 14469.

Periodicals: *Antique Radio Classified*, P.O. Box 802, Carlisle, MA 01741; *Radio Age*, P.O. Box 1362, Washington Grove, MD 20880; *The*

Channel Master, model 6511, green plastic case, AM, 12-1/4" by 5" by 6-1/4", $50.

Fada, model 1001, wood, Universal Superhelerodyne, AM/FM, restored, $60.

Horn Speaker, P.O. Box 1193, Mabank, TX 75147.

Advertising

Little Sprout 35.00
Miracle Whip, figural jar 30.00
Pepsi, figural bottle, decal 15.00
Polaroid Film, plastic, blue, sq, paper label 15.00
Tropicana, figural orange with straw 20.00

Character

Barbie, bust, plastic, remote speakers 25.00
Batman, torso, plastic 65.00
Big Bird, head, figural, paper decal front 15.00
Care Bears, plastic, semicircular, plastic bear sticker 10.00
Garfield, face, figural 40.00
Pound Puppy, stuffed dog on plastic radio 15.00
Smurf, head, figural, blue and white 20.00

Crosley

Model 3B, wood, large dial, five small knobs, 1923 ....125.00
Model 9-113, table, plastic, brown, elongated dial, 1949 ....15.00
9-119, Bakelite, brown, rounded corners, 1948 ....15.00

Emerson

Model 17, Bakelite, black, four tube, chrome trim.................75.00
Model 118, table, wood, five tube, AC/DC, c1936 ....55.00
Model 380, portable, Bakelite, sq, two knobs, leather strap 50.00
Model 511, table, Bakelite, white, clear plastic dial, gold tone metal grill . 35.00
Model 883, series B, table, blue, sleep timer 35.00

Model CX-284, portable, cloth covered, inner right dial, left louvers, slide-in door, handle, two knobs, battery, 1939 ....30.00

Motorola

Model 5H11, table, plastic, circular dial, metal pointer, 1950 ....25.00
Model 58R1, table, Bakelite, oversized dial, grill slots, 1948...........15.00
Model 63C, wood, clock, oversized oval clock face front, side knobs, 195325.00

RCA

Model 1R81, "Livingston," table, plastic, maroon, circular dial, pointer.... 15.00
Model 6K10, wood, painted, Art Deco-style, 1936.................250.00
Model 8BX6, portable, Bakelite, aluminum, 1948 ....50.00

Other

Adams-Morgan/Paragon, wood, large center dial, 1924 ....125.00
Admiral, Model 4A1, wood, dark panel, 1946 ....50.00
Admiral, Model 4X11, portable, plastic, semicircular dial, gold trim, 1952. 35.00
Air Castle, model 606-400WB, table, wood, right rect dial, left cloth grill with fretwork, two knobs, broadcast, battery, 1951 ....35.00
Airline, Model GSE-1620, table, plastic, large dial front right, 1956 ......15.00
American Bosch, "Amberola," table, six tube, wide metal dial front, 1925 . 75.00
Bendix, Model 55P2, table, plastic, imitation walnut, slide rule dial, vertical grill bars, rear handle, two knobs, broadcast, AC/DC, 1949 ....40.00
Bulova, Model 270, portable, transistor, leatherette, right round dial knob, plastic grill with crest, broadcast, battery, 1957 ....35.00

RCA Victor, model 40X-56, wood case, molded 1939 New York World's Fair motif, 9" by 6" by 6", $900.

Continental, Model 44, table, plastic, circular dial, 1955. . . . . .25.00

Fada, Model 110, table, wood, four tube, 1930s 65.00

Farnsworth, Model CK-111, console, Chippendale-style, 11 tubes, phono .150.00

Federal Telephone & Telegraph Co., Model B-30, table, wood, five tubes, three front dials, semicircular top 75.00

General Electric, Model 515, plastic, clock, 1951. . . . . .15.00

General Electric, Model H-500, table, Bakelite, circular center knob, 1940. . . . . .50.00

Howard, Green Diamond Eight, metal, painted top, three front knobs . . .75.00

Majestic, 5C3, alarm clock, circular clock face center, plastic louvers, 1952. . . . . .25.00

Olympic, Model 6-601, table, Bakelite, horizontal grill bars, elongated dial top, 1946. . . . . .50.00

Philco, Model 37-630T, table, six tubes, three bands, circular dial, three knobs, 1937. . . . . .75.00

Philco, Model 49-1606, console, AM/FM, four knobs, 1949 . . . . .35.00

Remler, Model 5500, "Scottie Pup," table, Bakelite, vertical louvers center, dog logo, 1947 . . . . .200.00

Sparton, Model 121, table, wood, sq, AM/FM, metal grill, four knobs, 1948. . . . . .25.00

Stromberg-Carlson, Model 61-H, table, wood, octagonal dial, three knobs, lever, 1935. . . . . .55.00

Westinghouse, Model 169, console, four band, phono, 1948 . . . . .15.00

Westinghouse, Model 350T7, table, wood, seven tube, AM/FM, semicircular dial 1951. . . . . .25.00

Zenith, Model 6D311, "Wavemagnet," table, Bakelite, Art Deco-style, antenna, 1939. . . . . .85.00

Radios, Transistor

In the early 1960s, transistor radios were the rage. Music was now both portable and convenient. Today, the transistor has gone the way of the early hand held calculator—both are clumsy and obsolete.

Newsletter: *Transistor Network*, 32 W. Main St., Bradford, NH 03221.

Novelty
Alarm Clock, round, pink and blue, Holiday Fair, 1968. . . . . .35.00

Bike Radio, Archer Road Patrol, orange and black, clamp-on style, Radio Shack, 1980s 12.00

Eiffel Tower, figural, metal, black base, two knobs, Japan 522, 1960s 45.00

Guitar, figural, Nashville Picker, red, Picker International, 1980s 40.00

Hairdryer, figural, Airwaves 2000, J&D Brush Co., 1990s 50.00

Little John, toilet, figural, Amico, 1970s 30.00

Newspaper Vending Machine-shape, Rocky Mountain News, 1980s . . 25.00

Piano, figural, wood, Lester Co., 1970s 95.00

Porsche Racer # 7, plastic, silver, 1980s 30.00

Washing Machine, figural, plastic, white, lift-up lid, Days Ease, 1970s 20.00

Other
Admiral, Model 528, turquoise, round dial, perforated chrome grill, top handle, volume knob, leatherette case, AM, battery, 1958. . . . . 50.00

Emerson, Model 888 . Titan, left peephole dial, perforated chrome grill, logo, AM, battery, 1963. . . . . 75.00

General Electric, Model H220A, wall mount, wood case, vertical slide-rule dial, left speaker grill, AM, AC, 1963 . . . . 7.00

General Electric, Model P851C, mini, top key ring, round dial, perforated chrome grill, AM, battery, 1962 . . . . 35.00

Hitachi, Model TH-650, peephole dial, right side thumbwheels, perforated chrome grill, AM, battery, 1963 . . . . 10.00

Hitachi, Model XH-1500, slide-rule dial, dual knobs, swing handle, perforated chrome grill, four top push buttons, AM/FM, battery, 1961 . . . . 25.00

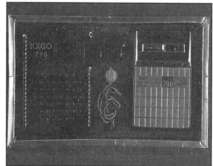

Americana Radio, 8 Transistor Super DX, Model FP80, leather case, earplug, instruction booklet and box, 8-1/2" w, 2" h, with radio station logo: $40; without logo: $30.

Box for Americana Radio Model FP80.

Motorola, Model AX4B, large round dial, two knobs, lattice plastic grill, crest, AM, battery, 1962 . . . . 20.00

Motorola, Model X29N, beige, flip-up top, slide rule dial, dual thumbwheels, dial light button, horizontal plastic grill, stand, AM, battery, 1962 . . . . 30.00

Philco, Model NT-600BK6, oval peephole dial, thumb-wheel tuning, perforated chrome grill, AM, battery, 1963 . . 10.00

RCA, Model 1BT58, Globetrotter, right and left knobs, top handle, perforated chrome grill, slide-rule dial, leather case, AM, battery 45.00

Realtone, Model TR-4250, top and front slide-rule dial, three top raised knobs, antenna, plastic louvered grill, four bands, multi battery, 1964 . . . . . . 25.00

Sharp, Model TR-222, half-moon dial, dual thumbwheels, perforated chrome grill, AM, battery, 1962 . . . . 20.00

Silvertone, Model 2207, gold, V dial, three transistors, perforated grill, AM, battery, 1962 . . . . 25.00

Sony, Model TR-6120, table model, ftd, top handle, plastic lattice grill, AM, battery, 1964 . . . . 15.00

Sylvania, Model 4P05, half-moon peephole, upper elongated V, perforated grill with crest, AM, battery, 1962 . . . . 25.00

Sylvania, Model 7058, Golden Shield, sq peephole dial, chrome paint, AM, battery, 1961 . . . . 25.00

Westinghouse, Escort, upper left watch, left side cigarette lighter, flashlight, AM, battery, 1968 . . . . 125.00

Westinghouse, Model H-698P7, checkerboard grill, round tuning dial, swing handle, bottom chrome inverted V, AM, battery, 1959 . . . . 40.00

Zenith, Model Royal 500N, slide-rule dial, perforated chrome grill, swing handle, AM, battery, 1965 . . . . 45.00

Railroadiana

Most individuals collect by railroad, either one near where they live or grew up or one for which they worked. Collectors are split fairly evenly between steam and diesel. Everyone is saddened by the current state of America's railroads. There are Amtrak collectors, but their numbers are small.

Railroad collectors have been conducting their own specialized shows and swap meets for decades. Railroad material that does show up at flea markets is quickly bought and sent into that market. Collectors use flea markets primarily to make dealer contacts, not for purchasing.

Railroad paper, from timetables to menus, is gaining in popularity as railroad china, silver-plated flatware and hollow wares and lanterns rise to higher and higher price levels. The key to paper ephemera is that it bear the company logo and have a nice displayable presence.

Clubs: Key, Lock and Lantern, Inc., 3 Berkeley Heights Park, Bloomfield, NJ 07003; Railroad Enthusiasts, 102 Dean Rd., Brookline, MA 02146; Railroadiana Collectors Association, Inc., 795 Aspen, Buffalo Grove, IL 60089; Railway & Locomotive Historical Society, P.O. Box 1418, Westford, MA

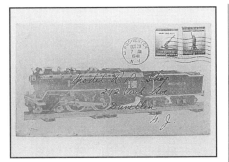

Envelope, first-day issue, postmarked 1941, $5.

01886; The Twentieth Century Railroad Club, 329 W. 18th St., Ste. 902, Chicago, IL 60616.

Periodical: *The Main Line Journal*, P.O. Box 121, Streamwood, IL 60107.

Booklet, Santa Fe Railroad, 1927 . . 15.00
Bowl, Union Pacific Railroad, china . 35.00
Butter Pat, 3-1/4" d, Atchinson, Topeka & Santa Fe Railroad,
　Sterling China 20.00
Catalog, Vulcan Gasoline Locomotives, Vulcan Iron Works, Wilkes-Barre, PA, 28 pgs, illus, 1926-27 . . . . 30.00
Cup and Saucer, Southern Pacific Railroad, Prairie Mountain Wildflower, Syracuse China 75.00
Hat, conductor's, Pennsylvania
　Railroad 60.00
Lantern, 17-1/2" h, Adlake Non Sweating Lamp, Chicago, yellow, red, blue and clear lights. 150.00

Mug, NYC, cream ground, rust color dec, stamped "Shenango China, New Castle, PA, Rim Rol Wel Rec T-14," $28.

Match Holder, Burlington Zephyr, stainless
　steel. 22.00
Napkin, Seaboard Railway,
　linen, pr 50.00
Pass, Erie Railroad. 8.00
Plate, New York Central Railroad, veterans, diesel engine dec,
　1951 . . . . 29.00
Playing Cards, California Zephyr,
　1950-60 . . . . 15.00
Print, Santa Fe Railroad, pictures Indians,
　framed, 1949 . . . . 35.00
Schedule, Pennsylvania Railroad Express,
　four-pg folder, June 21, 1885 . . . 20.00
Schedule, Philadelphia-Erie, framed,
　1869 . . . . 85.00
Sugar Bowl, cov, Burlington Railroad, silver, double handles,
　Reed & Barton. 75.00
Switch Key, Chicago & Northwestern. . . .
　13.00
Tablecloth, Baltimore & Ohio 20.00
Tape Measure, N&W Railroad,
　50 feet 23.00

Ramp Walkers

These comical toys have waddled their way into many toy collections. While you may find some ramp walkers made from metal, wood or celluloid, the majority of those available are plastic. Subjects vary from advertising figures to generic animals to popular television cartoon characters.

Astro and Rosey, plastic, Marx. 95.00
Bear, plastic, Marx 15.00
Big Bad Wolf and Mason Pig, plastic,
　Marx 40.00
Bull, plastic, Marx 15.00
Captain Flint Parrot, green, Long John Silver premium, 1989 . . . . 15.00

Badge, Penn Central R.R. Police Sergeant, lacquered brass, stamped "1969-1976," $75.

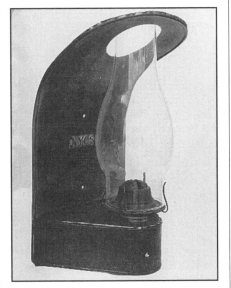

Lamp, NY Central, tin, oil, repainted, $45.

Chipmunks in marching band playing drum
   and horn, plastic, Marx 30.00
Clown, wood, Wilson 30.00
Cow, metal legs, plastic, Marx 15.00
Dachshund, plastic, Marx 15.00
Donald Duck, pulling nephews in wagon,
   plastic, Marx 35.00
Duck, plastic, Marx 15.00
Elephant, cast iron, lead legs, pat 1873,
   Ives, 3-1/2" l 125.00
Fred Flintstone and Barney Rubble,
   plastic, Marx 40.00
Goofy, riding hippo, plastic, Marx . . .45.00
Goofy Grape, Kool-Aid Funny Face,
   Pillsbury premium, 1989 . . . . . . .60.00
Horse, circus-style, plastic, Marx . . .15.00
Indian Chief, wood, Wilson 45.00
Jolly Ollie Orange, Kool-Aid Funny Face,
   Pillsbury premium, 1989 . . . . . . .60.00
Mickey and Minnie Mouse, metal legs,
   plastic, Marx 40.00
Monkey, wood, Czechoslovakian . . .30.00
Penguin, wood, Wilson 25.00
Policeman, wood, Czechoslovakian .35.00
Popeye, pushing spinach can
   wheelbarrow, plastic, Marx 25.00
Rabbit, wood, Wilson 40.00
Sydney Dinosaur, yellow and purple, Long
   John Silver premium, 1989 . . . . .15.00
Yogi Bear and Huckleberry Hound, plastic,
   Marx 50.00

Records

Most records are worth between 25
cents and $1. A good rule to follow is
the more popular the record, the less
likely it is to have value. Who does not
have a copy of Bing Crosby singing
"White Christmas"? Until the mid
1980s, the principal emphasis was on
78 rpm records. As the decade ended,
45 rpm records became increasingly
collectible. By 1990 33-1/3 rpm albums, especially Broadway show-re-
lated, were gaining in favor. To find out
what records have value, check *American Premium Record Guide: 1900-
1965* (Krause Publications, 1997).

By the way, maybe you had better
buy a few old record players. You
could still play the 78s and 45s on a
33-1/3 machine. You cannot play any
of them on a compact disc player.

Periodicals: *DISCoveries*, P.O. Box
1050, Dubuque, IA 52004; *Goldmine*,
700 E. State St., Iola, WI 54990.

Military, record blank,
U.S. Marines, cartoon
characters, $15.

Children's

Cinderella, TV soundtrack, Columbia,
   1965 . . . . 15.00
Hopalong Cassidy, Hoppy & Square
   Dance Hold Up, two-record set. . 65.00
Lady And The Tramp, 10", LP, Decca,
   1955 . . . . 50.00
Land Before Time, MCA, 1988 . . . . . 8.00
Mary Poppins, studio cast, Caedman,
   1968 . . . . 10.00
Mouse On The Mayflower/Little Drummer
   Boy, 1968 . . . . 50.00
Muppet Show, Arista, 1977 . . . . 8.00
Walt Disney's Song of Tomorrowland
   Golden Record, 6-3/4" by 7-1/2" colorful
   sleeve, yellow vinyl 78 rpm,
   1950s 30.00

Comedy

Bill Cosby, Boogie On Your Face/What's In
   A Slang, Capitol, 1977 . . . . 2.00

Phyllis Diller, Arthur Schwartz
   Revisited/Painted Smiles, 1984 . . . 5.00
Redd Foxx, Open the Door Richard, LP,
   Savoy, 1984 . . . . 6.00
Steve Martin, Let's Get Small, LP, Warner
   Brothers, 1977 . . . . 5.00
Groucho Marx, An Evening with Groucho,
   picture disc, A&M, 1976 . . . . 10.00
Martin Mull, The Days of Wine and
   Neuroses, LP, Capricorn, 1974 . . . 5.00

Cowboy

Gene Autry, two 10" d 78 rpm records,
   Okeh label, late 1930s 20.00
Lone Ranger, 7" by 8" cardboard dust cov,
   45 rpm Little Golden Record,
   c1958 . . . . 40.00
Roy Rogers, Pecos Bill, 10-1/2" by 12" rigid
   cardboard, three 78 rpm records . 75.00
The Restless Gun, 7" by 7" glossy paper
   slip case, 45 rpm, title song from 1957
   TV show 25.00

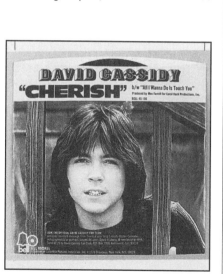

Rock 'N' Roll, 45 rpm, David Cassidy,
Cherish/All I Wanna Do Is Touch You,
Bell Records, $1.50.

Rock 'N' Roll, lp, The Best of the Doors,
Jim Morrison photo cov, $3.

Jazz

Count Basie, Dance Parade, Columbia,
    1949 . . . . .35.00
Dizzy Gillespie and His Orchestra,
    1956 . . . . .40.00
Benny Goodman, The Benny Goodman
    Trio, Capitol, 1952 . . . . .20.00
Quincy Jones, Around the World,
    1961 . . . . .6.00
Stan Kenton, Classics, Capitol, 195516.00
Sonny Rollins, Newk's Time, Blue Note,
    1958 . . . . .35.00

Movie

Close Encounters Of The Third Kind,
    Arista, 1977 . . . . .8.00
Mother, Jugs And Speed, A&M, 1976. . . .
    10.00
Little Shop of Horrors, Geffen, 1982 .20.00
Teenage Mutant Ninja Turtles, 1989. .8.00

Rock 'n' Roll, 45 rpm

The Lovin' Spoonful, Do You Believe In
    Magic?/On The Road Again, Kama
    Sutra, 1965. . . . . .1.50
The Mamas & The Papas, Monday,
    Monday/Got A Feeling,
    Dunhill, 1966 . . . . .1.50
The Platters, My Prayer/Heaven On Earth,
    Mercury, 1957 . . . . .4.00
Jerry Lee Lewis, Great Balls Of Fire/Sun,
    281 . . . . .20.00

Sports

Dallas Cowboys, Dallas Cowboys
    Christmas/Home Sweet Home,
    1985 . . . . .8.00
Hulk Hogan, Captain Lou's History of the
    World/Land of 1,000 Dances, 45 rpm,
    Epic, 1986 . . . . .1.50
Greg Luzinski, Grand Prix 207: Phillies
    Fever/Dancin' With the Phillies, 45 rpm,
    1977 . . . . .3.00

Red Wing

Red Wing, Minn., was home to several potteries. Among them were Red Wing Stoneware Co., Minnesota Stoneware Co. and The North Star Stoneware Co. All are equally collectible. Red Wing has a strong regional base. The best buys are generally found at flea markets far removed from Minnesota. Look for pieces with advertising. Red Wing pottery was a popular giveaway product.

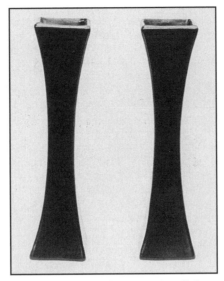

Bud Vases, pr, 7-3/4" h, black, relief mark, $40.

Club: Red Wing Collectors Society, Inc., P.O. Box 184, Galesburg, IL 61402.

Bobwhite

Beverage Server, stopper 95.00
Casserole, 1 qt. 40.00
Cookie Jar 60.00
Creamer. 35.00
Lazy Susan, stand 100.00
Mug 75.00
Platter, 20" l 90.00
Salad Bowl, 12" d. 85.00
Tray, rect 30.00
Tumbler 100.00

Round-Up

Creamer. 45.00
Cup 35.00
Plate, 6-1/2" d 15.00
Plate, 10-1/2" d,
    cowboys around fire 100.00
Platter, 13" l 50.00
Soup Bowl 55.00

Smart Set

Butter Warmer, stick handle, lid. . . . 40.00
Casserole, 1 qt. 55.00
Creamer. 18.00
Jug, 60 oz 85.00
Plate, 6-1/2" d 8.00
Plate, 7-1/2" d 12.00
Soup Bowl 18.00
Tray, 24" l 75.00

Tampico

Cake Plate, ruffled edge, ftd 45.00
Creamer. 20.00
Jug, 1 qt 95.00

Mug. 55.00
Plate, 6-1/2" d 5.00
Plate, 10-1/2" d 11.00
Platter, 13" d 25.00
Salt and Pepper Shaker, pr 35.00
Soup Bowl 18.00
Trivet. 75.00

Robots

This category covers the friction, windup and battery-operated robots made after World War II. The robot concept is much older, but generated few collectibles. The grandfather of all modern robot toys is Atomic Robot Man, made in Japan between 1948 and 1949.

Robots became battery operated by the 1950s. Movies of that era fueled interest in robots. R2D2 and C3PO from Star Wars are the modern contemporaries of Roby and his cousins. Robots are collected internationally. You will be competing with the Japanese for examples. When buying at a flea market, take time to make certain the robot is complete, operates (carry at least two batteries of different sizes with you for testing) and has the original box. The box is critical.

Hi-Bouncer Moon Scout, Marx, 11-1/2" h, battery-operated, litho tin torso, plastic arms, 1960s, $900.

Robot, Horikawa, Japan, 11-1/4" h, litho tin, battery-operated, walks, chest opens, gun shoots, body rotates 360 degrees, mkd "Made in Japan," $175.

Periodical: *Robot World & Price Guide*, P.O. Box 184, Lenox Hill Station, New York, NY 10021.

Acrobat Robot, Yonezawa, Japan, 9-3/4" h, plastic body, litho tin chestplate, battery operated, orig box, 1960s .285.00

Atomic Robot Man, Japan, 5" h, litho tin, pressed tin arms, windup, orig box 1700.00

Chief Robotman, KO, Japan, 12" h, tin, battery operated, silver, orig box 1800.00

Chief Robotman, KO, Japan, 12" h, tin, battery operated, white. 1200.00

Cone Head Robot, Yonezawa, Japan, 8-3/4" h, tin, plastic eyes, rubber antennae 2,800.00

Cragstan Astronaut, Japan, 14" h, litho tin, clear plastic helmet, battery operated, orig box 1,076.00

Dino the Robot, SH, Japan, 11" h, litho tin and plastic, battery operated, orig box 1,000.00

Dux Astroman, Dux, Germany, 12" h, tin and plastic, battery operated, orig box 1,400.00

Electric Robot and Son, Marx, 15" h, plastic, battery operated, orig box and cardboard insert, motor sluggish 595.00

Mechanical Robot, Linemar, Japan, 6" h, litho tin, plastic claw hands, windup, orig box 800.00

Mechanical Walking Spaceman, Tomiyama, Japan, 5-1/2"h, tin and hard plastic, windup, orig box and cardboard inserts 1,200.00

Mr. Atom, Advance Toy, West Haven, CT, 18" h, plastic, battery operated, orig box 700.00

Mr. Mercury, Marx, 13" h, litho tin, battery operated, remote control. 600.00

Mr. Robot The Mechanical Brain, Alps, Japan, 8-1/4" h, tin, windup, orig box and instruction sheet. 900.00

Planet Robot, KO, Japan, 9" h, tin and plastic, windup, orig box 285.00

Red Rosko Astronaut, Japan, 13" h, litho tin and plastic, battery operated 1,100.00

Robot, Linemar, Japan, 6" h, litho tin, battery operated, remote control, orig box 4,000.00

Robot, Yonezawa, Japan, 11" h, tin and litho tin, battery operated, orig box 1,600.00

Robot Lilliput, KT, Japan, 6-1/2" h, litho tin, key wind, laser copy of orig box 4,600.00

Robot ST1, West Germany, 7-1/2" h, silvered tin, key wind, orig box . 500.00

Smoking Spaceman, 12"h, tin, plastic dome, battery operated. 1,900.00

Television Spaceman, Alps, Japan, 11" h, tin battery operated, orig box . . 725.00

Video Robot and Dinosaur, SH, Japan, tin and plastic, battery operated, orig box 675.00

Rock 'N' Roll Collectibles

Most collectors focus on individual singers and groups. The two largest sources of collectibles are items asso-

ciated with Elvis and the Beatles. As revivals occur, e.g., the Doors, new interest is drawn to older collectibles. The market has gotten so big that Sotheby's and Christie's hold Rock 'n' Roll sales annually.

Periodicals: *Kissaholics Magazine*, P.O. Box 22334, Nashville, TN 37202; *The New England KISS Collectors' Network*, 168 Oakland Ave., Providence, RI 02908; *Tune Talk*, P.O. Box 851, Marshalltown, IA 50158.

Dolls

Cher, 12" h, Mego, 1976 . . . . 40.00
Elvis Presley, "Eugene," 12" h 50.00
Jerry Garcia, Cabbage Patch-style. . 70.00
Madonna, 3-1/2" h, "Breathless," Applause, 1990 . . . . 3.00
Mama Cass, 4-1/2" h, Hasbro, 1967 . . . . 90.00

Magazines

Creem Presents, #10, The Best of Metal Issue, December 1987 . . . . 4.00
People Weekly, Bob Dylan, Nov. 10, 1975 . . . . 4.00
Penthouse, Debbie Harry cov, February 1980. . . . . 10.00
Song Hits Yearbook, Captain & Tennille, Willie Nelson and Staple Singers, Summer, 1976. . . . . 2.00
Teen World, June 1962 . . . . 15.00
Tiger Beat, #2, October 1965 . . . . . . 20.00

Posters

Doors, 24" by 36", full color, green bottom border, white Doors logo, 1968, Doors Production Corp. 20.00
Fleetwood Mac, "Tusk," Germany concert photo 25.00

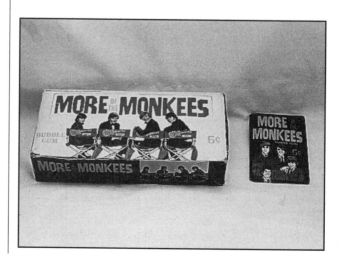

Bubble Gum, The Monkees, 24 packs, 1967 Raybert Productions, Inc., $100.

Puzzle, jigsaw, The Doors, black-and-white photo image, 10" by 8", $15.

Moody Blues, 18-1/2" by 25-1/2", stiff paper, April 1, 1970 concert, Terrace Ballroom, Salt Lake City, UT 50.00
Jim Morrison, 17" by 27" 10.00
Jimi Hendrix Experience, Soft Machine, The Paupers, 17" by 29" 10.00
Led Zeppelin, Jethro Tull, Fraternity of Man, Aug. 1, 1969 . . . . .15.00
The Who, 17" by 28" 10.00

Other

Backpack, MC Hammer, vinyl, 15" h, Bustin' Productions, 1991 . . . . . .15.00
Belt, Michael Jackson, leather, black, 2" photo, Lee, 1984 . . . . .15.00
Book, *Everything You Want to Know About Stevie Nicks*, Edith Ann Vare & Ed Ochs, Ballantine Books 5.00
Book, *Forever Hold Your Banner High*, Annette Funicello, 1976 . . . . .5.00
Book, *State Fair Mystery*, Donny & Marie Osmond, Whitman, 1977 . . . . .8.00
Calendar, Rod Stewart, coil bound, color photos, 1985 . . . . .15.00
Colorforms, Kiss, 1979 . . . . .35.00
Coloring Book, New Kids on the Block, Golden, 1990 . . . . .3.00
Diary, 4" by 5-1/2", Dick Clark American Bandstand Secret Diary, vinyl cov cardboard, gold colored metal lock, clear, orig price sticker, 1950s . . .60.00
Hand Puppet, The Monkees, talking, Mattel, 1966 . . . . .80.00
Hat, 9" l, Rock Around The Clock, blue felt, removable cardboard record on top, mkd "Manufactured by Bing Crosby Phonocards Inc.," c1950 . . . . . . .60.00
Jacket, tour, silver/gray satin, yellow and white embroidered couple dancing, black "Rock and Roll" above, embroidered 1963, back with gold, black and white "The Drifters On Broadway," tag inside mkd "Ragtime Collection" 150.00

Make-Up Kit, Kiss, Remco, 1978. . . 50.00
Mirror, Van Halen, 6" by 6" 5.00
Paper Doll, Rick Nelson, Whitman, 1959 . . . . 50.00
Record Case, 7-1/2" by 9", Tune Tote, vinyl cov cardboard, blue design, black, white, blue and fleshtone, black plastic carrying handles, paper sleeves for records, Ponytail, 1950s 25.00
Sheet Music, 9" by 12", Bill Haley and His Comets, Rock Around the Clock, two pgs, 1953 Myers Music. 18.00
Ticket, Eric Clapton, 2-1/4" by 3", 1975 Tampa, FL, concert, black and white, bluetone photo, stub 15.00
Ticket, Woodstock, 1969, three-day ticket, letter of authenticity. 125.00
Tour Book, Rod Stewart, 9-1/2" by 13-1/2", 1978-79 World Tour, 96 pgs. . . . 15.00

Rockwell, Norman

The prices in this listing are retail prices from a dealer specializing in Norman Rockwell and/or limited edition collectibles. Rockwell items are one of those categories for which it really pays to shop around at a flea market. Finding an example in a general booth at 10 cents on the dollar is not impossible or uncommon.

When buying any Rockwell item, keep asking yourself how many examples were manufactured. In many cases, the answer is tens to hundreds

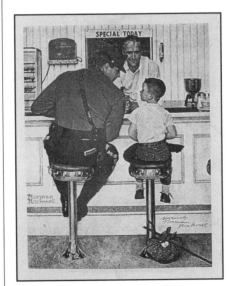

Print, The Runaway, sgd, 11" by 14", $40.

Stein, limited edition, Braving the Storm, 10" h, $125.

of thousands. Because of this, never settle for any item in less than fine condition.

Club: Rockwell Society of America, P.O. Box 705, Ardsley, NY 10502.

Bells

1975, Tavern Sign Painter 30.00
1987, Merry Christmas Grandma . . .33.00
1988, The Homecoming 38.00

Figurines

Day In the Life of a Boy, Gorham, 1980 . . . . .65.00
Little Mother, Rockwell Museum, 1981 . . . . .50.00
The Graduate, Dave Grossman, 1983 . . . . .30.00
Toy Maker, Rockwell Museum, 1979 . . . . .75.00

Collector Plates

Centennial, 1993, The Cobbler. 40.00
Centennial, 1993, The Toymaker . . .40.00
Christmas Legacy, 1993, Making A Wish 50.00
Christmas Legacy, Visions Of Santa 55.00
Rockwell Society, 1975, Angel with Black Eye 40.00
Rockwell Society, 1975, 1995, Filling The Stockings. 33.00

Magazine Cover

Boy's Life, 1951 . . . . .20.00
Saturday Evening Post, 1940. . . . . .20.00

TV Guide, 1970 . . . . .5.00

Others

Calendar, 1941, boy and dog illus, Hercules Powder Co., adv 175.00
Catalog, Sears, Roebuck & Co., cov art, 1932 . . . . .65.00
Coin, Ford Motor Co., 50th Anniversary 35.00
Ingot, Santa Planning a Visit, gold-plated silver, Hamilton Mint, 1975 . . . . .45.00
Magazine Tear Sheet, Country Gentleman, Jell-O adv, 1922 . . . . .10.00
Music Box, Between The Acts, Schmid 125.00
Poster, Freedom of Speech, WWII, 1943 . . . . .35.00
Sheet Music, Over There, 1918 . . . .45.00

Roof Glass

Roof glass was a Victorian house decoration created by Clark B. Nelson. Each piece is marked "Dec 1 91" (1891 patent date). Depending on the size of the house, scores to hundreds of individual pieces went atop houses from small gingerbread-style family dwellings to stately mansions, where the glass demanded attention.

The trim began at the edge of the house with a 14" upside-down "J" followed in metal tracking by 6" arrowhead shapes running from peak to peak. A double-wheel design marked the intersected roof peaks, and dormers sported the 4-1/2" arrowheads. Large fan-shapes were wedged into the front porch ceiling and support beams. Four fans could be formed into a circle and leaded into doors and windows. Unusual shapes, such as a prone lion, have been rumored to exist as well.

Decorative strap bracing, holding one or two undated glass globes with the same Swiss dot pattern, was often placed above the cresting. These braces were not grounded and served solely as decoration, not lightning protection. The balls were nicknamed "Burgoon balls" because they were first discovered in Burgoon, Ohio. Glass was shipped throughout the United States, with many caches found in Indiana, Michigan, Wisconsin and Iowa. Colors include white, green,

red, amber and cobalt, with sun-colored amethyst being the most common.

Advisor: Phil Steiner, 15832 S. County Rd 900 W, Wanatah, IN 46390.

Arrowhead 50.00
Burgoon Ball 500.00
Double Wheel 250.00
Fan-shape 125.00
Strap Brace 50.00
Upside Down J 200.00

Roseville Pottery

Roseville rose from the ashes of the J.B. Owen Co., when a group of investors bought Owen's pottery in the late 1880s. In 1892, George F. Young became the first of four succeeding generations of Youngs to manage the plant.

Roseville grew through acquisitions of another Roseville firm and two in Zanesville. By 1898, the company's offices were located in Zanesville. Roseville art pottery was first produced in 1900. The trade name "Rozane" was applied to many lines. During the 1930s, Roseville looked for

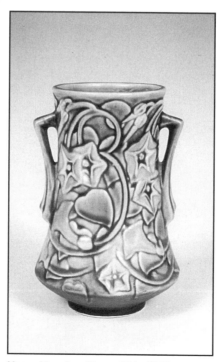

Vase, Morning Glory, 6" h, $230.

Vase, Bleeding Heart, 4-1/8" h, #961-4, $75.

new product lines. Utilizing several high gloss glazes in the 1940s, Roseville revived its art pottery line. Success was limited. In 1954, the Mosaic Tile Co., bought Roseville.

Pieces are identified as early, middle (Depression era) and late. Because of limited production, middle period pieces are the hardest to find. They also were marked with paper labels that have been lost over time. Some key patterns to watch for are Blackberry, Cherry Blossom, Faline, Ferella, Futura, Jonquil, Morning Glory, Sunflower and Windsor.

Clubs: American Art Pottery Association, P.O. Box 525, Cedar Hill, MO 63016; Roseville's of the Past Pottery Club, P.O. Box 656, Clarcono, FL 32710.

Periodical: *Pottery Collectors Express*, P.O. Box 221, Mayview, MO 64071.

Baskets

Bittersweet, #810-10 . . . . .180.00
Monticello, brown, #632 . . . . .550.00
Silhouette 135.00

Bowls

Apple Blossom, green, #326-6 . . . .120.00
Baneda 165.00
Ferella, 12" d 695.00
Florentine, 7" d 75.00
Pine Cone, brown, #278-4 . . . . . . .225.00

Candleholders

Clematis, brown, #1154-2 . . . . .50.00
Tourmaline, dark pink
    and turquoise 100.00
White Rose, pr 75.00

Vases

Cherry Blossom,
    two-handled, 5" h 225.00
Foxglove, pink, #54-15 . . . . .350.00
Fuschia, green, #895-7 . . . . .285.00
Ixia, #855-7 . . . . .75.00
Jonquil, squatty, 4" h 110.00
Magnolia, blue, #185-8 . . . . .135.00
Peony, tan, #171-19 . . . . .90.00
Pine Cone, blue, #840-7 . . . . .185.00
Poppy, pink, #873-9 . . . . .245.00
Primrose, #760-6. . . . . .90.00
Rosecraft, black, 5-1/2" h 40.00
Rozane, pansies, 5" h 150.00
Tourmaline, blue 75.00
White Rose, #994-18 . . . . .695.00

Wall Pockets

Bittersweet, green 295.00
Carnelian I, pink and blue 175.00
Cosmos, blue 375.00
Lotus, burgundy 145.00

Other

Ashtray, Imperial II, blue 245.00
Bookend, pr, Gardenia 165.00
Bookend, pr, Pine Cone, brown . . .195.00
Console Bowl, Freesia, brown,
    #568-12 . . . . .100.00
Console Bowl, Pine Cone, brown,
    11" d .295.00
Console Set, Calla Lily, 7"d bowl,
    pr of candleholders 100.00

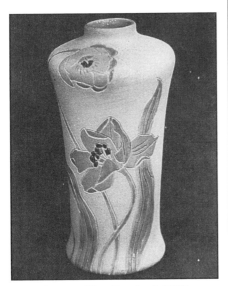

Vase, Rozane Woodlands, 6-1/4" h, $750.

Vase, Silhouette Nude, 7-3/8" h, #783-7, $185.

Console Set, Columbine, blue, 10" d bowl,
    pr of 2-1/2" h candleholders . . . 175.00
Cornucopia, Bleeding Heart, green,
    #141-6. 85.00
Cornucopia, Peony, tan, #171-8 . . 120.00
Creamer and Sugar, Zephyr Lily,
    blue. 105.00
Ewer, Clematis, #18-15 . . . . 295.00
Ewer, Freesia, blue, #19-6. . . . . . . 120.00
Flower Pot, matching underplate, Poppy,
    green. 245.00
Jardiniere, Normandy, 7" h 180.00
Jardiniere, Snowberry, green, 8" h 950.00
Jardiniere and Pedestal, Dahlrose,
    green. 500.00
Pitcher, Colonial, cream gloss, blue
    stripes, 8-1/4" h. 40.00
Pitcher, Holland, 6-1/2" h. 225.00
Planter, Magnolia, #388-6 . . . . 110.00
Planter, Poppy, blue 40.00
Urn, Florentine, brown, #463-5 . . . . 85.00

Royal China

The Royal China Co., located in Sebring, Ohio, used remodeled facilities that originally housed the Oliver China Co., and later the E.H. Sebring Co. Royal China began operations in 1934. The company produced an enormous number of dinnerware patterns. The backs of pieces usually contain the names of the shape, line and decoration. In addition to many variations of company backstamps, Royal China also produced objects with private backstamps. All records of these markings were lost in a fire in 1970.

In 1964, Royal China purchased the French-Saxon China Co., Sebring, Ohio, which it operated as a wholly owned subsidiary. On Dec. 31, 1969, Royal China was acquired by the Jeannette Corp. When fire struck the Royal China Sebring plant in 1970, Royal moved its operations to the French-Saxon plant. The company changed hands several times, until operations ceased in August 1986.

Collectors tend to concentrate on specific patterns. Among the most favored are Bluebell (1940s), Currier and Ives (designed by Gordon Parker and introduced 1949-50), Colonial Homestead (1951-52), Old Curiosity Shop (early 1950s), Regal (1937) Royalty (1936) and blue and pink Willow Ware (1940s). Because of easy accessibility, only purchase pieces in fine to excellent condition.

Club: The Currier & Ives Collectors by Royal, RD 2, Box 394, Hollidaysburg, PA 16648.

Colonial Homestead

Bowl, 5-1/2" d 3.00
Cake Plate, tab handles 12.00
Creamer and Sugar, cov 12.00
Cup and Saucer 4.00
Plate, 6" d, bread and butter. 1.50
Plate, 10" d, dinner. 3.50
Salt and Pepper Shakers, pr 12.00

Currier & Ives, blue and white

Ashtray 12.50
Bowl, Berry .4.00
Bowl, Cereal, 6-1/4" d. 12.00
Cake Plate, handled. 12.00
Casserole .65.00

Currier & Ives, blue and white, saucer, $1.

Currier & Ives, blue and white, bread and butter plate, 6" d, $2.50.

Creamer and Sugar, cov 17.00
Cup and Saucer 3.00
Gravy Underplate 2.00
Pie Plate, 10" d 15.00
Plate, 6" d, bread and butter 2.50
Plate, 10-1/4" d, dinner 4.50
Sandwich Plate 13.00
Soup, flat 7.50
Trivet, 7-3/4" d 14.00
Vegetable Bowl, 8-1/2" d, rimmed 7.00

Memory Lane
Berry Bowl 3.00
Plate, 6" d, bread and butter 2.50
Vegetable Bowl 18.00

Old Curiosity Shop
Berry Bowl, 5" d 3.00
Creamer and Sugar, cov 17.00
Cup and Saucer 4.00
Plate, 10" d, dinner 4.00

Willow Ware
Casserole, cov, 8" d 18.00
Sugar, cov 7.50

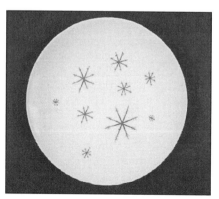

Star Glow, dinner plate, 10" d, $2.50.

Royal Copley

Royal Copley ceramics were produced by the Spaulding China Co., located in Sebring, Ohio. These attractive giftware items were most often marked with a paper label only, making identification a challenge. For hints on identifying unmarked Royal Copley, refer to Leslie C. and Marjorie A. Wolfe's *Royal Copley: Plus Royal Windsor and Spaulding*, published by Collector Books, 1992.

Newsletter: *The Copley Courier*, 1639 N. Catalina St., Burbank, CA 91505.

Ashtrays
Affectionate Birds 14.00
Bow and Ribbon 15.00
Leaf and Bird 7.00
Mallard 8.00

Banks
Pig, 7-1/2" h 28.00
Rooster, 7-1/2" h 35.00
Teddy Bear, 7-1/2" h 40.00

Figures
Angel, blue, 6-1/4" h 16.00
Angel, pink, 6-1/4" h 18.00
Black Cat, 8" h 24.00
Blue-Bird, 5" h 18.00
Cockatoo, 7-1/4" h 24.00
Dog, 6-1/2" h 16.00
Oriental Boy and Girl, 7-1/2" h 12.00
Sparrow, 5" h 12.00
Thrush, 6-1/2" h 14.00

Vase, 6-1/2" h, 3" d, black floral leaf and stem, pink ground, $12.

Vase, 8-1/2" h, 4" d, fish column, Essex assortment, #50, green and gray, $12.

Planters
Bamboo, oval, 4-1/2" h 6.00
Big Apple, 5-1/2" h 10.00
Big Blossom, 3" h 8.00
Coach, 3-1/4" by 6" h 12.00
Duck and Mailbox 35.00
Hen, 8" h 16.00
Kitten and Book, 6-1/2" h 18.00
Little Ribbed, 3-1/2" h 6.00
Running Horse, 6" h 10.00
Teddy Bear, 6-1/4" h 20.00
Woodpecker, 6-1/4" h 12.00

Vases
Bow and Ribbon, 6-1/2" h, ftd 10.00
Carol's Corsage, 7" h 12.00
Cornucopia, 8-1/4" h 18.00
Fish, cylindrical, 7" h 12.00
Floral, 6-1/4" h, handled 10.00
Harmony, 7-1/2" h 10.00

Other
Creamer, Leaf, handled 10.00
Lamp Base, cocker spaniel, figural,
  10" h 38.00
Pitcher, 8" h, pin, Floral Beauty 22.00
Sugar Bowl, Leaf, handled 10.00

Royal Doulton

Chances of finding Royal Doulton at flea markets are better than you think. It often is given as gifts. Since the recipients did not pay for it, they often have no idea of its initial value. The same holds true when children have to break up their parent's household. As a result, it is sold for a fraction of its value at garage sales and to dealers.

Figurine, Bonnie Lassie, #HN 1626, $325.

Check out any piece of Royal Doulton that you find. There are specialized price guides for character jugs, figures and toby jugs. A great introduction to Royal Doulton is the two-volume videocassette entitled "The Magic of a Name," produced by Quill Productions, Birmingham, England.

Clubs: Royal Doulton International Collectors Club, P.O. Box 6705, Somerset, NJ 08873; Royal Doulton International Collectors Club (Canadian Branch), 850 Progress Ave., Scarborough, Ontario M1H 3C4 Canada.

Periodicals: *Collecting Doulton*, 2 Strafford Ave., Elsecar, Barnsley, S. Yorkshire S74 8AA England; *Doulton Divvy*, P.O. Box 2434, Joilet, IL 60434.

Character Jugs
Large, Beefeater, 1947 . . . . .150.00
Large, Lawyer, 1959 . . . . .150.00
Large, Long John Silver, 1952 . . . .150.00
Large, The Sleuth, 1973 . . . . .150.00
Small, Beefeater, 1947 . . . . .85.00
Small, D'Artagnan, 1983 . . . . .85.00
Small, Graduate, 1993 . . . . .85.00
Small, Guardsman, 1986 . . . . .85.00

Figurines
Albert Sagger Toby Jug, 1986 . . . . .85.00
Appley Dapply, P2333, 1971. . . . . . .30.00
Benjamin Bunny with Peter Rabbit, P2509, 1975. . . . . .50.00
Cecily Parsley, P1941, 1965. . . . . . .50.00
Foxy Reading Country News, P3219, 1990 . . . . .55.00

Plate, 8-3/4" d, institutional ware, Canadian National System Railroad, $30.

Jemima Puddleduck Made a Feather Nest, P2823, 1983 . . . . 30.00
Mrs. Tittlemouse, P1103, 1948 . . . . 45.00
Old King Cole Tiny Jug, 1990 . . . . . 35.00
Timmy Tiptoes, P1101, 1948. . . . . . 30.00
Tommy Brock, P1348, 1955 . . . . . . 30.00

Plates
Accept These Flowers, 1985 . . . . . . 40.00
Christmas in Mexico, 1973 . . . . 25.00
Dad Plays Santa, 1991 . . . . 60.00
Kathleen and Child, 1978 . . . . 95.00
My Sweetest Friend, 1977. . . . . 40.00
Together for Christmas, 1993 . . . . . 45.00

Other
Child's Feeding Dish, Bunnykins in country store 135.00
Mug, Santa, 2nd ed 75.00

Rugs

You have to cover your floors with something. Until we have antique linoleum, the name of the game is rugs. If you have to own a rug, own one with some age and character. Do not buy any rug without unrolling it. Hold it up in the air in such a way that there is a strong light behind it. This will allow you to spot any holes or areas of heavy wear.

Hooked
Abstract, cross in center, colorful, 29" by 41" 27.50
Cat, folksy, lying on pillow, blue, black and white cat, salmon red and green pillow, dark gray and pink ground, salmon border, loosely hooked, fading, repair, 25-1/2"" by 35-1/2" 225.00

Cat, folksy, lying on rect platform, two shades of olive, red and white, gray-beige ground, multicolored foliage, wear, fading, some repair, 20" by 38" 275.00
Eagle, red, white and blue 100.00
Floral, red roses, black ground, leaf scroll border, rag and yarn, damage to border, 27" by 46" 82.50
Floral, unfinished, orig frame, browns, gray and faded pink, 26-1/2" by 33" . .55.00
Little Bo Peep, three sheep, faded colors, some wear, 18-1/2" by 37" 220.00
Morning Glories, pastel shades, ivory ground, deep purple border, slight color bleeding, 26" by 38". 27.50
Peacock, primitive, folksy, red, blue, yellow and green, black ground, edge wear and damage, 32" by 38" 55.00
Swan, cattails, water lilies, blues, greens, brown, black and white, braided border, modern, mounted on frame, 20" by 36" 70.00
Winter Landscape, house and trees, faded pink, blue, green, brown, white and black, 16-1/2" by 26" 72.00

Other
Chain Stitch, floral and diamond design, blues and pinks, black ground, 8" by 120" 55.00
Chain Stitch, floral design, blue, green and red, 4" by 72". 27.50
Character, Donald Duck and Nephews, cotton, mkd "Made in Belgium" . .35.00
Oriental, contemporary, Heriz pattern, red ground, 39" by 66". 195.00
Oriental, contemporary, Sarouk pattern, red ground, 37" by 65". 125.00
Rag, Pennsylvania, strip, bluish gray and white, blue warp, 3" by 180" 90.00
Rag, Pennsylvania, strip, Green and white, colorful string warp, one end frayed, partial orig factory label "Hollinger Mills Co., Carlisle, PA", 36" by 648". .440.00
Woven, ingrain, small floral design, red, greens and ivory, wear and damage, 3" by 264" 50.00

Russel Wright

Russel Wright was an American industrial engineer with a design passion for domestic efficiency through simple lines. Wright and his wife, Mary Small Einstein, wrote *A Guide To Easier Living* to explain the concepts. Some of his earliest designs were executed in polished spun aluminum. These pieces, designed in the mid

American Modern, creamer, $12.

1930s, included trays, vases and teapots.

Wright worked for many different companies, in addition to creating material under his own label, American Way. Wright's contracts with firms often called for the redesign of pieces which did not produce or sell well. As a result, several lines have the same item in more than one shape. Among the companies for which Wright did design work are Chase Brass and Copper, General Electric, Imperial Glass, National Silver Co., and the Shenango and Steubenville Pottery Companies.

Though most collectors focus on Wright's dinnerware, he also designed glassware, plastic items, textiles, furniture and metal objects. His early work in spun aluminum often is overlooked, as is his later work in plastic for the Northern Industrial Chemical Co.

Tidbit, two-tier, aluminum trays, bamboo handle, $50.

American Modern

Bread and Butter Plate, 6-1/4" d	3.00
Celery Dish	22.00
Child's Plate	30.00
Chop Plate	22.00
Coffee Pot	70.00
Cup	7.50
Pitcher	65.00
Plate, 10" d	6.50
Sugar, cov	10.00
Teapot	50.00

Iroquois

Bread and Butter	3.00
Butter Dish	45.00
Carafe	75.00
Casserole, 2 qt.	20.00
Cereal Bowl, 5" d	6.50
Gravy, 10 oz, with stand	25.00
Mug, 13 oz.	35.00
Plate, 9-1/2" d	4.50
Tea Cup and Saucer	10.00

Salt and Pepper Shakers

Hang on to your hats. Those great figural salt and pepper shaker sets from the 1920s through the 1960s have been discovered by the New York art and decorator crowd. Prices have started to jump. What does this say about taste in America?

When buying a set, make certain it is a set. Check motif, base and quality of workmanship. China shakers should have no cracks or signs of cracking. Original paint and decoration should be present on china and metal figures. Make certain each shaker has the right closure. Salt and pepper

Black Mammy and Chef, ceramic, $85.

shaker collectors must compete with specialized collectors from other fields, e.g., advertising and black memorabilia. I have been searching for a pair shaped like jigsaw puzzle pieces. So far I have neither seen a pair nor found a dealer who has seen one, but I will not give up.

Club: Novelty Salt & Pepper Shakers Club, P.O. Box 3617, Lake Worth, FL 33465.

Advertising

Esso Pumps	28.00
Firestone Tires	55.00
Greyhound Buses	75.00
Mixmaster, plastic, 1950s	25.00
Westinghouse, washer and dryer	30.00

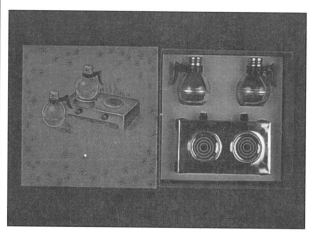

Glass coffee pots on metal hotplate, orig box, $18.

Black

Chef and Maid, chalkware 2-1/2" h . .40.00
Lady's heads .70.00
Leapfrogging Kids 75.00
Natives, baskets on heads 25.00
Porter and Suitcase 70.00

Character

Bud Man, blue shoes 230.00
Fred Flintstone and Barney Rubble .55.00
Kellogg's, Snap and Pop 65.00
Mickey and Minnie Mouse
    on Park Bench 195.00
Pillsbury Dough Boy 35.00
Pillsbury Dough Boy and Poppy,
    hard plastic, 1974 . . . . .60.00
RCA Nipper 25.00
Smokey Bear 100.00
Sneezy and Bashful 40.00

Other

Alcatraz Convicts 38.00
Amish Couple, white metal, painted . .6.00
Art Deco Woman,
    holding two hat boxes 95.00
Bananas, ceramic, yellow and tan . . .8.50
Bears, black and white 15.00
Begging Dog and Blue Bow 15.00
Boy and Dog, brown, Van Telligen . .65.00
Bride and Groom in Car 45.00
Cactus, Rosemeade 15.00
Cat, winking, Enesco 15.00
Cat and Fiddle 38.00
Cat Head, Lefton 25.00
Cats and Fishbowls, black cats 160.00
Caveman and Cavewoman 15.00
Chickens, Rosemeade 25.00
Christmas Trees 20.00
Colonial Couple, Erphila,
    Czechoslovakia 25.00
Conestoga Wagons, brown and black,
    white tops 10.00
Cow, purple 15.00
Deer, nodders 65.00
Donkey and Tipped Cart 15.00
Dutch Boy and Girl, Shawnee 60.00
Dutch Couple, large size 25.00

Elephants, gray, blue trim, trunks form
    letters "S" and "P,"
    Ceramic Arts Studios 35.00
Farmer Pigs, Shawnee 45.00
Fish, Rosemeade 35.00
Flamingos 15.00
Flying Saucers 45.00
Ghosts 20.00
Hammer and Nail 15.00
Humpty Dumpty, Regal 175.00
Jonah and the Whale, black 85.00
Jonah and the Whale, white 75.00
Kangaroo, Mother with Baby 22.00
Kangaroo, Nodders 95.00
Lobster, red, green base, claws held above
    head, attached by springs 25.00
Marilyn Monroe and Cake 35.00
Milk Cans, Shawnee 45.00
Miss Priss, Lefton 30.00
Mona Lisa and Picture Frame 25.00
Monkey and Palm Tree 20.00
Native with Banjo and Palm Tree . . 55.00
Pears 15.00
Penguins, ceramic, black, white and
    orange, 1930s 25.00
Rooster and Hen, Germany 25.00
Rotisserie, plastic 210.00
Sailor and Bo Peep, Shawnee 45.00
Sailor and Mermaid, huggies 225.00
Schmoos, Red Wing 100.00
Sea Lions 15.00
Surfer Boy and Surfboard 60.00
Surfer Girl and Surfboard 100.00
Telephone and Directory, ceramic, black
    phone, white book, black lettering 15.00
Turkeys, multicolored 15.00
Wrestlers, in wrestling position 25.00

Sand Pails

The illustrations found on litho tin sand pails are truly works of art. Innumerable child's themes from animals to cartoon characters have graced the sides of these seashore toys. Despite the fact that sand and salt water are natural enemies of tin toys, concentrate on pails in very good condition with little surface damage. Pails were mass-produced in large quantities, making condition an important part of value.

J. Chein & Co., 1930-70

3-1/2" h, cat family 150.00
4-1/2" h, Disney,
    Walt Disney Productions 175.00
5-3/4" h, cow and farm 75.00
7-1/2" h, Game Pail, orange and green,
    plastic hand hold, wire bail, 1961 75.00

7-1/2" h, Under the Sea, metallic blue,
    silver and white 125.00
8" by 8" h, tiger at beach 100.00

Ohio Art, 1930-70

3-1/4" h, children playing
    with puppies 125.00
4-1/4" h, Cowboy and Indian 125.00
4-1/4" h, Mexican children playing musical
    instruments 70.00
4-1/2" h, girl on beach 125.00
5-1/4" h, "FIRE" printed on both sides, red
    ground, yellow leaves,
    white lettering 100.00
5-1/2" h, calypso band,
    metallic purple 100.00
7-3/4" h, children picking
    strawberries 175.00

T. Cohn Inc.

3" h, boy pulling in fish with dog, mkd "#14
    Del-Ray Pops," Del-Ray Candy Co.,
    Wilmington, Delaware 175.00
4-1/4" h, children bathing animals . 125.00
4-1/2" h, children swimming 125.00

U.S. Metal Toy Manufacturing Co., 1930-70

5-1/4" h, Dutch children playing, yellow and
    blue 75.00
6-1/2" h, nursery rhymes 125.00
7-1/2" h, children playing pirates at sea,
    plastic handle 55.00
7-1/2" h, Treasure Island, pirates
    on bottom, scrap tin 150.00

J. Chein & Co., cowboy theme, 4-1/4" h, $100.

Siamese Cats, ceramic, 1960s, $8.

Safeguard Soap premium, paper label, $80.

Other

Advertising, Safeguard, 5" h, paper label reads "This Sandpail Free when you buy 2 bath or 3 complexion size bars of Safeguard".................80.00
Apex Safe-t-Play Pails, 5-3/4" h, rubber pail, shovel.................100.00
Ridley's, 3" h, Pinocchio, emb lobster bottom 175.00

School Memorabilia

"School Days, School Days, good old golden rule days." I've been singing this refrain ever since I moved into the former Vera Cruz elementary school in Pennsylvania.

Reward of Merit

Card of Honor, 1879, Diligency-One Hundred Tokens of Merit, multicolored chromolithograph 15.00
Excelsior, 50 merits, white and blue, gold trim, 1866...................10.00
Reward of Merit, schoolhouse illus, hp, reverse with student list, 1862 ....6.00
Toledo Public Schools Grade One Card of Worth, 1876, blue and red 8.00

Sheet Music

Little Old Red Schoolhouse, Wheeler & Durham, 1890 ....12.00
School Life, Charles L. Johnson, Respectfully Dedicated to All Schools, 1912......................15.00

Teacher's Pet, Allan Roberts and Jerome Brainin, 1937................5.00

Other

Bell, No. 7, brass, turned-wood handle....................40.00
Book, *School Memories*, 1920s, unused 18.00
Certificate, Teacher's Elementary School Certificate, Perry County, OH, 1905, sunrise over mountain vignette, 9-1/4" by 13"...............15.00
Calendar, 1960, The Travelers Co., adv, hanging...................11.00
Catalog, JB Clow & Sons, Modern Plumbing for Schools, 1916, 88 slick pgs, photos and names of schools as nationwide clients, 9-1/2" by 12". 45.00
Desk, student's, oak, 18" by 22" by 20", drawer under seat with pencil tray 75.00
Magazine, *Collier's*, School Days cov, Maxfield Parrish, 1908 ....85.00
Map, United States, hanging, orig wood case, varnished.............45.00
Photograph, black and white, school children standing in front of school, oak leaves cover bare feet, c1935, 8" by 9-1/2" 15.00
Pinback Button, Gaston Grammar School, 1" d, multicolored, c1915 ....2.00
Postcard, Lincoln Building, Quakertown Schools, PA, black and white 5.00
Report Card, Pupil's Report, neatly filled in, 1900 ....3.00

Schuetzen Memorabilia

Schuetzen vereins (shooting associations) were fixtures in many German- and Swiss-American immigrant communities from the 1860s until World War I; most eventually died out due to anti-German sentiment. The *schuetzen vereins* carried on the old European traditions and ceremonies, including the wearing of stylized uniforms and the liberal awarding of insignia, medals, pins, trophies, etc.

Target shooting matches were held locally, regionally and even nationally under the auspices of *bunds* (federations), each event generating its own prize medals, trophies, cups and other awards. All of this memorabilia is uncommon today, many of the gold and silver items having been sold and melted down during hard times.

Coin, Preisschiessen Chicago 1868, silver, orig chain loop, 46mm, $150.

Paper memorabilia, such as group photographs, membership certificates (diplomas), match announcements and regulations, posters, scorecards and targets, are all of value to collectors. The printing on any of these items will often be in German.

Advisor: Allen Hallock, P.O. Box 2747, San Rafael, CA 94902, (415) 924-1967.

Medals

Chicago Schuetzen Verein, 1904, gold and enamel, 1-3/4"..............125.00
4th National Shooting Festival 1904, silver and enamel, 3-1/2" 125.00
Kerrville Schuetzen Verein, 1914, gold, 1-3/4".....................50.00
San Francisco Schuetzen Verein, 25-Year Membership, gold and enamel, 2-1/2"....................200.00
6tes Nationales Bundes-Schiessen, NJ 1910, silver, tri-color ribbon, 3-3/4"....................125.00
Third National Shooting Festival, San Francisco 1901, 2-1/4", gold ...150.00
Third National Shooting Festival, San Francisco 1901, 2-1/4", silver ...85.00

Other

Beer Stein, Philadelphia Schuetzen Verein 60th Anniversary 1906, ceramic, 4-1/2" h 50.00
Book, *Philadelphia Schuetzen Verein 60th Anniversary*, 1906 ....75.00
Coin, souvenir, silver, Bundesschiessen, NY, 1868, 37mm 110.00

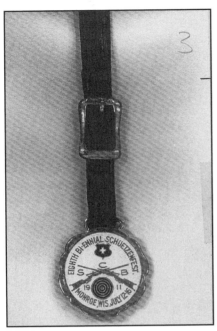

Watch Fob, Bi-ennial Schuetzenfest, Monroe, Wis., July 12-16, 1911, gold plate and enamel, leather strap, $50.

Coin, souvenir, silver, Preisschiessen
Chicago 1868, orig chain loop,
46mm.....................150.00

Diploma, New York Schuetzen Corps
1886, 13" by 17"..............50.00

Parade Banner, Nord-Deutschen-
Schuetzen Club, San Francisco, 1895,
hand painted blue silk,
30" by 48"..................650.00

Photograph, group, Dubuque Schuetzen-
Gesellschaft, undated,
16" by 21"..................110.00

Pin, CSB Dubuque 1899, gold and enamel,
1-3/8".......................75.00

Program, San Francisco Schuetzen-Verein
Golden Jubilee, soft cov,
4-1/4" by 5-3/4"..............95.00

Ribbon, membership, Hermann Scharf-
Schuetzen Verein, gold plate, tri-color
ribbon, 2-3/4" by 8"..........125.00

Token, Baltimore Schuetzen Park, brass,
19mm.......................15.00

Trophy Goblet, 2tes Nationales
Bundes-Schiessen, New York, 1898,
silver, 8-1/2"................225.00

Trophy Goblet, 5tes Nationales Bundes-
Schiessen, Charleston, 1907, silver,
8-1/4"......................150.00

Trophy Loving Cup, California Schuetzen-
Club Champion 1908, silver,
8-3/4".......................225.00

Watch Fob, souvenir, Eighth Bi-Ennial
Schuetzenfest, Monroe WI 1911,
gold-plate and enamel,
leather strap...............50.00

Secondhand Roses

This is a catchall category—designed specifically for those items which are bought solely for their utilitarian use. Anyone who regularly attends country auctions, flea markets or garage sales has undoubtedly seen his fair share of "recycled" household goods. Ranging from wringer washers to electronic video games, these products and appliances are neither decorative nor financially lucrative. They are strictly secondhand merchandise.

There is not much reason to focus on brand names, with two exceptions—Maytag and Craftsman. First, Maytag, widely regarded as the Cadillac of washers and dryers, consistently realizes higher prices than any other brand. Second, Craftsman hand tools, distributed by Sears, generally bring higher prices, due to the company's generous replacement policy.

As a result of advances in technology and space constraints in modern homes, several larger-sized appliances have little or no value on today's market. For example, console stereos and large chest freezers can often be had free for the hauling. All items listed below are in good, clean condition. All parts are intact and appliances are in working order. The prices are designed to get you in the ballpark. Good luck in getting a hit.

Club: Maytag Collectors Club, 960 Reynolds Dr., Ripon, CA 95366.

Appliances

Air Cleaner, less than 5 yrs old, single
speed, filter indicator.........15.00
Air Cleaner, more than 5 yrs old....2.00
Bag Sealer, electric..............4.00
Dehumidifier, 15 pt..............25.00
Dehumidifier, 30 pt..............35.00
Dryer, Maytag, 1-5 yrs old.......150.00
Dryer, Maytag, over 5 yrs old.....75.00
Other Brands, 1-5 yrs old........100.00
Other Brands, over 5 yrs old......65.00
Fan, exhaust, two-speed, 9" d......5.00
Fan, exhaust, three-speed, 16" d...10.00

Fan, exhaust,
hand-held, battery operated.....1.00
Freezer, chest,
5.0 cf, manual defrost.........35.00
Freezer, chest,
12.0 cf, manual defrost........75.00
Freezer, chest,
22.7 cf, manual defrost.......125.00
Freezer, upright,
5.0 cf, manual defrost.........40.00
Freezer, upright, 14.6 cf, frostless..75.00
Humidifier, floor model, plastic cabinet,
drum type, 11 gal.............12.00
Iron, electric, steam/spray.........2.00
Microwave, large, 1-5 yrs old......80.00
Microwave, small, 1-5 yrs old......55.00
Microwave, with electronic controls or
built-in turntable, add...........7.00
Mixer, counter top, two bowls......12.00
Refrigerator, compact, manual defrost,
1.7 cf.......................20.00
Refrigerator, draft-beer dispenser..85.00
Refrigerator, full size, 1-5 yrs old..175.00
Refrigerator, full size, over 5 yrs old110.00
Refrigerator, full size, side-by-side model,
deduct......................15.00
Refrigerator, full size, with ice maker,
add.........................20.00
Rug Shampooer.................15.00
Sewing Machine, modern, electric, cabinet
model, standard, no frills.......35.00
Sewing Machine, modern, electric, cabinet
model, standard, assorted attachments
and stitching variations........65.00
Sewing Machine, modern, electric,
portable, zig zag.............30.00
Small Kitchen Appliances (blender, corn
popper, electric knife, hand-held mixer,
toaster).....................5.00
Space Heater..................10.00
Tape Player, cassette.............2.00
Telephone, answering machine,
microcassette...............10.00
Telephone, cordless.............12.50
Television, 10", color, under-the-cabinet,
remote......................20.00
Television, 13", black and white,
portable.....................5.00
Television, 32", color, big screen..250.00
Vacuum Cleaner,
canister or upright............25.00
VCR, VHS, 40 channel...........50.00
Washer, Maytag, apartment-size,
portable.....................85.00
Washer, Maytag, full-size,
large capacity..............150.00
Washer, other brands, apartment-size,
portable.....................50.00
Washer, other brands, full-size,
large capacity...............75.00
Wringer Washer, Maytag,
stainless steel...............75.00

Wringer Washer, Maytag,
white porcelain 45.00
Wringer Washer, other brands,
white porcelain 25.00

Children's Items

Backpack Carrier 8.00
Bathtub, plastic 2.00
Carriage 5.00
Playpen, tubular steel frame,
mesh sides 12.00
Potty, plastic 2.00
Stroller 12.00
Walker 8.00

Entertainment and Recreation

Binoculars, miniature, folding 3.00
CD Player, personal 20.00
Computer, 486 . . . . .100.00
Dart Board, full-size, cork 5.00
Exercise Equipment, bicycle 15.00
Exercise Equipment, home gym . . .100.00
Exercise Equipment, Nordic Track . .75.00
Exercise Equipment, stepper 35.00
Exercise Equipment, punching bag,
small 5.00
Movie Projector, 8mm or Super 8 . . .15.00
Projection Screen 12.00
Slide Projector 20.00
Stereo, console, wood cabinet, record
player and radio combination 8.00
Stereo, headphones 3.00
Stereo, tape deck, dual cassette 35.00
Stereo, turntable, two speakers, name
brand 15.00
Video Game cartridge, Atari 3.00
Video Game cartridge, Nintendo 5.00
Video Game cartridge,
Super Nintendo 7.50
Video Game System,
full size, base, controllers
and accessories, Atari 15.00
Video Game System,
full size, base, controllers
and accessories, Nintendo 20.00
Video Game System, full size, base,
controllers and accessories,
Sega Genesis 30.00
Video Game System, hand-held, Lynx,
color, adapter 10.00
Video Game System, hand-held, Nintendo
Game Boy, headphones, adapter 15.00
Video Game System, hand-held, Sega
Game Gear, adapter 25.00

Miscellaneous Household Goods

Bread Box, metal 8.00
Canister Set, ceramic, figural 12.00
Clock, cuckoo 15.00
Curtains, patio door size 10.00
Dinnerware, service for four 25.00
Fondue Skewers, metal, set of four . .1.00

Television, portable, color, remote control, 20" screen, $30.

Linens (afghans, bedspreads, blankets)
like-new 8.00
Pots and Pans, eight-pc set,
aluminum 25.00
Pots and Pans, eight-pc set,
copper bottom 60.00
Pots and Pans, eight-pc set, stainless
steel 40.00
Venetian Blinds, mini, vinyl 3.00
Water Glasses, set of eight 3.00

Office Equipment

Computer Desk 25.00
Desk Lamp, gooseneck 2.00
Filing Cabinet, metal, two-drawer . . 25.00
Filing Cabinet, metal, four-drawer . . 40.00
Filing Cabinet, wood, oak,
four-drawer 250.00
Metal Shelving 7.00
Typewriter 2.00

Tools and Garden Equipment

Garden, blower, electric 12.00
Garden, edger, gas, 3 hp, four-cycle 75.00
Garden, hedge trimmer, electric . . . 15.00
Garden, hoe, rake, shovel 3.50
Hand Tools (hammer, pliers, saw,
screwdriver, wrench), Craftsman . 6.00
Hand tools, other brands 3.00
Ladder, extension, aluminum 45.00
Ladder, extension, wooden 25.00
Ladder, step, 48" 8.00
Ladder, step, 72" 12.00
Lawn Mower, electric 20.00
Lawn Mower, gas, purchased in spring or
summer 40.00
Lawn Mower, gas, purchased in fall
or winter 30.00
Lawn Mower, rotary 3.00
Pitchfork 4.00
Pruner, hand held 2.00
Power Tools (drill, grinder, saber saw,
sander) 15.00
Snow Blower, purchased in spring or
summer 45.00
Snow Blower, purchased in fall
or winter 60.00

Snow Blower, purchased during or after
major snow storm, double
fall/winter price
Weed Wacker, electric, 6 amp 15.00
Weed Wacker, gas, 32cc, 18" w cut. 45.00

Sewing Items

This is a wide-open area. While many favor sterling silver items, only fools overlook objects made of celluloid, ivory, other metals, plastic and wood. An ideal specialty collection would be sewing items that contain advertising.

Collecting sewing items received a big boost as a result of the Victorian craze. During the Victorian era, a vast assortment of practical and whimsical sewing devices were marketed. Look for items such as tape measures, pincushions, stilettos for punchwork, crochet hooks and sewing birds (beware of reproductions).

Modern sewing collectors are focusing on needle threaders, needle holders and sewing kits from hotels and motels. The general term for this material is "20-Pocket" because pieces fit neatly into 20-pocket plastic notebook sleeves.

Clubs: International Sewing Machine Collectors Society, 1000 E. Charleston Blvd., Las Vegas, NV 89104; Thimble Collectors International, 6411 Montego Bay Rd., Louisville, KY 40228; The Thimble Guild, P.O. Box 381807, Duncanville, TX 75138; Toy Stitchers, 623 Santa Florita Ave., Millbrae, CA 94030.

Box, Corticelli Spool Silk, cardboard, $7.50.

Needle Book, heavy paper, Japan, 1930s, 5" by 2-3/4", $12.

Newsletter: *Thimbletter*, 93 Walnut Hill Rd., Newton Highlands, MA 02161.

Advertising Trade Cards

Brainerd, Armstrong Co., spool cabinet, black and pink 110.00
Brooks Spool Cotton, folder, 1883 calendar .18.00
Clark's Mile End Spool Cotton, box of spools 50.00
Domestic Sewing Machine, Brownies 18.00
Eureka French Etching Silk, blue and sepia 8.00
J&P Coat's Spool cotton, lion covered by net 12.00
Merrick's Standard Thread For Machine Use, patriotic scene with two children 18.00P.T. Hoy & Sons Co., black sewing machine, red lettering. 18.00
Royal St. John Sewing Machines, little girl demonstrating sewing machine . .13.00
Singer, embroidered card of flowers, black ground .30.00
Wakefield Shuttle and Needle Co., black and blue, store vignette 28.00

Darning Kit, The Stocking Doctor Emergency Kit, matchbook shape, paper and wood, 2" w, $10.

Scissors, folding, "Compliments of The Home Insurance Co., NY," sterling silver, 2-1/4" l closed size, $85.

Catalogs

American Thread Co., 8-1/2" by 11-3/4", New York, 1921, 20 pgs 19.00
Butterick Publishing Co., New York, 1896, 104 pgs, patterns 34.00
May Manton Pattern Co., New York, 1908, 64 pgs, patterns for spring and summer 32.00

Other

Book, *History of the Sewing Machine*, James Parton, c1867, 44 pgs. . . 35.00
Calendar, Singer Sewing Machines, 1904, die-cut animal skin with Indian . . 85.00
Chatelaine, egg-shape. 80.00
Envelope, Singer Co., Pan American Expo, 1901, all-over color design 80.00
Jigsaw Puzzle, Singer Buffalo Puzzle, full color, 50 pcs, 1900 . . . . 35.00
Manual, Howe Sewing Machine, NY, 1872, 20 pgs, blue printed wraps 25.00
Needle Book, Army and Navy 15.00
Postcard, Singer Sewing Machine store, photo of employees and sewing machines, 1909 . . . . 38.00
Sewing Box, rattan, Victorian, 11" by 7" by 8" 120.00
Sewing Box, wicker, pink 48.00
Sewing Machine, Singer Featherweight, black and gold, case, instruction book and attachments 250.00
Sewing Machine, Willcox & Gibbs, lightweight, foot pedal 325.00
Sign, Clark's ONT Spool Cotton Thread, 14-1/2" by 25", 1890s woman and child, orig metal strips 250.00
Sign, Singer Sewing Machines, 14" by 24", grandmother and child using sewing machine 400.00
Spool Stand, 3-3/4" h chrome, center pin cushion 36.00
Tape Measure, figural, pig, copper . 60.00
Tape Measure, souvenir, Chicago World's Fair, egg, red 75.00

Shawnee Pottery

The Shawnee Pottery Company was founded in Zanesville, Ohio, in 1937. The plant, formerly home to the American Encaustic Tiling Co., produced about 100,000 pieces of pottery per working day. Shawnee produced a large selection of kitchenware, dinnerware and decorative art pottery. The company ceased operations in 1961.

Club: Shawnee Pottery Collectors Club, P.O. Box 713, New Smyrna Beach, FL 32170.

Periodical: *Pottery Collectors Express*, P.O. Box 221, Mayview, MO 64071.

Cookie Jars

Fruit Basket, mkd "Shawnee 84" . . 125.00
King Corn, #66 . . . . 135.00
Mugsey 425.00
Mugsey, gold trim 800.00
Puss 'n Boots, gold trim 395.00
Sailor, white, mkd "USA" 100.00
Smiley Pig, Cloverbud 450.00
Smiley Pig, Shamrock 295.00

Creamers

Elephant 30.00
Elephant, gold trim 285.00
Puss 'n Boots 60.00
Puss 'n Boots, gold trim 210.00
Smiley Pig, cloverbud 150.00
Snowflake, mkd "USA" 15.00

Pitchers

Chanticleer 85.00
Fruits, mkd "Shawnee 80" 65.00
Little Bo Peep 125.00
Smiley Pig, cloverbud 350.00
Yellow Tilt, mkd "USA 10" 35.00

Cookie Jar, Smiley Pig, 11-1/4" h, brown pants, #60, $500.

Teapot, Tom the Piper's Son, #44, $50.

Planters

Bear and Wagon 90.00
Buddha, #524 . . . . .15.00
Bird and Cup 12.00
Canopy Bed, #734 . . . . .95.00
Donkey with Basket, #772 . . . . .20.00
Elf Shoe, white with gold trim, #765 .15.00
Flying Goose, #707 . . . . .15.00
Giraffe, #521 . . . . .15.00
Oriental Girl with Mandolin, #576 . . .15.00
Piano, #528 . . . . .20.00
Squirrel, pulling acorn, #713 . . . . . . .40.00
Windmill, blue, #715 . . . . .20.00

Salt and Pepper Shakers, pr

Ducks 30.00
Flowerpots, gold trim. 25.00
King Corn .15.00
Milk Cans, paper label. 12.00
Owls, gold trim 40.00

Teapots

Elephant 250.00
Heart Flower 65.00
Pennsylvania Dutch, mkd "USA" 50.00

Other

Bank, bulldog 90.00
Butter Dish, cov, King Corn, #72 . . . .50.00

Teapot, Granny Anne, $175.

Coffeepot, cov, Sunflower Pattern, mkd "USA" 120.00
Match Holder, Fernware, yellow, mkd "USA" 25.00
Mixing Bowl, King Corn, nesting, set of three, mkd "Shawnee 8, 6," and "5" 85.00
Salt Box, cov, Fernware, yellow, mkd "USA" 30.00
Sock Darner, blue base, mkd "USA" 30.00
Sugar Bowl, bucket, blue trim, mkd "Northern USA 1042" 40.00
Sugar Bowl, fruit basket, mkd "Shawnee 83" 30.00
Syrup Pitcher, Valencia, orange . . . 12.00

Sheet Music

Just like postcards, this is a category whose 10-cent and quarter days are a thing of the past. Decorators and dealers have discovered the cover value of sheet music. The high ticket sheets are sold to specialized collectors, not sheet-music collectors.

You can put a sheet music collection together covering almost any topic imaginable. Be careful about stacking your sheets on top of one another. The ink on the covers tends to bleed. If you can afford the expense, put a sheet of acid free paper between each sheet. Do not, repeat do not, repair any tears with Scotch or similar brand tape. It discolors over time. When removed, it often leaves a gummy residue behind.

Clubs: City of Roses Sheet Music Collectors Club, 912 NE 113th Ave., Portland, OR 97220; National Sheet Music Society, 1597 Fair Park Ave., Los Angeles, CA 90041; New York Sheet Music Society, P.O. Box 1214, Great Neck, NY 11023; Remember That Song, 5623 N 64th Ave., Glendale, AZ 85301.

Newsletters: *Sheet Music Exchange*, P.O. Box 2114, Key West, FL 33045; *The Rag Times*, 15222 Ricky Ct., Grass Valley, CA 95949.

After The War is Over, 1917 . . . . 5.00
Alone, Marx Bros. cov, 1935 . . . . . . 10.00
Angel Eyes, Nat King Cole 5.00
Barney Google, 1923. . . . . 15.00
Bible Tells Me So, Roy Rogers and Dale Evans, 1940 . . . . 4.00

Battle in the Sky, c1915, $25.

By the Time I Get to Phoenix, Jim Webb, Glen Campbell cov photo, 1967 . . 3.00
Chicken Chowder, Irene Giblin, 1905 . . . . 15.00
Clicqout Club Fox Trot March, Eskimos playing banjos, 1926 . . . . 5.00
Dance Of The Fireflies, E.T. Paull and Sentenis 35.00
Down Among the Sheltering Palms, 1914 . . . . 5.00
Everybody Loves a College Girl, Kerry Mills, 1911 . . . . 10.00
For Me and My Gal, Judy Garland . . . 8.00
Give Me Liberty or Give Me Love, Claudette Colbert cov, 1933 . . . . . 5.00

Blue Suede Shoes, Carl Perkins, $10.

Woman Forever March, 1916, $25.

Good For Nothin' But Love, William Kernell
    and Harlan Thompson, from movie The
    Big Party, Sue Carol and Dixie Lee
    photo, 1930 . . . . .10.00
Hand Me Down My Walkin Cane, Calumet
    Music, 1935 . . . . .12.00
High & Mighty, John Wayne, 1954 . .20.00
I Got Stung, Elvis Presley 20.00
I'll Sing You a Thousand Love Songs, Clark
    Gable and Marion Davies cov,
    1936 . . . . .12.00
I Love You California, 1913 . . . . .7.00
I've Got the Profiteering Blues, Al Wilson
    and Irving Bibo, 1920 . . . . .10.00
Laugh Clown Laugh, Lon Chaney,
    1928 . . . . .30.00
Little Orphan Annie 15.00
Melody Time, Blue Shadows on the Trail,
    Disney, 1948 . . . . .30.00
Mona Lisa, Nat King Cole 5.00
My Buddy, Al Jolson, c1922 . . . . . . .10.00
Nothing More to Say, Big Slim,
    1946 . . . . .5.00
Oh Susanna, 1923 . . . . .45.00
Over The Rainbow, Judy Garland . . .15.00
Popeye the Sailor Man, Irving Berlin,
    1931 . . . . .75.00
Rum & Coca-Cola, Andrews Sisters,
    1944 . . . . .13.00
Silver Sleigh Bells, 1906 . . . . .30.00
Some Enchanted Evening, Richard
    Rodgers and Oscar Hammerstein II,
    from musical South Pacific, sgd Ezzio
    Pinza cov, 1949 . . . . .10.00
Tales My Mother Told to Me, 1911 . .17.50
The Grandpappy Polka, Johnny Giacoma,
    Gordon Jennings, 1947 . . . . .5.00
The Mary Pickford Waltz,
    Art Craft Pictures, 1917 . . . . .10.00

When I Dream About the Wabash,
    Roy Rogers, 1945 . . . . 10.00
You, the Great Ziegfeld, 1936 . . . . . . 5.00

Shoe Related Collectibles

This is a category with *sole*. Nothing more needs to be said.

Club: Miniature Shoe Collectors Club, P.O. Box 2390, Apple Valley, CA 92308.

Banks
Hushpuppies Shoes, vinyl, figural basset
    hound 25.00
Poll-Parrot Shoes, plastic,
    figural shoe 20.00
Red Goose Shoes, plastic, figural red
    goose, emb letters, 1960s 15.00

Figures
Ceramic, shoe, white, cherub figure on top
    15.00
Glass, Cowboy Boot, brown, c1965. . 4.00
Glass, High Button Shoe, c1970 . . . . 3.00
Glass, Boot, pincushion, blue, c1972 5.00
Metal, Boot with spur, silver,
    1-1/2" by 1-3/4", c1950 . . . . 65.00
Metal, Pincushion, silver, laced,
    2-1/4", c1852 . . . . 175.00
Metal, Slipper, wire, with bow,
    c1991 . . . . 20.00
Plastic, boot, pink, sachet holder,
    c1978 . . . . 4.50
Porcelain, baby shoe, 2-1/4" by 1-1/4", gold
    trim 15.00

Pinback Buttons
All American Shoe, eagle over inscription,
    white ground,
    blue and red lettering 15.00
Kirkendall Shoes, black-and-white
    high-button shoe illus, blue and white
    border inscription 18.00

Shoe Polisher, Ronson Roto-Shine, electric, 1970s, $5.

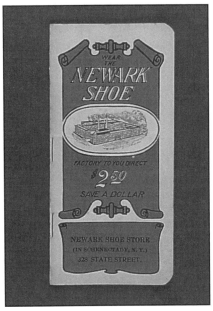

Tablet, Newark Shoe adv, 5-1/4" h, 2-1/2" w, $7.50.

Poll-Parrot Shoes, parrot illus 8.00

Other
Bookmark, Tappan Shoes Mfg., celluloid,
    die-cut, White & Hoag litho 48.00
Can, Ace No. 70 Boot Cement, 1 qt, ace of
    diamonds illus, screw top,
    contents 15.00
Catalog, Hamilton, Brown Shoe Co., 69
    pgs, 1929 . . . . 50.00
Charm, miner's knee boots, made from
    compressed anthracite coal, pr
    attached to orig card, c1930 . . . . 50.00
Coloring Book, Poll-Parrot Shoes,
    1950s 45.00
Comic Book, premium, PF Magic Shoe Ad-
    venture Book, Rocket Kids Moon Story,
    B.F. Goodrich, 1962 . . . . 22.00
Decal, Poll-Parrot Shoes, parrot illus,
    c1940 . . . . 10.00
Keychain, Newark Shoe Mfg., brass,
    engraved shoe illus, logo, 1900s. . 8.00
Mask, premium, Weathherbird Shoes,
    set of three 75.00
Match Holder, tin, die-cut, gold and black,
    nail hole top center 75.00
Miniature, cast lead, replica man's wingtip
    oxford shoe, bottom inscribed
    "Walk-Over, 90th Anniversary,"
    c1940 . . . . 12.00
Mirror, pocket, Cherry Blossom Boot
    Polish, product tin illus, 1920s . . . 60.00
Salt and Pepper Shakers, pr, figural shoe,
    sterling, "Geta," c1930 . . . . 200.00
Shoe Buttonhook, The Savings Store,
    Kalamazoo, MI 12.50

Shoe Horn, A.S. Beck shoes, metal,
    1940s 5.00
Shoe Horn, Queen Quality, 2" by 6",
    celluloid, curled handle, color portrait of
    lady, c1900, pr 35.00
Sign, Hamilton, Brown Shoe Co., tin, oval,
    two-sided, red, black and white . .25.00
Whistle, Poll-Parrot Shoes, cardboard,
    metal, orange and black, logo,
    1930s 30.00

Silver Flatware

Popularity of a pattern, not necessarily age, is the key to pricing silver flatware. Since most individuals buy by pattern, buy only from dealers who have done the research and properly identified each piece that they are selling. Deduct 50 percent from the value if a piece has a monogram.

If you are planning to buy a set, expect to pay considerably less than if you were buying the pieces individually. Set prices should be bargain prices. Alaska Silver, German Silver, Lashar Silver and Nickel Silver are alloys designed to imitate silver plate. Do not be fooled.

Cream Soups
Feliciana, Wallace 28.00
Festival, Lunt 20.00
First Frost, Oneida 28.00

Gravy Ladles
American Classic, Easterling 55.00
Grecian, Gorham 95.00
Southern Grandeur, Easterling 30.00

Lunch Forks
Buttercup, Gorham 17.00
Camelia, Gorham 19.00
Chantilly, Gorham 17.00
Chateau Rose, Alvin 19.00
George & Martha, Westmoreland . . .30.00
Manchester, Gadroonette 20.00

Cake Server, Malibu, 1934, Wm. A. Rogers A1 Plus, $25.

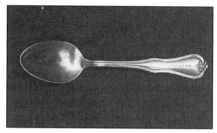

Teaspoon, sterling, monogrammed, Frank M. Whiting & Co., $8.

Master Butter
Celeste, hollow handle, Gorham . . . 14.00
Chapel Bells, flat handle, Alvin 13.00
Southern Grandeur, flat handle,
    Easterling 12.00

Sugar Spoons
Bridal Bouquet, Alvin 15.00
Camelia, Gorham. 13.00
Celeste, Gorham 16.00
Chateau Rose, Alvin 13.00
Marie Louise, Blackinton 35.00

Tablespoons
El Grandee, Towle 60.00
Estruscan, Gorham 45.00
Eternal Rose, Alvin 55.00
Lady Hilton, Westmoreland 55.00

Teaspoons
Bridal Bouquet, Alvin 13.00
Camelia, Gorham. 10.00
Celeste, Gorham 12.00
Champlain, Amston 13.00

Other
Berry Spoon, Feliciana, Wallace . . . 80.00
Bouillon Spoon, Feliciana, Gorham . 30.00
Butter Spreader, flat handle, Awakening,
    Towle 18.00
Cake Server, Georgian Rose,
    Reed & Barton 35.00
Cake Server, King Richard, Towle. . 40.00
Cheese Knife, Hanover, Gorham. . . 70.00
Citrus Spoon, Chased Romantique,
    Alvin 25.00
Citrus Spoon, Feliciana, Wallace,
    1969 . . . . 25.00
Coffee Spoon, Chantilly, Gorham . . 15.00
Demitasse Spoon 11.00
Dinner Fork, Bridal Bouquet, Alvin. . 23.00
Egg Spoon, Ivy, Gorham 32.00
Fork, Poppy, Gorham 75.00
Ice Cream Spoon, French Provincial,
    Towle 30.00
Jelly Server, Lasting Grace, Lunt. . . 35.00
Lemon Fork, Bridal Bouquet, Alvin . 14.00
Olive Fork, International, Frontenac 80.00
Oval Soup, Celeste, Gorham. 17.00
Pasta Scoop, Buttercup, Gorham . . 25.00

Pasta Scoop, Chantilly, Gorham . . .25.00
Pickle Fork, Chantilly, Gorham. 16.00
Pie Fork, Lancaster, Gorham 30.00
Pierced Tablespoon, Lancaster,
    Gorham .55.00
Place Spoon, Buttercup, Gorham. . .28.00
Preserve Spoon, Ivy, Gorham 110.00
Pudding Spoon, Grecian, Gorham . 150.00
Punch Ladle, Buttercup, hollow handle,
    Gorham .27.00
Salad Fork, Bridal Bouquet, Alvin. . .20.00
Sauce Ladle, Georgian, Towle 75.00
Sauce Ladle, Legato, Towle. 30.00
Seafood Fork, Medici Old, Gorham .22.00
Soup Ladle, Buttercup, Gorham. . . 155.00
Soup Ladle, Chantilly, Gorham. . . . 155.00
Steak Knife, Fairfax, Gorham 35.00
Steak Knife, Georgian Rose,
    Reed & Barton. 30.00
Tomato Server, Charlemagne,
    Towle. 95.00
Tomato Server, Charmaine,
    International. 95.00

Silver Plated

G.R. and H. Ekington of England are credited with inventing the electrolytic method of plating silver in 1838. In late 19th century pieces, the base metal was often Britannia, an alloy of tin, copper and antimony. Copper and brass also were used as bases. Today, the base is usually nickel silver. Rogers Bros., Hartford, Conn., introduced the silver-plating process to the

Sugar, 10" h, R&R Mfg. Co., $135.

Vase, 8-5/8" h, white iridescent glass holder, Derby, c1880s, $150.

United States in 1847. By 1855 a large number of silver-plating firms were established.

Extensive polishing will eventually remove silver plating. However, today's replating process is so well developed that you can have a piece replated in such a manner that the full detail of the original is preserved. Identifying companies and company marks is difficult. Fortunately there is Dorothy Rainwater's *Encyclopedia of American Silver Manufacturers*, 3rd Edition (Schiffer Publishing, 1986).

Ashtray, sq, shell handle, match holder top, emb human figures, Barbour 14.00

Basket, hexagon-shape, emb women, children and flowers, Barbour . . . 33.00

Bottle Opener, sterling handle, stainless opener, Frank M. Whiting 29.50

Calling Card Case, scroll design, etched monogram, Gorham 70.00

Candle Snuffer, emb floral design, Meriden 11.00

Chamberstick, ornate floral design, monogram, Meriden 25.00

Cigar Holder, 10-1/2" h, champagne bottle, beaded trim, engraved "CIGARS," Graham Silver 75.00

Cigarette Lighter, Ronson, oval, Art Nouveau design, ftd 18.00

Coffee Set, gold wash interior, monogram, Barbour 85.00

Corn Holder, ornate floral pattern, stainless blade, silk lined box, set of 12 . . . 85.00

Creamer and Sugar, mkd "Meriden" 100.00

Cup and Saucer, nautical engraving, Pairpoint 65.00

Dresser Set, mirror and brush, Art Nouveau-style, monogram 52.00

Flatware Service, luncheon set, 12 knives and forks, two crumbers, serving knife and fork, engraved blades, ivory handles 125.00

Gravy Boat, emb floral design, monogram 27.00

Ice Bucket, two handles, beaded rim, sq base, Gorham 35.00

Inkwell, pine needle design, white glass, Tiffany Studios 85.00

Jewelry Box, oval, ftd, cherubs with musical instruments dec, monogram, Victor Silver 33.00

Knife Rest, dolphin, mkd "Pairpoint" 35.00

Loving Cup, Masonic emblem dec, city and date, Van Bergh Silver Company 65.00

Mug, child's, etched design, Oneida . 6.50

Mush Set, plate and bowl, alphabet and "Hey Diddle Diddle" verse, William A. Rogers 85.00

Napkin Ring, Dog pulling sled, emb greyhounds on sides, engraved "Sara," Meriden 165.00

Napkin Ring, Floral Bouquets, Victorian 15.00

Nut Dish, squirrel on rim, pedestal base, Beacon Silver Company 21.00

Pin Cushion, heart-shape, velvet, Reed & Barton 35.00

Pitcher, plain, ice lip 29.00

Silent Butler, coat of arms design lid, wood handle, Reed & Barton 43.00

Stein, scroll and floral design, wood handle 65.00

Tea and Coffee Server, five-pc set, reeded base, American Sheffield 120.00

Thermometer Holder, small cherubs on corners 12.00

Thimble, gold wash, orig leather case 19.00

Tray, Georgian-style, sq, scrolls and flowers relief design, inner rim ribbing, Reed & Barton 32.00

Slot Cars

Aurora, the premier name in slot car racing, marketed its first electric slot car play set in the fall of 1960. Since then, slot cars have successfully competed with electric trains for their share of the model hobbyist's dollars.

Aurora, #1482, "Tuff Ones" Volkswagen, 1971-72, $40.

Accessories

ATM, steering wheel control unit, 1/24 scale 30.00

Gilbert, #19224, Railway-Highway Crossing, 1/32 scale, MIB 22.00

Strombecker, #9120, fence 1.00

Strombecker, #9160, Deluxe Overpass Support Set 2.00

Strombecker, #9195, straight track. . . 3.00

Strombecker, #9730, lap counter . . . 22.00

Cars

AFX, '57 Nomad, lime green 40.00

AFX, Rebel Charger, orange 80.00

Aurora, Thunderjet, #1366, Hot Rod Coupe, red and tan 60.00

Aurora, Thunderjet, #1384, Green Hornet, sticker 145.00

Aurora, Thunderjet, #1403, Cheetah, green 35.00

Aurora, Vibrator, #1542, Mercedes, yellow 55.00

Aurora, Vibrator, #1553, Hot Rod Roadster, green. 75.00

Cox, #9400, Ferrari, red, 1/24 scale . 70.00

Lionel, Corvette, tan, HO scale. 25.00

Marklin, #1317, Porsche Carrera Sportswagon, red, 1/32 scale . . 120.00

Revell, #R-3262, Ford Cobra Racer, body, burgundy, plastic, 1/24 scale. . . . 95.00

Strombecker, Ford GT40, yellow, 1/32, MIB 24.00

Race Sets

Aurora, #2071, Jackie Stewart Oval 8, HO scale, orig box 80.00

Aurora, #2703, Mario Andretti GP International Challenge, HO scale, orig box 50.00

Elden, #745110, Power Pack 8, 1/32 scale, orig box 45.00

Marx, #22635, Grand Prix Set, 1/32 scale, orig box 65.00

Strombecker, #9975, Indianapolis 5/1, 1/32 scale, orig box 120.00

Smokey Bear Collectibles

It is hard to believe that Smokey Bear has been around for more than 50 years. The popularity of Smokey started during the World War II, as part of a national awareness campaign for the prevention of forest fires. The National Forest Service ran slogans like "Keep 'em Green—Forests are Vital to National Defense" in an attempt to keep the public's attentions on the war effort.

From then to now, Smokey has been more the just a crusader for fire awareness and prevention; he has been a collectible character and a source of enjoyment to many admirers. There was a wide variety of Smokey collectibles produced: watches, radios, toys, posters and many games and books. Most had short production runs and were used as Forest Service giveaways or were sold by a select number of department store chains. Good luck in your collecting. Remember—only you can prevent forest fires.

Bank, figural, white, gold trim 65.00
Book, *Smokey Bear Saves the Forest* 5.00
Bowl, plastic, Arrowhead. 9.00
Coloring Sheet, pr, 8-1/2" by 11". 5.00
Costume, 1960s 35.00
Dakin Figurine, 8" h, vinyl, cloth,
    with shovel 40.00
Doll, cotton, stuffed, 6" h, Knickerbocker,
    1972 . . . . .18.00
Drinking Glass. 14.00
Figure, Aim Toothpaste premium,
    1960s 18.00
Flyer, colorful, 1959, 3-1/2" by 6" 5.00
Pinback Button, Keep America
    Green/Save A Tree, light green, black
    Smokey illus and lettering,
    1-1/2" d .10.00
Playset, Smokey Bear Patrol Kit Playset,
    plastic Smokey, plastic Ranger, metal
    jeep, iron-on transfer, 16-pg booklet
    Junior Forest Ranger Handbook, order
    form, orig box, Tonka, 1971 . . . .150.00
Ring, brass, expandable, figural Smokey
    with raised hand and shovel,
    1970s 25.00
Salt and Pepper Shakers, pr, china, yellow
    muzzle and hat, blue trousers, brown
    body, salt holding shovel, pepper
    holding bucket, 1960s, 4" h 20.00
Sticker Book, 12 pgs, color, Whitman,
    1970 . . . . .25.00

Snack Sets

The earliest snack sets (originally called tea and toast sets) were porcelain and earthenware examples manufactured overseas. Glass sets produced in the United States were a popular hostess accessory during the boom years following World War II. American dinnerware manufacturers of the time, such as Purinton and Stangl, also produced sets to match their most popular dinnerware patterns.

Newsletter: *Snack Set Searchers' Newsletter*, P.O. Box 158, Hallock, MN 56738.

Anchor Hocking
Blue Mosaic, milk glass 10.00
Classic, crystal. 1.00
Classic, milk glass 7.00
Fleurette, milk glass. 4.00
Golden Veil, milk glass 5.00
Soreno, avocado green 2.00
Soreno, iridized crystal 12.00

Federal Glass
Blossom, milk glass. 5.00
Crystal Leaf, crystal 1.00
Hawaiian Leaf, crystal 2.00
Yorktown, amber 3.00

Indiana Glass
King's Crown, amber 6.00
Smartset, milk glass. 3.00
Sunburst, frosted, plate only 1.00

Lefton
Golden Wheat 10.00
Gold Pine Cone 12.00
Silver Wheat 10.00

Other
Hazel Atlas, Simplicity, crystal 1.00
Laurel China, Japan, Rose Petal. . . . 6.00
Nasco Product, Japan, Delcoronado . 4.00
Noritake, oval, pink, orange and gray, floral
    dec 12.00
Purinton Pottery, Chartreuse, hp . . . 35.00
Stangl Pottery, Orchard Song 26.00
Steubenville Pottery, Woodfield,
    chartreuse. 5.00

Snow Globes

Most plastic and glass snow globes found at flea markets are imported from the Orient. A few are produced in France, Germany and Italy. There are no American manufacturers, but rather dozens of large gift companies who design and import an array of styles, shapes and themes. Enesco Corporation of Elk Grove Village, Ill., is one of the largest.

Club: Snowdome Collectors Club, P.O. Box 53262, Washington, DC 20009.

Newsletter: *Roadside Attractions*, 7553 Norton Ave., Apt. 4, Los Angeles, CA 90046.

Advertising
Atlantic Scaffold and Ladder Co. . . . 60.00
Flamingo Production Co. 14.00
Iran Air 15.00
Knorr. 12.00
Newsweek 65.00
Nickelodeon 12.00
Texaco 65.00
Urie's, Wildwood, New Jersey 8.00
Western American Insurance Co . . . 40.00

Aquarium
Marineland, porpoise 8.00
Mystic Marinelife Aquarium,
    Connecticut 6.00
Sea World of Florida, penguins 8.00

Character
Babar 12.00
Betty Boop, Bully, Germany, 1986 . . 15.00
Felix the Cat, Standing Ovations,
    1987 . . . . 12.00
Flintstones, Hanna-Barbera Productions,
    1975 . . . . 22.00
Little Mermaid, Bully, Germany 15.00
Marilyn Monroe. 35.00
Mickey Mouse, black and white, Bully,
    1977 . . . . 15.00
Snoopy, Willits, 1966 . . . . 15.00
Teenage Mutant Ninja Turtles, Christmas
    scene, Mirage Studios USA 12.00
Ziggy, Universal Press, 1980 . . . . . . .6.00

Commemorative
500th Anniversary of the Bahamas,
    1992 . . . . 15.00
Barcelona Olympic Games, 1992. . . 15.00
New York World's Fair 20.00
Seville Expo 15.00
Winter Olympics, Albertville, France,
    1992 . . . . 12.00

Figural
Bugs Bunny 85.00
Cat playing drum, plastic 18.00
Dolphin on top of dome 12.00
Frog, plastic, state
    name inside globe 12.00
Lantern, boy inside 15.00

Santa Claus, plastic, Santa on chimney
holding lantern 18.00
Snowman, ceramic, Applause, 1988.15.00

Glass Domes
Capitol Building, ceramic base,
1940s 40.00
Crucifix, ceramic base, Atlas Crystal
Works 35.00
George Washington Masonic National Me-
morial, plastic base, oil-filled,
1950s 30.00
Golfer, wood base 20.00
Niagara Falls, bakelite base 30.00
Star Trek, USS Enterprise, Willits . . .50.00

Holiday
Christmas, bell-shaped dome, Santa and
tree motif .8.00
Easter, rabbit, Dakin, 1988 . . . . .6.00
Halloween, skull, glass, wooden painted
base, orange lettering, battery
operated, Silvestri 20.00

Sports
Los Angeles Lakers 6.00
Notre Dame, Fightin' Irish 6.00
Pittsburgh Pirates 6.00
San Jose Sharks 6.00

Zoo
Birmingham Zoo 15.00
Greater Los Angeles Zoo 15.00
Hogle Zoo .10.00

Soakies

Soaky bottles are plastic bubble bath containers molded in the shape of popular children's characters. The first Soakies were marketed by the Colgate-Palmolive Co., in the 1960s and were an innovative marketing tool designed to convince kids (especially boys) that "Bathtime is Funtime."

As with any profitable idea, copycats soon appeared. One successful line produced by the Purex Company was called the Bubble Club. These containers were fashioned after Hanna-Barbera characters. The bottles included in this category are all plastic figural containers and range in size from 6" to 11" high.

Atom Ant 20.00
Augie Doggie 35.00
Baby Louie 22.00
Baloo 15.00
Bambi 22.00

Bamm-Bamm 29.00
Batman 50.00
Blabber, Quick Draw McGraw Show 12.00
Breezly, Peter Potamus Show 65.00
Bullwinkle 25.00
Bugs Bunny 14.00
Cecil, Disguise Kit 50.00
Cement Truck 24.00
Cinderella 16.00
Deputy Dawg 15.00
Dick Tracy 20.00
Droop-A-Long Coyote, Magilla Gorilla
Show 12.00
Felix the Cat 32.00
Fire Engine, with hose gun 29.00
Goofy 13.00
Huckleberry Hound 22.00
Lippy the Lion 20.00
Mickey Mouse 18.00
Morocco Mole, Atom Ant Show 20.00
Mr. Jinx 29.00
Mr. Magoo 20.00
Mummy 60.00
Mush Mouse 20.00
Musky Muskrat 24.00
Pebbles Flintstone, paint flecks 29.00
Peter Potamus 20.00
Pinocchio 14.00
Pluto 13.00
Popeye 20.00
Porky Pig 20.00
Punkin' Puss, Magilla Gorilla Show . 30.00
Ricochet Rabbit, Magilla Gorilla Show,
movable arm holds six-shooter . . 45.00
Robin 50.00
Rocky Squirrel 25.00
Santa, paint fleck 14.00
Secret Squirrel 25.00
Snagglepuss 25.00
Snow White 22.00
Smokey Bear 18.00
Speedy Gonzales, paint loss 15.00
Squiddly Diddly, Atom Ant Show . . . 20.00
Superman, Avon 10.00
Sylvester Cat, paint flecks 20.00

Felix the Cat, price each, $32.

Tennessee Tuxedo 29.00
Thumper 22.00
Top Cat 15.00
Touche Turtle, small flecks 32.00
Tweety Bird .24.00
Wendy Witch,
Casper the Friendly Ghost 39.00
Winsome Witch, Atom Ant Show 20.00
Wolfman 65.00
Woody Woodpecker 14.00
Yakky Doodle 20.00
Yogi Bear 22.00

Soap Collectibles

At first you would not think that a lot of soap collectibles would survive. However, once you start to look around, you'll see no end to the survivors. Many Americans are not as clean as we think. There is no hotel soap listed. Most survivors sell for 50 cents to $2 per bar. Think of all the hotels and motels that you have stayed at that have gone out of business. Don't you wish you would have saved one of the soap packets? You don't? What are you—normal or something?

Blotter, American Family Soap, Uncle
Sam, c1910 . . . . .15.00
Bookmark, Dingman's Soap, baby . . . 8.75
Box, Colgate's Fab, sample 15.00
Box, Fun-To-Wash Soap, black Mammy
wearing red bandanna, early 1900s,
3-1/4" h .25.00
Calendar, Snow Boy Washing Powder,
emb girl with dollhouse, 1901 . .125.00
Doll, Dynamo Detergent, dinosaur, green
and yellow, 11" h 15.00
Door Plate, Star Naptha Washing Powder,
porcelain 375.00

Advertising Trade Card, French Laundry Soap, die-cut, 3-5/8" by 2-13/16", $4.

Door Plate, Reuter's Soap, mother and child, green ground, c1910, 2-1/8" d .45.00

Pinback Button, Gold Dust Washing Powder, multicolored, late 1890s, 1-1/4" d .75.00

Pinback Button, Palmolive Soap, red, white and blue, 1930s 6.00

Playing Cards, Best Grand Laundry adv, "We wash everything with Ivory Soap" 5.00

Poster, Old Dutch Cleanser, fabric, product illus, blue and white ground, red border, 1930s, 15" by 20" 75.00

Pot Scraper, Babitts Cleanser 225.00

Ruler, Glory Soap Chips, celluloid, folding, blue and orange Swift & Co., trademark, 1919 calendar, 5-1/2" l 20.00

Sign, Colgate's Shaving Soap, cardboard, sailor giving another a shave 60.00

Sign, Ivory Soap, cardboard, creeping baby with bar of soap, matted, framed 50.00

Sign, Tulip Soap, paper, woman surrounded by tulips and various other vignettes, framed, 21-1/2" by 27-1/2" 55.00

Soap, Hanna-Barbera Bath Soap, Roclar, 1976, Yogi Bear, Yacky Doodle and Chopper on wrapper, 3" by 2" by 1" bar 8.00

Soap, Sinclair Oil, dinosaur-shape, MIB 15.00

Soap Dish, graniteware, hanging, cobalt blue swirl 110.00

Tape Measure, Fab Detergent, celluloid 20.00

Tin, Cashmere Bouquet, sample 30.00

Bath Soap, Flintstones Bubble Club Fun, 12 oz box, 1965, $65.

Tip Tray, Fairy Soap, girl sitting on soap bar, holding flowers, orange center, brown rim, c1936, 4-1/4" d 75.00

Social Cause Collectibles

Social cause collectibles are just now coming into their own as a collecting category. Perhaps this is because the social activists of the 1960s have mortgages, children and money in their pockets to buy back the representations of their youths. In doing so, they are looking back past their own protest movements to all forms of social protest that took place in the 20th century.

Great collections can be built around a single cause, e.g., women's suffrage or the right to vote. Much of the surviving material tends to be two-dimensional. Stress three-dimensional items the moment you begin to collect. As years pass, these are the objects most likely to rise in value.

Club: American Political Items Collectors, Labor History Chapter, 4025 Saline St., Pittsburgh, PA 15217.

Pinback Buttons

Black Folk Must Vote, black and white, 1960s 14.00

Boycott Lettuce, United Farm Workers, red, white and black, 1970s 10.00

Boycott Japanese Goods, litho, red and white, 1930-40 . . . . 25.00

Join UWOC, black and white, 1960s 14.00

Keep America Out Of War 25.00

Make Love Not War, 3-1/2" d, red, white and blue 35.00

Vote Socialist Workers in '72, Andrew Pulley for V P, browntone photo, blue rim 10.00

Young Americans For Freedom, red, white, blue and black, 1970 . . . . 12.00

Other

Advertising Trade Card, American Red Cross, Santa and Father time, printed, red and silver, undivided back, 1901-07 . . . . 20.00

Badge, Amalgamated Association of Iron, Steel & Tin, 9" h, ribbon, red, white and blue, brass hanger, celluloid insert, clasped hands illus, union logo, early 1900s 40.00

Booklet, IWW Song Book, 60 pgs, 4" by 6", Joe Hill photo cov, 1916 . . . . . . .75.00

Calendar, American Red Cross, 28" by 10-1/4", 1919 . . . . .35.00

Journal, The Official Organ of the White Ribbon Army, WCTU, 1887 . . . . .12.00

Clothing, T-shirt, extra large, cotton, blue, silk screened white peace dove on front, 1960-70 . . . . .40.00

Magazine, *Life*, Sept. 25, 1950, Swedish Red Cross girl cov 5.00

Postcard, Anti-Prohibition, "Why I Like the Orient," liquor bottles and gambling dice scene 16.00

Stickpin, figural hatchet, brass, "Carry A. Nation" inscribed on handle 30.00

Soda Fountain and Ice Cream Collectibles

The local soda fountain and/or ice cream parlor was the social center of small town America between the late 1880s and the 1960s. Ice cream items appeared as early as the 1870s. This is a category filled with nostalgia—banana splits and dates with friends. Some concentrate on the advertising, some on the implements. It is all terrific.

Clubs: National Association of Soda Jerks, P.O. Box 115, Omaha, NE 68101; The Ice Screamer, P.O. Box 465, Warrington, PA 18976.

Ice Cream

Advertising Trade Card, Dairylea Ice Cream, mechanical, Germany . . . 30.00

Booklet, Eskimo Pie, two pgs, premiums, 1952 . . . . 15.00

Container, Hopalong Cassidy, qt . . . 65.00

Decal, Mr. Softee Ice Cream Safety Club 10.00

Fan, Hoffman Willis Ice Cream Co., girl eating ice cream 15.00

Glass, Breyers Ice Cream, green logo, ftd 5.00

Mold, metal, Sealtest Ice Cream, pt . 17.00

Scoop, Coronet, metal 20.00

Scoop, Indestructo, #4 . . . . 45.00

Pinback Button, Semon Ice Cream, 1-1/4" d, red, white and gold, black lettering 14.00

Pinback Button, Skippy Ice Cream, 1-1/8" d, litho, red, white and blue, 1930s 12.00

Magazine Tear Sheet, *American Boy*, black and white, 1904, 11" by 14", $5.

Serving Tray, Benham's Ice Cream, tin, Palmer Cox brownies surround large dish of ice cream,
10-1/2" by 13-1/4" 150.00
Sign, Breyers Ice Cream, metal, white and green 60.00
Sign, Golden Rod Ice Cream, little girl eating ice cream. 90.00
Thermometer, Harington's Ice Cream, 12" h, wood. .35.00
Tray, Banquet Ice Cream,
10-1/2" by 15". 20.00
Whistle, Dairy Queen, cone-shape . .15.00

Soda Fountain

Bin, counter, Quaker Brand Salted Peanuts 40.00
Dish, Amber, banana split. 12.50
Blotter, Good-Grape, 1940 . . . . .18.00
Display Case, counter top, popcorn, wood and glass, hinged lid 45.00
Door Pull, Drink Hire's, tin. 50.00
Ice Cream Cone Holder, Vortex, patented 1916. . . . . .6.50

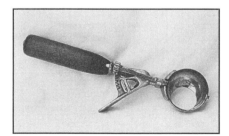

Scoop, No-Pak 31, $100.

Jar, Borden's Malted Milk, glass label. 175.00
Milk Shake Machine, Gilchrist, orig cup, c1926 . . . . 65.00
Napkin, Moxie, 1920s 25.00
Napkin, Pepsi, Pepsi & Pete illus, 1940s 50.00
Pencil Clip, Kramer's Beverages, celluloid, red and white 7.50
Sign, Bowey's Hot Chocolate, black logo 150.00
Sign, Orange Crush, tin with blackboard. 65.00
Spoon, Borden's, silver-plated. 1.50
Straw Box, Sweetheart, 1940s 45.00
Straw Holder, glass, clear, pressed design, four-sided, orig lid, 12-1/2" h. . . 100.00
Straw Jar, glass, frosted panel . . . 295.00
Straw Jar, glass, red, metal lid, 1950s 175.00
Syrup Dispenser, Hires, hourglass-shape, metal dispenser top,
7-1/2" d, 14" h. 325.00
Syrup Dispenser, Howell's Orange-Julep, paper label 65.00
Syrup Dispenser, Teem, paper label 25.00
Tray, Chero-Cola 65.00
Tray, Pepsi Cola, Hits the Spot, 1940s 15.00
Wafer Holder, Reliance 165.00
Watch Fob, Cherry Smash, celluloid, c1912 . . . . 275.00

Soft Drink Collectibles

National brands such as Coca-Cola, Canada Dry, Dr Pepper and Pepsi-Cola dominate the field. However, there were thousands of regional and local soda bottling plants. Their advertising, bottles and giveaways are every bit as exciting as those of the national companies. Do not ignore them.

Clubs: The Crown Collectors Society International, 4300 San Juan Dr., Fairfax, VA 22030; Dr Pepper 10-2-4 Collector's Club, 3508 Mockingbird, Dallas, TX 75205; National Pop Can Collectors, P.O. Box 7862, Rockford, IL 61125; New England Moxie Congress, 445 Wyoming Ave., Millburn, NJ 07041; Painted Label Soda Bottle Collectors Association, 9418 Hilmer Dr., La Mesa, CA 91942; Pepsi-Cola Collectors Club, P.O. Box 1275, Covina, CA 91722; Root Beer Float, P.O. Box 571, Lake Geneva, WI 53147.

Bottle, Pepsi-Cola, 12 oz, painted label, Duraglas 951-G, 9-3/4" h, $20.

Bottles

Double-Cola, 1952 . . . . .85.00
NuGrape, 1955. . . . . .65.00
Orange Crush, 1957. . . . . .75.00

Cans

Ma's Root Beer, steel-cone top 45.00
Nehi Orange, Happy Days series. . . .8.00
Pabst Cola .10.00

Drinking Glasses

Arctic Fruit-Ales 50.00
Banko 25.00
Dr. Brown's Celery Tonic 40.00
Fanta 15.00

Signs

Canada Dry, 10" by 14", 1950s 20.00
Cherry Smash, 6" by 11", 1920s . . 150.00
Chocolate Soldier, 9" by 27", 1950s. .100.00

Magazine Tear Sheet, Royal Crown Cola, *Life*, 1955, $15.

Playing Cards, Coca-Cola, 1943, $45.

Dr Pepper, 10" by 12", Lee Trevino,
    1980s 25.00
Julep, emb tin, "Drink Julep, Six Delicious
    Flavors," bottle illus,
    27-1/4" w, 19" h 105.00
Nesbitt's Orange Soda, cardboard, orange
    Grinch Monster, 1950s, 5" by 6" . .8.00

Thermometer
Dr. Well's: The Cooler Doctor, tin . . .45.00
Mason Root Beer, tin 65.00
Royal Crown Cola, 25" h 60.00

Toys
Kite, Pepsi Pours It On, 1960s 100.00
Paddle Ball, Dr Pepper, 1905 . . . . . .35.00
Truck, Pepsi, tin, plastic, 1970s 15.00

Trays
Ace-Hy, 1940s. 85.00
Canada Dry, 1950 . . . . .45.00
Orange Crush, 13" by 18",
    Mexico, 1940s 50.00

Other
Belt Buckle, Dr Pepper, enamel,
    1930s 200.00
Bottle Stopper, Hires Root Beer, metal and
    rubber. 12.00
Bottle Topper, Squirt, cardboard 18.00
Calendar, Orange Crush, 1941,
    full pad .325.00
Calendar, Royal Crown Cola,
    Wanda Hendrix pictures, 1950. . .35.00
Carrier, Donald Duck, 1950s. 35.00
Clock, Frostie Root Beer, cuckoo, Frostie
    swinging on pendulum 125.00
Clock, Teem 45.00
Coaster, Pepsi, cardboard, 4" d,
    1940 . . . . .15.00
Door Push, Pepsi-Cola, wrought iron,
    1960s 95.00
Door Push,
    White Rock Sparkling Water . . .100.00
Key Chain, Pepsi, 1908. . . . . .200.00

Mug, A&W, glass, map of U.S.
    and logo 8.00
Mug, Rochester Root Beer, emb . . . 45.00
Pitcher, Orange Crush, 1940s 100.00
Plate, Moxie, 10" d. 40.00
Poster, Orange Crush, colorful,
    1940s 65.00

Souvenirs

This category demonstrates that, given time, even the tacky can become collectible. Many tourist souvenirs offer a challenge to one's aesthetics. But they are bought anyway. Tourist china plates and glass novelties from the 1900 to 1940 period are one of the true remaining bargains left. Most of the items sell for less than $25. If you really want to have some fun, pick one form and see how many different places you can find from which it was sold.

Clubs: Souvenir Building Collectors Society, 25 Falls Rd., Roxbury, CT 06783; Statue of Liberty Collectors' Club, 26601 Bernwood Rd., Cleveland, OH 44122.

Newsletter: *Antique Souvenir Collector*, P.O. Box 562, Great Barrington, MA 01230.

Buildings
Arc de Triompe, Paris, copper finish . 5.00
Cologne Cathedral, Germany, antique
    pewter or silver finish 12.00
Rockefeller Center, New York City, 2-5/8"
    by 2" by 1", copper finish 25.00
Statue of Liberty, New York City,
    6" h 7.00

Playing Cards
Disneyland, castle illus, white ground. 5.00
Little Italy Festival, Outtio Stagioni
    Fountain, Clinton, IN, white, brown illus,
    green border 10.00
Pro Football Hall Of Fame, Canton, OH,
    building illus. 7.50

Postcards
Georgian Hotel, Athens 2.00
The Lake Mohonk House, The Testimonial
    Gateway, NY 3.50
The Touraline Hotel, Boston,
    hotel view 4.00

Trays, metal
Fort William Henry 7.00
Lake George, NY 7.00
Williamsburg, VA 28.00

Other
Album, New Orleans photos, 1885. . 10.00
Ashtray, Florida, shaped like state, brass,
    emb attractions 12.00
Ashtray, Leaning Tower of Pisa, Italy,
    3-1/2", silver finish 32.00
Book, Ohio Centennial, 1903 . . . . . .20.00
Bottle Opener, Brown Palace Hotel . 24.00
Card Folder, Yellowstone National Park,
    1928 . . . . .5.00
Compact, Hawaii, Elgin 30.00
Honey Pot, Belleville, KS 10.00
Ink Blotter, Yellowstone Park, metal. 35.00
Paperweight, New Salem State Park,
    glass, round, 2-3/4" d 30.00
Pinback Button, Detroit, multicolored,
    lighthouse scene, red slogan "Where
    Life Is Worth Living". 45.00
Pinback Button, Red Wing Street Fair,
    multicolored, masked jester,
    1899 . . . . .65.00
Plate, Clark House, Lexington, MA, four-
    sided 12.00
Plate, Ocean Pier & Fun Chase, Wildwood,
    NJ, pierced border. 8.00
Program, Rose Bowl Parade, 1940 . 20.00

Candy Dish, "Remember the Maine," pressed glass, 7" l, $75.

Canoe, white milk glass, 3-5/8" l, $15.

Shovel, Kearney, NE, glass, gold scoop
    and lettering, clear handle,
    6-1/2" l .20.00
Vase, Camp Lake View,
    Lake City, MN. 12.00

Souvenir Spoons

Collecting commemorative spoons was extremely popular from the last decade of the 19th century through 1940. Actually, it has never gone completely out of fashion. You can still buy commemorative spoons at many historical and city tourist sites, The first thing to check for is metal content. Sterling silver has always been the most popular medium. Fine enamel work adds to value.

Clubs: American Spoon Collectors, 4922 State Line, Kansas City, MO 54133; The Scoop Club, 84 Oak Ave., Shelton, CT 06484; Souvenir Spoon Collectors of America, 8200 Boulevard East, North Bergen, NJ 07047.

Algiers, sterling 20.00
Alma 30.00
Brooklyn Bridge, "New York" on handle,
    sterling .35.00
California, silver-plated 7.50
Camp Taylor, KY, WWII 8.00
Capri, Italy, emb bowl, enameled classical
    urn top, sterling 45.00
Checolah, OK, three figures on handle,
    sterling .20.00

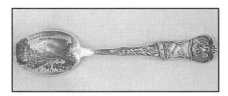

Canal Street, New Orleans, LA, sterling, 5-3/8" l, $15.

New York World's Fair, 1939, silver-plated, Oneida Community, $10.

Colorado, sterling. 20.00
Detroit, cutout handle, sterling 18.00
Harrisburg, PA, 1891, sterling 25.00
Helen, silver-plated 20.00
Honolulu, sterling. 25.00
Ithaca, NY, Cornell University Library,
    sterling 6.50
Mackinac Lake, sterling 30.00
Miles Standish Monument, sterling . . 8.00
New Year's, sterling. 35.00
San Francisco, sterling 18.00
St. Just, sterling 12.00
Uruguay, sterling 18.00
Washington DC, sterling 15.00

Space Collectibles

This category deals only with fictional space heroes toys. My father followed Buck Rogers in the Sunday funnies. I saw Buster Crabbe as Flash Gordon in the movies and cut my teeth on early television with Captain Video. My son belongs to the Star Trek generation. Whichever generation you choose, there is plenty to collect.

Club: Galaxy Patrol, 22 Colton St., Worcester, MA 01610.

Periodicals: *Space-Time Continuum*, P.O. Box 6858, Kingwood, TX 77325; *Strange New Worlds*, Box 223, Tallevast, FL 34270.

Battlestar Galactica
Figure, Mattel, 1978, Apollo. 8.00
Figure, Mattel, 1978, Gold Cylon . . . 15.00
Figure, Mattel, 1978, Ovion 8.00
Book, *Battlestar Galactica*, hardcover 3.00
Book, *Galactica Discovers Earth*, #5 . 1.00
Model, Base Star 30.00
Puzzle, Interstellar Battle,
    Parker Brothers, 1978. . . . . 6.00

Buck Rogers
Activity Paint Book, #679, Whitman 100.00
Badge, Solar Scouts Member, gold . 55.00

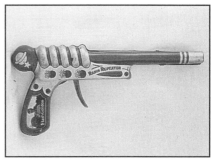

Flash Gordon, gun, radio repeater, litho tin, silver and red, Marx, $85.

Book, *Armageddon 2419 AD*,
    1979-87 . . . . 6.00
Book, *Buck Rogers in the 25th Century AD*,
    1933 . . . . 40.00
Book, *Rude Awakening*, 1990 . . . . . . 3.00
Game, Battle for the 25th Century,
    1988-90 . . . . 40.00
Pencil Box, 1934-38, American Pencil
    Company 150.00
Rocket Pistol, XZ-33, Daisy 125.00
Star Explorer Chart, 1936. . . . . 60.00
Telescope, Popsicle premium,
    1939 . . . . 90.00

E.T.
Book, *The Book of the Green Planet* . 1.00
Card Game, Parker Brothers 8.00
Cereal Box 10.00
Drinking Glass, Pizza Hut,
    "Phone Home". 2.00
Figure, 2" h, Holding Beer Can. 3.00
Figure, 2" h, In Robe with Telephone . 3.00
Watch, Melody Glow Alarm Watch. . 10.00

Flash Gordon
Book, *The Monsters of Mongo*, Big Little
    Book, Whitman, 1935 . . . . 50.00

Astronaut Daily Dime Bank, Kalon Mfg. Corp., $30.

Book, *The Time Trap of Ming* 2.00
Comic Book, Macy's giveaway,
    1943 . . . . .70.00
Figure, Dale 25.00
Figure, Dr. Zarkov 20.00
Figure, Ming 20.00
Kite 50.00
Lunch Box, plastic, color decals, Aladdin,
    c1979 King Features Syndicate,
    7" by 10" by 5" 65.00
Pencil Box, 1951 . . . . .35.00
Toy, Spaceship, die-cast metal, blue, white
    accents, orig display card, LJN Toys,
    c1975, 3" l 20.00
Toy, Starship, die-cast metal and plastic,
    sticker on each wing, Tootsietoy, c1978
    King Features Syndicate, 5" l 25.00
View Master, three reels, 1977 . . . . .10.00

Lost In Space, The Robinson Family
Comic Book, Gold Key, #8, 1968 . . .25.00
Halloween Costume, Ben Cooper,
    1965 . . . . .175.00
Puzzle, Milton Bradley, 1966 . . . . . . .33.00

Space 1999
Board Game, Milton Bradley, 1975 . .25.00
Book, *Breakaway* 1.50
Book, *Moon Odyssey* 1.50
Coloring Book, Saalfield, 1975,
    8-1/2" by 11", unused 10.00
Magazine, Space 1999 cov 1.00

Space Patrol
Apology Card 25.00
Badge, plastic 150.00
Binoculars, black 80.00
Handbook 70.00
Microscope, orig slides 175.00
Postcard, Cadet Happy 45.00
Space Helmet 150.00
Wristwatch, silvered metal case, black and
    red numerals, gray leather straps, U.S.
    Time, early 1950s 60.00

Space Exploration Collectibles

There can be no greater thrill than collecting an artifact of man's greatest adventure. Space exploration collecting covers a wide range of items from rocket models to autographs of men who walked on the moon! Autographs from astronauts can be had for free by writing to NASA and making a request. Autographs from former astronauts can be had by making a request to the astronaut or from an autograph dealer.

Mission patches from the earliest days of space exploration are also highly collectible. Mission patches are small works of art, depicting the goals and members of a particular mission. Mission patches can be found at flight museums or through mail-order or home retailers.

One of the most exciting areas of space collecting is that of items actually used to help send Man to the moon. These items include hardware, manuals and almost anything used in the quest for space. While these items can be hard to find, they can still be had from many of the people who were involved with, but have retired from, the space program. Other space items include presentation and manufacture models, art, books, space collector cards, postal covers, medallions, coin sets and collector pins.

Advisor: Dennis Kelly, P.O. Box 9942, Spokane, WA 99209, (509) 456-8488.

Club: Society for the Advancement of Space Activities, P.O. Box 192, Kents Hill, ME 04349.

Photographs, sgd, 8" by 10"
Armstrong, Neil 275.00
Aldrin, Buzz 125.00
Bean, Alan 75.00
Borman, Frank 80.00
Conrad, Charles 80.00

Magazine, *Newsweek*, man on the moon cov, July 28, 1960, $20.

Photograph, color, autographed by astronaut Joseph P. Allen, 8" by 10", $25.

Collins, Michael 200.00
Cooper, Gordon 110.00
Lovell, James 125.00
Schirra, Walter 100.00
Stafford, Thomas 65.00
White, Edward 425.00

Other
Flag, U.S., flown aboard Gemini V,
    6" by 4" 400.00
Food Packet, flown in space 300.00
Hard-hat, Richard Gordon, Gemini . 250.00
Mission Patch, Schirra, Walter, sgd,
    Beta Crew, 5" by 7" 200.00
Pen, Gordon Cooper, flown aboard
    Mercury 9 . . . . .110.00
Space Collector Card 2.00

Spark Plugs

More than 4,000 different plug names have been identified by collectors, the most common of which are Champion, AC and Autolite. Spark plugs are classified into six types: name plugs, gadget plugs, primer plugs, visible plugs, coil plugs and quick detachable (QD) plugs.

There is no right or wrong way to collect spark plugs. Some people collect a certain style of plug, while others grab any plug they can find. Use care when examining old spark plugs. Many have fragile labels which can be destroyed through improper handling.

Club: The Spark Plug Collectors of America, 2115 51st St., Apt. D, Lubbock, TX 79412.

Anderson, glass insulator, 18mm . . .45.00
Baysdorfer Affinity, orange porcelain,
    1/2"........................40.00
Beacon Lite, glass insulator, 7/8" . . .25.00
Bethlehem Fordson Tracor........25.00
BG Aviation....................5.00
Champion, super long reach.......15.00
Champion Gas Engine Special,
    #34, 1/2"....................15.00
Cloud 75, 7/8"................25.00
Cross Country, 7/8"..............5.00
Defender Deluxe...............10.00
Defiance, 4", five ribs, 7/8".......18.00
Dickson, 7/8"................25.00
Duval Automatic, intensified, 18mm .10.00
EKO, nickeled, blue, 7/8"/ld/......40.00
Everfire, porcelain, repaired, ...65.00
First American................10.00
Fouless.....................65.00
Fyrac Rockford IL..............15.00
Globe, picture of world, 1/2".......30.00
Hercules....................10.00
Herz Bougie Mercedes, heavy stone,
    7/8"........................30.00
Kingston, green top, 7/8"..........10.00
Liberty, bras, 1/2"..............45.00
Lodge Aero Plug, 6 fins, 18mm.....30.00
Lodge HNLP, 14mm.............5.00
Mosler Vesuvius, mica, 18mm.....18.00
MP 775, 7/8".................30.00
Oil Proof, old bottom, 1/2"........40.00
Oleo Magneto, brass, 18mm......50.00
PAF Non Fourls................10.00
Pasha, Rajah, 18mm............12.00
Prosper C....................7.00
Rex, mica, large plug, 18mm 18.00
Road King Non Foul, paper label,
    18mm.......................18.00
Splitdorf, aircraft, brass and mica,
    18mm.......................50.00
Tru-Fire.....................8.00

Lodge, 2HLN, 3/4", $5.

Tru-Test, Chicago type, 7/8" 5.00
Tungsten, blue porcelain,
    rough base 10.00
Tungsten Mica, large plug 25.00
Wards Standard Quality, #8, 7/8" . . . 5.00
Watkins, 1/2" 40.00
Watters All Spark............... 40.00
Westchester, Mosler origin, 1/2" . . . 60.00

Sports and Recreation Collectibles

There has been so much written about sport cards that equipment and other sport-related material has become lost in the shuffle. A number of recent crazes, such as a passion for old baseball gloves, indicates that this is about to change. Decorators have discovered that hanging old sporting equipment on walls makes a great decorative motif. This certainly helps call attention to the collectibility of the material.

Since little has been written outside of baseball and golf collectibles, it is hard to determine what exactly are the best pieces. A good philosophy is to keep expenditures at a minimum until this and other questions are sorted out by collectors and dealers.

Clubs: Boxiana & Pugilistica Collectors International, P.O. Box 83135, Portland, OR 97203; The Glove Collector Club (Baseball), 14057 Rolling Hills Ln., Dallas, TX 75240; Golf Collectors Society, P.O. Box 20546, Dayton, OH 45420; The Golf Club

Inkstand, bronze, tennis player, 7-3/8" l, $275.

Pinback Button, black and white, 1933 Bloomfield football team photo, 3" l, $25.

Collectors Association, 640 E. Liberty St., Girard, OH 44420.

Periodicals: *Boxing Collectors Newsletter*, 3316 Luallen Dr., Carrollton, TX 75007; *Sports Collectors Digest*, 700 E. State St., Iola, WI 54990.

Games

Dog Race, Transogram, deluxe edition,
    1937 .... 65.00
Donald Duck Pins and Bowling Game,
    Pressman, 1955 .... 50.00
Hounds & Hares Card Game, JW Keller,
    1894 .... 50.00
The VCR Hockey Game, Interactive VCR
    Games, 1987................ 12.00

Photographs

Canadian athlete wearing medals, wearing
    snow shoes, hand-colorized 60.00
Rocky Graziano, black and white, glossy,
    bold black marker autograph, 1947-48,
    8" by 10" 30.00
Yale, hockey and baseball teams,
    1900 .... 90.00

Posters

Larry Csonka, *Sports Illustrated*,
    1968-71.................... 20.00
Toronto Maple Leafs Media Guides,
    1975-76.................... 6.00
The Sporting News, Oct. 21, 1953,
    Rogers Hornsby 18.00

Other

Autograph, George Foreman, boxing
    gloves 145.00
Badge, copper-plated white metal,
    engraved front "1 Mile Run 1st Prize,"
    reverse "St. Patrick's Field Day May 30,
    1910"..................... 15.00
Book, *The Spectacle of Sports from Sports Illustrated*, 1957, 320 pgs, dj 25.00
Charge Coin, brass, emb, "Horace
    Partridge Co/Athletic & Sporting Goods"
    on one side, other with "Discount &
    Charge Coin," 1890s, 1-1/4" d . . . 18.00

Poster, cardboard, Harlem Globetrotters, 14" by 22", $25.

Comic Book, Blue Bolt, iceboat cov, June, 1940 . . . . .20.00

Clock, Joe Lewis souvenir, white metal, figural boxer, "Joe Lewis, World Champion," 9" w, 13" h 100.00

Dispenser, marbleized plastic bowling ball, chrome push-top, six glasses, figural bowler handle 60.00

Display, Holmes/Ali, Caesar's Palace, oil cloth, 17" by 17" 20.00

Figure, hockey, Brett Hull, mini, Gartlan USA 80.00

Figure, soccer, Pat Bonner, Kenner Starting Lineup, 1989 . . . . .37.00

Lapel Stud, multicolored James J. Corbett portrait, heavyweight boxing champion, white ground, red lettering, c1896 . . . . .50.00

Newspaper Adv, Max Baer, 1934 world heavyweight champion, endorsing premium physical development set from Quaker Wheat Crackels, from Sunday comic strip page, 10-1/2" by 15-1/2" 12.00

Pass, Sportsman's Park, 1943 . . . . .15.00

Pin, Kentucky Derby Festival, Pegasus pin, plastic, 1976 . . . . .65.00

Pin, Muhammad Ali, Sting Like a Bee, 3-1/2" d 20.00

Plate, Joe Lewis, 10-1/4" d 75.00

Plate, Tiger Williams, 8-1/2" d, sgd . .65.00

Stamps, Miscellaneous

Trading stamps were offered by retail stores to attract customers and increase sales. The more money spent,

the more stamps you could earn. The stamps could be redeemed for merchandise, either from the store that issued the stamps or from redemption centers that offered catalog merchandise. The first independent trading stamp company was set up in 1896. The use of trading stamps has declined, but some companies still give them out to stimulate sales. So far, a secondary market has not been established.

Other nonpostage stamps of interest to collectors include revenue stamps (often collected by philatelists), savings bond stamps and war ration stamps.

Clubs: American Revenue Association, 701 S. First Ave., Arcadia, CA 91006; Society of Ration Token Collectors, 3583 Everett Rd., Richfield, OH 44286; State Revenue Society, 22 Denmark St., Dedham, MA 02026.

Stamps, Postage

When I was a boy, everybody and his brother had a stamp collection. In today's high tech world, that is not often the case. Most stamps found at flea markets will be canceled, and their value is negligible. They can usually be bought in batches for a few dollars. However, there are rare exceptions. Who knows? If you look long and hard enough you may find an "Inverted Jenny." The following prices are for unused stamps.

Club: American Philatelic Society, P.O. Box 8000, State College, PA 16803.

Periodicals: *Scott's Stamp Monthly*, P.O. Box 828, Sidney, OH 45365; *Stamp Collector* and *The Stamp Wholesaler*, 700 E. State St., Iola, WI 54990; *Stamps*, 85 Canisteo St., Hornell, NY 14843.

Air Mail

1926-28, U.S. Postage, 5 cents, violet 8.00

1959, Jupiter, Lafayette, IN, 7 cents, blue and red 15

1980, Blanche Stuart Scott, Pioneer Pilot, 28 cents, multicolored 55

1991, William T. Piper, Aviation Pioneer, 40 cents, multicolored 80

Postage

1890-93, Abraham Lincoln, 3 cents, brown 50.00

1902-03, Benjamin Franklin, 1 cent, blue, green 6.00

1908-09, George Washington, 3 cents, violet 21.00

1924-26, Lexington-Concord, 2 cents, rose 5.00

1932-33, William Penn, 3 cents, violet 25

1938-54, Andrew Jackson, 7 cents, sepia 28

1940, Ralph Waldo Emerson, 3 cents, bright red violet 40

1943-44, Netherlands, 5 cents 15

1945, Florida Centennial, 3 cents. 15

1947, Everglades National Park, 3 cents, green 15

1948, California Gold Centennial, 3 cents, violet 15

1956, Labor Day, 3 cents, blue. 15

1957, Honoring Those Who Helped Fight Polio, 3 cents, red, lilac 15

1961, Nursing, 4 cents, blue, green, orange and black 15

1964, Register-Vote, 5 cents, red and blue 15

1966, Humane Treatment of Animals, 5 cents, orange, brown and black 15

1968, Walt Disney, 6 cents, multicolored .16

1971, Prevent Drug Abuse, 8 cents, blue and black 15

1972, PTA, 8 cents, yellow and black. . .15

1973-74, Zip Code, 10 cents, multicolored .18

1975, Apollo Suyoz Space Test Project, 10 cents, multicolored 18

1976, Alexander Graham Bell-Telephone Centennial, 13 cents, black, purple and red 24

Poster Stamps, 1939 New York World's Fair, $25.

1979, Robert F. Kennedy, 15 cents, blue,
28 cents

1983, Babe Ruth, 20 cents, blue 1.00

1985, Social Security Act, 22 cents, two-
tone blue 42

1986, Locomotive 1870s,
2 cents, black 15

1989, Lou Gehrig, 25 cents,
multicolored 60

1991, Abbott & Costello, 29 cents,
multicolored 58

1993, Buddy Holly, 29 cents 50

Postage Due

1879, 3 cents, brown 25.00

1917, 5 cents, red 8.50

1959, 30 cents, rose 55

1985, 17 cents, rose 40

Stangl Pottery

Stangl manufactured dinnerware between 1930 and 1978 in Trenton, N.J. The dinnerware featured bold floral and fruit designs on a brilliant white or off-white ground.

The company also produced a series of three-dimensional bird figurines that are eagerly sought by collectors. The bird figurines were cast in Trenton and finished at a second company plant in Flemington. During World War II, the demand for the birds was so great that more than 60 decorators were employed to paint them. Some of the birds were reissued between 1972 and 1977. They are dated on the bottom.

Club: Stangl/Fulper Collectors Club, P.O. Box 64-A, Changewater, NJ 07831.

Birds

Cockatoo, 6" h, 3405D 50.00

Drinking Duck, 1-1/2" h, 3250E 90.00

Feeding Duck, 1-3/4" h, 3250C 90.00

Love Bird, 4" h, 3400 . . . . .80.00

Oriole, 3-1/4" h, 3402S 125.00

Rooster, 4-1/2" h, 3285 . . . . .70.00

Dinnerware

Americana

Ashtray, 4" d 12.00

Coffee Pot 50.00

Creamer 6.00

Jug, 1 pt 20.00

Salt and Pepper Shakers, pr 16.00

Dinnerware, Ranger, plate, 6" d, mkd "3304 M.S.," $20.

Colonial, #1388

Ashtray, 3-1/2" d 12.00

Candle Holder, 3-1/2" h 12.00

Compote 15.00

Creamer 10.00

Jug, 2-1/2" h 12.00

Plate, 10" d 12.00

Relish, 12 " by 7" 20.00

Teapot 30.00

Country Garden

Ashtray, fluted 15.00

Casserole 60.00

Cereal Bowl, 5-1/2" d 15.00

Coffee Pot, 8-cup 55.00

Cup 13.00

Gravy Boat 20.00

Plate, 9" d 15.00

Server, two-tier 25.00

Teapot 50.00

Fruit

Bean Pot, 2 handle 85.00

Giftware, vase, brown ground, orange spots, $30.

Butter Dish 40.00

Cake Stand 25.00

Creamer 15.00

Pickle Dish 20.00

Pitcher, 2 qt 50.00

Tray, bread 40.00

Tray, condiment 22.00

Garden Flower

Casserole, Balloon Flower 25.00

Creamer, Calendula
and Morning Glory 10.00

Eggcup, Campanula 25.00

Pitcher, 1 pt, Rose 30.00

Saucer, leaves 5.00

Newport, #3333

Candle Holder 35.00

Carafe, wood handle 85.00

Cup 15.00

Plate, 8" d 20.00

Saucer 8.00

Teapot 100.00

Wild Rose

Butter Dish 35.00

Casserole, 8" d, handled 30.00

Coffee Pot, 4-cup 55.00

Gravy Boat 25.00

Pitcher, 1 qt 40.00

Plate, 6" d 6.00

Server, two-tier 25.00

Teapot 55.00

Stanley Tools

Mention the name Stanley to a carpenter and the first tool that comes to mind is a plane. While Stanley planes are the best documented and most widely collected planes on the market, Stanley also produced many other tools, many of which are becoming desirable to tool collectors.

Periodical: *Stanley Tool Collector News*, 208 Front St., P.O. Box 227, Marietta, OH 45750.

Catalogs

1863, Stanley Rule & Level Co., Price List,
46 pgs .250.00

1905, Stanley Rule & Level Co., Catalog
#34, 144 pgs 50.00

1922, Stanley Tools Catalog
#34, 128 pgs 50.00

1960, Stanley Tools Catalog, 64 pgs 15.00

1974, Stanley Tools Catalog
#34, 96 pgs 7.00

Hammers

Mallet, hickory, 10-1/2" l,
mfg 1863-1923 . . . . .10.00
Shoemaker's, cast iron, walnut, 12" l, mfg
1872 . . . . .75.00
Tack, cast iron, 12" l, mfg 1870 . . . . .35.00

Levels

Carpenter's, hardwood, brass, 24-30" l,
mfg 1911-17 . . . . .30.00
Mason's, softwood, brass, adjustable, 42"
l, mfg 1863-1942 . . . . .25.00
Machinist's, cast iron, 6" l,
mfg 1898-1958 . . . . .20.00

Other

Chisel Set, 12 butt chisels, sq edge,
hardwood box, steel shank,
hickory handle 150.00
Drill, breast, cast iron, steel, built-in level,
two-speed, 16" l, mfg 1911-35 . . .20.00
Drill, hand, cast iron, hardwood,
12" l, mfg 1925-35 . . . . .15.00
Gauge, reversible, cast iron, brass, 7" l,
mfg 1874-97 . . . . .75.00
Oil Burner, cast iron, 6" l,
mfg 1936-60 . . . . .10.00
Miter box, cast iron, 20" l,
mfg 1932-82 . . . . .50.00
Plane, block, cast iron, 7" l,
mfg 1888-1942 . . . . .50.00
Plane, tongue and Groove, cast iron,
rosewood, 10-1/2" l,
mfg 1876-1942 . . . . .35.00
Rule, carpenter's, boxwood, brass, mfg
1900-17 . . . . .75.00
Rule, pattern maker's, boxwood, brass,
lacquered finish, two-fold,
mfg 1884-1910 . . . . .100.00
Screwdriver, ratchet, steel, hardwood, 6" l,
mfg 1926-35 . . . . .20.00
Tape Measure, steel, 6' l, black finish, mfg
1935-57 . . . . .15.00
Tool Box, walnut, 22" l, mfg 1923 . . .50.00
Tool Cabinet, oak, 29" l,
mfg 1926-42 . . . . .50.00
Tool Chest, hard wood, enamel, blue and
yellow, 20" l, mfg 1927 . . . . .50.00
Yard Stick, maple, brass, 36" l,
mfg 1854-1958 . . . . .20.00

Star Trek Collectibles

In 1966, a new science fiction television show aired that introduced America to a galaxy of strange new worlds filled with new life forms. The voyages of author Gene Roddenberry's Starship Enterprise enabled the viewing audience to boldly go where no man had gone before. These adventures created a new generation of collectors: "Trekkies." From posters, costumes and props to pins, comic books and model kits, there is no limit to the number of Star Trek collectibles that can be found.

With the release of Paramount's "Star Trek: The Motion Picture" in 1979, the Star Trek cult grew. The Enterprise's new devotees inspired the inevitable new sequels: "Star Trek II: The Wrath of Khan," "Star Trek III: The Search for Spock," "Star Trek IV: The Voyage Home," "Star Trek V: The Final Frontier," "Star Trek VI: The Undiscovered Country," "Star Trek: Generations," and "Star Trek: First Contact."

In 1988, Trekkies demanded the return of the Enterprise to television and were rewarded with "Star Trek: The Next Generation." A new starship, manned by a new crew, retained the same desire to reach out into the unknown. More recent spin-offs include "Star Trek: Deep Space 9" and "Star Trek: Voyager." Whether you are an old Trekkie or a Next Generation Trekkie, keep seeking out those collectibles. May your collection live long and prosper.

Clubs: International Federation of Trekkers, P.O. Box 3123, Lorain, OH 44052; Starfleet, P.O. Box 24052, Belleville, IL 62223; Star Trek: The Official Fan Club, P.O. Box 111000, Aurora, CO 80042.

Periodical: *Trek Collector*, 1324 Palms Blvd., Dept. 17, Los Angeles, CA 90291.

Action Figure, Captain Kirk,
8" h, 1974 . . . . 48.00
Action Figure, Chief Miles O'Brien, Deep
Space 9 . . . . 10.00
Action Figure, Spock, 8" h, Mego,
1974 . . . . 55.00
Activity Set, Oil Paintings-By-Number,
#2109, Hasbro, 1974, MIB 60.00
Bank, plastic, 12" h, Kirk, Play Pal,
1975 . . . . 100.00
Belt Buckle, copper, 3-D, bust of Kirk and
Spock, 1979 . . . . 20.00
Cereal Bowl, plastic, Star Trek: The Motion
Picture, Deka, 1979 . . . . 15.00
Coasters, plastic, white, Star Trek & Fleet
emblem, Ritepoint 7.00

Greeting Card, Mr. Spock, Random House Greetings, 1976, 5-3/4" by 7-3/4", $10.

Clock, 20th anniversary, wall, logo, red on
white, Official Star Trek Fan Club,
1986 . . . . .40.00
Colorforms Set, 1975, MIB 40.00
Comic Book, Star Trek: The Motion
Picture, Marvel 6.00
Doll, stuffed vinyl, 12" h, Knickerbocker,
Kirk 45.00
Doll, stuffed vinyl, 12" h, Knickerbocker,
Spock .45.00
Game, Pinball, plastic, 14" l 30.00
Game, Star Trek III, West End, 1985 20.00
Greeting Card, Kirk and Spock, California
Dreamers, second series, 1986 . .3.00
Keychain, sq, two-sided, Lucite,
translucent pictures 5.00
Limited Edition Collector Plate, Spock,
Leonard Nimoy signature,
Ernst, MIB 135.00
Marshmallow Dispenser, Star Trek V, Kraft
promotion 25.00
Mug, Kirk, figural, sculpted,
3-D, bust illus. 15.00
Ornament, Galileo, Hallmark 20.00
Playset, Command Communication
Console, Mego, 1976 . . . . .80.00
Playset, USS Enterprise Bridge, vinyl,
fold-out, with chair, Mego, 1975 .80.00
Record, Leonard Nimoy Presents Mr.
Spock's Music From Outer Space, 11
songs, 12", LP, Dot Records 35.00
Record, Trek Bloopers, 12", LP, Blue Pear
Records 20.00
Snow Dome, musical, limited edition, Star
Trek Next Generation, plays movie
theme, 1993, MIB 100.00
Spoon, pewter, Star Trek Adventure
insignia handle, 1988 . . . . .20.00
Tie, silk, multicolored, Spock 14.00

Tumbler, plastic, red, Star Trek V, insignia,
    logo, black and gold, 1989 . . . . . . .5.00
Vehicle, Klingon cruiser, Dinky,
    1978 . . . . .20.00
Vehicle, Klingon Warship, Star Trek II,
    die-cast, Corgi, 1982 . . . . .18.00
Vehicle, USS Enterprise, 36" l. 50.00
Vulcan Ears, Franco, 1974 . . . . .10.00
Watch, Spock & USS Enterprise, digital,
    20th anniversary, Lewco, 1986 . .45.00

Star Wars Collectibles

It was in a galaxy not so long ago
that author/director George Lucas put
into motion events that would change
the way we think of space. In 1977, a
movie was produced that told the story
of an evil Empire's tyrannical rule over
the galaxy and of the attempts of a
young man from a distant world to end
this tyranny. Luke Skywalker's adventures became the Star Wars saga and
spanned six years and three separate
movies: "Star Wars," "The Empire
Strikes Back" and "Return of the Jedi."

The enormous success of the Star
Wars movies inspired the release of a
wide range of movie-related products
including toys, games, costumes,
records and comic books. As you travel through the flea market aisles in
search of Star Wars treasure, "May the
Force be with you."

**Action Walker, All Terrain Scout Trans-
port, MPC, windup, plastic, $12.**

Club: Official Star Wars Fan Club,
P.O. Box 111000, Aurora, CO 80042.

Newsletter: *The Star Wars Collection
Trading Post*, 6030 Magnolia, P.O.
Box 29396, St. Louis, Mo 63139.

Activity Books, Iron-On Transfer Book,
    Ballantine 15.00
Activity Books, Yoda's Activity Book . 5.00
Bank, ceramic, R2-D2 . . . . 40.00
Belt, leather, black, Obi-Wan and Vader
    pattern. 20.00
Blanket, Lord Vader's
    Chamber design 20.00
Book, *Han Solo's Revenge*, hardcover,
    Ballantine, 1979 . . . . 10.00
Book, *Star Wars*, George Lucas,
    paperback, first ed, Del Ray, December
    1976 . . . . 30.00
Bookmark, #1, Luke, Random House,
    1983 . . . . 8.00
Buckle, oval, Darth Vader bust 20.00

**Trading Card, Topps, 4th series, #207,
C-3PO, $25.**

Cake Pan, Boba Fett, Wilton 15.00
Calendar, 1984, Return of the Jedi,
    Random House 12.00
Calendar, 1991, Lucasfilm, 20th
    anniversary 10.00
Charm Bracelet, C-3PO, R2-D2, Darth
    Vader. 20.00
Coin, Imperial Stormtroopers,
    silver, 1 oz 90.00
Comic Book, The Empire Strikes Back,
    Marvel special edition 4.00
Cookie Jar, ceramic, figural C-3PO,
    Roman Ceramics. 100.00
Diary, My Jedi Journal, Ballantine . . 10.00
Game, Battle for Endor,
    West End Games 25.00
Game, Destroy Death Star, Kenner/Parker
    Brothers. 30.00
Hat, Yoda cap, ears 15.00
Limited Edition Plate, Hamilton Collection,
    Empire Strikes Back 45.00

**Action Figure, Tauntaun, Empire
Strikes Back, Kenner, $5.**

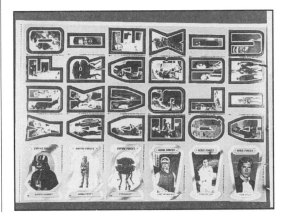

**Proof Sheet, Empire Strikes
Back bubble gum card stickers,
1980, 15-1/2" by 10-3/4", $30.**

Limited Edition Plate, Hamilton Collection,
Luke and Yoda 60.00
Lunch Box, plastic, blue, dome-shape,
design your own with stickers . . .30.00
Mask, Darth Vader, plastic, black 8.00
Mittens, 3-CPO, black 10.00
Mug, Han Solo, figural, Sigma 35.00
Music Box, Wicket and Kneesaa,
Sigman .75.00
Pinback Button, 3" d, Luke Skywalker,
Factors Inc. 6.00
Pinback Button, 3" d, Star Wars: The First
Ten Years, anniversary 6.00
Record, original soundtrack,
John Williams/London Symphony,
two-record set, two sleeves, liner-note
insert, poster, 20th Century
Records 20.00
Umbrella, plastic, clear, C-3PO and R2-D2
illus, Adam Joseph Industries . . .10.00
Underwear, boy's, Chewbacca, Union
Underwear/Underoos 15.00
Wallet, vinyl, Droids illus 10.00
Watch, digital, logo, black on silver, black
vinyl band, R2-D2 and Darth Vader on
opposite sides,
Texas Instruments 10.00

Stradivarius Violins

In the late 19th century, inexpensive violins were made for sale to students, amateur musicians and others who could not afford an older, quality instrument. Numerous models, many named after famous makers, were sold by department stores, music shops and by mail. Sears, Roebuck sold "Stradivarius" models. Other famous violin makers whose names appear on paper labels inside these instruments include Amati, Caspar Da-Solo, Guarnerius, Maggini and Stainer. Lowendall of Germany made a Paganini model.

All these violins were sold through advertisements that claimed that the owner could have a violin nearly equal to that of an antique instrument for a modest cost; one "Stradivarius" sold for $2.45. The most expensive model cost less that $15. The violins were handmade, but by a factory assembly-line process. If well cared for, these pseudo antique violins often develop a

nice tone. The average price for an instrument in playable condition is between $100 and $200.

Sugar Packets

Do not judge sugar packets of the 1940s and 1950s by those you encounter today. There is no comparison. Early sugar packets were colorful and often contained full color scenic views. Many of the packets were issued as sets, with a variety of scenic views. They were gathered as souvenirs during vacation travels.

There is a large number of closet sugar packet collectors. They do not write much about their hobby because they are afraid that the minute they draw attention to it, prices will rise. Most sugar packets sell for less than $1. It's time to let the sugar out of the bag. Get them cheap while you can.

Club: Sugar Packet Clubs International, 15601 Burkhart Rd., Orrville, OH 44667.

Sunbeam

Vintage Sunbeam mixers, although a novelty, are not limited by their function or performance. A 1933 Sunbeam beater will accomplish the same task as a 1955 or modern mixer/beater— with no difference in quality.

Bottom control mixers are difficult to find and command the highest prices, providing they are complete. Original attachments include mixer blades and green mixing bowls. They should be in working order and retain their egg-yellow paint finish and Sunbeam insignia and stickers. If cared for properly, vintage mixers will last a lifetime. Sunbeam also produced a myriad of small kitchen appliances, gadgets and related materials.

Advisor: Norman Hagey, 19672 Stevens Creek Blvd., P.O. Box 424, Cupertino, CA 95014, (408) 973-8129.

Mixer, complete with bowls and book
Model M4C 140.00
Model M4F, bottom control 130.00
Model M4H, bottom control 110.00
Model #1, top control 50.00
Model #3 .40.00
Model #3A 40.00
Model #3B 40.00
Model #5 .35.00
Model #5B 35.00
Model #5-1 . . . . .35.00
Model #5B-A 35.00
Model #7 .30.00
Model #7-B 30.00
Model #7-1 . . . . .30.00
Model #7B-1 . . . . .30.00

Mixer Attachments and Accessories
Apple/Potato Peeler 10.00
Basket Strainer 5.00
Buffer 4.00
Butter Churner 30.00
Can Opener 8.00
Coffee Grinder 12.00
Colander, Mix Master 10.00
Deflector Disc 3.00
Drink Mixer 5.00
Funnel, old type 2.00
Grape Fruit Reamer 4.00
Grater Disc 3.00
Ice Cream Freezer 15.00
Ice Crusher 5.00
Juice Bowl, green 10.00
Juice Bowl, white 3.00
Knife Sharpener 6.00
Meat Chopper 4.00
Mixing Bowl, aluminum, heavy gauge,
cov, 3 qt 15.00
Mixing Bowl, glass, green, large 18.00
Mixing Bowl, glass, green, small . . .12.00
Mixing Bowl, glass, white, large 8.00
Mixing Bowl, glass, white, small 5.00
Pea Chopper 12.00
Pea Sheller 5.00
Power Transfer Unit 5.00
Recipe Book, 1933-37 . . . . .8.00
Sausage Stuffer 1.00
Shake attachment, with glass 15.00

Toaster
Model #4, flat, patented turn over toasting
rack with expansion hinges for toasting
two whole sandwiches 70.00
Model B, flat, dated Jan. 30, 1923 . .80.00
Model T-1, automatic, two-slice, toaster
selector 35.00
Model T-9, automatic, two-slice,
round top 20.00
Model T-20C, end control 12.00

Model T-35, side control 10.00

Other
Cabinet, holds Mix Master and attachments, pull-out table top, drawer, ivory, 60-1/2" h, 24" w, 20" d . . .160.00
Clock, Model F-33, electric, green, white or ivory, 5-1/2" h 20.00

Super Hero Collectibles

Super heroes and comic books go hand in hand. Superman first appeared in Action Comics in 1939. He was followed by Batman, Captain Marvel, Captain Midnight, The Green Hornet, The Green Lantern, The Shadow, Wonder Woman and a host of others. The traditional Super Hero was transformed with the appearance of The Fantastic Four—Mr. Fantastic, The Human Torch, The Invisible Girl and The Thing. It pays to focus on one hero or a related family of heroes. Go after the three-dimensional material. This is the hardest to find.

Clubs: Air Heroes Fan Club (Captain Midnight), 19205 Seneca Ridge Ct., Gaithersburg, MD 20879; Captain Action Collectors Club, P.O. Box 2095, Halesite, NY 11743.

Captain America
Action Figure, 6" h, rubber, bendable, red and white, painted accents, plastic shield, 6" by 9" display card, Lakeside, 1966 . . . . .75.00
Bicycle Plate, 2" by 4", tin, color, raised image, Marx, 1967 . . . . .40.00
Book, *Captain America & the Great Gold Steal*, 118 pgs, paperback, Bantam Books, 1968 . . . . .35.00
Coloring Book, 8" by 11", Whitman, 1966 . . . . .30.00
Game, Milton Bradley, 1966 . . . . . .90.00
Kite, plastic, color illus, Pressman, 1966 . . . . .60.00
Lobby Card, 11" by 14", "Return of Captain America," black and white illus, Republic Pictures, 1944 . . . . .30.00
Pinback Button, 3" d, poly bag, carded, Button World, 1966 . . . . .30.00
Poster, Anti-Drug, 22" by 33", Captain America running, "Drugs destroy lives. Join the FBI and me in our battle against

drugs," Marvel Comics and the Department of Justice/FBI, 1989 . . . . 40.00
Ring, rubber, yellow, Captain America in running position with shield curved behind him illus, 1966 . . . . 40.00

Spiderman
Bicycle Siren, 4" h, plastic, red and yellow, decals, Empire Toys, Marvel Comics Group, orig box and attachments, 1978 . . . . 40.00
Book, *The Amazing Spiderman Collector's Album*, paperback, Lancer Books, 1966, Spidey's origin, exploits, enemies and secrets in comic form, black and white, 4" by 7" 13.00
Doll, 20" h, plush, red, white and black outfit, orig Knickerbocker tag, Marvel Comics Group, 1978 . . . . 20.00
Poster Puzzle, Aurora, 1974, 34" by 40", assembled, orig box in good conditions, puzzle complete 8.00

Superman
Card Game, plastic case, 45 cards, Whitman, 1966 National Periodical Publications 25.00
Game, 5" by 6", sliding square puzzle, black and white, Superman flying over buildings, orig display card 70.00
Glass, 4-1/4" h, Superman in Action, blue illus, peach color inscriptions, National Periodical Publications, 1964 . . . 50.00
Hairbrush, 2-1/2" by 4-1/2", wood, red, white and blue decal, c1940s . . . 75.00
Model, MPC, 1984, 100% painted . . 13.00

Paint Book, Superman to the Rescue, Western Publishing Co., 24 pgs, unused, c1980 DC Comics 15.00
Pencil Case, 3-1/2"" by 8", vinyl, zippered, red and blue illus and logo on yellow ground, Standard Plastic Products, National Periodical Publications, 1966 . . . . 60.00
Record Player, 1978 . . . . 65.00

Wonder Woman
Card Game, Russell's Mfg. Co., 1977, 1-1/2" by 3" by-1/2" color box, 40 cards with 10 different color illus 11.00
Glass, 6-1/4" h, clear, illus on front, logo and name on back, Pepsi issue, DC Comics, 1978 . . . . .18.00
Wall Hanging, 6-1/2" by 9", full color photo on cardboard backing, retains plastic seal 9.00

Other
Captain Marvel, EZ Code Finder, 4" d disk wheel, cardboard, Fawcett Comic premium, mid-1940s 125.00
Captain Marvel, puzzle, 13" by 18", "Captain Marvel Rides The Engine Of Doom," Fawcett Publications, 1941 . . . . .85.00
Fantastic Four, drinking glass, 7-Eleven, 1977, 5-1/2" h, wrap around scene of Fantastic Four about to battle Dr. Doom outside his castle 9.00
Flash Gordon, lobby card, 11" by 14", "Flash Gordon Conquers the Universe," Universal Pictures 50.00
Flash Gordon, lunch box, 7" by 10" by 5", plastic, color decals, Aladdin, 1979, King Features Syndicate 65.00

Captain Marvel, jigsaw puzzle, Captain Marvel Rides the Engine of Doom, $85.

Green Hornet, pinback button, 4" d, black, red, green and blue illus, 1966 Green-way Productions, copyright on rim 50.00

Green Hornet, Secret Print Putty, secret print book, magic print paper, Color-forms, unopened blister pack, c1966 . . . . .65.00

Incredible Hulk, model, Aurora, 1974, Comic Scene version, figure missing left foot, base with smoke plume, assembled, 85% painted 19.00

Marvel Comics Superheroes, lunch box, Aladdin Industries, 1976, 8" by 6-1/2" by 4", edge rusting, no thermos 9.00

Shazam, glass, Pepsi Collector Series, 1978 . . . . .10.00

Supergirl, book, *The Supergirl Storybook*, G.P. Putnam's Sons, 1984, movie photos, very fine condition 3.00

Superheroes, postcard book, DC Comics, 1981, full color, perforated postcards with miscellaneous superhero characters 10.00

Swankyswigs

Swankyswigs are decorated glass containers that were filled with Kraft Cheese Spreads. They date from the early 1930s. See D.M. Fountain's *Swankyswig Price Guide* (published by author in 1979) to identify pieces by pattern. Most Swankyswigs still sell for less than $5. If a glass still has its orig-inal label, add $5.

Club: Swankyswigs Unlimited, 201 Al-vena, Wichita, KS 67203.

Ducks and Horses, black, 3-3/4" h, $3.

Antique, #1, 4-3/4" h 5.00
Bands, blue and white, #3 . . . . 4.00
Bustling Betsy, blue, 3-3/4" h 3.00
Carnival, yellow 10.00
Circles & Dot, 3-1/2" h 4.00
Coin Design, clear, 3-3/4" h 2.00
Cornflower, 3-1/2" h, dark blue, #2 . . 3.00
Cornflower, 3-1/2" h, light blue, #1 or #2. . . . . 3.00
Daisy, red, green, white, 3-3/4" h. . . . 3.00
Dots and Diamonds, red, 3-1/2" h . . . 8.00
Forget-Me-Not, 3-1/2" h, dark blue . . 3.00
Forget-Me-Not, 3-1/2" h, red 3.00
Hostess Design, clear, 3-1/8" h 1.50
Jonquil, yellow, 3-1/2" h 3.00
Kiddie Kup, Bird and Elephant, red . . 2.00
Kiddie Kup, Pig and Bear, blue 2.00
Lattice & Vine, white and blue, 3-1/2" h 8.00
Lily of the Valley, red and black, 4-3/4" h 10.00
Posy, Violet, green and blue, 3 3/16" h 3.00
Sailboat, blue, 3-1/2" h. 10.50
Sailboat, green, red and blue. 12.00
Sailboat, red, white sailboats and stars, 4-3/4" h 18.00
Special Issue, red tulip, #1, Del Monte, 3-1/2" h 40.00
Sportsmen Series, Red Fox, black, 4-5/8" h 5.00
Star, black 5.00
Texas Centennial, black, blue, green and red. 20.00
Tulip, green, 3-1/4" h 4.50

Swizzle Sticks

They just do not make swizzle sticks like they used to. There is no end of the ways to collect them—color, motif, region, time period and so on. You can usually find them for less than $1. In fact, you can often buy a box or glass full of them for just a few dollars. Sets bring more, but they must be un-usual.

Club: International Swizzle Stick Col-lectors Association, P.O. Box 1117, Bellingham, WA 98227.

Afiliado al Diners Club, cowgirl silhouette, orange stirrer 3.00
Bellevue Casino, Montreal, plastic, figural mermaid 1.00
Die, figural, bakelite, on top of sq plastic stick. 3.00
Glass, plain, red base, set of six . . . 10.00
Golf, plastic, clubs and putters, lift-up cork screw bag holder, marked "1 oz PUTT; 1 1/2 OZ/IRON; 2 oz/DRIVE" 6.00

Howdy Revue, Greenwich Village, wooden, figural mallet 2.00
Jack Dempsey Restaurant, green and orange .18.00
Leaf, figural, black Catalin 5.00
Motel Multnoman, yellow plastic. 2.00
Palm Tree, figural 2.00
Seagram's Sea Breeze, plastic 20
The Royal Hawaiian—The Hotel on Waikiki Beach 1.50
Zulu-Lulu, plastic, 6" l, brown, transparent, set of six, orig display card 25.00

Taylor, Smith and Taylor Dinnerware

W.L. Smith, John N. Taylor, W.L. Taylor, Homer J. Taylor and Joseph G. Lee founded Taylor, Smith and Taylor (TST) in Chester, W.V. In 1903, the firm reorganized and the Taylors bought Lee's interest. In 1906, Smith bought out the Taylors. The firm re-mained in the family's control until it was purchased by Anchor Hocking in 1973. The tableware division closed in 1981.

One of TST's most popular lines was LuRay, produced from the 1930s through the early 1950s. Designed to compete with Russel Wright's Ameri-can Modern, it was produced in Wind-sor Blue, Persian Cream, Sharon Pink, Surf Green and Chatham Gray. Coor-dinating colors encouraged collectors to mix and match sets. TST used sev-eral different backstamps and marks. Many contain the company name as well as the pattern and shape names. A dating system was used on some dinnerware lines. The three number code included month, year and crew number. This system was discontin-ued in the 1950s.

Beverly
Butter Dish 20.00
Casserole .20.00
Cup. 5.00
Plate, 6-1/4" d. 2.00
Saucer 2.00

Empire
Butter Dish 20.00
Casserole .20.00
Cup. 5.00
Gravy 15.00

Golden Button, Ever Yours shape, dinner plate, 10-1/4" d, $5.

Plate, 6-1/4" d 2.00
Plate, 10" d 12.00
Platter, oval, 7-1/8" d. 8.00
Saucer. 2.00
Teapot. .35.00

LuRay
Berry Bowl, 5-1/2" d, pink 3.50
Bowl, tab handle, blue. 12.00
Casserole, 8". 85.00
Coffee Pot. .90.00
Demitasse Cup and Saucer, pink . . .25.00
Demitasse Sugar, blue 45.00
Dish, 5" d. 3.00
Egg Cup 12.00
Nappy, pink. 14.00
Pitcher, water, pink 48.00
Plate, bread and butter, pink, 6" d. . . .3.00
Plate, cake 40.00
Plate, dinner, blue. 13.00
Plate, grill, yellow 25.00
Plate, lunch, blue. 7.00
Plate, salad, 7" d, pink. 4.00
Platter, 11-1/2" l, pink 10.00
Platter, 13-1/2" l, green 18.00
Relish, green. 25.00
Salt and Pepper Shakers, pr, blue . .20.00
Teapot, curved spout 70.00
Vegetable, oval, yellow 16.00
Vegetable, round, 8" d, gray 28.00

Plymouth
Casserole 25.00
Chop Plate .12.00
Creamer 6.00
Plate, 9-1/4" d 9.00
Saucer. 2.00
Teapot, 2 cup 25.00

Teddy Bears

Teddy Bear collectors are fanatics. Never tell them their market is going soft. They will club you to death with their bears. Do not tell anyone that you heard it here, but the Teddy Bear

20" h, short gold mohair, straw stuffing, growler, folded ears, shoe button eyes, embroidered nose and mouth, swivel neck, humped back, jointed arms and legs, $500.

craze of the 1980s has ended. The market is flooded with old and contemporary bears.

The name "Teddy" Bear originated with Theodore Roosevelt. The accepted date of their birth is 1902-1903. Early bears had humped backs, elongated muzzles and jointed limbs. The fabric was usually mohair; the eyes were either glass with pin-backs or black shoe buttons.

The contemporary Teddy Bear market is as big or bigger than the market for antique and collectible bears. Many of these bears are quite expensive. Collectors speculating in them will find that getting their money out of them in 10 to 15 years will be a bearish proposition.

Club: Good Bears of the World, P.O. Box 13097, Toledo, OH 43613.

Periodicals: *National Doll & Teddy Bear Collector*, P.O. Box 4032, Portland, OR 97208; *Teddy Bear & Friends*, 6405 Flank Dr., Harrisburg, PA 17112; *Teddy Bear Review*, 170 Fifth Ave., New York, NY 10010.

Teddy Bear
3-1/2" h, golden mohair, metal frame, tummy opens to reveal oval mirror and powder puff tray, Schuco 325.00
5" h, Teddy Threesome, mohair, swivel head, stationary legs, collar with bell, felt paws, Steiff 65.00
5" h, white mohair, plastic brads, Schuco 65.00
6" h, Bedtime Bear, brown mohair, straw stuffed, glass eyes, sewn nose and mouth, jointed, Steiff, 1900s . . .150.00
6" h, Pouting Bear, brown plush, foam stuffing, molded face, sitting, Knickerbocker, 1950s 10.00
6-1/2" h, Berg Bear, gold plush, straw stuffed, Austria 85.00
7" h, Bear-at-Brunch, gold mohair, straw stuffed, stickpin eyes, sewn nose and mouth, jointed, swivel head, Germany 150.00
7" h, Scooter Bear, plush, windup, on wheels. 150.00
10" h, Cocoa Bear, white felt, stuffed, button eyes, 1940s 25.00
11" h, Riding Bear, stuffed, blue and white checked, metal tricycle, red wood wheels. 125.00
11" h, Brown Mohair, swivel head, gold muzzle, glass eyes, Zotty 130.00
11" h, Gold Mohair, glass eyes, Knickerbocker 250.00
11" h, Playmate Bear, gold mohair, stuffed, sewn nose and mouth, jointed, 1950s. .65.00
12" h, Smokey the Bear, Ideal, 1953 25.00
13" h, gold mohair, swivel head, glass eyes, Hermann 95.00
16" h, Gentle Ben, black plush, plastic eyes, pink mouth, red felt tongue, pull string, Mattel, 1967 . . . . .35.00
16" h, The Original Ideal Teddy Bear, 75th anniversary commemorative, brown plush, label, special-edition box, Ideal, 1978 . . . . .50.00
16" h, Yogi Bear, brown plush, stuffed, molded face, yellow paws, green felt tie, Knickerbocker, 1959 . . . . .85.00

Teddy Bear-Related Items
Bottle, Pour-a-Panda, James Beam Distilling Co., 1980 . . . . .15.00
Brochure, Teddy Bear's Baking School, Teddy Bear illus, 1906. . . . . .50.00
Doll Dishes, plastic, teddy motif, German, 1970 . . . . .10.00
Perfume Holder, metal, 1-1/2" h, back opens to reveal perfume, Max Factor, 1970s. .25.00

Teddy Bear Figurines
Anna-Perenna Porcelain, Adorables Collection, Bruno 15.00

Anna-Perenna Holiday Bear 35.00
Anna-Perenna Teddy Robinson 14.00
Boyds, The Bearstone Collection, Bailey
    The Cheerleader 16.00
Boyds, Grenville, red scarf 55.00
Boyds, Sherlock and Watson,
    in Disguise 16.00
Department 56, Upstairs Downstairs
    Bears, Mrs. Henrietta Bosworth . .25.00
Department 56, Nanny & Baby Arthur Off to
    the Park 45.00
Department 56, Winston 25.00
Enesco, Lucy and Me, two Bears Standing
    Next to Snowblowers, E2816 . . . .20.00
Enesco, Lucy and Me, four Bears With
    Shirts On, E3125 . . . . .20.00
Enesco, Lucy and Me, Bears Dressed as
    Pumpkin and Witch, E5412 . . . . .20.00
Enesco, Lucy and Me, Bear in Irish Suit,
    E4737 . . . . .20.00
Russ Berrie and Co., Teddytown Village,
    Aunt Eunice Bear 24.00
Russ Berrie, Love Heals All 28.00
Russ Berrie, Nurse 6.00
Russ Berrie, The Artist 5.00

Telephone Cards

One of the newest collecting crazes is telephone cards, commonly known as "telecards." They have been big in Europe for years. Look for an explosion in the United States during the last half of the 1990s. Telecards are credit cards issued by major telephone companies and many private companies. You purchase a card and then use up the credit each time you place a call. Once the credit value of the card is exhausted, you have an instant collectible.

Some telecards are produced as part of a series, some are limited editions. Most stand alone. The cards are issued in quantities that start in the hundreds and continue into the tens of thousands. Collector value rests in a card's graphics, issuing telephone company and the number issued. Prices are highly speculative. Only time will tell how this new collectible will "reach out and touch" collectors.

Prices listed here are from current sales lists issued by several individuals selling directly to collectors. The market has yet to determine if a premium is to be paid for cards unexpended credit balances.

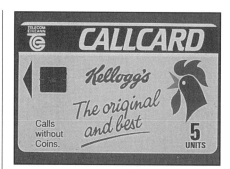

Kellogg's, Telecom Eireann, 5 units, $15.

Periodicals: *Moneycard Collector*, 911 Vandemark Rd., Sidney, OH 45365; *Phone Card Collector*, 700 E. State St., Iola, WI 54990; *Premier Telecard Magazine*, P.O. Box 4614, San Luis Obispo, CA 93403.

Access Telecom
Heineken Beer 23.00
Nabisco Snacker Cracker 20.00
NBC News Promo Card 20.00
U.S. Electronics-Call Home 15.00

ACMI
Birthday Card 12.00
Bozo Birthday 15.00
Endangered-Cheetah, $7 value 12.00
Endangered-Clinton, $3 value 10.00
Fed Ex 75.00
Ryder Truck Rentals 90.00

Ameritech
CardEx Conference Series,
    40-cent value 4.00
Phone Phair 1994 . . . . 31.00
Snowflake, $2 value, 1st ed 5.00

AT&T
Apollo Lunar Module, 10 units 25.00
Art Deco District-Miami Beach,
    25 units 70.00
E.T., 10 units, in envelope 55.00

Diet Coke, Watch Friends on TV, 15 minutes, $5.

Golden Gate Bridge, 10 units 17.00

Bell Atlantic
James Earl Jones, $2 value 5.00
Owners Meeting, $2 value 25.00
Trial Card-Green Phone, $5 value . . 10.00

General Electric
N.Y. Times Brooklyn Bridge,
    $50 value 15.00
Peter Max, set of four 40.00

GTI Telecom
Bud One Airship 7.00
Chamber of Horrors, set of five 30.00
Budweiser Clydesdale 8.00
Magic Minutes 8.00
Shell Motorist Club 10.00

Hallmark
Garden 15.00
House Illustrations 15.00
Moon Doggie 15.00
Personals, Sprint 25.00
Red Phone 15.00

NYNEX
Ballerina 18.00
College Graduate 42.00
Holiday Peace Card, $5 value 8.00
King Kong, $1 value 10.00

Pacific Bell
Christmas Cellular Santa 35.00
Christmas Holiday, $5 value 30.00

Smartel
Abraham & Strauss-Father's Day . . . 18.00
Call Me: I'm Sorry 14.00
House at Tanglewood 20.00
Newsweek 30.00
Norelco 10.00

Sprint
French Quarter, New Orleans,
    City Series 7.00
NBC Fall, Cosby Mysteries 85.00
Orlando Goofy Balloon 45.00
Popsicle Pup 40.00

Western Union
End of World War II 9.00
Transcontinental Railroad 9.00
Wright Brothers 9.00

Worldlink
Alligator 6.00
Concorde 15.00

Telephones and Telephone Related

If you ask people when they think the telephone was invented, most will give you a date in the early 20th century. The accepted answer is 1876, when Alexander Graham Bell filed his patent. However, crude telegraph and sound-operated devices existed prior to that date.

Beware of reproduction phones or phones made from married parts. Buy only telephones that have the proper period parts, a minimum of restoration and are in working order. No mass-produced telephone in the United States made prior to 1950 was manufactured with a shiny brass finish.

Concentrating on telephones is only half the story. Telephone companies generated a wealth of secondary material from books to giveaway premiums. Dig around for examples from local companies that eventually were merged into the Bell system.

Clubs: Antique Telephone Collectors Association, P.O. Box 94, Abilene, KS 67410; Telephone Collectors International, Inc., 19 N. Cherry Dr., Oswego, IL 60543.

Telephones

Desk, upright, Eiffel Tower, L.M. Ericsson & Co., c1890 . . . . .150.00
Emergency, Western Electric 100.00
Intercom, Stromberg-Carlson 75.00
Pay, 23J, metal,
Gray Manufacturing 150.00
Wall, Connecticut Telephone & Electric, watchcase receiver 25.00

Toy, figural, Bart Simpson, MIB 35.00
Toy, figural, Beetle Bailey 65.00
Toy, figural, Budweiser Beer Can . . 25.00
Toy, figural, Garfield, 1980s 35.00
Toy, figural, Pizza Hut Pete, 1980s . 50.00

Other

Almanac, Bell Systems Telephone, 58th anniversary issue, 1934 . . . . 14.00
Booklet, biography, Alexander Graham Bell, Bell Telephone, 32 pgs, Bell portrait cov, 1951 . . . . 6.00
Broadside, Atlantic Telegraph, Triumph of Science 20.00
Calendar, Tri-State Telephone Co., December 1916 . . . . 25.00
Fan, Bell System, logo, blue and white 12.00
Magazine, General Telephone Co., of Wisconsin News Lines, July 1956 . . . . 8.00
Paperweight, Bell System, New York Telephone Co., figural glass bell, dark blue, gold lettering, c1920, 3-1/4" h 70.00
Pen, Bell Telephone, Esterbrook . . . 45.00
Pencil, Bell Telephone, Auto Point . 25.00
Pin, Bell System, die-cut celluloid bell-shape hanger, blue, white lettering, "Local Long Distance Telephone" on front, reverse with "When in Doubt, Telephone and Find Out, Use the Bell", Whitehead & Hoag patent, 1905, 1" l 12.00
Pin, New England Telephone & Telegraph, service award, octagonal, 10k gold, raised Bell System logo above faux ruby, 1930s, 1/2" d 15.00

Pinback Button, Bell Telephone System, blue lettering and logo, white ground, "3 Sale Club" on center bell logo, "Plant Employee Sales, Go Get 'Em, Eastern Division" on rim, 1906-07, 7/8" d . 25.00
Pinback Button, Chicago Telephones, red ground, white lettering, 2-1/4" d . . 25.00
Pinback Button, New England Telephone & Telegraph Co., Bell System, blue and white 25.00
Playing Cards, Telephone Pioneers of America, blue and white, Bell logo 3.00
Pocket Mirror, Missouri and Kansas Telephone Co., Bell System, American Telephone & Telegraph, celluloid, blue and white, early 1900s, 2-1/2" l . . 65.00
Sheet Music, Call Me Up Some Rainy Afternoon, cover with woman making phone call and man walking in rain, 1910 . . . . 10.00
Sign, Indiana Telephone Co., Indiana Telephone Corporation, Local & Distance Service, 18" by 18", two-sided, porcelain enamel, black and white, late 1940s 65.00
Stock Certificate, American Telegraphone Co., District of Columbia, 1907 . . 13.00
Valentine, Love's Telephone, mechanical 40.00

Television Characters and Personalities

The Golden Age of television varies depending on the period in which you grew up. Each generation thinks the television of its childhood is the best there ever was. TV collectibles are one category in which new products quickly establish themselves as collectible. The minute a show is canceled, something that happens rather rapidly today, anything associated with it is viewed as collectible.

The Golden Age of TV star endorsements was the 1950s through the 1960s. For whatever reason, toy, game and other manufacturers of today are not convinced that TV stars sell products. As a result, many shows have no licensed products associated with them. Because of the absence of three-dimensional material, collectors must content themselves with paper, such as *TV Guide* and magazines.

Periodicals: *Big Reel*, P.O. Box 1050, Dubuque, IA 52004; *Classic TV*, P.O. Box 533468, Orlando, FL 32853; *Col-*

Candlestick, Western Electric Co., $90.

Wall, Utica Fire Alarm Telephone Co., $275.

lecting Hollywood, 2401 Broad St., Chattanooga, TN 37408; *Television Chronicles*, 10061 Riverside Dr., #171, North Hollywood, CA 91602; *Television History Magazine*, 700 E. Macoupin St., Staunton, IL 62088; *The TV Collector*, P.O. Box 1088, Easton, MA 02334.

Adventures of Superman
Activity Book, paint by number, 40 pictures, Whitman, 1966 . . . . .20.00
Belt, Kellogg's premium, plastic, aluminum buckle, "S" symbol, red and yellow, 28" l 150.00
Game, Calling Superman-A Game of News Reporting, Transogram, 1954 . . .60.00
Thermos, metal, red plastic top, King-Seeley, 1967 . . . . .40.00

American Bandstand
Diary, vinyl cov, metal fastener 40.00
TV Guide, Oct. 4, 1958 . . . . .15.00
Yearbook, 40 pgs, 9" by 12" 35.00

The Avengers
Book, *The Avengers*, 80 pgs, photos, hardcover, ABC Television Films, 1969 . . . . .25.00
Comic Book, The Mohawks, 68 pgs, black and white, 1966 . . . . .12.00
Game, Denys Fisher Toys, 1977 . . .30.00
Magazine, *Meet The Avengers*, 40 pgs, English version 25.00

Beverly Hillbillies
Book, *Beverly Hillbillies Annual*, 96 pgs, color, hardcover 20.00
Game, Standard Toykraft, 1963 . . . .30.00
Puzzle, 10" by 14", Jaymar, 1963 . . .20.00

Alf, puppet, plush, 1980s, $12.

Brady Bunch
Coloring Book, #1004, Whitman, 1974 . . . . 20.00
Puzzle, Whitman, 1972 . . . . 15.00
Record, Meet The Brady Bunch, Paramount, 1972 . . . . 52.00

Car 54, Where Are You?
Comic book, #1257, 128 pgs, Dell Publishing, 1962 . . . . 20.00
Coloring Book, #1157, 128 pgs, Whitman, 1962 . . . . 40.00
View-Master, #B568, Grand Canyon Adventure, GAF, 1971 . . . . 25.00

Family Affair
Doll, Buffy and Mrs. Beasley, 6" h Buffy, 3-1/2" h Mrs. Beasley, vinyl, fabric, boxed, Mattel, 1967 . . . . 60.00
Lunch Box, emb steel, metal thermos, King-Seeley, 1969 . . . . 50.00
Paper Doll, Buffy, cardboard, Whitman, 1968 . . . . 20.00

Happy Days
Doll, Fonzie, 8" h, vinyl, plastic, Mego, 1976 . . . . 20.00
Game, Parker Brothers, 1976 . . . . . 15.00
Pinback Button, Fonzie, color photo, 3-1/2" d, 1976 . . . . 8.00

Jackie Gleason Show
Game, And Awa-a-a-a-y We Go, Transogram, 1956 . . . . 125.00
Magazine, *Jackie Gleason-The Pictorial Story of TV's Greatest Star*, color cov, black-and-white photos, 1955 . . . 20.00
Record, Songs I Sing on the Jackie Gleason Show, 33-1/3 rpm, c1950 . . . . 25.00
TV Digest, Jan. 3, 1953, Gleason cov photo 20.00

Lassie
Coloring Book, Whitman, 1958 . . . . 20.00
Figure, plastic, orig cardboard tag inscribed "Lassie-Wonder Dog of TV," 1955 . . . . 50.00
Game, Adventures of Lassie, Lisbeth Whiting, 1955 . . . . 40.00
Lunch Box, steel, King-Seeley, 1978 . . . . 35.00

Lone Ranger
Binoculars, plastic, black neck strap, decals 50.00
Boots, leather, brown, red and white, orig 4" by 10" by 11" box, Endicott-Johnson 100.00
Hat, black felt, red vinyl stitching, chin cord, fabric label, Arlington Hats, 1956 35.00
Puppet, push-button, 3" h 25.00
Record, He Finds Silver, 45 rpm, LRG-17, No2 . . . . 20.00

M*A*S*H
Game, Transogram, 1975 . . . . .25.00
Costume, Corporal Klinger, vinyl, Ben Cooper, 1981 . . . . .30.00
TV Guide, Feb. 12, 1983 . . . . .15.00

Mr. Ed
Coloring Book, Whitman, 1963 . . . . .35.00
Comic Book, Mister Ed, The Talking Horse, #260, 16 pgs 18.00
Game, Parker Brothers, 1962 . . . . . .40.00
Hand puppet, vinyl and cloth, 10" h, Knickerbocker, 1962 . . . . .75.00

Partridge Family
Activity Book, paint and color, David Cassidy cov, Artcraft, 1971 . . . . .30.00
Colorforms, David Cassidy cov, 1972 . . . . .30.00
Coloring Book, #3997, Saalfield, 1971 . . . . .20.00
Game, Milton Bradley, 1971 . . . . . . .20.00
Puzzle, David Cassidy, life-size, APC, 1973 . . . . .70.00

Six Million Dollar Man
Activity book, #C2471, Rand McNally, 1977 . . . . .8.00
Game, Parker Brothers, 1975 . . . . . .10.00
TV Guide, May 18, 1974 . . . . .4.00

Other
Adventures of Ozzie and Harriet, coloring Book, David and Ricky, 11" by 14", Saalfield .35.00
Adventures of Ozzie and Harriet, *TV Guide*, May 15, 1953 . . . . .10.00
All in the Family, game, Milton Bradley, 1972 . . . . .10.00
All in the Family, mug, Archie Bunker For President, ceramic, white, 5" h, Archie portrait center, red and blue lettering, 1976 . . . . .8.00
Dennis the Menace, puzzle, frame tray, Whitman, 1960 . . . . .12.00

All in the Family, pinback button, 1-1/4" d, $5.

Dennis the Menace, record, The
Misadventures of Dennis the Menace,
33-1/3 rpm, Colpix, 1960 . . . . . . .25.00
Emergency, game, Milton Bradley,
1974 . . . . .20.00
Emergency, lunch box, emb steel, plastic
thermos, Aladdin, 1973 . . . . .55.00
Gilligan's Island, figures, Gilligan, Skipper
and Mary Ann, hollow, soft vinyl and
plastic 25.00
Gilligan's Island, game, Milton Bradley,
1965 . . . . .90.00
Gomer Pyle, USMC, game, Transogram,
1965 . . . . .40.00
Gomer Pyle, USMC, lunch box, emb steel,
Aladdin, 1966 . . . . .60.00
Green Acres, coloring book, Whitman,
1967 . . . . .25.00
Green Acres, paper dolls, Lisa and Oliver,
cardboard, six pgs uncut clothing,
Whitman, 1967 . . . . .35.00
Hawaii Five-0, book, *Hawaii Five-0: The
Octopus Caper*, 212 pgs, hardcover,
Whitman, 1971 . . . . .12.00
Hawaii Five-0, game, Remco, 1968 .40.00
Honey West, doll, 11-1/2" h, vinyl, fabric
outfit, Gilbert Toys, c1966 . . . . . .75.00
Honey West, game, Ideal, 1965 . . . .30.00
I Dream of Jeannie, doll, 6-1/2" h, vinyl,
fabric outfit, plastic pocketbook and
shoes, Remco, 1977 . . . . .75.00
I Dream of Jeannie, game, Milton Bradley,
1965 . . . . .35.00
Incredible Hulk, action figure, vinyl, green,
purple fabric shorts,
Mego, 1979 . . . . .30.00

Incredible Hulk, bank, plastic, green and
black, photo sticker,
AJ Renz, 1978 . . . . 25.00
Little House on the Prairie, doll, Laura, vinyl
and cloth, fabric clothing,
1978, boxed 25.00
Little House on the Prairie, lunch box, steel,
King-Seeley, 1976 . . . . 35.00
My Favorite Martian, coloring book,
Whitman, 1964 . . . . 25.00
My Favorite Martian, game, Transogram,
1963 . . . . 40.00

Television Lamps

What 1950s living room would be complete without a black ceramic gondola slowly drifting across the top of the television set? Long before the arrival of VCRs, Home Box and Nintendo systems, figural lamps dominated the tops of televisions. The lamps were made of colorful high gloss ceramics and the subject matter ranged from the relatively mundane dog statue to the more exotic (tasteless?) hula dancer.

A collection of 10 or more of these beauties will certainly lighten up the conversation at your next party. On second thought, it does not take 10. The pink poodle lamp on my television is more than enough to do the job.

Boot, brass 20.00
Buffalo, brown, standing on rocks . . 32.00
Fish, white, round metal base 18.00
Gazelle, black, jumping over
palm fronds 35.00
Male and Female Forms, plaster
composition, painted black, fiberglass
shade, price for pair 95.00

Panther, brown tones, $50.

Mallard, airbrushed, green and brown,
wings spread, planter base 35.00
Medusa, aluminum tubing, chrome,
52" h 300.00
Panther, stalking, black, white screen
background, green oval base . . . 25.00
Poodles, pink and black, black oval planter
base, price for pair 30.00
Rock, figural iron base, bamboo shaft,
paper shade, 53" h 110.00
Rooster, crowing, multicolored, standing
on brown fence, Lane & Co., Van Nuys,
CA, 13" h 45.00
Scottie Dog, pouncing, gold 18.00
Shell, figural, ceramic 90.00
Siamese Cats, 13" h 35.00

Televisions

Old television sets are becoming highly collectible. It is not unusual to see a dozen or more at a flea market. Do not believe a tag that says "I Work." Insist that the seller find a place to plug it in and show you. A good general rule is the smaller the picture tube, the earlier the set. Pre-1946 televisions usually have a maximum of five stations, 1 through 5. Channels 7 through 13 were added in 1947. In 1949 Channel 1 was dropped. UHF appeared in 1953.

To determine the value of a television, identify the brand and model number. See *Warman's Americana & Collectibles* for a more detailed list.

Club: Antique Wireless Association, 59 Main St., Bloomfield, NY 14469.

Admiral, Model 30B15, 10" screen, wood
console, 1948 . . . . 75.00
Air King, Model A-1000, 10" screen, wood
top, grill cloth, bottom knobs . . . 100.00
Andrea, Model C-VK12,
12" screen 100.00

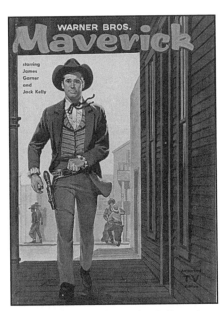

Maverick, **book, by Charles I. Coombs, Whitman Publishing Co., Alexander Toth illus, 1959, 282 pgs, $25.**

Gondola, ceramic, mkd "Premco Mfg. Co, Chicago, Ill, 1954," 16" l, 7" h, $25.

Olympic, Model TV-104, table model, wood case, Bakelite knobs, 10" screen, 1948, $125.

Crosley, Model 9-409M, 12" screen,
    double doors 35.00
DeWald, Model DT-120, 12" screen, wood
    top 60.00
Emerson, Model 614, 10" screen, bakelite
    top, 1950 . . . . .75.00
Fada, Model S-1015, 12" screen, wood
    top, four knobs, 1950 . . . . .35.00
General Electric, Model 16K1, 16" screen
    behind door, AM/FM,
    phono, 1950 . . . . .20.00
General Electric, Model 21T2420, 21"
    screen, portable 10.00
Hallicrafters, Model T-54, 7" screen, metal,
    13 channels, push-button tuner .150.00
Motorola Model VK-101, console, 10"
    screen, 13 channel,
    AM/FM, 1948 . . . . .125.00
Muntz, Model 24CB, 24" screen, wood
    console, tubular legs, 1959 . . . . .50.00
Olympic, Model TV-947, 16" screen,
    console, double doors, 1950 . . . .25.00
Philco, Model 51-T1634, 16" screen,
    console, wood top, four knobs, 1951 . .
    15.00
RCA, Model 9T246, 10" screen, grill,
    imitation mahogany finish, 1949. .25.00
Westinghouse, Model H-196, 10" screen,
    five knobs, rounded top, 1949 . . .85.00

Tennis Ball Cans

Tennis balls originally came in bags and cardboard boxes. In 1926, Wilson introduced the first metal tennis-ball can. It opened with a small key like a can of ham and had a flat lid that would not stay on the can after it was opened. After 1942, the lid was improved so that it could be put back on the can after opening to hold the balls securely. This lid was slightly dome-shaped instead of flat. Dome lid cans were also of the key wind opening type. Most English key wind cans had flat lids, regardless of when they were made and should not be confused with the rare U.S. flat-lid cans. However, the older English cans had a small solder spot either on the lid or the bottom of the can. The newer English cans had no solder spot.

Around 1972, the easy-opening pull-ring cans were introduced. The best cans are the big 12-ball cans, four-ball cans, flat-lid cans made in the United States and cans with a famous player on them. The newer pull-ring cans are still very common and are only worth 50 cents to $10. Some balls are still sold in boxes. Pre-1960 boxes are hard to find and are worth from $30 to $70. Boxes that predate cans are extremely rare and can cost $100 or more.

Advisor: Larry Whitaker, 2920 Jessie Ct., San Jose, CA 95124, (408) 377-8120.

Club: The Tennis Collectors Society, Gerald Gurney, Guildhall, Great Bromley, Colchester, Essex, England C07 7TU.

Wilson

Blue, white and gold, 12-ball can. . 100.00
Ellsworth Vines, blue and yellow or blue
    and green, dome lid 60.00
Ellsworth Vines, blue and yellow or blue
    and green, flat lid 75.00
Jack Kramer, red and white 40.00
Yellow, red, and, white. 15.00

Other

Bancroft, black, gold and white,
    "Winner" 25.00
Bill Tilden, black, white and red, Tilden on
    front, Tilden's record on back . . . 40.00
Chemold, Tony Roche on red can with
    Australian flag. 30.00
Chicago Sports Equipment, Henri Cochet
    pictured on can, blue, white and
    orange. 80.00
D&M, blue and red, flat lid 75.00
Dunlop, Vinnie Richards, red, white and
    black, dome lid 20.00
Dunlop, Vinnie Richards, red, white and
    black, flat lid 45.00
MacGregor, black,
    red and white plaid 25.00
Oxford, purple, 12-ball can 125.00
Pennsylvania, Allcort Championship,
    yellow and black, dome lid 25.00
Pennsylvania, Allcort Championship,
    yellow and black, flat lid. 50.00
Regent, Cannon Ball, green, black, red and
    white 30.00
Spalding, Pancho Gonzales, red or blue .
    20.00
Spencer Moulton, four-ball can, dark blue
    and light blue. 75.00
Voit, green and white, dome lid 25.00
Voit, green and white, flat lid 50.00
Wright & Ditson, white and red. 30.00
X-Pert, blue and red with white ball, dome
    lid. 38.00
X-Pert, blue and red with white ball,
    flat lid 65.00

Tennis Collectibles

One of the latest sports collectibles to receive attention is tennis memorabilia. The recent publication of *Tennis Antiques and Collectibles* by Jeanne Cherry (Amaryllis Press, 1995) has given collectors a much-needed and well-researched reference source. A Tennis Collectors Society has been in existence for several years, and the membership continues to grow, particularly in the United States. Collectors are seeking racquets, trophies, tournament programs, ball cans, prints, jewelry and anything else with a tennis or racquet motif. The earlier the better.

The single most popular symbol of the sport is the racquet. The most sought after models being those with unusual head shapes, i.e., lob or tilt-tops or flat-top frames. The earliest racquets usually had the maker's name incised or stamped into the wood. Decals usually indicate a post-1900 racquet. Handles of early racquets are wooden. Leather bound models first appeared in the late 1930s. Boxed sets for tennis included racquets, net, net posts, rules book, balls and a sturdy wooden box, with a lawn-tennis lithograph on the inside lid. Collectors dream of finding a complete matched set.

Trophies won by famous players at well-known tournaments or clubs command the highest prices. Trophies with tennis images are also desirable. Finally, the most sought-after collectible in the tennis field is original, period art; oils and stained glass, being two examples.

Advisor: Ken Benner, 217 Hewett Rd., Wyncote, PA 19095, (215) 885-5876.

Club: The Tennis Collectors Society, Guildhall Orchard, Great Bromley, Colchester, C07 7TU U.K.

Racquets
Dayton, wood handle, steel head, wire strings, no string breaks, diamond-shaped trademark decal on handle, 1930s 15.00
Harry C. Lee, Dreadnought Driver, big handle, c1903. . . . . .25.00
Hazell's Streamline, three-shaft construction, made in England, c1930s. . .90.00
Horsman, flat top, wood handle, model name and "Horsman" stamped into wood, thick original gut strings, c1890 . . . . .70.00
Prince Classic, aluminum, green throat piece, 1960s. 7.50
Spalding, The Hub, decals, wood handle, good strings, overall good condition, c1905 . . . . .20.00
Wilson, Famous Player Series, Don Budge, good condition, 1940s . . .10.00
Winchester, wood handle, clean trademark decal, c1930s. 40.00

Other
Annual, *Wright & Ditson*, soft cover, 1908, results of tournaments, rules, adv, etc. .12.00
Autograph, William T. Tilden, tennis book. 50.00
Book, *Match Play and the Spin of the Ball*, by William T. Tilden, hardbound, 1923, first edition 45.00
Box, wood, tennis lithograph on inside lid, held complete tennis set 100.00
Cigarette Cards, set of 50, each card with famous tennis player from 1930s, green 25.00
Fan, cardboard, wood stick handle, lady holding tennis racquet image, adv on reverse. .15.00
Magazine, *American Lawn Tennis*, 1920s 5.00
Magazine, *Harper's Weekly*, 1880s, full page print of ladies playing tennis in Prospect Park, New York City . . .12.50
Napkin Ring, racquet and ball, silver, c1890s .90.00
Net, with turned wood posts 50.00

Photograph, tennis players holding racquets, court in background, 1880s 20.00
Program, USLTA, Forest Hills, 1936 15.00
Program, Wimbledon, All England Lawn Tennis Club, player image on cover, 1950s 4.00
Trophy, 1905 Seabright Lawn Tennis and Cricket Club, silver, 10" h 90.00

Thermometers

The thermometer was a popular advertising giveaway and promotional item. Buy only thermometers in very good or better condition, which have a minimum of wear on the visible surface. Remember, thermometers had large production runs. If the first example you see does not please you, shop around.

Advertising
A. Tvarosek Oil Co., Berwyn, IL, cardboard, black lettering, 6-1/8" h 5.00
Borden Feed, orig box, 1952 . . . . . . 25.00
Cash Value Tobacco, tin 22.50
Champion Spark Plugs 20.00
Coca-Cola, bottle-shape, gold, orig box, 1950s 20.00
Dr Pepper, tin, 1960s logo, 20" h. . . 50.00
Dr. Pierce's Chemical Co., bakelite, 1931 . . . . 18.00

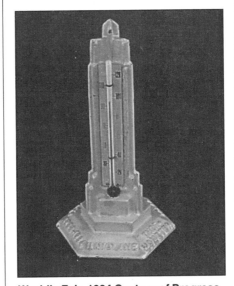

World's Fair, 1934 Century of Progress, Havoline Motor Oil adv, cast iron, $30.

First National Bank, Fremont, OH, wood, orig box .30.00
Georgia Real Estate Co., wood, 21" h, 1915 . . . . .70.00
Happy Jim Chewing Tobacco, 35" h 75.00
Kendall Oil, round. 25.00
Luminall, 39" h, 1950 . . . . .60.00
Naco Fertilizer Co., Charleston, SC . 22.00
Nyal Drugstore Service, 38" h 28.00
Old Dutch Root Beer, 27" h, 1940 . .65.00
Old Fashion Moxie, metal. 20.00
Pal Orange Ade, 26" h 40.00
Rislone 55.00
Rochester American Insurance Co., NY, porcelain. 27.00
Royal Crown Cola, cardboard, Santa Claus and bottle, 20" by 10", 1950s. . . .35.00
Salem Cigarettes 12.00
Sauer's Vanilla, wood, 1919. . . . . . .68.00
Snow Goose Flour, blue trim, white ground, 39" h 50.00
Standard Oil, tin, orig box. 20.00
Stegmaier Beer, glass, round. 43.00
Switch and Manufacturing Co., Carlisle, PA, frog, dark blue trim, white ground, 36" h 45.00
Washer Hardware, Sheldon, IA, wood frame. .24.00
World's Fair, 1934 Chicago World's Fair, octagonal, silver and blue dial symbol and lettering, brass rim, black metal back and hanging, 2-1/2" by 2-1/2" 50.00

Figural
Cat, bisque, 7-1/2" h, Bradly Japan label. 22.00
Negro, 1949 . . . . .25.00
Owl, plaster body, 6" h 75.00

Ticket Stubs

Next time you attend a paying event, don't throw away that ticket stub! It may be worth something in 20 years.

Entertainment
Beatles, Municipal Stadium, Kansas City, Nov. 17, 1964 . . . . .65.00
Cab Calloway & His Cotton Club Orchestra, 1935. . . . . .12.00
Eric Clapton, Tampa Stadium, Florida, 1975 . . . . .18.00
Elvis, San Antonio Convention Center, Oct. 8, 1974, unused. 50.00
Pink Floyd, Anaheim Stadium, Animals tour, 1977 . . . . .30.00

Sports, baseball, Montreal Expos, 1969, $5.

The Rolling Stones, Candlestick Park,
San Francisco, Tattoo You tour,
1981 . . . . .35.00

Political
National Progressive Party, 1912, Lincoln,
Jefferson and Washington front . .64.00
Republican National Convention, July
1992, with holograph,
orig envelope 6.00
Vice President Agnew's inaugural,
1973, 7" by 4" 5.00

Railroad
Boston and Main, 1900s 2.00
Northern Pacific, 1940s 2.25
Pennsylvania, 1940s 1.75
Wisconsin Central, 1910 . . . . .3.50

Sports
Auto Racing, Daytona 500, 1972, A.J.
Foyt 10.00
Auto Racing, Daytona 500, 1982,
Bobby Allison 4.00

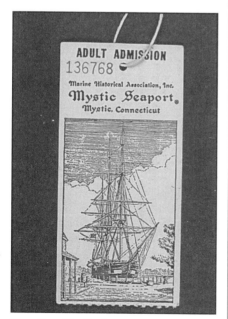

Vacation, Mystic Seaport, Mystic, CT, adult admission, $1.

Auto Racing, Indy 500, 1968,
Bobby Unser 25.00
Auto Racing, Indy 500, 1986,
Bobby Rahal 12.00
Baseball, 1969, All-Star Game,
RFK Stadium 6.00
Basketball, 1960, NBA All-Star,
Philadelphia 25.00
Boxing, 3/8/71, Frazier/Ali 75.00
Boxing, 6/19/92, Holyfield/Holmes . . . 8.00
Football, 1967, Sugar Bowl,
Alabama/Nebraska 12.00
Football, 1983, Gator Bowl,
Florida/Iowa 2.00
Football, 1970, AFC Championship . . 5.00
Football, 1977, Super Bowl XII 25.00

World's Fair
Centennial Exposition, Philadelphia, 1876,
admission 20.00
Columbian Exposition, Chicago, 1893,
General Admission 5 cent,
2" by 1" 27.50

Tins

The advertising tin has always been at the forefront of advertising collectibles. Look for examples that show no deterioration to the decorated surfaces and which have little or no signs of rust on the insides or bottoms.

The theme sells the tin. Other collectors, especially individuals from the transportation fields, have long had their eyes on the tin market. Tins also play a major part in the Country Store decorating look. Prices for pre-1940 tins are still escalating. Before you pay a high price for a tin, do your homework and make certain it is difficult to find.

Club: Tin Container Collectors Association, P.O. Box 440101, Aurora, CO 80044.

Cocoa
Baker's Breakfast Cocoa 10.00
Dunn's Chocolate 10.00
Hershey's Chocolate Cocoa, 5"
by 12-1/4" d. 25.00
Ovaltine, 8 oz. 10.00
Runkel's All Purpose Cocoa 10.00
Symond's Inn Cocoa, paper label . . 10.00

Coffee
Camp Fire, red. 100.00
Chase & Sanborn 10.00
Clover Farm 10.00

Cream Brand Roasted Coffee, milk pail,
handle .50.00
Diamond Brand. 100.00
Golden Sun, green and gray,
paper label. 25.00
Nash's, pail, red 25.00
Roasted Coffee, Sears,
Roebuck & Co. 100.00

Flat
La Belle Creole 100.00
Look Out. 100.00
Sweet Clover 100.00

Humidor
Boston Slice 50.00
Eutopia Mixture. 100.00
Surbrug's High Grade Smoking
Tobacco. 100.00

Lunch Box
Dixie Queen 25.00
Great West 100.00
King Koal 25.00
Plow Boy. 100.00
Rainbow Cut. 350.00
Skookum. 100.00
Tiger 25.00
Winner 100.00

Peanuts
Lotus Brand, white and pink 25.00
Pansies. .50.00
Squirrel Brand. 25.00

Peanut Butter
Armour's Veribest. 25.00
Gold Bond. 10.00
Peter Pan 25.00
Peter Rabbit, pail, Newton Tea & Spice
Co. 100.00

Tea
Banquet Orange Pekoe 25.00
Betsy Ross Orange Pekoe 10.00
Lipton 10.00
New Moon 25.00
Richeleiu .10.00
Sheba 25.00

Tobacco
Bill William 10.00
Cuban Seal. 10.00
Cupid Bouquet Little Cigars 25.00
Dutch Masters 25.00
El Verso .25.00
Good Cheer 25.00
Home Run Stogies 350.00
Justrite 25.00
Lady Churchill. 25.00
La Fendrich. 10.00
Little Tom 25.00
Muriel 10.00
Postmaster 25.00
White Ash 10.00

Upright and Vertical

Air Ship	.350.00
Crane's Private Mixture	.100.00
De Voe's	.100.00
Dial	.10.00
Half And Half	.10.00
King George	.50.00
Model	.25.00
Prince Albert	.10.00
Stag, oval	.25.00
White Manor	.50.00

Tobacco Related Collectibles

The tobacco industry is under siege in the 1990s. Fortunately, they have new frontiers to conquer in Russia, Eastern Europe, Asia and Africa. The relics of America's smoking past, from ashtrays to humidors, are extremely collectible. Many individuals are not able to identify a smoking stand or a pocket cigar cutter. Today, tobacco growing and manufacturing have virtually disappeared. Is it possible that there will be a time when smoking disappears as well?

Clubs: Cigar Label Collectors International, 14761 Pearl Rd. #154, Strongsville, OH 44136; International Seal, Label and Cigar Band Society, 8915 E. Bellevue St., Tucson, AZ 85715; Society of Tobacco Jar Collectors, 3011

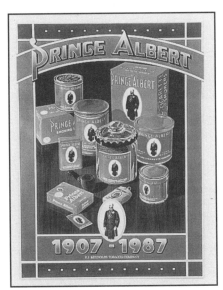

Poster, Prince Albert, R.J. Reynolds Tobacco Co., 1907-1987, 18" by 24", $15.

Tobacco Jar, glazed ceramic, $275.

Falstaff Rd. #307, Baltimore, MD 21209.

Cigar Boxes

Dolly Dollars	15.00
El Cedro	5.00
Hustler	20.00
Karl Marx	60.00
La Rosita	5.00

Caddy Labels

Sailor's Hope, nautical lady with binoculars standing dockside 50.00
The Diadem of Old Virginia, costumed woman with jeweled tiara holding spear 60.00
Welcome Nugget, miner holding nugget 50.00

Cigar Labels

American Empire	50.00
Caesar	125.00
Havana Beauty	30.00
King Alfred	40.00
La Rosada	100.00
Storky	75.00

Pipes

Briar, black man's head, white ceramic eyes, black pupils 70.00
Briar, skull with two capped teeth, carved open cuff, sterling band 70.00
Meerschaum, eagle, wings expanded, amber stem 150.00
Meerschaum, hunter with gun 100.00
Meerschaum, man sitting at desk smoking pipe, amber stem 150.00
Meerschaum, reclining nude youth with floral wreath 30.00
Meerschaum, two horses and giant flower 125.00

Meerschaum, woman carrying bundle of hay 125.00
Porcelain, barmaid and patron 125.00
Porcelain, deer in field 100.00
Porcelain, two hunters, domed metal cap bowl 100.00

Other

Ashtray, alabaster, owl center 15.00
Book, *Tobacco Joe's Almanac, 1922* . 7.00
Cigar Case, leather, set of five 10.00
Commemorative Medal, bronze, 100th anniversary R.J. Reynolds 25.00
Magazine, *Pipe Lovers*, October, 1946 . . . . 10.00
Thermometer, tin, emb, blue, Winston adv. 15.00

Tobacco Tags

If you've never seen a collection of tobacco tags, you've missed out on one of the most prolific, inexpensive and historically significant collectibles ever produced. Most tags were machine stamped from sheets of light gauge tin. They varied in size from tags the size of a match head to examples larger than a silver dollar. In the days before individual sanitary wrapping, when most chewing tobacco was sold in plug form, they were used to identify each manufacturer's product and to ensure repeat business. They were fastened to the plug by means of sharp prongs that were imbedded in the tobacco.

Plain galvanized tin was often used, but the most desirable tags were painted or imprinted, often with full-color lithography. Roughly grouped into about 25 different types and shapes, most aspects of turn-of-the-century life were depicted on tobacco tags, including various occupation, modes of transportation, sports and political figures of the day, popular slogans, etc. No documentation exists to verify the number of tags produced, but it is believed that at least 10,000 to 12,000 different examples exist. Due to the fact that most tags could be saved and redeemed for prizes, similar to S&H green stamps, huge quantities of tags survived to fall into the hands of eager collectors.

Prices listed are for tags in nice, average condition. Prices can vary according to supply and demand, geographic location, condition and crossover theme collectibility.

Advisor: Chris Cooper, Rt. 2, Box 55, Pittsburg, TX 75686, (903) 856-7286

Club: Tin Tag Collectors Club, Rt. 2, Box 55, Pittsburg, TX 75686.

American Navy, rect, red, white and blue, ship image 5.00
Arrowhead, die-cut arrowhead, white on blue, N&WT Co. 10.00
Battle Ax, die-cut ax, white on red. . . .1.50
Bailey's Big Horn, die-cut animal horn, emb words 10.00
Calhoun, oval, black on yellow, Vice President John C. Calhoun image, D.H. Spencer & Son. 7.00
Derby, oval, multicolor on yellow, jockey's cap image. 10.00
Early Bird, round, black and red on yellow, emb bird image 5.00
Fat Back, rect, multicolor, pig image, Lupfert Scales & Co. 10.00
Fried Cake, round, blue on red, white and blue, doughnut image. 7.00
Good as Wheat Plug, die-cut sheaf of wheat, black on yellow, Scotten Tob Co. 10.00
Hand-made, rect, multicolor, woman holding tobacco plug, Globe Tob Co. 25.00
Hiawatha, die-cut Indian figure, black on red 5.00
Hodge's Zebra, diamond, black on cream, running zebra image, Hodges . . .25.00
Kickapoo, round, black on orange, Indian chief image. 15.00
Little Joe, rect, black on yellow, Webb & Crawford. 7.00
Missing Link, oval, silver, emb chain links image 5.00
New Moon, die-cut crescent moon with emb face 7.00
Old Tom, oval, black on white, cat image 10.00
Parrot, round, yellow and green on red, parrot image, "Talks For Itself". . . .7.00
Rainbow, round, multicolor, rainbow image, Nall & Williams Tob Co. 10.00
Red Fox, rect, black and brown on white, fox image, Arnold & McCord Co. .15.00
Skylight, die-cut large crescent, red on yellow .10.00
Spur, die-cut spur-shape, emb 7.00
Tennessee Natural Leaf, rect, yellow on black, tobacco leaf image, East Tenn Tob Co. 15.00
Wax, found, black on yellow, honeybee image .7.00

Yankee Girl, rect, black and red on yellow, girl waving flag image, Scotten, Dillon Co. 5.00

Tokens

Token collecting is an extremely diverse field. The listing below barely scratches the surface with respect to the types of tokens one might find.

The wonderful thing about tokens is that, on the whole, they are very inexpensive. You can build an impressive collection on a small budget. Like match-cover and sugar-packet collectors, token collectors have kept their objects outside the main collecting stream. This has resulted in stable, low prices over a long period of time, in spite of an extensive literature base. There is no indication that this is going to change in the near future.

Clubs: American Numismatic Association, 818 N. Cascade Ave., Colorado Springs, CO 80903; Token and Medal Society, Inc., P.O. Box 951988, Lake Mary, FL 32795.

Boggs and Buhl, Pittsburgh, oval, white metal, knight's helmet between backward and regular B 15.00
Chemin De Fer Club, France, silver, 1930s 17.50
Fada Radio 15.00
Garden City Billiard Table Co., Chicago, brass, inscription on front, reverse with "Palace/Good For 5 Cents in Trade," 1880s 15.00
George B. Evans, Philadelphia, diamond-shape, white metal, drugs and gifts 15.00

Knights Templar, wood, $4.

E. Keller & Sons, Allentown, PA, $7.50.

Gimble Brothers, New York, oval, white metal 18.00
Goodyear Welt, Akron, Ohio and Toronto, aluminum, outer inscription reads "No Goodyear Welt Shoes Genuine Without This Trade Mark," 1890 . . . . .10.00
Hopkins Trans-Oceanic Co., brass. . .15.00
Horace Greeley, campaign, brass, portrait and "Sage of Chappaqua" on front, reverse with eagle and "Greeley, Brown and Amnesty 1872," 7/8" d 30.00
J B Brown, Newfoundland, silver . . .75.00
Josh Rouleau, Canada, copper, c1858. .100.00
Knights of the Golden Eagle, Washington, DC, brass 20.00
Knights Templars, Easton, PA, gilt brass, maltese cross and crossed swords on front, reverse with "36th Annual Conclave of the Grand Commandery of KT of Pennsylvania Easton May 28, 1889" .15.00
McDermott's Sunset Saloon, San Antonio. 30.00
McDonald's, wooden, Redwood City & Menlo Park, 50 cent, Neill, Philadelphia, sq, white metal 12.50
Newman's Clothing House, Bellefonte, PA, white metal 25.00
Ocean House, Cincinnati, clasped hands on front, Elm St. on back, 1883. .15.00
Palmer House Barber Shop, copper and nickel alloy, name and "10 cent 66" on front, blank reverse 15.00
Patapsco Fruit Butter Co., Baltimore, white metal 8.00
Pay Toilet, American Sanitation Lock Co. 3.00
Penn Mutual Life Insurance Co., Philadelphia, 1876 Centennial token, copper .25.00
Pennsylvania State Agricultural Fair, Philadelphia, gilt, 1880 . . . . .25.00

York Lions Club, 1921-1971 Golden Anniversary, brass, $15.

P.H. Lauber's Restaurant, New York,
  copper 40.00
Pocahontas Pioneer Garage, Philadelphia,
  oval, white metal, high relief Indian
  profile 17.50
Pony House Saloon, Dayton, OH, brass,
  name and address on front, reverse
  with "Good For 5 Cents In Trade,"
  c1900 . . . . .4.00
Remington, brass, "Shot With A Kleanbore
  Remington Cartridge" on front, reverse
  with "Shot With A Remington Rifle,"
  1-1/4" d. .8.00
R.H. Stearns, Boston, oval,
  white metal 15.00
R.H. White, Boston pear-shape,
  white metal 20.00
Richard F. Mason, Laurens, SC, brass,
  1870s 30.00
The Harbor, Aransas Harbor, TX,
  brass 30.00
Wm. Numsen & Sons, Baltimore,
  brass 8.00
W.H. Bradley Lumber Co., Tomahawk, WI,
  silver. .150.00

Tools

Every flea market has at least a half a dozen tables loaded with tools. The majority are modern tools sold primarily for reuse. However, you may find some early tools thrown in with the bunch. Dig through tool boxes and the boxes under the tables. Decorators like primitive tools for hanging on walls in old homes. Other desirable tools include those that are hand-wrought or heavily trimmed with brass. Names to look for include Stanley, Keen Kutter

and Winchester. Refer to the Stanley and Winchester listings for further information on these brand names.

Club: The Early American Industries Association, P.O. Box 143, Delmar, NY 12054.

Newsletter: *Tool Ads*, P.O. Box 33, Hamilton, MT 59840.

Periodical: *The Fine Tool Journal*, P.O. Box 4001, Pittsford, VT 05763.

Hammers

Farrier's, hand-wrought, claw-type, side
  straps 35.00
Figural, goat's head, cast iron,
  emb motif 50.00
Keen Kutter 20.00

Hatchets

Advertising, Kellogg's Toasted Corn Flake
  Co., emb, arrow head handle . . . 35.00
Boy Scouts of America 18.00
Goosewing-style, 9" iron blade,
  13" handle. 100.00
Keen Kutter, 5" hewing blade 35.00

Knives

Advertising, Kelly Tire and Boy, yellow
  celluloid handle, Remington 75.00
Advertising, Radio-Art Cabinets,
  switchblade, 3-1/4" l,
  Schrade Cutlery Co. 65.00
Jim Dandy, jack knife, three-blade, black
  handle, 3-1/2" l 10.00

Levels

Chapin Stevens Co., aluminum and brass,
  30" l. 30.00
Disston & Sons, mahogany and brass,
  1912 . . . . 55.00
Hall & Knapp, mahogany, imp eagle and
  shield, 29-1/2" l, c1853-58 . . . . . 40.00
Keen Kutter, #KK30,
  cherry and brass, 28" l 40.00

Saws

Bow, primitive, ash, old working repairs,
  12" by 156" 25.00
Hacksaw, hand-forged, English Lancashire
  pattern frame 45.00
Kitchen, Cortland Wood & Co.,
  double eagle, rosewood handle . 65.00

Screwdrivers

Billings & Spencer Co., wood handle,
  awl-shaped, Pat Feb. 4, 1896. . . 30.00
Booth Mills & Co., cherry handle, flat
  blade. 25.00
Miller Falls, #610A, ratchet, red handle,
  18" l. 15.00

Wrenches

King Dick, pocket, 4-1/8" l 35.00

Reed Mfg., pipe, 11" l 30.00
Rino Wrench Co., pipe, iron, elephant's
  trunk-shape 35.00

Other

Book, *Blacksmith's Account Book*, Carnes
  & Muzzey, 240 pgs, 1888-96. . . . 50.00
Book, *Tuck's Tool Catalog*, 48 pgs,
  c1910. . . . . 10.00
Carpenter's Mallet, burl, 13" l, worn . 30.00
Carpenter's Mallet, burl, 19" l, inserted
  handle 40.00
Chisel, Ohio Tool Co., socket handled,
  V-shape 25.00
Chisel, P. Merrill & Co., corner,
  13/16 . . . . 30.00
Hoopsetter, wood, concave base,
  handmade 45.00
Lathe, cast iron, black, 38" l, C A Mann,
  Providence, RI. 125.00
Leather Punch, brass base, hollow pins,
  9" l 15.00
Log Splitting Wedge, cast iron 15.00
Square, Craftsman, nickel-plated . . . 25.00
Square, Keen Kutter,
  cast iron handle 20.00

Toothpick Holders

During the Victorian era, the toothpick holder was an important table accessory. It is found in a wide range of materials and was manufactured by American and European firms. Toothpick holders also were popular souvenirs in the 1880 to 1920 period.

Do not confuse toothpick holders with match holders, shot glasses, miniature spoon holders in a child's dish set, mustard pots without lids, rose or

Glass, Flower & Peat, yellow stain, Pomona, 2-1/4" h, $45.

Plastic, mechanical, white log, red woodpecker picks up toothpicks, 4-1/2" l, 2-1/2" h, $25.

violet bowls, individual open salts or vases. A toothpick holder allows ample room for the toothpick and enough of an extension of the toothpick to allow easy access.

Club: National Toothpick Holder Collectors Society, 1224 Spring Valley Ln., West Chester, PA 19380.

Figural

Barrel, white milk glass, metal hoops 25.00
Beaver, wood, painted features, broad tail,
    hollowed out tree trunk 5.00
Boot, purple slag glass 50.00
Cat, bisque, wearing coachman's outfit,
    barrel holder 55.00
Cat and Bucket, silver-plated 65.00
Clown, brass, mkd "Jenning Bros." . .30.00
Donkey, pulling cart, china, Occupied
    Japan 8.00
Dwarf, bisque, 4-1/2" h 25.00
Egg, chick emerging, feet on branch,
    silver-plated, sq base, Hartford . .70.00

Silver Plate, dog, glass eyes, mkd "James W Tufts, Boston, 2693," 2-1/2" h, $175.

Rooster, silver-plated, engraved "Picks,"
    2" h 48.00
Top Hat and Umbrella, brass 20.00

Pattern Glass

Colonial, cobalt, Cambridge 25.00
Feather, clear 65.00
Heart, pink opaque 60.00
Iowa, clear 24.00
Hobb's Hobnail, vaseline 20.00
King's Crown, ruby-stained 38.00
Paddlewheel and Star, clear 25.00
Royal Oak, frosted rubina 125.00
Three Dolphins, amber 45.00

Souvenir

Custard Glass, Belvedere, IL 35.00
Ruby-Stained, Button Arches pattern,
    "Mother 1947" 20.00

Tortoise Shell Items

It is possible to find tortoise shell items in a variety of forms ranging from boxes to trinkets. Tortoise shell items experienced several crazes in the 19th and early 20th centuries, the last occurring in the 1920s when tortoise shell jewelry was especially popular. Anyone selling tortoise shell objects is subject to the Endangered Species Act and its amendments. Tortoise shell objects can be imported and sold, but only after adhering to a number of strict requirements.

Comb, side, cut steel, crown motif, late Victorian 185.00
Comb, Spanish, ornate design,
    5-1/2" l 45.00
Compact 12.50
Glove Box, domed lid, ornate ivory
    strapping, sandalwood int.,
    3-1/2" h 375.00
Hand Mirror, oval 110.00

Cigarette Case, hinged, snap closure, $200.

Letter Opener, silver fox-head handle,
    12" l 225.00
Match Safe, pocket, emb sides 65.00
Model, rickshaw, hinged hood, spoked
    wheels, metal poles, 8" l 110.00
Patch Box, rect, slightly domed lid, ivory
    trim 200.00
Pill Box, small ivory feet, 2-1/2" l . . .80.00
Pin, pique, yellow gold, silver, domed
    circle, flat hollow back, floral design,
    c1860 .325.00
Ring Box .110.00
Scent Bottle Case, Georgian, arched cov,
    convex front and back, 2-1/2" h. 110.00
Stickpin, carved fly perched on coral
    branch, gold-filled pin 75.00
Stickpin, Pique, yellow gold, domed disk,
    inlaid circles, c1880 . . . . .200.00
Trinket Box, rect, lacquered, hinged lid,
    single drawer, 9-1/2" l 250.00

Toys

The difference between men and boys is the price of their toys. At 30, one's childhood is affordable, at 40 expensive and at 50 out of reach. Check the following list for toys that you may have played with. You will see what I mean.

Clubs: Antique Toy Collectors of America, Two Wall St., New York, NY 10005; Diecast Exchange Club Newsletter, P.O. Box 1066, Pinellas Park, FL 34665; Majorette Diecast Toy Collectors Association, 1347 N.W. Albany Ave., Bend, OR 97701.

Periodicals: *Antique Toy World*, P.O. Box 34509, Chicago, IL 60634; *Collecting Toys*, P.O. Box 1612, Waukesha, WI 53187; *Toy Shop*, 700 E. State St., Iola, WI 54990; *Toy Trader*, P.O. Box 1050, Dubuque, IA 52004.

Amico, Highway Drive, battery operated, litho tin and plastic, 15-1/2" l, orig box, $100.

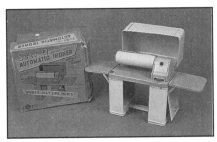

GW, Japan, Suzy-Q Automatic Ironer, battery operated, tin, pink and blue, 12-1/4" w, 7" h, orig box, $150.

Marx

Airplane, mkd "12", pilot wearing helmet and goggles, 6" l, 3-1/2" h 17.50
Butterfly, brightly colored wings, tumbles, 7-3/4" l, 2-1/2" h 30.00
Charlie McCarthy, walks, 8" h 165.00
Colonial Dollhouse, No. 4052, litho tin 60.00
Dishwasher K54, c1950s 60.00
Jumpin' Jeep, driver and passenger, two small wheels at front, two large wheels at center, 5-1/2" l, 4-1/4" h 100.00
Typewriter No. 1110, metal and plastic, c1950s-60s. 15.00

Other

Bandai, Japan, Chevrolet Convertible, friction, 9-1/2" l, 1956, orig box shows 1957 Chevy 475.00
Britains, toy soldiers, French Cuirassiers, set #138, orig box. 140.00
Coleco, Busy Box 6.00
Coleco, Horton the Elephant, sitting on egg, plush doll, 13" h, 1983 . . . . .35.00
Colorforms, Bozo the Clown, 1962 . .30.00

Irwin, Mechanical Walking Bear, #622, windup, brown plastic body, fabric cov, 5-1/4" l, 4-1/2" h, orig box, $175.

Playskool, Dairy Wagon, wood, $20.

Colorforms, Charlie's Angels, 1978 . 30.00
Cragstan, Japan, Ford Retractable, battery-operated, remote control, 10-1/2" l, 1959. . . . . 225.00
Gilbert, Mickey Mouse Club's Professor Wonderful's Wonder-Lab, science kit, 13" by 19" boxed set, 1964. . . . . 75.00
Hasbro, Mr. Potato Head, parts for faces, plastic car, boat trailer, 1950s. . . 75.00
Ichiko, Japan, Oldsmobile Rocket 88, two-door hardtop, gold trim, 13" l, 1960, orig box. 600.00
Ideal, Mr. Machine, 17-1/2" h, whistles, 1972 . . . . 30.00
Japan, Buick Roadmaster Sedan, friction, 11-1/2" l, 1951. . . . . 35.00
JNF, West Germany, Packard Convertible, working headlights and drive chain, wind-up and battery-operated, cardboard luggage in trunk, 11-1/2" l, orig box. 385.00
Kenner, Big Burger Grill, working electric grill, food mixes, 1967. . . . . 50.00
Kenner, Bubble-Matic, Bubble Shooting Gun, with 20 bubble-making tablets to load into gun with water, on card, 1965 . . . . 50.00
Kenner, Easy Bake Oven, 1960s. . . 35.00
Knickerbocker, Alvin (Alvin and the Chipmunks), puppet, stuffed body, vinyl head, 11" h 40.00
Knickerbocker, Bozo, Bend-'em doll, bendable body, rubber head, 8" h 30.00

Bird, windup, litho tin, unmarked, $35.

Lehman, Balky Mule, mule pulling three-wheeled cart and driver, 7-1/2" l, 5" h 110.00
Lehman, Wild West Bronco, bucking bronco with rider, 6" l, 7-1/2" h . 550.00
Lincoln Logs, 1947 . . . . 20.00
M, Japan, Dodge Gasoline Tanker, friction, 8-1/2" l, c1958 . . . . 110.00
Mattel, Herman Munster, doll, 20" h, 1964 . . . . 90.00
Mattel, Jack-in-the-Box, "Farmer In The Dell," tin, crank handle, 7" h, 1951 . . . . 85.00
Ohio Art, Children's Tea Set, tin, 14 pcs, 1950s. 75.00
Porter, Chemcraft Beginners Chemistry Set, No. 602, 1956 . . . . 20.00
Remco, Mr. Tricko, magic set, 1965 . . . . 120.00
Schuco, Ford four-door Sedan, Micro Racer, wind-up, #1045, 4-1/2" l, 1957 . . . . 150.00
TT, Japan, Jaguar, E-type, litho tin int., chrome accents, 11" l, mid 1960s, orig box. 325.00
Stevens, kaleidoscope, 1950s 15.00
Slinky, 1947, orig box 12.00

Trains, Toy

Toy train collectors and dealers exist in a world unto themselves. They have their own shows, trade publications and price guides. The name you need to know is Greenberg Books, now a division of Kalmbach Publishing, 21027 Crossroads Circle, Waukesha, WI 53187. If you decide to get involved with toy trains, write for a catalog. The two most recognized names are American Flyer and Lionel, and the two most popular gauges are S and O. Do not overlook other manufacturers and gauges. Note: The following prices are for equipment in good condition.

The toy train market has gone through a number of crazes—first Lionel, then American Flyer. The current craze is boxed sets. Fortunately, the market is so broad that there will never be an end to subcategories to collect.

Clubs: American Flyer Collectors Club, P.O. Box 13269, Pittsburgh, PA 15243; Lionel Collector's Club of America, P.O. Box 479, La Salle, IL

American Flyer, 630, caboose, 3/16 scale, orig box, $10.

61301; National Model Railroad Association, 4121 Cromwell Rd., Chattanooga, TN 37421; Train Collectors Association, P.O. Box 248, Strasburg, PA 17579.

Periodical: *Classic Toy Trains*, P.O. Box 1612, Waukesha, WI 53187.

American Flyer, Post-War, S-Gauge
Car, 752, Seabord Coaler, missing roof and two window inserts 132.00
Car, 23785, coal loader, three-button controller 363.00
Car, 23787, remote control Log Loader, missing man. 99.00
Set, 300 locomotive and tender, 639 reefer, 625 tank, 628 lumber, two 635 derricks, 629 cattle, 632 hopper, 630 caboose. 90.00
Set, 561 locomotive, 3/16th, 558 tender, 594 baggage, three 495 Pullmans 175.00
Set, 1494, The Lone Scout, 4685 locomotive, 4250 combine, 4251 coach, 4252 observation car. 3,750.00
Set, 3115 locomotive, two 3281 coaches, 3282 observation car, two-tone blue 350.00
Set, 3226 locomotive, AFL tender, 3216 lumber, 3208 box car, 3207 gondola, 3217 caboose Set . . . ., 450.00
Set, 3308 locomotive, 3189 tender, two 3171 Pullmans, 3172 observation car, buff and green 175.00
Set, 4006, 3/16th, 545 locomotive, 486 hopper, 480 Shell tank, 478 box car, two 484 cabooses 450.00
Set, 4684 locomotive, two Bunker Hill coaches, Yorktown observation car, orange roofs. 495.00
Set, Hiawatha Train Set, locomotive, tender, two coaches, observation car. 1,320.00

Set, Presidents Special Train Set, 4689 Commander locomotive, 4390 combine, 4393 diner, 4391 coach, 4392 observation, two-tone blue enamel 5,000.00

Lionel
42 Locomotive, standard gauge, single motor, thick rims, gray, minor dings . . . 450.00
52 Fire Car, orig box 300.00
60 Trolley, black letters, brakeman 465.00
164 Lumber Loader, orig box taped 300.00
203 Locomotive, 1941 high box coupler 525.00
215 Tank Car, standard gauge, pea green and brass, orig box 325.00
217 Caboose, standard gauge, orange and maroon, no box. 230.00
221 SF Alco, khaki, made for J.C. Penney. 300.00
255 Locomotive & 263W Tender, gunmetal. 775.00
419 Combine, standard gauge, mojave, maroon and wood-grain trim. . . 185.00
514 Box car, standard gauge, yellow and orange, no box 150.00
520 Searchlight Car, standard gauge, green and nickel, small chips near searchlight 230.00
629 Burlington 44 Tonner, orig box and insert 650.00
671 RR Turbine & 2046-50 PA Tender, some touch-up 325.00
751E City of Portland Train Set, 752E Power Car, 753 Coach, 754 Observation Car, silver, orig individual and set boxes 4,500.00
1350 Service Station F-3 Special Train Set, 8366 and 8365 CP F-3 AA, 9725, 9113, 9723, 9724 and 9165, orig set box 600.00
2338 Milwaukee GP9, sealed in orig box 1,200.00
6436-500 Girl's Train Hopper, small scratch 385.00
6464-325 B&O Sentinel Box Car, orig box 1,000.00
6464-500 Timken Box Car, yellow and white, tab-end trucks, orig box . 225.00
6517-75 Erie Bay Window Caboose, orig box 775.00
6556 MKT Two-Level Stock Car, orig box. 300.00

Marx
Allstate F9 ABA, NYC box car, NYC crane, Erie gondola, one container, Allstate flat with fuel tanks, Allstate bay-window caboose, open box car 295.00

112, Lehigh Valley, diesel switcher locomotive, red plastic, 1974-76 . 15.00
251, Canadian Pacific "Vancouver," maroon, gold lettering, black frame, four wheel, 6" l 60.00
396, Canadian Pacific, steam locomotive, streamlined, sheet metal, electric motor, black cab, copper boiler and sideboards, 1941. . . . . .20.00
548, Guernsey Milk, gondola, blue, cream int., four silver milk cans, eight wheel, 6" l. 35.00
551, New York Central, tender for steam locomotive, four wheel, blue, 1934-41 and 1950-55 . . . . .20.00
554, Northern Pacific, high side gondola, red, yellow int., silver frame, four wheel, 6", 1938-40 . . . . .7.00
567, New York Central, dump car, yellow, brown int., red and white frame, four wheel, 6" l 18.00
901 WP F9 ABA, gray and yellow . 250.00
1095 SF F9 ABA, with 4427 caboose. 100.00
1235, Southern Pacific, caboose, red and silver, 7" l, 1952-55 . . . . .5.00
1998, Rock Island, S-3 diesel, dummy, red and gray, 1962 . . . . .40.00
2002 NH F9 ABA, with NH caboose. 110.00
2124 B&M Budd car, orig box. 245.00
3824, Union Pacific, caboose, yellow and brown, black frame, four wheel, 6" l 3.00
4000, Penn central F9 AA, with 18326 Penn Central Caboose 285.00
4000, NYC F9 AA, orig box and insert. 200.00
4360, Cape Canaveral Set, 400 locomotive, red CCE tender, two Danger gondolas, rocket fuel tank, rocket launcher flat with red white and blue missiles, figure, RCC caboose, orig box 200.00
5532, Allstate, tank car, plastic, turquoise, eight wheel, 1962 . . . . .5.00
24235 Train Set, 490 locomotive, NYC tender, two chemical tank cars, PA gondola, Pacemaker caboose. . . 65.00
86000, Lackawanna, hopper, blue, red int., four wheel, 6" l, 1953. . . . . .3.00
131000, Seaboard Coast Line, gondola, yellow, four wheel, 1973 . . . . .2.00

Traps

When the animal rights activists of the 1960s surfaced, trap collectors crawled back into their dens. You will find trap collectors at flea markets, but they are quiet types. Avoid traps that show excessive wear and pitting. To be

Mouse, wood and metal, four spring, 4-1/2" d, $20.

Advertising, Ace-Hy Beverages, metal, 13" by 10", $35.

Advertising, Coca-Cola, 1961, $20.

collectible, a trap should be in good working order. Careful when testing one. You may get trapped yourself.

Club: North American Trap Collectors Association, P.O. Box 94, Galloway, OH 43119.

Bear, Kodiak, chain and swivel, Herter's
   #6 . . . . .425.00
Bee 40.00
Bird, Thayer. 700.00
Coyote and Fox, Verbail 100.00
Double Jaw, Sabo 90.00
Fish, broken trigger, Gabriel 210.00
Fly, Sears Farm Master. 50.00
Fly, Wee Stinky, fruit jar 10.00
Gopher, Crago 200.00
Gopher, Evans 200.00
Gopher, Gilson 400.00
Humane Trap, Cooper #2 . . . . .50.00
Ice Fishing, 15" l, walnut tip-up, attached
   brass reel, sliding break
   mechanism. 75.00
Minnow, handmade, 12" l, metal and mesh,
   hinged door 32.00
Minnow, Shakespeare, 1 gal, glass, pale
   green, metal lid, emb name 85.00
Mouse, CM Coghill, attaches to
   Mason jar 15.00
Mouse, Wire mesh, 9" l 40.00
Otter, coyote and bear, drag hooks, No. 14,
   Oneida .50.00
Partridge, Davenport. 110.00
Rat, Gladiator 35.00
Rat, Little Jimmy, wood and tin,
   live trap. 20.00
Save-a-leg, two sets of jaws 55.00

Trays

Tin lithographed advertising trays date back to the last quarter of the 19th century. They were popular at any location where beverages, alcoholic and nonalcoholic, were served. Because they were heavily used, it is not unusual to find dents and scratches. Check carefully for rust. Once the lithographed surface was broken, rust developed easily. Smaller trays are generally tip trays. Novice collectors often confuse them with advertising coasters. Tip trays are rather expensive. Ordinary examples sell from $50 to $75.

Advertising
Braumeister, man holding bottle
   and glass 45.00
Chero-Cola 65.00
Coca-Cola, Cotton Bowl Champs, tin,
   1976 . . . . 25.00
Columbus Brewing Co., 4-1/4" d, tip, early
   1900s 75.00
Cottolene Shortening, 4-1/2" d, litho tin,
   multicolored illus, black ground, NK
   Fairbank Co. 40.00
Deer Creek Ice Cream. 125.00
Dr Pepper, King of Beverage 35.00
Falls City Brewing Co., 13" d, topless girl
   on horse 250.00
Ferris Brick Co. 25.00
Franklin Life Insurance, tip. 30.00
Genessee Twelve Horse Ale 75.00
Geo. Ehret's Hellgate Brewery, NY, 13-1/2"
   by 16-3/4", oval, tin 25.00
Globe Wernecke 85.00
Hampdan's Ale, handsome waiter . 165.00
Hyroller Whiskey 25.00
Incandescent Light & Stove Co., tip. 75.00
Kenny's Tea and Coffee 40.00
Martha Washington Wine 95.00
Mascot Crushed Cut Tobacco 30.00
Moxie Centennial, 1984 . . . . 35.00
New England Brewing, stag illus . . . 65.00
Old Elkhorn Rye. 35.00
Parsely Salmon 40.00
Pepsi Cola, Hits the Spot, 1940s . . . 15.00
Round Oak Stove 18.00
Stollwerck Chocolate, tip 25.00
Union Pacific Tea 70.00
Wrigley's Soap 65.00

Commemorative
Kentucky Derby, 100th running, litho tin,
   color illus black rim, gold rose design
   rim 55.00
King Edward VIII, metal 95.00
Prince of Wales, 12" d, metal, purple
   ground, 1969 . . . . 35.00
Silver Jubilee, Queen Elizabeth II center
   portrait, metal, white ground 12.00

Kitchen
Aluminum, hand-wrought, fruit design,
   15-1/2" l 22.00
Aluminum, hand-wrought, tulip motif,
   handles, 14" l 35.00
Graniteware, mottled blue and
   white 125.00
Papier-mâché, rec, black ground, gold
   floral dec, mkd "Occupied Japan" . 8.00

Other
Change, Tom Moore Cigars 20.00
Character, Pinocchio and Gepetto, 8" by
   10", litho tin, c1940 . . . . 20.00
Pin-up, litho tin, model posed in martini
   glass, Beautebox, 1920s 150.00

Trolls

The modern troll craze was originally born in the 1960s. A second wave of popularity swept the nation in the 1990s, and trolls became popular with both boys and girls. Although trolls have been made in all shapes and sizes, their unique facial features and hair easily distinguish them from other dolls.

Newsletters: *Troll Monthly*, 216 Washington St., Canton, MA 02021;

Troll'n, P.O. Box 601292, Sacramento, CA 95860.

Dolls

Ace Novelty Co., Treasure Trolls, purple hair, blue eyes, shiny multicolored outfit, round, purple wishstone 7.00

Dam, Caveman, 12" h, 1964 . . . . . .115.00

Dam, Cow, 7" h, limited edition 65.00

Dam, Elephant, 6" h, limited edition, 1990 . . . . .65.00

Dam, Indian Girl, feather, belt 45.00

Dam, Princess, 6" h. 25.00

Dam, Santa, 7" h. 50.00

Norwegian, NyForm, pine-cone body, 3-1/2" h, mohair frame, painted lips and eyes, fur tail, pipe cleaner legs, block feet 11.00

Norwegian, NyForm, Viking, wooden, 3" h. 5.00

Russ, Aged to Perfection, 4-1/2" h, #18320 .7.00

Russ, Angel, 4" h, white dress, gold trim, wings 7.00

Russ, Baby Troll, 9" h, #2330, blue and white sleeper 13.00

Russ, Clown, 9" h, #3604, vinyl, fabric 17.00

Russ, Froggie, 12" h, #2412 . . . . . .20.00

Russ, Martian Girl, 4" h, #18531, silver dress 8.00

Uneeda Doll and Toy Co., Wishniks, Cowboy, 3-1/2" h, yellow hair, red checked shirt, blue jeans, tulip design scarf, plastic hat. 15.00

Uneeda Doll and Toy Co., Wishniks, Hunt-Nik, 3" h, red and black checkered flannel shirt, red pants, blue cap, red hair 20.00

Uneeda Doll and Toy Co., Wishniks, Naked Troll, 5" h, blonde hair, amber eyes, mkd on head "Uneeda Doll Co Inc., 1964" 15.00

Uneeda Doll and Toy Co., Wishniks, Pik-Nik, 5" h, bendable, orig package, 1982 . . . . .15.00

Other

Book, *It's a Dam Dam World*, Hal Goodman and Larry Klein, hardcover, c1965 . . . . .15.00

Case, Shanty Shack, plastic handle, Ideal 35.00

Charm, 1" l, sterling silver, mkd "NORGE" 10.00

Christmas Stocking, plush, fabric, red, white and green, Commonwealth Toy & Novelty Co.. . . . . .5.00

Cookie Cutter, aluminum, 3-1/2" h, Mirro. 25.00

Halloween Costume, Wishnik, flannel, satin, plastic mask, mkd "1965 D T.E. Uneeda, Ben Cooper," MIB 125.00

Nodder, Bobblehead Buddies, 8-1/2" h, vinyl, Chicago Cubs, mkd "Russ MLB 1992". 10.00

Nodder, Lucky Nik, 5" h, Japan, 1967 . . . . 30.00

Pin, 1" l, metal, mkd "REG. DES. 904-395" 35.00

Record, The Wishnik Family, Songs-Fun-Games, Little World Records, 1965 . . . . 75.00

Ring, 3/4" h, plastic, rhinestone eyes, yellow nylon hair 20.00

Trophies

There are trophies for virtually everything. Ever wonder what happens to them when the receiver grows up or dies? Most wind up in landfills. It is time to do something about this injustice. If you plan on collecting them, focus on shape and unusual nature of the award. Set a $5 limit—not much of a handicap when it comes to trophy collecting. Always check the metal content of trophies. A number of turn-of-the-century trophies are sterling silver. These obviously have weight value, as well as historic value. Also suspect sterling silver when the trophy is a plate.

Turtle Collectibles

Turtle collectors are a slow and steady group who are patient about expanding their collection of objects relating to these funny little reptiles. Don't you believe it! My son is one of those collectors and he's not at all slow when it come to expanding his collection. Turtle collectibles are everwhere. Like all animal collectibles, they come in all shapes and sizes. Candles, toys, storybooks, jewelry and ornaments featuring turtles can be found at almost any flea market. Watch out for tortoise shell items. This material is subject to the provisions of the Federal Endangered Species Act.

Bank, plaster, figural, 5" h, mkd "Freddy B. Turtle/Aviva Ent. Inc./Made in Taiwan/Republic of China" on bottom 4.00

Brooch, wood body, carved clear Lucite shell, 3" by 2". 50.00

Cookie Jar, figural Donatello, Teenage Mutant Ninja Turtles, Mirage Studios 35.00

Dish, cov, figural turtle finial, scroll base, two handles, 7-1/2" l 185.00

Dish, cov, two-piece, 10" l, L.G. Wright Glass Co.. . . . . .70.00

Doll, Touche Turtle, cloth and vinyl, Ideal. 80.00

Doorstop, cast iron, 3" by 8-3/4", Wilton .65.00

Doorstop, granite, hp face 12.00

Figure, amber, 5-1/2" l, Viking Glass 15.00

Flower Holder, crystal satin, 19 holes, 3-1/2" by 5-1/4", Cambridge . . .150.00

Paperweight, figural, cast iron, Fire Insurance adv on celluloid insert on hinged shell lid, int. mirror, early 1900s, 4" l 150.00

Planter, figural, white matte glaze, McCoy. .5.00

Plate, bowl and mug set, Teenage Mutant Ninja Turtles, MIB, 1989 . . . . . . .18.00

Salt and Pepper Shakers, pr, metal . 10.00

Servant's Bell, cast iron, figural, 2-1/2" by 7" 300.00

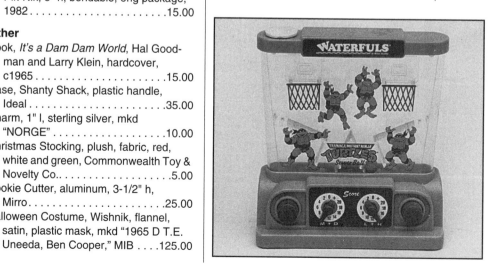

Water Toy, Teenage Mutant Ninja Turtles, Turtles Sewer Ball, Milton Bradley Waterfuls, $10.

Typewriters

The first commercially produced typewriter in America was the 1874 Shoels and Gliden machine produced by E. Remington & Sons. The last quarter of the 19th century was spent largely in experimentation and attempting to make the typewriter an integral part of every office environment, something that was achieved by 1910. Although there were early examples, the arrival of a universally acceptable electric typewriter dates from the 1950s.

The number of typewriter collectors is small, but growing. Machines made after 1915 have little value, largely because they do not interest collectors. Do not use the patent date on a machine to date its manufacture. Many models were produced for decades. Do not overlook typewriter ephemera. Early catalogs are helpful in identifying and dating machines.

Clubs: Internationales Forum Historishe Burowelt, Postfach 500 11 68, D-5000 Koln-50, Germany; Early Typewriter Collectors Association, 2591 Military Ave., Los Angeles, CA 90064.
Newsletters: *Ribbon Type News*, 28 The Green, Watertown, CT 06795; *The Typewriter Exchange*, 2125 Mt. Vernon St., Philadelphia, PA 19130.

Typewriters

Bing	130.00
Corona Folding	60.00
Demountable	80.00
Fox, No. 23	140.00
Harris Visible, No. 4	90.00
L.C. Smith, No. 3	25.00
Mignon, No. 4	150.00
National, No. 2-5	100.00
Noiseless	175.00
Oliver, No. 2	200.00
Rem-Sho	250.00
Remington, No. 10-12	50.00
Royal, No. 5	25.00
Smith Premier, No. 2-10	50.00
Standard Folding	250.00
Sun, No. 3	250.00
Underwood, portable	25.00
Wellington	150.00
Woodstock, No. 5	25.00

Typewriter Ribbon Tins

Beaver Brand	6.00
Burrough's	7.00
Carter's	8.00
Challenge Brand	7.00
Franklin Ribbon & Carbon Co.	7.00
Kleanwrite	7.00
Madame Butterfly	8.00
Midnight	5.00

Other

Advertising Trade Card, Simplex Typewriter, die-cut, Santa Claus holding typewriter, 1913	20.00
Booklet, Blickenderfer Typewriter, four pgs, Pan-American Expo giveaway, 1901	30.00
Booklet, The Typewriter: A Short History, Zellers, 1873-1948	7.00
Catalog, Oliver Typewriter Co., Chicago, 24 pgs, c1902	75.00

Umbrellas

Umbrellas suffer a sorry fate. They are generally forgotten and discarded. Their handles are removed and collected as separate entities or attached to magnifying glasses. Given the protection they have provided, they deserve better.

Look for umbrellas that have advertising on the fabric. Political candidates often gave away umbrellas to win votes. Today, baseball teams have umbrella days to win fans. Seek out unusual umbrellas in terms of action or shape. A collection of folding umbrellas, especially those from the 1950s, is worth considering.

Advertising, Japan Tea, floral designs and mastiff dog medallion, "Mastiff Extra Chop, Choicest Japan Tea, Abbott Grocery," 65" d open size, 40" h	100.00
Advertising, The Morning Call, Allentown, PA, newspaper, comic strip characters, unused	25.00
Beach	5.00
Golf, metal shaft	3.00
New York World's Fair, 1939, 28" d, child's, multicolored	40.00

Common, floral fabric, $1.

Disney, early, $150.

New York World's Fair, 1939, 32" d, green, blue and orange	35.00

Universal Pottery

Universal Potteries of Cambridge, Ohio, was organized in 1934 by The Oxford Pottery Co. It purchased the Atlas-Globe plant properties. The Atlas-Globe operation was a merger of the Atlas China Co., (formerly Crescent China Co., in 1921, Tritt in 1912 and Bradshaw in 1902) and the Globe China Co. Even after the purchase, Universal retained the Oxford ware, made in Oxford, Ohio, as part of its dinnerware line. Another Oxford plant was used to manufacture tiles. The plant at Niles, Ohio, was dismantled.

Three of Universal's most popular lines were Ballerina, Calico Fruit and Cattail. Both Calico Fruit and Cattail had many accessory pieces. The 1940 and 1941, Sears catalogs listed an oval wastebasket, breakfast set, kitchen scale, linens and bread box in the Cattail pattern. Unfortunately, the Calico Fruit decal has not held up well over time. Collectors may have to settle for less-than-perfect pieces.

Not all Universal pottery carried the Universal name as part of the backstamp. Wares marked "Harmony House," "Sweet William/Sears Roebuck and Co.," and "Wheelock Peoria" are part of the Universal production line. Wheelock was a department store in Peoria, Ill., that controlled the Cattail pattern on the Old Holland-shape.

Periodical: *The Daze*, P.O. Box 57, Otisville, MI 48463.

Ballerina
Cup 5.00
Platter, 13" d 10.00
Salt and Pepper Shakers, pr. 15.00
Teapot, 6 cup 25.00

Bittersweet
Casserole, 5 pt 25.00
Creamer 6.00
Cup 6.00
Plate, 7-1/8" d 5.00
Plate, 9" d 8.00
Stack Set, round, four pc. 45.00

Calico Fruit
Custard Cup, 5 oz 5.00
Jug, cov. 40.00
Plate, 6" d, bread and butter 5.00
Salt and Pepper Shakers, pr, range .20.00
Soup, tab handle 6.00
Stack Set, round, four pc. 45.00

Cattail
Casserole, cov, 8-1/4" d 15.00
Cookie Jar, cov 50.00
Gravy Boat .20.00
Milk Jug, 1 qt. 20.00
Platter, oval .20.00
Vegetable Bowl 15.00

Mount Vernon
Casserole, 7-1/2" h 25.00
Creamer 10.00
Plate, 9" d 3.00
Saucer. 1.50
Teapot. 30.00

Rodeo
Creamer 5.00
Plate, 6-1/4" h 2.00
Saucer. 1.50

Urinals

When you gotta go, you gotta go—any port in a storm. You have been in enough bathrooms to know that all plumbing fixtures are not equal. The human mind has just begun to explore the recycling potential of hospital bed pans. Among the uses noted are flower planters, food serving utensils and dispersal units at the bottom of down spouts. How have you used them? Send your ideas and pictures of them in action to the Bedpan Recycling Project, 5093 Vera Cruz Rd., Emmaus, PA 18049.

Valentines

There is far too much emphasis placed on adult valentines from the 19th century through the 1930s. It's true they are lacy and loaded with romantic sentiment. But, are they fun?

No! Fun can be found in children's valentines, a much neglected segment of the valentine market. If you decide to collect them, focus on the 1920-1960 penny valentines. The artwork is bold, vibrant, exciting and a tad corny. This is what makes them fun.

There is another good reason to collect 20th century children's valentines. They are affordable. Most sell for less than $2, with many good examples from 25 cents to 50 cents. They often show up at flea markets as a hoard. When you find them, make an offer for the whole lot. You won't regret it.

Club: National Valentine Collectors Association, P.O. Box 1404, Santa Ana, CA 92702.

Die-cut
Basket of violets, easel back, c1920 10.00
Girl in pink dress, easel back,
 c1910-20. . . . . 18.00

Honeycomb
Baby in basket with yellow honeycomb
 balloon, c1930 . . . . 15.00
Basket, cupid motif, c1925. . . . . 65.00
Blue pitcher, Lilies of the Valley and
 Forget-Me-Nots, 1900-15 . . . . . . 65.00
Red heart, cats and cupids easel back,
 4" by 6-1/2" h 45.00
Scout, "I'm Wig-Wagging I Love You To My
 Valentine," 1930 . . . . 7.00
Squirrel pushing red honeycomb heart,
 c1930 . . . . 15.00

Mechanical, Germany
Clown sitting on dog, 1930 . . . . 35.00
Kitten in basket, 1930s 15.00
Paper Lace
Do-it-yourself kit, die-cut hearts,
 envelopes, folders, paper lace,
 instructions, A-Meri-Card, 1945 . 45.00
Cupid, daisies and butterfly, rect, orig
 envelope, 1800s 55.00
Diamond, cupid and flower motif . . . 35.00
Winter landscape, silver lace, Dresden,
 19th C 65.00

Postcard, No. 265, printed in U.S.A, divided back, $2.50.

Pull-Out
Bridge covered with Forget-Me-Nots,
 Germany, 1933 . . . . .20.00
Forget-Me-Nots, ferns, rosebuds and
 doves, c1910 . . . . .45.00
Horseshoe, cherubs and roses,
 c1920-30 . . . . .65.00
Red hearts and roses, Germany,
 1910-20 .25.00

Ventriloquist Dummies

The most famous ventriloquists of all time are probably Edgar Bergen, Paul Winchell and Jimmy Nelson. At the height of their careers, mass-produced toys and other items were numerous. Many of them are now quite expensive and hard to find. However, beware! Because of their popularity, many dummies are still being produced today by the same toy companies.

One of the largest distributors of toy dummies is Juro (now called Goldberger Doll). The company produced many different dummies throughout its history, the most expensive of which are those earlier examples which are no longer being produced.

Advisor: Andy Gross, P.O. Box 6134, Beverly Hills, CA 90212, (310) 820-3308.

Charlie McCarthy
Effanbee, 1938, composition head, hands
 and feet or shoes, string behind neck
 operates mouth, 15" to 24" h, made in
 five different outfits including black tux,
 white suit and hat, white tails, overcoat
 and blue jacket, mkd "EFFanBEE" on
 lower part of neck block,
 with box 2,500.00
Same as previous, without box. . . . 650.00
Juro, may be marked "EEGEE" or "Larry
 Harmon," date behind neck denotes
 date of mold, plastic, string behind neck
 operates mouth, 24" to 30" h, modern,
 with box .50.00
Same as previous, without box. 25.00

Danny O'Day
Brooklyn Mass Co., composition, wearing
 Texaco Suit and hat with tag reading
 "Jimmy Nelson's Danny O'Day," mkd
 "Danny O'Day J.N.E." on back of neck,
 with box 1,400.00
Same as previous, without box. . . . 700.00
Juro, hollow body, head stick with string to
 operate mouth, black and white
 checkered suit with box 320.00
Same as previous, without box. . . . 270.00

Jerry Mahoney
Juro, plastic, hollow body, head stick with pull string to operate mouth, doll unmkd, orig box marked "Juro," green suit with tag reading "Paul Winchell's Jerry Mahoney," painted red hair, painted eyes looking to left, Deluxe Model, moving eyes, with box and booklet. 675.00
Same as previous, Deluxe Model, without box. .550.00
Same as previous, Standard Model, with box and booklet 500.00
Same as previous, Standard Model, without box. 375.00

Knucklehead Smiff
Juro, plastic, string behind neck operates mouth, red to brown hair, with box 1,250.00
Same as previous, without box 950.00
Paul Winchell, 1966, hard vinyl head, stuffed body, string behind neck operates mouth, mkd "Paul Winchell, 1966" on back of neck, with box.600.00
Same as previous, without box 500.00

Other
Clown Dummy, Pelham, England, head stick, mouth lever 125.00
Dummy Boy, Pelham, England, head stick, mouth lever, fur hair 125.00
Dummy Dan, late 1920s, composition, resembles Charlie McCarthy without monocle, string in back of neck operates mouth, various outfits including black tux and black and white checkered suit with checkered hat, various sizes, composition or stuffed cloth hands and shoes, unmkd 400.00
Dummy Dog, Pelham, England, head stick, mouth lever 125.00
Farfel, Jimmy Nelson's dog, Juro, used in Nestles commercials, with box. .300.00
Same as previous, without box 400.00
Mickey Mouse, Horsman, 1970-80s, hollow body, head stick, various outfits including red jack and black tux with tails, with box 350.00
Same as previous, without box 270.00
Moe, Three Stooges, Horsman, late 1970s, early 1980s, hollow body, head stick control with trigger for mouth movement, wearing red, white and blue plaid outfit with yellow shirt and red tie, with box 370.00
Same as previous, without box 300.00
Mortimer Snerd, Juro, may be marked "EE-GEE" or "Larry Harmon," date behind neck denotes date of mold, plastic, string behind neck operates mouth, 24" to 30" h, modern, with box 50.00
Same as previous, without box 25.00
Simon Sez, Horsman, 1980s, hollow body, head stick, shirt reads "Simon Sez" on front, with box. 225.00

Same as previous, without box . . . 300.00
Willie Talk, Horsman, 1980s, string at back of neck operates mouth, shirt reads "Willie Talk" on front, with box. . . 50.00
Same as previous, without box 20.00

Vernon Kilns

Founded in Vernon, Calif., in 1912, Poxon China was one of the many small potteries flourishing in southern California. By 1931, it was sold to Faye G. Bennison and renamed Vernon Kilns, but it was also known as Vernon Potteries Ltd. Under Bennison's direction, the company became a leader in the pottery industry.

The high quality and versatility of its product made Vernon ware very popular. Besides a varied dinnerware line, Vernon Kilns also produced Walt Disney figurines and advertising, political and fraternal items. One popular line was historical and commemorative plates, which included several plate series featuring scenes from England, California missions and the West.

Surviving the Depression, fires, earthquakes and wars, Vernon Kilns could not compete with the influx of imports. In January 1958, the factory was closed. Metlox Potteries of Manhattan Beach, Calif., bought the trade name and molds along with the remaining stock.

Newsletter: *Vernon Views*, P.O. Box 945, Scottsdale, AZ 85252.

Periodical: *The Pottery Collectors Express*, P.O. Box 221, Mayview, MO 54071.

Early California
Carafe, brown 25.00
Cup and Saucer, turquoise 5.00
Demitasse Creamer, dark blue 20.00
Platter, 12" l, orange 18.00
Salt and Pepper Shakers, pr, yellow 18.00
Vegetable Bowl, 8-1/2" d, orange . . 10.00

Gingham
Carafe 28.00
Chop Plate 10.00
Eggcup. 6.00
Pitcher, 11-1/2" h, ice lip 18.00
Plate, 10-1/2" d, dinner 6.00
Salt and Pepper Shakers, pr, range size 35.00
Soup Bowl, 8-1/2" d 12.00
Syrup 55.00

Gingham, salt and pepper shakers, pr, small size, $15.

Teapot, cov. 20.00

Hawaiian Flowers
Berry Bowl 14.50
Cup. 18.00
Plate, 6" d 8.50
Plate, 7" d 12.50
Plate, 8" d 16.00
Plate, 9-1/2" d 32.00
Plate, 10"d 24.00
Salt Shaker. 15.00
Saucer 10.00
Sugar, cov 26.00

Homespun
Butter, cov 55.00
Creamer 7.00
Coaster 3-7/8" d 8.00
Cup and Saucer 11.00
Demitasse Cup and Saucer 40.00
Fruit Bowl, 5-1/2" d 4.00
Gravy 10.00
Mixing Bowl, 8" d 16.00
Pitcher, 2 qt 30.00
Plate, 7-1/2" d 5.00
Plate, 9-1/2" d. 6.00
Salt and Pepper Shakers, pr 8.00
Sauce Boat, 6-1/2" l 10.00
Soup, lug handle. 7.00
Vegetable Bowl, 9" d, open 12.00

Modern California
Bowl, 6" d, orchid, handled. 12.00
Bowl, 9" d, azure blue. 35.00
Cup and Saucer, Pistachio green. . . 12.00
Cup and Saucer, Straw yellow 13.00
Fruit Bowl, 5-1/2" d, azure blue 8.00
Mug, azure blue 23.00
Plate, 6-1/4" d, bread and butter, azure blue 6.00
Plate, 6-1/4" d, bread and butter, Pistachio green. 6.00
Vegetable Bowl, oval, 9-1/2" l, azure blue 20.00

Organdie
Bowl, 7-1/4" d 5.00
Butter Dish, cov 35.00
Casserole, cov, individual. 15.00
Chop Plate, 12" d 12.00
Creamer 10.00
Cup and Saucer 7.00
Demitasse Cup and Saucer 25.00

Eggcup 25.00
Gravy 20.00
Plate, 6" d, bread and butter 2.00
Plate, 9-1/2" d, luncheon 6.00
Plate, 10-1/2" d, dinner 10.00
Platter, 14" l, oval 10.00
Salad Bowl, 9" d 15.00
Sugar, cov .14.00
Teapot, cov 65.00
Tidbit Tray, two tiers 24.00

Tam 'O Shanter
Casserole, cov, two handles 50.00
Plate, 6-1/4" d 5.50
Plate, 7-1/2" d, salad 8.00
Plate, 9-3/4" d, dinner 11.00
Platter, 12-1/2" l, oval 22.00

Tickled Pink
Butter, cov .36.00
Creamer 12.50
Cup and Saucer 12.00
Plate, 6" d 6.50
Plate, 7" d 7.50
Plate, 10" d 10.50
Platter, 9" l .16.00
Platter, 13" l 26.00
Relish, three-part 26.50
Sugar, cov .18.50
Vegetable Bowl, 9" d 18.50

Video Games

At the moment, most video games sold at a flea market are being purchased for reuse. There are a few collectors, but their numbers are small. It might be interesting to speculate about the long-term collecting potential of electronic children's games, especially since the Atari system has come and gone. The key to any toy is playability. A video game cartridge has little collecting value unless it can be put into a machine and played. As a result, the long-term value of video games will rest on collectors' ability to keep the machines that use them in running order. Given today's tendency to scrap rather than repair a malfunctioning machine, one wonders if there will be any individuals in 2041 that will understand how video game machines work and, if so, be able to get the parts required to play them.

Next to playability, displayability is important to any collector. How do you display video games? Is the answer to leave the TV screen on 24 hours a day? Video games are a fad waiting to be replaced by the next fad. There will always be a small cadre of players who will keep video games alive, just

Telstar, Coleco, $10.

as there is a devoted group of adventure game players. But given the number of video game cartridges sold, they should be able to fill their collecting urges relatively easily.

What this means is that if you are going to buy video game cartridges at a flea market, buy them for reuse and do not pay more than a few dollars. The more recent the game, the more you will pay. Wait. Once a few years have passed, the sellers will just be glad to get rid of them.

View Master

William Gruber invented and Sawyer's Inc., of Portland, Ore., manufactured and marketed the first View-Master viewers and reels in 1939. The company survived the shortages of World War II by supplying training materials in the View-Master format to the army and navy. Following World War II, a 1,000-dealer network taxed the capacity of the Sawyer plant. In 1946, the Model C, the most common of the viewers, was introduced. Sawyer was purchased by General Aniline & Film Corp., in 1966. After passing through other hands, View-Master wound up as part of Ideal Toys.

Do not settle for any viewer or reel in less than near-mint condition. Original packaging, especially reel envelopes, is very important. The category is still in the process of defining which reels are valuable and which are not. Most older, pre-1975, reels sell from 50 cents to $1.

Viewer, Sawyer's De Luxe Stereoscope, black Bakelite, 1948, $25.

Club: National Stereoscopic Association, P.O. Box 14801, Columbus, OH 43214.

Reels, packet of three, orig booklet and envelope
Alpine Wild Flowers, Sawyer's 12.50
Amazing Spider-Man, GAF #H-11 . .15.00
Archie, 1975 . . . . .30.00
Balance of Nature, Ecology,
    GAF #B-686 . . . . .25.00
Batman, GAF #B-492 . . . . .20.00
Brady Bunch, 1974 . . . . .45.00
Buck Rogers, GAF #L-15 . . . . .15.00
Buckaroo Banzai, GAF #4056,
    reels only 5.00
Butterflies of North America,
    GAF B-610 . . . . .10.00
Cowboy Stars, 1950s 20.00
Disneyland, 1960s/1970s, missing booklet,
    Fantasyland 18.00
Dracula, 1976 . . . . .20.00
Dr. Shrinker and the Wonderbug,
    Krofft Supershow No. 1 . . . . .30.00
Eight is Enough, 1980 . . . . .20.00
Family Affair, 1969 . . . . .50.00
Frankenstein, 1976 . . . . .20.00
Grizzly Adams, 1976 . . . . .25.00
Happy Days, 1974, The Not Making of a
    President 20.00
Harlem Globetrotters, 1977 . . . . . . .25.00
James Bond Moonraker, 1979 . . . . .30.00

Mickey Look Viewer Gift Set, plastic, six story reels, 1989, orig box, $8.

Jetsons, 1981 . . . . .20.00
Land of the Giants, 1968 . . . . .70.00
Lassie, Look Homeward, Sawyer #B-480,
    near mint 25.00
Laugh-In, GAF #B-497, mint, sealed.25.00
Lone Ranger, GAF Reissue 40.00
Man from U.N.C.L.E. Set, 1965, missing
    envelope 35.00
M*A*S*H, 1978 . . . . .25.00
MOD Squad 45.00
Mission Impossible, 1968 . . . . .50.00
Mork and Mindy Set, 1979 . . . . . . .18.00
Puss 'N Boots, GAF #B-320 . . . . . . .20.00
Roy Rogers 45.00
Seven Wonders of the World, Sawyer
    #B-901 .12.50
Six Million Dollar Man Set, 1974 . . . .30.00

Viewers

Model C, black plastic, reel inserted in top,
    1946 . . . . .25.00
Model D, lighted, focuses 35.00
Model H, lighted, round bottom, GAF logo
    on front, 1967-81 . . . . .15.00

Vogue Picture Records

Vogue picture records have been attracting the interest of collectors internationally for several years. They were invented by Tom Saffady and manufactured by his company Sav-Way Industries in Detroit in 1946 and 1947. These innovative, high-quality 78 rpm records were constructed with a central aluminum core for durability. A colorful paper illustration covering the entire record was applied to the core and then sealed in clear vinyl.

The beautiful multicolor pictures are often romantic, at times whimsical and frequently represent the song title. A small black-and-white photo of the artist appears as an insert at the margin of the illustration. The regular production Vogues were issued with a number in the range R707 to R786.

A wide variety of music can be found on Vogue picture records, including big band swing, jazz, country, Latin, fairy tales for children and even dance instructions. Eight albums, each containing two records, were released. Unfortunately, the record division of Sav-Way Industries was forced into bankruptcy after only 15 months of production, somewhat limiting the

R754, The Charlie Shavers Quintet, She's Funny That Way, $80.

availability of these highly collectible records.

Prices are for records in good average used condition. Premium prices can be obtained for records in excellent to near-mint condition.

Advisor: John Coates, 324 Woodland Dr., Stevens Point, WI 54481, (715) 341-6113.

R707, Sugar Blues/Basin Street Blues,
    Clyde McCoy & His Orchestra . . 40.00
R710, The Bells of St. Mary's/Star Dust,
    The Don Large Chorus 65.00
R714, Doodle Doo Doo/All I Do Is
    Wantcha, Art Kassel
    & His Orchestra 55.00
R718, Some Sunday Morning/In The Dog
    House Now, Lulu Belle & Scotty . 65.00
R719, Have I Told You Lately That I Love
    You/I Get A Kick Out Of Corn, Lulu Belle
    & Scotty 55.00

R776, Art Kassel Orchestra, If That Phone Ever Rings (And It's You), $65.

R721, You're Only In My Arms/When I
    Gets to Where I'm Goin',
    Patsy Montana 85.00
R725, Rhapsody In Blue-Part 1/Alice Blue
    Gown, The Hour of Charm All Girl
    Orchestra directed
    by Phil Spitalny 55.00
R733, Blue Skies/Seville, The Hour of
    Charm All Girl Orchestra directed by
    Phil Spitalny 55.00
R734, Sweetheart/A Little Consideration,
    Art Kassel & His Orchestra 75.00
R736, Out Where the West Winds
    Blow/Who's Gonna Kiss You When I'm
    Gone?, Kenny Roberts with The Down
    Homers 75.00
R737, Rhumba Lesson No. 1/Rhumba
    Lesson No. 3, Paul Shahin 55.00
R745, The Trial of "Bumble" The Bee-Part
    1/The Boy Who Cried Wolf-Part 1, The
    Jewell Playhouse directed by James
    Jewell 95.00
R753, At Sundown/Way Down Yonder In
    New Orleans, Clyde McCoy
    & His Orchestra 55.00
R754, She's Funny That Way/Dizzy's
    Dilemma, The Charlie Shavers
    Quintet 80.00
R760, So It Goes/The Minute Samba, Enric
    Madriguera and His Orchestra . . 65.00
R770, The Whiffenpoof Song/If That
    Phone Ever Rings, Art Kassel
    & His Orchestra 60.00
R771, If I Could Be With You/Jeannine, Art
    Kassel & His Orchestra 75.00
R774, Desert Fantasy/Save Me A Dream,
    Sonny Dunham & His Orchestra . 75.00
R780, Let's Get Married/Touch Me Not, Art
    Kassel & His Orchestra 55.00
R782, What Am I Gonna Do About
    You/Maybe You'll Be There,
    Joan Edwards 95.00

Wade Ceramics

Red Rose Tea issued several series of small Wade animals. Like many of my other collections, I will not be happy until I have multiple sets. "Drink more tea" is the order of the day at my office. How much simpler it would be just to make a list of the missing Wades and pick them up at flea markets where they sell in the 50 cent to $1 range.

Club: Wade Watch, 8199 Pierson Ct, Arvada, CO 80005.

Plates

Dominion of Canada, map and maple
    leaves illus 25.00
Nova Scotia, Canada, map, crest and
    provincial flower illus 25.00
Wellyphant, white, red and yellow. . .50.00

Posy Bowls

Barge, green 30.00
Caterpillar, beige. 90.00
Cherub, gray and yellow, white swan90.00

Vases

Art Nouveau-style, mottled, yellow, brown
    and green, Flaxman 244 . . . . . .150.00
Fantasia Series, gray, pink, black and
    white, "Fantasia by Wade of England-
    Walt Disney Productions"
    backstamp 160.00
Peony Series, hp, multicolored, Harvest
    Ware 313 . . . . .70.00

Other

Basket, emb basket weave design, emb
    flowers on front. 65.00
Butter Dish, cobbler, green and yellow . . .
    30.00
Cameo Dish, oval, emb rose design, brown
    and blue 10.00
Candles, porcelain, white, gold flowers . . .
    80.00
Cigarette Box, rect, copper, pink, yellow
    and green flowers and leaves . . .40.00
Flower Pot, Cherry Blossom, ftd, white,
    pink flowers 10.00
Frame, heart-shape, emb flower and
    leaves design 60.00
Jardiniere, two handled, oval, emb
    raindrop design bottom 20.00
Pin Tray, tailor, red, white and blue. .15.00
Wall Plaque, Sailboat, Yacht No. 7, blue,
    brown, white and gray 65.00
Wall Plaque, seagull, white, black
    and yellow 90.00
Wall Pocket, Gothic 159, triangular-shape,
    yellow, emb swirling leaves and tulips
    design. .60.00
Wall Pocket, three-sided, scroll design,
    yellow tulips, green leaves 90.00

Walgreen's Collectibles

What was your favorite drugstore? I have fond memories of hanging out at the local soda fountain—nothing could compare to the malted milk and ice cream concoctions of my youth. Unfortunately, most soda fountain counters have long been dismantled.

In the old days a trip to Walgreen's meant not only filling a prescription

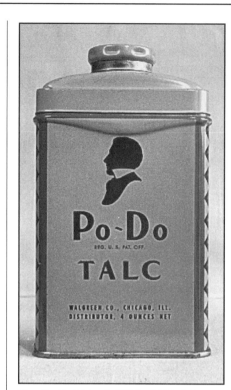

Tin, Po-Do Talc, 5-3/4" h, 1940, $20.

and picking up health and beauty care staples, it also meant taking a seat and ordering up your favorite soda fountain treat. Nowadays, when you take a trip to the drugstore, chances are you're sick, and the trip is a necessity. It certainly doesn't conjure up the pleasant memories it used to.

In business since 1901, the first store was founded in Chicago, by Charles R. Walgreen. A Walgreen has been in charge ever since. Today, there are more than 2,250 stores coast to coast; by the year 2000, there will be more than 3,000 in operation. Walgreen Drug Stores provide a vast range of items from which to choose, i.e., soda fountain accessories, drugs, toys, cosmetics and items from its exhibit at the 1933 Chicago World's Fair, just to name a few. In the 1950s, Walgreen's was the largest drugstore operation with soda fountains in the United States. They sold more ice cream malts and sundaes than any other retailer. For more information about Walgreen Drug Stores, refer to Herman Kogan and Rick Kogan's *Pharmacist to the Nation: A History of Walgreen Co.* (Walgreen Co., 1989).

Advisor: Gordon Addington, 260 E. Chestnut #2801, Chicago, IL 60611.

Soda Fountain

Dinner Plate, white, 1940, 6-1/2" w . 15.00
Malted Milk Canister, cream and light
    brown, 1935, 5 lbs, 5" by 4-3/4"
    by 9-1/2" 45.00
Malt Glass, clear, 1940, 16 oz,
    8-1/2" h 40.00
Mug, white and maroon lettering, 1950,
    3-1/2" by 4" h 12.00

Tins

Aspirin, flat, orange and brown, 1940, 12
    tablets, 1/4" by 1/4" by 1-3/4" . . .16.00
Aspirin, flat, orange and brown, 1940, 24
    tablets, 1/2" by 1/2" by 3-1/4" . . .20.00
Coffee, orange and black, screw top, 1 lb,
    1927 . . . . .350.00
Golden Crown Tennis Balls, cylinder,
    sleeve of three, 1938, 8" h. 75.00
Lady Charlotte Chocolates, colonial
    scenes, cream ground, 1940, 2-1/2" by
    4" by 7-1/2" 25.00
Milk of Magnesia Tablets, flat, light blue
    and cream, 1945, 1/2" by 1/2"
    by 3-1/4" 12.00
Quick-Strips Bandages, 1940, 1" by 2-1/4"
    by 3-1/2" 12.00
Theatrical Cold Cream, Tyson brand,
    round, blue, orange and black, 1930, 8
    oz, 4" by 3" 40.00
Throat Lozenges, Orlis, Valentine brand,
    flat, orange and cream, 1940, 1/2" by
    1/2" by 3-1/4". 12.00

Toys, Linemar, litho tin

Walgreen Cast Register Bank, red, gray
    and blue, 2-1/2" h 40.00
Walgreen Delivery Truck, white and red,
    7" l, 2-1/2" h. 75.00

Tin, Tyson Theatrical Cold Cream, 4" d, 1930, $40.

Toy, delivery truck, white and red, 7" l, 2-1/2" h, 1940, $75.

Walgreen Ice Cream Truck,
    white, blue letters, 1950,
    20-1/2" by 7" by 4" 200.00

World's Fair Souvenirs, 1933-34
Bracelet, copper, Walgreen building .45.00
Coin, copper colored, Walgreen building,
    2-1/2" d. 40.00
Drink Shaker, Art Deco-style, aluminum,
    black letters, 11" h 75.00
Napkin, auto dealership adv, lists four
    Walgreen store locations at Fair, 4-1/2"
    by 4-1/2". 15.00

Other
Bottle, paper label, Child's Witch Hazel,
    1928, 16 oz, 8" h 17.00
Bottle, paper label, Gay Cologne, Leon
    Laraine, green and white Art Deco-style
    bottle, 1941, 6 oz, 6" h 22.00
Canister, Calonite Powder, Research
    Labs, vertical cardboard cylinder,
    orange and blue, 3 oz, 4" h 22.00
Canister, Salted Peanuts, vertical cylinder,
    orange, cream and black, 1935, 16 oz,
    tin, 4-1/2" h. 35.00
Clock, soda fountain type, white and green
    adv insert above clock face, 1940, 25"
    by 25" h 150.00
Playing Cards, adv, red and black box,
    two-deck bridge pack 20.00
Pocket Mirror, 1938, Green Bay store
    opening 60.00
Sign, backboard type, 1938, Malted Milk,
    45" by 25" by 3" 400.00
Sign, stained glass, 1935, backboards,
    113" by 25", price for pair. 450.00
Talc Po-Do, light yellow, red and black,
    vertical, 4 oz, 4-1/2" 20.00
Toiletry Kit, includes talc, styptic powder
    and shaving cream, red box,
    1938. . . . . .125.00

Wall Pockets

The wall pocket; what can be said? What is a wall pocket? My mother used them for plants. A "rooter" she

Japanese, floral dec, blue luster band, 5-1/2" h, $20.

called them. Now they are used as match holders and places for accumulating small junk. Most common wall pockets were produced between the 1930s and 1960s, though some date to the Victorian era. Wallpockets can be made of wood, tin, glass or ceramic. Ceramic examples have been produced both domestically and abroad. Wall pockets come in all shapes and sizes, but all have a small hole on the back side for the insertion of the wall hook.

Dirt build-up and staining is very common, albeit most collectors prefer them to be neat and clean. Carefully check any wall pocket prior to purchase, dirt can hide cracked or broken areas, as well as common household repairs.

Club: Wall Pocket Collectors Club, 1356 Takiti, St. Louis, MO 63128.

Czechoslovakia
Bird and nest, 5" h 35.00
Parrot, 7" h. 35.00
Toucan, 7-1/2" h 40.00

Japan
Boy at stone wall, 5-1/2" h 12.00
Geisha, cone-shape, 8-3/4" h 20.00
Galloping Horseman, 5-7/8" h 12.00

Roseville, Dahlrose, 8-1/4" h, $100.

McCoy
Apple, 7" h 25.00
Bellows, bird handle, 7" h. 25.00
Flower, 6" h 15.00
Lily, 6" h, mkd "USA" 12.00
Pear, 7-1/4" h 25.00

Pennsbury
Cowboy. 30.00
Distelfink, 6" sq. 30.00
Tulip, 6" sq 30.00

Roseville
Bittersweet, 7" h 110.00
Columbine, 8" h 175.00
Corinthian, 8-1/4" h. 125.00
Magnolia, 8-1/2" h 115.00
Snowberry, 8" w 150.00
Wincroft, mkd "USA 267-5". 110.00

Royal Copley
Angel, 6" h 20.00
Lady, bare shoulders, 6" h 25.00
Colonial Old Man, 8" h 30.00
Oriental Girl with Flowers, 6-1/2" h. .20.00
Pigtail Girl, 6-3/4" h. 25.00
Rooster, 6-3/4" d 30.00
The Cornfield, 8" d 30.00

Shawnee
Birdhouse, 6" h, mkd "USA 830" . . .20.00
Floral, 5-3/4" h 20.00
Little Bo Peep, 5" h. 35.00
Teapot with apple, 6-1/2" h. 20.00

Weller
Flemish, 9-1/4" h 140.00
Florala, 9-1/2" h 75.00
Roma, 9-3/4" h 75.00
Wood Rose, 6-7/8" h 65.00

Wallace Nutting

Wallace Nutting (1861-1941) was America's most famous photographer of the early 20th century. A retired minister, Nutting took more than 50,000 pictures, keeping 10,000 of his best and destroying the rest. His most popular and best selling scenes included exterior scenes (apple blossoms, calm streams and rural American country-sides), interior scenes (usually featuring a colonial woman working near a hearth) and foreign scenes (typically thatch-roofed cottages). His poorest selling pictures, which have become today's rarest and most highly collectible pictures, are classified as miscellaneous unusual scenes and include: animals, architecturals, children, florals, men, seascapes and snow scenes. Process prints are 1930s machine-produced reprints of 12 of Nutting's most popular pictures. These have minimal value and can be detected by using a magnifying glass. Nutting sold millions of his hand-colored platinotype pictures between 1900 and his death in 1941.

While attempting to seek out the finest and best early American furniture as props for his colonial interior scenes, Nutting became an expert in early American Antiques. He published nearly 20 books in his lifetime, including his 10-volume State Beautiful series and various other books on furniture, photography, clocks and his personal biography. He also became widely known for his reproduction furniture. His furniture shop reproduced hundreds of different furniture forms, all clearly marked with a distinctive paper label glued directly to the piece or his block or script signature brand.

The overall synergy of the Wallace Nutting name—pictures, books and furniture—has made anything Wallace Nutting quite collectible.

Advisor: Michael Ivankovich, P.O. Box 2458, Doylestown, PA 18901.

Club: Wallace Nutting Collectors Club, 186 Mountain Ave., North Caldwell, NJ 07006.

Books

American Windsors, dust jacket . . .100.00
England Beautiful, 1st ed, green cov 55.00
Furniture Treasury, 1st ed, three volumes, green cov 300.00
Furniture Treasury, 1954 ed, Vol. I-II, blue cov 35.00
New York Beautiful, 2nd ed, tan cov 45.00

Furniture

#17, candlestand, Windsor, tripod base, block brand 525.00
#102, stool, Windsor, oval, paper label 250.00
#392, side chair, ladderback, four slat, block brand 475.00
#411, armchair, Brewster, script brand 1,000.00
#601, refractory table, oak, block brand 935.00

Pictures, good to excellent condition

Afternoon Tea, 14" by 17" 175.00
A Stitch in Time, 14" by 17" 220.00
Confidences, 13" by 16". 185.00
Five O'Clock, 11" by 17" 175.00
Going for the Doctor, 13" by 16" .1,100.00
Hollyhock Cottage, 13" by 16" 135.00
Larkspur, 11" by 14". 75.00
Mary's Little Lamb, 13" by 16" 250.00
Process Print, All Sunshine, 16" by 20" 25.00
Sea Ledges, 10" by 16" 265.00
The Meeting Place, 18" by 22". . .2,420.00
The Pergola Amalfi, 13" by 16" . . . 160.00
Untitled Interior, girls having tea, 8" by 10" 110.00
Watersmeet, 13" by 16" 125.00

Other

Catalog, Furniture, Supreme Edition, 1930 . . . . 110.00
Greeting Card, exterior scene, 4" by 5" 65.00
Silhouette, George and Martha Washington, pr 85.00
Silhouette, Girl by Garden Urn, 4" by 4" 40.00
Treenware, open salt, #28, 1-1/2", imp brand. 155.00
Treenware, pen and pencil tray, imp brand 250.00

Wash Day Collectibles

I keep telling my wife that women's liberation has taken all the fun out of washing and ironing. She quickly informs me that it was never fun to begin with. The large piles of un-ironed clothes around the house are ample proof. Wash day material is a favorite of advertising collectors. Decorators have a habit of using it in bathroom decor. Is there a message here?

Advertising Trade Cards

David's Prize Soap, 3-D illus 80.00
Lavine for Washing, folder, engraved 12.00
Maypole Soap, For Home Dying, three girls dying different colors 18.00

Irons

Box, cast iron, 1895 . . . . .40.00
Charcoal, tall chimney, 7" h, W.D. Cummings & E. Bless 75.00
Electric, Westinghouse, 1914. . . . . .40.00

Other

Box, Fab, sample 8.00
Brush, horsehair, wood handle. 20.00
Calendar, Snow Boy Washing Powder, emb girl with doll house, 1901 . .125.00
Catalog, Kirkman & Sons, Kirkman Premiums, 16 pgs, soap box coupons for household premiums, 1925 . .20.00
Clothes Dasher, copper and wood, 19" h 50.00
Clothes Dryer Rack, Dixiedri-Rack, steel, enamel, two tone, nickel-plated seat, rubber feet, Sommers Brothers Appliance Co. 20.00
Clothespin, spring type, Richardi & Bechtold. 2.00
Clothespin Bag, linen, "Clothespins" embroidered on side, green and yellow, homemade 10.00
Container, Peerless Hardwater Soap, glass ball-shape, metal lid, 10" h .120.00
Ironing Board, poplar, folding, one-board top, four turned legs, old green paint on base. 150.00
Laundry Basket, wicker, 11" by 24" h, 1924 .45.00
Laundry Basket, woven splint, oval, rim handles 35.00
Pinback Button, Gold Dust Washing Powder, multicolored illus, twins in tub, c1896. . . . . .50.00
Pocket Mirror, Star Palace Laundry & Dry Cleaners, 2-1/8" d 21.00
Sample, Gold Dust Twins Scouring Powder 125.00
Sign, Gold Dust Washing Powder, orange, black and white, c1900 . . . . .75.00
Soap Saver, tin frame, twisted wire handle, hanging loop, wire mesh container 20.00
Washboard, Columbus, wood 30.00
Washboard, National, wood frame, stenciled Pilgrim scene, brass scrubber. 30.00
Wash Stick, 36" l 12.00

Wastebaskets

Wastebaskets are not just for garbage. Many collectors are just beginning to appreciate the great lithographed artwork found on many character cans.

Character

Charlie Brown looking at report card, "Good Grief!", 13" h, metal, Chein Co., 1970s 20.00

Kiss 50.00

Return of the Jedi, litho metal, 1980s 18.00

Snoopy kissing Peppermint Patty, 13" h, metal, Chein Co., 1970s 20.00

Other

Sheet Metal, 1-1/4" h, oval, green fake leather, painted landscape and flower scene, 1930s 6.00

Sheet Metal, 16" h, stamped and slit, copper-plated, green paint, Dandee, Erie Art Metal Co., pat 1909 . . . . .50.00

Steel, 12" h, expanded, solid steel inside collar, white finish 30.00

Steel, 11-3/4" h, corrugated sides, raised bottom, green enamel finish 5.00

Tin, 11-5/8" h, perforated sides, white finish, Central Stamping Co., 1920 . . . . .40.00

Wire, 11-1/4" h, woven sq mesh, flared top, tin bottom, raised sides, looped swags top rim, The Wire Goods Co. 15.00

Wire, 22" h, openwork basketweave, sheet iron bottom 25.00

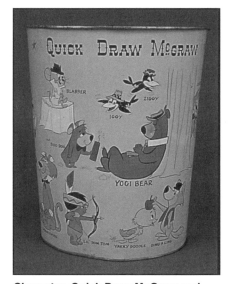

Character, Quick Draw McGraw and other characters, litho tin, $40.

Painted Tin, 11-1/2" h, $15.

Woven, 13" h, willow, colored straw braid, wooden bottom, ring handle, c1895 . . . . 20.00

Watch Fobs

A watch fob is a useful and decorative item attached to a man's pocket watch by a strap. It assists him in removing the watch from his pocket. Fobs became popular during the last quarter of the 19th century. Companies such as The Greenduck Co., in Chicago, Schwabb in Milwaukee and Metal Arts in Rochester, N.Y., produced fobs for companies who wished to advertise their products or to commemorate an event, individual or group.

Most fobs are made of metal and are struck from a steel die. Enameled fobs are scarce and sought by collectors. If a fob was popular, a company would order restrikes. As a result, some fobs were issued for a period of 25 years or more. Watch fobs still are used today in promoting heavy industrial equipment. The most popular fobs are those relating to old machinery, either farm, construction or industrial. Advertising fobs rank second in popularity.

The back of a fob is helpful in identifying a genuine fob from a reproduction or restrike. Genuine fobs frequently have advertising or a union trademark on the back. Some genuine fobs do have blank backs, but a blank back should be a warning to be cautious.

Club: International Watch Fob Association, Inc., RR5, Box 210, Burlington, IA 52601.

Advertising

American Old Line Insurance Co. . . . 40.00

Atlas Life Insurance 15.00

Banigan Rubbers, bronze, 1908 . . . . 30.00

Coca-Cola, brass, emb 95.00

Dead Shot Smokeless Powder, brass, celluloid 210.00

Dr Pepper, silver, 1910 . . . . 75.00

Fairbank's Gold Dust Washing Powder 40.00

George Worthington Co., silver, 1905 . . . . 20.00

Gooch's Best Macaroni, silver, 1915 50.00

Heinz Pickles, brass, pickle figural . . 50.00

John Deere, MOP 125.00

Joy Silver Streak Dual-Valve Rock Drills, silver 15.00

Keystone Watch Case Co., souvenir, 1893 Columbian Expo 40.00

Link-Belt Speeder, brass 22.50

Mack Trucks, bulldog 35.00

Miller Tires 45.00

Old Lincoln Whiskey Co. 45.00

Advertising, Cat Engines, Foley Machinery Co., brass, $20.

Advertising, Link-Belt Speeder Shovel-Crane, Allegheny Machinery Sales Co., brass, $22.50.

Penn Mutual Life Insurance 65.00
Piper Heidsieck Chewing Tobacco . .32.50
Red Goose Shoes, silver, 1912 . . . .75.00
Red Man Tobacco. 30.00
Rio Coffee, bronze, 1908 . . . . .35.00
Starrett Tools, silver, 1912 . . . . . . .30.00
Texas, arrowhead, saddle. 35.00
Walk-Over Shoes, silver, 1915 . . . . .25.00
Wards Tip Top Bread 50.00
Western Live Stock Insurance, silver,
    1910. . . . . .30.00

Organization
American Bowling Congress, 1915. .12.00
Canton Shriner's Club, bronze, 1908 12.00
Order of Moose, 1912 . . . . .15.00
PTA, Illinois-shape, bronze, 1910 . . . .8.00
The Rochester Club, bronze, 1912 . .10.00

Patriotic
Eagle with U.S. flag, bronze, 1917 . .10.00
Miss Liberty, red, white and blue, bronze,
    1918. . . . . .25.00
Woman's Relief Corp., bronze, 1908 10.00

Political
Al Smith, black and white, celluloid on
    emb silvered brass, 1928. . . . . . .60.00
Jimmy Carter, white metal, bronzed,
    1976. . . . . .5.00
Harding, brass, emb portrait, 1920 . .85.00
Kennedy/Welsh, enameled blue, brass,
    1962. . . . . .30.00
W.H. Taft, brass, raised portrait,
    1908. . . . . .25.00
Woodrow Wilson, black and white, celluloid
    on leather, 1912 . . . . .80.00

Sports
Baseball, silver, 1925 . . . . .10.00
Golf, bronze, 1910. . . . . .6.00
Horse Racing, Cincinnati, silver,
    1908 . . . . .35.00

Watthour Meters

Few people enjoy looking at watthour meters, those little monsters that stand constant watch, while tallying your electric usage. While their integrity is often questioned both verbally and physically, they remain one of the most accurate measuring devices known.

When electricity was beginning to be used for more than just lighting, a means to fairly calculate usage was needed. The "count the lamps" method was no longer practical. Early meters employed chemical plates and clocks that proved inadequate for widespread use. In the mid 1880s, the discovery of the induction principle led to the invention of electric motors and induction watthour meters, which have been in use for the last 110 years.

Prices listed are for meters dating from 1900 to 1930 in excellent condition.

Advisor: Tommy Bolack, P.O. Box 2059, Farmington, NM 87499, (505) 325-7873.

Duncan Electric
Model A 150.00
Model C, direct current,
    glass cover 500.00
Model D, top handle. 125.00
Model E 35.00
Model EK 150.00
Model ER, glass front 125.00
Model M. 40.00
Model M-2 . . . . 15.00
Model R, direct current 200.00

General Electric-Thomson
C-7 DC, metal cover 40.00
CP-4, metal cover 75.00
DF-2. . . . . 350.00
DS-5, glass cover 30.00
I 15.00
I-8. . . . . 15.00
I-10. . . . . 20.00
I-14, glass cover 15.00
I-14, metal cover 5.00
IP-5, prepay meter. 150.00
J-2, D-2, brass cover 100.00
J-2, D-2, steel cover. 30.00

Sangamo Electric
Alternating Current Type, two-pc glass
    cover. 150.00
D-5, mercury 25.00

Direct Current Type,
    two-pc glass cover. 125.00
NH Ampre-hour, five dial 35.00
Type H, oval, glass cover. 30.00
Type H, oval, metal cover. 15.00

Westinghouse Electric
OA, single phase, glass cover 18.00
OA, single phase, metal cover 5.00
OB, glass cover 20.00
OB, metal cover 10.00
OC, glass cover 20.00
OC, metal cover 10.00
Type A 150.00
Type B 30.00
Type B Prepayment 200.00
Type C, single phase, glass cover . .30.00
Type C, single phase, metal cover . .10.00

Other
Fort Wayne Electric, prepayment, wood
    device .375.00
Semco Electric, Model 1. . . . . .75.00

Watt Pottery

Watt Pottery, located in Crooksville, Ohio, was founded in 1922. The company began producing kitchenware in 1935. Most Watt pottery is easily recognized by its simple underglaze decoration on a light tan base. The most commonly found pattern is the Red Apple pattern, introduced in 1950. Other patterns include Cherry, Pennsylvania Dutch Tulip, Rooster and Star Flower.

Clubs: Watt Collectors Association, P.O. Box 1995, Iowa City, IA 52244; Watt Pottery Collectors USA, Box 26067, Fairview Park, OH 44126.

Double Apple
Baker, cov, #96, wire stand 399.00
Dip Bowl, #120 . . . . .250.00
Nappy, #05. . . . . .115.00

Apple (left) #60 ribbed bowl, $125; (center) #73 salad bowl, $80; (right) #7 ribbed mixing bowl, $55.

Open Apple, mixing bowl, #7, 7" d, 3-7/8" h, $100.

Salad Bowl, #73 . . . . .150.00

Open Apple
Creamer, #62 . . . . 1,500.00

Red Apple
Baker, open, #96. . . . . .85.00
Creamer, #62 . . . . .85.00
Mug, #121. . . . . .220.00
Nappy, cov, #05 . . . . .175.00
Pie Plate, #33, adv 175.00
Pitcher, #16, three leaf 130.00
Pitcher, #17, ice lip 175.00
Platter, #31 . . . . .475.00
Salad Bowl, #73 . . . . .80.00

Starflower
Bowl, # 5, five petal 40.00
Bowl, #54 . . . . .125.00
Casserole, cov, #18, four petal,
    tab handle 125.00
Cookie Jar, #21. . . . . .199.00
Dip Bowl, #120 . . . . .95.00
Grease Jar, #47 . . . . .385.00
Ice Bucket, #59, five petal 250.00
Mixing Bowl, #8. . . . . .40.00
Mug, #510 . . . . .110.00
Pitcher, #15 . . . . .90.00
Salad Bowl, #73, 4 petal 75.00
Salad Set, #73 serving bowl, six #74
    individual bowls 475.00
Salt & Pepper Shakers, pr, #117 and #118,
    four petal, raised letter 205.00

Tear Drop
Bean Pot, #76 . . . . .175.00
Canister, #72. . . . . .429.00
Nappy, cov, #5 . . . . .300.00
Nappy, cov, #6 . . . . .32.00
Mixing Bowl, #7, ribbed 45.00
Refrigerator Pitcher, #69 . . . . .499.00

Tulip
Creamer, #62 . . . . .225.00
Deep Mixing Bowl, #65 . . . . .135.00
Pitcher, #16 . . . . .245.00

Wedgwood

It is highly unlikely that you are going to find 18th, 19th and even early 20th century Wedgwood at a flea market. However, you will find plenty of Wedgwood pieces made between 1920 and the present. The wonderful and confusing aspect is that many Wedgwood pieces are made the same way today as they were hundreds of years ago.

Unfortunately, Wedgwood never developed a series of backstamps to help identify a piece's age. As a result, the only safe assumption by which to buy is that the piece is relatively new. The next time you are shopping in a mall or jewelry store, check out modern Wedgwood prices. Pay 50 percent or less for a similar piece at a flea market.

Clubs: The Wedgwood Society, The Roman Villa, Rockbourne, Fordingbridge, Hants, SP6 3PG, England; Wedgwood Society of New York, 5 Dogwood Ct, Glen Head, NY 11545.

Basalt
Candlestick, classical figures, scroll design, 7-3/4" h. 100.00
Figure, seated raven on oval base,
    4-1/2" h 165.00
Pitcher, classical figures and putti,
    7-3/8" h 160.00
Tea Service, partial, glazed floral design,
    six pcs. 100.00
Vase, ram's head and swag design,
    7-3/8" h 110.00

General
Chop Plate, Kutani, 12-1/2" d 75.00
Creamer and Sugar, Old Vine 20.00

Creamer and Covered Sugar, imp "Wedgwood, Made in England," blue ground, white classical figures, 2-1/2" h #20 creamer, 3-3/4" h #30 sugar, price for pair, $150.

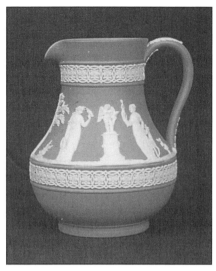

Pitcher, #36, imp "Wedgwood, Made in England, 1951," blue ground, white classical figures, 4-3/4" h, $75.

Honey Pot, attached underplate,
    beehive-shape, 4" h,
    white stoneware 130.00
Pitcher, copper grapes, cream ground,
    6-1/2" h 42.00
Plate, Boston Library, blue transfer,
    c1900. 40.00
Plate, Bunker Hill Monument, blue and
    white, 9-1/4" d 25.00
Plate, "Rebecca Repelling the Templar",
    blue transfer, Ivanhoe series,
    9-1/2" d 80.00
Platter, Kutani, 18" l 75.00
Vegetable Bowl, cov, Patrician 55.00

Jasperware
Biscuit Jar, white classical cameos, women and cupids, dark blue ground, SP top, rim, handle, ball ftd base, mkd "Wedgwood" 150.00
Bowl, white cameo, mythological figures,
    dark blue ground, 4-3/8" d 70.00

Tile, King's Chapel, Boston, light brown, 3-3/8" by 4-3/4", $200.

Cache Pot, white classical figures, green ground, restored 75.00

Chocolate Pot, white classical cameo, dark blue ground, 6" h 135.00

Jar, cov, white cameo, classical figures in medallions, leaves on cov, dark blue ground, 3" h, marked "Wedgwood, Made In England" 95.00

Pitcher, white classic cameo, dark blue ground, 6-1/4" h 125.00

Vase, white cameo, four seasons, blue ground, 5-1/8" h 88.00

Weller Pottery

Weller's origins date back to 1872 when Samuel Weller opened a factory in Fultonham, near Zanesville, Ohio. Eventually, he built a new pottery in Zanesville along the tracks of the Cincinnati and Muskingum Railway. Louwelsa, Weller's art pottery line, was introduced in 1894. Among the famous art pottery designers employed by Weller are Charles Babcock Upjohn, Jacques Sicard, Frederick Rhead and Gazo Fudji.

Weller survived on production of utilitarian wares, but always managed to produce some art pottery production until cheap Japanese imports captured the market immediately following World War II. Operations at Weller ceased in 1948.

Periodical: *Pottery Collectors Express*, P.O. Box 221, Mayview, MO 64071.

Bonito, flower pot and saucer, 4-1/2" h, 5" d, stamped mark, artist sgd, $70.

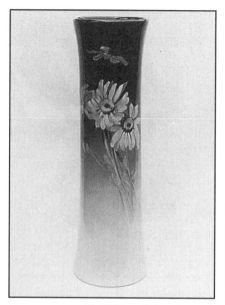
Eocean, vase, 12-5/8" h, mkd, artist sgd "Leffler," $550.

Burnt Wood
Bowl, 3" h 70.00
Candlestick, 8" h 70.00
Mug, 4" h 100.00
Vase, 5-1/2" h 50.00

Coppertone
Candleholders, pr, 2" h 50.00
Cigarette Stand, frog, 5" h 100.00
Figure, frog, 4" h 130.00
Figure, turtle, 4-1/2" h 150.00
Dupont, vase, 6-1/2" h 70.00
Eldora-Chelsea, vase, 5" h 60.00

Louwelsa
Ewer, 6-1/4" h 150.00
Jug, 4-1/2" h 120.00
Vase, 6-1/2" h 120.00

Presidential Plaque
Grant 65.00
McKinley 75.00
Washington 100.00

Warwick
Bud Vase, 7" h 50.00
Flower Insert, 5-1/2" h 60.00
Vase, 4-1/2" h 50.00

Zona
Baby Ware, dinner plate, 7" d 50.00
Baby Ware, Pitcher, 3-1/2" h 40.00
Utility Ware, creamer, 3-1/2" h 35.00
Utility Ware, vase, 9" h 50.00

Other
Art Nouveau, shell vase, 6" h 250.00
Bo Marblo, bowl, 2" h 50.00
Blue Cameo, bowl, ftd, 4" h 40.00

Hudson, vase, 11-1/4" h, imp mark, $185.

Blue Cameo, vase, rect, 8-1/2" h . . . 40.00
Flemish, bowl, squirrel design, 3" h . 75.00
Flemish, planter, reeded design, 4-1/2" h 70.00
Floretta, ewer, 4-3/4" h 80.00
Floretta, vase, 7" h 80.00
Forest, jardiniere, 4-1/2" h 80.00
Fru Russet, vase, 5-1/2" h 150.00
Greenbriar, vase, 5" h 50.00
Novelty Line, ashtray, 5" h 75.00
Novelty Line, wall Pocket, Egyptian, 10" h 150.00
Orris, vase, 10-1/2" h 50.00
Parian, wall pocket, 7-1/4" h 90.00
Sydonia, vase, 9" h 60.00
Tivoli, bowl 75.00
Wild Rose, cornucopia, 5-1/2" h 30.00
World's Fair, souvenir, vase, 3-1/2" h 150.00

Western Collectibles

Yippy Kiyay, partner, let's get a move on and lasso up some of those Western goodies.

The western collectible is a style or motif as it relates to the object. The Western theme presents itself in the decorative imagery of the item. The use of Western materials for construction of the item also defines it as a possible Western collectible; i.e. cattlehide carpets and wall hangings or items constructed from bull horns.

The Western motif may also be defined as any item that relates to the Western frontier culture. Native American Indian and Mexican cultures are also part of the Western collectible theme. It is these cultures that contribute so much of the color to the Western heritage.

Club: National Bit, Spur & Saddle Collectors Association, P.O. Box 3035, Colorado Springs, CO 80934.

Periodicals: *American Cowboy*, P.O. Box 12830, Wichita, KS 67277; *Collectors West*, 741 Miller Dr. S.E., Ste., D-2, Leesburg, VA 20175; *Yippy Yi Yea Magazine*, 8393 E. Holly Rd., Holly, MI 48442.

Newsletter: *Cowboy Guide*, P.O. Box 6459, Santa Fe, NM 87502.

Watch Fobs

Bronco with cowboy 75.00
El Paso Saddlery. 140.00
Holster with gun 85.00
Long horn with saddle. 150.00
Los Angeles Saddlery & Findings . .135.00
Hamley Round-Up Saddle 175.00
Star Brand Los Angeles Saddlery . .125.00
Van Patter's Flying Vee
    Eff Saddle Ranch. 140.00

Other

Bandanna, West High Cowboys, silk 23.00
Book, *Woman Trapper*, Beadle's Frontier
    Series, pulp novels, 1908-09 . . . .20.00

Magazine, *Arizona Highways*, rodeo issue, February 1960, $1.

Book, *The 2nd William Penn Treating With
   Indians on the Sante Fe Trail 1860-66*,
   W.H. Ryus, 1913. . . . . 50.00
Catalog, Harness Leather, square-rigged
   saddle, copper-block plates, Rockford,
   IL, established 1862 . . . . 50.00
Cookie Jar, cowboy boots, American
   Bisque. 150.00
Gloves, buckskin, Northern Plains Indian,
   glass-beaded columbines 450.00
Pin, Texas Cousins Farm
   and Ranch 30.00
Print, Northern Pacific North Coast,
   Montana Roundup,
   orig shipping tube 100.00
Program, Houston Rodeo Magazine,
   features Gene Autry World
   Championships, 1944. . . . . 50.00
Program, Silver Jubilee of Old Trail Driver's
   Association of Texas, 1940. . . . . 35.00
Ribbon, Fredonia Texas Rodeo, bucking
   horse illus, 1929 . . . . 42.00
Ribbon, Salt Lake City Cattlemen's
   Convention, 1901 . . . . 85.00
Saddle, cowboy 40.00
Saddle Horse Bit 25.00
Salt and Pepper Shakera, pr, Rod's Steak
   House, Williams, AZ 35.00
Scarf, silk, cowboy motif 12.50
Scarf Slide, bronco and cowboy . . . 22.50
Spur Straps 30.00

Westmoreland Glass

Westmoreland Glass Co., made a large assortment of glass. Some early pieces were actually reproductions of earlier patterns and are now collectible in their own right. Other patterns have been produced for decades. Expect to pay modest prices. Flea market prices are generally much lower than contemporary department store prices.

Clubs: National Westmoreland Glass Collectors Club, P.O. Box 625, Irwin, PA 15642; Westmoreland Glass Society, 4809 520th St. S.E., Iowa City, IA 52240.

Newsletter: *The Original Westmoreland Collectors Newsletter*, P.O. Box 143, North Liberty, IA 52317.

American Hobnail

Ashtray, round, 4-1/2" d. 5.00
Candleholders, pr, 5" h 30.00
Creamer and Sugar 20.00
Mayonnaise, bell rim, ftd 17.00

Beaded Grape

Candlesticks, pr 32.00

Quilted Block, candy dish, cov, $20.

Honey, cov, roses dec 35.00
Sugar, 3-1/2" h 10.00

English Hobnail, milk glass

Goblet. 7.00
Nappy, 4" d. 4.00
Salt and Pepper Shakers, pr,
    barrel-shape 25.00

Paneled Grape

Basket, oval, 6-1/2" h 22.50
Bowl, scalloped, 9-3/4" d 50.00
Cake Salver, ftd 85.00
Cup, coffee 9.00
Goblet. 18.00
Jug, qt. 35.00
Pitcher 30.00
Plate, 6-1/2" d. 20.00
Plate, 8-1/2" d. 24.00
Salt and Pepper Shakers, pr, ftd . . .16.00

Other

Animal Dish, cov, duck, cobalt blue, yellow
    eyes. 65.00
Animal Dish, cov, hen, milk glass,
    3-1/2" h 15.00
Beaded Edge, nappy, oval, painted
    strawberries, 6" l 10.00
Beaded Edge, tumbler, fruits dec, ftd 15.00
Bramble/Maple Leaf, compote, crimped,
    ftd 25.00
Bramble/Maple Leaf, creamer
    and sugar 20.00
Della Robia, nappy, crystal, orig label,
    4-3/4" d .9.00
Della Robia, water, 8 oz 10.00
Egg Cup, chick 8.50
Roses and Bows, Wedding Bowl, small,
    "Best Wishes" 45.00
Salt Shaker, chick. 15.00
Toothpick Holder, owl. 15.00

Zodiac, platter, blue, red and gold,
16" l 95.00

What's in the Case?

After years of wandering around the country visiting flea markets of every shape and size, there is one phrase I hear over and over again, "What's in the case?"

What's in the case? deals with items found in glass-covered tabletop showcases. Their numbers are infinite. Their variety limitless. They are in the case because they are the smallest of the small, too delicate or expensive. Showcases have also helped to discourage the unfortunate, but all-too-common disappearing act performed by many pocket-size collectibles.

Items under glass are generally valuable. To handle them without a dealer's permission is practically a sacrilege. Arrangement in the case may be haphazard or organized, depending on the dealer's selling methods. Don't be surprised if you find a number of cases packed to overflowing.

Whiskey Bottles, Collectors' Editions

The Jim Beam Distillery issued its first novelty bottle for the 1953 Christmas market. By the 1960s, the limited-edition whiskey bottle craze was full blown. It was dying by the mid 1970s and was buried sometime around 1982 or 1983. Oversaturation by manufacturers and speculation by non-collectors killed the market.

Limited-edition whiskey bottle collecting now rests in the hands of serious collectors. Their Bible is H.F. Montague's *Montague's Modern Bottle Identification and Price Guide* (published by author, 1980). The book used to be revised frequently. Now five years or more pass between editions. The market is so stable that few prices change from one year to the next.

Before you buy or sell a full limited-edition whiskey bottle, check state

Luxardo, basket of fruit, 1969, $15.

laws. Most states require a license to sell liquor and impose substantial penalties if you sell without one.

Club: National Ski Country Bottle Club, 1224 Washington Ave., Golden, CO 80401.

Jim Beam
Beam on Wheels, Cable Car, 1968 . . 5.00
Centennial Series, Key West, 1972 . . 6.00
Clubs and Conventions, Akron-Rubber
  Capital, 1973. . . . . 22.50
Customer Specialties,
  Antique Trader 20.00
Executive Series, Sovereign, 1969 . 12.00
People Series, Buffalo Bill, 1971 . . . . 7.00
Political Series, football,
  elephant, 1972 . . . . 12.50
Regal China Series, Franklin Mint,
  1970 . . . . 8.00
Sport Series, Bing Crosby 33rd National
  Pro-Am, 1974 . . . . 27.50
State Series, Florida, Shell, pearl,
  1968 . . . . 4.50
Trophy Series, owl 20.00

Ezra Brooks
Animal Series, Bear, 1968 . . . . 6.00
Automotive/Transportation Series,
  Motorcycle, 1971 . . . . 12.00
Heritage China Series, CB Convoy,
  1976 . . . . 8.00

Institutional Series, American Legion,
  Hawaii, 1973 . . . . 15.00
People Series, Court Jester, 1971 . . . 9.00
Sports Series, Ski Boot, 1972. . . . . 10.00

Lionstone
Bicentennial Series,
  Valley Forge, 1975 . . . . 22.50
Bird Series, Love Birds, 1/2 pt, 1979 20.00
Mr. Lucky Series, music,
  Dentist, 1980 . . . . 35.00
Wildlife Series, Falcon & Rabbit, miniature,
  1978 . . . . 10.00

McCormick
Bicentennial Series, Betsy Ross. . . . 25.00
Bird Series, Wood Duck, 1980 . . . . . 30.00
Great American Series, Henry Ford,
  miniature, 1977 . . . . 12.00

Ski Country
Christmas Series, Ebenezer Scrooge,
  1979 . . . . 40.00
Circus Series, circus wagon, giraffe,
  1977 . . . . 30.00
Waterfowl Series, Swan, black, Australian,
  1974 . . . . 30.00
Wildlife Series, Bear, brown, 1974 . . 25.00
Wildlife Series, Elk, 1979 . . . . 80.00
Wildlife Series, Skunk Family, 1978 . 40.00

Other
Cabin Still, Deer Browsing, 1967 . . . . 7.00
Cabin Still, Mallard, 1966 . . . . 10.00
Cyrus Noble, Animal Series, Mountain Lion
  & Cubs, miniature, 1979 . . . . 15.00
Cyrus Noble, Sea Animal, Penguin Family,
  miniature, 1980 . . . . 18.00
Double Springs, Bicentennial Series,
  Washington DC 12.00
Double Springs, Car Series, Cale
  Yarborough, 1974 . . . . 25.00
Luxardo, apple, figural 15.00
Michter's, Pennsylvania Dutch Hex,
  1977 . . . . 15.00
Pacesetter, Corvette, red, 1975 . . . . 40.00
Wild Turkey, Lore Series, #2 . . . . . . 20.00

Whiskey Related Collectibles

Whiskey and whiskey-related items are centuries old. Normally, the words conjure up images of the Western saloon and dance hall. Since the taste of similar whiskeys varies little, manufacturers relied on advertising and promotions to create customer loyalty.

Shot Glasses
Live Oak Whiskey. 20.00
Old Grand-Dad Whiskey. 10.00

Old John Henry Whiskey, etched . . .10.00
Old School Rye 20.00
Sunny Brook Whiskey 20.00

Sign

Calvert, tin, cigarette on ashtray with two
    bottles and jigger, 1930s 90.00
Four Roses Whiskey, tin, oval 150.00
Green River Whiskey, tin, black man
    beside horse. 175.00
Seagram's Rare Old Whiskies, tin and
    cardboard 25.00

Other

Ashtray, Jim Beam, 9-1/2" d 125.00
Back Bar, Jim Beam, miniature, figure
    holding glass miniature bottle, Regal
    China, 1978 . . . . .18.00
Badge, Seagram's Whiskey, red, white and
    blue, c1940. . . . . .14.00
Blotter, Green River Whiskey adv,
    cardboard, black man beside horse
    illus. 3.00
Cookie Jar, bisque, International
    Association of Jim Beam Bottle Clubs
    front, 9-3/4" h, Regal China,
    1976 . . . . .30.00
Decanter, Old Crow Whiskey, ceramic,
    Royal Doulton, 1955. . . . . .45.00
Figure, Old Crow Whiskey, plastic, black
    crow, 11" h 40.00
Flask, gold, 14 oz, "I Love Jim Beam" front,
    outline map of Washington back,
    6-1/2" h, Regal China, 1976. . . . .40.00
Glass, Paul Jones Whiskey, clear, gold and
    red logo, set of 4 . . . . .28.00
Match Holder, Old Judson Whiskey/JG
    Stevens, tin, multicolored, girl offering
    Dad a glass 180.00

**Jug, Meredith's Diamond Club,
Knowles Taylor, 7-1/2" h, $95.**

Pitcher, White Horse Scotch, 8" h, $15.

Paperweight, Queen Mary Beam Bottle &
    Specialties Club, 10th birthday
    commemorative, 7" h, Regal China,
    1978 . . . . 90.00
Pitcher, Seagram's 7, white, emb, red
    ground. 8.00
Pocket Mirror, Duffy's Pure Malt Whiskey,
    round. 20.00
Pocket Mirror, Garrett's Baker Rye, oval,
    celluloid, woman in veil holding bow
    illus 185.00
Print, Green River Whiskey, black man be-
    side horse standing before brick wall,
    frame. 25.00
Token, Green River Whiskey 10.00
Tray, Old Barbee Whiskey, oval, girl in
    plaid coat and feathered hat . . . 150.00

Whistle

Webster defines a whistle as an instrument for making a clear, shrill
sound. No wonder children love them.
Collectors can whistle a happy tune at
virtually every flea market. The most
desirable whistles are those associated with well-known characters and
personalities. They can command
prices that are hardly child's play.

Advertising

Cracker Jack, plastic, ocarina 8.00
Cracker Jack, plastic, rocket 8.00
Dairy Queen, ice cream cone figural,
    plastic 12.00
Good & Plenty, Choo Choo Charlie, plastic,
    two tones 12.00

**(Top) German police, pocket chain,
1920s, $45; (bottom) German military,
lapyard, 1930s, $20.**

McDonald's Tootler, plastic, five tones,
    1985 . . . . 3.00
Nickelodeon, made for McDonald's . . 3.00
Snap! Crackle! Pop!, vinyl, Kellogg's,
    1985 . . . . 8.00
Trix, plastic, three tones 15.00

Character

Donald Duck, vinyl 1.00
Mickey Mouse, bubble pipe, plastic,
    Lido 10.00
Ollie, plastic 20.00
Santa Claus, plastic 1.00
Snoopy, plastic 60.00

Police

English-style, brass, mkd "Municipal Police
    Reg. U.S. Pat. Off," c1920 . . . . . .50.00
English-style, lead, Japan. 15.00
Traffic, bakelite, c1930s 25.00

Scouts

Boy Scout, with compass, Germany. 30.00
Girl Scout, plastic, green, logo 15.00

Train, figural

Mighty Steam Whistle, plastic, three tones,
    Sound Toys Unlimited 5.00
Keychain, plastic. 10.00

Pistol, figural, litho tin, Japan, $5.

Whistle For Culligan Soft Water St. 2-7171,
plastic.....................25.00

Wood
Bird, two tones, Yugoslavia........10.00
Clown, hp, Sevi, Italy.............8.00
Pipe, wooden bowl, plastic stem....15.00

White Knob Windups

White-Knob Windups are small, plastic mechanical toys. They arrived on the market in the mid 1970s. Their name is derived from the small white ridged knob found at the end of the metal rod that extends from the body and winds the motor.

Club: White Knob Wind-Up Collectors Club, 61 Garrow St., Auburn, NY 13021.

Character
Barbie, Mattel, 1986 ....2.00
Cabbage Patch Kids, crawler,
Tomy, 1985 ....5.00
E.T., LJN, 1982.................9.00
Muppets, Kermit the Frog, swimmer,
Tomy, 1983 ....10.00
Pac Man, Inky Ghost, blue, Tomy,
1982.....................12.00
Pink Panther, Bandai-America, 1981 10.00
Popeye, Durham, 1980...........15.00
Smurf, walker, blue knob, Galoob,
1982.....................12.00
Snoopy, Aviva, Swimmer 9.00
Snoopy, Aviva, Walker, Red Baron...5.00
Snorks, swimmer, Tomy, 1984 ......9.00
The Chipmunks, hopper, Simon
with guitar, Imperial, 1983 ....9.00
Tom & Jerry, Multitoys, 1989 ......5.00
Wizard of Oz, witch, Multitoys, 1988..6.00

Other
Bathtubbies, Tomy, 1983 ....3.00
Curious Critters, cat, Tomy, 1984 ...10.00
Game, Bumbling Boxing Game, Tomy,
1982.....................10.00
Game, Home Run Homer Game, Tomy,
1982.....................12.00
Get Along Gang Rollers, Dotty Dog on
handcar, Tomy, 1984...........9.00
Hilarious Hats Walkers, police, Tomy,
1983......................8.00
Inch-A-Longs, Bandai-America, 1981 .6.00
Major League Baseball, hoppers, team
logo, Russ, 1989 ....6.00
Mini-Tools, jigsaw, Galoob, 1980 ....5.00
Mity Machines, bulldozer, Galoob,
1984.....................7.00
Pocket Pets Hoppers, Tomy, 1983 ...2.00
Rascal Robots, Tomy, 1977 ....6.00

Scurry Furries, owl, Tomy, 1982 ... 10.00
Snow Funnies Rollers, bunny on skis,
Tomy, 1981................. 3.00
Ugh-A-Bug Crawlers, tarantula, Tomy,
1981 .... 8.00

Wicker

Wicker and rattan furniture enjoyed its first American craze during the late Victorian era. It was found on porches and summer cottages across America. It realized a second period of popularity in the 1920s and '30s, and a third period in the 1950s. In truth, wicker has been available continuously since the 1870s.

Early wicker has a lighter, airier feel than its later counterparts. Look for unusual forms, e.g., corner chairs or sewing stands. Most wicker was sold unpainted. However, it was common practice to paint it in order to preserve it, especially if it was going to be kept outside. Too many layers of paint decrease the value of a piece.

Chairs
Desk, Art Deco, 16" h 135.00
Funeral Parlor, 37" h 95.00
Side, Art Deco, 37" h 175.00
Window Seat, 34" by 18" by
29-1/2" h 350.00

Tables
Coffee, 30-1/2" by 16-1/2" by 16" h,
c1940s 85.00
Parlor, 31" by 21" by 30" h...... 260.00
Rect, magazine shelf 145.00
Round, braided edge base shelf .. 250.00

Other
Basket, 10" by 11", c1920 .... 35.00
Clothes Hamper, 22" by 17-1/2"
by 25-1/2" h................ 65.00
Comb Case, 13" by 14" h 55.00
Doll cradle, willow, open weave,
18" h 150.00
Footstool, 20" by 12" by 12-1/2" h . 155.00
Headboard, Victorian-style, 36"
by 50" h.................. 125.00
Lamp, table, 14" h 85.00
Log Carrier, reed, 24" by 12"
by 18" h.................. 165.00
Magazine Holder, 18" by 14-1/4"
by 24-1/2" h............... 110.00
Pie Caddy, sea grass, 13" by 27" h 125.00
Plant Stand, reed, 30-1/2" h...... 130.00
Potty Chair, c1900 .... 75.00
Rocker, child's, c1910 .... 150.00

Rocker, sewing, with pocket...... 265.00
Shoeshine Kit, 11" by 6" by 9" h.... 65.00
Top Hat, 13" d, 6" h 45.00

Willow Ware

The traditional willow pattern, developed by Josiah Spode in 1810, is the most universally recognized china pattern. A typical piece contains the following elements in its motif: willow tree, apple tree, two pagodas, fence, two birds and three figures crossing a bridge.

Willow pattern china was made in almost every country that produces ceramics. In the 1830s, more than 200 English companies offered Willow pattern china. Buffalo China was one of the first American companies to offer the pattern. Japanese production started about 1902, around the same time Buffalo made its first pieces.

Since the Willow pattern has been in continuous production, the term "reproduction" has little meaning. However, the Scio Pottery, Scio, Ohio, is currently producing an unmarked set that is being sold in variety stores. Because it lacks marks, some collectors have purchased it under the mistaken belief that it was made much earlier.

Clubs: International Willow Collectors, 2903 Blackbird Rd., Petoskey, MI 49770; Willow Society, 39 Medhurst Rd., Toronto, Ontario M4B 1B2 Canada.

Bowl, flow blue, mkd "Willow," 6-3/4" d, Doulton-Burslem, $75.

Newsletter: *The Willow Word*, P.O. Box 13382, Arlington, TX 76094.

Ashtray, fish figural, 5" l, Japan 25.00
Baking Dish, two temples, line border, 3" h, 8" d, Hall China 20.00
Bank, stacked pig figures, 7" h, Japan 40.00
Biscuit Jar, two temples, cane handle, 4-1/2" h 125.00
Bowl, pedestal base, 9-1/4" d, 5" h .125.00
Butter Dish, cov, 8" d, 3-1/2" h 150.00
Cake Plate, Mandarin pattern center, Dagger border, 9-1/2" sq 50.00
Candle Holder, chamberstick-style, scalloped edge, gold trim, 5" d, Gibson & Sons 150.00
Casserole, cov, 9" d 50.00
Cheese Dish, Wiltshaw & Robinson, English 150.00
Child's Toy Tea Set, plastic, 15 pcs, traditional center, butterfly border, Ideal 40.00
Clock, tin, mkd "Smith's, made in Great Britain" 100.00
Coaster, Tennent's Pilsener Beer adv, 4" d 20.00
Cocktail Shaker, metal lid, six tumblers, 3" h 125.00
Coffee Jar, instant, 6" h, Japan 40.00
Coffee Pot, 6" h, granite ware 70.00
Dresser Box, porcelain, 1-3/4" h, 3-1/2" d .75.00
Egg Cup, pedestal base 15.00
Glass, ceramic, Japan 15.00
Gravy Boat, scalloped edge, attached underplate, 7-1/2" l 100.00
Honey Dish, 4" d, Midwinter mark . . .30.00
Ladle, 7" l .100.00
Match Safe, 2" h, Shenango China . .65.00
Mustard Pot, barrel-shape, 2-1/2" h .60.00

Oil and Vinegar Bottles, set, 6" h . . . 50.00
Pepper Mill, metal top, 3" h, Brown Willow 35.00
Pie Plate, unglazed base, 10" d, Japan 50.00
Pitcher, scalloped border, 5" h 100.00
Salad Fork and Spoon, ceramic, SP 150.00
Spoon Rack, rolling pin-style, open pocket top, 9-1/2" l 70.00
Spoon Rest, double-style, 9" l, Japan 35.00
Toothbrush Holder, 5" h, Doulton . 125.00
Tray, SP, 11-1/2" d 75.00
Trivet, wrought iron frame 30.00
Wall Plaque, brass, oak, 7" d, 2-1/4" w 80.00

Winchester

Mention Winchester and the first thing that comes to mind is the Wild Wild West and the firearms used to tame it. Today, the Winchester name is collectible, whether it is found on tools and cutlery or advertising and sporting goods.

Club: The Winchester Arms Collectors Association, Inc., P.O. Box 6754, Great Falls, MT 59406.

Belt Buckle, pewter, limited edition, Proof Series, 1977 . . . . 70.00
Booklet, Retail Price List, 1958 . . . . 30.00
Booklet, Rifle & Price Guide 35.00
Booklet, Tools 30.00
Bullet Mold, #44-WCC 70.00
Calendar, 1961, reproduction of 1895 calendar, mounted in plastic, foam back 120.00
Calendar, 1976 . . . . 30.00
Calendar, 1978 . . . . 35.00

Carving Set, 2 pc, stag handles 90.00
Catalog, 1920, component parts . . . 35.00
Christmas Card, with envelope, unused 20.00
Coin Slug 15.00
Flashlight, focusing 40.00
Hatchet, broad-style, raised lettering 40.00
Ice Pick 85.00
Kitchen Saw 40.00
Meat Grinder, W-32 . . . . 65.00
Oil Can, with contents 45.00
Postcard, Smith-Winchester factory . 35.00
Roller Skates 40.00
Screwdriver, #7113, 4" l 45.00
Screwdriver, #7160, 1-1/2" l 30.00
Shears, 6" l 45.00
Shot Glass, horse and rider, "Best Shot in America" 35.00
Straight Razor, #8531, silver end caps 95.00

Wood Collectibles

There is something great about the grain, patina and aging qualities of wood. This is a catch-all category for wooden objects that had no other home in the book. The objects are utilitarian, yet classic for their type.

Barrel, stave constructed, laced wood bands, refinished, 10" h 100.00
Bell, wood, cow, 7" h 40.00
Book Rack, carved, painted sleeping Mexican, adjustable width 15.00
Boot Jack, pine, 17" l 12.00
Bowl, pine, carved, dipper type, tool marks, 13-3/4" l 150.00
Bread Board, pine, one board wide, applied ends, old red paint on back 50.00
Bread Box, carved, "Give Us This Day," 12-1/2" h 80.00

Creamer, pitcher-style, 2-3/8" h, Shenango, $12.50.

Pinback Button, $15.

Table, miniature, burl walnut, 9-3/4" l, $195.

Whimsey, with egg-shaped darner, turned, 4-1/2" h, $45.

Butter Churn, stave constructed, wooden
    bands, old patina, no lid,
    15-1/4" h 115.00
Butter Paddle, curly maple, worn finish,
    8-1/2"l 50.00
Candle Dryer, sq chamfered post, "X" top
    with holes, 34" w, 24" h 60.00
Funnel, 7-1/4" h, 4-3/4" d 75.00
Ink Well, turned, gold trim on black ground,
    glass liner, 2-1/2" d, printed paper label
    reads "S Sillman & Co., Chester,
    Conn" 20.00
Keg, stave constructed, split sapling
    bands, worn paper label, "Rifle Powder,
    Rustin Powder Co., Cleveland, Ohio,"
    13" h 125.00
Knife Box, pine, divided, shaped center,
    cutout heart 115.00
Match Holder, beehive-shape, tartan
    decoupage, 3" h, ivory top socket holds
    burning match 75.00
Pestle, curly maple, sturdy turned handle,
    refinished 40.00
Rolling Pin, maple, 14" l 25.00
Scoop, birch, 11" l 195.00

Sock Stretcher, 14-1/2" l 12.00
Spice Box, scalloped frame, six open tin
    canisters, 8-3/4" d, 3" h 110.00
Spoon, rope twist handle, turned ivory
    finial, 8-1/8" l, treenware 40.00
Sugar Bucket, stave constructed, iron
    bands, swivel handle, dark finish, pitted
    bands, 5-3/4" h, 6-1/2" d 95.00
Whisk Broom, wooden Mammy handle,
    4-1/2" l 18.00
Window Box, primitive, worn finish,
    heart-shaped handle 65.00

World's Fair Collectibles

It says a lot about the status of world's fairs when Americans cannot stage a fair in 1993-1994 that is even half as good as the 1893 Columbian Exposition in Chicago. Was the last great World's Fair held in New York in 1964? Judging from recent fairs, the answer is an unqualified yes. Although it is important to stress three-dimensional objects for display purposes, do not overlook the wealth of paper that was given away to promote fairs and their participants.

Clubs: World's Fair Collectors' Society, Inc., P.O. Box 20806, Sarasota, FL 34276; 1904 World's Fair Society, 529 Barcia Dr., St. Louis, MO 63119.

Periodical: *World's Fair*, P.O. Box 339, Corte Madera, CA 94976.

1893 Columbian Exposition, Chicago
Advertising Trade Card, American Ceramics Co., Manufacture building, 5 1/2 h"
    by 3-1/2" w 20.00
Booklet, advertising, "A Foot of Facts
    About Cleveland,"
    opens to about 14" l 19.00
Change Tray, multicolored 45.00
Cigar Box Label, multicolor litho, Columbus
    being welcomed by Black and Indian,
    woman with U.S. flag in front of Expo
    bldg, 4-1/2" sq 11.00
Knife, "World's Fair," globe engraved on
    blade, white bone handle 80.00
Medal, "Drink Jackson's Napa Soda for
    Health," Columbus landing on rev,
    aluminum, 1-1/2" 40.00
Paperweight, Ferris Wheel 75.00
Pin Tray, Miss Columbia, aluminum, round,
    bas-relief with floral border 3" d . 30.00
Plate, ceramic, "World's Fair Chicago,
    1893," exhibition grounds panorama,
    7" d 75.00

1905 Lewis and Clark Centennial, souvenir medal, brass, 1-3/8" d, $35.

1898 Trans-Mississippi Exposition, Omaha
Napkin Ring, engraved 10.00
Vase, porcelain, "Machinery & Electricity
    Building, Omaha, 1898," black transfer
    on white, 4-3/4" 45.00

1901 Pan-American Exposition, Buffalo
Advertising Trade Card, bust of Nellie Bly
    and factory scene, black print on
    aluminum 30.00
Elongated Coin, Temple of Music,
    McKinley assassination info
    on reverse 20.00
Letter Opener, brass, figural buffalo . 35.00
Miniature Lamp, glass, pink,
    two globes 430.00
Purse, small 13.00

1904 Louisiana Purchase Exposition, St. Louis
Acorn, wooden, Acorn Stoves and Ranges,
    3/4" by 1" 50.00
Advertising Trade Card, Junket Booth, St.
    Louis World's Fair, geisha on front,
    junket adv on back, 3-1/4" by 5" . 12.00
Belt Buckle, Geronimo, DC Seltzer, brass,
    2-1/8" by 3-7/8" 200.00
Bookmark, "World's Fair 1904 St. Louis,"
    blackened aluminum, heart-shaped,
    1-7/8" by 2-1/4" 25.00
Candy Dish, china, "Palace of Arts, St.
    Louis Exposition, 1904," bottom mkd
    "Victoria Carlsbad Austria," multicolor,
    gilt border and floral pattern, 6-1/8"
    by 6-1/8" 100.00
Cup, Palace of Manufacturers decal,
    Germany 25.00

Egg, tin 65.00
Fan, "A Deed of the Pen," multicolor illus on silk, wood rib handle, 7-1/2"" by 13" 150.00
Hatchet, cast iron, 12-1/2" l 65.00
Hatchet, glass, "Peace and Prosperity," 10" 85.00
Inkwell, Palace of Electricity, white metal, 3" by 4-1/2". 50.00
Pinback Button, "Apple Day, World's Fair, Illinois Apples," red apple, black lettering, 1-1/2" d 25.00
Shoe, brown bisque, souvenir, man's-style, "St. Louis 1904" across toe, 2" by 4 3/8". .200.00

1915 Panama-Pacific International Exposition, San Francisco
Auto permit 12.00
Coin Purse, suede, silvered brass closure, 2-1/2" by 3-1/2" 25.00
Sheet Music, "Hello, Frisco, Hello" . .25.00

1926 Philadelphia Sesquicentennial
Handkerchief, cotton, black on white illus of Liberty Bell, "Produced for celebration of the Sesqui of Signing of Dec. of Ind., Bureau of Eng. & Printing," 17" sq 15.00
Pinback Button, "Sesqui-Centennial, Philadelphia," Colonial ringing Liberty Bell, 3/4". 20.00
Tape Measure, John Warren Watson Stabilators, "Sesqui-Centennial-Philadelphia 1926," company building illus 55.00

1933-34 Century of Progress, Chicago
Book, *Official Photographs of the Century of Progress*, Century of Progress Pub., 1933 . . . . .14.00

1933 Century of Progress, Chicago, miniature booklet in walnut shell, $30.

Bracelet, Elephant and Buddha 25.00
Candy Tin, De Mets Chocolates, Miss Liberty and Scenes from Chicago World's Fair, 8-1/2" d, dark blue and gold 30.00
Cigarette Case, lady's 35.00
Coasters, set of four 20.00
Compact 30.00
Lamp, ceramic, hollow, figural base of Travel Building 3-1/2" h, white lampshade 5-1/2" h, with black transportation motif in silhouette. 80.00
Mirror, "Hall of Science," 3", oval, multicolored 45.00
Needle Case 12.00
Pin Tray, Skyride and Ft. Dearborn, rounded square, emb brass finish, 3-1/2" 15.00
Poker Chip 15.00
Program, opening week 35.00
Puzzle, "Scrambled Eggs," 3-D wooden puzzle, "A Century of Progress" decal 35.00
Sewing Kit 20.00

1939-1940 New York World's Fair
Ashtray, Trylon and Perisphere, Syroco. 12.00
Bank, Remington Typewriter, miniature, orig box 255.00

1964 New York World's Fair, drinking glass, $24.

Book, *American Art From the New York World's Fair* 1939, 344 pp 300.00
Flipbook, hula girl 15.00
Pennant, Trylon and Perisphere, blue with white lettering, 9" 31.00
Pitcher, ceramic, Hull pottery, asymmetrical, Trylon and Perisphere, blue and orange on white 45.00
Toy, Sailboat Souvenir, white metal, World's Fair symbol attached to main sail, on 3" l base, boat is 3-1/2" l, 4-1/2" h 40.00

1939 Golden Gate Exposition, San Francisco
Bandanna, rayon, large five-point star, illus of various types of transportation on border, blue, pin, green, white, 18" h" by 19-1/2" w 35.00
Book, *Weller: Magic City, Treasure Island-1939-1940*, history of fair, 380 pgs, eight color plates, 1940 . . . . 30.00
Puzzle, "Fair Faces," faces lithographed on four cardboard sections, multicolored, make 256 different faces, 6" h" by 5" w 30.00

1962 Century 21 Exposition, Seattle
Booklet, "Your Adventure on Seattle's Space Needle," black and white and color photos, 4-1/4" by 8-1/2" 8.00
Bottle, Jim Beam, Space Needle . . . 20.00
Cigarette Lighter, chromed metal, tower-shape, "Seattle USA Space Needle," 9-1/4" h 55.00
License Plate, colorful 35.00

1964 New York World's Fair
Milk Bottle Cap 5.00
Salt and Pepper Shakers, pr, glazed ceramic, illus of Unisphere 25.00
Tumbler, set of five, Pool of Industry, World's Fair Circus, New York State Exhibit, Unisphere, William Shea Stadium, each 6-1/2" h 50.00
Viewer and Slides, square plastic viewer case, four slides, pop-up magnifier, 2-1/2" sq 15.00

1982, Knoxville World's Fair
Cap, sailor type, black and red inscription on brim 5.00
Coloring Book, With Cut-Out Postcards 5.00
Elongated Cent. 1.50
Poster, Sunsphere 20.00

Wrestling Memorabilia

Collecting wrestling memorabilia can be a very frustrating activity. There

Arcade Card, Ruffy Silverstein, sepia tint, 3-3/8" by 5-3/8", $6.

are no price guides, and most sellers I have encountered profess to having little or no knowledge of any aspect of professional wrestling. In recent years, wrestling has continued to lose the respect it had decades ago. From the 1800s to the 1950s, the results of important wrestling matches could be found in your local newspaper on page one of the sports section. Not anymore. Today, many fans and collectors do not like to admit to following the sport or collecting memorabilia pertaining to this wonderful slice of Americana.

Prices for wrestling memorabilia can vary tremendously. Sellers usually have no idea what to charge when they come across odd wrestling pieces. Pay only what the item is worth to you.

Advisor: John Pantozzi, 1000 Polk Ave., Franklin Sq., NY 11010, (516) 488-7728.

Books

Complete Book of Wrestling, 1988, hard cov 10.00
Fall Guys, Marcus Griffin, 1937, hard cov .20.00
World Champion Wrestler, Gotch, 1913, hard cov .15.00

Figures

Hasbro, Dusty Rhodes, 8", MIP . . . 100.00
Hasbro, Sgt. Slaughter, 8",
    mail premium 35.00
LJN, Bret Hart, 8", MIP 150.00
LJN, Hulk Hogan, 8", with stand . . . 35.00

Other

Beer Glass, wrestler, 1950s. 10.00
Board Game, Verne Gagne Wrestling,
    1950s 25.00
Calendar, wrestling, promoter Fred Kohler,
    1954-57. . . . . 10.00
Cigarette Card, Allen & Ginter,
    1887-88. . . . . 35.00
Halloween Costume, Hulk Hogan . . 10.00
Limited Edition Collector Plate,
    Hulk Hogan 35.00
Magazine, *Sports Illustrated*, Danny Hodge
    cov, April 1, 1957 . . . . 12.00
Magazine, *Sports Illustrated*, Hulk Hogan
    cov, April 29, 1985 . . . . 5.00
Movie Poster, Gorgeous George, Alias The
    Champ, 27" by 41" 25.00
Mug, Hulk Hogan, 32 oz 10.00
Peanut Butter Glass, WWF, 6 oz 6.00
Postcard, Gorgeous George Orchid 10.00
Salt and Pepper Shakers, pr,
    figural wrestlers 13.00
Sign, early wrestlers, Oertels Beer adv,
    cardboard, 1950s, 13" by 20" . . . 75.00
Statue, Ideal, wrestlers, 18", 1971 . . 50.00
Statue, Rittgers, three-pc set, two wrestlers
    and referee, 1941 . . . . 40.00
TV Guide, Gorgeous George cov, Feb 25,
    1950 . . . . 20.00
TV Guide, Lou Thesz cov,
    Apr 15, 1950 . . . . 20.00
Wrestling Revue, Vol. 1, #1,
    Fall 1959 . . . . 25.00

Wristwatches

The pocket watch generations have been replaced by the wristwatch generations. This category became hot in the late 1980s and still is going strong. There is a great deal of speculation occurring, especially in the area of character and personality watches.

Since the category is relatively new as a collectible, no one is certain exactly how many watches have survived. I have almost a dozen that were handed down from my parents. If I am typical, the potential market supply is far greater than anyone realizes.

Club: National Association of Watch & Clock Collectors, Inc., 514 Poplar St., Columbia, PA 17512.

Newsletter: *The Premium Watch Watch*, 24 San Rafael Dr., Rochester, NY 14618; *The Swatch Collectors Club*, P.O. Box 7400, Melville, NY 11747.

Periodical: *Comic Watch Times*, 106 Woodgate Terrace, Rochester, NY 14625.

Advertising

Big Boy, Swiss Analog 30.00
Budweiser, Swiss, 1972 . . . . .40.00
Ernie Keebler, Quartz-Analog,
    1980s. 25.00
McDonald's, Lafayette Watch. 25.00
Raid, Jewels-Swiss, 1975. . . . . .25.00
Scrubbing Bubbles, Marcel, 1975. . .20.00

Character and Personality

Abbott & Costello, Bradley, 1986 . . .50.00
Adolph Hitler, colored dial, 1976. . . .50.00
Annie Oakley, Muros Watch Factory,
    1950 .150.00
Archie, Swiss Analog, 1972 . . . . . . .60.00
Barbie, gold tone top, metal back, Mattel,
    Bradley, 1981 . . . . .25.00
Batman, black plastic case,
    Gilbert, 1966 . . . . .90.00
Betty Boop, King Feature Syndicate,
    1983 .45.00
Buffy & Jody, Sheffield, 1973 . . . . . .25.00
Casper, Swiss-Analog, 1974 . . . . . .65.00
Cathy, Bradley, 1982 . . . . .40.00
Cinderella, Webster, 1972 . . . . .25.00
Flipper, Swiss-Analog, 1974. . . . . . .30.00
Heathcliff, Bradley, 1981 . . . . .40.00
Lucy, United Features Syndicate,
    1952 .40.00
Masters of the Universe, "Skeletor,"
    Bradley, 1983 . . . . .15.00
Mickey and Pluto, digital, Walt Disney
    Productions, 1983 . . . . .20.00
Robin Hood, Bradley, 1956 . . . . . .100.00
Winnie The Pooh, Bradley, 1933 . . .30.00

Elgin

Avigo, manual wind, black dial, luminous
    hands. 60.00
Doctor William Osler, manual wind. 100.00
Shockmaster, 17j, gold filled. 60.00
Townsman, manual wind, applied gold
    studs 100.00

Character, Hoppy, $140.

Political

George Wallace, "The Fightin' Lil' Judge,"
    Bill Dinken Time, Inc. 80.00
Jimmy Carter from Peanuts to President,
    Goober Time, 1976 . . . . .70.00
Ronald Reagan, 40th President,
    1976. . . . . .60.00
Spiro Agnew, Swiss, 1973 . . . . .55.00
Trickie Dickey, "Now Let Me Make This
    Crystal Clear," Caricature Watch Co.,
    1974. . . . . .85.00
Uncle Sam, calendar, Swiss, 1972 . .45.00

Sports

Muhammad Ali, Bradley, 1980 . . . . .70.00
National Football League, Bradley . .25.00
Rocky Marciano, HK Analog, 1976 . .50.00

Other

Bulova, Accutron, gold-filled 125.00
Doric, fancy lugs, two-tone case, 17j,
    c1935. . . . . .70.00
Girl Scout, Timex, 1950. . . . . .40.00
Illinois, Off Duty Engraved, manual wind,
    silvered dial, water-resistant,
    c1927. .100.00
Longines, rect, manual wind, drop lugs,
    outer seconds ring, c1946 . . . . . .70.00

Mimo, manual wind, hour, minute and sec-
    onds windows, chrome head,
    c1931 . . . . 110.00
Roamer, auto wind, date, 17j. 50.00
Technos, "Sky Diver," auto wind, 17j, SS,
    1970 . . . . 50.00
Timecraft, 17j, SS, c1950 . . . . 150.00
Zentra, ladies, auto wind, 24j. 90.00

Yard Long Prints

Yard-long prints cover a wide variety of subject matter. Desirability rests
not so much with subject as with illustrator. The more recognized the name,
the higher the price.

American Beauty Roses, 1894, sgd "New-
    ton A. Wells," Art Interchange Co., NY,
    8" by 28". 110.00
Assorted Fruit, 1897, Jos. Hoover & Sons,
    Philadelphia, 7" by 36" 120.00
A Study of Violets, 1900, sgd "Mary E.
    Hart," Art Interchange Co., NY, 8" by
    36", unframed 60.00
A Yard of Roses, 1898, sgd "Newton A
    Wells," 10" by 35" 120.00
Carnation Symphony, 8" by 35". . . 130.00
Foot Rest Hosiery, 10" by 27" 135.00
Honeymooning in Venice, 1922, Pompe-
    ian, sgd "Gene Pressler,"
    7" by 26" 175.00
Lady on balcony overlooking body of water,
    14" by 39", unframed 135.00
Montage, banquet of game birds, fruit and
    rabbit, 10" by 36" 110.00

The Bride, 1927, Pompeian, sgd "Rolf Arm-
    strong," 7" by 26", unframed 75.00
Vertical Roses, "The Great Atlantic & Pacif-
    ic Tea Co., NJ" on leaf at bottom left, 10"
    by 38" 135.00
Yard of Dogs, sgd "C.L. Van Vredenburgh,"
    9" by 34" 155.00

Zoo Collectibles

I have been trying for years to find
"Z" categories to end antiques and collectibles price guides. Finally, a book
in which zoo collectibles are not out of
place!

Game, Fun at the Zoo, 1902 . . . . .200.00
Game, Marlin Perkins Zoo Parade,
    Cadaco, 1955 . . . . .90.00
Game, Zoo Hoo, 1924 . . . . .55.00
Limited Edition Collector Plate, Zoological
    Gardens, Kern, 1983, Elephants, M.
    Carroll .55.00
Little Golden Book, *A Day At The Zoo*,
    1949 . . . . .10.00
Little Golden Book, *Albert's Stencil Zoo*,
    1951 . . . . .25.00
Playing Cards, Wild Animal Park, San Di-
    ego, lion, zebras, elephant, hippopota-
    mus and rhinoceros, color. 6.50
Stein, Endangered Species Series, 1992,
    Giant Panda 30.00
Stein, Endangered Species Series, 1995,
    Cougar. 35.00

PART THREE

A Flea Marketeer's
Annotated Reference Library

You Cannot Tell the Players Without a Scorecard

A typical flea market contains hundreds of thousands of objects. You cannot be expected to identify and know the correct price for everything off the top of your head. You need a good, basic reference library. As a flea marketeer, there are two questions about every object that you want to know: "What is it?" and "How much is it worth?" A book that answers only the first question has little use in the field. Titles in the "Books About Objects" list contain both types of information.

The basic reference library consists of 50 titles. I admit that the number is arbitrary. However, some limit was necessary. Acquiring all the titles on the list will not be cheap. Expect to pay somewhere between $1,250 and $1,500 (you can occasionally find some of these books at clearance prices—25% to 75% off—through the publishers or at discount book sellers).

The list contains a few books that are out of print. You will have to pursue their purchase through used-book sources. Many antiques and collectibles book dealers conduct book searches and maintain "wants" lists. It is not uncommon to find one or more of these specialized dealers set up at a flea market. Most advertise in the trade papers, especially *The Antique Trader Weekly* (P.O. Box 1050, Dubuque, Iowa 52004) and "Books For Sale" in the classified section of *AntiqueWeek—Central Edition* (P.O. Box 90, Knightstown, IN 46148). One dealer that I have found particularly helpful in locating out-of-print books is Joslin Hall Rare Books, P.O. Box 516, Concord, MA 01742.

Many reference books are revised every year or every other year. The editions listed are those as of Spring 1997. When you buy them, make certain that you get the most recent edition.

One final factor that I used in preparing this list was a desire to introduce you to the major publishers and imprints in the antiques and collectibles field. It is important that you become familiar with Antique Publications, Antique Trader Books, Avon, Books Americana (an imprint of Krause Publications), The Charlton Press, Collector Books, House of Collectibles, Krause Publications, L-W Book Sales, Schiffer Publishing, Tomart Publications, Wallace-Homestead (an imprint of Krause Publications) and Warman (an imprint of Krause Publications).

General Price Guides

Rinker, Harry L., *The Official Harry L. Rinker Price Guide to Collectibles* (New York, NY: House of Collectibles: 1997). This listing is totally self-serving. I firmly believe I author the best price guide to post-1920 collectibles and that you should own it. This guide is truly comprehensive, containing dozens of collecting categories not found in other "collectibles" price guides. The introduction to each category contains a brief history, list of reference books, names and addresses of periodicals and collectors' clubs and information about reproductions. It is the perfect companion to *Price Guide to Flea Market Treasures*.

Does a flea marketeer need a general antiques and collectibles price guide? The realistic answer is no. As each year passes, antiques play a smaller and smaller role in the flea market environment. General antiques and collectibles price guides tend to be heavily weighted toward the antiques portion of the market. Most flea marketeers, whether buyers or sellers, deal primarily in 20th century collectibles.

Yet, I believe every flea marketeer should maintain a multiple-year run of one general antiques and collectibles price guide for the purposes of tracking market trends and researching and pricing objects that fall outside their knowledge level. The worst mistake a flea marketeer can make is to buy a different general antiques and collectibles price guide from one year to the next. Find the guide that best serves your needs and stick to it.

The following four price guides are listed in the order of frequency that I see them being used in the field:

Huxford, Sharon and Bob, ed., *Schroeder's Antiques Price Guide, 15th ed.* (Paducah, KY: Collector Books: 1997).

Kovel, Ralph and Terry, ed., *Kovels' Antiques & Collectibles Price List for the 1997 Market, 29th ed.* (New York, NY: Crown Trade Paperbacks: 1997).

Schroy, Ellen, ed., *Warman's Antiques and Collectibles Price Guide, 31st ed.* (Iola, WI: Krause Publications: 1997).

Husfloen, Kyle, ed., *Antiques and Collectibles Price Guide, 13th ed.* (Dubuque, IA: Antique Trader Books: 1997).

Identification of Reproductions and Fakes

Hammond, Dorothy, *Confusing Collectibles: A Guide to the Identification of Contemporary Objects.* This book provides information about reproductions, copycats, fantasy items, contemporary crafts and fakes from the late 1950s through the 1960s. Much of this material appears in today's flea markets. Some is collectible in its own right. The best defense against being taken is to know what was produced.

Hammond, Dorothy, *More Confusing Collectibles, Vol. II* (Wichita, KS: C.B.P. Publishing Company: 1973). Out of print. *Confusing Collectibles* took a broad approach to the market. *More Confusing Collectibles* focuses primarily on glass. It contains all new information, so you really do need both volumes.

Lee, Ruth Webb, *Antiques Fakes and Reproductions* (published by author: 1938-1950). Out of print. Note: This book went through eight editions. The later editions contain more information. A good rule is to buy only the fourth through eighth editions. Dorothy Hammond followed in Ruth Webb Lee's footsteps. Lee's book chronicles the reproductions, copycats, fantasy items and fakes manufactured between 1920 and 1950. While heavily oriented toward glass, it contains an excellent chapter on metals, discussing and picturing in detail the products of Virginia Metalcrafters.

Antique & Collectors Reproduction News. This is not a book, yet it belongs on this list. This monthly publication tracks the latest reproductions, copycats, fantasy items and fakes. An annual subscription costs $39, an amount you are certain to save several times over during the course of a year. Consider acquiring a full set of back issues. Write Antique & Collectors Reproduction News, P.O. Box12130, Des Moines, IA 50312.

Books About Objects

Action Figures. I desperately wanted to include a title on this list for action figures. The problem is that there is none that I can recommend. As a result, I suggest your subscribe to or buy an occasional copy of *Lee's Action Figure News & Toy Review* (556 Monroe Turnpike, Monroe, CT 06468. Sample issues are $6.45, postage included.).

Baker, Mark, *Auto Racing Memorabilia and Price Guide* (Iola, WI: Krause Publications: 1997). Auto racing collectibles have replaced baseball collectibles as the hot sport collecting category of the 1990s. Collecting auto racing memorabilia, from dirt track to Indy cars, has shed its regional cloak and become national in scope. Baker's book is the first off the starting line. James Beckett and Eddie Kelly's Beckett Racing Price Guide and Alphabetical Checklist only covers trading cards and diecast cars. A checkered flag for Baker because he includes these and much, much more.

Barlow, Ronald S., *The Antique Tool Collector's Guide to Value, 3rd ed.* (El Cajon, CA: Windmill Publishing Company: 1993). Out of print. This is the book for tools. Barlow has compiled auction and market prices from across the United States. Since this book is organized by tool type, you need to identify the type of tool that you have before you can look it up. There are plenty of illustrations to help. Treat the pricing with caution. If Barlow does not publish a new edition by the next edition of this book, I plan to drop this reference from the list.

Bagdade, Susan and Al, *Warman's American Pottery and Porcelain* (Radnor, PA: Wallace-Homestead: 1994). Recommended because of its wide range of coverage. As with other Warman titles, the category introductions provide a wealth of good information, including a large number of drawings of marks. Pricing that is auction-based is clearly indicated. Use to cross-check information in Duke's *The Official Identification Guide to Pottery and Porcelain.* The Bagdades also authored *Warman's English & Continental Pottery & Porcelain.* While most ceramics found in American flea markets are American in origin, a few European pieces do slip into the mix. If you encounter English and Continental ceramics on a regular basis, consider adding this second Bagdade book to your library.

Bunis, Marty and Sue, **Collector's Guide to Antique Radios, 4th ed.** (Paducah, KY: Collector Books: 1997). There is a wealth of radio books in the market place. This one is tuned in to a wide band of radios. Organization is by manufacturer and model number. Although heavily illustrated, the book does not picture the majority of the models listed. The book also covers radio parts and accessories.

Collectors' Information Bureau's Collectibles Market Guide and Price Index, 13th ed. (Barrington, IL: Collectors' Information Bureau: 1995). The best thing about this book is that it covers a wide range of limited-edition types, from bells to steins. It serves as a collector's checklist. The worst thing is that it is industry-driven. Important negatives and warnings about the limited-edition market are missing. Field-test the prices before paying them.

Cornwell, Sue and Mike Kott, **House of Collectibles Price Guide to Star Trek Collectibles, 4th ed.** (New York: House of Collectibles: 1997). There is no question that Star Trek collectibles will "live long and prosper." This price guide covers more than 5,000 items licensed for the initial Star Trek television program, the movies and television spin-off series, "Star Trek: The Next Generation," "Star Trek: Voyager" and "Deep Space 9." Includes some foreign licensed materials. Alas, a chapter on convention souvenirs is nowhere to be found.

Cunningham, Jo, **The Collector's Encyclopedia of American Dinnerware.** (Paducah, KY: Collector Books: 1982) 1995 price update. This is a profusely illustrated guide to identifying 20th century American dinnerware. In spite of the fact that many new companies and patterns have been discovered since Cunningham prepared her book, it remains a valuable identification tool, especially since its pricing is updated periodically.

Dale, Jean, **The Charlton Standard Catalogue of Royal Doulton Beswick Figures, 5th ed.** (Toronto: The Charlton Press: 1997). This is one in a series of four books edited by Dale, covering the products of Royal Doulton Beswick. The others are: **The Charlton Standard Catalogue of Royal Doulton Animals** (1994); **The Charlton Standard Catalogue of Royal Doulton Beswick Jugs,** 3rd ed. (1995); and **The Charlton Standard Catalogue of Royal Doulton Beswick Storybook Figurines** (1996). A feature of each of these books is that pricing information is provided in English pounds, Canadian dollars and American dollars. Americans should pay more atten-tion to books published by The Charlton Press. The title list includes books on Chintz and hockey trading cards.

Duke, Harvey, **The Official Identification and Price Guide to Pottery and Porcelain, 8th ed.** (New York, NY: House of Collectibles: 1995). This book is dinnerware, kitchenware and accessory oriented. As such, it is the perfect companion to Cunningham's guide. Duke covers many of the companies and lines of which Cunningham was unaware when she first published her book in the early 1980s. Illustrations are minimal, making it necessary to know the name of your pattern before looking anything up. The book is well-balanced regionally. Many West Coast pottery manufacturers finally receive their due. Its major drawback is the lack of an index; hopefully, this will be corrected in the next edition.

Florence, Gene, **The Collector's Encyclopedia of Depression Glass, 12th ed.** (Paducah, KY: Collector Books: 1997). This is the Depression Glass collector's Bible. Among its important features are a full listing of pieces found in each pattern and an extensive section on reproductions, copycats and fakes. One difficulty is that there are hundreds of glass patterns manufactured between 1920 and 1940 that are not found in this book, because they do not have the Depression Glass label. Supplement the book with Gene Florence's **Kitchen Glassware of the Depression Years,** also published by Collector Books.

Foulke, Jan, **12th Blue Book Dolls and Values** (Cumberland, MD: Hobby House Press, Inc.: 1995). Foulke is the first place doll collectors turn for information. The book is high-end, turning its back on many of the post-World War II and contemporary dolls. Within the doll field, it sets prices more than it reports them. Cross-check Foulke's prices in Dawn Herlocher's **200 Years of Dolls: Identification and Price Guide** (Antique Trader Books).

Franklin, Linda Campbell, **300 Years of Housekeeping Collectibles** (Florence, AL: Books Americana: 1993). Books Americana split the second edition of **300 Years of Kitchen Collectibles** into two separate volumes, albeit retaining the edition number for one of the spin-offs. Now, instead of paying $10.95 for a handy-to-use single source, you have to pay $45.90 for two volumes at $22.95 each. Hopefully, a publisher will see an opportunity and once again put this information in a single volume. Until such time, it makes sense to buy the two Franklin volumes.

Franklin, Linda Campbell, *300 Years of Kitchen Collectibles, 3rd ed.* (Florence, AL: Books Americana: 1993). The second edition of this book was well organized, had a readable format and was easy to use. The third edition provides ample proof that bigger is not necessarily better. The new format is incredibly awkward. The wealth of secondary material may be great for the researcher and specialized collector, but it is a pain to wade through for the generalist. Franklin joins the Coca-Cola Company as someone who failed to recognize that they had created a classic. For now this is better than nothing, but it provides a real opportunity for a challenger.

Gibbs, P.J., *Black Collectibles Sold in America.* (Paducah, KY: Collector Books: 1987, 1996 price update). Black collectibles have gone through a number of collecting cycles in the past 15 years. Popular among both white and black collectors, Black memorabilia is likely to cycle several more times in the years ahead. Because of this, prices in any Black collectibles book have to be taken with a grain of salt.

Gilbert, Ann, *40's and 50's Designs & Memorabilia: Identification and Price Guide* and *60's and 70's Designs & Memorabilia: Identification and Price Guide* (New York: Avon Books: 1993). The plus of this two-volume set is that it provides a chronological approach not found in other price guides. The negative is that the coverage is spotty, and many prices are no longer valid. Hopefully, new editions will fill in the gaps and provide a much needed price updating. Still recommended because of the set's fresh organizational approach, one that continues to increase in popularity among collectors and interior decorators.

Hagan, Tere, *Silverplated Flatware,* revised 4th ed. (Paducah, KY: Collector Books: 1990, 1995 value update). You do not see a great deal of sterling silver at flea markets because most dealers sell it for weight. Silver-plated items are in abundance. This book concentrates only on flatware, the most commonly found form. While you can research silver-plated hollowware in Jeri Schwartz's *The Official Identification and Price Guide to Silver and Silverplate, 6th ed.* (House of Collectibles, 1989), disregard the prices. The market has changed significantly.

Hake, Ted, *Hake's Guide to...* series (Radnor, PA: Wallace-Homestead). In the first half of the 1990s, Ted Hake authored a five-book priced picture-book series focusing on material sold in Hake's Americana Mail Auction. Each collecting category is introduced with a brief history, often containing information not readily available to the collector. The series consists of: *Hake's Guide to Advertising Collectibles: 100 Years of Advertising From 100 Famous Companies* (1992); *Hake's Guide to Comic Character Collectibles: An Illustrated Price Guide to 100 Years of Comic Strip Characters* (1993); *Hake's Guide to Cowboy Character Collectibles: An Illustrated Price Guide Covering 50 Years of Movie and TV Cowboy Heroes* (1994); *Hake's Guide to Presidential Campaign Collectibles: An Illustrated Price Guide to Artifacts from 1789-1988* (1992); and *Hake's Guide to TV Collectibles: An Illustrated Price Guide* (1990). Several titles are out of print. Allowing this series to die was one in a long list of mistakes made by Chilton Books in the company's final years as publisher of Wallace-Homestead and Warman titles. Hake's latest effort is *Overstreet Presents: Hake's Price Guide to Character Toy Premiums* (Gemstone Publications, 1996). Check it out.

Heacock, William, *The Encyclopedia of Victorian Colored Pattern Glass,* nine volumes (Marietta, OH: Antique Publications). One of the major gaps in the antiques and collectibles literature is a general price guide for glass. On the surface, the subject appears overwhelming. Heacock's nine-volume set covers glass manufactured from the mid-19th through the early 20th century. Actually, some volumes extend deep into the 20th century. Book 1 on toothpicks, Book 2 on opalescent glass and Book 9 on cranberry opalescent glass are among the most helpful. Antique Publications has issued revised pricing lists for Volumes 1 (1996), 2 (1993/4), 3 (1991/2), 4 (1992/3), 6 (1992/3) and 7 (1993/4). Volumes 2, 5, 7,and 9 are out of print. Volume 8 was never published.

Herlocher, Dawn, *200 Years of Dolls: Identification and Price Guide* (Dubuque, IA: Antique Trader Books: 1997). Doll identification and pricing information presented in a fresh, new and extremely usable format. Covering 125 doll manufacturers, the book features a mix of antique and collectibles dolls. Use to cross-check the information and pricing in Foulke's *Blue Book of Doll Values.*

Huxford, Bob, *Huxford's Old Book Value Guide, 8th ed.* (Paducah, KY: Collector Books: 1997). There are always piles of old books at any flea market. Most are valued at less than 50 cents. However, there are almost always sleepers in every pile. This book is a beginning. If you think that you have an expensive tome, check it out in the most recent edition of *American Book Prices Current,* published by Bancroft-Parkman.

Martinus, Norman E. and Harry L. Rinker, **Warman's Paper** (Radnor, PA: Wallace-Homestead: 1994). The paper market is hot and getting hotter. Paper is available and affordable. The market already has dozens of specialized shows. **Warman's Paper** is organized into 75 collecting topics and more than 200 subject topics. Of all the books with which I have been involved, this title ranks number three on my "most proud" list, right behind **The Official Harry L. Rinker Price Guide to Collectibles** and **Warman's Furniture.**

Melillo, Marcie, **The Ultimate Barbie Doll Book.** (Iola, WI: Krause Publications: 1997). Barbie—the vinyl goddess, the billion dollar baby—has become so important she deserves a separate listing. There are dozens of Barbie price guides available. This is my favorite full-coverage guide. When I want information on contemporary Barbies, my choice is Jane Sarasohn-Kahn's **Contemporary Barbie: Barbie Dolls 1980 and Beyond** (Antique Trader Books, 1996). Also consider adding a Barbie price guide that includes information on costumes and accessories, two hot Barbie subcollecting categories in the late 1990s.

Morykan, Dana Gehman and Harry L. Rinker, **Warman's Country Antiques and Collectibles, 3rd ed.** (Radnor, PA: Wallace-Homestead: 1997). This is the general text-oriented price guide to Country that has long been needed. A special feature is the names and addresses of reproduction craftspersons and manufacturers. For those who still feel the need for a picture-oriented guide, check out Don and Carol Raycraft's **Wallace-Homestead Price Guide to American Country Antiques, 15th ed.,** due out in fall of 1997 (Iola, WI: Krause Publications).

Morykan, Dana G. and Harry L. Rinker, **Garage Sale Manual & Price Guide.** (Dubuque, IA: Antique Trader Publications: 1995). The only price guide that covers recyclables, objects whose value rests primarily with their reuse and not collectibility. Includes more than 100 categories, from adding machines and artificial flowers to umbrellas and video game systems and cartridges. Are garage sale objects sold at flea markets? You bet they are and in large quantities. Just the coverage you need for low-end material. If you can make a buck, why not sell it?

Osborne, Jerry, **The Official Price Guide to Records, 12th ed.** (New York: House of Collectibles: 1997). This is the book to which everyone refers. It lists every charted hit single and album from 1950s through 1990. Alas, it provides minimal coverage for pre-1940 records. Today, record collecting is highly specialized. There are dozens of specialized price guides to records, many of them published by Krause Publications. Write for a catalog of available titles to: Krause Publications, 700 E. State St., Iola, WI 54990.

O'Brien, Richard, **Collecting Toys: A Collectors Identification and Value Guide, 8th ed.** (Iola, WI: Krause Publications, 1997). The reason that there are no specialized toy or game books on this list is that you have no need for them if you own a copy of O'Brien. The book dominates the field. It is not without its weaknesses, especially in the area of post-World War II toys. However, each edition brings improvement. O'Brien has enlisted the help of specialists to price many of the sections, an approach that greatly strengthens the presentation.

Overstreet, Robert M., **The Overstreet Comic Book Price Guide, 27th ed.** (Timonium, MD: Gemstone Publishing, Inc.: 1997). Distributed by Avon Books. Long live the king. The challenge to the throne by Alex Malloy's **Malloy's Comics Values Annual** has ended unsuccessfully. Although focused too heavily on Golden and Silver Age American comics and not heavily enough on contemporary American comics, foreign issues and underground comics, Overstreet is clearly the price guide of choice among adult collectors. This book sets the market more than it reports it.

Petretti, Allan, **Petretti's Soda Pop Collectibles Price Guide: The Encyclopedia of Soda-Pop Collectibles.** (Dubuque, IA: Antique Trader Books: 1997). This is the latest offering from the King of Coca-Cola collectibles. This priced picture guide is organized first by object type and then alphabetically by soda company. As this book goes to press, Petretti is putting the final touches on the 10th edition of **Petretti's Price Guide to Coca-Cola Collectibles,** the first edition to contain Petretti identification numbers. Once available, it is a must-add to your library.

Rinker, Harry L., **Dinnerware of the 20th Century** (New York, NY: House of Collectibles: 1997). This book provides detailed information on the 500 most popular dinnerware patterns sought by replacement buyers. Each pattern has an illustration of the plate from the set and a comprehensive checklist of the forms available. There are two other titles in this series: **Stemware of the 20th Century** covers the 200 most popular stemware patterns and **Silverware of the 20th Century** includes the 250 most popular flatware patterns.

Romero, Christie, **Warman's Jewelry** (Radnor, PA: Wallace-Homestead: 1995). The best general price guide to jewelry available. It uses a time-period approach, is well illustrated and features highly detailed listing descriptions. The book also is loaded with historical information, hallmarks, manufacturer's marks, reference source referrals and a time line chronicling the history of jewelry. Appendices include a listing of American costume jewelry manufacturers (with dates of operation) and a glossary.

Schroy, Ellen, **Warman's Glass, 2nd ed.** (Radnor, PA: Wallace-Homestead: 1995). The most comprehensive guide available to the traditional glass market. While heavily American focused, it does include information on major English and European glass collecting categories. It has a balanced approach, covering everything from the finest art glass to household utilitarian glass. Includes all the features expected in a Warman's title, including category introductions that have historical information, references sources, addresses of collectors' clubs and reproduction alerts.

Shugart, Cooksey and Richard Gilbert, **Complete Price Guide to Watches, No. 15.** (Cleveland, TN: Cooksey Shugart Publications: 1995). Although this book has been distributed by four different publishers during the past seven years, it has never failed to maintain its high quality. It is the best book available on pocket- and wristwatches.

Sports Collectors Digest, **Baseball Card Price Guide, 10th ed.** (Iola, WI: Krause Publications: 1996). This book has become a superstar. It is more comprehensive and accurate than its competition. Supplement it with the **Sports Collectors Digest 1997 Standard Catalog of Baseball Cards,** 6th Edition (Krause Publications, 1996). The one-two hitting combination of these two books relegate James Beckett's **Sports Americana Baseball Card Price Guide** to benchwarmer status.

Sansweet, Stephen J. and T.N. Tumbush, **Tomart's Price Guide to Worldwide Star Wars Collectibles** (Dayton, OH: Tomart Publications: 1994). Who is going to win the battle of outer space collectibles—Star Trek or Star Wars? For years, I bet on Star Trek. Time to admit I am wrong. This is one of many titles issued by Tomart Publications. I have a problem with Tomart titles. They use such broad price ranges that I feel the pricing information is almost meaningless. Others disagree.

Swedberg, Robert W. and Harriett, *Collector's Encyclopedia of American Furniture*: three volumes: Volume 1—**The Dark Woods of the Nineteenth Century: Cherry, Mahogany, Rosewood and Walnut** (1991, 1996 value update); Volume 2—**Furniture of the Twentieth Century** (1992, 1996 value update); Volume 3—**Country Furniture of the Eighteenth and Nineteenth Centuries** (1994) (Paducah, KY: Collector Books). The Swedbergs write about furniture. While their most recent work is done for Collector Books, Wallace-Homestead, their previous publisher, still keeps their series on oak furniture in print. It is worth a referral from time to time. Also do not ignore the **Swedbergs' Furniture of the Depression Era: Furniture & Accessories of the 1920's, 1930's & 1940's** (Collector Books, 1987, 1996 value update). All books utilize a priced-picture approach. Text information, including descriptions for individual pieces, is minimal. Sources are heavily Midwest. The plus-factor is that the books feature pieces for sale in the field, not museum examples.

Mark Books

Lehner, Lois, **Lehner's Encyclopedia of U.S. Marks on Pottery, Porcelain and Clay** (Paducah, KY: Collector Books: 1988). This is the best reference book for identifying the marks of U.S. pottery and porcelain manufacturers. It contains detailed company histories and all known marks and trade names used. When possible, marks and trade names are dated.

Rainwater, Dorothy T., **Encyclopedia of American Silver Manufacturers, 3rd ed.** (Atglen, PA: Schiffer Publishing: 1987). This book focuses on hand-crafted and mass-produced factory-manufactured silver and silverplate from the mid-19th century to the present. It is organized alphabetically by company. Each detailed company history is accompanied by carefully drawn and dated marks. A glossary of trademarks is another welcome feature.

Business References

Hyman, Dr. Tony, **Trash or Treasure: How to Find The Best Buyers of Antiques, Collectibles and Other Undiscovered Treasures** (Pismo Beach, CA: Treasure Hunt Publications, 1997). Tony Hyman is one of the most magnetic radio personalities that I have ever heard. He writes and compiles. Most importantly, he hustles what he has done. This is a list of people who buy things. One good contact pays for the cost of the book. It is also a great place to get your collecting interests listed.

Johnson, Don and Elizabeth Borland, ***Selling Antiques & Collectibles: 50 Ways To Improve Your Business*** (Radnor, PA: Wallace-Homestead: 1993). In a flea market era, when there is a proliferation of dealers and fierce competition for customers, this book gives you the competitive edge. It shows you how to stand out from the crowd, increase clientele and keep customers coming back. The advice is practical and budget conscious.

Maloney, David, Jr., ***Maloney's Antiques and Collectibles Resource Directory, 4th. ed.*** (Dubuque, IA: Antique Trader Books: 1997). This is the one reference book to buy if you are only going to buy one. It is a comprehensive directory to the antiques and collectibles field containing about 9,000 entries (names, addresses, telephone numbers and a wealth of other information) in approximately 2,700 categories. It is fully cross-referenced. It covers buyers, sellers, appraisers, restorers, collectors' clubs, periodicals, museums and galleries, show promoters, shops and malls and many other specialists.

Vesely, Milan, ***Money From Antiques*** (Iola, WI: Krause Publications: 1997). This is one of a number of books that explains how to establish a small business selling antiques and collectibles. In previous editions, I recommended Robert G. Miner's ***The Flea Market Handbook*** (Wallace-Homestead, 1990). Although the information in this book remains the best there is, relative to establishing a flea market business, it is out of print and difficult to find. Jacquelyn Peake's ***How to Open and Operate A Home-Based Antiques Business: An Unabridged Guide*** (The Globe Pequot Press, 1995) offers a bit more traditional business approach than Vesely. I recommend locating and reading all three books.

Wanted to Buy, 5th ed. (Paducah, KY: Collector Books: 1995). This is another book listing individuals who want to buy things. If you are a serious collector, write to Collector Books and see if your name and interests can be included in subsequent editions. The book differs from Hyman's ***Trash or Treasure...*** because it contains several dozen listings and prices for most categories.

General References:

Kovel, Ralph and Terry, Kovels' ***Antiques & Collectibles Fix-It Source Book*** (New York, NY: Crown Publishers: 1990). Many flea market treasures have not withstood the test of time well. While they should probably be passed by, they all too often wind up in the hands of a collector. This book provides the options available to have these objects fixed.

Rinker, Harry L., ***Rinker on Collectibles*** (Radnor, PA: Wallace-Homestead: 1989). Out of print. This book is a compilation of the first 60 test columns from my column, "Rinker on Collectibles." Many are now classics. The book allows you to delve into the mind-set of the collector. It deserves textbook status. I bought the remaining warehouse stock. If you would like a copy, send $10 to: Harry L. Rinker, 5093 Vera Cruz Rd., Emmaus, PA 18049. I will even autograph it for you.

Werner, Kitty, ed., ***The Official Directory to U.S. Flea Markets, 5th ed.*** (New York, NY: House of Collectibles: 1997). My opinion of this book is clearly stated earlier. Nothing has changed in my mind since I wrote that section (see Chapter 2).

Just for the Fun of It

Gash, Jonathan, *The Sleepers of Erin* (New York, NY: Viking Penguin: 1983). If you are unfamiliar with Lovejoy the antiques dealer, it is time you make his acquaintance. You will not regret it. I had a hard time picking a favorite. I could have just as easily chosen ***The Judas Pair, Gold by Gemini, The Grail Tree, Spend Game, The Vatican Rip*** and *The Gondola Scam,* all in paperback from Viking Penguin. ***The Tartan Sell, Moonspender*** and ***Pearlhanger*** are in hardcover from St. Martin's Press. Also, check out the "Lovejoy" television series (starring Ian McShane) that airs on the A&E network

Rinker, Harry L. ***The Joy of Collecting with Craven Moore*** (Radnor, PA: Wallace-Homestead: 1985). Out of print. Try never to become so serious about your collecting or dealing that you forget to laugh and have fun. Find out if you are Craven or Anita Moore or Howie and Constance Lee Bys. Trust me, you are in *The Joy of Collecting with Craven Moore*. I guarantee it. Although it is out of print, I still have a few copies around. I will sell you one for $6. Send a check or money order to: Harry L. Rinker, 5093 Vera Cruz Rd., Emmaus, PA 18049.

Antiques & Collectibles Trade Newspapers

NATIONAL

The Antique Trader Weekly
P.O. Box 1050
Dubuque, IA 52004
800-334-7165

Antique Week
   (Central and Eastern Edition)
27 N. Jefferson St.
P.O. Box 90
Knightstown, IN 46148
800-876-5133 or (317) 345-5133

Antiques & the Arts Weekly
Bee Publishing Company
5 Church Hill Rd.
Newtown, CT 06470
(203) 426-3141

Collectors News
506 Second St.
Grundy Center, IA 50638
(319) 824-6981 or 800-352-8039

Maine Antique Digest
P.O. Box 1429
911 Main St.
Waldoboro, ME 04572
(207) 832-4888 or (207) 832-7534

Warman's Today's Collector
Krause Publications
700 E. State St.
Iola, WI 54990
(715) 445-3775, Ext. 257

REGIONAL

NEW ENGLAND

Antiques & Collectibles and the
   Long Island Arts Review Magazine
P.O. Box 33
Westbury, NY 11590
(516) 334-9650

Cape Cod Antiques & Arts
(Register Newspaper)
P.O. Box 39
Orleans, MA 02653
800-660-8999

The Hudson Valley Antiquer
P.O. Box 561
Rhinebeck, NY 12572
(914) 876-8766/fax (914) 876-8768

MassBay Antiques/
   North Shores Weekly
2 Washington St.
P.O. Box192
Ipswich, MA 01938
(508) 777-7070

New England Antiques Journal
4 Church St.
Ware, MA 01082
(413) 967-3505

New Hampshire Antiques Monthly
P.O. Box 546
Farmington, NH 03835-0546
(603) 755-4568

Unravel The Gavel
P.O. Box 171, Rt. 126
Ctr. Barnstead, NH 03225
(603) 269-2012

The Western CT/MA Antiquer
Antiquer Publications
P.O. Box 561
Rhinebeck, NY 12572
(914) 866-8766/fax (914) 876-8768

Treasure Chest
P.O. Box 245
North Scituate, RI 02857
800-557-9662 or (212) 496-2234

MIDDLE ATLANTIC STATES

American Antique Collector
P.O. Box 454
Murrysville, PA 15668
(412) 733-3968

Antique Country
Ultra Graphics
P.O. Box 649
Berryville, VA 22611
(703) 955-4412/fax (540) 665-9430

Antiquer's Guide to the
   Susquehanna Region
P.O. Box 388
Sidney, NY 13838
(607) 563-8339

Antiques & Auction News
P.O. Box 500, Rt. 230 West
Mount Joy, PA 17552
(717) 653-4300

Northeastern Antique Buyer's Guide
Edinburgh Enterprises
97 Edinburgh St.
Rochester, NY 14608
(716) 546-6383

The New York Antique Almanac of
 Art,   Antiques, Investments
 & Yesteryear
The N.Y. Eye Publishing Company
P.O. Box 335
Lawrence, NY 11559
(212) 988-2700

New York–Pennsylvania Collector
P.O. Box C
Fishers, NY 14453
(716) 924-4040 or 800-836-1868

Renninger's Antique Guide
P.O. Box 495
Lafayette Hill, PA 19444
(610) 828-4614 or (610) 825-6392

SOUTH

Antique Gazette
6949 Charlotte Pike, Ste. 106
Nashville, TN 37209
(615) 352-0941

The Antique Press
12403 N. Florida Ave.
Tampa, FL 33612
(813) 935-7577

The Antique Shoppe
12055 S.E. Hwy. 441
Belleview, FL 34420
(904) 347-3384

Carolina Antique News
Print Communications, Inc.
P.O. Box 241114
Charlotte, NC 28224
(704) 563-1168

Cotton & Quail Antique Trail
205 E. Washington St.
P.O. Box 326
Monticello, FL 32345
(904) 997-3880

The MidAtlantic Antiques Magazine
Henderson Daily Dispatch Company
304 S. Chestnut St.
P.O. Box 908
Henderson, NC 27536
(919) 492-4001

The Old News Is Good News
 Antiques Gazette
P.O. Box 305
41429 W. I-55 Service Rd.
Hammond, LA 70403
(504) 429-0575

Southern Antiques
P.O. Drawer 1107
Decatur, GA 30031
(404) 289-0054

20th Century Folk Art News
5967 Blackberry Ln.
Buford, GA 30518
(770) 932-1000/fax (770) 932-0506

MIDWEST

The American Antiquities Journal
126 E. High St.
Springfield, OH 45502
(513) 322-6281/fax (513) 322-0294

Antique & Collectible News
P.O. Box 529
Anna, IL 62906
Fax (618) 833-5813

The Antique Collector and
 Auction Guide
Weekly Section of Farm and Dairy
P.O. Box 38
Salem, OH 44460
(330) 337-3419

Antique Review
12 E. Stafford St.
P.O. Box 538
Worthington, OH 43085
(614) 885-9757

The Collector
204 S. Walnut St.
Heyworth, IL 61745
(309) 473-2466/fax (309) 473-3610

Collectors Journal
1800 W. D St.
P.O. Box 601
Vinton, IA 52349-0601
(319) 472-4763

Discover Mid-America
400 Grand, Ste. B
Kansas City, MO 64106
(816) 474-1516 or 800-899-9730

Great Lakes Trader
132 S. Putnam
Williamstown, MI 48895
(517) 655-5621

Indiana Antique Buyers News, Inc.
P.O. Box 213
Silver Lake, IN 46982
(219) 893-4200

Midwest Illinois Antiques Gazette
4 S. Hill St.
Winchester, IL 62694
(217) 742-3595

Old Times
4937 Xerxes Ave., South
Minneapolis, MN 55410
(612) 925-2531 or 800-539-1810

Yesteryear
P.O. Box 2
Princeton, WI 54968
(414) 787-4808

SOUTHWEST

The Antique Traveler
P.O. Box 656
115 S. Johnson
Mineola, TX 75773
(903) 569-2487

Antiquing Texas
P.O. Box 7754
The Woodlands, TX 77387
(713) 364-9540

Arizona Antique News
P.O. Box 26536
Phoenix, AZ 85068
(602) 943-9137

ROCKY MOUNTAIN STATES

Mountain States Collector
P.O. Box 2525
Evergreen, CO 80439
(303) 987-3994

WEST COAST

Antique & Collectables
Californian Publishing Co.
1000 Pioneer Way
P.O. Box 1565
El Cajon, CA 92022
(619) 593-2925

Antique Journal
1684 Decoto Rd., Ste. #166
Union City, CA 94587
(510) 791-8592 or 800-791-8592

Antiques Today
Kruse Publishing
977 Lehigh Cir.
Carson City, NV 89705
800-267-4602/fax (702) 267-4600

Antiques West
3450 Sacramento St., #618
San Francisco, CA 94118
(310) 276-4544
East Coast (207) 797-7749

Cochran's Art, Antiques
  & Collectibles
P.O. Box 750895
Petaluma, CA 94975
(707) 769-9916

Country Pleasures Magazine
202 B N. Tower St.
Centralia, WA 98531
(360) 736-9534

The Flea Market Shoppers Guide
P.O. Box 400
Maywood, CA 90270
(213) 587-5100

Old Stuff
VBM Printers, Inc.
336 N. Davis
P.O. Box 1084
McMinnville, OR 97128
(503) 434-5386

West Coast Peddler
P.O. Box 5134
Whittier, CA 90607
(213) 698-1718

INTERNATIONAL

CANADA

Antique Showcase
103 Lakeshore Rd., Ste. 202
St. Catherine, Ontario
Canada L2N 2T6

Antiques and Collectibles Trader
P.O. Box 38095
550 Eglinton Ave. West
Toronto, Ontario
Canada M5N 3A8

The Upper Canadian
P.O. Box 653
Smiths Falls, Ontario
Canada K7A 4T6

ENGLAND

Antique Trade Gazette
17 Whitcomb St.
London WC2H 7PL
England

INDEX

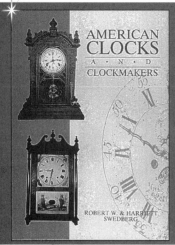